PRAISE FOR...

ART BUSHING:
His Diary, Letters, & Photographs of WWII

"As I read through this text, one word continually flashed through my mind: 'Amazing.' Amazing that this much-in-love couple continued correspondence throughout their long separation brought on by war. Amazing that they were able to resume their storybook life after WWII. Amazing that the letters, cards, pictures, et al, remained intact down through the years. Amazing that we are privileged to follow virtually every aspect of their day-to-day lives— from Dotty's humorous description of squirming into a girdle to Art's visceral depictions of combat. Amazing that their observations from the 1940s parallel many situations in the 21st century, particularly pertaining to (a) the cruelty of racial and ethnic discrimination and (b) the pall of uncertainty for the future —be it war in the Bushings case, or the unknowns about COVID-19 today. Indeed, here is a truly amazing book, on oh-so-many fronts!"

Sam Venable, author and Knoxville News Sentinel columnist

"This book features two parallel stories. One is the enduring romance and love of the featured character and his wife. The other, the guiding story, deals with the service of Art Bushing in the U.S. Army during and after World War II. Following his graduation from college, Bushing entered the Army and, after basic training, received language training. He was deployed to Europe as an infantryman, as part of Patton's 3rd Army, fighting all the way to Austria. This is an enjoyable book, easy to read. The story pulls the reader along, anxious to find out what will happen next, both in Europe and at home in Tennessee. It is an interesting and informative look at one man's journey through the final years of World War II and after."

Michael F. Dilley, Major, U.S. Army (Retired), Military Historian and Author

"Art Bushing: His Diary, Letters, & Photographs of WWII is a must-read for anyone interested in WWII and the effect it had on individual soldiers. The information contained in the book as well as the pictures, capture one man's journey through the war as seen through his eyes and experiences, and captures his personal relationship with his wife during the war through his letters. His father, Arthur Bushing, was my Grandfather's secretary and teacher after my Grandfather returned from WWI. For our family, this made the book even more personal but I would encourage everyone to read this outstanding book."

Gerald York, COL (ret), USA, and Grandson of Sgt. Alvin C. York

"This collection of thoughtful letters is a road map for how to build a Christ-centered marriage that will endure. While Dotty and Art are rooted in the unfolding events of WWII, their unwavering hope for the future, their careful nurturing of their love, and their trust in God's oversight are all timeless. Their letters are a compelling example of how history intersects with theology, philosophy, and psychology."

Dave Tabler, publisher, AppalachianHistory.net

"This is several books in one. It is a love story, a window into civilian and military life in the 1940s, and a tribute to a wonderful school in Tennessee. The correspondence ranges in subject from theology to literature to geology, include descriptions of current events and reminiscences of happy times together, and describe the mundane details of life. In short, these letters are windows into what it means to be human, in love, and dedicated to making the world a better place. May we all be inspired by them to find our own version of this experience."

Tom Bogart, 11th President, Maryville College

"Art Bushing had long been a legend at Maryville College when I met him nearly thirty years ago. I had just moved into the President's Office in Anderson Hall, and was looking for advice when some wise staff member suggested: "You should talk to Art Bushing." Art accepted my invitation to go to lunch, and the hour-plus that we spent together was just what I needed. He gave me a crash course in Maryville College history and frank counsel that served me well throughout my presidential watch.

"Those who read *Art Bushing: His Diary, Letters, & Photographs of WWII* will be similarly well-served. They will discover a diarist, a philosopher, a photographer, a warrior, a contemporary historian, a teacher, an aficionado of the arts, a travel journalist, and a man of faith. Art was, in sum, a multi-faceted, multi-talented son of Maryville College. Readers of this book, even those who think they knew him, will likely find in its pages the revelation of a breadth and depth of thought beyond their expectations.

"They will also discover a wonderful love story. The affection that Art Bushing and Dotty Barber Bushing had for each other comes through in page after page. Their mutual commitment is there in every letter throughout Art's Army days. Whether in combat in Europe or on furlough in Paris or England, he keeps his pledge to write to Dotty and waits impatiently for her warm letters to find him overseas. The reader comes to share their frustration with the Army's interminable delays when the war has finally ended and Art is waiting anxiously to come home to Dotty.

"On a mild afternoon in November of 2008, I had the sad privilege of conducting Art Bushing's graveside service. Dotty was there, along with their adult children. My heart was heavy for them, and the sadness would surely have been much heavier for me had I read those letters beforehand. Yet I am comforted now by having shared their loving correspondence and knowing that it had survived not only WWII but through more than six decades of marriage. God bless you, Art Bushing!"

Gerald W. Gibson, 10th President Emeritus, Maryville College

"*Art Bushing: His Diary, Letters, & Photographs of WWII* is a must-read to get a behind the scenes look into the lives of the 'Greatest Generation' and the momentous sacrifices that were made to defeat tyranny and preserve freedom. Following the experiences of Art Bushing with his entry into the Army, and his eventual combat deployment into the European Theater of Operations (ETO), and his wife Dotty, this book captures the essence of what soldiers and their loved ones endured both on the Home Front and the Western Front. This is a timely work of one of the most consequential epochs in American History and a must-read for the next generation to understand that indeed freedom is not free."

Doug Mastriano, PhD, Senator (Pennsylvania), Colonel (US Army, Ret), and American military historian

———

"Mahatma Gandhi once said, 'In a gentle way, you can shake the world.' Arthur and Dotty Bushing filled a 24 hour day with 36 hours of life! A smorgasbord of service—to our country, to our community, to our lives, and to our Lord God. This close-up and personal view into their lives, their story, will paint a picture of the 'earthquake' they created in their lifetime proving the difference we can all make in the lives of one another. A national hero serving a local world."

Joanie Latorre, East TN Historian, PBS Antiques Extravaganza

———

"This is an interesting collection that informs our understanding of the American experience during World War II."

Charles Hubbard, PhDm Professor of History, Lincoln Memorial University & Abraham Lincoln Historian

Art Bushing

His Diary, Letters, &
Photographs of
WWII

Art Bushing

His Diary, Letters, & Photographs of

WORLD WAR II

Climbing Angel Publishing

ART BUSHING: His Diary, Letters, & Photographs of WWII
    Written by Arthur Story Bushing
Primary letters written by Art and Dorothy "Dotty" Bushing
Other letters from a variety of close family and friends

Art's "Memories of WWII" diary (1945 & 1946) edited by Dorothy "Dotty"
    Bushing and Martha Hess. Additional notes added by Art Bushing.
Book transcribed, compiled, and edited by Lisa Soland
    Tonya Hobbs, assistant to editor

Published in 2020 by
Climbing Angel Publishing
PO Box 32381
Knoxville, Tennessee 37930
http://www.ClimbingAngel.com

First Edition, July 2020
Printed in the United States of America
Photos contributed by Dorothy "Dotty" Bushing
Cover design by PrintEdge, Knoxville
Interior design by Climbing Angel Publishing

Volume II, ISBN: 978-1-64370-028-1
Library of Congress Control Number: 2020909691

I would like to dedicate this book, written by my deceased husband Arthur Story Bushing, to my children Arthur Stuart Bushing, Barbera Bushing-Rose, Kathy (Bushing) Banfield, and Jennifer (Bushing) Hill, with the fond hope that they will pass it down to the next generation.

Dotty Bushing

CONTENTS

Dotty & Art Bushing with Karen Eldridge's sons,
Robbie and Drew Eldridge.

FOREWORD

"$\mathcal{H}$ e's such a nice man."
"He's so smart."
When I arrived on the Maryville College campus in the fall of 1990, I found both descriptions of Arthur Bushing, Jr., to be true. They had come from my great aunts, Frances Beaty McDonald and Margaret Beaty Echols, then Nashville residents who remembered "Art" as a dear childhood friend from Jamestown, Tenn., some 50 years earlier.

Frances and Margaret were two of eight children born to Dillard Osborne Beaty and Martha Ellen Smith Beaty. The Beaty siblings' birth years stretched from 1915 until 1932, so Art, born in 1922, fit right in and likely was fascinated by visits to the loud, busy Beaty household that was unlike the home he shared with only a mother and father.

Art was my teacher only once (English 162: Interpreting Literature in the Spring semester of my freshman year), but he always greeted me and my older sister, Ann (also a Maryville College student) like relatives whenever we saw him on campus and frequently asked about Frances and Margaret; their brothers and sister who were still living; our father and mother; our grandmother, aunts and uncles; and Jamestown. It wasn't long after I started at Maryville College that Art proudly proclaimed to me that Ann and I were the fifth generation of the Smith-Beaty family he had known. I was as equally touched that he had bothered to count it as I was impressed that life expectancies allowed such an achievement.

As a student, I experienced Art's generosity and intellect, but it wasn't until I was hired as director of the College's Alumni and Parent Relations Office in 1997 that I began to know and appreciate Art as a devoted alumnus, 50-year employee and campus legend. He seemed to know everyone connected to Maryville College, and he helped his alma mater in any way he possibly could.

This impressive breadth of service began just after his graduation in 1943, when Art, an English major/math and physics minor was hired to teach physics. His appointment was interrupted by service in World War II, but he returned to his beloved Maryville College in 1947 as an assistant professor of English. By that time, he had studied for a summer at the Sorbonne in Paris and had begun work on a master's degree at the University of Tennessee.

Over the next half-century, he would not only earn a master's degree and continue his education at the University of Iowa, Duke, and other universities, he would become a rock in the English Department. His teaching load frequently included courses in 17th and 18th Century British Literature and an upper-level course entitled "The Novel in English." He chaired the department on two separate occasions.

And whether they had him as a professor or not, Maryville College students across the decades knew him for his Manual of Outlining and Research, which taught undergraduates how to organize information and properly cite sources for papers.

In 1957, Art was asked to divide his time between academics and administration when he was tapped to become the College's Dean of Men, a position he held for eight years. He was asked to direct the College's Summer School in 1968, a position he held for nine years. In 1973, he initiated the Continuing Education Program, directing it for five years. And for three years, faculty looked to him to coordinate the Freshman Inquiry Program.

In the early 1990s, Art spent January Terms as a history professor, leading a class on World War II. He supplemented the text with his own stories and invited veterans into the classroom to share their wartime experiences and lessons.

A model for lifelong learning, Art was always studying something. His research subjects included William Shakespeare, Henry Fielding, and World War I hero Alvin C. York, whom Art knew personally in Jamestown.

Art retired in 1996 but walks to campus from his home on nearby Jones Avenue weren't over. For more than a decade after he graded his last final examination, Art was a frequent visitor in the Advancement Offices at Willard House and the Communication Office at Fayerweather Hall, helping with reunions and other gatherings on campus and sharing news from classmates and former students. He kept up with people and often relayed the goings-on of longtime friends like Ted Kidder, Ted Pratt and Ellis Burcaw. He and Dorothy Barber Bushing, his wife of more than a half-century and also a Maryville College alumna, seemed to be present at almost all college functions.

In 2000, Art was recognized with the College's highest honor, the Maryville College Medallion. In presenting the award at the Founder's Day Banquet that year, President Gerald W. Gibson said of the 1943 alumnus: "His devotion is unceasing and his support untiring. He did far more than was asked of him and far more than could have been expected."

———

I married just months after the 2000 Founder's Day, and as a wedding present, Art and Dotty gave me a blank guest book with a note of advice to begin a tradition of recording all the friends and family members who visit my new home. It might have been an unusual wedding gift from anyone else, but not the Bushings. After getting to know them in those 10 years, I knew that they valued personal relationships and time spent with loved ones above most material possessions. And I knew theirs was a marriage on which I should pattern my own.

One of the last visits I made to the Bushing house was in 2007 to introduce Art and Dotty to the sixth generation of the Smith-Beaty family, my sons Robert Harrison and Andrew Blake. Dotty took our picture, and I took one of her holding Drew while Art and Robbie looked into the camera. In a sweet moment that I'll never forget, Art took Robbie out in the backyard and showed my 3-year-old his garden and water hose. Seeing the water shoot out of the nozzle, Robbie connected the moment to his favorite superhero. He asked Art if he liked Spiderman, and Art replied in the affirmative. A friendship was made.

With this publication of *Art Bushing: His Diary, Letters, & Photographs of WWII*, I am introduced, alongside thousands of members of the Maryville College family, to yet another dimension of Arthur Bushing, Jr.—that of decorated soldier, philosopher, poet, writer, Christian disciple, and devoted son, friend, fiancé, and husband.

Twelve years after his death and 74 years after he penned the last entry in his wartime diary, Art offers a final class in life, love, and the power of words.

He was such a nice man. He was so smart. But Arthur Bushing, Jr., was so much, much more, and I'm thankful for this book—yet another opportunity—to be reminded of that.

Karen Beaty Eldridge
Executive Director for Marketing &
Communications, Maryville College
Maryville, Tennessee
May 2020

Art and Dotty Bushing on their wedding day

INTRODUCTION

My Maryville College Wedding!

$\mathcal{I}$ t all started in the Maryville College woods, a beautiful section of the woods with huge trees and a brook running through them. I was a year ahead of Arthur Story Bushing in school, so I was no longer bound by the college rules which would have horrified the matrons if they had known that I went to the college woods at night with a man. That was a "no, no." But I had already graduated.

And so, one summer while "Art" was still a student there, the two of us went for a walk in the college woods, and there among these glorious old trees, we pledged our troth. But alas, the week after he graduated, Art enlisted in the army and was swept off to California to be in what they called the Army Specialized Training Program. His parents ran the local draft board and I'm sure Art did not want to have special exemption so he took responsibility and did his part by signing up. While with the Army Specialized Training Program, he was given training in the Dutch language which was used in the Dutch Islands in the Pacific where he might be called upon to go to help the top brass make decisions.

Art was first sent to camp Roberts. Then after a period of time, he was sent on to Stanford where the unit of the ASTP was held. While there, he decided he would like to send me a special ring. He made a deal with my mom to take the package inside when it arrived, and on Christmas morning, as I was waking up, my mother brought me this package wrapped neatly in Christmas paper. So, Art had sent the ring to me through the mail and I was delighted!

Later when he received a little bit of leave from the program, it was planned that Art would come to Knoxville so we could be married. But, the army cancelled that leave. Then suddenly it was back on again, but now we had less time so I was to travel to him instead. With those last minute changes, I had no berth on the train—nowhere to sleep—and so I traveled from Knoxville to California sitting up. But I was on cloud nine because I was going to be married, so a little inconvenience did not bother me at all!

When I arrived to Chicago, Union Station was a madhouse, so I was unable to get on the train that I had originally scheduled. Instead, I took one that was an hour later because it was the only train available, and after three days of rocking back and forth in the seat, I arrived to San Francisco, California. I disembarked and stood on the platform. All the other passengers took off. And no sign of Art. Help! There I was; I traveled 3,000 miles to California to get married and no spouse in sight.

Finally, I called one of my Maryville College classmates, Helen Pratt Tapp, who lived with her mother nearby. Her husband was already fighting in the war overseas. Helen had been busy making arrangements for our wedding to take place in her church. She said to me on the phone, "Now Dotty, I want you to go to the Greyhound Bus Station to wait for Art. He'll pick you up there." When Art had not found me at the train station at the appointed time, he called Helen as well and she instructed him to do the same.

I went to the station and I waited and I waited, but Art did not appear. It turns out that in San Francisco there were two Greyhound Bus Stations, and he had gone to the wrong one. Finally, after all these mishaps, in walked Art with a bunch of wilted flowers and an explanation of what had happened with him. What a relief! And to finally know that nothing unfortunate had happened to him!

My arrival was on a Wednesday and the wedding was scheduled for a Thursday, the following day. My friend Helen served as my maid-of-honor, and a classmate of Art's, Van Cise, served as his best man. Would it be redundant of me to mention that Phil Evaul, the man who performed most of the ceremony, was also a Maryville College graduate? Phil just happened to be in California studying at the Presbyterian Seminary at San Selmo, so that made every member of the wedding party a Maryville College graduate.

We were married on April 6, 1944, in Helen's church in San Jose on the Maundy Thursday of Easter week. The church was wonderfully decorated with fragrant Calla lilies so we didn't need any other flowers at all. And that's my Maryville College Wedding story.

What you are now holding in your hands is the written and photographic work of the wonderful man that I married in California during World War II.

Art served in the United States Army and was not supposed to keep a diary, but like Sergeant Alvin C. York, he did anyway. My husband's father, Arthur Samuel Bushing, was Alvin York's personal secretary following the Great War. Father Bushing, as we called him, was never fully accepted in Jamestown, Tennessee, because he was a Yankee, having spent his youth growing up in Brooklyn, New York. I don't believe that Art's father was ever fully recognized for the role he played in Sergeant York's life. My father-in-law wrote much of the lectures and speeches York delivered. Father Bushing was a writer too, and because he worked and lived in Jamestown, Tennessee, that is where my husband, Art, spent most of his childhood.

When I think back to those early days when I first met Art at Maryville College, I was charmed by his personality, yes, and his great big smile, as this book's cover gives witness. But it was his concern for others, the fact that he always put other people first that grabbed hold of me and would not let me go. This compassion showed itself primarily in his volunteer work in the church, and in the classroom when he taught.

After World War II, my husband returned to Maryville College, his alma mater, and was hired as an Assistant Professor in the English Department, teaching his beloved subject of writing. He eventually served as chair for that department, and before he retired in 1996, he had greatly impacted the lives of so many students. He even kept up with them after they had graduated, continuing to encourage them in their lives. Following my late husband's death, I'll bet I received close to 200 sympathy cards from former students, writing that Art was the best teacher they ever had.

I hope you enjoy Art's WWII diary, looking at his snapshots, and reading some of the letters we exchanged. Art loved to write. I was only a fair writer myself, but throughout the war we corresponded daily. He never swore, smoke or drank, which were activities that were typical of young men at that time. To me, Art was the most wonderful person in the whole wide world. Simply put, God sent him to me, and together we always felt that God was most significant in our lives.

Dotty Bushing
Maryville, Tennessee
February 2020

Arthur Story Bushing

PREFACE

*T*he path to progress is littered with the remains of those who have dreamed and yet who have been unable to fulfill their dreams. Appalling figures are given to discourage returning vets from launching out into business ventures of their own. The divorce rate is rising, and literary trends in America seem to point to mass production of trash.

Nevertheless, progress is made only as a result of someone dreaming. Individuals only make individual progress as they dare to dream and make plans by which their dream may be realized. I would sometime like to count up the number of plans which I have dreamed, and which have fallen by the wayside of all dreams. There have been many and yet there have been a few which have been realized. I still believe that one must "hitch one's wagon to a star." We never reach all of the goals which we set, and yet should we fail to set goals as a result, we would accomplish very little.

All of this rambling leads me to my point, of course, that I have another plan in mind. This one just occurred to me this morning while I was writing another letter to you. For some time I have been wondering just how I should attempt to put some of my experiences overseas into writing. I had thought of short stories as being perhaps the best medium for me during the next ten years or so since I will need at least that much time if not longer to develop my own style. The idea which suddenly popped into my head was to rewrite my letters to you—that is the letters written since I came into the Army, perhaps since I came overseas.

My idea would be to comb my letters for pertinent passages from my letters reflecting my experiences, my thoughts, conditions in the Army, etc. Within a letter-medium, I would have more latitude for putting across views and observations, and my novice style would not be so prominent. In additions to my letters to you, I could use my journal, letters to Mother and Dad, and an overflowing journal of notes, I think that I would have a wide choice of source material. The big job would be to choose and delete.

Such a compilation might have more of a chance as a book than anything else I would be likely to produce for some time to come, and yet that is of minor importance. I do hope to find some success in writing—someday, but I know full well that I have absolutely no talent for writing. I have that feeling way down inside of me that I will find myself in writing someday, but I suppose most people experience the same thing at one time or another. To work over our letters and put them in some sort of consolidated form would be to at least provide a source for my own use at some future time....

Letter from Art Bushing
to wife, Dotty
Mainburg, Germany
March 30, 1946

PEACE

Perched upon the muzzle of a cannon
A yellow butterfly is slowly opening and
shutting its wings.

by Amy Lowell

[A poem found among Art's artifacts.]

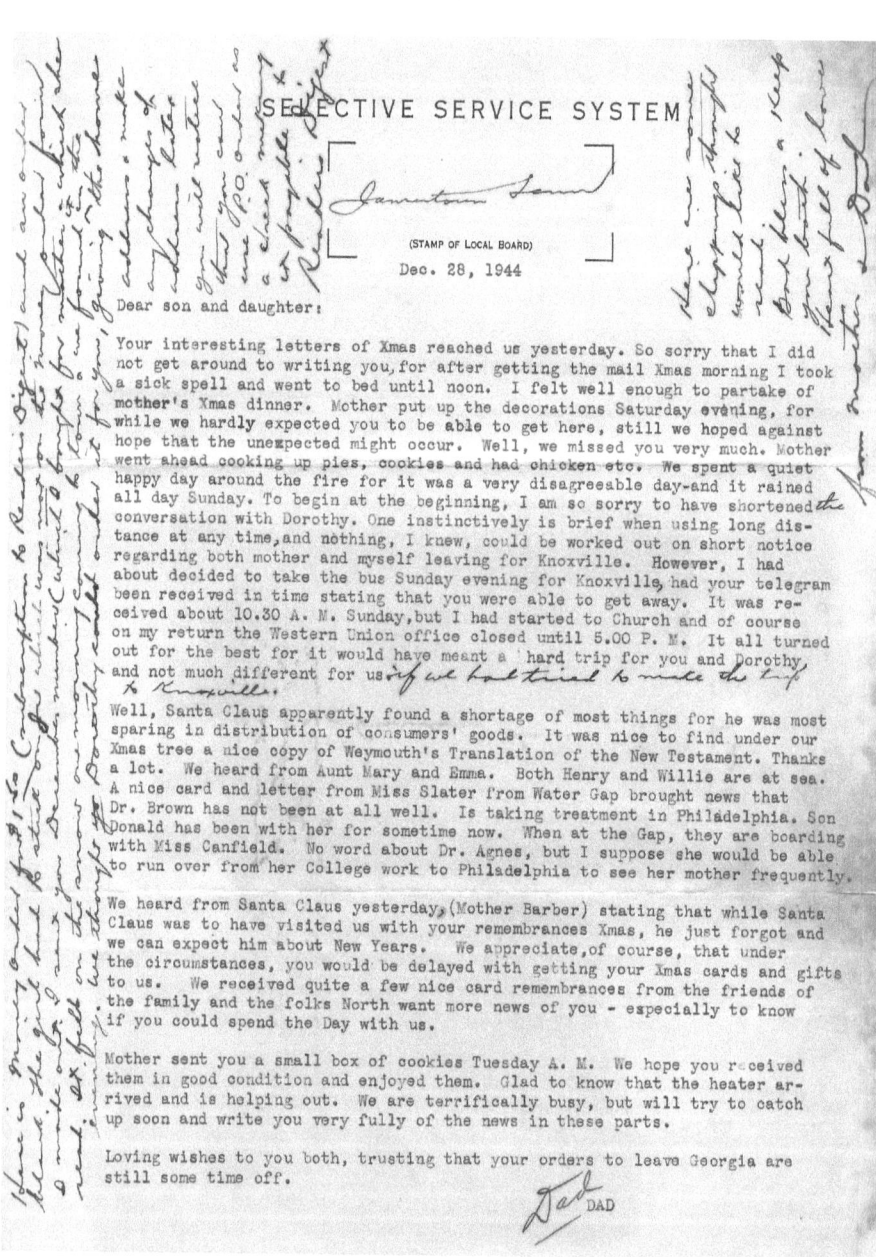

SELECTIVE SERVICE SYSTEM

(STAMP OF LOCAL BOARD)

Dec. 28, 1944

Dear son and daughter:

Your interesting letters of Xmas reached us yesterday. So sorry that I did not get around to writing you,for after getting the mail Xmas morning I took a sick spell and went to bed until noon. I felt well enough to partake of mother's Xmas dinner. Mother put up the decorations Saturday evening, for while we hardly expected you to be able to get here, still we hoped against hope that the unexpected might occur. Well, we missed you very much. Mother went ahead cooking up pies, cookies and had chicken etc. We spent a quiet happy day around the fire for it was a very disagreeable day-and it rained all day Sunday. To begin at the beginning, I am so sorry to have shortened the conversation with Dorothy. One instinctively is brief when using long distance at any time,and nothing, I knew, could be worked out on short notice regarding both mother and myself leaving for Knoxville. However, I had about decided to take the bus Sunday evening for Knoxville, had your telegram been received in time stating that you were able to get away. It was received about 10.30 A. M. Sunday,but I had started to Church and of course on my return the Western Union office closed until 5.00 P. M. It all turned out for the best for it would have meant a hard trip for you and Dorothy, and not much different for us if we had tried to make the trip to Knoxville.

Well, Santa Claus apparently found a shortage of most things for he was most sparing in distribution of consumers' goods. It was nice to find under our Xmas tree a nice copy of Weymouth's Translation of the New Testament. Thanks a lot. We heard from Aunt Mary and Emma. Both Henry and Willie are at sea. A nice card and letter from Miss Slater from Water Gap brought news that Dr. Brown has not been at all well. Is taking treatment in Philadelphia. Son Donald has been with her for sometime now. When at the Gap, they are boarding with Miss Canfield. No word about Dr. Agnes, but I suppose she would be able to run over from her College work to Philadelphia to see her mother frequently.

We heard from Santa Claus yesterday,(Mother Barber) stating that while Santa Claus was to have visited us with your remembrances Xmas, he just forgot and we can expect him about New Years. We appreciate,of course, that under the circumstances, you would be delayed with getting your Xmas cards and gifts to us. We received quite a few nice card remembrances from the friends of the family and the folks North want more news of you - especially to know if you could spend the Day with us.

Mother sent you a small box of cookies Tuesday A. M. We hope you received them in good condition and enjoyed them. Glad to know that the heater arrived and is helping out. We are terrifically busy, but will try to catch up soon and write you very fully of the news in these parts.

Loving wishes to you both, trusting that your orders to leave Georgia are still some time off.

DAD

December 28, 1944, Letter from Art's dad to Art

1

THIS IS THE ARMY, MR. JONES

Basic Training

$\mathcal{O}$ n the 6th of August 1942, I enlisted in the United States Army. When I had investigated various programs with the Navy, the Army Air Corps, even the Marine Corps, I discovered that poor eyesight and/or color blindness were enough to keep me out. My enlistment with the Army provided an opportunity to complete my college work and earn my degree at Maryville College in TN.

In early 1943, when Dr. Lloyd asked me to teach college physics to the newly arrived Army Air Force Cadets, he hoped that the Army would release me from my enlistment or postpone my active duty in order to continue with the teaching. After some correspondence, the Army denied the request, and so on 1 June 1943, I reported to Fort Oglethorpe, Georgia, for active duty. About two dozen of us from Maryville reported at the same time. During the processing, I saw written on my papers the word "Meteorology," a program for which I had earlier applied. It happened, however, that the Army was setting up the Army Specialized Training Program (ASTP), a requirement for which was to be college trained. The minimum was two years of college or university experience. Apparently, ASTP had priority over meteorology because I and sixteen others were shipped to California.

We were loaded on a special car with private rooms and an observation section at one end—by all means the most luxurious travel conditions that I was to have during the next three years. On the way

West we sometimes passed troop trains with officers and other soldiers of rank who looked with wonder and envy at our quarters. Other times, we were put on a side track for priority trains. With a corporal as our leader, we stopped in St. Louis, Kansas City, Salt Lake City, and San Francisco, each time being able to get off the train to eat and often to wander a bit waiting for the next move. I have a vivid memory of crossing the Great Salt Lake with a full moon reflecting on the waters. Our destination was Camp Roberts, a basic training camp near Paso Robles and roughly halfway between Los Angeles and San Francisco.

With a bit of the confusion that we learned to expect—the GI slang was SNAFU, situation normal, all fouled up—we soon discovered that a full complement of men had not arrived. To begin a training cycle, we needed 1,000 men; we had perhaps 700. Those in charge knew of nothing to do but to start basic training. After six weeks the remainder came, and so we began right and left face by the numbers, repeating everything that we had already covered. Late in this cycle of training, I was hospitalized for three or four days, returned to the unit, made up everything that I had missed. Nevertheless, I was sent to another group that was a few weeks behind mine, "This is the Army, Mister Jones...."

On the positive side, I was with a number of friends from College including Ken Cooper, Ted Kidder (both classmates, Bob Hunter (older son of Dr. Hunter, English Dept. Head), Dean Stone, Ken Talbot, and Peter Van Blarcom. All of the trainees were college men, and for the most part we had army career officers in charge of training. The drill sergeant was a very strict German, for whom there was nothing but intense discipline. Morale was high, a fact that I appreciated even more when I found a relaxed and demoralized group when I went to my second unit.

Camp Roberts was located in a desert area. In the hot summer sun, the parade ground temperature often reached 120 degrees. Even so, at night the temperature cooled quickly so that we needed all the cover available. Sometimes the early morning fog that rolled in from the Pacific did not burn off for two or three hours. In light of the fighting going on in North Africa, we were on strict water rationing, often being restricted to one canteen per day. We trained hard, ate like horses, slept like logs. After six months of training, I was probably the healthiest I had ever been.

Basic training was intended to put army recruits into top physical condition. We were on a rigorous daily routine involving calisthenics, close order drill, marches, obstacle courses, field operations in which we simulated a combat problem. By all odds the worst part of all for me was the bayonet drill. We had to run through a course in which dummies were posted with grotesque faces, almost always Oriental. With yells and inflammatory words, those in charge tried to arouse our adrenalin as we ran the course and slashed our bayonets through our opponent. Hand-to-hand combat was included. The psychological conditioning was far worse than any physical demands. We had training films and lectures, again part of the mental conditioning. We had experience with firing most of the small weapons of combat: large and small machine guns, two sizes of mortars, bazookas, hand grenades, and the M-1 rifle. At one point we crawled through a barbed wire entanglement with live machine gun fire a few inches above our heads. Some of the training did simulate combat, but nothing can be compared to the real experience. Night projects were dangerous, in part because the ground in the areas where we trained often had long cracks wide enough to sprain or break an ankle or leg.

We lived in two-story barracks, sleeping on double bunks with forty men making up one platoon and occupying one building. I slept on a top bunk with a bare light bulb shining in my face and giving me a lifetime habit of sleeping with a pillow over my head. We were aroused at an early hour to fall out for reveille and then marched to the dining hall. At least once when we were slow to line up in the allotted time, all passes were revoked and we spent all day Saturday scouring the barracks. That process involved moving all bunks and footlockers out of the building and, on our knees, scrubbing the floor with hand brushes. The Army had many methods to condition green recruits. Every hour was scheduled, but a ten-minute break came at the end of every fifty minutes. I thought that was one of the smartest things the Army did. I learned to sleep for most of that break. When we had nothing else to do, we were lined up to "police the area," i.e., picking up cigarette butts and all other trash in our area.

We did have movies and an occasional USO entertainment group came through, which included Bob Hope and his troupe. Each area had a chapel and weekend worship services. I came to know a fellow GI who had majored in philosophy at Notre Dame and another who was a devout Jew. We had many ten-minute discussions about our faiths, and I occasionally went with the Catholic friend to mass. He, however, could not attend Protestant services with me.

For the first few weeks, we were not allowed weekend passes. I recall that my first one was to go with Ken Cooper, a Maryville classmate, to Santa Cruz, a resort town on the coast. My habits were such that I recall feeling guilty when we went to a movie on Sunday afternoon—I think it was one starring Bob Hope. Another pass was with Ted Kidder going to visit one of his aunts, who took precious gasoline to drive us around to see some of the sights. Civilians were very kind to us, and usually we could hitchhike and beat the bus schedule.

Army Scheduling

Although I never fully adjusted to the condition, I soon discovered that Army life involves constant rumor and thus constant uncertainty. Since our training at Camp Roberts began, we were told that we were destined for special assignments. Upon completing my basic training I was sent to Santa Rosa Junior college, a few miles north of San Francisco. We were put in classes to occupy our time and held there until early January. My friend Ken Cooper and I were invited to a home for Christmas dinner. I recall that a son from the family was overseas, and they gave us an opportunity for a festive meal. They took us for a drive through the Valley of the Moon, made famous in Jack London's writings. The area is famous for its wine production. I was also near San Anselmo Seminary, where my college friend Phil Evaul was enrolled. Ken and I were able to visit with Phil and wife Peggy and enjoy Phyllis, their new baby.

During this period Cooper was shipped back East to enroll in medical school, and after the holiday I was sent to Leland Stanford University in Palo Alto, south of San Francisco. After V-E Day (Victory in Europe), I was selected to attend the Sorbonne (the University of Paris) for summer courses. I describe that experience in later journal notes from that period.

Stanford University

Many thousands of men and women in uniform received special training in a wide variety of fields. Since I was among a few chosen for language study, I was diverted from meteorology to Dutch studies at Leland Stanford University in Palo Alto, south of San Francisco. Opening in early January, 1944, the program was headed by a lady who had escaped the German invasion of Holland. Her staff was made up of people from different parts of the world with varying degrees of competence in teaching. One male came from the South Pacific who had learned English from missionaries from the southern part of the United States. His accent revealed his training.

4

I don't recall the numbers, but I estimate that the enrollment was about sixty, all college graduates from a variety of fields. One of my roommates was trained as an engineer from Cornell. We were housed, of course in the school's dormitories. For my last quarter I was with a man of Jewish faith from Brooklyn and a Greek Orthodox believer from Chicago. The program was designed for three quarters of intense study of conversational Dutch. In addition to mornings filled with instruction, we spent additional time in practicing our conversational skills.

At the end of the first term, we decided that my fiancé, Dotty Bushing, would come out from Tennessee for our wedding, an event planned mainly by the efforts of Helen Pratt Tapp, a classmate of Dotty's at Maryville. The date was set for Maundy Thursday of Easter Week at Helen's church in San Jose. Phil Evaul (another Maryville grad.), who was studying for the ministry at nearby San Anselmo, performed the ritual except for pronouncing us husband and wife, which only an ordained minister could do. With Helen acting as Matron of Honor, and Oliver Van Cise (still another Maryville classmate stationed nearby) serving as Best Man, all members of the wedding party were Maryville College graduates! Most unusual for a wartime wedding three thousand miles from home.

The schedule at Stanford was rigorous. Classes, physical education, and movies (which I don't remember) filled the days and hours to the brim. Except for weekends, I was not allowed off campus during the week, which was a little tough for newly-weds. But finally, during the last quarter, I had some small duty (exchanging sheets and towels once a week) which gave me the privilege of going home each night. My classmates joked constantly that I didn't have enough energy for the calisthenics. In reaction, I redoubled my efforts and was rewarded in the third term with my choices for exercise—swimming, tennis, etc. After one strenuous afternoon of the latter, I developed intense pain, which was first mis-diagnosed. After attending classes the next day, I reported to the clinic and was found to have a very high level of white corpuscles. Thus I had an emergency appendectomy, was in bed for a week and in the hospital for thirty days. I was given a chance to make up my classes, obviously an impossible task. At any rate, at the end of the third term all of us were graduated and then shipped to various army units.

I was sent to the 71st Infantry division stationed at Fort Benning, outside of Columbus, Georgia. Dotty came down from Knoxville, where she had been living with her parents. She joined newly married

5

Cordelia Kidder; both girls found jobs at Tom's Toasted Peanuts factory along with other transient army wives. After three months of maneuvers in very cold, snowy weather, the 71st Division was sent to Fort Dix, N.J. for shipment overseas, still lowly PFC's, having been given no credit nor ranking for their months of training in the Army specialized Training Program.

1945

2

EN ROUTE

Jan. 1, 1945, Jamestown, TN

D otty and I arose at a late hour to find a snow falling. Snow! The first real snow I had seen since the winter of '42-'43. Mother and Dad had already gone to work, but Dad came back to report difficulty in finding a ride for us to Crossville. The roads are covered with snow and ice. After a wonderful breakfast which Dotty prepared, we went to town to check on schedules and to eat dinner in the Mark Twain Café. Saw and talked with a number of people whom I have not seen for a long time.

Dad found a fellow who lives a short way outside of Crossville, and he agreed to take us over. However, we had to leave about 2:30. It was difficult to say goodbye, especially when I knew that it was the last time for a very long time to come.

Jan. 11, 1945
Ft. Benning, GA

This morning one of the minor crises of my life came like a dark cloud on a winter day. For more than a week, I have been thinking that each night at home would be my last. Last night we were told that our restriction would begin today. Dotty had packed most of her stuff and planned to leave today.

Dotty was brave as we said goodbye—she has amazing fortitude. My spirits have been very, very low today. I will have to adjust to the separation, of course, but will not be easy.

Fort Benning, Art & Dotty before Art left for overseas.

January 12, 1945

In the middle of the afternoon, I found myself in possession of a pass. Naturally I hesitated very briefly in getting into town. Beul Root and I went in together to do a bit of needed shopping. Found a much needed jack knife (with gadgets) and a leather bag for toilet articles. Good knives are almost extinct, but mine seems to be fairly serviceable at the very sensible price of $3.00. Good dinner at SS with pleasant memories of former meals when our wives graced the table. Back early and tried to call Dotty, but no one at home.

On our way into town this afternoon, two or three fellows indulged in a bit of wishful thinking concerning civilian life. "I intend to do absolutely nothing for the first six months," said one.

'Tis a bit strange mayhap, but I feel just the opposite. I want to do twice as much as I have ever done when I am released. One of the reasons that I have had great difficulty in adjusting to life here has been the tremendous amount of time utterly wasted. There are hours on end when I can do nothing. I try to review my Dutch as much as possible, which helps. I try to read but even so I have too much time when there is nothing but very idle thoughts to fill my time. No, I look forward to being really creative and accomplishing much.

Letter from Art to Dotty
Jan 13th 1945

My Dearest,

'Tis both interesting and curious the reaction of individuals to crises and eventful moments in their lives. In civilian life control conditions are far more difficult than in the Army where large numbers are subjected to the same experiences. Of course, the obvious variable is the individual's background, and herein lies the key to the multitudinous reactions.

When I returned to the barracks last night, the place was in an uproar. Though the hour was late, men were talking, laughing, and in general doing everything but sleep. Beer was being consumed by the gallon. Whiskey came late and was consumed rapidly. A couple of days ago, I watched men shoot dice and play cards after their hour for departure. Games raged all day. A few men read their Bibles.

I am beginning to evolve a theory explaining a bit more clearly to me the GI who is winning this war. But not only does it explain the every day GI but the applications are wider.

Men seek to escape the present and reality by various means. The poet creates a world around him to shut off the cruder elements outside. Some of us find comfort and assurance in our Bible reading and in prayer. The G.I. (the average G.I.) finds that liquor lifts the weight of reality from his shoulders and dice help pass the time more quickly.

How long will it take mankind to find constructive activity? How long will it take men to find the answer to their questions concerning the deeper values?

I wish that I could pursue the subject further, but I have no more time. My next letter will be written en route.

I am awfully glad to have been able to talk with you tonight,
Darling. May God bless our deep and abiding
Love,
Bushy
P.S. I shall try the second word rather than the letter. Same order.

Letter from Art to Dotty
[January 13, 1945]
USO
Columbus, GA
Fri Night
My Darling,
I have five minutes before I go to catch my bus back to dear ol'
sand Hill. Yes, I did get in again.
I could spend many a rainy afternoon attempting to describe the
intense longing which I have for you since you went away. As though
you were gone a month, as though my sun had disappeared and I
existed merely in darkness.
By the time this arrives, in fact, long before, I shall have left. Ted
was right.
Nothing new but lots of rumors. I shall try to call you tonight, but
fear it will take too long. Lots to do when I get back.
All my love
Bushy

Letter from Art to Dotty
Friday Night, Jan. 12-1945
My Dearest,
This will prove that I tried to call you even though I may not
succeed. However, I feel rather confident that I will be successful
though there be a probable hundred men here tonight on a similar
mission. A steady bus is heard—the latest rumors perhaps, speculation
as to the future. A few like your husband are writing their loved ones
and a few sit and gaze at the perpendicular walls (how extremely so
they are tonight).
Beul and I just returned from the USO in town where I dashed off
a brief note to you. By one of those freaks of chance which come my
way every now and again I managed to get a pass for a few hours this
afternoon. Beul and I caught a convenient ride and were able to finish
our shopping by supper time. By the way, upon my return to Bentley's I
did find the leather bag for $2. It is just what I wanted. Now don't

apologize, my Lovely, you couldn't help it if the little boy knew nothing of the stock he carried. I also found a good pair of shower slippers suitable for folding up in small spaces. And to continue the story of "eureka's" I found the knife I wanted. It cost more then I had wanted to pay, but I consider it a "must" to have.*
*Refer here to the essay on values which I intend to write.

After our buying spree, we went to the S and S for a very satisfying supper. I splurged just a bit there too, by buying three vegetables and a salad, but it was so wonderful after eating in mess kits out of doors for a few meals. I dashed down to 510 just to check on the time of your departure. Mrs. Barfield was very surprised to see me and told me that you had taken care of all the minor details such as telephone bills, electric light bills, etc.

Darling, I love you. I also miss you terribly. According to all good psychologists, that is poor psychology. However, I am a poor psychologist so I am excused. I do miss you and I am beginning to realize a little of how deeply interwoven have been our lives during the past nine months.

"As the bow unto the cord is
So the man unto the woman
Useless each without the other."
But remember:
"For everything that we have lost, we have gained something; and for everything that we have gained, we have lost something."

Our separation will deepen our love far beyond the depths we thought possible. We shall find a new dependency upon hidden sources, strengthen, upon prayer, upon daily Bible reading, upon God.

There is almost nothing that is new with us. We are to wear our overcoats which is definitely to our own advantage. Our work during the last couple of days has been made up largely of details of one sort or another.

By the way, I was just called over to the deck and told that my number did not answer. I wish I could wait, but I have a great deal to do and it is now 9:30. I fear that—well. As usual, I changed my mind. I have just placed the call again, and plan to wait. Beul smiles at me.

I think that I shall spend the next hour or two waiting writing a letter to Bill. He deserves one and it may be a long time before I will find the time again.

Ever Thine,
Bushy

P.S. Darling it is now 10:20 and 2-6363 still does not answer. I must go back to the barracks. I wanted so much to call you, but I fear that I can't wait longer.

Goodnight my Lovely.

Bushy

Jan. 13, 1945
En Route

The big day dawned with the rain pouring down. We arose an hour early in order to wait an hour longer.

The action and reactions of men to similar experiences is of more than passing interest. Today and tonight drinking and gambling were rampant. Almost everyone seemed to want to take the "final fling" at Sand Hill [section of Ft. Benning]. It seems that liquor is the only source of escape for most of the men. Dice and cards help pass the time away. Especially at such times does it seem almost impossible [for me] to feel a vital and integral part of 1st Platoon, Co. K.

We were released about 5:30. I went down to the now-empty chapel for a last period of meditation. Later down to the telephone station to call Dotty. Connections were made very quickly and it was good to hear her voice again. Her job with Dr. Peyton [minister at Fourth Presbyterian Church] begins as soon as she wants it.

Roll call at 21:15 (9:15 p.m.) and the CO called us to attention for the last time at Sand Hill. Route step [order which allowed conversation while marching] was given but few talked. One or two men made half-hearted jokes. Someone began humming the Air Corps song. Down by the RSO (Regimental Supply Office) we marched and on down the hill to the trucks. Our heavy overcoats and two blanket rolls made a comfortable load. Stars shone and the night was warm.

Behind the Q.M. Bldgs. we marched and were told to ground equipment (in the mud). We waited. One fellow wished for a hundred rounds of ammunition to pour into Columbia. (Many fellows have developed a strong dislike for GA and the South in general.)

With much puffing a train brought the long line of cars to the stop. First platoon drew car 13. The date—Jan. 13th. (Really, I'm not superstitious.) The band began to play "The Jugglers." I have never cared for the song but I stepped a bit more lively as it played. An off color clarinet brought discord. Someone snickered. I thought about the poor band playing for 21 trains—three or four a day. One of the three generals (from the artillery I think) watched us march by. I hoped that we looked good. We halted by our car and awaited the signal to board. In brief minutes the train began to move. This was the beginning of a long trip.

Letter from Art's parents to Art
[Arthur "Art Sr." Bushing was
Alvin C. York's secretary.]
Sunday Night
Jan. 14 ⌈1945⌉

Dear precious son:

We received you welcomed letter this a.m. Beautiful, rather mild sunny day. Church services was well attended. Mother cooked nice dinner; big frosted cake—it looked just like your wedding cake—how we wished you were here with us. So the break has at last come—your separation from dear Dorothy—your sweet capable & loving wife whom we have truly learned to love, as opportunity comes, but not too frequently as yet, to know her better. Many precious ties are being broken, as many have already been broken the world over, on account of this cruel and senseless war. Would that men could & would accept the love of God in their hearts as the only guarantee of an abiding peace. My dear boy, as the time approaches for you to enter upon more active duty, as soldiers understand that term, our prayer shall continue & deepen in sobering thought that our Father protect and lead you and be your comfort or stay. Lean on the everlasting arms, dear son, and what ere befalls, yours the glorious assurance that you are not alone. I have prayed for you, as you know I have daily, but constrained to bear to the throne of grace in earnest plea to God, the remembrance of all the boys & men called into service and separated from loved ones, many of whom lie wounded & sick in hospitals. These all I have prayed for also. Surely our Father will understand our concern that you be spared to testify to your faith in His power & goodness in a life of service & usefulness to His glory. So be trustful and face the future confidently knowing in your heart of hearts that He doeth all things well.

One of the hard things to hear will be the separations coming by delayed correspondence; yearning for some word of how you are getting on—where you might be, in any given day or week. Dear boy, we shall never forget you, but think of you; comforting each other daily that your Uncle Sam is offering you every protection. We'll buck up to the situation, and never neglect, under any but impossible conditions to try to write you every week of your now soon to be real absence.

I trust Dorothy is bearing up well and with an understanding & brave heart is accepting what has to be. Our love shall follow her likewise, in no diminished correspondence. We shall want to hear from her regularly & share all the news of & about you, and of those items of news from here that might interest her. I'll try to write her at Knoxville, when we learn that she definitely returned there. We shall hold everything in strict confidence. Board meeting tomorrow—always a ragged day for us; plenty of reclassifications lately. God bless you, dear precious boy, come the day of Peace & your return—never forget that Dad can be counted on to see that the dreams you have of a little home is realized; pending any final settling down, because of other plans, you & Dorothy come & stay with us. All our love goes out to you—as long as life lasts, years through eternity.

Dad & Mother's love forever Mother & Dad

Before mailing this—we received your address A.P.O 360 @ New York, NY Co K 14th inf. Again God bless you & keep you safe—Dear precious son.

Note to Art from Dad
Monday P.M.

Dear precious son:

Just to add a few lines after a hectic day. Board meeting, long drawn out, after we had gotten off call for 88 men. I was down in Courthouse at 4.45 A.M. helping on checking. We were delighted to get your first letters yesterday A.M. Hope you can see Mary and Emma before leaving for your service destination. We shall follow you and think of you continually. It was nice to hear from Dorothy. Will keep in close touch with her. I promise without fail to send Encore your new address. Your first copy at least must have gone to [Ft.] Benning. I got my first copy of Saturday Review of Literature ordered at same time today. God bless you and keep you.

Always
Dad...

Letter from Art to Dotty
1-14- (15 & 16) [1945]

My Dearest,

I left behind all ideas of writing for the duration when I was given my uniform and gun. I felt, and rightly so, that the time and quiet required for creative writing would not be found. So far I have been right except for three or four bits produced at Roberts. However, Saturday the climax for a short story came to me in a flash. I have been playing with the idea for two days, and the details are well in mind.

Time: Night—beginning about ten o'clock and extending into the morning hours (Dec. 16-17). Place: An undisclosed position near Stavelot [Belgium] where the recent German offensive began. Situation: the experiences of a G.I., in this area for a rest, faced with the full tidal wave of German fury as it burst on an unsuspecting Allied line. I get some of the ideas from a detailed article in last week's Life and from other reports.

Pete, the central figure, is in a rest area, where his company is relaxing after four weeks of fighting on the front lines. He relaxes in his tent after after a day of football and exercise when at ten p.m. the unexpected order comes to move out. [Reminder to reader, letters have been typed exactly as they were originally written.] At first there is surprise among the men and then anger at the seemingly unnecessary order. The point that I would try to develop particularly in the first portion and actually throughout the story would be the reactions, thoughts, and feelings of the G.I.

The outfit begins the approach march, still feeling that the "brass" is trying to be funny. Before the line of departure is reached, an enemy patrol (which turns out to be a full regiment) is sighted and the company halts near a crossroad. As the action develops, the men dig in and realize that they are in for real fireworks.

First the company is isolated from the rest of the battalion and then Pete's platoon is isolated on the flank. A desperate call for ammunition before the unit was cut off brings up worthless 60 mm mortar shells, which are obviously useless to the rifle squad. The enemy is closing in, but are far enough away to allow their artillery to shell unmercifully the position. The platoon's casualty list includes 50% of the men.

In desperation Pete takes the only grenade launcher to be found and adapts the 60 mm mortar shell to it. The expedient works for a short time and the attack is held off momentarily.

A brief lull gives the men time to take account of their situation. Twenty rounds of ammunition are left in the squad, now reduced to five men. The supply of mortar shells is still adequate; but as the attack begins again, the overworked launcher breaks and is useless.

The last portion of the story is the climax, all that goes before being merely a build up for it. My ambitious idea would be to give a Shakespearean study of a modern fear driven to insanity by a chain of events. The early portion of the story would reveal the delicate balance of Pete's mind. The poem idealist has never adjust fully to the rough ways of the Army.

Throughout his Army life, he was subjugated his deeper feelings and tried to be a good soldier. So far he has survived, even through four weeks of fighting. Now, however, just as he begins to relax from the tension of battle, he is snatched up again and thrown into a critical situation. He realizes that the German push is more than a local patrol action.

When the grenade launcher breaks, the ammunition for the rifle is almost gone, Pete and the remaining men are at the mercy of the enemy. Pete breaks, he shouts, he goes completely wild. A kind friend leaps from a fox hole to knock him down with a swinging rifle. As he falls, a bullet pierces his helmet. He regains sanity as life ebbs slowly, and remembers nothing of what has happened except the raging battle. Disconnected thoughts come quick and fast. His mind settles for a moment on a high school play in which he played "…….To die; to sleep; No more; and by a sleep to say we end the heartache, and the thousand natural shocks that flesh is heir to, 'tis a consummation devoutly to be wish'd. To die, to sleep; to sleep: perchance to dream; ay, there's the rub; for in that sleep of death what dreams may come, When we have shuffled off this mortal coil Must give us pause: there's…there's."

He falters. He feels the sensation of being lifted up and away. The final artillery garage sounds, but not for Pete.

Well, Darling, there are a number of details that I must work on, with particular care being taken with the final scene. I'm not sure that I can do it justice, but I shall try. Hope that I can get around to it soon. If you can keep this outline, I can do it much later in case I fail to do it sooner.

Loving wishes,
Bushy

East Coast
Jan. 16 - 45

Darling,

I no longer have to dream of whiteness and snow. Since we arrived, winter has shown the full power of her windy blasts. Today pellets of icy snow drove almost on a horizontal plane to make its victim's faces look, for all the world, like round, red steaks. Luckily, we were not in such weather all day.

My trip was a pleasant one and I hardly minded the KP which I had on Monday. Ted and I are together tonight and we are located very close together. The situation looks good for passes and I hope to get in to see a few folks while I'm around.

The PX here contains practically everything, and I hope to get a fountain pen before I leave. Good old Peter Paul Mounds are here in abundance, and I found some small bags for toilet articles.

The cold is intense, but I find my clothing sufficient so far. I find the new surroundings invigorating to say the least.

As I grow accustomed to this idea of censorship, I suppose that I shall be able to write more. At first, I find it hard. More tomorrow.

All my love,
Bushy
Write Mother and Dad

Jan. 17, 1945
East Coast [Camp Kilmer]

Our trip from the south was more pleasant than I had expected even though we were traveling by troop train. I drew K.P. [kitchen police] on the second day, but there was little to do. We arrived in Camp Kilmer in good spirits and found a covering of whiteness to greet us. Smokeless coal is used which offers a decided improvement to the landscape when compared with our former surroundings.

I began immediately to search for Ted. K. [Kidder] who had arrived two days before. Unable to find him, I ended up by going to the show with Ash Blumenstein and [Buel] Root. Saw Keys of the Kingdom which was very well done. Acting throughout was good and interpretation of Chinese far better than usual. After the picture, I continued my search for Ted's outfit. Someone had heard that it was in S.C. Each unit here is complete within itself and each one is almost entirely ignorant of the other. I finally found his company and left a note for him. Last night we were together for two or three hours.

Our processing continues on apace. Strict rules on censorship outlined to us and new gas masks received yesterday. Weather very bad yesterday. Snow driven by very hard wind, with the icy pellets making mince meat of the poor victim's face. At times the snow flew almost parallel to the ground.

My Dearest,

I have the feeling of being in a world apart tonight. I found the post library! It is always a thrill to be able to find the cloistered walls of books surrounding me; to be able to reread a bit from Shakespeare, a poem by Jeffers; to have Harper's on my left and Webster on my right; to know that at least some of the men around me are interested in ideas rather than things.

By the way, my search for the haunting line "Tis colder now..." remains fruitless. The lines are even more appropriate now and I shall not be satisfied until I find the rest of the poem. I wonder if you could question Dr. Hunter concerning my ghost the next time you see him.

By the way, the current issue of The Atlantic contains an article by Owen Lattimore on Japan ("The Sacred Cow of Japan," Jan. 45, pp 45-52.) There is to be a sequel on China in the Feb. issue. Hope that you can read them. I intend to ask Dad to save them for my files. Lattimore was one of the minor gods at Stanford. His opinion was considered very highly.

Although I have been unable to keep up with all the details of the week's news, it does look good. The long awaited Russian drive drives on. In the Pacific the current attacks on the coast of China are coming with more rapidly than I had expected. I still hold out for the attack on Formosa (by attack, I mean invasion), but a direct landing around Amoy or one of the other port cities might well come first.

I wonder if you have noticed the new wave of optimism that comes as a result of the good news of the week. We Americans are so prone to follow the tail of the kite—blow as the wind blows. We are still a young people and this is a sign of youth and immaturity. Nevertheless, I wish we could grow accustomed to the ways of manhood, it's responsibilities, it duties.

I have had no letters as yet, but I hope that tomorrow will bring with it the sunshine of your letter. Another adjustment will be the infrequency of mail, but that too will have to be borne with fortitude. I miss so very much those nights when I could leave the things of the Army: work, sweat, cursing, low and vile thinking—and return to the haven called "home" where peace, love, purity and beauty abounded.

Darling, I can not describe the happy anticipation I have of our future years; our middle age, our old age. Perhaps my conservative nature is already creeping out but those later years can be filled with so much that is beautiful and serene!

The hour is late but our love is young. We have the myriad hours of a lifetime to grow and prosper in

Our Love,

Bushy.

P.S. See article "Gateway to Victory" by Gen Somervell in Collier's Jan 20th. Also "The Week's Work" in the last page of the same magazine.

Letter from Dotty's Mother to Art
Jan. 17 '45

Dear Bushy,

Whew! I feel like I'd be been struck by a cyclone. After a whole months vacation Mary Ruth would discover last night at seven o'clock that she had to be back this morning in time for chapel [at Maryville College]. She hadn't packed a thing—everything she had practically she had brought home to be cleaned—so you should see us scurrying around getting them packed. As Dottie emptied a suit case Mary Ruth filled it up—Ann had come in at 2:30 yesterday morning so she was here to go over this morning. We went up to Carol & Wests last night on account of how Mary Ruth is trying to make a match between Ann & Dean so the family wanted to meet her. Dotty spent the night with Flo and hasn't come home yet—Misery loves company you know so she & Flo will be seeing a lot of each other I imagine. Its so good to have her home but doggonit we would love to have you too. We shall do our best to take good care of her so don't worry on that score. She loves her work at the church and it will be good for her to keep busy.

I have been spending about half of each week away from house and its good to be back for a spell. Mary & Tom are some better but not strong enough to do anything yet so are a great care. Well I better catch up on back "house work" so bye now. Good luck & God bless you.

Love

Mom.

Letter from Art to Dotty
Jan. 18, - '45

East Coast

Dearest Heart,

Excitement and rejoicing! Your first letter arrived today—the one written last Saturday. I'm hoping that the mail will be a bit more frequent now, but I can easily understand if it isn't. By the way, the

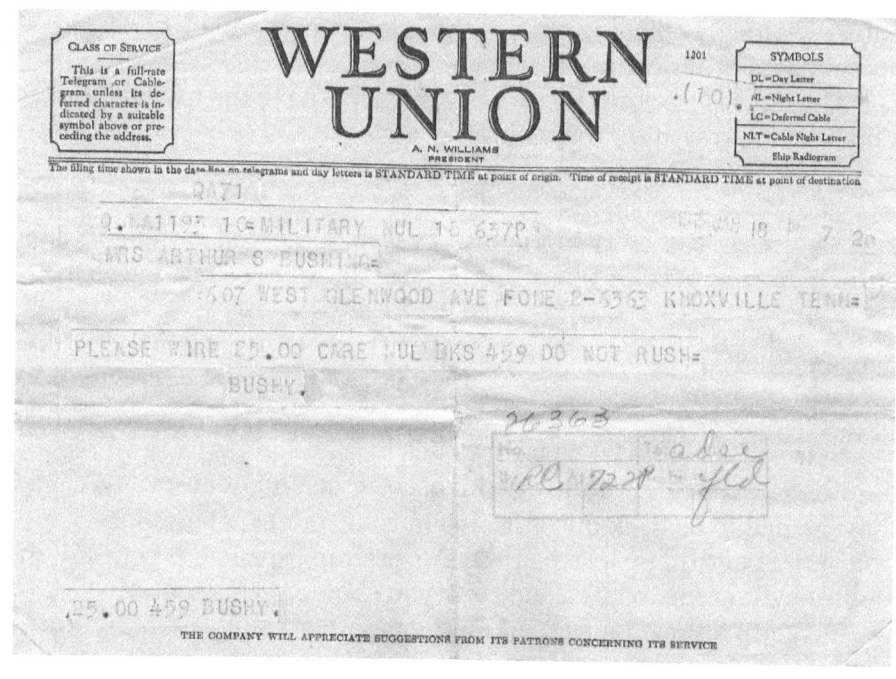

Telegram from Art to Dotty on January 18, 1945 at 7:20 pm

Army was supposed to send my new address by V-Mail. I wonder if it came through (the splotch comes from my new pen. It's peculiar that way.)

Today I made a change in my pay allotment which may interest you. As soon as we get aboard ship our pay is automatically boosted 20%. Thus I will be getting $64.80 for my base pay. Since $10-$15 is considered sufficient for expenses over there. I needed to find some way in which to take care of the money. I cancelled Mother's bond for $7.50 per month and made out a new bond allotment for $18.75 per month for you. I don't think you will object and I know that she will not.

Started to tell you a joke but don't have time. Intended to write tonight and went to show with Ted, "Can't Help Singing" with Diana Durbin. Beautiful coloring and good music. Picture lousy otherwise. Sent telegram for money just to tide me over until I leave. Passes beginning and I hope to see Aunt Emma tomorrow. Ted & Cordy hoping to get together.

More Tomorrow. Goodnight & God bless
    Our
    Love
      Bushy
P.S. How does airmail compare w. regular mail.

Letter from Dotty to Art
[January 18, 1945]
Thursday nite

My Own,

    Your telegram came tonight, and I have been trying and trying to read some secret message into it. I think you are trying to tell me to come, but wish I were sure of that. You probably do need the money, but if you didn't need it right away ("do not rush") why wire, I say to myself. And then I look again and the words "do not rush" must indicate that you will be there long enough to make it worth the long expensive trip to see you.

    Tomorrow morning (but early) I shall go to Western Union to pick up the telegram and wire you the money. If I can see it and inspect it myself, perhaps I can see the hidden message. I realize that a wire for money is about the only sort of wire you are allowed to send, so there must be a message. Oh, darling, maybe "do not rush" means don't come at all, don't do anything drastic, don't rush up here I'll be gone. Yes, no? There are so many interpretations. Presently I shall open my Bible and pray for direct guidance in this matter from what I read therein.

    Tonight I made biscuits for supper, and they turned out quite well. I'm learning, hey, I'm learning.

    This morning in town I purchased some material and a pattern for making your mother a blouse for her birthday. Do you think I'll have time to make it?

    Darling, I love you. Maybe I shall see you soon. How wonderful it would be to more fully express
      Our Love,
        Dotty

I am leaving tomorrow on the 6:50 train arriving Phila. Sat. nite. Hope I interpreted wire correctly.

Letter from Art's Mother, Arza, to Dotty
January 19, 1945

Dear Dorothy:

Thanks a lot for your letter which came this a.m. We were beginning to wonder if you had gone along with your husband, and yet we knew you would have a lot to do to get back into civilian life so to speak.

Glad you got the job, for keeping busy is the only way to be able to carry on when faced with the fact that there really is a war going on and we must give up, for a while, the one most dear to us.

You must have had a job getting all those boxes packed and on the train. You should have left the jars. Don't send them on to me, as I have plenty, and would probably not use them again. There isn't much need of my making so much juice now, as we don't drink much of it when I do make it. Of course I shall always keep a supply in the event the war should be over and your husband comes marching home. I say that flippantly, but God grant that it may be true.

We are delighted with the pictures. Thanks so much for them. We were not able to get the full beauty of the tiny ones you sent, as the projector was not so good. These are real good we think.

So far we have been able to keep the work up, but we don't have a minute to spare. We get off over 100 men next week, and on Monday and Wed. we get up at 4:30, and see that they have breakfast before leaving. We don't complain for some of our boys don't even get to go to bed.

Of course we can't expect to hear soon as to the destinations of the 71 division, but I hope we can in some way be able to know just where they are stationed. Somehow it helps to know, but sometimes they are not permitted to tell. Our two neighbor boys who sailed about 4 weeks ago have landed in India. Their A.P.O No. is New York.

Please say to your mother that I'm sorry not to have written her about receiving the shrubs, but we have been so terribly busy. I appreciate her help in getting them. They came in good condition.

Believe it or not my Calla which you brought is beginning to bloom.

Love & best wishes from us both.
Mother B.

Dear daughter Dorothy:
So glad to hear of your safe arrival home. Wrote our sonny boy and your sweetheart a long letter last Sunday after his last letter written last Friday. Before mailing some Monday A.M. we had card giving new address N.Y. so sent letter air mail to that point. How we shall miss those intimate weekly letters which for over 5 years came so packed with all his hopes and doings. God grant he may return to us safe and well. Excuse short line. Kind and loving regards to Dad and Mother Barber

>Daddy Bushing.

Letter from Art to Dotty

East Coast

Jan 20, 1945

My Dearest,

It seems as though I am rapidly slipping. When I returned from N.Y. last night I found one letter from you and today I received two. Should have written I arrived, but it was rather late and I was extremely tired. I was happy beyond words to began to get letters direct.

Oh yes! My pass. Twelve hours is the best we can do (My what construction!), but that is enough for a good visit into town. Beul and I went in together, although we separated soon after arrival. I wanted, of course, to visit Aunt Emma & Aunt Mary, so Beul visited Radio City most of the day. Without too much difficulty, I made my way to Brooklyn and took Aunt Emma completely by surprise. Her youngest, Cousin Willis, is home from the sea; but he expects to go out again very soon. Many a tall tale he tells of excitement and hair-raising adventure on the seven seas. He's first asst. to Chief Engineer in Merchant Marine; and has been sailing for years. Uncle Henry is on a short run to S. Am. now and will probably come in for the last time. Aunt Mary, too, was completely surprised to see me;—she has her sister with her and seems to be getting along. Everyone wanted to know about you, and I proudly showed them your picture.

With almost no other activity, I returned with Beul to camp. He had an enjoyable time even though part of it was spent in waiting for me.

(I just realized that I am not supposed to write on the reverse side of these pages!)

Passes are not at all certain, but I hope for another in the next couple of days. If and when, I shall attempt to get into Philadelphia to see Ken, Arlene, and perhaps Mr. & Mrs. Hargrave. Ted has seen Cordy and I think they are together in N.Y. tonight (I think I mentioned that Ted is only two hundred yards away from my barracks.)

Sunday Morning

Spent part of my time last night listening to "The Firebird" by Stravinsky. Find that the library has a group of records, and I shall investigate them immediately. This morning I went to church with MacIntosh. The scripture was 91st Ps., and the text was taken from the first verse. The entire sermon was a re-statement of "He that dwelleth in the secret pace of the most High shall abide in the Shadow of the Almighty."

By the way, (I am writing this in snatches), I just happened to think of Mother's desire in regard to a couple of books we have at 607. Hope you have sent her <u>A Tree Grown in Brooklyn</u> and <u>The Robe</u>. As yet, I have not received the little game combination. Letters have arrived very slowly from [Ft.] Benning and the package may be returned to Mom. In such case, I would like to have it sent on here. I suppose that it will reach me eventually. I think that when I get beyond the reach of post office facilities, you can send airmail stamps, three or four at a time, to me. I intend to stock up with a number of them.

Tuesday Night.

Wrote to Jenks address today. Hope it arrived in good time. Wrote home tonight but left details of your trip to you to describe. The hour is late, but I shall try to write again tomorrow. Mail will be delayed for a few days, but I shall continue to write and then mail them when I can. Nothing of news to relate: So glad that our misunderstandings worked out to such a successful conclusion. I love you with a love that is eternal. May God bless us in His own Wisdom.
    I love you,
    Bushy

Jan. 21, 1945
East Coast

A seeming consummation of eighteen months of pain circles round and round within my brain. My old headaches have returned with a new lease on life to plague my every waking hour. I suppose that the cold has reawakened my sinus, for I often find it difficult to contain a scream. I withdraw within myself to hide the turmoil of my seething brain. I sincerely believe that the day will come when I can no longer hold back. I sometimes feel the uncontrollable urge to throw things, to break things—anything. I have always prided myself in holding sway over anger and tempestuous rage but I know not how long my record shall remain unmarred.

For the past two weeks I have been [partially] nauseated with food. My sleep is often fitful and I have lost much of my former ability for concentration. I wonder how long I can go on without a break. I wonder.

Perspective seems terribly hard for the human mind to maintain. We are so easily blown in one direction and then another by the winds and eddies of current opinion. We have a first Sgt. (Mauser by name) who is well-known for inefficiency. He hath the "lean and hungry look" of a G.I. Caesius. When I first inquired concerning OCS [Officer's Candidate School] at Benning, I was assured that he wanted to see "the boys get every possible break"; and yet I know for a fact that he deliberately held up my papers and papers belonging to others until the openings were closed.

To get to the point, he has more than once put a penalty on those who go on sick call. One fellow was given K.P. because he asked to go to the dispensary shortly before we moved. When I asked to go today, he mentioned that men on sick call would not get passes. I was on sick call more than once in Benning for poison ivy, a strained shoulder, etc. I deliberately did not go complaining of my headaches because of the stigma attached to going. Now the pain is to the stage where I must break the bonds of petty feeling. It is never good to be on the wrong side of the fever with the First Sgt., but the necessity for finding relief is the greater of the drives. I intend to try every possible way to obtain some sort of cure or alleviation, even if it means that I shall receive no more passes from this station.

A telegram from Dotty today indicating that she is visiting Jenks [Marian Jenkins, Dotty's roommate at Maryville College, who was living nearby]. I had no intention of planning for her to come to Philadelphia, since my situation is so very uncertain. Nevertheless, I am extremely happy that she is near and will bend every effort to see her. She reports that our efforts to increase the family have failed. Both of us had fully decided three or four months ago that we should go ahead with plans for a third member in our family. We prayed earnestly that our union might be blessed with a child. It is hard to accept the fact that so far we have failed, but there is no help for it. We believe that a Power greater than ours guides our lives and our plans. "The Lord giveth...blessed be the name of the Lord." My, but I love children and how I long for the day when I can proudly look upon my own!

Jan. 21, 1945
East Coast

Old Shadows

Out-lived shadows fill the corners of my mind,
And dash upon me in an unexpected hour.
How can we escape the wisps of passing memory?
Now and again the present with new shadows formed
Comes upon me when I least expect.
I seek to reach the mountain top
Where shadows come not from on high, but
No!
There are rivers to cross and mountains to climb
And shadows, old shadows that fill my path worn mind.

Look Upon This Upturned Face

Look upon this upturned face:
A dreamer's eye
The unwrinkled brow and pleasant smile.
You do not know and they do not know,
But I know.
I know the turmoil in that seething brain,
The wakeful hours of blackness and despair,
The secret calling to the understanding stars,
The heart that seeks to find itself in a lost eternity.

Letter from Art's Mom & Dad to Art
Sunday Jan 21 [1945]

Dear Son:

Your letters of 16 & 17 came this a.m. and we have already gotten. Colliers mentioned in one of them, so I guess we pretty well know your story. So glad Ted is with you, and its also good to know that the food is good. Hope you can visit Emma and Aunt Mary.

We are ok. Got our work in good order for the two groups going tomorrow and Wednesday morning. As Harry Lauder says: "It's nice to get up in the morning but it's nice to lie in bed," only on these two mornings there's no lying in bed, but getting up at 4:30 We don't mind so much for after all its not as hard as it seems—just like your troupe train ride—one can do a lot of things which seem hard.

It's going to be hard not to be able to hear all about what you are doing, where you are and etc. but it's going to be interesting hunting for hidden messages in your letters, and I'm sure are able to write some riddles which the censor will not be able to read.

Glen and Fay are in India and Fay's first letters since landing came today. They have N.Y. A.P.O. Nos. but they sailed from the Pacific Coast. If by chance you should retrace the trip you made in Oct. you can write for John B's address and visit him while you are waiting to sail—anyway you can write for it.

Manza wrote that she had a letter from Fred last week also one the week before. Said he was O.K.

Clayton Crovens is home from the South Pacific. He went to Australia over two years ago and this is his first furlough. He looks real well but says that he wants to go across again. I think he has 30 days here. Seems that Fred ought to get to come home. He has been on foreign soil 3 years.

The Frogge girls are here for the week end. Seems that their Dad has bought a ranch near Reno, Nev. We had a change of address form him, so it looks like he's there for some time.

There isn't much local news of interest, but we are intensely interested in the war news from the Eastern Front. There isn't anything which lasts forever so it looks like there might be a turn in things in the not so distant future.

We have the Atlantic magazine you mentioned and I read "The Sacred Cow of Japan." Will save it for you. Both your Dad and I have finished "My Son My Son" and thought it real good. I'm glad he wasn't My son.

Do you remember the Beaty boy nicknamed "Tar baby?" He has been a prisoner of the Japs on the Philippines for over two years, and they had never heard from him until a few days ago. He wrote his mother that he was getting on O.K. and that he had gotten all her letters. His brother Bill is over sea and Bill's wife (a texas girl) has come here to live. Loma Beaty Boles has given up her job of nursing and is here.

We had a letter from Dot few days ago. Said she had begun her new job and was very much pleased with it. She sent us some enlarged colored pictures of the "wedding pictures" and we appreciate them very much. I've shown them to several people, and everyone has something nice to say about them.

"Believe it or not" my Calla bulbs are beginning to bloom. You may not know it, but I've never seen a white Calla bloom only in funeral sprays, and I'm so glad these are blooming. I had a white one for years but it never bloomed. And the little cuttings (Azalea) on the kitchen window sill are forming buds! Can you imagine plants so tiny doing their bit toward making the world brighter?

Today was a regular Spring day for a change. We have been having rainy weather for nearly a week, and the days seem so damp and foggy at night it's like I imagine a London night to be—for fog.

We always anxiously away any message you have time to send, and will try to write as often as we can. Do you know if our letters will be censored?

Love and our prayers for your safety. Mother

Letter from Art to Dotty
East Coast
Jan. 23, 1945 Tues.

Dear Dotty,

I was so glad to have had the opportunity to see you again, even though the time was of necessity, limited. It was good also to meet John and see Jenks again. They have a lovely place and certainly have a full measure of happiness. My trip back was uneventful and I managed to remain on two feet despite the condition of the pavements and sidewalks.

After thinking more about your situation I think that you are entirely right in regard to your work. As pleasant as a prolonged vacation would be, visiting Harriet, Sam, & Mae, you are wise to return to your job. Dr. Peyton needs you and your mother can certainly use your help.

Give my best regards to Jenks & John and thank them for their many kindnesses. I will write again soon.
As ever.
Bushy
P.S. Received letter from Mrs. Hargrave sent to the South.

Jan. 24, 1945, East Coast
Camp Kilmer, New Brunswick, NJ
In Retrospect

Sunday afternoon I returned from Ted's barracks to find a telegram awaiting me. To my complete surprise it indicated in a roundabout way that Dotty was in Philadelphia visiting Jenks [Marian Jenkins '42] and her husband. The plan had been that I would send for her only if I thought I would have time to see her. I had not given the word since my situation would hardly warrant it. Nevertheless, I was excited that she should be near again. I had hardly hoped that another pass would be forthcoming although I had put in for it. Monday came and to my joy and surprise a pass came. (We were told that these passes were definitely the last.) I caught the first train possible out of town and then made my way after some delay to Huntington Valley. As I rode the bus on the last leg of my journey we stopped for couple of passengers. Who should it be but Jenks and Dotty! We rode happily along to our destination and Jenks' home. A lovely neighborhood and a comfortable little house (wonderful fireplace). What utter joy and contentment to spend even a few hours with my dear wife. For more than sentimental attachment, there lies between us a deep bond of complete oneness that makes life with her complete; without her, empty.

Jenks and John seem very happy together. Although he is her senior by a number of years, her maturity seems to bridge the gap very successfully. She gave up work as of Jan. 1, and has taken up the full responsibility of a dutiful housewife. John is a chemist, a scientist as it were, and is inclined to recount many personal exploits. I am sure that his evident pride is justified for he does seem to be a very capable person. Both he and Jenks belong to a church following the doctrine of Swedenborg. As I told Dotty, if she is around there three more days, I think she will become a convert. They gave me a couple of his books to peruse. With due respect for the right of every man to

31

worship as he sees fit, I oft times regret that more Protestants are not able to fit their ideas into one of the long established sects. Our many divisions on very petty differences do little to offer a united front against the foes of the church and the inroads made by our Catholic brothers. I hold no grudge against the latter either, but it is possible for them to out-general us through better general-ship.

As I was saying before I interrupted myself, it was a thrill to be with Dotty for a few hours again. Such moments are golden nuggets in memory's chest to be brought out and reflected upon again and again.

"Gateway to Victory" pp. 12-16, by Lt. Gen. Breton Somerville [CO ASF], Colliers, Jan. 20, 1945, includes the following news:

"More than 24,000 ship tons of Army cargo were sent overseas in six months through the New York Port of Embarkation. Fourteen tons of ordnance equipment alone— artillery, rifles, ammunition, automobiles—leave our eight ports of embarkation every minute of every day.

"The Port of New York is the world's largest. Within it are an airport, a great hospital for American soldiers wounded overseas, an ammunition loading area, railroad yards, the world's largest military warehouse and a plant where all types of military vehicles are processed for shipment. Nearby are the staging areas for troops in transit overseas.

"It requires ten tons of organic equipment—such as trucks, clothing, and weapons—to get one soldier into the European theater of operations. Sixty pounds of supply are needed each day to keep him there. In combat he needs a ton of ammunition, food, clothing, and medical equipment each month...."

(Contained further in this article were the first pictures to be released by NYPE). In the column "The Week's Work" (P.73 op. cit.) the three camps in the NYPE are listed as Camp Shanks, at Orangeburg, N.Y.; Camp Kilmer, at New Brunswick, N.J.; and Fort Hamilton, Brooklyn.

My time in this "benoemed" (Dutch) NYPE is seriously limited. Tonight I came down to the Service Club to spend my last evening in the library. There is something about a library that takes me away *from the routine of Army life. What release to find myself in a world apart.*

Although it is extremely difficult to be so, I think that this is an excellent time to attempt to analyze my feelings toward the Army, toward the prospect of a gangplank, and perhaps toward life in general.

In the first place, I think that I am basically an individualist. I am not inclined to go along with the crowd unless the crowd is going my way. Even at Maryville [College] when I was among my own, I often preferred to stay in my room or in the library or studying rather than attend a social function. [Sometime in the early '90s my old friend John Hawkins wrote me that he and others used to laugh at me for spending so much time studying.] Thus, in the Army, although I believe that I have been generally well-liked, I have made few friends with deep friendship ties.

While being an individualist, I am also an "optimistic realist" as one friend said, or better, an idealist. I may find it otherwise, but do not believe that I could or would ever make a good infantry rifleman. The wheels of a wrist watch were not made to run the hands of Big Ben, nor were the petals of a rose intended to follow the path of the sun. A square peg does not fit the proverbial round hold. I believe that as a duty to my country and to those I love, I would put my heart and soul into hundreds of jobs in the Army. I sincerely do not feel that I can ever be fully reconciled to the requirements of killing the enemy. Nevertheless, as I have always felt (both before I entered the service and afterward) when the time comes, I shall gladly lay down my life if necessary to serve the country I love, that country that has given me and 130 million others all that we have. I suppose that thousands share my feelings; it has become almost an axiom in discussing the GI [with others]. We don't want to fight, but we do want to end the bloody mess.

In regard to facing the gangplank, I can never recall looking forward to it; but I can truthfully say that I think it will be one of the thrilling moments of my life. It is as though one were stepping out into another world, knowing that anything and everything could happen. It is as exciting as the Crusades or the Overland Trail of 1849. Perhaps it is not so adventurous as the voyage which Columbus took (the famous one, I mean), but I do expect to discover a short route to a land of riches, perhaps a new land—a land within myself in which I shall find God and Christ in a very new and different way.

I still have a spark of red blood left though I am a conservative old fossil at twenty-three.

Letter from John "Squawky" H. [Hawkins] to Art

Andover Newton Theol. Sch.
Newton Centre, Mass.
24 Jan. '45 [handwritten]

Dear Bushing,

Mighty glad to recieve your letter, dear Friend. Did you get a card from me Christmas? Hope so. I'm surprised and not at all pleased to hear of your present location: position, I might better say. It would seem to me that the Army is most efficient in misplaceing and improperly evaluating its personnel. A man of your calibre should by all odds be an officer, preferably a chaplain. I can't blame them for your not being a chaplian, but I most certainly call the blasphemy of Heaven on their abysmal aberitions and blunderings in regard to use and appraisal of manpower and potential! I don't want to seem fecicious or braggadocio, but it would seem from my limited experience that the Navy is 100% more considerate and efficient than the Army.

I'll not tarry long over this as I have a New Testament comprehensive to study for this evening for the morrow. I do wish to inquire concerning your and Dotty's well being and present plan of action regarding the future. It seems evident that you are definitely inhibited in your ability to give any information regarding your activities. I would judge from what you indicate that you are or will soon be P.O.E. or stageing area; that you will be among those in the European theatre of activity; that you will possibly manicure a rifle from now on out: that Dotty is not with you at the moment; that you are not too far from New York, perhaps Maryland or Virginia—no— New Jersey, more likely. (I'm not pumping you, by the way).

Yes, I could come down to meet you at any time you might indicate. If you can wire me or let me know by 'phone I'll hop the first train for N.Y, out of Boston and be with you in 5 or 6 hours. There are many things I need to talk over with you. I am engaged now, Bushing, to a lovely girl doing her masters in R. E here at school. She is the daughter of a Dr. in a near by town, one of five sisters and one brother. She is a wonderful and a lovely woman, 22, large—that is, like John Hellums, not at ALL fat—she is a Bates grad in sociology and psych., very athletic and robust, healthy; Dark skinned, eyed and of dark hair.

She is a yankee from 'way back: taciturn, full of dry wit and mighty good sense of humor; keen intellect, <u>lovely</u> singing and speaking voice; almost black, naturally curly hair; light and graceful on her feet, MIGHTY well put together, 'though she tips the scales at 150, and more usually; She is deeply religious and highly idealistic and sensetive. But she is practical and has her many faults of one or another nature as well. We complement each other, in fault and in virtue. We love each other. We'd like to be married next summer after summer session; we'll see!

Now I must close, Hope we can get together soon! I'll anticipate and pray for a call from you. Call Boston: Lasell 9453, ask for Squawky or leave a message. Wire: same Address. Aufwiedersehen, John

Letter from Bill [maybe Hargrave] to Art

1-25-45

[USS Alpine APA 92 USNR c/o FPO S.F. Calif.]

Dear Art,

Most amazing! A really long talkative letter from you. I was afraid had almost forgotten me! Well, well, so they've really got you rifle lugging huh? Are they going to turn you loose on this side of the world with your Dutch and a rifle, or on that side with just rifle. On second thought, that's where the Dutch originate isn't it? Maybe you'll be holding down a desk job in Holland yet, amongst the Piedmont letters! Wherever you end up I wish you the best of luck and success and a rapid trip back. Do hope it is over there, though, because there is nothing—and I do mean nothing, over here but filth and mud, plus some lunatic Japs, who try anything.

This won't be very long cause I haven't much time. As usual your letter (and all your mail) didn't get here till the last minute again and that means no time for long, lengthy answers. If the mail would come when we arrive, maybe we'd have ample time to scribble returns. Meantime they are keeping us plenty busy in all ways. Now that some more men have been transferred I have added work to do. Oh well, also time in the sack. May do me some good!

Remember back in school when I told you I had a Dottie, too? Well, I have, and the situation is gradually clearing. A few more months out here and it should be clear. At least I'm hoping so. With any kind of luck at all and a lengthy enough leave (plus maybe a wee bit of shore duty) and perhaps I can join your vaunted ranks. Only trouble is you are a year ahead of me! Meeting Dot, was well worth the wait though. She's everything all the rest of the girls I've known put together plus something else—herself! One of these times when I can tear myself away from one of her pictures, I'll send you one. If you ever manage to hit Philly & Drexel Hill, you'll get a chance to see some of her pictures. I remember all your raving about Dot, and now I wish I could remember the exact phrases you used so I could use em.

Say, what do ya know. I'm taxable this year—by 26 dollars!!! Don't feel any different though.

Sorry I haven't time for more elaborate letter at present, but I shall call quits with a few more of our newly optimistic predictions. I think Germany's downfall will be in April or May—tho spring drive you know —provided the Russians don't put an end to it with this drive of theirs.

Over here, we will have reached most of our goals before the year is out. Possible by the middle of the year. However, Japan itself, plus plenty of small satellites will remain to be pounced upon and completely demolished. At present, I really favor that. I don't relish another one of these conflicts, for I fear the next one may be the beginning of the end—and we'll revert back to something else instead of progressing ahead. Maybe that is unduly pessimistic, but the new ranges and power of the weapons now formed and planned, give every indication of said destruction!

So with that morbid piece of thought I cease. Sure am glad you were able to get home and do all of the things. I'd love to have a crack at once more myself. I've promised myself that same jaunt my first opportunity. Mt. LeConte, The Chimneys [trails in the Smoky National Park], Jamestown and Maryville. Only hope you and Dot are available to enjoy the trip with us "note the plural."

Bye for now, take care of yourself and Dottie. Say "hello" for me.
Your Ex, Bill
P.S. When I find out you've really left, I shall try dropping Dot a line every now and then, when feasible.

Letter from Art's parents to Art
Thursday 1-25-45

Dear Son:

Your Jan 21 letter came today and we are glad that you got to see Mary and Emma. Do hope you get to see Ken Cooper and the other friends in Phila. We don't know why our letters are not reaching you. We send them Air Mail and hope you have received them by this time.

We are O.K. Our report on 70 men sent to camp came back showing 41 rejections, and of the 18 transferred to other boards, we will no doubt get a similar report. We are keeping up the work by keeping busy most of the time but we don't mind.

Eaton is here for 10 days. I haven't seen him but your Dad says he looks thin and the Captain's bars are the most glistening thing about him. Fay is in Assam India and has written for a pound of Maxwell house coffee, which they plan to send to him. Say he's already killed a snake.

We have had notice that Shelby Turner has been discharged to accept change in status. He got an honorable outright discharge; and we will have to reclassify him and send him back. If he didn't get something done about the change before he got out he may find himself in the infantry—where they are putting everyone now. The discharged men tell us that the Army is breaking up Units all over and putting the men in the Infantry.

We had hoped to hear that you were going to get to make use of your Dutch, and here's hoping that the opportunity will still come for you to do so.

Am anxious to hear about your watch. It will be too bad if you have to sail without being able to have it with you.

We've only had one letter from Dot. She wrote that she was sending the heater as soon as she got time to pack it. We will be glad to read the books you mentioned, when she sends them to us. Am glad that she got the job, for being busy helps an awful lot. I'm wondering if I will be content to go back to regular routine house work when this is over.

From the news we are getting now, it looks like this war can't go on forever, and sooner or later we can all be back home.

We have had nice weather all week, and I was very much surprised to see my early jonquils through the ground. Jonquils mean Spring. Hope to again hear from you as to how things are going.

Lots of love from us both
Mother.

[Art's father wrote the following in the top margin.]
Dear boy: Sure nice to hear from you. Awful busy today. Do hope you got my first letter to you (air mail) January 14. We'll try to keep a record of letters mailed you. Of course, will be wondering often when we'll hear from you & on acct of delayed mail you will wonder about our letters to you. God bless & keep you safe—dear son, is my daily prayer for you & all the brave boys & men everywhere.
Dad

Art Bushing's Unit overseas (left side of photo)

Art Bushing's Unit overseas (right side of photo)
Art is in the 2nd row from the top, 10th from the right

Marvin P. Breeden — Stanardsville, Va Route 1 Box 29
Frederick H. Price — Indianola, Miss.
Wilbur R. Giesking — 2702 N. Penn. St. Indianapolis, Indiana
Richard G. Carson — 1136 Rosedale Ave, Glendale, Calif.
William Pomair — New Orleans, La
Jesse Taylor — Forest City, N.C.
John O'Connell — Bayonne N.J.
Edward R. Utrup — Watervliet, Mich. R.R.2
Loyle R. Armstrong — Versailles, Ohio R.H.2
Erman Moore — 191 Reynolds St. Rochester, New York
Robert W. Crimi — Moorestown, N.J.
James A. Long — Aley 12. N.C.
Kendall P. Bates — 1901 N Court St. Rockford, Illinois
Alex Miko — P.O. Box 140 Convoy Ohio
Paul W. Harper — Norfolk, Va.
Daniel J. Lindow — Owensboro, Ky.
Dan M Howle — Darlington, S.C.
Eugene K. Oak — Eureka, Calif.
John B. Hall — Banner, Ky.
Carl L. Soderstrom — 615 E. Amherst, Ave. Englewood Colo.
George Shaffer — Phila., Pa.   (Art's Unit Overseas)
Anthony L. Sinisi — Altoona, Pa.
James J. Kelley — Chicago
Kenneth F. Curtis — Gardiner, Maine
Walter Wlodyka — Buffalo, N.Y.
John W. Pratt — Leaksville, N.C.
Bill Welch — Balto. Md.
Emil Root — Muskegon, Michigan (876 Wood St.)

O. + Bushing — 17th from Left,
2nd Row from Top

3

ATLANTIC VOYAGE

JAN. 25, [1945], EAST COAST

T he night of departure has arrived and in another hour we leave our barracks. The day passed swiftly for me. I was on detail [Army term for a job assignment] first to clean up officers' barracks and in the afternoon on the trash truck. With the exception of a few details and a "dry run" practice entrainment, the company did nothing. The general feeling among the men seems to have vacillated considerably—one time up, one time down. Part of the time, a quietness filled the squad room; at other times, songs and forced laughter met the ear. The rapid advances of the Russians since Jan. 12th (the date the big drive began) are very encouraging. Today they are reported to hold a 57 mile front on the Oder [River] with two crossings, and also a large German pocket isolated in East Prussia. However, the intense cold (1 degree above o in New York today) foretells a cold crossing and probably a very rough sea. For the past hour, many of the men have either participated [in] or watched the "Transport Sweepstakes." This, which I will describe in great detail at a later day, is very popular with the platoon and consists of horse racing with all the betting and excitement of Bay Meadows of Santa Anita.

My spirits are unusually high. One reason is perhaps that my sinus pressure has been relieved by nose drops from the hospital.

Another reason is the adventure of the unknown which I referred to in a discussion last night.

Jan. 26, 1945
At Sea

We fell out [another Army term for an order to exit] of the barracks last night; and, contrary to usual practice, we waited only about twenty minutes before marching to the train. As we stood in formation out in front of the company area, a few of us sang one song after another just to improve the general morale (including our own). The moon was almost full and a few fleecy clouds adorned the heavens. Directly under the moon hung a giant V which for me portended Victory.

In a fast electric train we sped to New York, boarded the ferry, and pushed and shoved through the ice to the other side. Three or four of us continued to laugh and crack jokes in an attempt to cheer the gang. Many refused to respond. We learned that one man from 2nd Plat. was not present for final roll call. Fine time to go "over the hill." Very soon he would have to go over the side of the ship.

Lt. Carol (2nd Plat.) and Lt. Thomas (3rd Plat.) seemed strangely like enlisted men tonight. Lt. Thomas was very sleepy and seemed just a bit apprehensive. Carol's jokes seemed intended to cheer himself as much as anything else.

As we stood in line on the dock waiting to go on board, Red Cross ladies gave us welcomed hot coffee, doughnuts and chocolate bars. They were very kind. At 12:20 A. M. a man on the dimly lit dock yelled, "Bushing, Arthur S.," I replied and my foot was on the gangplank. My duffel bag, pack, rifle, etc., were a bit cumbersome, but I was on board. The ship, a navy vessel, has better accommodations than I had expected. With a minimum of confusion we were assigned bunks and our life on board had begun. I went directly to sleep but was awakened about three to hear the men on the bunk above me still playing cards. After a couple of suggestive remarks, I convinced them that it was time good little soldiers were abed.

July 24 (1946)
Added later from Paris

At the time the above was written, certain details were left out for obvious reasons. I boarded the "General Brooks" [we were told that it was a navy transport] at 12:20 on the morning of Jan. 26. To the best of our knowledge, about sixty ships of all types are in our convoy. The entire 14th Regt. [about 5,000 men] was on our vessel, including part of Div. Hdq.

Letters from Dotty to Art
607 W. Glenwood,
Friday
[January 26-30, 1945, excerpt]

Darling,
Home again, home again, jiggety jog; Dottie is home again all in a fog! Pome.
Tues. I wrote you, Wednesday Jenks and I went into town and saw a show, and yesterday I left. All night no sleep, so tonight am a little sleepy. Just a little. Whew, golly. The "Fall of the House of Usher" is on the radio, and I am in the house alone. Shghaaa. Gives me the creeps. Mother and Dad went to Record Breakers, but I thought I'd just stay home—write you a letter, then get into bed early....
I must go now, to dream of our love. It makes me so happy all the time. People who know the circumstances look at my smiling face and ask if tears wouldn't be more appropriate (no one has put it quite that boldly), but I merely smile some more & shake my head. The present separation cannot touch the deep well of my complete happiness in sharing our lives together.
Such is the solid foundation of
Our love,
Dotty.
P.S. The stork is charged with a lot of things which should more properly be alarmed on a lark.
P.P.S. "STORK TRUTH"—three Polish soldiers were practicing Eng. They were discussing wife of a colleague who was unhappy because childless. "She is unbearable," said one. "No, inconceivable," corrected 2nd. "You are both wrong—she is impregnable," said 3rd. Courtesy of Ladies Home Journal.

Monday
[Jan. 29, 45, excerpt]
My Dearest,
Wonder where you are tonight, what you are doing, what you are thinking. I am at home, just finished a huge washing with Dad's help, and I am thinking of you, you, you. I also washed my hair and will do another little washing of stockings when I finish this. I worked all day today, as every Monday, working mostly on the revision of the church roll. I run into some interesting things in the process, also some puzzling things. I call somebody to find out about somebody and learn lots of things about somebody else. It's a great system. I am jealous of all these gals that are gonna be mothers. There are at least ten of my friends and relatives who are due to have babies this spring. Never saw anything like it. Don't know what this younger generation is coming to. Tsk, Tsk. Wonder what they got what I ain't got? All of which reminds me of a couple of—No. I told you those. Skip it....
Our love,
Dotty

Tuesday Night
[Jan 30 '45, excerpt]
My luscious, lonely, lovable, Lumpkin—
Li love lu. Lere's la loundest, liggest, lretettiest lmoon loutside lonight lat li've leen lin la llong lime!
Bob Hope is rattling away on the radio with his nonsense and more nonsense.
I've really had a churchy day today. I told you about the meeting this afternoon & who was to be there. It was held at Jimmy Smith's church. Dr. Bates & Dr. Case were there, but I didn't get to speak to them on account of I left early to go to the 2nd Presbyterian church for supper and the young people's meeting with speech by said Miss Rachel Benfer, who will speak at our church tomorrow night, goody. She is a lulu. She bounces with vivacity, almost. It is easy to see why she was chosen as sec'y for young people's work for Board of National missions.
You know, I've come to conclusion that the church work doesn't really grip you, nor do you have a very good idea of the work that is being carried on by your church locals—national—entire, if you just go to church on Sunday morning. You get lots of spiritual nourishment on Sun. morns, but you have to be a part of some organization in the church before you find out what really goes on, before you become a

44

part of what is going on. It is really doing my heart good to be getting back into the work and becoming a part of it....

The news looks better and better, or worse & worse depending on which side you favor. Me, I favor the Allies.

Russians within 73 miles of Berlin. Looks as if the Germans are bound to crack soon. Before you get there, I hope. If you are going there. Wherever you are going, my dear, my love follows you.

Your loving wife,
Dotty

Jan. 26th, 1945
First Night, At Sea

It was a soul-shaking thrill tonight to go aft and stand in the bow of the boat; to watch the golden path of the moon, wavering upon the water; to see the growing swell rise and fall; and to feel the steady north wind beat salt spray into the pores of my face. I knew tonight that I loved the sea, that I had always loved it but had never known how much.

I skulked along the shadows of the deck (I was not supposed to be out here) and climbed up on the poop deck. A full moon shone on the water; I spread my feet and let my imagination run full sway. The wind had increased considerably; white caps rode high on the crest of a wave and then slipped with a receding sigh into a great valley. The boat rolled back and forth and spray flew over the rail. Black shadows could be seen on either side, but not a light gave away the fact that other ships were near. Far out in front I could see a small boat, a cutter I believe, crossing back and forth before our bow. We counted many ships today, and there are surely many more over the horizon.

Standing there on the deck, my arms akimbo and my legs wide apart, I could easily imagine the thrill that Drake, Magellan, and a hundred others knew. I could imagine what it was to have almost nothing but the stars and a compass to steer by. (I think that we have lost sight of the stars since we found "more advanced methods" for following our course.). They had nothing but the dim unknown ahead, knowing not whether the next wave was friend or foe. I love the sea.

Dearest Heart,

The ship rolls gently from side to side; the sun shines down on the full well of the ocean; brisk and invigorating air sweeps the deck, but here below it is warm, very warm. Most of us are feeling a peculiar sensation deep down in the pit of our stomachs, but so far no one has found it necessary to stagger to the rail. Our first day at sea has been a very beautiful one, and we can only hope that succeeding days will be similar. Darling, the ocean is wonderful! I now know what prompted Byron to write, "Roll on thou deep and dark blue ocean, roll, Ten thousand fleets sweep over thee in vain...."

We left our camp in the light of a moon almost full. Fleury clouds made the sky even more beautiful and just beneath the moon was a giant "V." portentous, I thought, of the new future. The night was cold but our clothing was warm. A few of us sang to liven up the party but many of the fellows were solemn. The face of the future is clouded in uncertain and it is a natural instinct to look upon it with trepidation and apprehension....

My spirits have been high for the past few days and I am looking forward with a great deal of expectation to the future. The food is good and to my joy, we get three meals a day. I hope I can report as good a day tomorrow as today.

With each passing day I find new meaning to the depth of
Our love,
Bushy
P.S. Beautiful sunset tonight with myriad colors.

Jan. 27, 1945
Second Night, At Sea

There was quite a marked change in this second day at sea as compared with the first. We rolled a great deal last night and during the daylight hours it was worse. White caps covered a very green sea, giant swells rose and fell and a strong wind blew salt spray over the rail. The day was cloudy, visibility was poor, and the convoy moved closer together. Once on the bow and once on the starboard I was doused thoroughly. The second time the water broke all the way across the ship.

Beginning at breakfast and increasing as time went on, more and more [men] were affected by the roll and sway. Men could be seen hanging onto the ropes next to the rail—their heads low. Others never reached the deck. No one laughed because no one knew who would be next. Sgt. O'Connell, my squad leader, was very sick, with a very bad sinus and running a fever. I have avoided most of the ill effects so far, although my stomach felt less than good. I ate two meals and slept a great deal. Fresh air is one of the best treatments that I have found. I still find the greatest thrill to go aft and stand on the forward deck. There I stand and watch the great waves rise and fall, the wild waves lift up fiery dragon heads and then hesitate, be struck by a larger wave, recede. The sea has a strange, intriguing power.

I am reading Sandburg's Abraham Lincoln, the Prairie Years and find it excellent. Sandburg's prose is merely extended poetry it seems. As I read into the character of the man, I find a new kinship with him. Sandburg develops the dreams of a dreamer, the stirring of action still hidden in the womb. I too have known the stirring of purpose and [the] future within my inner being. As a small boy I felt that there must be vast realms of knowledge beyond my reach. I felt that there must be a key to open the doors of wisdom, but I knew not where to find the key.

When I was twelve I walked to school one morning with my classmates. I was told of the many who had gone up to the altar in the revival at my church [Methodist Church in Jamestown]. Without knowing why, I began to cry softly. I knew that I should go up to the altar that very night and confess Christ as my Savior. I did. I had found the key but the key presented only the threshold to my anxious desires.

For years I have felt that there was some divine purpose behind my existence. My prayer is often a prayer that I be shown the way for me. "Lord, I believe that somewhere in the giant catacombs of life there is a niche which I was intended to fill. Direct my path to that niche and help me to fill it to the utmost of my ability and talent."

My belief and conviction have been confirmed at every turn. In elementary school I tied for second place at graduation. In high school, by a turn of fate I graduated at the head of my class. [Hannah Vaughn, who had led the class for four years, moved to California sometime after Christmas in our senior year, so the turn of fate left me in first position by default.] It was in high school too that I learned to mix socially. I was active in dramatics, in music, in sports. In college I continued to take part in a wide variety of social activities, and it was *there that I found myself intellectually. In high school the encouragement of Mary Ellen Roberts, my [third year] English instructor, gave me impetus to my long-standing interest in literature and especially poetry. This led to my majoring in English literature at college, and there I also achieved some degree of success. God was good to me. Especially did I feel that He was guiding me when I met my future wife and enjoyed her companionship for the remainder of my college days. [We first met in Pearsons Dining Hall at 6:00 p.m. on March 10, 1940, and we began immediately to date.] In the Army I have had some so-called breaks (even though at this moment I am in the infantry going "over the pond").*

One of the reasons that I was so definite in answering a question put to me on my way home, Dec. 31st, was this deep faith in the purpose of God for my life. I found a certain Ike Conaster in Crossville who had brought his mother over from Jamestown for dental work. He agreed to take Dotty and me home. His mother asked me in the course of my trip if I thought that I would return from overseas. "Of course," I said, as though the question were rudimentary. I do believe that I will return from the war. I believe that I will return to fulfill the purpose of a Divine Planner. I believe that my field is in the classroom and that God will direct my path in service to Him and to my fellow man.

Letter from Art to Dotty
Third Day At Sea
1945

Dearest,

I fear that no letters will be mailed until we arrive at our destination, but I shall try to write a bit every day in order to keep with my thoughts and events insofar as I can relate them. 'Tis strange the working of the mind. There are days when my pen flows effortless across the page, and there are days when it is only with concentrated effort that I write that the weather was cloudy, the sea calm today. I am still unable to do much of value during the day except sleep. I never tire of going "top side" and enjoying to the utmost the sea and the sky. Today most of the fellows have recovered their sea legs and I think that we will have less and less difficult. I am discovering certain tricks to getting around on the boat that are proving of value. One of these consists of falling up the steps. It really happens that when the ship rolls starboard (right), one may run with almost no effort up the steps toward the starboard side. Another similar occurrence is noted when

48

one is walking along the deck and the boat rolls. It seems as though one could fly merely by lifting the arms.

We can buy candy and cigarettes on the boat but only by the box and the carton. Yesterday peanut bars (not Tom's) were sold. And today it was chocolate. A box sells for 80¢ and the cigarettes for 50¢. I guess I will save a number of half dollars. The regular food continues good and a candy supplement is hardly necessary (even for me). I especially enjoy the hot coffee we have. Almost always hereto for, coffee has been cold by the time I got it. I still wish there was something else to drink. With every meal I could drink a quart of milk, nicht wahr?

By the way, a few ocarinas, flutes, (small plastic type) and harmonicas were issued today. I was not around at the time and so failed to get one. Hope to be luckier next time. Would like to have either or both. From the Red Cross we received "diddy" bags containing a book, stationery, pencil, sewing kit, etc. I think that my personal PX is rather well stocked for the nonce.

Jan. 28
Third Night, At Sea

Today for the first time in my life I tasted communion wine. In fact I suppose that it is the first time that I have ever tasted wine. With all due reverence, I thought that it tasted like cough medicine. The service was very short, but it was none the less meaningful. I enjoyed the singing very much.

Yesterday we were issued five large boxes of silhouette model airplanes for the company to assemble. We are wondering just when we will get paper dolls to cut out. Also received phrase books in French and German. It would seem that my former hopes concerning our destination are entirely off. A few harmonicas and more ocarinas and flutes were issued, but I was not lucky. We are able to buy candy and cigarettes, but only by the box and carton: 80¢ for the former and 50¢ for the latter. Glad I can save my 50¢.

The sea was relatively calm today, and most of the cases of seasickness have more or less recovered. My constant headaches persist. The weather is not a friend of sinus even though I do love it otherwise.

The thoughts of home and love are long, long thoughts. Dreams of Dotty fill my mind, and I look for a clear sky and fair winds.

Letter excerpt from Art to Dotty
Fourth Day – At Sea

Dearest Heart,

'Tis quieter now. I can feel the steady vibration of the powerful motor below, a heating pipe pops with irregular cadence, and the ventalor inhales the air with an unmannerly noise. All else is silent. The ship rocks gently with a motion that is almost caressing and the boys sleep. Yes, it is a good time to think, and read, and write....

By the way, in case water has no effect on telepathy, I received your monogram tonight and I was greatly helped by it. My entire outlook is made bright by my faith in your faith. Your belief in me is far greater than my belief in myself. God was very kind when He gave me such a perfect complement to my nature. I need you, Darling, when we are together, and when we are separated by leagues.

I ran into Kinsey today and we spoke Dutch for half an hour. We hope to get together every day and converse a bit. Saw Mac tonight and he is agree. It feels good to limber up my tongue again with a few g-g-g's etc. I find, that though a bit rusty in spots, I have little difficulty in expressing my ideas. One reason is perhaps that I have attempted to think in Dutch a little each day.

Jan. 29
Fourth Night, At Sea

It was a consoling thought to find today that Abe Lincoln was once a mere private in the U. S. Army during the time of the Indian Wars. Of course, the consolation is merely rationalization because at another time he was Capt. Lincoln.

Passing thought: The pessimist has almost all of the past to prove his pessimism; the optimist has all of the future to prove his faith.

I slept late this morning. Sleep, when I can get it, is my only escape from the intense headaches with which I continue to be troubled. More than once (I am ashamed to admit) I look at the rail and wonder what it would be like to measure the distance in one leap. The intense pain thus often blots out all that I have to live for (I have everything) and causes me to lose that most valuable of all virtues— perspective. I ask the question, "How long, O Lord, how long?"

One of the most beautiful of the scenes upon the sea is the mystical effect of the moon as spot light, shining upon a certain portion of the water. It happens in this way: When there are clouds in the sky, often entire areas of water will be dark, save for one. Through the clouds shines the moon to make bright this single spot. If a ship is in the lighted area perchance, the observer has all the more reason to exclaim, "The heavens declare the glory of God, and the firmament showeth His handiwork."

In one of my last visits with the Evauls (College friends, Phil '40 and Peggy '39), a rousing discussion developed when I asked Phil for his interpretation of a portion of the scripture for the day: "Be kindly affectioned one to another, with brotherly love, in honor preferring one another" (Rom: 12:10). The last phrase brought forth the question. The meaning to me was that a fellow Christian would be given preference, that is that his company should be sought before that of others, a favor to him before a favor to one who is not of the faith. Dotty and Phil derived a somewhat different meaning, and they were substantiated by several commentaries. One, I believe, backed my contention. When Dotty and I were at home in Oct., I brought the subject to Dad's attention, and he gave his interpretation in almost the same words as I had used. On Sunday while the Communion text was being read, I was struck by this passage: "As we have therefore opportunity, let us do good unto all men, especially unto those who are of the house-hold of faith" (Gal. 6:10). I believe that a large Bible has Rom. 12:12 as a cross reference, but this I must check. At any rate, it is an interesting point, and one which the fellows at Maryville in our [study] Group stressed over and over.

Jan. 30
Fifth Night, At Sea

Had my first pass overseas tonight. However, it was only to the officers' mess for a concert. The place was crowded and I sat on the floor with Buel Root and Carl Soderstrom, (friends). Interested and interesting groups. The good program included "Variations on a Theme" by Paganini; Mozart's "Symphony 39 in E-Flat"; Dvorak's "Symphony for the New World"; and "Nutcracker's Suite," by Tchaikovsky. Such a program does take one away, and I enjoyed it very much. I found that Buel also enjoys classical music a great deal. At his invitation I attended choir practice this morning. About twenty of us met for an hour and a half. Good leader and some good voices. Hope I can continue to go.

51

Letter excerpt from Art to Dotty
Fifth

Dearest,

Although I failed to make connections with Kinsey today, I did practice something besides Dutch. Beul attended a choir practice yesterday and told me about it. Well, why not? I know, I can't sing but I just love to try. Every morning at nine-thirty is the practice. It is not only fun but also a break from the tortuous monotony of having nothing constructive to do. I was one of three first bases today. Yes, it is a bit high for me.

I also furthered my horizon today by obtaining a pass—my first overseas.... I had to hold your hand; hope you didn't mind. I lost myself very completely in the music, and felt your presence. By the way, didn't we see a movie in which the "New World Symphony" was played as background? I can't place where it was.

We get a smattering of the news, but little more than highlights. I suppose that it will be very hard to know what goes on from now on except through the reading of Time.

I am tired and the hour is very late. I must to bed to sleep, and aye, perchance to dream. I dream of you almost nightly now and it is as though I were with you a few hours each day. I love you, Darling, and miss you.

Goodnight, My Love.
Bushy

Letter excerpt from Art to Dotty
At Sea
6th (8)

Dearest Heart,

For the first time today, we saw a bit of the Navy's fire power. Nothing but a bit of target practice, but plenty good—both powerful and accurate. I'm certainly glad that it's on our side rather than against us.

Most of the afternoon was taken up by seeing a very lousy movie, "Johnny Eager" with Robt. Taylor. Very conventional, but it did help to pass the time. This morning I sang again and tomorrow we broadcast over the ship's PA. system. Actually the choir wouldn't be half bad with a couple of week's practice. I very seldom have had occasion to take part in the renowned "full session" in the Army, but here on board there is so little space for activity that it is some time unavoidable. Tonight we discussed everything from radar and the speed of our ship to wild mixtures of drinks and unusual American dishes such as rattlesnake and pig's feet. What a life!

Pardon me if I wander, but my mind is prone to be like that in these days....

Jan. 31
Sixth Night

Our motors were out and we drifted behind the convoy for a bit of gunnery practice today. Big 5'ers and ack-ack fired on flares shot up and did a very accurate job. Glad they are on our side. Counted a large number of ships in our convoy including a number of troop ships of varying sizes.

Very marvelous sunset tonight reminding me of sunsets seen at Maryville long ago with Dotty. Those days do seem far away. Reading in Time *tonight, I find that records reveal that 3/5 of the men in the Armed forces have four years of college or more. College grads who are doing their bit in the dear old infantry, many led by men with less than an eighth grade education. I'm really not bitter.*

Feb. 1
Seventh Night

For some time I have felt that Truth was, that Truth is, an entity. For hundreds of years science and philosophy (including religion) have gone along seeking ultimate Truth—each in its seemingly separate fields of thought. I am convinced that the ultimate for each will be found in one single conclusion. Truth is of God and the final discovery in science and religion will be found in an identical answer.

Some of us follow one line in search of ultimates until we build for ourselves a modern leaning tower of Pisa. Bits of knowledge are like blocks which we build up bit by bit. When only one line is followed, we build into the air until finally the tower falls. It falls unless we are broad enough in our perspective. If we can see only the unity in the final analysis of Truth, then we have the secret of following the true line of research. We build on a broad base in the style of the Pyramids —a base broad enough to provide a firm foundation.

Today the sea was delightfully calm and reminded me of the fame of the Blue Mediterranean. The afternoon was very warm and the sun made the deck a very pleasant place to spend the time. I talked to Bill

53

Kinsey (Stanford friend) from noon until supper and then worked with him on the recorded program for tomorrow. He's on detached duty doing that.

Sgt. Carl Soderstrom is one of the interesting personalities that I have encountered in the Army. From Colorado, "Sod" was in the 82nd Battalion in Camp Roberts about the time I was there. He made cadre and went to [Camp] Blanding, Fla. He was there in IRTC for several months and came to Fort Benning the day before I arrived.

In a very short time we found that we had something in common and became friends in short order. "Sod" is deeply religious, perhaps displaying as much fervor and conviction as anyone I have ever met. I think that he is also as dogmatic in his fundamental beliefs as anyone I have ever known.

His beliefs concerning the Bible and religion are extremely fundamental. He believes that the prophecies are being fulfilled and that the judgment is near at hand when Christ will return. He is a follower of the Moody Bible Institute, Frank Norris, Schofield and other fundamentalists.

I fear that I might be classified as a lost heathen if he but knew some of my deeper beliefs and convictions.

Letter from Art to Dotty
At Sea 1945 (9)

Darling,

I left off last night before I had a chance to finish all that I wanted to say. You see, the system I have been using has been to make notes of what I intend to write and then enlarge upon it, as I write. Last night I managed to get the notes written, but before I could complete them in letter form I was too sleepy to hold a pen. I'll have much to write about next letter if I can only continue the system during the interim when no letters can go out. At any rate, I shall begin now where I left off last night: For some time I have felt that Truth, was that Truth is an entity. For hundreds of years science and philosophy (including religion) have gone along seeking ultimate Truth—each in its seemingly separate fields of thought. I am convinced that the ultimate for each will be found in one single conclusion. (This enables one to see the necessity of perspective in any field of interest. By perspective, I mean the placing of proper values and proportions on values.) Truth, is of God and the final discovery in science and in religion will be found in this single answer.

In regard to this generalizing, there are those who, of course, seldom search for knowledge; and yet I suppose no man fails at one time or another to put two and two together to get an answer. Some of us follow one line in search of ultimatum until we build for ourselves a modern leaning tower of Pisa. Bits of knowledge are like blocks which are build up bit by bit. But eventually, when only one line is followed, we build into the air until finally the tower falls. It falls unless we are broad enough in perspective. If we can only see the unity in the final analysis of Truth, we have the secret of following the true line of research. (I do not mean research in the technical sense that it is commonly used, but rather in a very broad way, meaning to include the every day think of John Doe and family.) By varying our interests, by seeing other points of view, by examining findings of Truth in fields other than our own, we build on a broad base in the style of the Pyramids—a base that provides a firm and lasting foundation.

Yesterday afternoon the sea was as calm as Norris [Norris Lake in Knoxville]. The sun shown down and a slight breeze blew across the deck. I sat with Kinsey next to the rail and we talked from noon until time for supper. As he mentioned, it feels good to be able to talk with some one known before. It will be swell when I can talk with Ted again. By a very strange coincidence I ran into an old friend from Roberts today. He was a corporal who befriended me in the 80th Bn. When I went to that outfit, he saw fit to put me on all the ammunition loading details. He came to this unit about the same time I did. Speaking of friends, Beul and I are spending a lot of time waiting in chow lines together, going to choir practice, etc. We find that we have more and more things in common. Hope you can keep in touch with Dorcas now and then. Just in case you can get George Kahin's address, I think we should write him too.

By the way, I think you know that I cannot put dates on these letters at sea for obvious reasons. I have put the year for the sake of history, when we reread these ages and ages hence. With the exception of the first letter which I wrote, I have put down page numbers for the sake of continuity. I hope the letters arrive in some semblance of order. Until I find out more concerning our supply of paper, V-Mail, etc. I shall limit letters to you and the folks, (with one or two exceptions—an overdue letter to Hal, "Mom" Pratt, Tom, etc.) I hope everyone will understand my situation. By a foolish mistake, I sent your first letter "free",—I thought it was to go off the boat the first day. Thus it may take some time to arrive. I shall send succeeding letters airmail and will also write a V-Mail, hoping that it will go quickly in case the airmail doesn't. As you get news, perhaps you can exchange it with Mother & Dad, just in case their letters do not come through. Another passing thought, we have been told that in case we are reported missing in action our folks at home are urged <u>not</u> to attempt to contact us through the American Red Cross. In case we were behind enemy lines and not captured, this would only give away the fact that we were at large. That's just in case of an emergency.

When I was at POE, I made out the new allotment as I told you. When the record was checked with me later, it seems that my old $7.50 was not cancelled, but my new $18.25 was taken out. Thus two bonds will be coming until I can correct the mistake. Perhaps it is just as well for I doubt that I shall have a great deal of use for money for some time.

In rereading these letters (I still have all but the first), I see that on the third day I failed to mention a new experience for me. In all the communions that I have taken all over the country, I had never before tasted communion wine. We had a very simple but impressive communion service, and I was glad that I could take part. We have continued choir practice each day and that too has helped a great deal.

A couple of nights ago I saw one of the most beautiful sunsets I have ever seen, excepting only a few of the outstanding ones which we saw from behind the chapel [on the Maryville College campus]. The entire sky was filled with color. On one side were long streaks of blue sky with interlaced strips of delicately tinted bluish-pinks (That combination sounds very strange, but it is the only way I know to describe it.) I have never seen such color. The west was filled with ever changing golden hues and I watched as the sun sank silently into the depths of the sea. I silently thanked God for the view, and squeezed your hand a bit tighter.

Darling I don't know what I would do if I did not have the little folder with me. It means a great deal to be able to look upon your face even though an ocean and thousands of miles separate us. After these letters arrive, there may be more long delay. I hope not, but it may be expected. I shall be strong in the knowledge that our faith in each other and in God shall overcome all hardships and difficulties that face us. Our months of fellowship and love together built a bulwark that can withstand any eventuality. I kissed you goodnight and goodbye with the conviction that our union has been as perfect as a Divine and Loving God could have planned for two of His children whom He has blessed.

My prayers are for you and for our Love which is eternal. Nothing can destroy the strength of
                    Our Love, Bushy

Letter excerpts from Dotty to Art
Friday Morning
Feb. 2

Dearest Hussyband,

The groundhog saw his shadow today, so we are warned of six more weeks of winter weather. I wonder what those six weeks will bring forth on the battle fronts. The big three are new in secret session discussing peace plans, the Russians are a little over thirty miles from Berlin and still going strong, and American-British forces are meeting a little less resistance on the Western German lines. Yesterday came the joyful news that 510 American prisoners in a prison camp on Luzon (the fellows were taken prisoners on Bataan) had just been freed. All this news will no doubt be quite stale by the time this letter reaches you, but one never knows, does one. I am almost afraid to let the wild hopes of near peace raise themselves in my mind, but I am having a struggle with said hopes....

There isn't much of news here since yesterday, except dat I dot a dasty code in da head. I bind drickig red medecid ad fruit juice for all ib worth. Last dite Mother bade be go to bed early. I put so many nose drops in my nose that it came out my ears!... Love, Dotty

---

Feb. 2
Eighth Night, At Sea

Tonight we were told our destination along with a few other bits of information. It is hard, I suppose, for every GI to realize for the first time that he is at last within a combat zone, to realize that in a very short time he will face that for which he has been training for long months, perhaps even years. Along with everyone else, I have never been able to picture myself in combat. I wonder how I will react.

[YEARS LATER I REALIZED THAT WE WERE IN A COMBAT ZONE AS SOON AS THE CONVOY LEFT NEW YORK. AT THE TIME, I HAD NO IDEA THAT THE GERMAN SUBMARINES WERE SO SUCCESSFUL IN SINKING OUR SHIPS.]

Those mad Russians are at it again. They are reported within 45 miles of Berlin, although the Germans declare the reports false to the effect that the Red forces are in Frankfort (50 miles from Berlin). Nazi reinforcements are being rushed to Danzig in an effort to save it. The Americans are still pushing against the Siegfried line but no decisive gains are reported.

All indications are that the Big Three Conference (long awaited) is either in progress or very close at hand. This meeting should prove to be history making in its results.

Feb. 5
Eleventh Night, At Sea

On Saturday night I spent the entire evening writing Dotty, Mother and Dad, Tom [Jones], "Mom" Pratt [mother of Helen and Ted, and the one who did much for us when we were married in San Jose], and Mary Ruth [my sister-in-law]. Tomorrow is the last day for mail to be taken on the boat. Have written Dotty every day for a total of sixteen pages plus a V-Mail. Also three letters home plus V-Mail.

[Since mail arrived in the States at uncertain intervals, I kept an account of consecutive pages that I wrote Dotty. I also had devised a simple code based on the numbers in the date. When I used only numbers, she knew that each one identified a key word in each paragraph of the letter. Taken together, she could determine information that otherwise would not get by the censor.]

Sunday proved to be perhaps the most eventful day of the trip. I have been practicing with the choir every day and have enjoyed it greatly. As one of the three or four 1st basses, I have contributed little; but the experience was good for me, and I am a good listener. We sang two numbers in the worship service Sunday morning and heard a good sermon, "The ship of Zion" by Chaplain Hail. Many nautical terms and references were made, but it was not, in the non-nautical sense, "all wet." (Low humor!)

At noon on Sunday I found that another concert was to be presented in the afternoon; however, I also found that there would be one ticket per platoon. Later Soderstrom found an extra one and very kindly gave it to me. Feeling a bit guilty, I nevertheless went on my way. I got there late but in time to hear most of "The Emperor's Waltz" (Straus). During the next number, "Shostakovich's Fifth," I let my mind wander thru the porthole. Fog was heavy, as it has been for the past two days, but I could see the gentle rise and fall of the ocean as the boat rolled from side to side. The mysterious deep seemed a particularly appropriate setting for the playing of the deep and moving symphony. I was held enthralled by the music and by the sea. (The third movement is by far the most beautiful for me.) In addition to the view of the ocean in the distance was the view reflected in the porthole glass suspended above the aperture. In this I could see the swift rush of the foaming brine alongside the boat. That too seemed to hear the music I heard and dancing in a fast beat with the same time. The following number, Franck's "D. Minor," was interrupted by a perfunctory physical examination for all enlisted men. We took up later to complete this symphony and also hear a collection of Offenbach themes. These were delightful in their lilting quality and added a final bon-bon for our complete menu of satisfying music. As I told Dr. Mack, the ship's dentist, who presented the program, it is always a rare thrill to listen to good music in the Service.

After supper I visited the Troop Office to obtain application blanks and more information concerning the Armed Forces Institute. Met an elderly fellow named Ludman (Pfc.) who seems to have enlisted. He is certainly over age. Very nice and helpful. Knows Maryville, having had two sisters and a brother attending. Interested in my ASTP training and may prove helpful. [College records show that Mary C. Ludman was in the class of 1933; Mayme Carol Ludman, in class of 1937].

[Because of censorship rules, here and elsewhere I omit names of locations. At this point we anchored in Portsmouth Harbor.]

We anchored Sun. night and I went to lower deck rather late. Lights were visible, but were probably ships' lights. We had entered the Channel, possibly the most influential body of water in the entire world. The water was quiet now and lapped steadily against the ship's side. The fog-filled air gave nothing to the sight. It was another of those great moments in the history of one dreary-eyed GI. I know that back of that mist-filled beyond lies the glory of a King and the grandeur of England herself. I thought of the cold and unseeing eye of Caesar as he approached the shores of this "uncivilized isle," sixteen centuries ago. Little did he know or perhaps care concerning the vast role that his faraway corner of his empire would play in the future of the world. And did St. Augustine, bringing Christianity to this pagan land, know as he neared its shores that Pilgrimages would be made famous by Chaucer, that Henrys and Georges would rise and fall, that Shakespeare would come and remain, that a nation would grow slowly but surely into manhood and withstand the tempests of men and nature? Did he know as he peered into this dim unknown, into the haze of the horizon, that it was England?

Old William the Conqueror in 1066 must have looked upon England as a vassal state to be added to his Empire. "What a rich gem

Vol. 2 No. 9   Sunday 4 February 1945   Aboard Transport

EASTERN FRONT

In Silesia, Nazi resistance has stiffened to the extent that Marshal Konev's 1st Ukrainian Army reports few gains save for added pressure to the northwest of Breslau in an attempt to strengthen a junction with forces of Marshal Zhukov.

The Nazis are also offering fierce resistance to all Russian thrusts in the vicinity of Frankfurt and it is possible that Zhukov and Marshal Rokossovsky are planning a twin drive on Stettin, German port on the Baltic, in order to divert German forces from Zhukov's main front.

WESTERN FRONT

Gen. Hodges' 1st Army has advanced 3 miles in the vicinity of Monschau, taking several German towns, while Gen. Patton's 3d Army is advancing on Prum. Marshal Von Rundstedt's armies are reported to be re-grouping for a stand against the allies along the Siegfried Line, though any such attempts are being severely hampered by allied Air Force attacks on German transportation systems, mainly railroads in the Ruhr.

Troops from the U.S. 7th Army and from the French 1st Army have entered Colmar and are clearing the city of the enemy, who is fleeing back across the Rhine.

The 6th German Panzer Division which took part in the German counter-offensive, and was badly mauled by U.S. troops in the Ardennes Forest, is reported as being shifted to the Eastern Front, but as yet has played no part in recent action against the Russians, due to being delayed en route by the ever increasing attacks by Allied Air Forces.

PACIFIC AREA

In the Philippines, Japanese troops in northern Luzon have been divided from those in the South by the advancing U.S. 6th Army. Advances on Manila are being made slowly due to difficult terrain.

In Burma, British troops continue their drives on Mandalay from new landings off the Arakan peninsula and from the British 14th Army Front about 12 miles west of Mandalay.

HOME FRONT

Joseph Grew, former Ambassador to Japan, and newly appointed Under-Secy of State, states that the U.S. has come to the aid of France in the forming and supplying of 4 French Divisions, and 300 supply and Air Corps units. It is planned to form at least 8 more French Divisions with U.S. aid. 100 ships have been overhauled and modernized, including the battleship, Richelieu.

Leo Crowley, Economic Administrator, announces that millions of tons of ammunition and supplies are being sent from the U.S. to the Russians to aid them in their current drive on the Eastern Front.

****

Flashes --

Jap troops lost in defense of Leyte more than 131,000.

Washington -- Singapore, Jap held Naval Base, bombed by 100 B-29s, in 90 minute raid.

Washington--- The nomination Henry Wallace, former Vice-President, to be Secreatary of Commerce, remains unsettled.

- -SOUVENIR COPY TO MY VALENTINE- -

The Jungleer, Atlantic Edition, page 1 (Feb. 4, 1945)

Souvenir Copy

Adviser--------Capt. Jacob L. Goldstein
(Regimental Information and Education
Officer)
Editor------------Pfc. Henry W. Ladman
Production--------Pfc. James G. Graham
Production----------Pfc. Will Gorsold
Special--------------T/4 William Grogan

DISTRIBUTED THROUGH THE COURTESY OF
YOUR FIRST SERGEANT.

PLEASE SHARE YOUR COPY------THE SUPPLY
IS LIMITED.

THIS IS IT

This is it!

In a few days we disembark.

Only time can tell what the future
holds for us.

Whatever that future is we are ready
to face it. Maybe it isn't by choice
that many of us are here and possibly
we don't like the thoughts of going
through what we know may be in store
for us.

But we'll do what is necessary------
others have gone ahead of us. We can
profit from their experiences. What
others have done we can do.

We are not super-men---- we're not
fighting to propagate a 'Master Race'.
We are fighting for America and the
right for men to live in peace.

We don't ask that bands welcome us--
we don't expect a hero's acclaim;

All we ask and hope for is that peace
may soon come to a war-torn world and
that we may soon return home.

We are well trained and do not lack
clothing, food or equipment.

We are here because we have a duty to
perform.

Let us do more than our best.

APPRECIATION TO THE NAVY

We all want to thank the United States
Navy for the complete sense of security
that we have felt on this trip.

But for the untiring efforts of Naval
Personnel, not only at Sea but on land,
our trip could not have been successfully completed.

SOMETHING YOU MAY WRITE HOME

The American Red Cross is in the field
to help you in many ways. One of those
services concerns vital communications
between you and your home. We can give
better and faster service to you in this
matter if you will write to your wife or
folks NOW telling them that if there is a
vital message for you they should give
it to the nearest Red Cross Chapter in
their home town. The Chapter will get
the message through faster than they
could.

The Chapter will wire the message to
Washington, D.C. where in turn it will
be sent by radio or cable to the Field
Director's Office where you are stationed. From there the message will be forwarded to you through your unit. What
often happens is that some well meaning
person will misinform you or will send
a vital message by slow mail, or you
might get a wire with inadequate information such as, "Mary is very ill." How
much better if your Red Cross Chapter
had been called and all the information
given so that you really know the situation. Also this would constitute ver-
ification if an emergency furlough is in
order.

Your Field Director is Mr. Grimm and
Asst. F. D. is Mr. Eads. We will continue to be with you wherever you go
and will do our best to help you with
your problems which come up back here.

HATS OFF

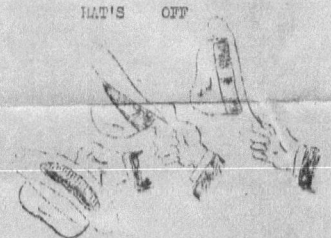

To the men of The Transportation Corps,
The Medical Administrative Corps and Special Service, all of whom saw to it that
our trip was completed comfortably, he-
althfully and enjoyably.
To the Ship's radio operators, who provided us with up-to-the-minute wireless
reports.
And to all the others who had a part in
bringing us here.

THE JUNGLEER MAY BE MAILED HOME
This copy of the Jungleer, as well as

The Jungleer, Atlantic Edition, page 2 (Feb. 4, 1945)

GERMAN DEFENSIVE CAPABILITIES (East Front)

In general, flat approaches along her eastern border make assault upon Germany from this area relatively easy. But several rivers make the attack more complex - the Warthe, Bober, Obra, and Oder. Main Nazi defenses are built upon the last - a 500 mile long, slow-moving stream, which bends west at one point deep into Germany, to within 50 miles of Berlin. But, supplemented by the ingenious fixed defenses constructed by captive labor, it can still prove a formidable obstacle. Soviet bridgeheads across the Oder (2 in number) are along its southern reaches in Silesia and do not immediately threaten the capital. The mountainous terrain of the Silesian coal-mine district can be defended by a stubbornly intrenched foe, unless rendered isolated by a flanking thrust to the northwest.

Western Front

German positions in the Netherlands are buttressed upon the Maas and Waal Rivers and designed to prevent any turning of the northern flank of the Siegfried Line in the neighborhood of Kleves and the Emmerick Gate. With the exception of the major American indentation beyond Aachen the Siegfried Line has not been breached, unless in its buffer outposts. In Alsace, between Strasbourg and Mulhouse, the artificial barriers of the Siegfried are protected by the Vosges Mountains and heavily forested areas that extend even north to Luxembourg and Belgium, as in the Ardennes and Monschau Forests. In the extreme south, the Siegfried Line, backed by the Black Forest, abuts on the gigantic wall of the Swiss Alps. Behind the maze of pill-boxes and dragons teeth (in some places 40 miles deep) flows the Rhine, 540 miles long and, in places, as much as 1500 feet wide.

Italy

The Italian Front is practically a self-contained theater as far as the Nazis are concerned. It has formidable natural barriers on all sides and harbors within such big industrial cities as Milan, Turin, Padua and Bologna. With his reported 28 divisions, Marshal Kesselring is reputed to be able to continue the war there alone after the defeat of Germany elsewhere and thereby prove Germany's ace bargaining asset at the Peace Conference. The line of defense now runs from Viareggio on the west coast, through the northern foothills of the rugged Appenines, to the impassable marshes of the Lagoon di Comacchio on the Adriatic. It is protected on the west, north, and northeast by the Swiss, Italian and Austrian Alps, respectively. The Brenner Pass, approximately 4,000 feet high and easily defended, provides excellent communication with Germany. The Po River, and the last network of modern highways ...

Italy (cont'd)

of troop movements and logistics in this area.

****

CONCERT THIS AFTERNOON

Dr. Mack, the Ship's Dentist, will again present a concert of recorded music this afternoon in the Troop Officers' Mess Hall at 1345 hours.

All those with passes are invited.

The program will include:

Shostakovich --	Symphony #5
Franck --	Symphony in D Minor
Offenbach --	Gaite Parisienne

****

CHOIR SINGS THIS MORNING

The choir is pleased to announce that they will sing on the Boat Deck this morning.

The times will be announced later.

WARMING THE BENCH - by Sgt Frank Deblois, ONS

Although nearly everyone admits that Marty Marion is the greatest shortstop in baseball, fans from Cleveland, Ohio, have presented a pretty strong case for Lou Boudreau, shortstop-manager of the Indians ----- Boudreau won AL batting title last year and set a fielding record of .944. His 122 double plays, 32 more than Marion made, set another record. Tops in runs-driven-in with 109 in AL was Junior Stephens, of Browns, another shortstop .....

The boxer of the year was Beau Jack, lightweight windmill from Atlanta, Ga., according to Ring Magazine ... Jack lost, won, lost the lightweight title last year... Now he's in the Army -- Interviewed in Paris, Cpl Billy Conn said he liked Joe Louis' fists better than Nazi bombings. "The Brown Bomber is the only boxer I'm anxious to meet again," said he ...More than 400 prominent American athletes have been killed since Pearl Harbor, according to a recent survey. Most famous were Sprinter Charlie Paddock, Polo Ace Tommy Hitchcock, All-American back Nile Kinnick and Track Star Lou Zemperini. ---- Sgt Joe DiMaggio recommends Honolulu as a post war training camp for the New York Yankees. He also says that Ted Williams is a better hitter than he (Joe DiMaggio) ever was ... Could be ..... Cincinnati Reds' Ed Heusser's 2.38 mark was best ERA for either league last year. Dizzy Trout was tops in AL with Detroit teammate Hal Newhouser right behind him. Trout and for my royal chest!" he must have announced to his henchmen as the coast of England met his gaze for the first time. I can see him standing in the prow of his boat, brandishing his long, thin sword in the light of the English sun: "A new province for my France!" He did not know that England would rise as inevitably as the rising of the morning sun. England would rise to lead the world, not for an instant, but for an age.

As I continued to gaze into the impenetrable fog, I thought of the great turning point in England's "Adonic" history, 1588, and the defeat of the famed Spanish Fleet. In these very waters, the English Navy turned to sail proudly for home, the laurels of victory, of supremacy hers. I wonder if a man aboard the victorious fleet, even at this decisive moment, knew as the coast of his native land appeared, if a single man knew the part that he had played in changing the history of his country and thus the history of the world.

Finally the thought of 1940 came to my mind, "The Battle of Britain." Hitler and his henchmen must have seen this land as a sunken star (stone), a mere stepping stone to be used in his plan for conquest. But the dim mist contained more than a sunken stone. Out of its depths arose a rock of faith, in her own past and in her own future. England preserved her life and thus preserved the life of the world. Truly the life that freedom-loving men know today would have been destroyed had England bowed. But England stands as a monument centuries old to the lamp of truth and freedom. May her glory remain and may her example live in the annals for all ages.

I was thrilled tonight to gaze into the impenetrable fog and know that behind that fog lay "England, the Unknown Isle."

Letter from Art to Dotty
At Sea, Cont.
(13)

My Darling,

"Tis Sunday and I believe the day has been one of the most pleasant of the journey. This morning I attended church service and we of the choir rendered two numbers. The sermon, a good one, was filled naturally enough with many references to the sea, the ship, and sailing in general. At lunch I found that another concert would be presented this afternoon but I also found that only one ticket was allowed for each platoon. Beul luckily was able to get that. By a bit of unexpected luck, "Sod" was given a pass and offered it to me. A real break indeed! As I told Beul, there would have been but two ways that I would have spent a more pleasant two hours—one with Mother and Dad; the other with you, my very lovely creature. We begin with the "Empire Waltz," the Shostakovich's Fifth, Franck's "D Minor," and an arrangement of Offenbach themes. As I sat listening to the great Russian symphony, my eyes wandered out a port hole to the open sea. Heavy fog shortened my sight, but I looked out on the gentle rise and fall of the swell in a quiet sea. This view was visible each time the ship rolled and the movement seemed to keep a certain beat with the mood of the music. The dim mystery of the depth corresponded also the depth of feeling and mystic quality of the moving music. From time to time I glanced up at the reflection of the water close to the ship in the mirror of the port hole glass suspended above the aperture. Here I could see the swift white foam rushing past the ship. Everything seemed in keeping with the beautiful music that came to my ear. I love the sea.

4

FRANCE BEFORE COMBAT

DEBARKATION

*M*ist and rain came down most of the day. The fog hung low. Usually we gripe about such conditions, but during the past few days we have welcomed the overcast. Bombs to not drop under such conditions, and our Captain is supposed to have reported that Nazi bombs fell here within the past few days.

A subdued feeling pervades the ship although a forced lightness of feeling is noted. We have a growing sense of being within the combat zone. Formerly, for five long years, Europe and World War II have been far away. Now we are at the very door, at a port, like all others, which was leveled in the passing cyclone of war.

I have been thinking lately of how eternally old each new experience is. We look forward with mixed feelings to the things of which we have heard but as yet are outside our realm of contact. At times we wonder just how we can possibly get through with some of these things. And yet experiences that seem most new and startling have occurred to others during endless ages.

I think of my first impression of England. Many millions have sighted her shores for the first time. I think at the moment particularly of our first stop on the shores of Europe and the startlingly new experiences to follow. Since D-Day, Fred [Story] (my uncle) and millions like him have waited just as I am doing with a feeling of perplexed wonder. What will the next day, the next week, the next month bring? Millions, I say, have been in my shoes; this experience is as old as the invasion day landing. Yet we still crane our necks, we still feel a bit lost, we still will count this as one of the high points in our experience. Human nature is an interesting study.

Five Hours Later

Even while I was writing the above we moved from our anchored position into the harbor [Le Havre]. I went on deck to see with my own eyes for the first time the destruction brought about in this war. At first I saw a long jetty completely bare. From what I saw later, I take it that this section had been cleaned of all debris in preparation for rebuilding. Some of the other men reported seeing sunken ships in the outer harbor, but I did not see these. We turned around in preparation for docking, and another view presented itself. I saw another long jetty, but this time the destruction of war was fully evident. A long skeleton of a warehouse told the tale. Twisted and bent in some places to the ground, it looked as though fire and bombs had eaten away everything but a few bones of a giant dinosaur. A few large pieces of machinery lay idly by as though tossed carelessly aside. A few concrete pillboxes were on the waterfront, battle scarred. Directly behind stood even more evidence of the fighting made necessary by the German suicide units holding such ports as this one. Of course, I had seen pictures of these houses being gutted, but here it was. In one place an entire second story was blown away, one end wall remaining. In another section not a single house stood without showing great gaps in the [exposed] rooms and walls. From our ship we could see two buildings that seemed singularly free from battle marks. These were the spires of two cathedrals.

A few carts typical of the region wandered about among the rubble, clearing and cleaning. Natives of the region worked with the GIs, the Seabees, etc. In the front of the twisted wreck in front of us was a giant eagle with wings widespread. It seemed strangely out of place. Feathers were gone but the spirit of the bird seemed to remain to be symbolic of the spirit of France.

I suddenly had a new concept of this war. I suddenly felt glad that I was here; I suddenly knew that all my thinking concerning the war is in the abstract until one has seen its effects, of course. I haven't seen the effects. We have held this port for months and much work has been done. However, it is a beginning of far more terrible pictures to come. (How terrible I cannot know.).

Monday Feb. 5, 44

Dear Son:

Some how we didn't think it would come to us—the days of waiting and wondering where you were, where you would land and when we would hear again, but there isn't a thing one can do to hasten the time when we'll have an answer to all the questions. We anxiously await news as to your destination and hope that you will be able to tell us just where you are.

We got some news today which seems hopeful concerning Fred. Members of Patton's 5th division are getting a furlough home and the places mentioned as to where we know Fred has been. I'm sending the clipping on to Manza. She came out here week ago today and stayed two days and nights. She is not so well but got a tooth taken out and some medicine from Sloan.

We are O.K. Our work is going along nicely and unless the regulations regarding 4-F's change we are not going to be so rushed.

Sgt. [Alvin C. York] is sick—nothing more than usual but was in bed a couple of days last week, and didn't come to the Bd. meeting today....

Lots of love and our prayers follow you.

Mother

[Written in the margin.]

P.S. Dear Arthur boy!

Our prayers & love follow you daily & constantly. We look for that good word that you are well. You are seeing some of that great world. May your experiences add to your stature and faith in that better world to come after the fighting ceases & good will toward all men again brings the happiness & peace we long for. Will follow this more detailed & definite news. Keep up a good heart. God bless you & all your companions is my daily prayer. We are looking for a long letter from Dorothy soon again   Dad

---

Camp #1
Feb. 8

We left our boat about midmorning and loaded on large trucks. We rode through the port city and out into the country. There was evidence everywhere of fighting. Many windows and roofs were absent. I saw several cathedrals that had been hit in many places. I

was immediately impressed by the attractiveness of the architecture. Tile roofs and multicolored walls, along with very clean yards and well-kept gardens gave the evidence of pride in appearance and a long culture of refinement. Barbed wire entanglements, pillboxes, trenches, and foxholes dotted the country side. Everywhere we saw the native people walking or riding their wheels (bicycles). Almost invariably they waved and smiled at us, and each time we saw them walking, they carried with them a piece of bread, a cabbage, or some sort of food. In one town, the third we passed through, a lady threw a long loaf of bread into our truck. It was whole wheat and very good. Several times when the truck stopped, we saw children who often came up to the truck. Thin-legged and shivering, they smiled and pleaded, "Cigarette pour pa-pa?" Although we have orders to the contrary, many fellows gave them packs of cigarettes and money. We could easily see the effects of malnutrition in the thin spindles that served as legs.

We stopped for a couple of hours and ate chow—my first meal and first "K" rations. ["K" rations were packaged in a small box about the size of a crackerjack box.] I liked them very much. We had a chance to inspect a defense position of trenches and pillboxes. The rain had begun earlier in the morning and it continued intermittently. We moved on.

All of us were amazed when we found that we had large tents at our first camp. We also received new cots and, most amazingly, sleeping bags. We were lucky to have a dry tent; that is, dry by comparison with the others. Some poor fellows were knee-deep in mud. We had carried everything we own on this side [of the Atlantic] on our backs, and everyone was tired. We were in bed and asleep by eight o'clock.

My first day on land on this side! The very fine farm land, the picturesque thatched roofs, the great care in taking care of home and gardens, the poverty and destructiveness of war, the spirit of friendliness, of determination—all of these things made a lasting impression on me.

Letter from Dotty to Art
[February 9, 1945]

Bushy dearest,

I've been having more fun making your mother's birthday present blouse. Last night I cut it out and sewed, all this morning I sewed, and tonight at Record Breakers I did a little more. Soon it will be finished and I can send it to her after her birthday is all over. Dogonnit. My trip to Phila. sort of retarded me on stuff like that. Don't you think I'm a retarded child anyway? Don't answer that!

Don't believe I told you what I bought when Mother and I went shopping a couple of days ago. I bought a new dress, a "thank you present" for Jenks, a cup and saucer to our china, and a "pantie" girdle. The girdle is to wear mostly with my new dress and others. My tummy is nice and flat (now) but you know what my behind does! It needs subduing a bit for some dresses. My new dress is a pretty combination of white, lavender, and purple, but don't jump a [to] conclusions just because I said purple. It isn't a bit loud. Anyway, it is made of a material that sort of clings to the body—hence the girdle.

You may be interested in know that I am joining a modern dance class which several friends attend. "T", Lois Durman (don't think you've met her, and Jessie Dempster are all in it. It will be wonderful exercise for me, as well as satisfying my prancing instincts a bit. It meets once a week at the "Y.H." Sounds like fun to me!

Between work and R.B. tonight I went to the Boy Scout banquet, so I can write it up for the papers. They had a covered dish supper, and a very nice program followed. Mr. & Mrs. Duggan were there. Mrs. Duggan brought one of her inimitable cakes. Are you acquainted with the Duggan cakes? Brother! They melt in your mouth. The one tonight was chocolate with chocolate icing, and so big that I it into thirty pieces! M-m-m-m-m-m. Yumee, tummee. Now. Is your mouth watering yet?

There was a program and a sing and a speech and a movie, but I didn't stay for the movie, because I wanted to get to Record Breakers.

Had a grand time there—heard Rachamaninoff's [Rachmaninoff's] piano Concerto No. 2. Mmmmm. After that Flo played and Dean sang (yeah, Dean is here for a few days) and Lois Ann sang and Ruth Lane sang, and I sang and then we all sang together.

Here is a joke Dad copied from something. Sorta of cute but a trifle shady! "The Treasury Dept. checked up on the sales of war bonds and found that folks down in the hills of Tenn. were not buying them. They sent a special representation down to work on the job. He approached a tumbled down shack, saw a man on the porch, walked up to him and introduced himself. 'I'm from the Treas. Dept., sent down to sell War Bonds - - you've heard of War Bonds, haven't you?' 'Can't say as I have,' answered the man. 'Well, maybe you've heard of Roosevelt?'—'Nope, never heard of him.'—'You must have heard of Pearl Harbor?'—'Nope, never heard of her, either.' 'Surely, you've heard of Churchhill?' —'Nope, never been on that thar hill.'—'Good Heavens, man, you surely must know theres a war going on and the whole world is in a lot of trouble!' Just about that time a voice from the house called out, 'What's goin on out thar?' The man of the house replied, 'There's some fellow out here by the name of Roosevelt, says he took Pearl Harbor up on Church Hill and got her in trouble and now the fool wants me to go his bond!'"

Here's to our love. Long may it wave.
Your affectionate wife
Dotty

Feb. 10 '45

Last night I made my debut into a French villa. Beul [Root] and I went in and walked around with a couple of others. The streets were completely dark except for an occasional G. I. truck or a horse and buggy. All cafes and inns were curtained so that very little light came through. Groups of five and six soldiers could be seen wandering from shadow to shadow and entering the doors as they found wine and beer. These were the only items to be found. Cigarettes are the much desired medium of exchange—50 francs ($1.00) per pack. One of the fellows with me wanted to get rid of two packets and I undertook to use my halting French as middle man. I thought of what changes had taken place since war began five years ago. These quiet little inns and cafes, now filled to overflowing with GIs, are hardly the quiet rooms in which Frenchmen once gathered to sip their wine and discuss the current politics. One of the fellows used the German "Danke schoen" upon receipt of two bottles of beer. "Bosche?" questioned the Frenchman behind the counter, with a sudden hardening of his features. The poor GI could almost feel cold steel down his back.

Letter excerpt from Art to Dotty
At Sea

Dearest,
Here is a copy of our regimental paper published daily aboard ship. The news herein is exceptional in detail since usually there was but one shut. Thought you might enjoy seeing it. Also enclosed is a

shack of my upper story wheat. Knowing how short my hair was before, you may well imagine what it looks like now. But practical, my dear, practical! [Art actually enclosed a lock of his hair for Dotty.]

Letter from Art to Dotty
Somewhere in France
Feb. 10 1945 (Sat.)
(14)

My Dearest,

This is the first time that I have been able to put a date on my letter since I left the states and also the first letter I have been able to write since arrival. My hands are cold and the light is growing dim, but I shall try to get this off. It must be in shortly to get in the first mail going out. Your letter of the 29th describing the Japanese dinner came today. This was our first mail and most welcomed. Also heard from Squawky, answering my letter written in the states. I am sure that there are letters written before yours of the 29th.

There is much to say and describe but I will have to wait until later for details. We arrived after a very safe trip. We have bad rain, heavy rain, every day since arrival; but the weather is not far different from that with which we are familiar. We are very lucky in our facilities although the bath room gets a bit cold now and then. Yesterday I washed for the first time. Washed, shaved, and washed my dirty clothing in the same water—half a helmet full. Our food has really been good and my old appetite has returned in full force. Luckily, we get <u>Stars and Stripes</u>, G.I. overseas newspaper every day and in this I will be able to get much of the news.

By the way, I have already found the need for a couple of things— although it may take a very long time to get here. I need a flashlight very badly. You probably will not find one in Knoxville, and if not, ask Dad if he needs the one I left with him. Get an extra set of batteries and a bulb if possible. Also need the lock which I left in my things at home (607). Since I seldom have chance to brush teeth, better send some dental floss (1). I think Daddy can get some emery cloth (or similar substance for me. I don't know whether or not you could find a small hunting knife with about a six inch blade, thin style. I would have gotten one, but I didn't realize the real need. This should also include sheath suitable for carry on a belt. Better include my bond ointment also. I wonder if you find any Hoppe's No 9. gun oil (bore cleaner). If you can, perhaps in a hdw [hardware] store, send it for I need it badly. We can always use a few candles and these would be welcomed in any package. I suppose that by the time I could get wristlets, it would be warm, but I wish I had a pair right now. That is a long list and more than can be included in a five pound package. Perhaps Dad & Mother could send one with part of it. However, they can't get some of the things. Canned meats and non-perishable items (dried fruits perhaps) would always be welcomed as fillers for packages.

Darling, my morale went up to a new high when your letter arrived today. I shall attempt to spend most of the morrow writing to you, describing some of the things I have seen and thought since I wrote last time. I think of you constantly and dream of the future, our future. I love you from the very depth of my being. May God bless

Our Love,

Bushy

P.S. Will send above list which may be necessary for sending

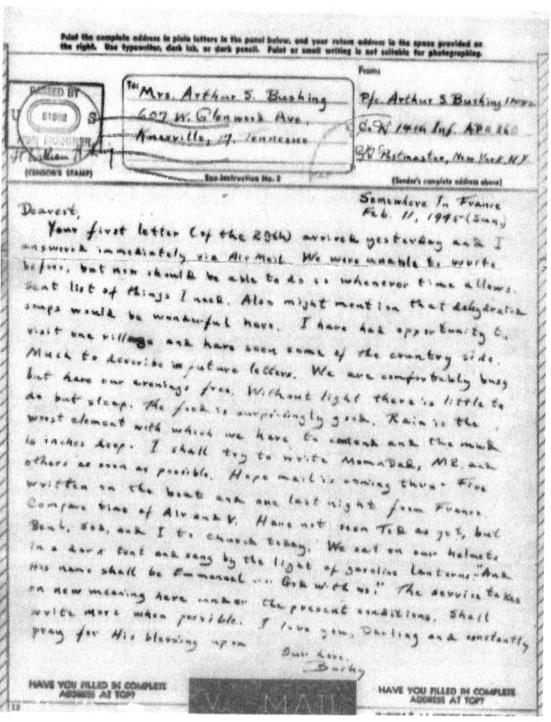

V-Mail from Art to Dotty dated Feb. 11, 1945, postmarked Feb. 21.

Little Man,

I've had a busy day, also a busy yesterday. Nearly all morning I spent cleaning this room, and I do mean cleaning! Putting things away, cleaning out boxes and drawers, peeling off the inches of Knoxville soot, wiping the windows, etc. After lunch I cleaned the bathroom in the same sort of fashion, then went to town to get the invitations for Y.P. banquet from the printer, etc., etc. Came home, ate supper, and went to Flo's to help work on service-men's newspaper I told you about, and stayed there till pretty late. Got home finally and Dad, Dean, and Ann demanded that I take Mary Ruth's place in Rook game, so I did. Er, bid.

Did I tell you Dean was home? Well, he definitely is. He got a little bit of furlough gas, so he & his family yesterday went by Maryville to pick up Mary Ruth and Ann, then went to mountains. It was warm & sunny, 1st day like that we've had, so it was made to order for their trip. The Ann-Dean situation is progressing nicely, just as we hoped it would. They make a good looking cupple (?), and sort of couldn't help liking each other.

[typed] Hope you don't mind if I finish this on the machine. 'Tis quicker and writes more. Betcha. Bob Ogden and wife are home—he did graduate from OCS, is home for short furlough, then goes to Fla. Helen says that a girl in Columbus got a letter from 71st guy from Seattle, Wash.! I somehow don't believe it. Both the Lt's. (Dean & Bob) sang in the choir this morning, and Dean sang a duet with Troy Bell Lane at the evening service.

Aunt Carol and gang came to 607 for Dinner after church today, Ann and Mary Ruth still here being partly the reason. M-m-m-m. Best ole dinner. Afterwards, Flo and I typed all afternoon on the newspaper. Then more church 2½ hours, come home, call members of the Every-member-canvass-committee to a meeting tomorrow night, and finally at last I can write my beloved a letter. But I had to work pretty hard for the privilege. This has got to stop. No, no, Not the letter writing---This being so busy every Sunday. After all, wherein is it a day of rest? I want to know? Saturday is my day off, but seldom is it a day of rest! Now Darling, I am not too busy, I sleep till 8:00 or more every morning. I've just fallen into the habit of griping, and it is a nasty, nasty habit. Slap me, won't you? That will teach me to gripe about nothing. That is all it is. Nothing.

The February meetings are now in session at the college. The speaker is pres. of Louisville Seminary, and the girls say he is wonderful. I shall try to attend at least one of the meetings this week, between now and Wed. when they end. Also I have been praying for their effectiveness.

Oh, darling, darling, darling. I have been praying for you, and for our love. And it gives me the most wonderfully serene feeling to know that you are safe in God's hands. I am waiting so eagerly for your return and the infinite progress of

Our love,
Dotty

Letter from Art to Dotty
Somewhere in France
Feb 11, 1945 (Sun. Night

My Dearest,

The tent shakes and the poles creak. The wind blows up a real storm outside. Our little stove throws out heat and our little squad huddles about. We have a piece of rope stuck in a can full of dubbin (used for shoes) and the light flickers up and down, reflected against an opened tin can. You are probably in the middle of your Sunday meal as I write, and I think of the Sundays we have had together. I shall try in the days to follow to catch up on past experiences.

Feb. 12 Monday

Sunday was truly a miserable day, with rain and wind all day. Went to Church in the morning in the 1st Batallion area. The tent was a large one and lighted by two mantle lanterns. We sat on our helmets in the dampness and sang. The sermon was based on a passage from Matt.: "And his name shall be called Emmanuel, which is interpreted 'God with us.'" Was glad to see Lt. Moberg (Plat. Leader) attending. In the afternoon I took a sponge bath—my first since I left the boat. Feels good to be halfway clean.

The wood situation has been one of the most serious shortages that we have had. Transportation has been difficult and we have had but about two rations of coal. These have been entirely insufficient. As order has been repeated time and time again forbidding the cutting of wood, of bringing in trees, etc. It has been impossible to enforce such regulations because the officers themselves are "hurting" for wood. Tonight [Sgt.] O'Connell (my squad leader) and four more of us went out on a raiding party to find something to burn. We had to spend most of the day sitting on the stove to keep warm. Just at dusk we went out, passing long lines of men returning with loads of wood. We found a pond surrounded by small trees. Tonight we have plenty of wood and the axe has been busy for most of the evening. Some of the fellows have been talking with some of the French in the area. Rather than staying in their tents, the Germans were billeted [soldiers lodging in a civilian's house or nonmilitary facility] with the [French] people. When they wanted wood they took it from the woodpile. At least we cut our own. Men have to keep warm and GIs will if it is possible to do so.

All indications are that a general push is on up at the front. The Germans have just flooded a large portion of the Ruhr, slowing down advances, but the British have entered Cleve, the northern anchor of the Siegfried Line. The Russians continue their advance on Stettin [German post city]. A break seems inevitable in the very near future.

We have a few replacements going out. I don't like that but I understand it is only to get rid of a few "bolos" [misfits, goof-offs]. One fellow is going to medical school to become a platoon medic (Fred Price). O'Connell says that something is coming up for me. I am sweating it out—to use the current GI vernacular. I wonder what it can be.

Feb. 13, '45

We are allowed two or three passes per squad per night, and so most of the squad sits around the fire from the time darkness falls until bedtime, usually about ten o'clock. One of the most interesting experiences for me is to sit around our little stove and observe the individuals in our squad. For the past two nights we have been blessed with a candle. Formerly we have burned dubbin [an oily substance to be applied to boots], bore cleaner, lighter fluid, and almost anything which we have at hand. As the light flickers and the shadows play tag on the walls of the tent, I look into the faces of my fellows and think.

From all walks, representing almost all strata, we come. We have a "racketeer" [Giesking from Indianapolis, who claimed to be a former gangster], a college instructor, a factory worker and a college student. A truck driver and a worker from the Naval yards, S/Sgt. John O'CONNELL is accepted by the platoon as the best squad leader and no questions asked. He has been in the Army about two and a half years, having taken his training in a regular division—the 89th. He received a rating after four months and has continued up to Staff [Sergeant]. He came to our outfit at the same time I did.

John grew up in New Jersey and was working at a defense plant prior to entering the Army. Although he has never attended college, he was offered an athletic scholarship and has gone to night school.

A large number of points indicate that men may have been held for an extended period of time. [Garbled but apparently a reference to points that GIs accumulated for overseas duty—one point for each month. After the war was over, these points determined the order in which men would be sent home.]

Feb. 13, '45

I had an interesting experience tonight in attempting to wash my "long handles"—woolen underwear. I walked over to our source of clean wash water—about four hundred yards away in a hedge row (our other source is any hole in the ground around our tent). I brought it back in my all-purpose bucket (the steel helmet), and heated it in a bucket on the stove. I poured my hot water in my all-purpose wash basin (my steel helmet), and started to wash. I found all the water soaked up in the woolen tops. With much difficulty I poured more water in and finally succeeded in getting it thoroughly wet. I can't say that it was clean, but perhaps some of the sweat washed out.

Nine Nazi paratroopers were dropped near Rouen last night dressed in the clothing of French civilians with forged papers. Four have been captured and the others are still at large. Such things give us cause to realize that war is not far away.

We have also been told that a group of four thousand Germans is still in a pocket in a famous port in this vicinity. There are many of these pockets all up and down the coast of France. They are suicide units, naturally, but they hold up the use of these ports for our supplies.

Letter from Dotty to Art
Tuesday, Feb. 13 [1945]
Baldwin 223

Darling,

I am having a wonderful time here among all the old familiar sights and sounds and people and things. Outside, at the end of the hall, harmonious voices caroling hymns indicate prayer meeting in session; across the table Mary Ruth sits engrossed in studies; footsteps and voices, the distant tinkle of a radio crowd the building with life.

It was the February meetings that brought me over. And a nice little sister, of course. Caldwell, pres. of Louisville Seminary is speaker —I think you've heard him before—I had—in chapel, perhaps. He is tall, gray-haired, fine featured, and has a wonderful voice, rich and deep. Tonight he talked about the "Gamble Magnificent." It reminded me somewhat of Thompson's sermon on "Every Bottle Shall be Filled With Wine." He spoke of how most forms of gambling are sinful, but that "betting your life on God" is quite the opposite, and is a venture that pays big dividends. If we were as daring and venturesome in our Christianity as we are in some other phases of our living, if we had more of the bold spirit of Peter, what an utterly different world this would be!

I met Mary Agnes (Cordy's sister) tonight. She looks a little like Cordy, especially the eyes. She seems to think Cordy has heard from Ted already, but I ain't heard from you, so how could that be? Or does Ted have some pull you don't have?

I am staying overnight, will attend the morning meeting, then to home. Or rather to Maryville and work. I won't get to open my valentine till tonight Dggnnt.

Got a letter from Dorcas today. She sent me a snapshot of her and Beul taken in Columbus, so I'd better send her one of us. Hmmm? She is also working and attending a number of outside activities, just like me.

I still haven't received a letter from Cordy. I'm trying to persuade her to live with me and work in Knoxville—hope I can succeed. There is nothing for her in Crossnore, and I feel sure she could find work along her line in Knoxville.

Darling, every time I look out the window, go out the door, or look across the campus I expect to see you there. You are not there, you are here, I feel your presence by my side and know your spirit in my heart. It is wonderful to be again in the birthplace of

Our love,
Dotty

Feb. 14

As taps sounded tonight, seven members of our squad finished the last of a half loaf of French wheat bread. Although we are getting

sufficient food, all of us feel that we are not getting enough. We procure extra food at every opportunity. Last night one fellow came in with a long loaf of bread. We cut it up and put it on the hot stove top. To us it tasted like cake.

We also obtained a small lamp for our squad. One of the fellows bought it for 600 francs ($12). Before the war it was worth about 20 francs. This one belonged to the Germans when they were garrisoned here. It is small, but very serviceable and will burn anything.

Second mail call today. I received three letters from Dotty, and one from home, and one from Mary Ruth (Dotty's sister). All were greatly welcome. Fay Qualls is in Assam, India, and has killed a snake. Wants a pound of Maxwell House coffee. Shelby Turner has been discharged from the Army. Mary Ruth writes of a talk by Dr. Orr [religion/philosophy teacher at Maryville College]—the Good Life is not an "it." It is a series of stepping stones leading from one to the next.

Letter from Art to Dotty
Somewhere in France
Feb 14th. 1945
(23-28)

My Dearest,

Today, appropriately, enough on Valentine's Day. I received five big letters. One from Mother and Dad written Jan 25th, one from Mary Ruth, Feb 3rd, and three from you. Oh joy! The first was written from Huntingdon Valley on the 24th, and the others on Feb 2nd and 3rd respectively. I was, of course, overjoyed to get the various items of news including the Victory Ship for Maryville. Also appreciated a great deal getting the church bulletin which I thought unique. I also opened the lovely Valentine today. It was very, very nice one, Darling. Thank you.

Last night our situation was improved a great deal by the purchase of a little lamp from one of the Frenchmen in the neighborhood. Fellows in our squad bought it for 680 francs or $12. That sounds like a terrible price, but values are topsy-turvy here. (It was worth 20 francs before the war.) The value of an article depends upon its utility value. The little lamp will burn almost any fuel and is very serviceable. It belonged to German soldiers who were here before we came. We can carry it with us wherever we go and I shall now be able to write at night without completely ruining my eyes. I will also be able to read a bit more now with a source of illumination after darkness falls.

78

Last night, I went to town with O'Connell, my squad leader, and Beul. We first found the new "Jungleer Service Club." It consists of an old building with wooden benches, electric lights, and a stage with a screen. A number of old magazines were to be found all around the room. We found that we were just in time for the movie—"San Diego, I Love You," so having nothing better to do we decided to stay for it. The movie began with a couple of news reels from last Nov. and boxing reels of the early 20's. Just before the main picture began, the lighting system went flooey and we were in complete darkness. We had planned to attend the regular French "Cinema" in town, so off we went to that. There we were in time to hear the last number by a Negro Jazz Band. No French movie! After wandering around a bit, we ended up by returning to camp before nine.

Just as taps sounded at ten, seven of us sat around our little stove toasting French bread with butter right on top of the dirty stove. It tasted almost like cake, and I think was appreciated far more than most cake eaten in the States. (If you have difficulty reading this it is because my hands are so cold I can hardly write. The sun is warm, but the air is cool.) Later in the evening, some of the fellows returned with ten eggs and we fried them over the fire in a G.I. mess kit. "Oh the joy of the soldiers' life!" Our food is good and we get enough (I guess); but a bit extra is always a luxury. All look forward with much anticipation to that first package from home with food....

In reference to your questions concerning postwar compulsory military training, I say to begin with that I favor it. I'm glad that you brought up the question for there are many points that I want to think about. I was reading today in York a comment that the year of training should could be divided so as to be made up during summer months between school terms. That may prove a good suggestion. I think that the experience is thoroughly worth while for the individual, and there is no question in my mind that we should have the potential to back up our world commitments. I see the church viewpoint concerning waiting until after the war, and tend to agree. Waiting will give those who oppose the measure a better chance since the vast majority favor it at the moment. Reactionary forces will set in, but also a more rational viewpoint will be held by that time. There is less likelihood of regret and less likelihood of a perverted law being passed. The latter point I think is the most important one. The law will be more rational I think and more according to what it should be if it is discussed and made up later.

By the way, I am having an opportunity to observe first hand the workings of the famed French Black Market. Gen. Eisenhower has said that it is a bigger problem than the fighting at the front. When we came here, a packet of cigarettes sold for 50 francs or $1. Due to this sudden influx of supply, the price has dropped to about 30 francs. <u>Stars and Stripes</u> carried the story last week that cigarettes were selling in Paris for 550 francs $10 per pack. Chocolate candy is supposed to be worth 750 francs per box. That seems impossible and yet that is the way the Black Market works.

By the way, Darling. I think 'twould be better if you could date your letters. I can always check the outside postmark, but I am not going to be able to keep the envelopes. Thus to know about when events took place, it would be of upmost assistance to have the date thereon.

I don't mean to harp on the subject of the package I asked for, but there is always the chance that one letter will not come through. In regard to the emery cloths, Dad will know about it. I want it very fine to be used for removing rust. I do not need very much. In regard to the knife, I want a thin blade about six inches long. I was very much mistaken when I failed to get one before I left: Hope Dad can sharpen it for me before you send it, for I will have trouble putting an edge on it. A few candles in each package that you send will always be appreciated, as will dehydrated soups. I think I mentioned that cigarette lighter. I'm not smoking, but a lighter would be a very valuable item. An item such as a knife is far more important, but if you can find one for a reasonable price I would like to have it. Three or four bottles of malted milk tablets (10¢-25¢ size) will offer a very fine addition to my vitamin needs. I shall include a list of these things in my letter since a request is necessary I believe before you can mail it. I also think that there is a five pound limit per package. I mention everything I can think of because it will take literally weeks to arrive. Stationery could always be included in packages from time to time. In regard to the watch in Calif., I hope you have heard something about it. Write the Glathes about it again if you still haven't heard. I really don't think that you should buy one until my situation is more stable. Later perhaps I can send for one. If you haven't bought one as yet, don't.

Tomorrow we are supposed to get our PX rations (candy, cigarettes, etc.) and if the weather is nice we will probably play a bit of softball. I hope I get to pitch. I could really use a bit of exercise of that nature.

Darling, the hour is late and I could write for pages: However, "there are miles to go before I sleep," as Frost [poet] says. I have much to do tonight and part of it is sleeping. I look forward with the dawn of each new day to the letters from you which may come. I dream of you far more than ever before. Only a few nights ago we walked together in a field of flowers up to our waists. These dreams of [are] very, very real and they bring you ever closer to me. The constant driving force behind me each day is the knowledge and power of

Our Love,

Bushy

P.S. I enclose

2 francs note

5 " "

10 " "

Please mention receipt of these.

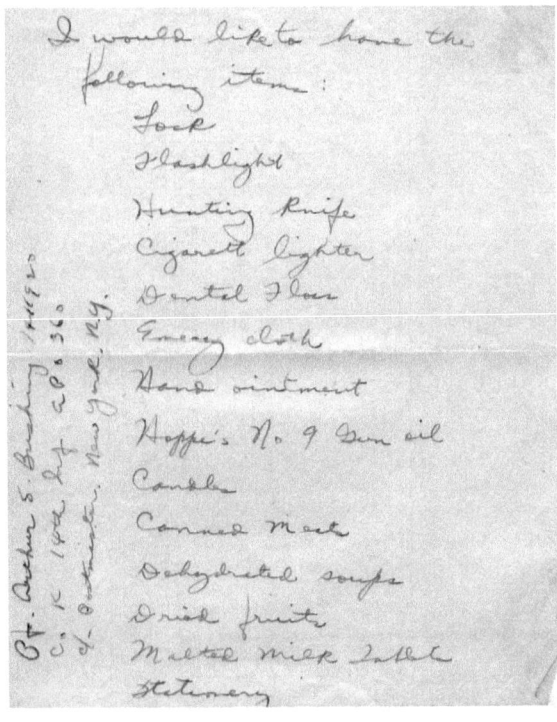

List of requested items needed by Art
in Feb. 15, 1945 letter to Dotty.

Dear Valentine? Er-,

Really, there is no question about it. You are very definitely my valentine. Please excuse the slip of this drip. Also, I love you, my dear. In the springtime. Alla time, in fact. Darling, you are so sweet and so wonderful, and your valentines were so cute and so beautiful! Respectively! And if you were here I would give you such a hug and a kiss as would prove my words beyond the shadow of a doubt. The fascinators are lovely. I've been hankering for one for a long time. And you have me not one, but two! Darling, you're wonderful! (I repeat.) Shall I say it again? 1000th verse, same as first. And the card—it is not only cute, it is utterly adorable.

There was another wonderful session of Feb. meetings in chapel this morning. The talk was on love (my favorite subject), on how there should be the element of loyalty in love, otherwise is becomes mere sentiment....

Goodnight, my love, I shall go now to dream of
OUR LOVE,
Dotty

Feb. 16

For the second successive morning the sun came out bright and clear. A few clouds in the Eastern sky provided a beautiful sunrise and last night was a marvelous sunset. Spring seems to be definitely in the air and the trees are beginning to bud. It reminds me of an April morning in the Cumberlands—a morning when I would go out to clean off the garden preparatory to plowing or to work among the flowers. Anything to be outside in the invigorating air.

Fri. night

My afternoon was spent in one of those grand and glorious experiences in the Army—a detail. The entire company was called out to perform a very simple task of spreading some gravel and draining our ditch line. The job could have been performed effectively by twenty men and one Sgt. Soon after we began, a major something or other (our new Batn. Exec.) came along with some very crazy ideas in regard to drainage. Everything was thrown into confusion and the entire project was halted. Time passed and we stood. Two 2nd Lts. And Capt. Long were around, and finally something was decided. As Lt. Carol (2nd Plat.) muttered under his breath, there were too many blankety-blank bosses. The same is true so often in the Army. Every man has his own idea as to how something should be done, and every man with an extra stripe or a higher ranking piece of brass can enforce his personal viewpoint. The result is far too often confusion, with waste of manpower and efficiency, and complete disgust among the troops. Before the little incident of the afternoon was finished, everyone, including the non-coms and Lieutenants, were cussing and discussing the Major who had caused all the extra grief. Men say that soldiers are often careless with their ammunition at the front.

Another interesting incident in a French camp occurred tonight in the chow line. Chow works in this manner: pots of food are placed along-side the walk way in front of the mess tent, and we march by [the] platoon to receive our food. At each meal, the order of the platoon is rotated. One very unpopular cook among the men is T/4 Finnigan, who long ago seems to have turned sour on the world. Tonight, each man in the first three platoons received two hot dogs. Men eating in the fourth and fifth received five and six; and, when seconds began, there were still a very large number of dogs left. A great deal of unequal distribution developed. Everyone was unhappy, and much griping went on. The matter was taken up with the officers, since this is but the climax to a series of similar occurrences when our friend Finnigan serves the meat. Oh, the joy of the soldier's life. It would not be worth living if one did not have something to gripe about.

Our week began with a two-hour hike each morning, which I welcomed. We have had almost no training for more than six weeks, and all of us need the conditioning. Wed. morning we hiked for the last time, and all drivers were pulled out (supposedly to go after our vehicles). We also learned that certain men were to be pulled out to go to Belgium as replacements. These were supposedly the "bolos" in our outfit. Tonight we hear that next week we have a regular training schedule with night patrols included. There is no secret to the fact that we (the Allies) are preparing for a big Spring offensive. I believe that all of these bits fit into the larger pattern concerning our future. Of course, there is no question as to what our ultimate objective is. We came here to aid in defeating the Germans. I think that perhaps the secret desire of almost everyone has been that we would make up part *of the Army of Occupation and that the fighting would end before we reached the front lines. During these days we live, as it were, in suspended animation. When will we move? Where? How? How soon will the war end? What will happen when the Russians reach Berlin? These and a thousand other questions play hide and seek in the back of our minds as we work a bit from day to day, gripe about the chow, stand in line, and gold brick [make up excuses to avoid a job] on detail.*

Letter from Dotty to Art
Fri., Feb. 16 [1945]

My Darling,

Hello. How are you? That's good, so am I. And how is your cold, your sinus, your headache, your poison ivy, your whatnot? Well, I am really glad to hear that your whatnot is getting along so well. That compensates for all the rest, doesn't it? You know mine was acting up not long ago, but when it got well I felt so good!

The first issue of the "Hearthlog" came off the press yesterday afternoon, so I want to send you one soon. If you were only a member of the church it would be sent to you anyway.

Last night I went to a linen shower for Frances Gilmore. The gang there was mostly made up of the church girls. We gabbed, played games, etc, and had a big time. Frances' gifts and [had] been hidden in various places all over the house, so she really had to work for them.

I christened the white fascinator by wearing it for the first time last night.

Rosemary Johnson (daughter of S.S. teacher) is majoring in English at U.T. and she was interested when I told her of your ambitions. She wants to teach also, and wants to know what advantage there is, if any, to getting M.A. & Phd. All at once. I didn't think there was any.

Gotta get Dad's lunch now. Be good to yourself, darling, and don't forget that

      I love you,
      Dotty

Feb. 17

Yesterday I read a masterpiece of descriptive writing in an excerpt from Hardy's Tess of the D'Urbervilles. It is a description of the death of the child of Tess: "So passed away Sorrow the Undesired—that intrusive creature, that bastard gift of shameless Nature who respects not the civil law; a waif to whom eternal Time had been a matter of days merely, who knew not that such things as years and centuries ever were; to whom the cottage interior was the universe, the week's weather climate, new-born babyhood human existence, and the instinct to suck human knowledge."

This single paragraph is enough to make the difference between an artist molding the image which he wishes to present and a pseudo-artist putting mere words together in a vain attempt to create artistry. This is creative art, while so much writing is purely mechanical. I feel a deep longing to return to the company of such friends as Hardy, Shakespeare, and half a hundred others.

Letter from Art to Dotty
Somewhere in France
Feb. 17, 1945 (Sat.
(29-34)

My Dearest Heart,

Today proved to be a rather exceptional one for your husband. One of the things that helps our morale perhaps more than anything else was exceptional chow. You have no idea how much chow can mean to men living and working as we are.

(Sun. Afternoon

Although I lost most of my appetite on the boat, I regained it very quickly when I began to get exercise and plenty of fresh air. Almost all of us return for seconds every meal (if seconds there are.) Well, chow was only one item. We also received our PX supplies. These are rationed and we get equal amounts of cigarettes, candy etc., regardless of what we prefer. After getting it, we can trade around as we please. I have plenty of trade materials in the form of cigarettes, cigars, etc. A third morale builder was our afternoon pass which I spent observing French life. However, the most important thing to make me feel good was mail call. Chow, candy, passes—none of these in any amounts can mean half so much as just one letter from you, my Dear. Yesterday, I received four wonderful letters from you and one from Van. Today, I received another from you, mailed the 8th (the latest), and one from Mother. It's almost worth while going without letters for a few days just to have the joy of receiving a stack of them when the mail does come through. But never worry about failing to write one day of course, I hope you will: but always consider yourself forgiven.

As far as I can determine, I have received all of your letters up to and including the 8th, with the exception of the 7th. However, that is sure to come through soon. I believe that I mentioned before how much it would help if all letters had the date on the inside. When I receive them in such disorder, I always like to go back and read through as they are written. Funny thing happened in regard to Van's letter. It was mailed to my former address (pre N.Y.) via "Free" mail on Feb. 4th. It arrived with your Air Mail of the 1st. Some time you could try a regular mail just for comparison of time. Van was blessed with a three day pass during Xmas and a 15 day furlough in Jan. What a life! Says Tally is doing well and writing often. Hope they are off for a long road of happiness. Mother and Dad speak always of being delighted to hear from you, and I am glad that at least your letters to them will be regular even though mine are not.

Darling, in case you did not know, your letters are wonderful. I enjoy particularly your discussions of the news and your comments on the church, your work, etc. Bits of thought from your letters are taken by me and thought about from every angle. There is so little chance here to come in contact with "thoughts". A wife of old Encore's and my Bible are almost the only other sources I have for deeper inspiration. Interested to hear of Dr. Peyton's remark concerning my future. That too I think about.

I am still in the process of analyzing just what the effect of this new life, these new contacts are going to have upon me. I really don't know. I am sure I will be the stronger for it. I am sure that I am learning many things I never knew before concerning my fellow men, concerning human relations, and things of the spirit. I am finding out the level of thought that the average American maintains. I wish that I could see something noble in it and see intrinsic values underlying a surface roughness. Perhaps I will later on, but at the moment I can't. Base thinking, evil minds, intolerance—these things I find. No, Darling. I'm not turning sour on the Army and the world, but I do think that I can see with a bit more perspective. I hope that I can attain "optimistic realism" (as Lillywhite turned my outlook). I can better understand the intolerance of the Germans and the Japanese when I find the innate hatreds that crop up as soon as the word "Jew" or "Negro" is mentioned. How can we who have lived in America discredit individuals because of their race or creed? I cannot answer my own question, but I know that it is justified in being broached.

I should not leave the picture all black. I must say that there is a co-operative spirit in my squad which I never thought potentially possible. Our squad is becoming known as the best in the outfit. This is almost entirely due to the leadership of Sgt. O'Connell, our squad leader. I think that I have commented on him before. He has a special way of handling men that reveal true qualities of leadership. I am glad that I am working under him. Just a comment in passing: I note that generally speaking the older men who have been in the Army three and four years are more tolerant than others. However, even this is only relative.

By the way, I should have mentioned earlier that my headaches have been greatly relieved since I saw you. I was given nose drops containing ephedrine and these opened up the sinus to relieve the pressure. Please do not worry. I should never have allowed you to see those notes I took. One thing leads to another and I happen to think of other notes. I am getting a chance to do a great deal of writing that I have never been able to do before. I want to reflect something of the G.I. life and point of view. My experiment is proving satisfactory. I just hope that I can continue as I have started.

I had intended to explain why I failed to write last night. After supper Price, the other college man in my squad, and I went out looking for water. We finally found it and came back with our all purpose helmets filled. With the aid of a hot fire, I heated it and took a pleasurable bath. The remainder of the evening was spent in doing minor repairs on clothing.

Glad to hear about Bruce Evans. I shall attempt to look him up when it is possible to do so. I still have had no chance to see Ted, but perhaps I will soon. I have had no opportunity write Time or Hal as yet, but I still have hope. Perhaps you have written Time. I hope so. In regard to the airmail stationery which you suggested, I would be more than glad to get it. As yet I have discovered no source of supply for paper and using only one side depletes my stock.

I am happy beyond words that you are working with Dr. Peyton in the church. I can already see that you are going to be absorbed in your work and that means that you will be occupied constantly. Glad you are taking on the dancing, but please don't overwork. We still have a scrapbook and a photo album to fill.

Was very sorry to learn of the death of Aunt Lora's husband. However, I know that it must be a release as you say. Thanks for explaining who Aunt Lora is, but you taught me well in my first lessons. I think I can place almost all of our relatives.

I fear that your letter of the 31st ("Thurs. morning but Wed's. letter") arrived with at least one page missing. It was typewritten she [and] with no close. The envelope had been opened on the way. Hope there was nothing of very special importance that I missed. Glad to hear about The Hearth Log and hope plans are going ahead. Hardly know what you could quote from my letters but I could hardly object. Remember you are biased!

The news continues good particularly in the Pacific. The fall of Bataan yesterday and Corregidor being taken today is something of a surprise to me. I had expected lengthy resistance at these strong points. The long awaited invasion on the China coast cannot be far away and direct attacks on Japan itself seems in the offing! Surely by the time this reaches you something will break on the Western Front. Our offensive too cannot be far away. We are getting a very limited flow of political news in the Stars & Stripes. Wish you would clarify the Wallace-Jones conflict which had just begun when I lost contact with a daily newspaper.

Darling, as usual, I wish that I could continue to write to you ad infinitum. It always happens that I spend my time writing you, and have no time for anyone else (I really don't mind a great deal). However, this must be "good night." I love you with the strength of my soul and mind and heart. May the God we know and love bless and strengthen in eternity

> Our Love,
> Bushy

Letter excerpt from Art to Dotty
Somewhere in France
Tues. 2-20-45

Mother writes that Fred, who is over here, may get a furlough home. He has been overseas for 3½ years and in Europe since D-Day. I certainly hope that he can get home. She also writes that Uldene and her husband have a car and furniture all paid for and are now looking for a home. Hearing such things and also hearing about Peggy Murrian and the other infanticipators makes me long for the time when we can get a little planning done ourselves. I'm counting on that bank account. I think that I shall leave my bonds as they are, for I see that money is no use. However, we have heard that furlough to England are not outside the realm of possibility. I would give a great deal for a visit there. Who knows, the chance may come!

Don't let this influence the box you send, but we had a wonderful meal yesterday—southern fried chicken, brown gravy, mashed potatoes. I think it was probably the best I have had in a long time. Saw "Pin-up Girl" today, but thought it thoroughly lousy. Of course, the band was good, but I don't care for bands of that type.

Darling, I live not in the present but always in the future, in our future. I long for the day when we can settle down, away from the rough and sordid side of life, when dreams will be fulfilled and God will complete the blessings of

Our Love,

Bushy

P.S. Shall try this one "Free" just to compare time taken to get through.

Letter excerpt from Dotty to Art
[February 19, 1945]
Monday at the Office

"I was to wear my new dress and the new griddle which I had never worn before. You would have laughed, I am sure, to see me struggling with the exasperating garment. I finally manage to get into it, and by dint of much effort got the thing fastened. All should have then been fine, but alas I attempted to bend over for to put on my stockings and found to my dismay I wasn't bendable. (You might say I was exbendable) There were stiff metal stays in the front of it which jammed into my ribs and stomach at a great rate upon any attempt at bending. After cutting into the seam and removing these stays, I had then only to hitch my stockings to it and the ordeal would be over. But I had not reckoned with the fact that the supporters ended with a type of fastener with which I had never dealt before. After much fastening and re-fastening I finally discovered how it worked. Whew! The girdle was on!"

Feb. 20, '45

On Saturday last, I experienced full participation in the famed French Black Market. We received our PX [Post Exchange] rations including six packs of cigarettes. Since we arrived cigarettes have been selling

for 50 francs, but the value, of course, has depreciated as a result of the large influx of GIs. I went to town on Sat. having been told that I would not be able to sell my six packs. I wandered the streets for some time and finally sold to two boys of 16 or 17 eager to get them. Later one of the S/Sgts from my platoon (Taylor) told me that we could sell them in a certain café. Five or six of us entered the place and sat down as though to order drinks. Taylor went into the back room and made the connections. He called me and I too went back. I was told to slip my packs into an empty ice box. The Frenchman wrote the figures on the table top with his finer—40 francs per pack. We returned to our table after receiving our money. Cider was ordered but when I brought the glass to my lips I thought it was vinegar. I finally pushed the drink aside. I'm far too young to begin drinking now.

The experience of selling cigarettes as I did had a tang of excitement that was out of the ordinary. I believe that it is basically wrong to participate in Black marketing. However, there are two or three reasons that I think of in rationalizing my action. For one thing, I wanted to have the experience, the subdued thrill if you will, of taking part in such an affair. Thousands of GIs are doing it, and many on a large scale. The French Black Market will go down as a black page in the annals of this war. This is not excuse in itself and certainly is not justification. In the second place, I felt that I needed the money. We have had no full payment since Dec. and only one partial payment of $5. Most of us are penniless. Our squad has been getting bread, butter, and eggs, and they have used up most of their loose money. I have contributed little. However, I could have waited to make it up to them later. I did not have to have money. In the third place, all of us dislike seeing others make money when we can't or don't. Some of the men brought cartons of cigarettes to sell. Others sell their rations, but almost everyone has participated in one degree of another.

In Coronet (Dec. 44) I found a condensation of A Tree Grows in Brooklyn, the very popular book by Betty Smith. The following passage is interesting:

"Francie has heard swearing since she had heard words. Obscenity and profanity had no meanings as such among those people. They were emotional expressions of inarticulate people with small vocabularies; they made a kind of dialect. The phrases could mean many things according to the expression and tone used in saying them."

This is not fine writing in the best sense of the word, but it has particular significance and meaning for me in regard to certain Army associations.

Letter from "S. Beulah" to Art
[from Mary Ruth, Dotty's sister]
Feb. 20, 1945

Dear Bro. B.,

How are the whales? Or did they ever show up? You should have been a whalethy man when you got there. (Ha!) (Oops! I just discovered you can take that 2 ways! Take your choice.)

You really have a clean little sister tonight. Right after supper I went down and did one more huge washing; then I came up and changed my bed (and on Tuesday, too!) then I took a nice leisurely bath. Now I'm cleaning up my correspondence (ha! ha! Oh, Beulah, you're sharp tonight.)

My letter life? Ugh. Your you don't know how welcome letter and one from your sweet wife today were the first I've had for over 2 weeks now. Maybe the jinx is broke. Do you reckon so? Letters from the Philippines are (be)coming mighty few and far between lately, but I 'low as how that there must be a pretty busy place right now, eh? Anyway, I was more than glad to get

Morning, Feb. 21

it – I was tickled to pieces. (Put me back together fast & in an hurry, roommate—I have a class in a few minutes!)

Today a War Bond Queen will be elected. Each class nominated a girl, and the class which buys the most war stamps (percentage basis, of course) will be the one whose queen is elected. My roommate almost got the sophomore nomination, but didn't.

There seems to be no news now, so I sorta think this letter will be a shorty. I'll try to do better next time. Be a good Bushy, and don't do anything my brother-in-law wouldn't do.

Your lurvin' sis,
S. Beulah

P.S. – Your valumtime was so cute [three hearts drawn here]!

P.S.S. – I suppose Dot told you about the Feb. Meetings? If not, let me know, and I'll try to supply a little information.

Letter excerpt from Art's Parents to Art
February 20, 1945

Dear Son:

The long awaited message, meager as it was, came last night. We accepted it as notice of your safe landing somewhere, and we are so glad and thankful for that much news. We also know that more will be forthcoming when you have time to write. We are hoping you can tell us where you are for it helps a lot not to have to imagine so much.

We are OK and for once in a long time we are not rushed with work. Unless "work or fight" bill is passed (and we don't think it will be) we are going to have easy going for a while. What a change!

Your Vmail address was postmarked 2-17-45 and reached us 2-19. Of course we have no way of knowing where it was mailed or when you wrote it, but when your first letter comes we will be able to judge how long it will take for us to hear.

We had a letter from Dorothy last week in which she said she was waiting patiently for a letter. She sent us "The Robe" which I'm reading and enjoying it very much. She seems to be keeping busy, but is coming over to see us some weekend when she has some free time....

Your Dad has had a recurrence of his kidney trouble and for several days he had difficulty getting up or down on account of his back, but as suddenly as it comes, it goes and at present he is OK again. At least its a reminder that he must be careful and take care of himself.

We are thinking of you, praying that you will not be called upon to do a harder job than you are able to do, and patiently waiting the word which will let us know how you are.

Lots of love
Mother & Dad

[Written in top margin.]

Dear precious son: Must make real effort to write you a long letter soon. God bless & keep you. Hope the going isn't too tough. You are doing your part I am sure. May God sustain, strengthen & keep you for the final victory. A heart full of love. Dad.

Letter excerpt from Dotty to Art
Wednesday
Feb. 21, 1945

Last night after work I rushed home to get supper for Daddy and me (Mother is staying with the sick folks for a few days), and after it was over we picked up Mother and all of us went to see the show "Since You

Went Away", starring Claudette Colbert, Jennifer Jones, Shirley Temple, Monty Wooley and a few other stars that made a pretty wonderful cast. You can imagine what the story was about. The main characters were a mother and her two highschool age girls and the poppa who had been called into the Navy and was overseas, didn't show up in the picture at all. Rather the picture was concerned with the very human and moving events that happened to the family he left behind. Everybody in the theater (except Daddy) wept in spots, because it hit so many tender spots. The father was missing in action for a long time, and the boy friend of the oldest girl was killed in action, so you can see why it hit tender spots. Having heard so much about the picture and how sad it was, I was very interested in discovering what my reaction to it would be. I found that rather than depressing me or overwhelming me with doubts and fears as to your welfare, rather than that it served to strengthen my belief which I have held all along that your faith is what counts in this situation, your faith is what pulls you through, your faith is what enables you to know a peace that other people sometimes do not have. He who puts his trust in God need have no fears of any kind. Well, that was free preachment. I didn't intend to delve this far into the matter.

Feb. 22, '45

Today was a red letter day in my Army experience. It began this morning when we arose half an hour early. I awoke an hour early and built a fire. We started out at 8:30 on one of the hardest hikes for some months. Ten miles in about two hours and a half. Soldiers seem never to learn to keep the line closed up and thus those in the rear are forced to run. We were in the rear for one hour and we ran.

We came back for a swell meal, and I had tremendous seconds. After lunch we were waiting to wash our mess kits when distinguished visitors arrived. The enlisted men stared in wild amazement; the officers dashed wildly. Our own CO., of course, accompanied the men, and the party entered one of the tents along the company street [the kitchen]. In a few moments, they came out and, miracle of miracles, they came into our tent—three shoulders of brass, big brass. When [we] were called to attention, we stood with eyes glued upon our first visitor.

Sgt. O'Connell reported. "Where are you from"? he was asked. "What is your job? How many experts? [reference to a rating usually made on the rifle range in basic training] (Ans. 'none') This is a rifle squad, isn't it? How many sharpshooters?"

"I'm not sure, Sir."

With a series of expletives that are hardly suitable for reprinting, he gave a suggestion to John: "When you get up there, know everything about your men. When there is a job to do, know what every man can do."

I received every impression of efficiency, business, interest in the individual, and realization of the job to be done. Many reports concerning the men were verified. Both of the big boys showed effects of work, of lack of exercise. It was a unique experience to have so distinguished a visitor in our tent, talking to our squad leader. When he left, he patted John on the left shoulder, smiled, and walked out. I shall not forget the experience of this day.

[THE DISTINGUISHED VISITOR WAS GEN. DWIGHT D. EISENHOWER. FOLLOWING WARNINGS OF CENSORSHIP, I REFRAINED FROM PUTTING HIS NAME IN THE NOTES I MADE. IN LIGHT OF THE FACT THAT OUR SQUAD DID NOT TRAIN TOGETHER AND THAT SGT. O'CONNELL HAD NOT BEEN WITH THE MEN VERY LONG BEFORE WE CAME TO EUROPE, IT WAS HIGHLY UNLIKELY THAT HE WOULD HAVE KNOWN OUR MARKSMANSHIP RATINGS FROM BASIC TRAINING. MY MEMORIES OF THE GENERAL'S PERFORMANCE WERE NOT VERY POSITIVE.]

The climax of the day came tonight when I had a long talk with Sgt. Christenson on philosophy and religion. Happy to find that he has a renewed interest in religion. After much thought in regard to Utopian plans, he has decided that religion is the one thing lacking. He reached the conclusion by way of the political avenue. 'Tis highly interesting that [Frank] Brink, Bob Schwarzwalder, Dick Boyd, Dr. Orr, and I discussed this very thing over and over again at Maryville College. We approached from the other avenue, but we reached the same conclusion. Truth is an entity!

Letter from Ted to Art

22 Feb 45

Dear Art,

Received your letter yesterday in the quick time of one day and was plenty glad to hear from you. Naturally enough, I was figuring on how we could get together. And that's rather a tough preposition—we're a little too far apart for walking purposes & as for getting off to get up there is also a problem of certain proportions. As for getting a pass I've never heard of such things! We are allowed into nearby towns in the evenings, but the curfew doesn't allow for a very extended tour! When something comes along which calls for a trip into your area I really don't believe it is possible for us to get together. If I should even get there, I'll be sure to look you up & there's always the chance that the possibility will occur. Maybe if we move we'll be more conveniently located to each other. However, I like this & am quite willing to stay. I don't doubt but what you feel the same way. I'll bet your rumors are good & thick over there—ours are juicy enough, too though I've been surprised that there aren't more than there are. That sure was a good one about hearing that we were going overseas!

That trip was good, wasn't it? Generally warm & smooth & as pleasant as such a trip could be. Wish we could see some of this countryside together. Some of it certainly is fascinating & the villages & churches so unique & old looking. Have taken up about a half roll of film so far, but really haven't had the chance to do what I'd like along those lines. These last few day since the rain cleared up have really made it quite worthwhile living & pleasant at times!

Glad you get those "frequent letters from the wonderful wife." Nothing quite like them for a morale booster. And the mail service is pretty good too. Up till now, letters from Cordelia have averaged 9 or ten days, but tonight brought in a batch of old mail from home written a month ago. With nothing much else to do in nights I've written letters galore. We get a movie every third night which I faithfully attend when not on h.q. c.q. or KP. The latter I've pulled once, & the former is my second night on tonight. Obviously scrape the new power bottoms for both! Neither is bad out here. Cordelia said she had a letter from Dottie who liked her job very well & wanted Cordelia to come down & live with her & work in the hospital.

Have you heard from Pratt recently? I have & he's over here somewhere. He says he was at the same POE we were at the same time. I'll bet he crossed at the same time, too. By the way, Art, any address over here if you know the APO is in the European Theater of Operations just write it local, U.S. Army instead of the c/o PM, N.Y. stuff—as of this envelope. Pratt's address is APO 15754, C/o PM, N.Y.

Glad someone heard of or about Jack. Believe I'll endeavor to get the correspondence going again—it would probably do him good if I know Jack Feldman. He'll probably get in on what I think will be a big push for the Coast of China. Maybe we'll get in on the invasion of the coast of England! But this is a peaceful place, all right. The longer we hold out here the better off we are. I believe even the brass is starting to think that, too.

By the way, it was French that you were proficient in, if I remember correctly! You aught to keep from rusting up too much then. Sure is not much to do with the money I hear we might be getting—and the rations are precious. We've got to get together for a session some time—have lots on my mind too. Cordelia is substitute teaching off & on, but no steady job yet, she had a scare (which would have pleased you, had it been your wife) & haven't heard from her since. Certainly don't want to be a papa this time of year!

Take it easy, Art, & we'll make the connections sooner or later.
Ted.
P.S. The censors like words spelled out so I went thru & spelled out C.

V-Mail from Art to Dotty
February 21, 1945

Sing out sweet songs, ye skies above,
Of yearning hearts, and tell of love
Fast through the hourglass runs the sands
So let our hearts go hand in hand
And if the clouds should hide the sun
Making shadows as of night, then one
Bright ray that none but I could see
Would shine from love you gave to me
And on this silver path I'll stand,
Come, let our hearts go hand in hand.
All My Love,
Bushy

Letter from Arza Bushing (Art's mom) to Dotty
Friday Feb. 23 1945

Dear Dorothy

We too feel like saying "Yippee." Yesterday we received an Air Mail letter written at sea and a Vmail one written from "somewhere in France" so there is no more wondering about where he is. He had a good trip considering the situation and we are so glad. We think he is taking a very sensible view of the whole thing, and feel sure that he is being guided by the Divine Hand.

"Believe it or not" or work is beginning to lighten up, and for the first time in months and months we feel caught up. We were interested in all you wrote about your work, and hope you continue to find it interesting. Keeping busy is one sure way to keep from worrying—too much.

We will be glad to have you come over any weekend you are free; but inconvenient as it is, there is no bus but the 4:30 P.M. (Well we do have a 9:30 A.M.) Just send me a card and I'll have some of the dust taken up.

The past few days have been real spring like and I'm getting anxious to dig in the dirt. I have plenty of leaves to take up when the days get a bit longer. My Crocus are blooming and they make quite a bit of color among the dull gray leaves.

Yesterday afternoon I reset some shrubs, and today I hope to get home in time to do some pruning on the grapevines. I don't know how we are going to plan about a garden, but I do know that I can have the plot which I planted last year. That I can prepare myself, but this labor shortage is something to be reckoned with.

We are writing Air Mail letters—as the Air Mail came just as fast as the V. Mail and we can write so much more by Air Mail. From the news it looks as though some day the whole thing will be over and we won't have to depend on letters.

I've nearly finished reading "The Robe" and am enjoying it very much. I recently read "My Son, My Son" and enjoyed it also.

We both send love and best wishes and hope to see you in the near future.

Mother B.

Do you think Ted was on the boat going over? He said one of his Stanford friends was with him and I'm hoping it is Ted. They've been together so long.

[Written in top margin]

Howdy Dorothy dear! Come over whenever you can. If work continues to slacken off a bit I am coming over a spend week-end. Kind & loving wishes to Pa & Mother Barber.

A.S. Daddy Bushing

Am sending Arthur a supply of Air-Mail stamps. ASB

Dearest Heart,

Much of my faith in things of the spirit was renewed last night and tonight by separate experiences. I was on K.P. yesterday, but was relieved last night in time to go to Wednesday evening services in town. "Sod," Beul, and I had a special pass and went in to find about ten men present. Both Chaplains were present and we had a good song service and Bible study discussion of John 15.

2-23-45

The service was led by Chaplain Webb of whom I have spoken before. It was like a refreshing shower to enjoy the fellowship in the meeting. The second thing that I intended to mention last was a talk which I had with Sgt. Christenson. (Remember me speaking of him when we were in C_____?) I had never discussed religion with him before, but we had a big discussion last night. He says that in recent months he has taken a new interest in religion and is anxious to find out more. After talking for some time and with some hesitation, he mentioned that he had arrived at a rather radical conclusion. I urged him to continue. He began by saying that after studying a number of the utopian plans for a future world, he felt that all lacked something. That something was religion. I hastened to tell him of the Group at Maryville and how much we had thought along exactly the same lines. I was overjoyed to find another thinker who had reached the same answer from an entirely different avenue of approach. Chris studied social science for four years at U.C.L.A.

'Tis encouraging, these incidents in helping me over rough spots, just as your wonderful letters are encouraging—though in no way to be compared with the strength that comes from your faith. It seems that the process is extremely slow, but someday perhaps people will be led to see the simple truths that a carpenter preached two thousand years ago. I am more firmly convinced as time goes by that Christ is absolutely the only answer. But winning people to this point of view involves the passing on of understanding in the "Orean" sense of the word. It involves the individual being led to know truly in his own mind that the first commandment is to "Love thy God..." and the second like unto it.... Dick, Ken, Bob, Brink and the rest of the fellows had reached this point in their thinking, and, of course, there are many others. God grant that more and more of us may see the Light of Spiritual Truth before Scientific investigation over balances the scale and our entire civilization topples as a result of its top-heavy condition.

On K.P. the other day I had the glorious job of smashing cans—(the cook over seas must know how to open cans—that is all; K.P.'s smash them!) As events ran, I was given a half a can of pan-cake batter to empty. Instead of following orders, I obeyed my established Scotch nature and hustled the can off to my tent. With butter saved from our meals, our little squad greased the top of our stove and fried pancakes. Mixed with bits of coal and ash from the stove top, the cakes tasted like the finest to be obtained in any café in gay Paree. We also have the habit of toasting our bread on the stove top, and that too tastes delicious.

Going from food for the stomach to food for thought, I quote an interesting passage which I found in a condensation of A Tree Grows in Brooklyn, appearing in Coronet (Or: 44): "Francie had heard swearing since she had heard words. Obscenity and profanity had no meanings as such among those people. They were emotional expressions of inarticulate people with small vocabularies; they made a kind of dialect. The phrase could mean many things according to the expression and tone used in saying them." This is not fine writing in the best sense of the word, but it has particular significance and meaning for me in regard to certain Army associations. There are two things, yes three, which drive me very close to the explosion point time and time again. I abhor the low and vile interest in sex that the majority of the men display; I am completely disgust at the constant use of profane language used by the "inarticulate people with small vocabularies;" and I am filled with pity and alarm at the strong racial feeling and hatred that exists among American soldiers.

Your letter of the 26th was the last to arrive, but the one of the 8th was the latest which I have received. Should have a sizable stack tomorrow. I hope that soon I will hear that my letters from the boat have begun to arrive.

Tonight, Beul, Sod, and I came to town to write letters in the little service club in town and listen to a short wave radio which we have in the club. We have been listening to everything from German propaganda to original Swiss yodeling. The former is rather interesting. American jazz is played, and from time to time news broadcasts are given from the Gen. point of view. We have listened to Swedish broadcasts, Russian music, French, Italian and good old U.S. The latter sounds always the sweetest.

The Valentine Art sent to Dotty via V-Mail on February 14, 1945

Darling, the sands run apace. My hands are cold and the hour is late. I love you with a love that springs from a deep spiritual unity. The culmination is in eternity for
      Our Love,
      Bushy

Letter from Dotty to Art
Friday, Feb. 24 [1945]

My darling, darling Bushy,

How utterly wonderful! What joy, what bliss! How happy I am! Oh rapture, oh contentment beyond compare! O.K., O.K. I'll tell you what I am raving about—I got <u>four</u> letters from you today! Four! What a thrill it gave me to stand beside you on the deck in the moonlight and at sunset, enjoying to the full the wondrous things that God has wrought, and squeezing your hand <u>almost</u> as hard as you squeezed mine. The letters that came were the two airmail affairs that gave a complete account of your trip, and two V-mails—one the valentine (how sweet) [below] and the other written "somewhere in France" and telling of mud and going to bed with the chickens and of the communion service.

This game with the postman makes life very exciting. I always seem to know when I am going to get mail. Today the postman hadn't come when I left for the office, so I phoned Mother soon after I got there, but mail still hadn't come. I had to go to town to pick up some mimeographed letters to be mailed to members of the church, and as soon as I returned from that mission I called again to find out about the mail situation. She nearly floored me when she told me I had five letters! Four from you and one from Jean Kaelber. Joe is about to get a medical discharge on account of his hands. In fact, the doctors at the hosp. where he is now can't figure out how he ever got into the army with such a condition existing. Clinton was discharged some time ago, is now attending Stanford as a civilian student! The Ritchie boys are slowly drifting into the infantry. They've graduated at Ritchie and are just waiting around for something to happen. Borgis & somebody else have entered Inf. OCS, Katy has applied for it, and that's how things stand there.

I didn't get a good chance to read the letters till after Record Breakers tonight. Mother brought them to me at work, but I was very busy getting those letters out, and immediately after 5:00 I went to town to mail the letters and then on to the Y.H. for the Modern Dance class I have joined. It is lots of fun, and splendid exercise, but oh, I'm gonna be sore tomorrow! After class dash (?) home, eat supper, clean up, and go to R.B. We had a very interesting lecture on the "scherzo." I made five buttonholes on your Mother's blouse during the evening.

And now I've read & reread your letters my dear. It thrills my soul to know that my puny faith has helped you some. It may help some more to know that my faith is growing stronger every day we are separated. I feel that God has a plan for us, and that part of the revelation of that plan lies in the beauty and depth of the love we have known, which has so enriched our lives and souls. Perhaps he means for us to feed the poor in heart from the riches of
Our Love,
Dotty.
Saturday –
Oh, brother, am I sore. And getting sorer. But I'm happy on account of said mail (male) situation. 'Tis most time for the postman. God bless you and
Our Love, Dotty.

Letter from Dotty to Art
Sunday, Feb. 25 [1945]

My Darling,

I've got spring fever! What we are having now may prove to be a false spring, but it is certainly nice while it lasts. Perfectly balmy weather, perfectly balmy. Warm breeze, warm sun, warm me. As I looked up at a blue sky and white, fluffy clouds, and the warm breeze tugged at my hair, I pressed your hand, gazed into your eyes, and said "How wonderful" without opening my mouth except to smile at you.

In fact, you seemed quite near to me all day as I enjoyed nature, communed with God, and went about observing the Sabbath Day. Mrs. Johnson's class was even more inspiring than usual. The lesson was of "Jesus, The Son of God." In it Jesus was asking the 12 who men that [thought] he was, and of course Peter gave the classic answer "Thou art the Christ, son of the living God." She worked that around to asking what answer we would give if asked that question, and in asking the question, she made it weigh on each person personally. Dr Peyton made me squirm a little by his sermon. If each person in the church brought one other person into the church per year everybody would belong in no time! I regret to say that I have never won one single solitary soul to Christ that I know of. Have you? We're slippin. And that ain't good.

It is now Monday morning, and I must to work. One fellow wrote from Paris that potted ham on doughnut makes a swell combination—I thought you should know about it!

God bless
        Our Love,
        Dotty

P.S. Mizpah

P.S.2 Ruth Duggan is in town on leave, and is coming over for supper tonight.

Letter from Art to Dotty
Somewhere in France
Feb. 25, 1945 (Sun.)
(39-44)

My Dearest Heart,

'Tis Sunday now. Most of the men are out on pass or playing ball. Three of us remain in the tent and I welcome the relatively quiet period in which I can write and think. These opportunities seem all too rare these days. I miss terribly the hours that we had together in which we could pursue thought on the plane of our own choosing.

After my discussion with Christenson, which I mentioned in my last letter, I decided to attend the Mormon service this morning. And so, at nine o'clock, while you were still dreaming sweet dreams, Beul and I went to the little French school building at the crossroads which is being used for services. On our way, we were picked up by Col. G., our Battalion Commander, who happens to be a member of the Mormon faith. A small group was present and the service soon began. Communion is taken each Sunday and consists of bread and water. There is no ritual but two prayers accompanying the passing of the elements. We sang from a Mormon song book made up for the most part of hymns written by members of the faith. The lesson was a discussion of the 13th Article of Faith, corresponding closely to the 13th Ch. of I Corinthians. I enjoyed the service as a whole and hope to attend again.

One point which was merely mentioned this morning struck me with interest, and that was in regard to celestial marriage. It seems that the Mormons include in their marriage ceremony a passage which indicates an eternal bond. My first thought was to question why other rituals did not include this. It would seem to be a beautiful inclusion. However, as I began to write of this just now, I recalled Luke 20:34, 35. "....they which shall be accounted worthy to obtain that world, and the resurrection from the dead neither marry nor or [be] given in marriage." I wonder what you think of this question and how Dr. Peyton would interpret it. If you recall, this answer by Christ was regarding a woman who had married seven brothers. It does not apply direct to two people, although a general principle I suppose could be drawn. I still have a deep feeling that the love that exists between us has an eternally spiritual quality which will transcend the physical world we know. Let me know what you think regarding those points.

After the Mormon service, we stayed for the regular Protestant Service under Chaplain Webb. The sermon "On Forsaking our Birthright" was based on the story of Esau and Jacob. I find that Webb is a deep thinker and very much to my liking. He spoke of the great potential for each man and the necessity for reaching God's level. I hope that you have had the chance to read the book on Presbyterian Doctrine. I would like very much for you to summarize it in your letters.

Yesterday came your letter of the 11th and I am glad to hear about the Deann situation. It does my heart good to hear about these young people. Takes me back to my early days—long years ago. I hope you can cut down on the Sunday schedule, Darling. It should be a day of rest insofar as possible. And don't apologize for griping. Goodness knows I do enough of that for both of us. Glad to hear that the February Meetings are doing well. I too shall add my prayers to yours for their success. I well remember how much they can mean. Mom's letter, written the 25th of Jan., arrived only last week and I was glad to hear from her. She suggests that I can now really accuse you of chasing me all over the country. Hmm! I wrote "Mom" & Dad a few days ago and will try to write as often as possible.

What does Flo hear from Carl? I thought that I had his address with me, but I don't. Include it in a letter some time. Also tell me what's new with Samarriet and give them my loving wishes.

All indications are that the big push is on in Europe as of yesterday. I cannot help feeling that this must be the beginning of the end, for Germany cannot possibly withstand the full onslaught of the combined strength of the allied countries. The news from the Pacific is also most encouraging, although we are only receiving the highlights of that theater of activity. I still have had no second class mail in the form of magazines, etc. Am looking forward to that first package from you. By the way, I understand that a list is not necessary item by item for a package, but a general request for something is enough. I shall from time to time mention that food from home is wonderful to receive. You can use the requests as you wish but don't feel that you must send them every time I mention package. To send them at intervals will be much better. I just thought of something else which I should have and that is a laundry stamp. You should be able to get it (along with a pad and ink) at one of the office supply stores in town. The number I want is B-9120. As to the size, I would like to have one suitable for carrying around and yet not too small. I think that some near ¼" (one fourth inch) letters would be about right. This G.I. laundry takes indelible pencil right out of clothes and I should have a permanent mark.

I am trying to keep up with my notes reflecting something of the life of the G.I., my surroundings, and my own thoughts and feelings regarding these things. Insofar as possible, I shall try to copy bits from these notes in my letters, just in case I lose my journals. However, I hope that I shall be able to return with my little black book filled to the brim. The squad already expects me to publish what I am writing and they are extremely curious as to what I put down. I hope that it will prove of interest to our little ones.

Speaking of "the substance of things hoped for," I think a great deal about our responsibilities as parents and the task that we will face in training our children. I am convinced that a minimum amount of money tends to bring a family close together and solidify the bonds binding them together. For to have a minimum amount of money means that great care must be taken in the spending thereof and sacrifices will have to be made by all. Sacrifice invariably tends to unify the bonds of union.

There is a great deal of G.I. equipment that we could use for camping after the war. I want to get at least one pup tent (with closed ends), two muisette bags for carrying equipment on our back, mess equipment, cantines [French spelling], cantine cup, cover, a pair of combat boots for hiking, and a couple of pairs of woolens. All of these things will be swell to have for camping and also for that cabin we shall have in Emerts Cove. All of these things should be selling at very reasonable rate. We shall see.

Luckily our weekly PX rations have been coming through and we get a little candy along. Supplies of ink and papers are extremely limited so I shall be glad to get either or both now and then. Really, Darling, I don't mean to plague you with things to send; but there is always a chance that some of these letters will be lost. If I refer to articles more than once, it is merely to insure getting it eventually. I hope that my system of number the pages consecutively will be of help.

I was wondering today if it would be practically for me to have a subscription to the Journal. How much would it cost? Don't do anything until I find out more about it. As I mentioned before, we are still waiting for second class mail, but I shall investigate the prospects.

I must bring this to a close just as the moon appears over the Eastern horizon. I can see it appearing on the horizon in Emerts Cove with all the glory that is Le Conte rising to meet the sky. I hope you are able to visit the cabin often, my Love. I have many happy memories of our visits there. I also think of the grand lake in Oct. with you, Dr. Peyton, & Dad. I am far below that mountain top at present, but the thought of it give me strength and light for the shadows. I live in the faith of

      Our Love,
      Bushy

Feb. 26, 1945

Last Wed. night [Sgt.] Soderstrom, Root, and I received passes to attend the mid-week service in town. The rest of the company went out on patrols, but we were lucky enough to be able to get away. The attendance was not large, but we had a good discussion of John 15: 1-10. Chaplain Webb is a provoker of thought. I always enjoy singing. Afterward we stayed in the little service center and listened to the short wave radio. We heard everything from Swiss yodeling to German propaganda. We also heard Russian Folk music, French, Italian, and German music. Sweetest to our ears was American jazz.

Saturday we completed the second big hike of the week. This one was scheduled for fifteen miles, but it must have been eighteen. My leg muscles were still stiff from Thursday. In the vernacular of current expression, I was "hurting" every step of the way. During the third hour, I had a return engagement with my old headaches, which cause me to wonder how long I can continue to control my action. I wonder if the Doctor in Camp Roberts was correct. When I go days without sleep, with little food, with all the physical and mental strain that will accompany combat, I wonder what my reaction will be. I sometimes think that if I would only break loose—griping with each irritation— that the tension would be released. However, that is against my nature. I shall hold myself in restraint as long as it is possible to do. I hope and pray that I shall not break under strain.

On Sunday morning I brushed up my rifle for inspection and left it on my bunk. I then left with Root and Christenson for the Mormon service. On our way we were picked up by Lt. Col. G—'s jeep. (He is our Btn. Co.) Upon arrival at the little ecole at the crossroads, a small group was present and Bro. G—(as he was called) led the service. Communion (with water) is held each week and this we took without the usual reading but accompanied by two prayers. Later a Sunday School lesson was discussed by a Lt. whom I had never seen before. The discussion was based on the 13th Article of Faith, closely paralleling the 13th Ch. of I Cor. There seems to exist a very fine feeling of brotherly affection. However, I sensed a self-conscious feeling of oppression. Perhaps it is thoroughly justified. I was left with a lukewarm feeling, but I do want to find out more about the faith.

I was interested in a reference to celestial marriage. It seems that the Mormon ceremony includes a reference to the eternal bond of love. The idea struck me as being a very fine one. However, I later began to think of Christ's admonition in this regard in Luke 20: 34-35: "...but *they which shall be accounted worthy to obtain that world, and the resurrection from the dead, neither marry, nor are given in marriage." This, of course, was in answer to the query concerning the woman with seven husbands. I find it difficult to apply this to but two people. I somehow must feel that the deep and abiding love that exists between Dotty and me will extend far beyond this physical existence. Our Love has reached a spiritual level that transcends the physical. God is truly Love, and our relationship is a divine one reflecting in part the Love of God. Thus, to me, our Love cannot and will not die when the end of our physical life comes but will extend on into the dimness of the afterlife.*

Beul and I remained for the regular Protestant service led by Chaplain Webb. Using the story of Esau and Jacob, he discussed "Foregoing our Birthright." One of the points that impressed me was the potential for each individual—either angel or devil. He spoke of God's plan for every individual and the necessity of reaching God's level not by wishful thinking but by striving.

Letter excerpt from Art to Dotty
Somewhere in France
2 – 27 – '45
(45-46)

Glad that you are sending Mother the birthday blouse. I, of course, could send her nothing at the time, but I will send something when I can. She mentioned receipt of your birthday letter. The incident of the girdle is not precisely distressing, but I shall await a final verdict until I see you.

Somewhere in France
Feb. 28, 1945
(47-50)

Dearest Heart,

The hour is late and I must hasten to bed, but I shall at least be able to start a letter tonight. I just returned from the Wednesday night service which was very fine. Chaplain Webb discussed a portion of the Sermon on the Mount and I was particularly impressed by the comments on two familiar phrases: "Ye are the salt of the earth... Ye are the light of the world..." He brought this down to our own situation and how the Christians in our outfit uphold the light of Christian Truth. But the point that impressed me more was another comment he made. He made reference to God's promise that if ten righteous ones were found in the cities of the plain that the cities would be spared. The few Christians scattered through out the world have been the salt that has savored the world (no pun intended), he said, and they have given light to a dark and troubled to mankind.

I have a new understanding of Christ and the money changers, Darling. I expect to write you sometime telling of an experience not far different. There are times when I want to smash noses with all my physical strength, and yet I know that it is useless. Prejudice cannot be driven out nor wisdom and understanding driven in by a blow of the fist. Nevertheless my righteous indignation has been aroused more than once in recent days.

March 1 – Thurs.

Today we had another rare occurrence in the Army—excellent steak, mashed potatoes and brown gravey, peas, and peach cobbler. Slurp, slurp! It was really an exceptional meal. We have been receiving far better chow in recent days, but it can always stop as suddenly as it began. We have had real spuds of late—not the dehydrated kind, and many other vegetables have been fresh. Since I arrived here, I have tasted powdered milk for the first time. I was surprised how good it is and I like it almost as much as the real thing. We get it for cereal every morning and sometimes it is our beverage. Coffee, of course, comes twice a day, but we usually have a juice for the third meal. Some one in our squad (Brelden, a farm boy from Va.) received the first box today. Whoosh! When twelve men begin on a box it doesn't last long. Remember that any box to me is to the squad and will go twelve ways. That is the way things work over here. Before registrations were clamped down, some of the fellows were able to get French bread, butter, and sometimes a few eggs. These have been shared equally no matter who paid the bill. It was a picturesque picture to see twelve men gathered around the little stove, a dim light throwing grotesque shadows on the walls of the tent, with eggs frying on the stove lid. Almost every meal we brown are bread right on the stove top after pushing most of the dirt off. What a life!

I signed up for the regimental choir today and we had our first practice. The leader is the same fellow that directed the choir on ship board. It seems that the regimental C.O. is desirous that we have a choir and we are to give a command performance for the General in a few days. Beul is also attending and so is Fred Price (Miss.) We should have a lot of fun and the training could accidentally help me. I am reaching the point where I get along with my bass [brass] far better than formerly. Wish you could see the little portable organ that the chaplains have. It is only slightly wider than than a regular suitcase and a few inches longer, but when opened up it pours out an amazing volume of music.

There has been a growing indication that something may eventually break on the western front as the tidal wave of the Ninth and Third Armies drive on toward Cologne. I have been able to follow the events as they have unfolded so far, and the situation certainly seems satisfactory. The weather is still bad but I don't think that it will be so cold from now on. The mud is terrible but even that should disappear before many weeks. I think that part of my optimism was dampened long months ago, but I can't see how the Germans can withstand this present onslaught. I can't see how they can possibly hold out until June 1st. A break before then would not surprise me in the least. Although I have not been able to follow the Pacific war in as much detail, I have, of course, noted the present trend of strategy. Our vast power in that theater is at last being unleashed. Today Japan reported that an island (Pelawan (?) has been invaded just north of Borneo. If so, this may be that thrust into the N.E.I. Hmm! I feel free to make another little prediction in that area. I think you recall the cabinet situation in Japan. When things go wrong, this body accepts the flame and usually resigns. This has already taken place two or three times with each succeeding cabinet being less and less radical. I think that the New Party spoken of recently will eventually put in its own cabinet. The new cabinet will claim to be against the military cliche and will seek peace. It may take more than one cabinet change but it will come, "So sorry," they will say. "Evil Japanese forced us to fight our good friends, the Americans. We never wanted to fight!" How soon they will accept unconditional terms is perhaps another question, but it will come sooner or later.

Dearest, my mind is filled with thoughts of our Love, of our Future. I think of you constantly and long for the day when we can continue our plans. I wonder just when we can take up those plans again. May we prepare our hearts and minds for the tasks that are ahead. May God bless

   Our Love,
   Bushy

Letter excerpt from Mother Bushing to Dotty

Jamestown Tennessee

Mar. 1, 1945

"No word from our soldier since the one V-Mail letter saying he had landed in France. We await patiently more news of his reaction to real military life, and any other news he is permitted to write. He wrote that he had asked you to send him some things including a flashlight. If you can't get one there, we will be glad to give up the one he left with us. We can very well get along without it if he needs it. If there is anything else we can furnish please let us know. Isn't it too bad he can't have all the juices stored in our basement? I bet he could make way with every bit of it.... Love and best wishes from us both Mother B."

Mar. 1, 1945

The first day of March dawned with a clearing sky and the promise of a change in the weather. We were glad, for every clear day means better bombing weather to support the big offensive up front. However, clouds soon arose and temperature dropped. It turned cold and miserable. A forced march of four miles in an hour had been scheduled, but this was canceled—supposedly because there were too many blisters resulting from yesterday's 15 miles. We cleaned weapons all morning.

Yesterday we took the second long hike, and I took 26, 800 paces doing it—c. 15.2 miles. I paced it just to satisfy myself in regard to the total distance. We did the same thing on Sat. and it seemed at least 18. Interesting to note the difference in pace near the front and the rear of the column. On Sat. we were next to the last company in a battalion of seven companies, and we were almost running for the entre march. Yesterday we were the second company in the battalion and the pace was even. The difference was caused in the falling back and closing up all along the long length of slugging lengths. In the forward positions, the variation is not noticeable.

Saw Kinsey last night and he says that a few men have been pulled out of the outfit who speak German, French, or Dutch. Yesterday a list was taken in our company of the men with language background. Today the First Sgt. checked again on our languages. I shall keep my fingers crossed.

Had a good letter from Ted Kidder yesterday. My letter reached him in one day and his took four days to reach me. He is doing well and hopes to maintain the status quo. Another one of those amazing coincidences has occurred with Ted Pratt. He was in the same POE [Post of Embarkation] as we when we were there and he sailed about the same time. Probably the same convoy. Is over here now. Dotty has invited Cordelia to come to Knoxville, live with her and work. Think it would be good for both of them. Lt. Moberg promised me a pass for Sunday to visit Ted. He is only four miles away. 'Twill be good to see and talk with him again.

March 2, '45

This morning we fell out at 8:30 and marched to town to see what I suppose was the lousiest picture I have ever seen—"Atlantic City." After it was over, we took the four mile speed march which we expected yesterday. It was not bad and we completed it in about fifty minutes. We had only rifles, belts, and raincoats, but my belt was loose and it dragged behind.

When we reached camp, poor Miko (truck driving Texan in our squad—34 yrs. old) on his bunk completely exhausted. His lungs are in bad shape as a result of his being weakened by carbon monoxide, and it took real guts for him to stick it out as he did. With attention from a medic and warm coffee, he soon recovered but remained abed.

I learned a trick in regard to treating exhaustion. It is caused by a lack of sufficient carbon dioxide in the blood. If a paper bag is placed over the nose and mouth, carbon dioxide will be replaced rapidly and recovery is hastened.

We had a good short [movie] this morning on "GI Sports," showing some of the games played in the combat area by GI Joe. One relay was a new version of the wheelbarrow walk with three men instead of two. [A drawing of three stick men follows]

Another was a relay in which volley balls were pushed with the head. A dizzy one involved the boys running out to a stake, placing their forehead upon the stake, and circling around it seven times. The return was a "zig-zag" as the French call a drunk. Two or three games were adapted from baseball. One of these was played with a volley ball and kicked rather than batted. The ball must be thrown around the bases, and the batter tries to reach home before the ball can make the rounds.

Mar. 3

Perusing through an old <u>Newsweek</u> I found a discussion of <u>Puritanism and Democracy</u> by Ralph Barton Perry, 688 pages, Vanguard, $5. Perry has analyzed the two dominant traditions of our American Culture, and in it he blends history and philosophy. "Puritan ideas," Perry says, "were acquired before and during the colonial period, and democratic ideals before and during the Revolutionary period, so that both may be said to have molded the American mind from the beginning. They originated in the prenatal phase of American Life and predetermined the whole of its later development." Other ideals were introduced by the Catholic settlers of the Southwest and the great 19th [century] wave of immigration from non-puritan and non-democratic European countries. However, the Puritanism implanted in the 17th century and the democratic creed disseminated in the 18th century furnished a background for a large part of the distinctly Am. tradition.

Perry's main thesis is that America, having been founded upon these two ideals, can develop only as long as the American people continue to seek a synthesis of both traditions. He does not, however, ask us to accept the "distorted Puritanism" that most of us think of when we use the word "puritan."

On the contrary, the author lashes out at prudishness, canting humility, censoriousness, hardness, intolerance, and that "aversion to joy, especially the joy of other people" which are the hallmarks of the spiritual descendants of Jonathan Edwards.

"Man," Perry says, "derives dignity from his inalienable capacity for joy and suffering, from his capacity for self-determination, and from his tragic but faithful and age-long effort to live and to live better through intelligence and cooperation." That, in essence, is the definition of the meaning of democracy.

Perry is no blind worshiper of democracy per se. Frequently he finds that democracy has forgotten that "a government must govern and that government implies obedience. Democracy has been too often "an exponent of vulgarity rather than of eminence." It has allowed its name "to be used as a cloak for greed and exploitation." In politics and economics it has been "too easily satisfied with the minimal rather than the real," and that its triumph was written in the stars, and that progress and universal peace were guaranteed merely because they were reasonable and good.

To rectify these faults Perry urges an acceptance of the moral good of Puritanism and the political good of democracy for the ideal state, which he calls a "puritan democracy." But he does not think this ideal can or will be quickly reached.

————

Letter from Art to Dotty
Somewhere in France
March 4, 1945 (Sun.
(51-54)

My Dearest,

Perusing through an old Newsweek, I found a discussion of a new book, Puritanism and Democracy. By Ralph Barton Perry. In it he has analyzed the two dominant dominant traditions of our Am. culture, and in this analysis he blends history and philosophy "Puritan ideals," Perry says, "were acquired before and during the Colonial period and democratic ideals before and during the Revolutionary period, so that both may have been said to have molded the American mind from the beginning. They originated in the prevatal phrase of Am. life and predetermined the whole of its later development.'... Perry's main thesis is that America, having been founded upon these two ideals, can develop only so long as the American people continue to seek a synthesis of both traditions. He does not, however, ask us to accept the "distorted puritanism" that most of us think of when we use the word "puritan".

"On the contrary, the author lashes out at prudishness, canting humility, censoriousness, hardness, intolerance, and that aversion to joy especially the joy of the other people' which are the hallmarks of the spiritual descendants of Jonathon Edwards.

"Man," Perry says, "discover dignity from his inalienable capacity for joy and suffering, from his capacity for self-determination, and from his tragic but faithful and age-long effort to live and to live better through intelligence and cooperation: That, in essence, is his definition of the meaning of democracy.

"Perry is no blind worshipper of democracy per se. Frequently he finds democracy has forgotten that a government must govern and that government implies obedience". Democracy has been to often "an exponent of vulgarity, rather than of eminence." It has allowed its name to be used as a cloak for greed and exploitation." In politics and economics it has been "too easily satisfied with the nominal rather than the real, and that its triumph was written in the stars, and that progress and universal peace were guaranteed merely because they were reasonable and good."

"To rectify these faults Perry urges on acceptance of the moral good of puritanism and the political good of democracy for the ideal state, which he calls a "puritan democracy." But he does not think this ideal can or will be quickly reached."

Darling, I had no intention of going into such detail when I began the discussion of this book. However, I was attracted by the report on it and hope that sometime I will have a chance to read the entire book. I shall write Dad about it, and I would not be surprised if he has it already.

Mon 5th [excerpt]

Good to know that you are enjoying your dancing classes. I too find myself a bit sore at times but not from dancing. Tell me more about the class and what you are doing in the class. We have been playing a little volleyball after supper lately and now and then we have a softball game.

Dearest Heart, your faith is an abiding rock of strength for me each day. It is not "puny" but very, very strong and it upholds me when the future seems dark indeed. I wrote "Squawky" the other day concerning our plans—four years at Yale, four children, background material for a book, a good rest, etc., etc.,—these things is a matter of the first few years after release from the Army. It does seem that we are shooting for the stars, but we shall achieve much of it. Truly, our future is a bright one.

The first flowers are appearing among the leaves. A few buds are to be see on the trees. The days are a bit warmer now and the daylight hours are noticeably longer. Spring is just around the corner, and with spring comes new life and new hope. Suffering mankind throughout the world will see in the signs of spring a hope for a better world in the months just at hand.

Good night, My Love
Your own
Bushy
P.S. No time to check for mistakes.

Letter from Dotty to Art
Sunday, March 4 [1945]

My Dearest,

I sit by the fire, the great big fire, the only noise which strikes my ear is that of rushing waters and a few odd whistles from the fire.

Scene: The Cabin. Setting: The Mountains. What bliss, what joy—except for the absence of your dear self. There has been quite a bit of rain lately, and the river is a mighty, rushing torrent. The rocks in the river are not visible at all, only splashes of white spray here and there indicate the presence of something disturbing its smooth (?) flow.

Flo and I are here alone—everyone else has wandered off somewhere. Uncle West and some of the gang went hiking, Aunt Carol & Aunt Lois (Mrs. Cain) are out. We came up yesterday, two cars full, nine in all. It was raining, and the roads were muddy and slick, but we made it and had fun besides. We always have fun here. And on the way here. You know. I love this mountain!

Friday night Mother and Dad & I went to supper and a show. We saw a "Thin Man" picture, featuring Wm Powell & Myrna Loy as Mr. & Mrs. Charles. It was good!—a murder mystery with lots of laughs and a stack of suspicious suspects of who might have did the awful deed. There was a train sequence in it that was extremely funny and very true to life.

At last (Friday) I got the letter that should have come first—the one you sent free. In fact, none of the letters have come in their proper order, but at least they came, and I am very grateful for that, Darling. Your letters are so descriptive, and so full of you that I just love 'em to pieces. Yup, to pieces.

Also got a letter from your ma and pa Friday. Their work is lighter now, thank goodness. They send a couple of cartoons which I consider cute and am sending them on to you. Also saw a cute one in the Sat. Eve. Post. The man in the pot said to the Cannibals standing around: "Would you mind stirring me a little? I think I'm burning on the bottom."

I'm gonna burn on the front if I don't get away from this fire, Darling, I constantly discover new depths and new heights to
    Our love,
        Dotty.
P.S. And always in this place I feel very near to you, whether we are together or apart.
P.P.S. Mizpah

Monday, Mar. 5

Darling,
"I like March...." quoth I. The wind, it is gusty. My hair, she goes whoosh and falls on my nose. The forsythia and the jonquil, they bloom out very yellow. March—she is here!

Today came a letter from you. I am so pleased that it is becoming almost a daily occurrence, but I expect there will be times——. I hope my mail is coming through to you in similar fashion. To date I have received 11 letters from you—seven the first week, three last week, and one already this week. I shall try to mail the box containing most of the things you wanted tomorrow or next day. We have a flashlight here if I can find batteries to put in it. I may not be able to put everything in one box. If not, you can look forward to two of them.

Darling, it is extremely regrettable but apparently necessary to have hatred and race prejudice during a war especially among the soldiers—otherwise they wouldn't get mad enough to fight (so reasons the army). Men of the calibre you mentioned perhaps cannot be made to view the thing as idealistically as you. Hate and prejudice are almost as alarmingly rampant among the folks here at home. Take Mary's case for instance. She joined our church not long ago, and is well accepted by the majority of people in the church. But one couple, who used to be very stauch members of the church, and whose son was recently killed in the Pacific, now refuse to enter our church again as long as Mary remains there. And there may be others who feel the same way. Such attitudes on the part of those who call themselves Christians will do a great deal of harm to the progress of The Church universal. The sad part of it is that most everybody regards Mary as Japanese, but she regards herself as American.

Where has our democracy gone to? There is going to have to be a lot of educating and uneducating when this was is over, my fine college professor. And you will get to help with it. Great opportunities await you, my dear!

Three times I have dreamed that you appeared on the scene in civvies. Wishful thinking, maybe? Ahhh. I think and dream of you constantly. There is no escaping our eternal
       Love,
       Dotty.
P.S. Who'd want to, anyway? Not me, huh, not me.
P.S. Mizphah

Letter from Dotty to Art
Tues, March 6 [1945]

My Dearest Hubby,

This just can't last, but oh, how wonderful. A letter yesterday and two today. From you, of course. Just ask me sometime do I love to get your mail. The answer to that, of course, is a military secret. But you can draw you own conclusions. From now on I shall try to put more "thoughts" in my letters for you to mull over.

I suppose working closer to the church enables me to see people as I've never seen them before. Or perhaps I am becoming more critical. At any rate, people I've always thought very well of seem to be changing —for worse instead of better. It worries me no end. Little pettish features seem to crop up that I didn't know (they, we) had. Surely church people should be freer from those things than anyone else.

Wed. March 7

As you can no doubt tell, I was sleeping when attempting to write the above—it shows in my writing!

To continue about the (our) church. Another thing I have noticed is that besides the lack of unity there seems to be a great lack of spirit and zeal. People come to church, and work there, but there isn't a great deal of vitality in evidence. I think perhaps war-weariness is partly to blame for it, also the fact that everybody is doing more than ever before, and so there isn't as much energy and vitality to put into church work as formerly.

Thurs., March 8 [excerpt]

Dearest,

...Yesterday I mailed the package to you, darling, and I hope to goodness it gets there in a hurry & O.K., because it has just about all your eggs in one basket. It contains the flashlight, compliments of Aunt Mary. By the way—she doesn't want to hear of your killing any Japs whatsoever. But to go back to the flash—Aunt Mary furnished the case, and I was able to get batteries and an extra bulb, which I placed inside the empty case of the flashlight. Also in the package were: your hand cream, a lock (mine) some stationery, a lot of food, some candles, and your birthday present. So, if the package doesn't reach you it will really be too bad. One thing I forgot to put in the package was dental floss, so I am enclosing some with this letter.

Also enclosed is a clipping concerning the Wallace – Jones situation, and I think it will clear things up considerably for you. That was some pow-wow. And so Democratic. Tsk, tsk.

Jenks and John have a pretty good answer from their religion about eternal love, being wedded in the hereafter, etc. etc. We are wedded physically, and we are wedded spiritually and mentally, and the two are part of the same thing, the same love. The more our spirits become one, the more spiritually wedded we become, and this spiritual marriage continues in the life to come. If our spirits are one, and it is our spirit that continues life when we die, how then can they be separated in life after death? This reasoning is partly mine and partly Swedenborg's, mostly Swedenborg's. Wish I could quote. At any rate, I do know that Swedenborg is quite definite on the point, whether I put it down correctly or not.

Japs are still fighting hard on Iwo Jima, but now they hold less than a third of the island, so it is a last ditch stand. <u>German defeat seems imminent</u>, and their morale seems almost completely crocked. Darling—it <u>can't</u> be long now!

Deep, deep within my heart, and shooting up throughout my entire being, our love burns with a bright and steady flame. The fire gives light to my days and warmth to my actions. With all of me

I love You,

Dotty.

P.S. Mizpah.

Mar 7, '45

On Sunday I attended church in the little brick school house at the crossroads, with Chaplain Webb conducting the service. After lunch I obtained my pass and hastened away. Fred Price and Christenson had planned to visit with me, but both were on guard [duty]. I walked to town and attempted to get a ride at the M.P. [Military Police] station but had no luck. So, with head high and an unusual lightness in my feet, I began the walk. I knew only that Ted K. was in the vicinity of St. Lo. After walking about eight kilometers, a lone truck came along and a kind-hearted GI saw fit to give me a lift. I arrived in St. Lo, and to my complete surprise saw Marvin Flowerman (an old Stanford roommate) marching by. We yelled greetings and he gave me directions for finding Ted. My destination was another mile farther away. I continued on, only to find that Ted was out on his first afternoon pass. His outfit has been very busy in recent weeks and [they] have no breaks during the work day. I parked on his bunk, read a bit, and soon fell asleep. He returned in a short time and we had a good talk. Ate supper with him and left shortly before darkness fell. Ted has a number of good rumors and a few facts of general interest. It seems for one thing that the original plans for our outfit have been altered. It seems that we are definitely a part of the 15th Army which is called the "Victory" Army. According to the best information which

Ted has, we are not likely to see the front lines, but there is much mopping up to be done in pockets left behind. All indications are that we will not remain in this vicinity for long. Ted has had opportunity to take a few pictures and write a number of letters. My letter writing has consisted largely of letters to Dotty, but 'tis as well. I think my friends will understand.

My return was uneventful, but I regretted having left so late. Darkness came quickly and I walked alone along the shadowy road. I was not frightened in the least, but I knew that it was not wise to be alone in the French countryside at night. I was picked up about four kilometers outside of town by an MP in a command car. My Sunday afternoon stroll was for a total of about nine miles, but it was very worthwhile to talk with Ted. I arrived in camp about 20:15 (8:15 p.m.) to find a long, wonderful letter from my loving wife. She received four letters from me on the 24th of Feb., the first mail to arrive since I reached the Old World.

Monday night our platoon went on detail at the motor pool from 21:00 to 03:00. It rained and misted most of the night. We had to unload gravel from trucks, and they came at the rate of five every thirty or forty minutes.

———

* Letter from Art to Dotty
Visit from Gen. Eisenhower
Somewhere in France
March 7, 1945 Wed.
(55-60)

Dearest Heart,

I have just found out that I can now mention a rather outstanding event which arrived a few days ago. Our division was honored by the visit of an outstanding man—none other than our commander-in-chief-"Ike" himself. We had completed a hike in the morning and had returned for a big chow. Our little squad sat in our tent with the sides up (it was a warm, clear day). We had no warning whatever but someone said that Gen. Eisenhower was in the vicinity. The word spread like a prairie fire in a strong wind. We saw company officers running right and left. Suddenly, we saw the General himself and he was coming toward our company area. We craned our necks with mouths agape. Coming up our street was the General accompanied by Gen. Lear, his new executive, our own Gen. W—— and plenty of lesser brass. They entered one of the tents across the street and we continued to gaze. Movie cameras clicked and pictures were snapped. I hastened to clean my rifle which was lying dirty on my bunk and there [I] was inside the tent by my bunk (Everyone else was seated along the front of the tent just inside, with the dirty mess kits lying on the ground.) The party came out of the tent across the street and came toward us. We held our breaths; we waited. Our squad leader called attention and we stood riveted. The conversation was, of course, brief. I shall not quote it directly, but it sparkled with the personality and colorful language of "Ike". There I stood within six feet of the man who has written, and continues to write, a very long page in the history of the world. I must admit that I was deeply impressed. Before leaving, he reached over and patted O'Connell (my squad leader) on the shoulder. He walked out; the spell was broken. Everyone in the tent began talking at once. I shall not soon forget the experience of seeing and hearing my Commander.

Darling in the past few days, I have had a new experience. I have never had a fear of combat and the thought of fighting has never preyed upon my mind. However, in a subconscious way, I suppose the reality of the prospects are always present with one who has trained as an infantry soldier. However, in the last few days I have had a new sense of confidence and of power. I belief [believe] with all my heart that it is a closer realization of God's presence with me. I belief [believe] also that it arises from your faith and your prayers. It is as though a load were lifted from [my] shoulders, and I almost look forward to the experience of combat. I shall never look forward to killing, but all of the experience that accompany combat, other that [than] killing, are unique in the wide range of human experience. I believe that whatever happens in the days ahead that God will be close beside me, and beside me will be your towering faith.

(3-8-1945) [excerpts]

I learned a little trick a few days ago that is of interest and may prove useful someday. On the return from a recent speed march, one of the older fellows in our squad fell on his bunk completely exhausted. When the medic came, he asked for a paper bag. The trick is this: exhaustion results from a lack of carbon dioxide in the blood. When a paper covers the nose and mouth, the patient breathes an excess of CO_2. Thus the recovery is speeded. We may need that trick on a hiking club trek sometime....

I missed the popular show "Since You Went Away," but have heard much about it. Glad to get your full report and especially to get your reaction. It is truly more than a coincidence that in this very letter I discussed the matter of faith and my feeling regarding the future. I had not realized that the strained relationship had existed. The papers or rather, the paper makes little mention of such things for obvious reasons.

It certainly sounds like old times to hear that Helen and Roland will be visiting you soon. Yes, Darling, I am glad that you will have the chance to return a little of the hospitality which they showed us in the past. My heartiest welcome is extended as of now to them when they arrive. Have had no opportunity to write Ted P. yet, but will do so.

I cannot help noting the approach of a very memorable date—two in fact. The first, of course is none other than March 10th. Just in case you have forgotten, my Dear, "J" Gillette introduced us just five years ago. I shall be thinking about you in a very special way on that day. But there is another date that I shall also remember and that, of course, comes on the 6th of April. I fear that I shall have no opportunity to buy an anniversary present for some time, but when I do I shall try to make up for it. [Upon typing this letter for publication, the editor mailed an anniversary card to Dotty, at the time, 99 years old.]

This letter is being written by a series of starts and stops. I have just found out that my bond situation was thoroughly confused back in the States. I tried to cancel my $7.50 bond and take out an $18.75. I signed the payroll tonight and found that both of them will be taken out of my check each month. $6.50 for insurance and $22 for your check is added to that. This means that I shall receive exactly $10.05 when nothing is taken out for laundry. Well, that is enough. I need very little over here, but the time may come when I will. I don't think that I will send very much home, but rather will save up and have when the need arises. At the moment, about all I need is 30 francs (60¢) per week for PX rations.

Our love is more than a mere attraction, largely physical in character. Our love wells from the very depth of our spiritual existence and is a part of that Great Love, Divine in its source, which was exemplified in the life of our Lord. I love you, Dear Heart.

   Ever thine
   Bushy

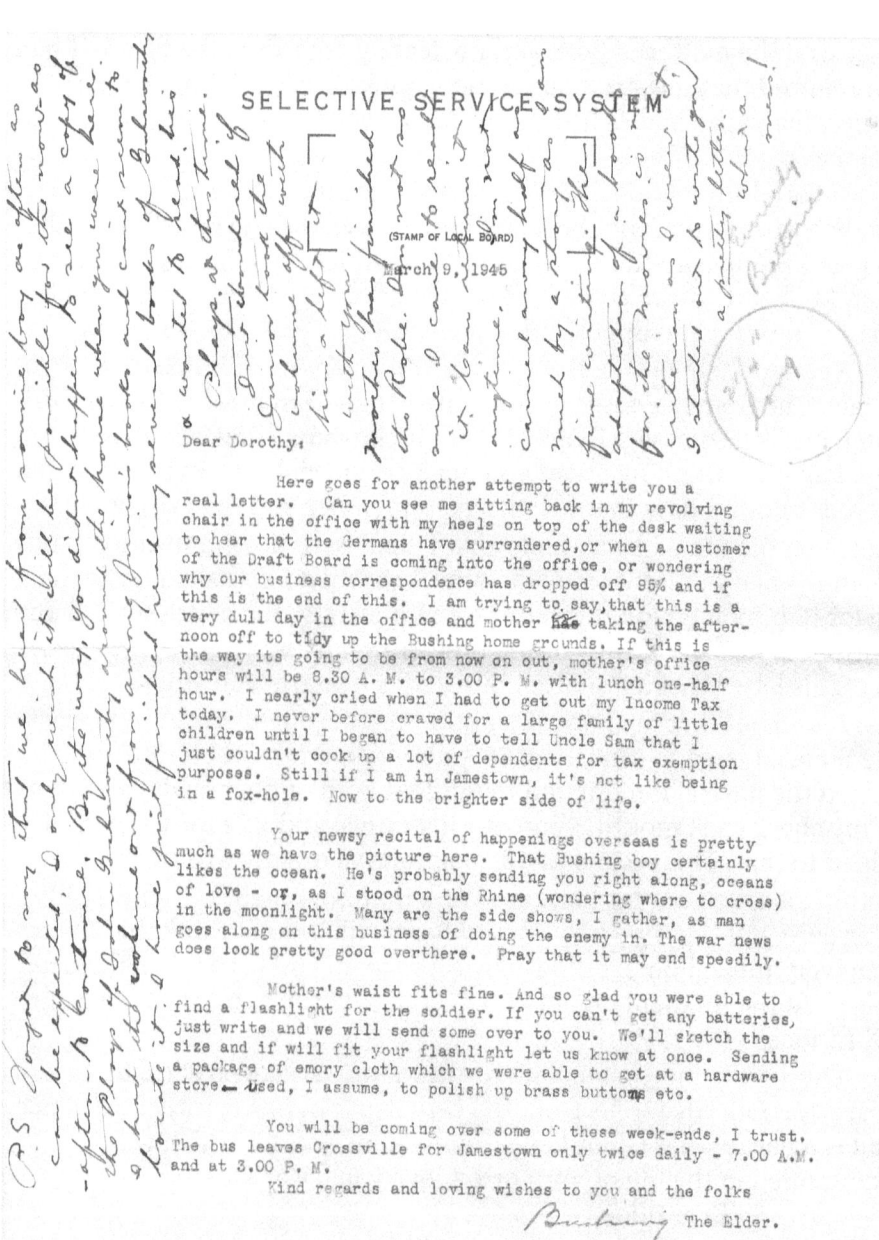

Dear Dorothy:

        Here goes for another attempt to write you a
real letter. Can you see me sitting back in my revolving
chair in the office with my heels on top of the desk waiting
to hear that the Germans have surrendered,or when a customer
of the Draft Board is coming into the office, or wondering
why our business correspondence has dropped off 95% and if
this is the end of this. I am trying to say,that this is a
very dull day in the office and mother has taking the afternoon off to tidy up the Bushing home grounds. If this is
the way its going to be from now on out, mother's office
hours will be 8.30 A. M. to 3.00 P. M. with lunch one-half
hour. I nearly cried when I had to get out my Income Tax
today. I never before craved for a large family of little
children until I began to have to tell Uncle Sam that I
just couldn't cook up a lot of dependents for tax exemption
purposes. Still if I am in Jamestown, it's not like being
in a fox-hole. Now to the brighter side of life.

        Your newsy recital of happenings overseas is pretty
much as we have the picture here. That Bushing boy certainly
likes the ocean. He's probably giving you right along, oceans
of love - or, as I stood on the Rhine (wondering where to cross)
in the moonlight. Many are the side shows, I gather, as man
goes along on this business of doing the enemy in. The war news
does look pretty good overthere. Pray that it may end speedily.

        Mother's waist fits fine. And so glad you were able to
find a flashlight for the soldier. If you can't get any batteries,
just write and we will send some over to you. We'll sketch the
size and if will fit your flashlight let us know at once. Sending
a package of emory cloth which we were able to get at a hardware
store. Used, I assume, to polish up brass buttons etc.

        You will be coming over some of these week-ends, I trust.
The bus leaves Crossville for Jamestown only twice daily - 7.00 A.M.
and at 3.00 P. M.

        Kind regards and loving wishes to you and the folks

                                     Bushing The Elder.

March 9, 1945, Letter from Art Sr. to Dotty

**[From the letter dated March 9, 1945,
written in the margins,
from Art Sr. to Dotty.]**

P.S. Forgot to say that we hear from sonnie boy as often as can be expected. I only wish it will be possible for the now-as-often to continue. By the way, you didn't happen to see a copy of the Plays of John Galsworthy around the house when you were here. I had the volume out from among Junior's books and can't seem to locate it. I have just finished reading several books of Galsworthy & wanted to read his <u>Plays</u> at this time. Just wondered if Junior took the volume off with him & left it with you.

Mother has finished the Robe. I'm not so sure I care to read it. I can return it anytime. I'm not carried away half as much by a story as I am fine writing. The adaptation of a book for the movies is no criterium as I view it. I started out to write you a <u>pretty</u> letter, what a mess! [and this in pencil] Eveready Batteries 2 1/4" long

5

FORWARD MARCH TO THE FRONT

French Train Station
40 and 8 [40 men and 8 horses]
March 10, 1945

ast night we were allowed no fires—in fact we were allowed none since 09:00 yesterday. About 18:30 a tent caught fire, and the order was issued immediately that no open flames would be allowed. Since most of us had open lamps, we were hurting. The rest of the fellows rolled blankets and made up their roll, intending to sleep in sleeping bags only. I maintained that the night would be cold enough to warrant the use of the blankets and that we would have time to roll the blankets in the morning. More than one fellow unrolled his pack in the course of the evening. I was a bit cold but I slept.

We are learning many tricks in regard to making up sleeping bags. We find that it is most important to have plenty of insulation between the body and the ground. Paper or cardboard is a good insulator. A shelter half, raincoat, and over coat are best under the bag with two blankets folded inside. This gives two layers on top and two on the bottom. The new cover [for the bags] which we have helps retain the body heat and is very satisfactory.

Many rumors flew today concerning our destination, but one predominated. It seems as though we have much to expect. We have had a partial blackout on the front line news, but the bits that have filtered through sound spectacular. We [i.e., American troops] crossed the Rhine on Wed. after taking Cologne about Tues. On our way to the train the "Top-Kick" (1st Sgt.) said that we were 37 miles beyond the Rhine. That sounds like a Russian communiqué.

Mar. 11, '45
En Route
Outside the city of Rheims

I was unable to do much writing yesterday, but I did have time to think a great deal about yesterday's date five years ago. It was just five years ago that I was introduced to Dotty and asked to take her home [i.e., walk with her to her dorm at Maryville College]. I thought of the events of those years and of the advances in certain respects. Dotty seemed very close to me as I curled up in the straw, made my bed, and prepared for sleep.

We found our car not so terribly bad. It is one of the famous "40 or 8" cars from the last war. It will hold 40 men or eight horses. We had only 25 men and equipment, but when we stretched out in our sleeping bags there was hardly room to twitch a muscle. There was plenty of straw on the floor, and when we closed the door we were extremely warm.

I intended to list the items which we carried from outo the Railroad station. I want to record it, for it would be hard to believe twenty-five years from now. Our packs were made up of two blankets, and the sleeping bag and cover [all of which] went into a horseshoe shape. On our pack was the usual raincoat, trowel and shovel. Each man had 80 rounds of ammunition in his belt, and I had an additional 10 magazines (200 rounds) of ammo for the Baring Automatic Rifle (BAR). We also carried our gas mask, two days' rations (K and C), rifle and bayonet, overshoes, extra boots, and full canteens. We wore our long woolens [underwear], O.D.'s [Olive Drab heavy woolen pants and shirts], sweaters (I had two), field jackets and overcoat. Not a bad load for a donkey.

I slept much of the afternoon—the train [having] pulled out about 12:00. We were passing through country more rolling now. I was reminded of the terrain in East Tenn. between Knoxville and Bristol. The fields were much larger in this area, and more wooded areas were to be seen. Many of the hedge rows were of the small hedge type rather than the trees which made up the rows in the western part we were leaving. Many of the bridges and intersections over which we passed had been bombed a great deal, as shown by the craters on either side. In a place or two we saw entire trains wrecked and burned along the tracks.

About seven o'clock we came to the first large city that we had seen in France—A [Amiens].

Although there was evidence of much bombing, there were many signs of activity. Along the RR was a parkway where couples walked and held hands. Smoke came from the chimneys of factories, and the station itself showed activity.

Later Same Day

We stopped here for about an hour and a half. Some of the fellows went over to the latrine which consisted of nothing more that holes in the floor and a means of flushing. Actually, the station appeared rather up-to-date. We left about 8:30 and soon crawled in our "sacks," as our sleeping bags are called. I slept very soundly through the night and was awake only a few times. We arose about eight and found ourselves on a flat plain with the city of R—[Rheims] in the hazy distance. Here we ate our breakfast and waited until about eleven. With the aid of a very excellent GI map which Mike, a friend in the next company, had left me, I have been able to follow our route rather accurately.

The morale of the men when we left was perhaps as high as it has been any time of leaving from any previous station. Our last day at D —was a beautiful one; this perhaps was a contributing factor. The very excellent news coming from the front, the taking of Cologne, crossing the Rhine, etc., were also items involved. We felt good. Even on the train yesterday and today, the general feeling has been high, but naturally the wear of travel was beginning to become apparent. It seems strange that we should be living and sleeping here in a box car, floor covered with straw, enjoying the scenery as much as though we were in the observation car of a streamliner.

I just wonder when I will enjoy a shower again. The last one I had was a poor substitute for a shower in salt water on the ship. The last real shower was in POE [Port of Entry] about Jan. 25. I hardly know when I took my last tub bath. It must have been when we lived with Mrs. Grimes back in Columbus, GA. That seems long ago and far away.

Mar. 12
Camp #2

Had another good night's sleep last night in the boxcar. Before we awoke this morning we passed through the large city of N—[Nancy]. When I first opened my eyes, I saw new destruction—destruction that was far more recent than anything we saw around D— [Deauville]. Large craters were on either side of the tracks. One track had been torn up and stood intact on its side, reaching fifteen feet into the air. We soon reached our train destination [Luneville], and here we ate our breakfast, preparatory to detraining. In this area we find that the French are just returning, but already they are getting back to the business of tilling the soil. At one place we saw an ox and horse hitched together with a second horse leading. As we came East , we found an increasing warmth in the attitude of the civilians toward us. After gathering our equipment together, we made ready to leave. The clock on the tower of the station was stopped-four past four, it said. We loaded into trucks--twenty-three to a truck. Later we learned that the station had been strafed
only ten days ago and a big dog fight occurred over it day before yesterday. As we rode to our new home we passed through some of the worst devastation that we have seen yet. Entire hillsides had been blown apart with artillery and mortar fire. Buildings were leveled. In some of the villages we saw the sides of buildings gone. The faces of a few war-worn Frenchmen were to be seen around the houses. Ammunition lined the highways over which we passed, and lines marked the path cleared of mines. I had no desire to wander outside of the cleared paths. The terrain through which we passed reminded me very much of the rolling hills around Camp Roberts [Calif.]. As we moved further, we see more and more trees, and finally we passed through a heavily wooded area. Small villages dotted the landscape. We reached our new home—the village of T--.

Mar. 13

Our village, in the shape of a Y, is made up of about fifteen houses. Here again, the French are just returning after having been driven out by the Germans. The people here worked for the "Count," living in the nearby manor. We were told that all of the surrounding land belonged to the Count before the war. Our platoon was billeted in one of the better houses in the village, and our squad has the best room.

Although small, it is situated on the second floor with windows on two sides. Only one pane is entirely gone, and in this too we are very lucky. The second platoon has not a single window. A small chapel is located in the village with the typical circular tower. The date, 1840, is engraved on our front door, and I rather imagine that the entire village dates from about that period. I hope to draw a rough sketch of the chapel just for the record.

So far no "booby" traps have been found, and perhaps there are none. However, I intend to be as careful as possible. One mine can make this GI harmless for the duration.

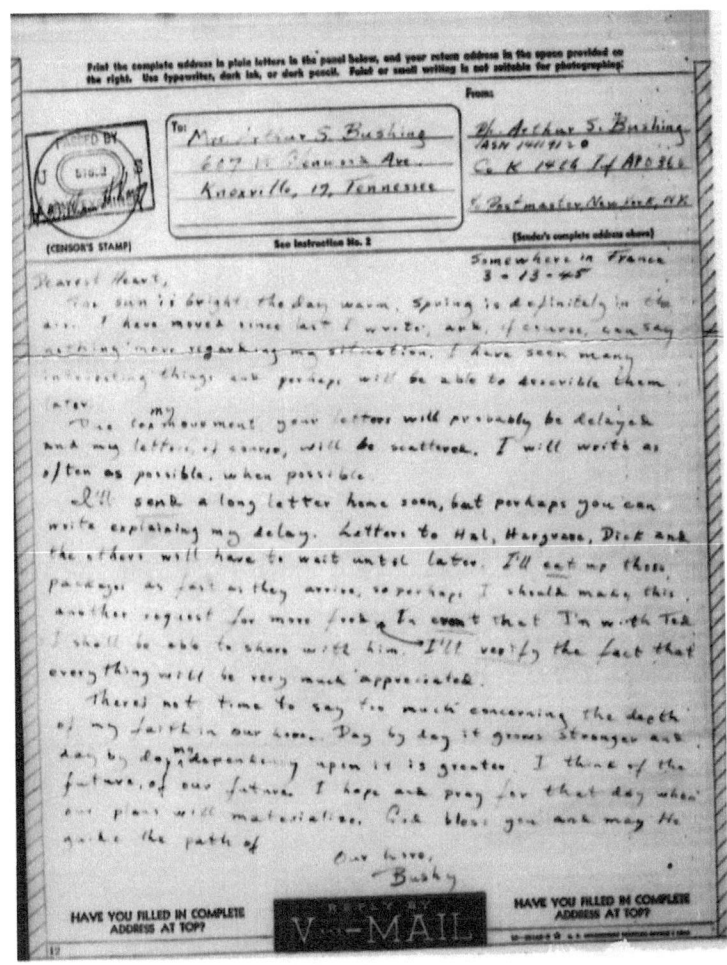

V-Mail March 13, 1945, from Art to Dotty [62]

Saturday Afternoon May 5

Dear sonnie boy:
It is a quiet afternoon. Mother has gotten off quite early after a nice chicken
dinner at restaurant, with work in nice condition to enter upon next week's work.
It should be one in which mother can take off most of the afternoons—certainly
no later than 3. P. M.
This last week has been one of the most disagreeable of the season - cold and
rainy with overcoats necessary and at home a fire every evening. It would seem
after today, for the sun is shining and it has warmed considerably, *that it will fair up*
Nothing new here on the home front, but plenty as you too know, over the radio
as to the sudden collapse of the German Wehrmach. The news has been good in your
sector as we can judge of General Patch's Army. I am wondering if you were in the
push which entered the Hitler Redoubt - or as some has said, the redoubtable redoubt.
Or am I forgetting that you are now with the famous Patton Third Army. We are all
awaiting announcement of V-E Day. We had a nice letter from Dorothy since her return home. Mother and I both wrote of how much we enjoyed her short stay.

Oh, yes, he 's some news from and on the home front. Sgt. bought out the Brook's
Store property at Pine Haven. George ork and Jr. York as the ("York Brothers"
Store) are operating said store. From the firm name I take it that Sgt. and
George are the Brothers in the deal. On April 16, Sgt. told the Board that he
thought it would be a nice thing to T raph our new President congratulations
and pledge him the Boards' support - the following was sent: "The President,
The White House - Washington, D. C.
            The members of the Fer ess County Local Board
            Selective Service con tulate you on your ele-
            vation to the Presiden y and pledge you our loyal
            support in the great sk which still lies ahead
            of our beloved Country.

                    signed   Sgt. Alvin C. York, Chm.,
                              W. H. Voiles
                              W. H. Sewell
        personel
Comes the/reply by letter:

                        The White House
                        Washington

                            April 25

My dear Sergeant York:
            I want to thank all of you for the message which you
sent me pledging loyal support in the tasks ahead. This assurance of
confidence and cooperation means a great deal to me and you have my
deepest gratitude.
                    Very sincerely yours
                        Harry Truman
Sergeant Alvin C. York
Pall Mall,
Tennessee

The Board will be pleased to read reply at their meeting tomorrow, I feel
sure.

We long for yourreturn but we know that there will be much remaining overthere before all of you boys board ship for home. It does look like early
peace, but with half of the job completed. Next the Pacific, but that should
not be a matter of years to clean up. Let us continue to pray for the real
final day of victory, and world peace. God bless and keep you, dear son,
you and all your pals. A heart full of love and longing from *Do hope you are*
Thanks so much for writing - as opportunity allows, DAD in good health and holding up.

Letter from Art Sr. to Art Jr., dated May 5, 1945
[Discovered after initial publication and inserted out of order.]

130

6

NOTES FROM COMBAT
IN ETO & LATER COMMENTARY

I N MARCH 1943, DR. EDWIN R. HUNTER, DEAN OF CURRICULUM AT MARYVILLE COLLEGE, ASKED ME TO TEACH INTRODUCTORY PHYSICS TO THE ARMY AIR CADETS, WHO WERE COMING TO THE COLLEGE. I HAD TWO SECTIONS WITH SIXTY MEN IN EACH CLASS, MEETING DAILY. ALTHOUGH THE COLLEGE APPEALED TO THE ARMY TO ALLOW ME TO CONTINUE IN THAT POSITION, THE REQUEST WAS DENIED, AND ABOUT THE 1ST OF JUNE I REPORTED TO FORT OGLETHORPE GA. SHORTLY THEREAFTER I WAS SENT TO CAMP ROBERTS, CALIFORNIA, FOR SIX MONTHS OF BASIC INFANTRY TRAINING. IN JANUARY 1944, I WAS PLACED IN THE NEWLY FORMED ARMY SPECIALIZED TRAINING PROGRAM (ASTP), ONE LOCATION FOR WHICH WAS AT STANFORD UNIVERSITY. AFTER WE HAD NINE MONTHS OF INTENSIVE STUDY OF DUTCH, MALAY, AND THE SOUTHEAST PACIFIC, THE PROGRAM WAS ABANDONED.

IN OCTOBER OF 1944 I WAS ASSIGNED TO THE 71ST INFANTRY DIVISION, WHICH WAS TRAINING IN FORT BENNING, GA. I REMAINED IN THE RANK OF PRIVATE, FIRST CLASS (PFC.) UNTIL AFTER THE WAR ENDED. LATER I WAS ASSIGNED A CLERK'S JOB IN A SERVICE COMPANY, WAS GIVEN CORPORAL'S STRIPES, AND EVENTUALLY MADE TECH SERGEANT (T-4). I WAS DISCHARGED IN 1946 WITH THAT RANK.

DURING COMBAT I WROTE THE FOLLOWING IN A SMALL NOTEBOOK. A LARGER JOURNAL CONTAINS MATERIAL THAT I BAGAN SHORTLY BEFORE LEAVING THE STATES, CONTINUED UNTIL WE MOVED INTO COMBAT, AND PICKED UP AFTER THE WAR ENDED IN THE ETO [EUROPEAN THEATER OF OPERATION].

AFTER ADDITIONAL CONDITIONING IN OUR FIRST CAMP, IN FRANCE, WE LOADED INTO WWI BOXCARS (40s AND 8s, i.e., 40 MEN OR 8 HORSES) AND WERE TAKEN TO LUNEVILLE, IN THE EASTERN PART OF THE COUNTRY. FROM THERE WE MOVED TO THE COMBAT AREA.

WE HAD BEEN WARNED NOT TO CARRY INFORMATION THAT WOULD, IN THE EVENT OF BEING CAPTURED, REVEAL ANYTHING VALUABLE TO THE GERMANS. THUS, I HAVE VERY FEW REFERENCES TO OUR LOCATION. FOR A SHORT WHILE WE WERE NEAR THE CITY OF SPEYER ON THE RHINE. AFTER BRIEF SKIRMISHES, WE WERE TRUCKED NORTH TO CROSS THE RIVER ON A PONTOON BRIDGE NEAR DARMSTADT. PERHAPS IT WAS AT THE POINT THAT OUR 71ST DIVISION WAS ASSIGNED TO THE 3RD ARMY UNDER THE COMMAND OF GEN. GEORGE PATTON.

A FEW EXPLANATORY NOTES ARE IN CAPITALS AND BRACKETED. EXCEPT FOR AN OCCASIONAL ADDITION OF PUNCTUATION THE MATERIAL IS AS IT WAS WRITTEN.

"Watch on the Rhine"
March 13, 1945
Somewhere in France
2nd Camp

The 13th seems to have played a prominent part in our activity: [Box] Car numbers, train numbers, dates of departure, etc. The day dawned cloudy, but it soon cleared and we found the 13th to be the most balmy of any time thus far in France. Break-fast was our first kitchen-prepared meal in six days. After eating some of these "kitchen meals" we sometimes think that "C" or "K" rations are to be preferred. Soon the order came to turn in almost everything that we have with the exception of what we wear. Only personal items were left in our duffel bags. These will be sent home in case anything unfortunate occurs. My personal things still amounted to half a duffel bag. With much misgiving I left my little black notebook in my bag. I trust that I will have it again with me soon. Left to take with us is very little. We have our blankets, our sleeping bag, one set of O.D's. [OLIVE DRAB, WOOL PANTS & SHIRT] (those on), two sets of woolen underwear, all the socks we have--these things and little more. We are traveling light.

Tonight while waiting to leave, I went into the little chapel here on the village square. The beauty of the inside was in marked contrast to the bleak poverty of the surrounding houses. There was a quiet beauty in the sanctuary. I knelt in meditation and prayer. There is a calm assurance that prayer gives which nothing else offers. I am very glad that I have found this well-spring of power.

The excitement of the day was climaxed by a minor flurry earlier in the evening. I was cleaning up a rock sink preparatory to clearing the building. The window in front of me shook with two explosions; but, since we have heard constant firing of artillery today, I thought little about it. I heard a terrific clatter as [SGT] O'Connell and [PFC] Littlefield raced down the stairs. The crowd swayed out the door; the crowd swayed inside again. The first reports were that it was a Nazi plane. Someone saw the insignia! Other reports said English; others American. Best reports seem to indicate that some plane dropped extra fuel tanks which exploded upon hitting the ground. It was interesting to note the reactions of all of us. [PFC] Giesking quickly shoved a magazine into his BAR [Browning Automatic rifle] and headed for the open. Most of us raced around, hardly knowing what was going on. I hope that we can now settle down, and that right early.

We have had no news for several days, and the rapid advance on the northern sector remains veiled in secrecy for us. Rumors say that we have a bridgehead across the Rhine, 30 miles deep and 100 miles wide, [The Ludendorff Bridge] over the Rhine at Remagen was captured intact on March 7th]. Not bad for so short a time! Remarkable, in fact! FDR is reported to have predicted the end of the war in ETO [European Theater of Operation] in three weeks, and Marines are supposed to have landed on Japan proper [a false rumor]. And thus the rumors, "zonder neues berichten," [without reported news] continue.

A beautiful sun has just dipped below the horizon; the evening star, very bright and clear, shines through the twilight; I feel a comforting calm as we await trucks which will move us forward in another stage of our long journey to the front.

The above was written in the small feudal town of Tarquimpol, near Dieuze, France. Located on a low hill, the dorf [village] was surrounded by swamps and marshlands. We moved out of the area by truck, and by devious routes approached the front. After a long, cold ride, we debarked shortly after midnight and began to march. As we unloaded we could hear artillery crashing nearby and see the bright flashes. We thought that we were traveling light, but when we began to carry everything that we possessed on our backs we could hardly call the loads light. We marched at a swift pace and with but one break until four o'clock. Our destination was another small town called Mizenthal (near Bitche). I cannot put into words the depth to which the human spirit can sink when the body is driven to the seeming limit of endurance. This march was only the beginning of many, many more to come. The entire company was put into the crowded space of a small school building. The dust was inches thick in the attic, but I found a small space in which to place my sleeping bag. I fell into a deep sleep while a cold wind poured through the holes in the shelled roof. Men were sleeping on steps, on tables, in the attic, outside—anywhere the space could be found to place a blanket. I awoke about eight the following day and went downstairs to heat my "C" ration over a small fire. When we arrived we were told that the front line was only about a thousand yards away, but when daylight came the artillery seemed farther away. Most of the day was spent in washing, shaving, resting. Beul Root and I slipped away from the rest to think about our wives and eat a can of peanuts that I had carried from the boat. In the early afternoon orders came to load up and prepare to move. We moved out of town and over the nearby hills. This section is especially mountainous, and we always seemed to manage to climb all of them. At last we arrived at the crest of a long ridge. With much caution a reconnaissance by our platoon was made; and, as dusk fell, we dug into position. We learned that we were still in a reserve, and that the big push was about to begin. The Company CP [Command Post] received word that 44 battalions of artillery were to open up at midnight. Giesking and I were joined at our foxhole by Sgt. O'Connell and we covered out retreat [position] with logs and dirt. By later measurement we found that the width of our foxhole was three hands, or about twenty-seven inches, and we slept in this space. *Of course, most of the night, one of us was standing guard. We were supposed to have one fellow in each hole awake all night, but we were very close to the other holes and so we rotated in the squad. The artillery bombardment was very heavy, but I doubt that 44 Bns. [Battalions] were involved.*

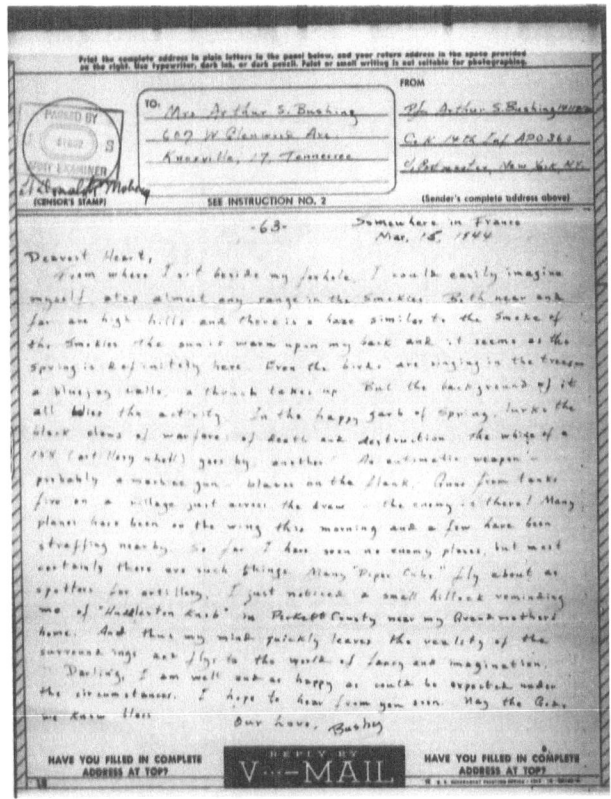

V-Mail March 15, 1945, from Art to Dotty [63]

March 15, Thur.
[Near Meisenthal]

From where I sit, I could easily imagine myself atop almost any range in the Smokies. Both near and far are high hills, and there is a haze similar to the smoke of the Smokies. The sun is warm upon my back, and it seems as though Spring is definitely here. Even Birds are singing in the trees nearby—a blue jay calls, a thrush take up. But the

135

background of it all belies the activity. In the happy garb of spring lurks the black claws of warfare—of death and destruction. The whine of a 155 goes by, another! An automatic weapon—probably a machine gun—blazes on the flank. 75's mounted on tanks fire on a village just across the draw—the enemy is there. Many planes have been on the wing this morning, and a few have been strafing nearby. So far I have seen no German planes, but I presume that there are such things, though few in number. Many "Piper Cubs" fly about as spotters for our artillery. (The innovation of these grasshoppers must have been revolutionary for the big guns.) I just notice a small hillock reminding me of "Huddleston Knob" in Pickett County, TN. And thus my mind quickly leaves the reality of the surroundings and flies to the world of fancy and imagination.

[AT THIS POINT SPRING WAS NEAR, BUT MOVING INTO HIGHER TERRAIN WE WERE AGAIN IN WINTER CONDITIONS. AS WE ADVANCED THROUGH THE SCHWARZWALD (BLACK FOREST) WE HAD SNOW, SLEET, AND RAIN. WE SELDOM HAD SHELTER AT NIGHT. ONCE IN A HOUSE, AFTER MANY NIGHTS OUTSIDE, I RECALL THE FLOOR BEING MUCH HARDER THAN THE GROUND, AND FELT CLAUSTROPHOBIA. I COULD NOT OPEN MY EYES AND SEE THE STARS.]

March 16

At last the order has come. We have been waiting and watching the progress of the fight for two days. We have the news this morning that the 7th Army is advancing on a 50-mile front. The artillery has blazed intermittently since we came forward. A large town (B--) [Bitche] is partially in our hands—we are moving forward to clear it. At the moment we sit beside the road with our heavy, full field packs. We must drop them. Each man is lost in his own thoughts and there is little talk. I think of the 23rd Psalm and the 91st. Dotty read the latter to me in our last meditation together. "He that dwelleth in the secret place of the most high. . . ." I suppose that everyone wonders what his reactions to combat will be. My stomach has been upset all day, but I slept a couple of hours and it seems better. Even though I feel a calming hand and a source of strength from above, I must admit that I have felt more calm and collected on a Spring day in former times. "I believe, help Thou my unbelief." Three wonderful letters from Dotty and one from Mother helped my morale a great deal last night. Their faith is very strong.

Yesterday we moved our location slightly and found ourselves in possession of fine positions that were already dug in. It appeared to have been a part of the line which was stalemated for so long – 70 days, I believe. We discovered an old CP [Command Post] that had been hurriedly evacuated and found a number of cans of rations of various sorts. I found a new type shelter half [canvas, half of a two-man tent] to replace my old one, and there was equipment of various sorts strewn about. There was a certain amount of pleasure, perhaps boyish pleasure, in making such a haul.

Dotty writes concerning a letter of mine on race hatred, and comments that the same situation exists at home, citing Mary Hirabiashi, our Japanese friend, as an example. [WEST AND CAROL BARBER, DOTTY'S UNCLE AND AUNT IN KNOXVILLE, TOOK MARY INTO THEIR HOME FOR MOST OF THE WAR, THUS ENABLING HER TO AVOID THE DETENTION CAMPS OUT WEST.] She suggests that perhaps I can do something about this after the war. I sincerely hope so.

Last night I had a long talk with Giesking, the former Indianapolis gangster and BAR man to whom I am an assistant. I think I pierced his outer shell and saw something of the inner man. Like most of us, these two "selves" are not the same. Perhaps I will have time a bit later to discuss my findings at greater length.

["ON THE NIGHT OF MARCH 22-23, THE 5TH DIVISION BEGAN TO CROSS THE RIVER AT OPPENHEIM, SOUTH OF MAINZ" (Ambrose, Citizen Soldiers, p. 433.) Shortly thereafter my unit crossed the Rhine at this point.]

Letter excerpts from Dotty to Art
Friday, March 16

Darling, are you allowed to tell me which Army you are in? So many people ask me, and I don't know what to tell them. Seems to me there was some talk of your being in the 3rd before you left, but I'm not sure.

My darling, I love you with all my heart.
Dotty

Sat., Mar. 17, 1945
My Dearest,
I wish I could paint up a picture of our back yard with colors instead of words. It is a veritable carpet of violets, with a patch of deep

violet ones here and another over there, while in between there are other patches of pale blue ones, violet ones, and white ones with blue centers. All over the back part of the back yard, and some are spilling through the archway and and in front of the fence.

But I can't spend the whole letter going on about the violets, after all, there were other things that happened that bear going into ecstacies about. I went to Maryville this afternoon. Several things made it memorable. Flo and I went over on the 3 o'clock bus. It was raining pitchforks when we went to town, but the skies were clearing as we boarded the Maryville bus. The countryside was a symphony of white yellow, and pink blossoms. The fruit trees are out—I hope they don't all friz later....

Oh, darling, the campus still casts its old spell. My trip to the campus was almost on the anniversary of the momentous meeting of Dotty and Art Bushing. Being on the campus brings up sharply all the poignancy and wonder of

> Our Love,
> Dotty

> Sabbath
> Mar. 18, 1945

Beaurtifurl Bushy,

Springnnnnn is here. Today should be Easter. New life of every kind pulses in the very air. The boidies is boisting their throats yapping and yapping. All sorts of trees and bushes are thrusting out either buds or blossoms. The air is warm and longorous but vibrant as can be. My soul is like to burst with Spring! I want to shout and sing and dance and play all to once. And then I want to throw my arms around you and squeeze till you - - - uh - - - all right—I'll let you squeeze me instead. Mmmmmmm. (Words spoken during long kiss)

Do you know what Paul Revere said at the end of his ride? Nope, guess again. No, that's not right either. O.K., I'll tell you. He said, quote "Whoa!"

From the ridiculous to the sublime go I. Dr. Peyton's sermon this morning was excellent. The title of it was "The Eternal Question" The same question which Pilate asked himself and the people is a question which each of us must ask ourselves—What shall I do with this man? Pilate settled it by sending him to be crucified. Will our answer to the question serve to crucify Christ or will it enable Him to live through us? The sermon included a number of digs about race prejudice.

This afternoon we went canvassing for the youth

"Your letter of the 8th, was postmarked the 12th, arrived the 20th, just eight days. And wonderful it was, too. That was very interesting about Eisenhower. I imagine the visit did a great deal for the morale of your outfit. Did you by any chance get in any of the newsreels you spoke of? Or do I have to see every movie that comes to town from now on just to make sure?

"How thrilling that you feel a renewed faith, a deeper sense of confidence and power, a closer realization of God's presence. That presence is all things to you—power, protection, love, life itself. Hang onto it, Darling. My constant prayer is that it hangs on to you. And not only hang onto it but use it, use it! It can do great things for Christ."

Letter from Art to Dotty
Somewhere in France
Mar, 20 1945 (Tues.
(66-74)

Dearest,

A cool wind blows and the morning sun remains behind the clouds. My hand is cold as a write but I do want to make this a long letter if I can. It has been more than a week now since I wrote anything more than a V-Mail. As you well know, I have little choice in these things.

One of the little instances that breaks the monotony of this life occurred Sunday night and perhaps it is worth while to relate. Our supper comes at a very late hour and Sgt. O'Connell ask me to round up the men of our squad to eat. I had reached the last foxhole and was on the point of spreading the good word. The next thing I knew, I was floundering in water up to my waste [waist]. Seeing steps in the shadows a few feet away, I made my way to them and managed to reach the ground level again. The night was very cold and I stood shaking like the leaf of an aspen. But fate was kind. A jeep was standing not twenty-five yards away. I was put into it, given a blanket to throw around me, and rushed into the Battalion Hdq. area. In the company kitchen, I found that I had not a dry thread on my body. I stripped and put on dry woolens. After getting thoroughly dry, I piled into a stack of blankets and slept. It was the soundest, the warmest, and the longest sleep that I have had in a long time. Being located in the kitchen was a decided advantage on the following day. My clothes were so wet that I spent most of the day drying them. By a bit of luck I found extra clothing and shoes to wear while this process was going on. While helping a bit around the kitchen, I managed to make up in part for a few meals lost in the rush of preceding days.

At another time in recent days, we had opportunity to observe first hand a great deal of enemy equipment. Knowing the collector's instinct that most of us possess, you can imagine with what interest we rummaged among the various piles of things left when their outfit moved—in a hurry. We have no desire to carry any more weight than is absolutely necessary, but I suppose everyone managed to find one or two small articles to supplement our [or] improve his stock.

These items serve to illustrate how seemingly insignificant happenings color our present mode of living. Parts are drab, parts exciting, and parts are unpleasant. Nothing leads me to feel any special longing to find my career in such a life. Even so, I learn something new each day. One must learn under such circumstances. Our home is carried on our back—our life on our shoulders (no connection with "heart on sleeves"). Everything that we need for living from day to day goes on our back when we move and thus such items are cut to the minimum. There is no handy closet, drawer, or corner. Almost every night we learn something new about keeping out the frost, the dew, the penetrating cold. To have a dry board on which to sleep at night is a luxury.

And yet there are times when Prometheus seems truly unbound. In one position two of the fellows were located in a dug in position with heavy walls, even a door, and on the inside a makeshift stove had been set up. An old mattress was found and they sleep like kings. On that same night, I too found an old mattress. I shared it with another but separately. We split it down the middle and paced it in our respective fox holes. I proved to myself that night that I could sleep in an upright position.

Somewhere in Germany

3-23-45

Well, three days have passed since I began this letter. I only hope this time I shall be able to finish all that I wish to say.—Not that that is possible! I am still unable to mention everything that I would like to mention, but we can say that we are now on Germany soil. The first day of Spring marked my the time of my fist step on the soil of the Reich. We are seeing more and more activity all of the time, but the Germans are rather active on their legs and we find it difficult to keep up. Perhaps we will be able to find enough trucks to catch up.

This morning as I write I am sitting at a table in the sunshine. The day is so warm that I have just finished washing and am still stripped to the waist. The weather here must be at least a month ahead of E. Tenn., for we have been enjoying a delightfully warm time recently. We are now in a small German village which we entered last night. I slept under a roof for the first time in ten days. We had plenty of hay and straw and it was almost heavenly. There is nothing pleasant about the cold damp that seeps through the body after a night in a hole in the ground, and we really appreciated the opportunity of having four walls around us.

Recent days have not been so bad, but the hiking is not the most exhilarating that I have ever done. I am on the verge of losing my old taste for climbing hills. Joe North passed me the other day on a truck and I certainly envy his job. ~~I am in the mood right now to join the Navy for the next war.~~ (Censored) But of the two experiences, I suppose that mine is more varied. The "bitch" (pardon the term) that one hears most now concerns the chow. Moving as we are, we often have difficulty keeping contact with the kitchen. Those times, we "hurt".

Your V-Mail of the 27th Feb. arrived a couple of days ago. Funny that my V-Mail should come quicker and yours slower than via Air. I received your letters of Mar. 5th & 6th already. Good to hear that Tom came around to see you. I shall try to write him some time if time allows. There are so many letters I would like to write! Including about three or four per day to my very beautiful wife.

Darling, "when it's dark enough, we can see the stars." There are times, I must admit, when things look black. I put one foot in front of the other and wonder how long I can continue to do it. Those times come but they only bring closer the dreams I have of our future. I think often of the home that will be ours, the children, trips to the mountains, days when our lives will be our own. I am learning to hate even the business of being told every move, every thought that I make.

I cannot end this by complaining. I can always say that the weather has been truly wonderful while we occupy the great outdoors. I hope that it will continue this way. I look forward to the coming of the first packages that come. I will be glad to get more.

I must try to write a note to Mother and Dad. Will also try to get a V-Mail off to you today. Remember, Darling,
　　　I love you,
　　　Bushy

March 23, '45
Germany

Well, these notes have suffered during the past few days. We thought when we left M—[Meisenthal] that we would be sticking our bayonets in the Nazis within a few hours. It hardly turned out that way. We have been in combat of sorts, but it has been nothing that we expected. We hiked about eight miles and rode several more to reach our destination. Passing through a town which had been cleared only hours earlier, we moved on into a bivouac area. We were dog-tired, having been carrying all of our equipment. (This included extra boots, overshoes, overcoat, shelter half, bed roll, extra woolens, toilet articles, extra ammunition, etc.). Out leaders seemed to have no regard for our load as we marched. Very few breaks were taken, and a great many men fell out. Much time was lost in reorganizing—far more than two or three five-minute breaks would have taken. We arose at 2:30 and moved out with our full equipment again. This was really a "rat race" and we continued on for two hours without a break. This time we reached the city of B--[Bitche], which had just been taken. Dumping most of our equipment on the other side of town, we replaced the—[100th] div. which had been fighting all night. By the time we reached our position, eleven men were left in our platoon [normally 40 men]—including non-coms and officers. The first thing that happened was the surrender of a Nazi. This was only the beginning. In our position we found a great deal of German equipment. Many blankets were lying around, and these we utilized (our squad blankets have been lost for more than a week). We found a light machine gun with plenty of ammo, and this we set up in our defensive position. We spent the day here and moved on to take up new front line positions just outside of LB [Lager-Bitche]. Here again we expected to encounter momentary firing from the enemy. This was to continue for several days, but as is now apparent, the enemy was and is in full retreat in this area. According to the latest rumor, resistance has been virtually wiped out to the Rhine. If so, this is a terrific break for us. By the 21st we had reached the German border after marching about twelve miles from B—[BITCHE]. Geisking is in the hospital with a bad foot [IT PROVED TO HAVE BEEN BROKEN – 3 BONES – ON THE MARCH, THE RAT RACE INTO BITCHE], and so I carried the BAR. [THE BROWNING AUTOMATIC RIFLE TOGETHER WITH THE BELT FILLED WITH AMMO CLIPS WEIGHED FIFTY POUNDS. EVERYTHING ELSE THAT I OWNED

WAS ON MY BACK ALSO. I CONTINUED AS THE BAR MAN FOR THE REMAINDER OF THE WAR.] My feet were killing me, and I limped almost all of the way on the hike. The bones in my feet seem to be giving way. I have great difficulty maintaining a rational viewpoint on these hikes. I awoke on the morning of the 21st with a sick stomach. Part of our "C" rations have been of the old type and some of these have been spoiled. I still have my bad stomach and still toss up part of my food – the little that I eat.

[AFTER CROSSING THE RHINE, WE HAD ONLY ONE MEAL FROM THE KITCHEN UNTIL THE WAR ENDED. I CONTINUED TO HAVE PROBLEMS WITH MY "C" RATION DIET. FROM THIS POINT ON I WILL ADD PERTINENT NOTES AS RECORDED IN PATTON'S THIRD ARMY BY CHARLES M. PROVINCE AND INDICATED BY THE # SIGN. SUBJECT IS 71ST INFANTRY DIVISION UNLESS OTHERWISE NOTED.]

[3/28 "ORDERS . . . THAT VERY SHORTLY THE THIRD ARMY WOULD HAVE . . . CONTROL OF . . . 71ST INFANTRY DIVISION (#231).]

Letter from Dotty to Art
March 24, 1945

Happy Birthday, Darling!

I never have been able to celebrate your birthday like I wanted to, dogonnit. But the day will come when I can—you mark my words. The day will come when I won't have to mail your gift to you and worry over whether it will arrive at the right time or not. The day will come when I can give you something you want instead of need. The day will come when I can say "happy birthday" with a kiss and a few other appropriate gestures of affection. The day will come when I can bake a cake for you on March 24, and have ice cream, and make a party of the occasion. The day will come when the rest of the family (ahem) will add their gifts to mine. Yes, The Day Will Come! I know it. I feel it.

May you find something this day that makes you happy—the song of a bird, or the smile of a friend, or (now I'm bragging) the message of my love for you which I am constantly sending over the thought waves. May God bless you and keep you and make His face to shine upon you, and give you peace. May He lift His countenance upon you and be gracious unto you.

"Grace be to you, and peace from God our Father, and from the Lord Jesus Christ. Blessed be thy God and Father of our Lord Jesus

Christ, who hath blessed us with all spiritual blessings in heavenly places in Christ."

"Now the God of hope fill you with all joy and peace in believing, that ye may abound in hope, through the power of the Holy Ghost," All my love—Dotty

Letter from Art to Dotty
Somewhere in Germany
March 25, 1945
(76-79)

My Dearest,

Again the sun is warm and I am able to relax a few minutes. "Tis Sunday afternoon and I can almost hear the Philharmonic playing. I think of you, of the church service which you attended this morning, of the Sunday meal at home with "Mom" and Daddy, of the Sunday afternoons that we enjoyed of old. Your good letter of the 11th (Sun.) arrived today to make the day seem all the more like Sabbath. After finishing this letter, I shall read my testament and hold a period of meditation. Yes, darling, I do find opportunity for worship even here. I find myself drawn more and more to idealism and idealistic ways of thought, and I know that I am not the soldier that is to be desired for this type of work.

Yesterday, my birthday, I began atop a G.I. truck load of gasoline moving forward. We passed through many German towns and saw many varied impressions on the faces on the civilians. One of the fellows on the trucks had found an old top hat—the type I used in the ministrels. With this cocked on the side of his head, he received laughter from almost everyone. Old women seated in their front yards ceased to face the thought of the second defeat in their memory and smiled at this crazy "Yank". Children, standing along the highway, were excited by the sight of all the soldiers (a different type of soldier from what they were accustomed) and laughed merrily. They looked on with resignation, they looked on and smiled, and many, of course, had gleams of hatred that come now and then to the corner of the eyes then withdrew. These people on which I gazed had come very near to knowing world conquest. They had certainly traveled far with their leader along that road. Now, perhaps with a new realization, they were beginning to know utter defeat. What a tremendous swing for the pendulum of human emotion to make!

At one place, an intersection of routes, we saw long streams of people pushing and pulling carts, leading children, carrying all that they could, attempting to escape the bombings that accompany war. If it were not so terribly tragic, it would verge on stark comedy. Here they were, Germans! Fleeing their homes, carrying a few personal items, crying, cursing, wondering what had happened to the vain promises that "no bombs would every [ever] touch German citizens," wondering where their invincible "Fueher" and his invincible Wehrmacht could be. Since 1939, Sept. 1st, other peoples, not Germans, had been doing this very same thing. They too cried, were perplexed, cursed their enemy soldiers that passed by swiftly on trucks. Now the pendulum of human misery has swung. Yes, it is ironical. I recalled passages from the Sermon on the Mount which I had read only a short time before. We humans cannot learn the simplest lessons it seems.

While I was yet writing I was called for a squad meeting, at which place I received your good letter of the 13th (mailed on the 15th). Just after this I was able to go to church service for the first time in two or three weeks. Here again I must describe the marked contrast. A Catholic service was held within the Cathedral and the Protestant service just outside in the "Adolph Hitler Platz" (there is one in every town in seems, and, is merely a town square). We were seated, about a dozen of us, on our helmets in front of the chaplains jeep and the little portable organ. There in town stood just in front of a monument dedicated to the German soldiers of the I World War. The people gathered on the streets on four sides and watched. We sang, we prayed, together, we listened to the words of the chaplain. The buds on the trees around were bursting with bloom and the birds were accompanying the tenor soloist who proclaimed that "Day was dying in the West." The situation was strangely unreal.

3-26-45

As usual, one thing or another interrupted my writing yesterday but luckily I am able to continue today. This morning, clouds continued to roll in and the rain began just as we finished making our fox hole family waterproof. Just as in E. Tenn. however, after two or three hours of steady down pour, the clouds disappeared and the sun began to shine. What a wonderful thing warming sunshine is! As we spread our equipment to dry, we saw one of the most impressive sights of Am air force that I have yet seen. With long vapor trails behind them, bombers in countless numbers roared on toward the heart of Germany. A feeling of pride and security wells up within the heart of the "lowly" foot slogan when such a sight he views from his foxhole home.

Yesterday was of course, Palm Sunday. I thought it appropriate that I should receive nine long letters from "Mom" Pratt and also one from Helen on that day. It was just a year ago on Palm Sunday that I attended church with them while awaiting that wonderful telegram telling me that you would arrive in San Francisco at "10 o'clock Thursday morning." It was certainly swell to hear from them and they gave me news concerning Ted. I hope to write him over here. Glad that you heard from Jim G. and hope you will write him for me. Also, Darling, for heaven's sake, try to stop make excuses to Hal for me. I still devote all of my writing time to you and Mother & Dad. I think it is justified, but I do wish I could do better in regard to my friends.

We here are taking renewed hope at the turn of events reported in every paper that arrives. I am wondering, along with you and everyone else, just how long "Jerry" can hold up under the present pressure. One thing we know and that from everyday experience right here—the German soldier is more than willing to yell "Kamerade" and does so with hearth warning regularity. But the amazing thing is that they continue to fight even as they do. The Rhine has now been crossed in many places and all that we need to do is continue to throw men and material across our established bridgeheads. Again, on the other hand, as they get closer home there is the psychological factor of "home defense." It is a sordid but not hopeless picture.

I have a long letter to write on values again, but I must save it for later. If I do not soon wind this up and get it in the mail, you will think I have deserted my post as a husband. I shall try to start another letter, if time allows. Oh yes, you mentioned, in a backhand sort of way (which I had a devil of a time reading) that you could not find a cigarette lighter. That is all right, Darling. This reference is the only one I have received concerning a package sent, but I am sure other letters will make reference to them. Unless radical and unexpected changes occur, I shall always leap with joy when I receive boxes from you. Food is ever a critical items so do not hesitate to send it. Be sure that the box is <u>very</u> securely tied for it receives rough handling en route.

Although I often wait until the last to mention it, the presence of Our Love is with me at every moment during the day and night. I look up at the moon each night with while on my vigil of watch and ask that she "whisper my Love." I feel your prayers with me and the Guiding Hand of our Heavenly Father is ever clasped in mine. I feel His presence with new comfort and I feel secure. May He ever bless
Our Love,
Bushy

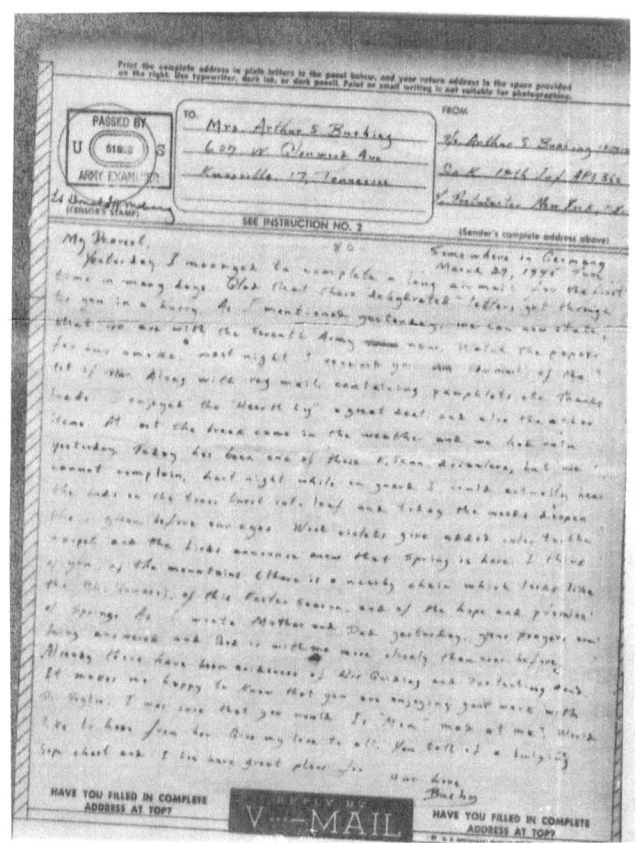

V-Mail March 27, 1945, from Art to Dotty
"Last night while on guard I could actually hear the buds on the trees..."

March 28
4 o'clock

The first Purple Heart was earned in our platoon today by Pratt. He was on an outpost when a shrapnel caught him. A second man [Carson, from another squad] was hit when a buddy fired accidentally while cleaning his rifle. And so the numbers decrease. It is only the beginning.

Last night my team [BAR team of three] held an LP [Listening Post] on the river.

Somewhere in Germany
Mar 28, 1945 Wed.

My Dearest,

My morale shot to a new high yesterday when I was the proud recipient of eight letters! Five from my dear wife, one card from Mom, Dad and one from Tom. Three of yours were mailed on the 19th and arrived on the 27th. Not bad. Your notes on Spring sound strangely similar to those I have written in recent days. What a telepathic, (or is it "telepathetic") pain! The backyard description was good but the Maryville incident even better. My worries are at last over concerning "'tis colder now," but can you find a copy? Tanks, bud.

By the way, I wonder if you were able to get a note off to Dr. Felix Kessing concerning the bibliography. I still must get that for Dr. Peyton. Glad to get the addresses and shall certainly try to write Ted and Carl. Have seen Ted K. only the one time. Must write him also. Good to know that Helen and Kerr are on the right road, but the "poignancy and wonder" brought about by your visit was of greater interest. Perhaps you can note by the papers that there still exists a good deal of activity over here. We seem to encounter more every day, and I already have a couple of late rations [?] to file away. I am more positive than ever that the Camp Roberts "Dad" was all wet. Much to say but little time at the moment. With the meager aid of inadequate words. I say

I love you,
Bushy

P.S. Beautiful Easter card.

March 29th

Our squad of only nine men was stretched over an area of about six hundred yards. Some of the fellows were too nervous for sleep, for crossings [by Germans] were being tried. On the third shift Moreau, [third member of my team] sighted boats about fifteen minutes after he began his watch. According to plan, Breeden [second member] and I were awakened, and we prepared for action. At first I could see nothing and was certain that the others were seeing things. After fifteen minutes the shadows began to change, and I was willing to say that boats were there. We were agreed that there were at least two of the two-man type. After hearing a muffled cough repeated five or six times, and as one of the boats appeared about ten feet from shore, we opened fire with one rifle. Moreau fired five shots, and I did the same with the Breeden's M-1. For reasons of security we withheld firing of the BAR [STANDARD PROCEDURE WAS TO HOLD THE WEAPON IN RESERVE. FOR THIS REASON, I WAS CALLED ON INFREQUENTLY TO FIRE.] As far as we know, we scored no hits, but the boats disappeared. I assume that they moved along the shadows down stream. After firing, we sent Breeden back with word of our activity, and Lt. Moberg [our Platoon leader] and [Sgt.] Romair returned to investigate, After viewing our LP, it was decided that we should stand watch nearer the bank, and so we froze for the remainder of the night. No more boats appeared.

Saturday night we pulled into our dike position out of O— [OTTERSTADT?] [ON A 1991 MAP OF GERMANY I FIND OTTERBACH AND OTTERBERG WEST OF MANNHEIM AND HEIDELBERG IN THE SARRLAND.] Monday afternoon we received fire from 88's. After the barrage ended, we found that a shell had landed only twenty-three paces from our dugout. We were not even aware that it had hit there since it landed just over the top of the dike on the forward slope while we were just over the top on the reverse side. Yesterday afternoon we also received fire near our positions. The guns were probably searching for our mortar positions. It is a comforting feeling to have a nice deep hole to dive in when that lonely whistle sounds overhead. All of us learn to eat dirt.

On Sunday night our squad drew its second patrol. I missed the first but was asked to go on this one. Our mission was to make a reconnaissance to the Rhine (about a mile away), and find if enemy was still to be found. Five of us advanced about a thousand yards, moving forward a few yards, then stopping to listen. Sgt. O'Neill and Price [Fred Price was our Point Man] were in front, and they thought that they heard a cough. They hit the dirt as did we. O'Neill challenged twice and there was no response. He opened fire, after which we withdrew. The CO was not pleased with the results of our patrol, and yet there was little else to be done under the circumstances. The patrol at best was little better than a suicide if the enemy wished to disclose its presence. Because of the dense brush, we could not afford to advance through the woods, and thus we were forced to move along the open road with no cover but a shallow ditch line. Later in the night Lt. Moberg took a patrol of non-coms (including O'Neill) all the way to the Rhine without encountering enemy.

Letter from Art to Dotty
Somewhere in Germany
3-31-45 (81-86)

My Dearest Heart,

We are enjoying a new experience as I write that is a pleasant change to put it mildly. For the past two nights we have had a roof over our heads, other than a tent. Today I had a good bath, washed my hair, shaved, washed a few dirty articles, and washed and combed my hair. I am beginning to feel like a white man again.

There is only one thing that mars the pleasure of this activity (our rather partial inactivity): we are here, occupying a German home, the people forced out, we are here as conquerors and will become the role. The family in this particular place seem so frightened that they scurry around trying in every way to please us. For most Americans this experience is new, different, and I might say, uncomfortable. To misquote Emerson, every man likes to be served, but few men likes to be served very much. Old Andy Jackson, another Tennessean, claimed that "to the victor belongs the spoils." Well, to a small extent, perhaps. As I mentioned in a previous letter, I am a poor soldier for the very reason of my attitude in this situation. I am soft when it comes to dealing with people even though they be enemy, even though I know that, given the opportunity, they might easily stick a knife in my back, or pick me off with a sniper's bullet at the first opportune moment. No my Dear, I fear that your husband fails in certain respects to measure up to the full standards (may I say "down to the standards") that mark a conquering soldier.

The Rhine is the topic of conversation now which flows like the very river itself. Days go by when the only news we have consists of veiled rumors, but we do catch up with a full account of events now and then. "Rhine crossed All Along Western Front" was certain a headline that thrilled the hearts of the G.I.'s all over Europe. We near ultimate victory without question. The Frankfort breakthrough is being considered near rout in the last paper (Thur.) which we have seen. What rejoicing there will be when that final shot is fired. Surely even these German people will be glad that bombs & shells will cease to fall.

In reference to my present abode, I failed to mention a significant factor. Our squad at present occupies a very sedate German bar. I doubt that I will be so fortunate as to spend the famed ten nights here, but for me one night in such a place is a new experience, especially when that one night is spent flat on my back, my senses numbed to my surroundings.

Needless to say, our location in such a place was not without recompense for those who have a taste for the stronger types of drink. (I think that there are three in my platoon, including myself, who do not touch liquors.) Several occasions have already arisen when there has been drinks for everyone and we three (Sod, Beul, and I have stood apart). It is not particularly difficult, for I have been under social pressure before, and it seems to make not a great deal of difference in my relations with the others.

In recent days I have been able to offer slight service as mediator between my Lieutenant and the Germans. I have not too much difficulty in making myself understood and it is good practice for my German. Even if we wish, we are not allowed to "fraternize" with the people, and so this is almost the only opportunity I have for contact with them.

Tomorrow is Easter. How different from the Easter I knew just a year ago. I have no way of knowing even what the next hour may bring, so I cannot know whether or not I will be able to attend services or not. I certainly hope so. My fervent prayer is that a new meaning of Christ's Life will come to the hearts of men everywhere as the war draws near an end. I would pray that the simpler life of Love which He taught might be understood as the only way for peaceful and happy pursuits. With prophets of old, I would say "How long, Oh Lord, How Long?"

For days at a time, as I think I have mentioned, we eat from cans —"C" rations as they are called. One meal is contained in two cans. In one is found the solid part of the meal—meat and beans, stew, hash, spagetti and meat, meat and noodles, etc. The other can is a bread unit containing four or five biscuits, a drink powder (coffee, cocoa, lemonade or orangeade), and candy. Always nourishing and tasty when one is hungry, these rations do get a bit monotonous at times. Thus we attempt to vary them insofar as possible. I have become known for the crazy concoctions which I make from my rations. I shall mention only one as an example. Eating my meat unit without the biscuit, I save these for a separate dish. In the little can which holds the unit, I heat water and make a very strong cup of coffee. In this, I place one of the daily 1 oz. bars of chocolate and melt it. In this, I crumble my biscuits and add sugar. This I heat, cooking it down to a mush. I consider it one of my best puddings, and many of the fellows have copied it. And so, Darling, you must not allow me to challenge the position you hold as the chief cook in the Bushing household. (By the way, how are you getting along with your cooking these days? I'm expecting very big things when I return.)

Unless I find myself occupied, I shall attempt to write a long letter tonight on values which I have promised for some time. By signing off now, I may be able to get a letter written to Mother and Dad and perhaps even one to Mary Ruth.

A deep current of strength and courage comes to my heart from the well-spring of

Our Love,
Bushy

April 1st
(Easter)

Wed. night our platoon was asked to volunteer for a patrol to go across the Rhine and accomplish a rather hazardous mission. Two (or more) machine gun nests have harassed our patrols for several days, and several casualties have resulted from their activities. The mission assigned to this patrol was to float down the river, circle to the rear of the guns, wipe them out, and return by way of the 5th [division] further down the stream. Lt. Moberg refused to volunteer his men, but offered to lead the patrol, as did Sgt. [Edward] Utrup. By a very happy coincidence, our entire unit was relieved a few hours before we were to go on the patrol. If made, this would have been by far our most hazardous job to date.

[WE WERE TO MOVE OUT AFTER DARK, AND SO WE HAD A FEW HOURS OF DAYLIGHT TO ANTICIPATE OUR ASSIGNMENT. MORE THAN FIFTY YEARS LATER, I STILL RECALL WRITING LETTERS TO MY WIFE AND TO MY MOTHER, REALIZING THAT THIS WAS IN FACT A SUICIDE MISSION. SHORTLY BEFORE DARK, ANOTHER UNIT REPLACED US.]

With lightened hearts we moved back under the light of a moon almost full to an assembly area outside the site where the 88's had been falling. Here, in a pine wood to be likened to pine woods of GA., we dug our holes and slept. [WE HAD TRAINED FOR THREE MONTHS AT FORT BENNING, GA., PRIOR TO SHIPPING

OVERSEAS]. We were supposed to leave at four o'clock the following morning, but here we spent the day, moving out in the mid-afternoon.

[4/2 THE 71ST "MOPPED UP" NEAR FULDA (#239)].
[4/3 " ... CLEARED THE WOODS FOR TWENTY MILES SOUTH OF LAUTERBACK" (240)].
[4/4 " ... COMPLETED THE CLEARING OF ITS ZONE AND THEN MOVED NORTH TO ASSUME POSITIONS ALONG THE LINE FROM SCHLUCHTERN TO FULDA" (#241)].
[4/6 " ... WENT INTO AN ASSEMBLY AREA AT HOF-BIEBER" (#244)].
[4/7 " ... MOPPED UP AND PROTECTED THE SOUTHERN FLANK" (#245)].
[4/8 "2ND CAVALRY WAS RELIEVED FROM CONTROL BY THE 71ST ..., WHICH WAS SANDWICHED BETWEEN THE 11TH ARMORED AND 26TH INFANTRY DIVISIONS" (#246)]
[4/10 FOLLOWING THE CAPTURE OF COBURG, "THE 71ST DIVISION, HOT ON THE HEELS OF THE 11TH ARMORED, KEPT MOPPING UP" (#248)].
[PRESIDENT FRANKLIN D. ROOSEVELT DIED UNEXPECTEDLY ON APRIL 12, 1945. SEE LETTER REGARDING HIS DEATH AT END OF CHAPTER.]
[4/12 CROSSED THE HARLACH RIVER (#250)].
[4/14 " ... THE 71ST ... RELIEVED THE 11TH ARMORED DIVISION IN BOTH THE CITY {OF BAYREUTH} AND TO THE NORTHWEST" (#252-53)]

Letters from Dotty to Art
Easter Sabbath
April 1, 1945

My Dearest,
How beautiful was today. True, it rained, it was cloudy and gloomy looking most of the day, but how beautiful it was. I arose at 6:00, and at 6:30 I was on my way down the hill to the church. The sun had just just come up, and appeared near the horizon as a blazing, brilliant, deep orange mass. Soon, however it disappeared, and the morning became gray and misty. Despite the somber background, however, the early services glowed with a beauty all its own. Do you remember the stove fireplace in the garden? The fireplace part had been draped in a white sheet, and a white cross leaned against the chimney. In front of

the cross an open Bible was propped up, and either side of which stood a pot of white lilies. A worship center such as this created a very favorable atmosphere for the service. A young people's choir, robed, sat on the ledges on each side of the fireplace. An organ (the kind you pump with your feet) had been brought out & set on the hill beside the fireplace. After a few numbers by the choir and readings by a couple of the young people, Dr. Peyton delivered a short meditation, the essence of which was experiencing the reality of Easter. Until we actually experience in our spiritual life the truth of the resurrection, it will not seem like truth to us. Truth experienced is real truth. (of Dr. Orr's preachments on truth). After the service the young people served breakfast. There was the usual array of new clothes & corsages present this morning. Except for a new blouse, I wore exactly the same outfit as a year ago Easter (our first Sunday together as man & wife). Mother had bought me a couple of yellow roses, so I added some lily-of the-valley from Aunt Mary's garden and made my own corsage. I thought you would want me to wear some, and knew you would have sent me some if at all possible.

The congregation for the morning service spilled over into the S.S. room. The junior choir, which had been well trained by Mrs. Peyton, sang quite well. Our choir sang an anthem and a hymn. We were to have sung two anthems, but decided at the last minute to omit one of them because there were not enough copies to go around. The one we omitted was the one in which I was to have sung a solo.

Mary Ruth came home, so I visited with her most of the afternoon. Too soon it was time to go to church again. My new group of Intermediates is going to be a joy to work with,—they are so full of life.

Darling, I have thought of you constantly all day long. My thoughts were a continuous stream of praying for you, thinking of you remembering you, wanting you, talking to you. How glorious it is to think and pray for
Our love,
Dotty

Monday
April 9, 1945
Darling,

As I do more and more reading about national and international affairs, the more convinced I become that the world is indeed in a mess, and that this world and all that in it is must look pretty ugly to God. How can he keep on forgiving us the high level of evil we allow to flourish? There is plenty of it right under our noses—it isn't all in

Germany and Japan. The papers this morning were full of several stories and articles about the horrible things that have been going on in German prison camps, death camps, etc. Things like that don't engender much love in the hearts of the allies. It looks as if the big nations are going to quibble over trifles at the peace conference and leave vital issues untouched. Coming even closer home this city's gov't is as corrupt as corrupt, and anybody who tries to change things for the better is either fired or smeared. How can men hope to build lasting happiness and enduring peace through strife, bloodshed, trickery, and dictatorial policies? WE MUST ALL REPENT AND RETURN TO GOD, FORSAKING OUR EVIL WAYS. If we don't I truly fear the consequences.

I didn't mean to go on so about it, but it was sort of boiling up inside, so I had to let off a little steam.

I wrote four letters tonight, but still have a lot to answer. If I could write that many every night I'd soon be caught up, but alas that is not possible. Tomorrow night I go to a circle meeting & a concert (an arrangement of Hansel & Gretel by the Knoxville Symphony).

Darling, I wondered how long it would take you to inquire about "Mizpah." In the Bible Jacob & Laban, at a site called Mizpah, terminated a pact with the following words: "May the Lord watch between me and thee, while we are absent one from another." This quotation has become known as the Mizpah Benediction, and is often repeated in unison of the close of religious meetings. Thus when I terminate our letters with this Mizpah, I am really asking God to be with us during our separation.

According to the latest reports from my private gremlin you look like a cross between Chew Fu and great-uncle-Albert. Thus you may find the enclosed clipping suggestive and it is to be hoped, beneficial. (Urgent note from my conscience—"Now Dotty, you know the poor fellow probably has neither water, time, nor equipment for shaving. Why rub it in?) I'll bite—why?

Darling, I constantly think and pray for
      Our love,
        Dotty
P.S. Mizpah!

[Their one year wedding anniversary.]
April 6, 1945

My Dearest Husband,
Darling Bushy,
Sweetheart,
Most adored one,

And all the other precious names in the world—select the one you like best and tell me which one it is, so I can call you that more often.

Darling, this has been a rather peculiar anniversary, and I must confess—a bit lonesome. My first thought upon waking was of you, my beloved, and of how much the day meant to me, and vivid recollections of April 6, 1944. The morning was spent in finishing your letter begun the night before, practicing my music, and preparing lunch for Dad & me. Then off to work, meeting the postman as I went out the door. But he had nothing for me at all, not even from Jamestown. Nothing. My spirits went a bit lower. I know in my heart that you were thinking of me just as longingly and intently as I was thinking of you, but I wanted some tangible message from you on this special day, and not having had any mail from you at all in over a week made it even worse. But the atmosphere of the church calmed and soothed my spirits as usual, and lifted them from the valleys wherein they had fallen. Afterwards I came home, ate supper, then went to the "Y", which held open house tonight. It was like a four-ring circus, what with a swimming exhibition, the fashion show, volleyball, and some dancing (square & modern) going on simultaneously! We put on our modern dance act four times with a different crowd for audience each time. Before I knew it the evening was over, and our anniversary was over. Mother gave me this paper (isn't it cute?), and Helen & Roland sent us a card last week, and those were the only remembrances we got.

Darling, I had meant to spend this entire letter recounting my love for you, what marriage to the most wonderful guy on earth means to me, and what a glorious year this has been. But how can I begin to tell you how much you mean to me? How can I find words to tell of my love for you? There are no adequate expressions. But I can still say that you are everything to me; that this has been the most joyous, the most complete year of my life; that the closer you are the closer God is; that my faith in Him is strengthened and made finer by your faith; that sharing life with you gives it infinitely more meaning than formerly.

Oh, Darling I love you so. Wherever you are and whatever you are doing tonight, I hope you feel   My love for you, Dotty.

Somewhere in Germany
April 7, 1945 (88-95)

My Darling,

I have perhaps but a few moments in which to write and even these are the first that I have been able to utilize in the past week. Not even yesterday on our first anniversary was I able to sit down and talk with you on paper. Nevertheless, I did speak to you many times during the day. You were very close, my Dear.

I have so much to say and so little time to say it. Your wonderful letter written on my birthday came two days ago and I do believe that it is the finest letter I have ever read. You are close to me always, but that letter brought you even closer. You will never know just how much strength your love and faith aids me during these days. There are times when my spirits sink to new depths. There are times when my body seems strained to the breaking point and I wonder how it is possible to take another step. It is then that I call upon God for His aid and it is then that I think of you and of your faith in me. Thus I go on.

Sunday Afternoon
April 9th

Sunday afternoon and at last I may have a few moments in which to write. I believe that this has been the longest delay in my writing since I landed. I wrote on the 31st (two letters, I believe), but not since then have I been able to write. Such is life—life in the Army.

I shall attempt to go back a bit and tell you something of my Easter. It was truly far more like Easter than I had ever hoped. In the first place, my activities were such that I was able to have a clean shave and a haircut. The latter was my first in almost two months. By coincidence, the Quartermaster had field showers in the next town and I was lucky enough to be able to load on a truck and go over. This, My Turtle Dove, was my first hot shower since Jan 24th. Sponge baths have been my only luxury since that time. At the showers were also able to get clean underwear and socks. I dare not say how long it had been since I had had the former. To make the day complete insofar as rest and worship was concerned, I was able to attend Easter Service in a little German theatre. The service was simple, but impressive; and I felt that we were experiencing true worship. I was able to attend with MacIntosh and this too was an added event. The Chaplain took the names of our families and promised to write telling of our attendance. I trust that he did. Events in the latter part of the day were not so pleasant—we did the usual, almost diurnal, thing—we moved. All of us regretted that we had to leave our barroom home, but our gypsy life demands such things. I suppose that in the rush of present day activity, two nights in a barroom is sufficient.

Much of my life during the days that followed must remain veiled in a cloak of secrecy. We had no houses, but we had much rain. I never before knew how cozy & well-built pup-tent could be. After several moves and much climbing, we are at a higher altitude now, and thus a colder one. However, on such a day as this one, it is very pleasant. The sun is warm upon my back even though the air remains crisp and birds continue to sing. I am ever thankful that my winter was not spent as it might have been. I have been very lucky, Darling.

On one of the days last week, I think it was Wed. or Thur., I received a very old letter written March 9th. In this you described the contents of the first package all of which sounded quite wonderful. I shall report immediately upon its arrival. We expect long delays on these packages, but they are certainly wonderful to look forward to.

So far you have made no mention of receiving the bonds which I made out. The new one was for $18.75 and the old one for $7.50. Today I was paid for the first time in two months. It seemed a bit paradoxical to receive German marks (instead, of course, by AMG.) but I had no qualms about taking them. My total pay was only $20.00 and it remained in my hands about two minutes. I turned it in immediately to be sent to you, along with a few francs from my last pay. You should receive a money order for $30 or almost that. Be sure and tell me when this comes.

Pardon the rapid change of subject, but as I sit here I watch large convoys of equipment and materials pass by. It just occurs to me how utterly wasteful this business is. All of these trucks, all of these weapons, & everything will be thrown away when this thing is over. This is not literally true. Perhaps some of this will be shipped to the S. West Pacific, but for the most part the equipment will be cast aside. I have seen entire towns, large towns, demolished. I have seen Frenchmen and Poles just released from German prisoner camps who have been held since 1939, on foot with a few clothes on their back trying to find their way home. I have seen Germans too, trudging along the highways, seeking to escape the ravages of war. I truly hate this more and more each day. What needless suffering and waste and to what avail? I know, or think I know, why I am fighting, why we

Americans are fighting. But how utterly tragic that the race of man should allow the necessity for war to arise.

I must tell you, Darling, that certain ideas and outlooks of mine are changing. In recent days I have built up a growing dislike for the requirements of my daily living. I am doing my job as a soldier, but there is no matter of choice. I have distaste for both the physical and the mental. However, there has arisen on the other hand, a counter outlook. I believe that I am learning things that would have been otherwise impossible to know. I am beginning to feel in a new way that He who has reason for all things has reason for this also. "Let this cup pass from me, yet not my will but Thine." I try to go on without questioning too much. I find that every march, every watch, every job has an end, and Time, the eternal balm, moves ever onward.

I must write Mother and Dad today also. Had a good long letter from both today. I gather that Dad suffered far more from his recent illness that I had been led to believe. I do hope that you can write the folks often for your letters mean much to them. I am terribly glad that their work is lighter now.

How can I hope to tell you with my faltering pen how much I think and dream of our future together? There are rivers to cross and mountains to climb, but God will continue to bless

Our Love,
Bushy

P.S. I enclose 2 Franc notes } for M.R. [Mary Ruth]
5 " "
1 Mark "

Letter excerpt from Art's mother to Dotty
April 10, 1945

"I really didn't realize that we had not been writing, but maybe we haven't and again maybe time is going by a lot faster than we realize. We haven't been real sick, but we have both had colds. Arthur got one and handed it over to me, and I'm still sniffling and a snuffing. I've been alone since Sunday. Arthur had to be in Nashville yesterday in a case of a Delinquent registrant, but will be home sometime tonight."

Letter excerpts from Art's dad to Dotty
April 9, 1945

"Now going overseas, we have been writing Arthur every week. It appears that while we have been hearing from him pretty regularly, our letters to him have not been getting though as we had hoped. We have sent two 5 lb packages which we do trust will not be delayed. So glad to hear he is still safe and well. Our prayers go up daily for his safe return.

"Well, here I am in Nashville—a witness for the Government in a delinquency charge against one of our registrants who refuses to answer Instructor Call for Army service. He says he isn't going to war—just like that—so he is in jail here awaiting his trial in June. I was surrounded before Federal Grand Jury this A.M. as one in charge of S.S. records. I left Jamestown yesterday afternoon and will leave for home tomorrow afternoon....

"We hope you are getting along nicely. Mother and I have had heavy colds. I left her feeling pretty miserable yesterday. Fortunately we were not afflicted at the same time, for I was recovering my spell of "Flu," as the doctor called it—when she caught miserable cold....

"Tell us about your work—your health. We know, with us, you miss our precious boy—your sweetheart. I do hope you find his letters cheerful in spite of the terrible privations he and the boys suffer in these closing and terrible days knocking out the enemy."

Letter from Art to Dotty
Somewhere in Germany
April 11, 1945
(97-105)

My Dear,

When I tell you my present situation, will think I enjoy a permanent vacation. However, the other side of the picture is veiled in military secrecy and so I can only describe the happier side. Perhaps it is as well. A few moments ago I finished a shave, a real, honest-to-goodness bath (as distinguished from a shower) and a general clean up. At least two hours of my sleep last night was spent on a bed—my fist since the States. Again we are privileged to occupy a house.

I write from a bench in a small garden. The sun is warm and I sit in my undershirt. Just now a middle-aged German woman came up to the long bench and sat down. Perhaps it is her house which we are in at the moment. As I watch these people from day to day, I try to pierce the veil that hangs between the countenance and the inner mind. Any opinions of such things are always products of observation plus imagination, and so how can I be sure? However, certain facts seem evident.

Perhaps I can categorize my impressions under three or four heads in good Floydian style: surprise, fear, resignation, acceptance. As we move on from town to town we often pass through where no G.I.'s are to be seen. Often the streets are crowded with startled faces. "What on earth can you be doing here?" the expressions seem to voice, "It can't happen here!" "But Adolph said...." "The newspaper yesterday said the Americans were twenty miles away. Today....! Yes, these people are undergoing a new surprise as we roll even farther into the heartland. When the first shock of realization passes, I see fear written upon the faces of many. A horrible picture of the American soldier must have been painted by Nazi propaganda. Some seem to think that rape, murder and thievery are life functions for us. They expect the worst and hardly understand when we ignore them or treat them indifferently.

Later

Pardon the break but this is a scene that I must record. Beul and half a dozen of us are sitting around a table with a real electric light (not a candle) lending light. Some write, some read, some listen. We are tuned in on an Allied Expeditionary Force's radio program with hot jazz. You know how I detected jazz back home, but here all of us listen as though we were listening to heavenly songs. It really sounds wonderful to our homesick ears. This scene seems so foreign to those which we have known of late—it is almost like a college frat house.

Thur. - April 12

To continue the theme upon which I was writing before I interrupted myself last night—The third phase as I see it of the adjusting attitude of the German people is that of resignation. General traits change but little and it is well known that Germans are not slow in falling in line with military rules. After surprise and fear register, one sees a saddened and resigning look upon the faces of the people upon the street. They hurry to and fro as they attend to their daily activities. There seems little hatred in the average face but there are also few smiles. I think that perhaps children foretell the trend more quickly than older folk. Already their curiosity is getting the better of them, and they come around to gaze and wonder, and accept. Even a few of the elders seem to accept our presence. There may be a fatalism in this; I don't know. But these impressions strike me forceably —surprise, fear, resignation and finally acceptance.

I must make mention of one or two instances to show that many variations exist within my artificial labels. More than once a civilian has been quick to assert that he has no connection with the Whermarcht (Army) or again that he is not a Nazi. The other extreme was exemplified yesterday by a very opposite incident. I was reading a copy of Time when a very old lady hobbled up. She seemed intensely interested in the picture of Stalin on the cover. With much elaboration she carried on and seemed to want to see more of the magazine. Thinking I might make a sale, I began to point out all the fine features including pictures and maps. I stopped at a map of Europe and began to point out the towns which were falling thick and fast. —Hanover, Bremen, Vienna, etc. She nodded, "ja, ja!" But when I had finished, she placed her hand over central Europe including much of the conquered territory, "Allies in Deutchland!" she cried in quavering tones.

I have a short play in mind which I shall try to outline soon. It is just forming in my mind but it is based on much the same thing as that which I dealt with above. I will attempt to portray a few of the attitudes and impressions of these people under the present conditions. More about his later.

Another bit of news I reported in a V-mail last night pertained to our new status. We are now assigned to the 12th Corps, 3rd Army. Perhaps you can follow my activities in the paper. Of course, as you know our division status is not likely to change, but we are shifted from one Army Group to another.

From a point of financial increase, you may be interested to know further that I have received the Expert Combat Infantryman's Badge entitling me to $10 more per month for the remainder of my stay in the Army. Unless I am far wrong, this brings our total income from the Army to $103.80 per month. That should cause a sizable growth in that little nest egg, My Love. As I mentioned in a letter of Sun., I am sending $30 via Money Order—or I should say, the company clerk is sending it. Tell me when the order arrives. In all probability, I will be able to send a little every month as a result of the new increase.

I am finding a wealth of thought provoking material in my copy of Encore. This along with Time provides wonderful companionship, and how I long for such company. Often I allow myself the luxury of reminiscing over past days of intellectual activity and I find my only cheer in the knowledge that those days, even far brighter days lie ahead. I am writing even now in a kitchen where we have been cooking. Our quarters consist of a middle-class apartment. How easy to close my eyes and imagine that you are here, the home our own, the future ours to plan.

Darling, I love you. I would jump at the chance to ask you to become my wife if the job had not already been done. Gee, I guess I am romantic tonight! I still have much work to do before I sleep and so I must say, "sweet dreams!" and if you don't mind, I repeat,

I love you,

Bushy.

P.S. My latest concoction: ¼ bar chocolate dissolved in one cup of coffee (minus milk). We seldom have the milk or cream and this makes a delightful substitute.

* Letter from Art to Dotty
[President Roosevelt's death]
Somewhere in Germany
April 14, 1945 (Sat. Even.
[106-113]

My Darling,

On Thursday night as I was being relieved from my post of duty the news of the death of our Commander-in-Chief came. As was true I suppose in the case of almost everyone, I received the news with more than a little shock. Just at the moment when the Allied Nations are poised for the final victorious battle in Europe the tragedy of his death is but the more tragic. Of course, the foundation for peace has been established and for that we can be thankful. Nevertheless there will be decisions in which the voice of Mr. Roosevelt would have weighed heavily. It would matter little who stepped into his place. No one could have the world influence, the world prestige which he possessed. Perhaps not even history itself will be able to reveal just how much its own pages will have been changed by the President's untimely passage.

With every respect for the magnificent job which Mr. Roosevelt has done, not only during the critical war years but also in his earlier New Deal Administration, I am forced to make one small critical observation in view of the present situation. It has been no secret that the President has never allowed any member of his party to become prominent nor to rise to a challenging position. More than one individual has been restrained by one means or another when his prominence became pronounced. It was by this method that nominations for a third and a fourth term were secured. The ends sought were accomplished, but the aftermath is now to be reckoned with. The Democratic Party is without a real leader, behind which the majority will fall. But more than that, the leadership of our country as a whole, and thus, in part, the world, is in the hands of an inexperienced an almost unknown man. (I was tempted to say "politician," but the term is rather strong.)

I devoted a page to critical comment which should have been praise, but one small generalization I wanted to draw. In all his greatness, and he was great; in all of his foresightedness, and he did see into the future, a loophole was left unguarded which may or may not prove costly to the cause of a just and lasting peace. As my friend Emerson was wont to say, "Every man is wanted, but no man is wanted very much." We should plan with the thought in mind that at any moment another may replace us. I labor the point and just pursue another topic before my page and pen run out.

For reasons of censorship I have been unable to mention my crossing of the Rhine, but now I can relate the experience. (As I mentioned in my last letter, I am now with the 12th Corps, 3rd Army— still same division, of course.) We approached the famed river shortly after the first bridgeheads had been established in our sector. The rain was falling and the clouds lay in low clusters over our heads. As our trucks moved nearer the pontoon bridge we could easily see the destruction wrought by bombs, shells, and demolition. The bridge formerly spanning the river lay in twisted ruins as though frozen in a death struggle. The long pontoon boats lay side by side and supported the iron runways. Water rushed between these pontoons and the entire structure rode up and down as the heavy trucks made the crossing. At last we were on the other side and rolling onward. The Rhine had been crossed.

In our recent moves from town to town I have had opportunity to observe various things concerning the peoples here. Some of them I discussed in my last letter. One commentary which I failed to mention concerns their industrious nature. Much of the time as we see them, their daily routine has been broken by the surrounding conditions of war. However, now and then we pass through valleys tucked in the mountains where the devastations of war seem to have left the people untouched. Here we see entire families working the fields. Of course, there are no men. Even men of middle age seem to be prominent by their absence. Old men with white hair, grandmothers, young girls, and women, little boys—all are at work sowing and planting. Man must seek bread no matter what the tides of war may bring.

As a result of our moving about our mail has been held up and I have had no letters for four or five days. However, the stack will be all the more wonderful to read when they do reach me. I am also hoping that my first package will get here soon. I did receive another copy of the Echo a couple of days ago and I read every word with the same nostalgic feeling that overwhelms me each time. I think of The Hill. It just occurred to me that the recreation center in Bartlett climaxes the plans which we began at Retreat at Lyons Springs four years ago. Thus our plans bear fruit.

Today I was able to get a couple of packages in the mail for the first time. One to you contained the chess-checkers set which was a present from Bill. I have carried it over half of Europe and I would like to keep it for cold winter nights by the open fire. The second package was a souvenir knife which I mailed Dad. I have been unable to get anything in the way of a suitable present or souvenir for you, my Love, but I shall do the best I can when the opportunity comes.

As the days pass, some swiftly, some slowly, I know that each sunset marks a day nearer the time when we will be together again. I pray constantly for that day to come.

Goodnight and pleasant dreams. May His Peace follow always

Our Love,
Bushy

April 16, 1945
Monday Morning
[typed]

Miner thrill of minor thrills! I have my hands on a keyboard once more. It is a German make, of course and some of the keys are different (for instance that "y" is where the "z" should be and vice-versay.) But you can hardlz imagine how much fun it is to be able to sit down and dash off a couple of lines with a machine.

I began this letter on Saturday night, and here it is Mondaz morning. Circumstance prevented mailing it sooner but I hope to get it off this time. As you no doubt guess we are situated in a German home at present; and we have been thus lucky for past week. This is one of the nicest places that we have found, and it is the first time that we have found a typewriter. (Why don't we do this more often?") Probably the one single thing most appreciated by the most of us is achance to sleep in a real bed. Last night I slept with a sheet under me for the first time since I left our little spot with Mrs. Barfield. What a luxury! Perhaps the second thing most appreciated by us is the chance to use a kitchen stove for cooking. In addition to our rations, we often find potatoes (and now and then a stray chicken—Shh!) You have no idea what a chef I am turning out to be.

I have in mind a long letter concerning the actions and reactions of men in combat. This is a pity that I do not have time to go into a lengthy discussion of the subject this morning because from long practice I think better when my fingers are on a tzpewriter. (that is, when I do not have to worrz about that doggone "y".) Sufficient to say at the moment that I have been very much surprised at the way individuals have reacted. more than one case, men that I thought would possess utmost calm and poise have gone literally to pieces. Men who possessed every outward quality of leadership have proven excitable and nervous under the strain of battle conditions. Naturally enough, I was especially interested in my own reaction. As I have mentioned before, I have found a deep and satisfying calm which has been with me even under the greatest strain. It is a calm resulting from a complete abandonment to a Higher Will. Although not basically a new experience, it is one which I have found in a new way since I landed on this side. I believe that I shall not soon forget my experience.

Another result of my present mode of living as I have mentioned before has been to see into the working minds of the other individuals. The men with whom I work and fight and live are not at all the type with whom I associated at Maryville. I do not mean to put myself on another plane, but the fact is that they are different. The knowledge gained and the accompanying insight gained will not be without recompense.

My wandering thought has led a bit astray, but perhaps it is just as well. I do love to sit down and talk at random, especially when thee is no way that my loving wife can stop my chatter. In the hope that my letter will not require too many extra stamps upon arrival, I enclose a copy of the order in which I received the CI Badge. I believe that I mentioned before the fact it entitles me to an extra ten dollars per month for the rest of my Army life.

Darling, I cannot count the ways I love you. I only know that my body, mind, and soul yearns for you presence. Our future will be but the more wonderful for the separation which is so hard to bear now. May we always face life's various situations with a smile and an utter faith in
      Our love
      Bushy

April 15 (Sun.)

Just two weeks ago I wrote the above notes, and now it is Sunday again. [Art's referring to April 1st's diary entry.] Much has happened in the interim, and I hope to write concerning these past days in later notes. There is one development which has begun during this two week period. I have developed new and growing discontent with my situation. I saw combat and did not hesitate. I heard the whine of 88's and I did not shake with fear. [IN HIS EXCELLENT DESCRIPTIONS OF THE INFANTRYMAN IN COMBAT, BILL MAULDIN DESCRIBES THE 88mm AS "THE TERROR OF EVERY DOGFACE" (93)]. I found comfort and protection in a Higher Trust. As has been true throughout my life, I have felt that I was following a Divine plan, and it was not my will but God's. Suddenly within the past two weeks I have begun to feel that it is time for me to do something. I believe that if I so try that I will be able to find a position somewhat different from the one which I now occupy. True enough, the physical side of my activity is one of the things which causes this new feeling (my feet have been giving me trouble and my old sinus trouble is returning). [I HAD CONTINUED TO CARRY THE BAR, AND VIRTUALLY ALL OF OUR NIGHTS WERE SPENT IN THE OPEN IN WINTER CONDITIONS. WE NEVER PITCHED TENTS DURING COMBAT BUT WRAPPED OUR SHELTER HALF AROUND OUR SLEEPING BAG.] However, there is a mental and a spiritual depression which I cannot seem to overcome. My friend [SGT.] Soderstrom is experiencing the same feeling. [OF COURSE, NOTHING CAME OF THIS DESIRE TO GET OUT OF FRONT LINE DUTY UNTIL THE WAR ENDED].

My job at the moment is one which I detest as much as perhaps anything I have had to do in the Army. Because I can usually make myself understood in speaking with the Germans [ALTHOUGH MY TRAINING AT STANFORD HAD BEEN IN DUTCH ONLY], I am often asked to secure a house for the squad or the platoon. With all of the destruction which the Wehrmacht has spread, with all of the untold suffering caused by the fanaticism of the Nazi Party, with the experience of combat which I have had behind me, I still am unable to feel hatred for the German people. It runs counter to my entire being, and I now seriously question whether or not I am capable of hatred. Perhaps there is a lack of perspective on my part; I cannot help my innate feelings.

Entering Austria. Note the white flag which was supposed to
save a house from artillery fire.

April 16, 1945
From *Stars and Stripes*

*"Northwest of Bayreuth, the 71st Inf. Div. cut the Berlin-Munich
highway, the main escape route from the capital into the Bavarian
hills."* [AFTER THE FIGHT OUTSIDE OF BAYREUTH MY UNIT
RODE THROUGH TOWN IN TRUCKS. ONE TRUCKER HAD PLACED
A NUDE FEMALE MANNIKIN ON TOP OF HIS CAB. SOLDIERS
WHO WERE OCCUPYING THE CITY HAD FOUND A SUPPLY OF
NAZI FLAGS, AND THEY WERE TOSSING THEM ONTO TRUCKS AS
WE PASSED. IN NEED OF HANDKERCHIEFS, I TORE PART OF
ONE FLAG INTO SMALL SQUARES AND USED THEM THE REST OF
THE WAR.]

[4/18 Near Bamberg, 71st advanced two miles (#258)].
*[4/19 " ... gained eight miles due south of Bayreuth and captured
Pegnitz" (#259)].*
[4/20 " ... captured Velden and Auerbach (#160)].

168

Darling,

Another tragic death occurred today—Ernie Pyle. He is receiving almost as much publicity as Roosevelt! One commentator, in speaking of his writing and writing in general, said: "The art of writing is not so much the art of words as it is the art of feeling." I think that is true, to a large extent.

Tonight I shall go to town after work, eat supper there, and roll bandages. Ruth Lane says she will go with me to roll bandages, then come home with me to spend the night. That should be fun.

Darling, I've been trying to keep up with your activities by means of the newspapers, but I have not seen the 71st mentioned yet nor the 14th Inf., and I have scoured the papers every day. Of course, the 7th Army is almost always mentioned, but that gives me only a very general idea. Victory seems very near, and oh how I am praying for your speedy return. After all, will have a great deal to catch up on in

Our love,
Dotty

April 20

From time immemorial man has possessed fear and dread of the unknown. Much of his religion and mystic belief has been based upon this inborn instinct. Modern man has dissolved much of the mystery which surrounded the life of early man, but new causes for fear have developed. Perhaps one of the oldest and deepest causes for apprehension is that which precedes entry into battle. I can imagine the cave man wondering just what gods had been sought against him as he prepared to wage an attack upon his neighbor. Or the unanswered questions which filled the mind of the knight as he mounted his charger in preparation for the assault. What thoughts filled the minds of the men at Bunker Hill or the boys at Lookout Mt.?

Today we are again waiting to move forward into the unknown of battle. What lies ahead we do not know. Almost certainly we will encounter sniper fire. [IN THE LATTER DAYS OF THE WAR, AS WE APPROACHED VILLAGES AND SMALL TOWNS WE WOULD OFTEN SEE WHITE FLAGS FLYING FROM WINDOWS. WE SOON

LEARNED THESE DID NOT PREVENT SOME LONE SNIPER FROM SHOOTING AT US].
[4/21 "Near Neumarkt … attacked and gained seven miles" (#262)].
[4/22 " … advanced southeast and captured Amberg, Illschwang, and Rosenberg during … eleven mile gain" (#263)].
[4/23 " … cleared Schwandorf, going forward seventeen miles" (#264)].
[4/24 " … the 5th and 14th Regiment (I was in the 14th) crossed the Regen river near Regenstauf and then continued on their way to the Southeast toward the Danube River" (#266)].
[4/26 " … completed treadway bridge across Danube near Sulzbach. Advanced 5 miles beyond bridgehead (#268)].

Letters from Art to Dotty
Somewhere in Germany
4-20-45
[115-199]

My Darling,

What a grand feeling! This morning I removed my long woolens for the first time (except for washing) in long months. The days are very warm now although the nights are still cool. We are still wearing our O.D.'s so I think that I shall manage. The feeling is comparable to that of a bear when he comes out of his winter hole.

Censorship still prevents my saying very much but at least I can quote an excerpt from <u>Stars and Stripes</u> (Ap. 16th.) "…Northwest of Bayreuth the—Inf. Div. (my own) cut the Berlin Munich into the Bavarian hills." The city of Bayreuth was leveled as was no German city that I have seen. Four and five story buildings with the entire side removed. More than once I saw this when pictures on the opposite wall remained unbroken. It is as though one were looking at a giant stage already set. You know, as I wrote Dad and Mother yesterday, I cannot reconcile the present paradoxical situation. We are told that the Germans are planning to go underground and carry on their plans for world conquest. We are told that great stores of munitions and supplies are being stored to be used in guerrilla activity. Nevertheless, by failing to come to terms they are merely bringing more compete destruction to their land. We are in a town at the moment in which far more than half of the houses were burning, Roads, bridges, factories, and installations —all are being leveled. It seems to me that if the Nazi leaders are planning a return engagement they are defeating their own purpose. It seems more likely to me that Hitler and his gang know that all is lost. Germany can never hope to become a world power (or world menace) again. Since all is lost, they are fighting to the last to be certain that nothing is left.

Companies of Germans are being encounter which have been formed for only a few days. These are made up of everything from Boy Scouts to Lufftwaffe pilots. They have little effective fighting power but they do harass. Yesterday I overheard a conversation with a sixteen year old German. (He spoke very good English as many do.) When asked if he had ever been in the Army, he said no, but that if we had come a week later he would have had to don a uniform. Young boys, old men—these make up the German Army today.

April 28 Sat.

Darling,

Day before yesterday I wrote a V-Mail hoping to alleviate your fears concerning this long delay in writing. It has been the longest period of delay since I came over but I hope that you can understand. Five days ago the pupils of my eyes were dilated and they have not returned to normal. Thus I can hardly see what I write here and I have a whole pile of mail which came last night that I can hardly make out. However, reading them will be all the more pleasurable later on. On my pile of mail, I have letters from Phil, Ted P., and a wedding announcement of Dave B.'s marriage. Letters from Mother & Dad mention your long expected visit, but as yet I have received no report. I do hope that you made the trip and had a good time. I'm sure that you were able to tell the folks bits of news that they would not be able to receive otherwise.

My second package arrived last night and I appreciated it no end. The lighter is just what every G.I. is desirous of having. We were able to get extra rations last night and so I am saving the cake for a lean period. The fruit tastes wonderful. Our fruit supply is extremely limited due to extended supply lines.

Darling, when I fail to write, it doesn't mean that I am not thinking of you constantly. I can but call upon your patience and understanding to bear with me. Soon, soon I hope that I will be able to write with more regularity. My constant prayer is that God may bless
      Our love,
      Bushy

My Dearest,

This is a bad way to start off a letter to you, a cheerful letter to you, but I miss you so. You have seemed very close to me all day, and in seeming close my longing for you is all the more acute. I love you. I miss you. I hope you back soon, Darling, soon.

Enough on that note. We had a swell time yesterday with Mary Ruth's gang. There were five girls (including Mary Ruth) and five fellows. They were all nice kids, all lots of fun, and they really did! Have fun. They came over early in the afternoon and played badminton and pit before supper. We had a picnic supper in the back yard. After supper they all went skating. After I got the dishes done I went up to Flo's to spend the night—you see, all five of the girls stayed here for the night. The days went back to Maryville. Just like old times. Took me back. Wish I were, sometimes. One of the boys wanted to know if I went to Maryville and when—he just wondered whether the brand of corn was the same. Seems it is. Will it always be? That is something to think about.

Dr. Peyton preached a wonderful sermon this morning—on prayer. The text for it is a wonderful promise for this day. "If my people, which are called by my name, shall humble themselves, and pray, and seek my face, and turn from their wicked ways; then will I hear from heaven, and will forgive their sin, and will heal their land." (2 Chron: 7:14) Isn't that wonderful? If only we will turn from our wicked ways, if only we will humble ourselves, and pray, pray, PRAY. It accomplishes so much, not only in objective results but in the transformation of our hearts resulting in ourselves through the act of prayer.

Just heard on the radio—the Germans in Berlin are complaining because the Americans have not arrived to save them from the Russians!...

Good night, Darling. With all my heart I
    Love You
    Dotty.

April 24
Pirkensee (S. of Amberg c. 30 miles)

During the past two weeks I have had the experience of passing out three times. One of the these came after a long day of climbing. When we stopped for a short break, I went out completely. The second time, we had been marching at night out of Bayreuth for about four hours. While marching up a long hill, I fell on my face—flat. Tuesday we moved from Amberg by truck to Pirkensee, preparatory to moving upon Regensburg, where the 2nd Bn was attacking. We were eating our dinner around a fire when I began to feel a little weak. I sat down and almost immediately passed out. When I regained consciousness, I was breathing heavily and my heart was palpitating. Pulse ranged between 90 and 100....

[MY RECORD BREAKS OFF AT THIS POINT. DURING A HALT IN OUR ADVANCE, I SUDDENLY FELL TO THE GROUND. I HAD A BRIEF OUT-OF-BODY EXPERIENCE WHEN I HEARD CONVERSATION AND SEEMED TO BE LOOKING DOWN ON MY PRONE BODY. I WAS TAKEN BACK TO A HOSPITAL UNIT WHERE I REMAINED FOR THREE OR FOUR DAYS. I WAS EXAMINED, GIVEN TIME TO REST, AND LEFT MUCH TO MYSELF. I HAD AN OVERWHELMING FEELING OF GUILT THAT I WAS NOT WITH MY SQUAD. SHORTLY THEREAFTER I WAS RETURNED TO MY UNIT TO FIND THAT OUR COMPANY HAD BEEN ENGAGED IN THE LONGEST AND MOST INTENSE FIRE FIGHT OF OUR COMBAT EXPERIENCE IN THE CAPTURE OF REGENSBURG, A MAJOR CITY ON THE DANUBE. LATER, REFLECTING ON WHAT HAPPENED, I ATTRIBUTED IT TO PHYSICAL EXHAUSTION, INSUFFICIENT NOURISHMENT, AND PSYCHOLOGICAL REACTION TO THE JOB I WAS EXPECTED TO DO. NEITHER THEN NOR AT ANY OTHER TIME DID I HAVE AN OVER-WHELMING SENSE OF FEAR. DURING THE REGENSBURG ENGAGEMENT, TONY, A SQUAD MEMBER, HAD HIS HELMET OPENED UP AS THOUGH A CAN OPENER HAD BEEN USED. ALTHOUGH HE WAS NOT WOUNDED, THE TRAUMA WAS SUCH THAT HE WAS NO LONGER FIT FOR THE FRONT LINES AND WAS SOON SENT BACK TO A HOSPITAL. WE NEVER SAW HIM AGAIN. ONCE MORE I HAD A STRONG SENSE OF GUILT THAT I HAD NOT BEEN WITH MY BUDDIES. "BONDING," OR "ESPRIT-DE-CORPS" ARE TERMS USED TO DESCRIBE WHAT I LEARNED WAS A COMMON EXPERIENCE.

"THE GREAT COMBAT HISTORIAN OF WORLD WAR II, S. L. A. MARSHALL, WROTE THAT FEAR AFFECTS <u>ALL</u> [sic] MEN, EVEN THOSE IN THE MOST HIGHLY MOTIVATED UNITS. MARSHALL FOUND THAT NO MORE THAN A QUARTER OF THE MEN ACTUALLY FIRED THEIR WEAPONS ON THE BATTLE-FIELD.

RELIGIOUS SCRUPLE AGAINST KILLING WAS ONE REASON. A BIGGER FACTOR WAS SHOCK. IN ONE STUDY OF A DIVISION THAT SAW HEAVY FIGHTING IN WORLD WAR II, A QUARTER OF THE SOLDIERS ADMITTED THEY HAD BEEN SO SCARED THAT THEY VOMITED. ALMOST A QUARTER LOST CONTROL OF THEIR BOWELS. TEN PERCENT URINATED IN THEIR PANTS.... ARMY PSYCHIATRISTS IN WORLD WAR II FOUND THAT <u>EVERY</u> [sic] MAN HAD AN ABSOLUTE LIMIT OF PSYCHIC ENDURANCE, AT MOST ABOUT 60 DAYS OF CONTINUOUS COMBAT OR AGGREGATE OF 200 TO 240 DAYS."
(Evan Thomas. "At the Front." <u>Newsweek</u> (Feb, 3, 2003), 37.)
I was in a combat area for approximately four months, front line duty for about sixty days. I was not aware of any one vomiting, urinating, or failing to fire weapons. The BAR, which I carried, was considered a reserve weapon, and during several engagements I was ordered not to fire.

[ALTHOUGH WE HAD OTHER SKIRMISHES, THE REGENSBURG BATTLE WAS THE LAST MAJOR ENGAGEMENT FOR OUR UNIT. AS WE CONTINUED TO MOP UP, WE RECEIVED LARGE GROUPS OF GERMANS WHO STREAMED WEST TO AVOID BEING TAKEN PRISONER BY THE RUSSIANS. WHEN THE WAR ENDED, WE WERE NEAR LINZ, AUSTRIA. SOLDIERS OF THE 71ST DIVISION MET THE RUSSIANS IN VIENNA AND WERE CREDITED WITH REACHING A POINT FARTHER EAST THAN ANY OTHER AMERICAN UNIT.

[MY SQUAD WAS ASSIGNED THE JOB OF GUARDING A BRIDGE ACROSS THE KREMS RIVER NEAR NEUHOFEN, WHERE WE STAYED FOR SIX WEEKS. HERE WE PITCHED OUR TENTS, SERVED GUARD DUTY 24 HOURS A DAY, AND HAD OUR FOOD BROUGHT TO US FROM THE UNIT KITCHEN (WHICH I NEVER SAW).

[IN ADDITION TO THE WELCOME LEISURE, TWO LUXURIES CAME WITH THIS ASSIGNMENT. FOR ONE THING, WE WERE ABLE TO PITCH OUR PUP TENTS FOR THE FIRST TIME SINCE WE CAME TO THE ETO. SECOND, IN AN ABANDONED VEHICLE I FOUND A PADDED SEAT THAT BARELY FIT INTO MY SIDE OF THE TWO-MAN TENT. ALTHOUGH MAKING THE SPACE A KIND OF SPLIT LIVEL, IT PROVIDED AN ALMOST-FORGOTTEN COMFORT.

[WE HAD NO DIFFICULTIES; LOCAL FARMERS CROSSED THE BRIDGE REGULARLY, AND WE PRETENDED TO READ THEIR

Art alone on his boat ride in Gemunden.
[Referred to in diary entry April 24, 1945]

*IDENTIFICATION PAPERS CAREFULLY. THOSE COULD HAVE
BEEN IDs FOR SS MEMBERSHIP AS FAR AS WE WERE
CONCERNED, BUT WE ACTED AS THOUGH WE KNEW WHAT WE
WERE DOING. THE WOMEN CAME OUT SHORTLY AFTER
DAYLIGHT TO WORK IN THE FIELDS. LATER IN THE MORNING,
A MALE OWNER OR SUPERVISOR APPEARED IN HIS LEATHER
SHORT PANTS, FEATHERED HAT, AND PIPE ON HIS WAY TO
CHECK ON THE WORKERS.*

*[DURING THE SIX WEEKS IN AUSTRIA, I WAS GIVEN ONE
WEEKEND PASS TO VISIT THE RESORT TOWN OF GEMUNDEN,
AN ARTIST COLONY ON A BEAUTIFUL LAKE, ALL I REMEMBER
FROM THE WEEKEND WAS A BOAT RIDE. THAT WAS MY FIRST
OPPORTUNITY FOR REST AND RELAXATION SINCE THE
CHRISTMAS PASS I HAD IN THE STATES.*

[AFTER OUR SIX-WEEKS STAY IN AUSTRIA, THE 71ST MOVED BACK TO GERMANY, AND FOR A SHORT TIME MY COMPANY WAS STATIONED IN GUNZBURG, NEAR ULM, ON THE DANUBE. OUR DIVISION HEADQUARTERS THEN MOVED TO AUGSBURG WITH MY COMPANY LOCATED IN ITS PERMANENT OCCUPATION IN MEMMINGEN TO THE SOUTH. BEFORE VJ (VICTORY IN JAPAN) DAY WE EXPECTED TO BE SHIPPED TO THE PACIFIC TO TAKE PART IN THE ANTICIPATED INVASION OF JAPAN.]

[5/6 Consolidated position along the Enns River, south of Steyr (#282-83).
5/7-8 Processed large numbers of German troops (#286).]

Letter excerpt from Art to Dotty
Germany, April 27 [1945]
Sunday [120-125]

...There was something that I wished to write about more than a week ago, but I had no opportunity. It concerned an incident which occurred in the large city of A_____. We entered one night while there were still German soldiers roaming the street, but luckily we encountered little resistance. The following morning I had occasion to walk past a business section where a window had been broken. The shop was one selling cameras and photo supplies and it had been looted thoroughly. Even as I passed, GI's were coming out with film. My blood raced and I became as angry as I usually manage to get. This is a side of the story which is seldom told, but one that is sadly true. The Am. G.I., when given a chance, will loot and raid like a barn thief. Actually the incident above is extreme. It is the only case that I have known where a window had been deliberately broken and a business establishment entered. But the G.I. does loot, does raid, and does act at times in a way which appears more like the action of a Nazi trained fanatic than an Am. soldier . Only tyranny claims that "to the victor belongs the spoils." I know. How well I know. When a G.I. fights, stares death in the face, sees friends die, he seeks to take some revenge some where. Naturally enough he deserves some small pleasure if it is nothing more than a jar of jam or fruit, a few potatoes, a chicken, or a warm blanket. I think that to take something useful, something needed (perhaps a pair of socks, or a towel) is justified. But it is never right from a moral or ethical standpoint to destroy property needlessly or to take valuables merely because one can. You know, it has often been said that the difference between a fearless man and a forceful man is a gun. When one has a gun in his hand and the Allied forces behind him, he need have little fear of poor helpless civilians. I know one instance in which a soldier took a large radio from a house—a radio totally impractical to carry, especially by an infantryman. Another fellow helped himself to a silverware set and I have seen innumerable clocks & watches taken. How I hate and despise the low level to which human standards sink when forced with the crisis of war. I cannot but fear that we are weaving strains of discord into the patterns of peace for which we fight. But enough of that.

I stopped long enough to glance at a list of "must" letters. Only eleven in addition to another to my dear wife and one to Mother & Dad. Probably, if I do have time for more writing today, I shall spend it in catching up on a bit of sleep. What an endless circle in which I move! This circle will be broken but the one which is endless & eternal is the one in which our Love moves as it ascends upward toward the heights of God's Divine Oneness. I can but say,

I love you.

Bushy

Letter excerpt from Dotty to Art
Sabbath
April 29, 1945

My Darling,

At last (11:00pm) I have a few minutes in this day when I can talk to you, my love. 'Tis rather a busy Sabbath I have had. There was a short space between the time when I finished the dinner dishes and time to go to a meeting, but I used it for reading the paper. But more about today's schedule later.

It was yesterday that was really exciting. The day looked rather inauspicious—dark, gloomy, and rainy all day long. I did my usual Saturday work and cleaning. Then started in cleaning the wallpaper in my room. About 5:30 I was just finishing this task, and I had promised Phyllis I would go to the show with her at 6:00, so I did some tall scurrying to bathe and dress and eat in just a half hour! Just barely made it. All day long the radio had been buzzing with the news that Himmler had made an offer of unconditional surrender to Britain and America, but that it had been refused because Russia had not been included. The show was a very light comedy with a mediocre plot, but I enjoyed it after working hard all day. We got in in the middle of the picture, and had seen part of it plus the newsreels & shorts when suddenly the film stopped and the lights came on and some men came and on the stage and picked up a mike and started to make an announcement, but didn't get very far. He had no sooner said "Germany—," when the whole theater was in an uproar, and the rest of what he said was drowned completely out. But we knew that he had said "Germany Surrendered!" After the dramatic announcement a blue and red combination of lights was flashed on the screen while the "Star Spangled Banner" was played several times. Then came a selection showed on the screen about how war was not over merely because victory had been declared, that Japan was yet to be overcome, and that one must not quit our jobs, blah, blah, blah. Finally we settled calmly (?) down in our seats to see the rest of the picture. The show must go on! As one emerged from the show shouts of extra were heard, and Phyllis and I both managed to grab one from an old lady selling them right & left in front of the Tennessee Theater. During all this time the impulses to pray and shout and laugh and cry were seething in mixed confusion with men.

But alas, even before we reached home we discovered that there was no reality to the glad news, that it had sprung from an unconfirmed rumor. Owattale—tdown! If I were Jean Kaelber I would now make an extremely comical gesture, give a couple of snorts, and say "Can't those news guys find anything better to do than to get one all flustguberated like this?", beating my head against the wall betimes. The papers today were full of the furor caused all over the nation by the release of the startling (but false) news. It took the voice of the president himself denying the validity of the news to calm the nation and set it back to normal. Only I don't think we are back to normal yet —we are still on the edges of our seats waiting for the real news to come through just any minute. All I got to say is—they better make it good next time!...

There isn't nearly enough room in which to speak of
      Our Love
      Dotty
Tis Eternal. [arrow drawn here to "Our Love"]

Jamestown, Tenn.

My dear precious son: Friday, April 27, 1945
It was good to get your V-mail letter this A.M., together with a nice long letter
from Dorothy. We are watching developments over on your side with anxious interest,
praying that the end in sight may not be delayed much longer. Cannot repeat too
often,our longing to see you return safe and undiscouraged and in good health so
that after the needed rest and refreshing you will need,can be spent with us.
We will do everything we can to make you and Dorothy happy and comfortable. We
enjoyed her visit very very much - which was all too short. She was looking well
though a bit tired. I am so disappointed that I have not been able to get over
to Knoxville. I am awfully anxious to make the acquaintance of Mother and Mr.
Barber. I know I am going to like them,and when we get a new car I picture us
making many trips over to Knoxville to visit them every so often,and then have
them come over here. I am enjoying many hours reading evenings,and it is then
that I think of you longing that you could share in the comforts of home with
all of the implications of this long and terrible war)as in the past and re-
sumption of normal life for us all; but especially that yourinterrupted and
what might have been so happily possible for you in beginning your life of useful
service and happiness with Dotty. We hope, we pray,that in God's good providence
these things may yet work out in a better and peaceful world.

I continue to improve in health. There are times when I feel rather done in and
I am restive at these times at not being able to do more about the place when
mother finds so much about the place that needs to be done. I help some of
course, and as I feel stronger I shall render a more telling service. My kidneys
are pretty much normal as I can judge. I certainly am not bothered enough to
even suspect that might be what makes physical effort such a bother. It is
enough to say that I am being very careful in my diet and exercising such precaution that a breakdown is unthinkable-as long as I consciously am taking care
of myself.

As to mother: she has never felt or looked better. She seems very happy and
as always,interested in those household activities as her flowers, the garden,
and the culinary art as only a mother can be perfect in. Such cakes and pies
How we think and long for you Sundays when we sit down to dinner and so sorely
miss you. Dear boy, what a day that will be when you come home: our looks
will portray the stirrings in our hearts,in some degree, of what we feel just
to look at you,in thanks to almighty God for this wonderful reunion - after
such interminable separation. God grant that you be not denied - that we be
not denied, realization of what Home may mean to you and to us, so desolate without you.

So glad to hear that Encore is beginning to reach you. I shall have all the copies
If any should miss reaching you. The Saturday Review of Literature is very fine.
I just received z copy of "American Chronicle", The Authbiography of Ray Standard
Baker (pen name David Grayson) He wrote, as you may remember, Woodrow Wilson,
Life and Letters. He wrote in Woodrow Wilson's time many magazine articles
in McClure's Magazine; an able writer and fine character, having made a fine
contribution to American life in fine reporting. He is in the sunset of his life,
and this recalling of the past lends itself to many hours of enjoyable reading.
I said above that I had justreceived the book but as a matter of fact I have
received it some ten days ago as a book dividend from the Literary Guild. This
was a surprise gift to termination of my four book subscription - my agreement
to take at least four books this year.

The mail is about to leave and mother wants her letter to get off in this mail.
So good-bye and God be with you, dear precious son. I long to come over and
see you,and if you are to serve in Europe for any long period after the war,
I shall long if it were deemed impossible, that I might make the trip or send
Mother and Dorothy over to see you. A heart full of love, dear boy.
                                                              DAD

Letter from Art's dad to Art, dated April 27, 1945

Letter excerpts from Dotty to Art
Wednesday
May 2, 1945

"The day is cold and damp and rainy outside, but inside I am always warmed by thoughts of you. Oh. Too mushy. I should say Hi, Butch. What have you done with Hitler? But if I did, then you might never know how much I was loving you and thinking of you. Take your pick.

"The news continues to be exciting most of the time, now. Yesterday Hitler was "proclaimed" dead and radio Tokoyo says we have landed on Borneo! Today at noon we heard that all German armies in Italy had surrendered unconditionally to the Allies. That should take a load off your mind. Who knows what tomorrow will bring? If you know what I mean and I don't see how you could help but. Thought you would be particularly interested in Borneo, but by the time this reaches you you will probably have read all about it in the Times. I am jealous—I think Time gets to you much sooner than my letters do. Poutpoutpout. Only please don't take the above sentence too literally, please."

Letters from Art to Dotty
Somewhere in Germany
May 3, 1945 [26-31]

Darling,

Again delays mark my letter writing. The wonderful news concerning the war is music to my ears but it seems to effect our activity but little. The last few days have been long and rather difficult. I recall that many weeks ago I wrote concerning the coming of Spring. Beginning on May 1st and for every day thereafter we have had snow and very cold rain. This I think has tended to damper the full impact of the full break that has finally come. I can never put over in words the way in which one's spirit and feelings can be numbed and deadened by long hours of walking up and down hills of hours on guard from a damp fox hole.

5-4-1945 [typed]

Dearest,

After a good night's sleep, hot food, and the warmth of a warm sun which we have not seen for several days, I have a much better outlook on life than I had last night when I began this letter. I have missed writing for so long that I hardlz know where to begin to catch up. Again we are lukz enough to be under a roof and a verz nice one at that.

Perhaps I can explain a little of the reason for my attitude last night when I mention a little of our activity in recent dazs. On Wednesdaz we covered between twentz-five and thirty miles afoot up hill and down dale.

Austria, May 6th Sun.

This letter has been most difficult to even get started. I do hope that I will be able to finally finish it today. I have just returned from Church Services, my first since Easter Sunday five weeks ago. It was wonderful to sing and worship in group service again.

I sit in the kitchen of an Austrian peasant family; a date over the ancient stove reveals that the walls were erected in 1869. The people hardly seem to know what is going on as we eat, sleep, clean our weapons and carry on our routine. Some one asked this morning if we were German troops. These people know little of war, of chaos, and world confusion. (I hope I have time at the end of the letter to give a rough drawing showing the fort-like-plan of the house and barns.) [posted at end] In the distance I can see the snow capped foothills of the famed Bavarian Alps. and I am reminded of the Rockies. How little I knew that I would learn of the war's and near the Bavarian Alps in the home of Austrian peasants.

The news is not confirmed but it is reported that all hostilities have ceased. Yesterday we heard that it was all over except in our sector. If I had been writing regularly, I would hesitate to write today even though the occasion is a momentous one. Again I feel depressed and my outlook seems very dark—hardly a mood in which to write my dear wife. Nevertheless I shall write and hope tomorrow I shall see the silver lining not apparent today. When we heard yesterday that all was over, I felt more like crying than rejoicing. I was tired and cold and wet. The past few days have been trying from a physical standpoint. But more than the physical numbness was the feeling of depression caused by the happenings of recent days. The war over, I felt as though we had lost everything for which we fought.

In our sector prisoners have been walking in for several days. Yesterday was a climax and the number must have run into the hundreds. Naturally, the possibilities for looting were excellent. Wrist watches and pocket watches were taken by the dozens. Many pistols and field glasses were found. Today comes the order that there will be no more looting but it had become a phobia with some of the men. Not satisfied with one or two watches, some of the fellows would take every one that they found. There was actually unhappy feelings caused by

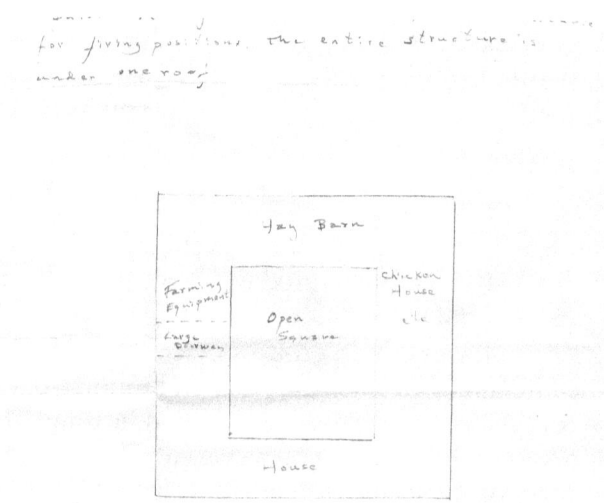

Fort-like-plan of the house and barns, May 6, 1945

men competing with each other other for worthless items. Hatreds, prejudices, unmannerly, unsoldierly conduct—everything black seemed to pile up before my eyes and how could I be glad. Of course, I realize now even as I knew then that my depression resulted from a loss of perspective. I was to blame for my failure to rejoice at the news. However, there was no help for it.

Censorship will be more lax now and of course everything will be more pleasant. (Today we had our fist chow served by our kitchen in more than five weeks.) In succeeding letters, I hope to go back to my first landing in France and recount our activities in some detail. I shall wait for a bit more time to go into detail, but I shall mention a few towns which perhaps you have noticed in the paper. While still in Germany, we passed through Bayreuth shortly after it was taken. My company was one of the first to enter Ambery and the city of Regensburg surrendered to our Regimental Commander along with a reported eighty thousand troups. As I say, I shall go into a bit more detail in later letters.

We have a great of mail which perhaps will catch up with us now and when we finally settle down a bit it should be rather regular. There is so much that should be more regular now!

Along with millions of other G.I.'s, my thoughts now turn to the end of the war in the Pacific. Will we be sent? Will we remain in Europe or AO (Army of Occupation)? Will we be in civilian clothes a year from now? I suppose that from now on the time will pass far more slowly than formerly because before we were too busy to think of these things. But, Darling, never in the long days and weeks of combat was I too busy to think and plan and dream of our future. What a glorious day when we shall be together again to go ahead to make our dreams become reality.

Meanwhile we can but continue to work and pray for that day. I find with each passing day a new strength from the depth of our abiding Love.

I love you,
Bushy

Letters from Dotty to Art
Saturday
May 5, 1945

My Darling,

Well—it seems that it is all over in Germany but the shouting, and your dear 3rd Army is the only one still fighting. It would happen that way. However, you haven't been there nearly so long as some of the others, so perhaps it is only fair. My mind is full of questions as to what is to happen to you all when it really is over and

Oh Darling—a special news flash just came over the radio from Paris—all the German Armies in Southern Germany have surrendered!!!!!! Thank God—your fighting days are over—for a while at least! There is so much I want to say, so many prayers of thanks to raise, but I must hurry to get this in the mail by the time the postman gets here.

I am mailing your third box to you today. It contains mostly food, some candles and stationery, and some literature. I hope you get it, Darling, and all the other four boxes on their way to you.

Last night I went to dancing class, then "T" and Lois Ann & I ate in town, then came out to the High School to join Dad, Uncle West & Flo to hear the Knoxville Male Chorus concert. It was good to hear male voices! But you know—twas a funny thing—they were either too young or too old! I stopped off at Ruth Lane's and spent the night with her— she was alone in the apartment.

Mary is leaving shortly for school to take post-grad work in dietetics, so we are giving her a surprise "going away" party tonight.

Got to go—I love you—God has been answering my prayers—he has been taking care of you—I'm more than glad the fighting is over— above all—

I love you, Dotty

The Sabbath
May 6, 1945

Dearest,

I hope you won't mind if I think about you all the time. You are almost never out of my conscious thoughts, and always in my subconscious mind there is an awareness of youness. That awareness frequently takes the form of anticipation of delicious things, things in the future, our future. As I say—I hope you don't mind.

Today's paper, besides answering that victory in Germany was very near, carried an article on the Army's plan for reduction of forces and transfer of forces from East to West. The chances don't seem to good for your being discharged, but they seem excellent for your coming thru the States and getting a thirty-day furlough en route! Yes, really! I know it is months too early to make any plans, but I like to think about how we would spend it if we did have that heavenly month together, such as two weeks in Jamestown, one in Knoxville, and one at the cabin all by our lonesomes. Well, I can dream can't I?

If you are still part of the 3rd Army, I suppose you are still fighting. Wish I knew. Patience. Patience is a virtue, Dotty.

May 7, 1945
VICTORY!!

Darling—!

This has been rather an exciting day, to put it mildly. Before I had finished my breakfast they began interrupting programs on the radio to bring us the unofficial news that German had surrendered completely. I found it difficult to tear myself away from the radio to go to work at 9:00, but go I did, and could only wonder about the events that were taking place. Home for lunch I learned that the news was so, but that Truman and the other big 3 had not proclaimed it so formally. I learned that New York and London were jubilant in an audible fashion, but here the news was very quietly received. I learned that Truman's official VE Day proclamation would probably come tomorrow so that it may be simultaneous with the proclamation in England, Russia, and the other European countries. The general reaction everywhere seems to be one of quiet joy sobered by the thought of the terrible sacrifice that has been paid and the terrific job that lies ahead.

As for myself, my feelings go too deep for words. All I can do is call God's name and your name, look at you both mutely, and pray that you will know what is in my heart. How can I write my thanksgiving that you are safe, that God has answered my prayers, that Europe's peoples can look for a period of freedom from combat, tyranny, and oppression? How can I tell you of my deep, deep joy that you can lay down your rifle and head (slowly but surely) for home, perhaps to remain, perhaps only to stop for a while? How?

Tonight we went to Maryville for Florence's joint recital with Frances (Harris) Grosch. They hath performed splendidly. Flo wore a corsage of pink roses which I made from those on our arbor. Mary Ruth was one of the ushers, sweet gal. She says Hi. Saw Dr. Hunter & Mrs., and enjoyed a chat with them. Dr. Hunter says he told you wrong about the title of the poem containing "'Tis colder now." It is "An Epistle to the Buried in the Earth," rather than a Poem. Dr Dr. Hr.

Flo looked happier than I've seen her for ages. It has been nearly four weeks since she has had a letter from Carl, so that has been keeping her spirits down. I hope he is [letter ends]

Letter from Art to Dotty

32 V-Mail
dated May 6th

Austria
May 7, 1945, Mon.
[33-37]

My Darling,

Yesterday I managed to write two letters to my most adorable wife. Wish I could do as much every day. The news is confirmed that the war is over and we rejoice. It seems so hard to realize the full import of the news. I was thinking the other day how much has happened in our lives since this gigantic struggle began. It was Sept. 2nd, 1939, when Germany invaded Poland. I believe that Maryville opened four days later, on the 6th. I was still a country kid, away from home for the first time. Knowing little and caring little for international affairs. How few of us realized our lives were to be changed by current events. Well, I spent four years at college where I gained the beginnings of an education. I pass through the transition stage from boyhood to manhood, and, my Lovely One, I met you. We smiled, we held hands, we kissed, we joined our lives in holy union. There was the Army, of course. There still is! Two years, a soldier. Or has it been two years a civilian in G.I. clothing? Not until I joined the 71st did I experience the full impact of contact with the Army, the old Army, the "line" out fit. I once thought that I had done a good job of adjusting to my surroundings, but I was wrong. I do think that I did a terrific job of fooling myself. I hate this life—all of it! I have gained in understanding but lost respect for many of my fellowmen. I have found new sources of strength, new companionship in solitude, walking and talking with a Higher One. If I had not been able to share my thoughts and feelings with "Sod", Fred Price, and Beul, I hardly know what would have happened during the past three months. Now that the war is over, at least in this theatre, we can look forward to the next phase—the end of the Pacific war, and then———! The finally [final] phase will be the transition into clothing which is not G.I.

Pardon this stream of thought writing, but I am in one of those moods this morning. The company barber just arrived—a pleasant little Italian boy who cut hair for many years in Pittsburgh. There will be our first cuts since Easter.

You know, I was seriously tempted last night. In fact I virtually gave way for I intended to taste champagne. In all of my life I have never tasted wine, whiskey, beer, rum, gin or any of the other strong drinks. Many times, particularly over here, I have been the only one in the crowd who did not take a drink, but I have always stood firm. The temptation of last night was not a sudden fancy, but a conclusion arrived at after much deliberation. I can't find where Paul says it, but somewhere he states that it is not that which entereth the body which defileth the man but that which cometh out. In the 14th Ch of Romans the subject is dealt with again and I can find no teaching which forbids the tasting of wine.

Lapse of 15 min.

I do not believe in drinking but I am led to believe that from the ethical and moral viewpoint it is not wrong to drink a glass of wine or other light drink. Thus I planned to taste Champagne in celebration of victory. As it so happened, by the time I started to get a cup, everything was empty. During the lapse of 15 minutes, my opportunity came. Beul and I gingerly poured a small amount of champagne in a cup. We sipped. I am told that the quality is poor and I am convinced. The taste seems similar to cider slightly sour. I was so disgusted with the sip that I had that I think I shall not soon again try, but the issue is no longer a moral or ethical one.

Perhaps, Darling, my thinking is perverse. Perhaps I have fallen into an ethical fallacy due to a constant poll from the less ethical influences around me. Please give me your very frank opinion. Understand, I have by no means become a drunkard or a drinker overnight. I have nearly reached the point where I do not consider it wrong for me to taste a light drink. Read Rom: 14 and anything else you happen to have at hand. Tell me what you think.

Many of the fellows are sending packages this morning—all sorts of odd trinkets and useless items. Somehow I have little desire to send such junk home. Some of the men have three and four watches, two or three pistols, field glasses, cameras, etc. etc. Beul gave me a pair of field glasses and Price gave me a pistol. Some one else gave me a pocket watch. That makes up my loot. I do hope to be able to find something nice for you but I shall wait until I do find something nice.

It is almost time for another hot chow. We had hotcakes this morning) I hope to write a few more letters this afternoon and perhaps another to you, My Love. Gee, it feels good to be able to sit down and talk with out rush. Why don't I do this more often! I will!

Ever thine,
Bushy

P.S. Another $10 on the way.

I enclose more souvenir money from Germany

1 mark 50 mark
10 "   100 "
20 "

Letters from Dotty to Art
Tuesday, May 8,1945
V-E Day

Darling,

This is the day of victory, official now because Truman and Churchill have proclaimed it so. I got up early so as to be sure of hearing Truman's broadcast at 8:00. Oops. Out of ink. [Dotty changes to write in pencil.] This will do just about as well. As I was saying—I got up to hear the broadcast and got my head stick in the radio and couldn't get it out till noon. Had to eat then, and go to work. There wasn't much to do, and I was too exciting (what am I saying—) too excited anyway. Mostly I prepared the decorations for tonight's meeting.

Tonight was an appropriate time for devotions, anyway. The meeting referred to was a circle (ladies') meeting—my very first. For the devotions we sang "O God, Our Help, in Ages Past", then I read portions of the 1st, 2nd, & 3rd chapters of Ephesians, Weymouth Translations, followed by a period of silent prayer. I had called for sentence prayers but nobody voiced any, so I finally had to close it with one of my own. Capt. Marker, Chaplain at Alcoa, made a lengthy but interesting speech about his work. He served as a missionary in Iran for 14 years, and asked to be sent there for duty, but no soap. You know the

Army, alas too well when it comes to placing a guy where he is fitted to go! I asked Capt. M. if he by any chance knew the Fishers while in Iran, and what do you think? He worked in the same school with them! Small world, ain't it? And that is how I spent VE Day—listening to the radio, working, going to Circle Meeting, and offering up endless prayers for you, for me, and for all people everywhere. Not very exciting, huh?

Wednesday
May 9

Dearest,

No letter today. Nor' yesterday, nor any day for a week and a half. This makes the second long period with no mail. Now that the fighting has stopped and there is no longer any news of your activity in the paper, it seems twice as hard to go without mail. But I should kick— Florence finally got a letter yesterday—her first from Carl in almost a month! However, it was written on the 23rd of April, so I suppose all the letters in between must have been held up or lost. His letter was very interesting (yes, we pass some letters around), and talk of his being taken prisoner by the Germans, held for a day, then liberated by Americans. I have been wondering if you were O.K, Darling. For [letter ends]

Letter from Art to Dotty
Austria
May 7, 1945 [40-43]
V-E Day

My Darling,

The hour is late and I should be in bed but I feel like talking a bit more before I sleep. The official news came this afternoon that the Armistice became effective at 2:35 P.M. today. We continue to rejoice as we relax and rest. Tonight I celebrated by sharing my last piece of that wonderful fruit cake with Beul and Sod. Beul said that he would remember you in his will, and also mentioned that if he had met you first he probably would have beaten me to the draw (or rather the altar.) I felt properly complimented. Both boys appreciated the cake very much as did your husband. He always appreciates good food. Another bit of celebration was to have a long talk with Sod tonight such as I often had with John, Dick, Bob, and many others at Maryville. It was indeed refreshing.

The past two months have been almost like a spiritual desert in certain respects. I have had little chance for reading or for discussing religious points as I was so accustomed to doing. However, as I have said before, I most certainly reached a new depth of faith and abiding comfort from a new closeness to God. I do hope that in the days ahead I will be able to read my Bible with greater regularity, will be able to attend services regularly and talk with others of like mind. Christianity (or rather Christian Living) cannot be a static thing. It must move onward or it disappears.

I had intended to discuss the reasons why I oppose compulsory military training but I need more time for that. I shall mention a couple of things I need while they are in my mind. I began a letter to the Glathers today only to realize that the address was uncertain in my memory and I had only a hazy idea as to the initials. Please send both. I would also like to have an address book with all the addresses what you think I would want. Mine was lost in some distant corner of Germany. All of which reminds me that I should make a request now and then for food so that you can continue to send those wonderful boxes. Please send another box when it is convenient to do so. I have received to thus far.

It is with acute longing that I miss the readings, the meditations, prayers and discussions which we enjoyed so often together. How wonderful it will be when we can enjoy those things again together. I think too of the happy times we shall have training the little ones as they grow up. My friends show pictures of their children and I turned bright green with envy. Patients, Bushing! Those things will come. Meanwhile I constantly think and pray for
Our Love,
Bushy
P.S. Thought you might like the enclosed souvenirs.

Letter from Art to Dotty

VICTORY IN EUROPE DAY [VE-DAY], MAY 8TH 1945
Austria, May 8, '45 [44-51]
Darling,
A lilting Scotch ballad I hear on the radio. One boy plays with a broken guitar string across the table from me and others wander in and out. We are sitting in a small bar room in a small town or rather village in Austria. At least we do not have a manure pile in the front door. I have a new appreciation of the so-called squalor of S.E. Europe after seeing some of the conditions under which these people live. As we

found in Germany, the barn and home are almost always under one roof. Usually only a wall separates the one from the other. In the plan where we first heard the news of peace, stagnant water and manure was piled outside the door. It must be terrible in the heat of summer weather. At least in this new place we have much cleaner conditions than those before. This bar room in which I sit is very clean and the walls are finished in natural wood. On high shelves are rows of old dishes adding an ornamental touch and a deer's antlers adorn a post of honor over the door. Outside the sun is sinking in beautiful spring fashion. What a relief it is to look at an area of woods, a stone wall, or a fox hole and know that one need have no fear of a German uniform appearing with a "burp" gun.

By the way, I have never described the German "burp" gun, have I? The name is well chosen for when it is fired there is a but a blur of sound. It is an automatic weapon something like our machine gun. However, it fires between 1200 and 1400 rounds per minute. We heard them first while still down on the Rhine and the first reaction was the lasting one—a cold chill down the spine.

Well, I had intended to discuss last night my views on compulsory military training. To begin with, I'm "agin' it". For a very long time I accepted it as a foregone conclusion, giving the subject little thought. Then I read of the discussions and debates at Maryville I began to think seriously concerning the issue. With celebrating G.I.'s on one hand and a blasting radio on the other. I may have difficulty organizing my discussion, but here goes.

From all that I can find out, the purpose of the purported program is to provide a corps of well trained men as a reserve to be used in case of aggression. The training would be for the physical training and the military lore. These are the only two values that I can see from it. Now, as far as the second is concerned, I discount any lasting value from this. After having gone through twenty-four weeks of basic training and then after having gone through combat I consider the former time almost wasted. We spent hours in close order drill, arm and hand signals, sighting and aiming of weapons—untold hours of blood, sweat, and perhaps even a few tears. Useless—utterly! We were told that those things are for purposes of discipline, but I also disagree with that. Very little discipline that assists in combat did I gain from all of those things which were drilled into me so many times. Thus would I discount any real and lasting values from the military point of view. Further, training received in the post war period would be outdated and forgotten by the time their services would be needed. If anything, this world struggle

Gi's enjoy the luxury of a bath in an Austrian Stream May '45

has shown that military tactics change even before the eyes. What use
is there of training now for a war ten, twenty years from now—one
which may never come? The men now trained would never see combat.
Now, regarding the physical training. That I admit is a strong point for
argument. However, I believe that there is a better plan which could be
substituted. I would propose a nation wide physical training intended
to embrace every able bodied male. This could be put on through the
medium of the high schools, colleges, Y.MEA's etc. The cost would be
one-fifth to one-fourth of that of compulsory training and would effect
far more. The spirit of co-operation, the team work, the opportunity for
developing leadership—all of these things would be developed far more
through sports such as football, basketball, soccer, etc. than through
the squad problems which the Army could conceive.

May 10th

The primary difficulty as I see it in this plan would be to include
everyone. However, it appears that this problem could be solved with a
little study. In the schools and colleges the program of physical
education could easily fit in as it did at Maryville. With a bit of
Hollywood build up and the proper push behind it, I believe that the

191

entire nation could be brought into the swing of the thing. Thus those otherwise unaffected by compulsory military training would be helped including the female populace.

Be in no hurry to answer, but let me know what you think of them scattered ideas. Perhaps Dr. Peyton has formed some opinions along those lines.

Our latest move has been into the field again. We are now lined up on dress parade fashion in pup tents. For the nonce the weather is delightful. I have my finders crossed.

Our news is scattered but I have a feeling of optimism creeping slowly over me in regard to the return to the States for the stranded "G.I's." Will say more of that later. I am told that the city of Linz is the most beautiful in all of Europe. I do wish that I could see it, but no opportunity as yet.

May 8

I can't finish the rest of the discussion on military training but I do want to take time to describe the scene around me. We have just captured a Volkatrum trooper with a truck. Three cases of drinks were found therein and the boys are preparing to celebrate the end of the war—only 37 minutes from now. Hot jazz is playing and now & then we can here [hear] the noise of rejoicing tells us that the World is happier tonight.

10th again.

Last night came your letter of the 22nd—the first I have received in almost ten days. Should be a pile somewhere. Will send this along and try to begin another letter tonight. I too miss you acutely, my Dear. I long for you more each passing day and yet I know that our future will be the sweeter for our separation. God will surely bless us in
Our Love,
Bushy
P.S. Please send package when convenient.
Just recd letters 2 ct (2), 30th, Daddy letter and the big package from home—Joy!!!!!!

My Darling,

Today has seemed more like the Sabbath than any Sunday I have spent for a long time. I arose at the leisurely hour of 7 o'clock for a breakfast of eggs and cereal. Our single duty of the day was to police up the paper around our tents. I washed and shaved with honest to goodness hot water and cleaned up my tent (sweeping and dusting where necessary). After this I read a bit and then to Church Service where I heard a very fine Mother's Day sermon. After lunch I wrote Mothers in honor of the occasion (Tis a pity there was not a third mother to whom I could write on Mother's Day!) The afternoon has been an extremely hot one, contrasting sharply with the cool appearance of the snow-covered Alpine region within our Ren. There was little activity around camp as we sweltered beneath our pup tents. I lifted the sides to catch any breath of wind that now and then stirred the surrounding clover field. The afternoon was broken by the coming of a Red Cross truck with hot coffee, doughnuts, and two Am. girls. The sight of the latter was also welcomed. Later MacIntosh came by and we talked for two and a half hours. It is the first time that we have had a real chance to talk since we left Doudeville, France. It was good to talk with him.

Last night Beul and I went for a long walk just as the sun was going down. Oddly enough, this was the first chance that we had had for a long talk in many weeks. You have difficulty understanding why I can't see Ted and yet here is an example of the same difficulty even within my platoon (containing only forty men).

While we were in combat we were so busy that such things were almost out of the question. Once or twice I think that I passed through the town in which Ted was located but for the most part we were separated by many miles. I fear now that even when we are semi-permanently located, I will be too far away from Ted to see him.

Last night came your two letters of the 26th & 27th. Mother reports the same two week delay in my letters, but I do hope that no such hold up will be repeated. It shouldn't be from now on. Wish I could be there to hear the reports on the S.F. Conference. The Stars & Stripes carry far too little news of such nature & my Time will be delayed. So, I welcome any comments which you make. I anxiously await the final outcome of the Conference for I do feel that its outcome in the final analysis will foretell the success or failure of the plans for peace.

[now letter is typed] Well, this time I am not in a German home but I do have access to a machine, poor as it seems to be. I think that I can say more, faster in this manner, and so I will attempt to use it at any rate. For some time I have planned to begin a series describing in some detail my activities after landing. I shall start now, and hope to finish eventually.

As zou no doubt guessed, we came over in a large convoy, the size not even we knew. Our ship was named the "General Brooks," and was a Naval vessel. This was a decided advantage for these are notably more clean than Army boats. We had a lay over a few hours off the coast of England at Fortsmouth, but of course did not go ashore. I think I described in some detail my first sight of England. We crossed the channel during the night, but spent most of the following day getting into the port of Le Harve. From there we moved by truck to our home in France, none other than Doudeville. We set foot on European soil on Mother's birthday and our stay in Doudeville was for about a month. The camp made up entirelz of tents was entirely new, and we spent much time in building up the place. We hauled rock and dug in mud long hours at a time. Before we left, we had built up a very nice place, and the rains were ended. Before leaving, we did do a bit of training, mainly road marches. For the most part we merely kept busy, saw a few movies, and played softball and volleyball. From there we moved in the famous boxcars, the "40's and 8," from Doudeville through Amiens and Riems to a small station near Duneville, France. Passing through the latter city (Riems) managed to catch a glimpse of the famous cathedral there. The spot where we detrained had been straffed ten days before our arrival and dogfights had occurred on the preceding day. We felt that we were getting near the front. From this point we moved about four miles from Deuze into a small village call Tarquimpol (probably found on no map in the States.) Here we stayed only a couple of days, long enough to rid ourselves of a great deal of excess equipment, including most of our personal belongings.

Tuesday May 15th

My Darling,

Monday came and passed and I was unable to continue my letter. I worked all morning yesterday and in the afternoon we moved. Much to our surprise our situation is greatly improved. We (the squad) are located on the banks of a delightful stream flowing swiftly through the valley. Our work is negligible and most of our time is our own. I arose at the frightful hours of 10:15 and cleared my brain with a cool dip in the deep. S Wonderful!

Before moving yesterday we had time to enjoy the better half of a show put on by one of the Service Company units. The orchestra was fair and the diversion welcomed. There are growing indications of a decided effort on the part of the Army to provide profitable entertainment for us. One of the major projects will be a gigantic sports program designed to include almost every G.I. in Europe. Built along the lines of our Intramural Program at Maryville, it will be climaxed by a G.I. Olympics to be held in one of the larger stadiums over here—perhaps in Nurnberg.

A second program and one which interests me far more is the educational opportunities for those men who stay here in the Army of Occupation. As yet, we do not know whether or not we will be able to take part, but if we do. Oh boy! Certain general courses will be given within the unit but most of those I have had. However, there is a chance that I might be able to teach some of these since instructors will be picked from our own division. This has only a second rate interest to me because of another part of the program. This is the university training. Certain qualified individuals will be detached from their unit and allowed to attend selected universities throughout Europe. Military duties would be replaced by study and the subjects studied would be of the students own choosing. The only catch as I understand it is that if the unit were retuned to the States, the individual would have to remain until his course was completed.

As far as I am concerned, it seems to be a grand opportunity for those interested in pursuing further studies, and all A.O. troops will have an opportunity to take advantage of it. Those who do not take part in the educational program in one way or another will have a training schedule involving close-order drill, and a dozen other subjects designed to fill up the time with activity.

Darling, with each passing day I feel a growing sense of need and longing for you. I long to hold you close in my arms, to whisper in your ear the feelings of my heart, to know the relaxing balm that your presence brings. I know now as never before how much I need you to make life complete. The day will surely come soon when our lives will continue as one life, together. May God hasten the day.

Ever Thine,
Bushy
P.S. Mizpah

P.S.II Letter came from Mother and Dad last, arriving in 8 days. Also good letter with picture from Sis.

Letter from Dotty to Art
Wednesday
May 16, 1945

Darling,

Joy, oh joy! Today came your V-Mail of Apr. 26, and it made me so happy! I hope you will forgive me for having been a trifle worried, but it had been almost three long weeks since I had received any mail from you. You said it had been 11 days since you had a chance to write, and it took the V-Mail three whole weeks to travel from you to me, so you can see how the delay affected the situation at this end of the line. Needless to say, I am greatly relieved. I knew your letter would come, but I found it harder to be patient than ever before.

So very glad that your packages have started arriving. Do you think it advisable to mail any more—do you think you will remain in Europe long enough to get them if I did mail any more? Probably so.

Darling, it was mean of me to send you the "stubble trouble" clipping when I knew that you probably couldn't shave for weeks on end (don't take it too seriously), but I thought you might get a laugh out of it.

Also in today's mail came your check for $30 which you said you were sending. I'll put it in the bank.

Mrs. Grimes writes that she is better and can get around on crutches now. I think I wrote you some time ago that she had broken her leg.

Uncle Sam's funeral was this afternoon. It was held at the McCamman—Cammans Funeral House in Maryville. Four ministers took part—Miles, Bradley, Crothers, and Graham—and it was a very nice service as funerals go. Most funerals are such miserable affairs. Those closest to the departed are embarrassed and miserable on account of their grief, and all the others are embarrassed of having to witness the obvious grief of the aforenamed. Thus it is bad all the way around. Uncle Sam is survived by his wife Ava, and one son, Wallace who is married & has one son. The grandson is 13 yrs. old, and has always been very devoted to Uncle Sam. The poor boy shook with uncontrollable sobs as the close of the service.

When the whole thing was over, part of the folks went back to Uncle Sam's house, but I went to the campus with Mary Ruth. We sat on a bench in front of Baldwin looking toward the chapel and town,

and the slanting rays of the setting sun viewed from that angle brought back a flood of memories. Extremely pleasant memories they were too, Darling. Joyous, beautiful memories of the beginnings of
> Our Love,
> Dotty

P.S. I forgot to tell you that I got Keesing's bibliography Saturday, and with it came a note containing his greetings to you.

P.S.#2—Mizpah

Letter from Art to Dotty
Austria May 16, 1945 (Wed.
[61-68]

Dearest Heart,

With more than the usual thrill I received your letters of the 24th and 4th this morning. In the first place, I had received no mail from you since about Sat. In the second place, I look forward more and more to each letter from you. Someday, Dorothy, I shall become bold enough to hold your hand and whisper into your ear the secret of my heart. Perhaps I shall ever find the courage to hold you in my arms and kiss you. And, yes, I may even stumble to my knees and ask for your hand in marriage. (Naturally, I prefer the one with the ring!) Well, if you insist, give me the whole arm and we'll call it a deal. Ah-lack-a-day! Another day, another rose!

Did fish are not biting so well, (we ran out of hand grenades) and the water is too wet for swimming (I am a bit lazy to tell the truth). The beautiful Austrian women are not around at the moment (they never were around here I don't think) and so I took my pan in hand (I find difficulty writing with my pen in any other position).

After a blood counter and a pulse rating I think that I suffer from a sun stroke—would that it were your stroke instead. But the sun is warm, and we have hot chow for two meals today rather that "C" ration (how we hate them now!), and there is nothing pressing to be done (except you), and I feel so lazy and almost contented—almost but not quite. I shall never be contented while this Army life lasts. And how it does! Oh well, son day I'll have sun body to stroke my sun stroked-head (if it isn't too late!)

I was delighted to hear that another package is in the making. Just a few moments ago I finished the last fig from one of Mother's boxes. The stationery will be welcomed along with the other items. There are times when I almost have to use the reverse side of some of my old letters. I suppose that very soon our PX supplies will be regularly supplied, but not yet. Mother has a habit of including three of four sheets from time to time and these have saved the situation more than once. The "MA" stationery was "loot" swiped at one of the high points of my shortage. Such things are necessary to the pursuit of the war effort.

Your comments concerning the direction of the rushing (not Russian) German brings to mind stories that I had intended to relate earlier. During the last days of the war and even after peace was officially declared, we had the experience of having large bodies of German soldiers march toward us ready to give up. Part of the time we were riding on trucks and the throngs actually became so great that we merely waved them to the rear rather than place guards on them. The popular expression which all G.I.'s immediately took up was (and still is to an extent) "Alles ist Raput!" "Everything is done for." This was yelled at almost every German soldier which we saw, often they smiled, gesticulated with their hands, and repeated the phrase, "Alles ist Raput." Over and over again these Germans expressed their fear of being prisoners under the Russians.

During one of my "jobs" of guarding a group of PW's, I encountered a German Lt. who spoke very excellent English. Before the war he had studied medicine in Vienna and there had many English speaking friends. He too anxiously questioned the possibility of being placed in a Russian prison camp. In the course of our conversation I asked him at what point did he think that the average German soldier knew the continuation of the war useless. "When the Fueher died," quoth he with a reverence that sounded strange to my unaccustomed ear. Trying to dig deeper, I asked when he himself knew that the war was over. "When the Fueher went to Berlin," said he. "I told my commander that that was the beginning of the end." I remained dissatisfied and so attempted to probe deeper. "But why did you wish to continue when continuation only meant further destruction of German cities, railroads, bridges, and industries?" "We had hope," he answered, again in reverent tones. "Hope even after we swept passed Cologne and onward toward Berlin?" I queried. "Yes, you see I was in Vienna when your planes came. First, they dropped sheets—er—pamphlets, I believe you call them, telling us that you came to liberate. Then came the bombers and you bombed civilian homes and military installations alike." (Imagine a German having the nerve to say this.) I then reminded him of the Cologne instance when the Cathedral was left untouched when everything was leveled. He had no answer for that one.

How much of this the Lieutenant actually believed, I have no way
of knowing. He seemed very intelligent, and yet we know that the
German propaganda was powerful. Whether conscious or unconscious
his mind was filled with perverted ideas and he was more than glad to
spread his propaganda. To make a mere guess, I think that my friend
the Lieutenant was like thousands of other German officers and
enlisted men who held a fanatic faith in der Feuher and who will form
the core of any attempt to revive the National Socialist Party and
Nazism. The conversation was extremely interesting and I think that it
is something for the records.

Here is something else for the records, my Love. During these days
when I have time to think more than two thoughts for myself, my
longing for you is more and more acute. I feel the need for your
companionship, for the touch of your hand, your lilting laugh, your
bright smile. Life apart from you is at best a mere existence. I long for

the day when our lives will flow into a union which not even death can separate—a union in which our individual lives will cease to exist and a single life will evolve. That to me is the future of
Our Love,
Bushy

Letters from Art to Dotty
Austria
May 17, 1945 [70-81]
My Dearest Heart,
Again there is a question in my mind as to whether or not the page number is correct. I hope that it is. By the way, does numbering the page assist in any way? [in upper right corner, 70-81]
As I write, most of the squad sits a few yards away imbibing in drink. I have a P.S. to add to my lengthy commentary on drinking. While I see no reason to change my original conclusion that no moral or ethical wrong is involved in taking a light drink, I am so disgusted with the drinking that goes on around me that even the sight of the stuff is repulsive. I tasted champagne and was so disgusted that I have no desire to even taste champagne again.
I am trying to discover why men drink. It is not a simple answer but I think that I am finding a partial solution. When I mentioned that champagne had a horrible taste, one of the fellows answered by saying that none of the drinks appeal to the taste. "It's the effect," he said. I think that men, unable to find release from the hum drum of living, turn to drink to get away from reality. From observations of the men around me who drink, they are usually those who know only a limited number of ways to occupy themselves. As soon as work is slack, they find time heavy on their hands. I remember a remark by Joe Kaelber to the effect that a few drinks tended to make for sociability. That is the trouble. These people turn to drink because they cannot break down the inhibitions that stand in the way of enjoying the presence of others.
I wonder if people have still failed to learn to think. When not occupied with a specific job, they are unable to think in a creative way and so occupy their time. That is a very crude expression of what I mean and I think that it is worth thinking through more thoroughly. If true and valid this theory could be applied to other vices including the seeking of physical pleasure in the unbecoming manners.

The past two days have brought me perhaps as close to heaven as I shall get on this side of the Atlantic. Friday night I moved from my squad location to the company C.P. (Commander Post). There, Beul and I slept. Saturday morning we arose and after breakfast loaded on a truck off to the mountains! How familiar that sounds. By ten o'clock we had arrived, found our area, disposed of our equipment, etc. and were ready for twenty-four hours of freedom. (To my regret I had to give up my writing last night as I almost fell asleep over my pen.)

We have finished breakfast and are now awaiting the trucks which will take us back. The clouds are low this morning. Even the hills around are capped by clouds. From where we sit (Beul and I); I see across the lake for perhaps four miles. The water is calm and but one lone boat is to be seen.

Tues. Evening (22nd)

Dearest,

I seem to have a great deal of difficulty writing this letter. 'Tis now Tues. and I began on Friday. There is a great deal to write about and I think that the only thing to do is to start at the beginning (which, after all, is the only logical place to start.

About ten days ago the 71st took over the facilities for recreation on Lake Gmunden (also called Lake Troun) near the town of Gmunden. At this time a few men were sent up for a "rest". The arrangement was for each group to remain twenty-four hours.

Friday night I found that my turn had come and I managed to get Beul in on the trip through a vacancy from our squad. Upon our arrival at the Lake, Beul and I rushed down to the boat house. Luckily we found a boat, but unluckily it was an G.I. landing craft. Nevertheless we had fun struggling with it for two hours.

The Lake is very large and holds all the beauty for which the Alps are known. Its shape is roughly that of a pear—eight miles long, two and a half miles wide and a hundred and fifty feet deep in places. Directly across from our location was a peak rising almost straight up to the height of more than 3,000 feet. A snow capped range nearby rose to a height of 4500 feet. The city of Gmunden was off limits to the G.I.'s but we did pass through it.

It was a real pleasure to be able to put my rifle, belt, and steel helmet aside and forget about the Army for a few hours. We were under almost no restrictions, and our time was our own. The vacation was doubly gratifying since I was in the mountains again and what mountains! Darling, I thought about you constantly and felt your presence as I enjoyed one scene after another. The full enjoyment was only added to by the fellowship with Beul. With only one other fellow over here could I have enjoyed it more and that would have been with Ted.

Saturday afternoon Beul and I took a couple of rides in motor boats provided for our enjoyment. These had been brought by the engineers and were handled by them. There were also sail boats on the lake but we didn't mange to get one of them. Since snow was still melting and running into the lake, the water was rather cold but I enjoyed a dip none the less.

To add to our list of lucky breaks, we had two cameras and plenty of film. I think we caught some good snaps, although it may take weeks to get the prints developed. Sat. afternoon we caught Gen. Wyman in a close up as he looked over the facilities.

Everyone was supposed to sleep in the field but Beul and I found an old bed in an upstairs room in the boat house. Here we slipped, after dark, and enjoyed the comforts of a roof over our heads (even though it was a single bed). Before going to sleep, we went out on our private porch (much like the upper deck of the boat house at Stanford). I happened to have an extra "K" ration and so we enjoyed a midnight snack. It brought back many memories of college days, but the moon did more than this as its light illuminated the lake, the snow capped mountains, as the water lapped gently against the shore, I was carried away by a flood of memories of the nights of yesteryear. I [It] was lovely!

Sunday morning we arose, expecting to return to "the other world" after breakfast. To our glad surprise, we found that we "had" to stay another day due to the fact that the camp was soon to move to another site. Our morning was taken up with a two our [hour] trip up the Lake and back in an old Diesel-powered tug. The scenery was magnificent. After lunch we took a hike—being true infantrymen—climbing in the Alps! From the vantage point of a high ridge we had a marvelous view of the lake & the surrounding county and here we obtain some good shots (I hope).

I failed to mention one important thing. On Saturday afternoon there was a heavy rain. Afterward the sun came out and a perfect rainbow was formed over the great peak rising across the lake. Above this rainbow were formed three others.

I have never seen such a sight. I stood in awe and reverence as I saw the glorious array of color. The great mountain was for the most part a mass of barren gray rock but there were splotches of green, (trees) dark red (vein of ore) and gold (a sand rock quarry). The sight was truly a memorable one.

I shall have other comments concerning my vacation but I must bring this letter to a close. I have your letters of April 24th, May 2nd, 5th, 6th, 7th, 10th, & 13th. I surely hope that my mail is coming through now. Mother has not heard from me from April 14th to May 12th. With the exception of one break of about eight or ten days, I have written three to four letters per week. Be patience, Darling, for nothing can change

Our Love

Bushy

Letter from Art to Dotty

Kremeten, Austria

May 23, '45 Wed. [82-91]

My Dearest.

The letter which I finished last night was written piece-meal and though long (12 pages) took five days to complete. I hope to do better this time. In my haste to cover everything, I fear that I missed several points which I wanted to mention. Perhaps I can do better and cover them now. As I write I am delightfully disturbed by two small Austrian children. How I love it! One is ten and the other six—both extremely intelligent. I am learning more German every day from these kids. I love to play with them, give them chocolate and chewing gum. You have no idea how the German children long for chocolate. They must think that we have it growing on trees for everywhere we go we hear "Give me chocolate", part of the time in German, part of the time in English. Even the older people crave it and its trade value is very high. These children are so cute & it is so much fun to play with them. I wish —but in time!

On the evening prior to my trip to the mountains I received a long letter from Ted K.—the first in many weeks. He is located only a short distance away (about 15 mi.) but as yet we cannot get together. Perhaps in a short time we will be located more closely together and can get passes together. I certainly hope so. Ted expects to remain here for some time but all that we have are rumors. Everything is expected and nothing is known for certain. I still await a letter from Pratt but I guess he is busy. Another thing is the long delay in getting our mail. My letter to Ted took more than ten days and here we are in the same division. I am sure that Pratt is "sweating out" the C.B.I.

Today we were told that censorship has been lifted and I should be able to speak with complete freedom now. Our platoon has had a real break since V-E day. We have been guarding bridges to prevent sabotages and pick up German soldiers without proper identification. Our squad has been luckier still in being located two and a half miles from the rest of the platoon. Thus we are left almost entirely alone. Our duties require our attention only a few hours each day. Tomorrow we begin a sports program and so our time will be taken up in part with that.

You spoke of being jealous of Time—Never that, Darling. Time is always at least two weeks late while I am receiving your letters in from eight to ten days. My back Encores are coming and yesterday I received the Echoes for the first semester.

One of the minor points which I had intended to mention in regard to my mountain trip was the opportunity I had to observe the interesting blends of architecture. I would give a great deal to be able to sketch some of them. There is a definite influence from the Middle East as seen in many church steeples. Getting away from the Gothic characteristics found farther west, these steeples are rounding... I noted many rooves were slightly curved at the eves. Many of these I saw on my way to and from the Lake, but around the shores were many more interesting styles to observe.

Beul and I snapped at least one picture of a quaint house but I wish that we could have taken a couple of pictures of some of the native costumes. One old gentleman sticks in mind. Slightly weazened (sp?) his skinny legs stuck out strangely from leather shorts. A jacket, highly ornamented adorned his shoulders and a long pipe clung to his teeth. The picture was completed by a large plume in his hat. This plume I saw often and shorts were very popular with the men.

May 24, Thurs.

I think I mentioned that Ted is located at Steyr just now. When he wrote he was still billeted in a house but he expected to go into tents shortly.

During the first part of our stay here, the weather was perfect; but now the rain is with us again. Luckily we have found a sentry box to sit in on guard and it is certainly a great help. We have been able to supplement our food supply with fish from the stream, obtained by tossing in hand grenades. Although not the sporting way, the method is certainly affective. The rains have probably brought many more fish down stream and so luck should be good.

In waiting of daily events and incidents, I often have difficulty in going back and picking up the thread of events which occurred during the days of combat. However, eventually I hope to complete the story. I believe I stopped the last time with our arrival at Tarquinpal after crossing France. It was here that I went into the beautiful little chapel where I knelt for prayer and meditation. It was in this town (or rather village) that another incident occurred worthy of note. About noon we heard the approach of a plane and soon heard the scream of a power dive. This was quickly followed by a series of explosions. We ran out, rifles in hand, someone yelled "German Plane!" We never knew exactly but some guess that the explosions were caused by auxiliary gas tanks being dropped. At any rate, they landed a safe distance away, and we had experienced our first flurry of excitement.

After witnessing a beautiful sunset we crowded on trucks about nine o'clock the second day. For hours we rode in cramped positions, and finally we de-trucked. We could hear artillery bursts and see the flashes as we began our march. Extra boots, overshoes, two blankets, sleeping bag, ammunition, extra woolen underwear etc., etc.—all of this was on our backs. We marched on and on. Many fell out. At four o'clock in the morning we arrived in the town of Mizenthal and were put to bed in a school building. The front lines were just over the ridge a thousand yards away. The building in which we were placed was terribly crowded and many remained outside. I found a dusty corner in the attic, falling immediately into sound slumber. We spent most of the following day sleeping and cleaning up. Beul and I slipped away from the rest to eat a small can of mixed nuts which I had saved from the boat. We looked at the pictures of our wives, talked of the past, and wondered what the ensuing hours might bring.

Late in the afternoon we "saddled up" (to use the Army vernacular) and began a long climb out of the valley in which the town was located. Shortly after our arrival at our destination we were given our positions to dig in and were told the situation. We were purely defensive, being in reserve behind another division. We knew that artillery or mortar fire could easily be laid on our hill position so we gladly dug in. It was this night that three of us slept in hole measuring twenty-seven inches (three hand spans) wide. Don't ask me how. On the following day I wrote you two V-Mails describing the coming of Spring. We moved again but it was only a few hundred yards and this time we were in

Kematen, Austria, June 45

positions that had been held by the 42nd Div. for ninety days. Fox holes were deep and many comfortable dug outs had been built. Just as we came up the push began, the artillery poured in on the positions, and the boys of the 42nd moved forward. Long columns of men and material passed us on the way to the front and ambulances and jeeps came back with the wounded. We knew that this was "it."

We pulled out from these positions on the second day. (By the way it was here that I slept sitting up on my fox hole for one night.) and then began a march which was to go down in our history as the "death march to Bitche". I must wait until later to describe this.

Yesterday I was given the little badge which we officially received several weeks ago. I also received a bronze battle star and according to today's <u>Stars & Stripes</u> our unit gets another. More points!

Well, someday we will have to worry no more about points, about an uncertain future, about a million and one things in the Army. Then will we plan and work and fulfill the dream of
Our Love,
Bushy

Dearest Heart,

For three or four days I have been without mail from you. I know that is nothing in comparison with the long periods during which you have waited for mail, but some of the fellows are getting mail in six days. That isn't bad! On three successive days I received three copies of Time and so I am catching up with the news. How wonderful it is to be able to read and write almost as much as I want. (Since there are but twenty-four hours in a day, I suppose that I will never be completely satisfied.) This morning I completed an eight page letter to Dr. Hunter, which was long overdue. If I only had a few addresses, I could soon be completely up with correspondence. But really that day will never come. If I could write three twelve page letters per day to my very wonderful wife!

By the way, did I remember to tell you I love you. For a brief time last night the full moon shown from out the clouds. I walked by the river and I squeezed your hand. Once again we walked in the shadows of the College Woods. The moonlight reflected on your beautiful hair, your enchanting face. I pressed you close and kissed you. Our hearts kept time to the racing music of Our Love. We are one.

This morning as I still slept a truck came by with Beul and "Sod". They were going to the mountains and I could have gone. However, I was too sleepy to know what was going on and also it turned very cold last night. The ride on the open truck and the night's sleep in the open would have been very uncomfortable. These rationalizations are true but I think that I would have gone anyway had I been given time to get ready. You know me—and the mountains.

I wrote in a previous letter asking for an address book with all the addresses which you think I might want. I have been thinking that from now on I should be able to carry a book or two along. Perhaps you could send The Pocket Book of Verse in the next package. I miss my poetry a great deal. As per usual a little candy and food will be greatly appreciated by all concerned.

Yesterday we signed our point record and to my surprise I have more than I thought. The difference came when I received credit from the date of my enlistment (Aug. 6, '42) even though ten months of this was on inactive status. Thus I have a grand total of 42 points—just half enough. Of course, if I could only claim three children that would 36 additional points or a total of 78. If we get another star for Germany, that would be five more. Well, what's undone can't be done, to use an old Bushing saying. We have not been blessed with triplets—yet!

By the way, Mother was delighted with the stationery which you sent and she always enjoys your letters. My mail to them has also been delayed and they love to get any news that you may have. Do write them as often as you can. I am wondering if "Mom" is with Harriet by now. I hope that she can make the trip for I know how much it will mean to both of them. When is the big event expected?

Your plans for our thirty days sounds very wonderful. I too dream but—well, I still have my fingers crossed. Our situation remains so unchanged but it can not remain so for long. With the exception of Doudeville, this has been our longest stop since Ft. B.

I was interested to hear of Carl's experience. I shall try again to write him soon. Have you heard anything at all from Bob or Arlene. I should like to establish contact with them. I answered Ted K.'s letters but still await word from Pratt.

I knew there was something I wanted to describe—I have no way of knowing how much it is discuss in the papers at home, but "fraternization" is a big topic over here. The Army is encountering new difficulties all the time and stringent rules are being clamped down. I know of one instance of a man being sentenced to four months, fifteen days, for merely being caught in conversation with an Austrian woman. Conditions of war bring with them abnormal sex life, along with every thing else; (Some doctor claims that European women are suffering from mass sex frustration.) and far too many men have not the moral courage or the will power to abstain from physical gratification. My knowledge of human individuals expands, as, I hope, does my understanding.

Yesterday I received a form letter from Maryville along with a request for Alumni dues. I hope you can pay mine since I have no way of sending money in such amounts. By the way, I have not heard that you received $30 which I sent many weeks ago. I also sent $10 which was probably sent only a few days ago. The system is a very poor one under which we are able to dispose of our pay. Only last week we received our pay for April although I had signed up to send it home in the first days of May. I feel very guilty because I have been unable to make proper recognition of certain events—our wedding anniversary and such. However, under the prevailing conditions there seems to have been no help for it. I promise to make up for everything, My Love.

Again tonight, no mail. I shall be patience as you were. Outside the sky is overcast, the clouds hang low. A slow steady rain has begun. My spirits, I must confess are a bit low. Do you realize that in six more days I will have completed two full years of active service in the Army. I have risen to the height of Private, First Class, after diligent effort, etc, etc. This rank I have held for almost seventeen months. With the exception of a few cadet positions at Stanford, the total responsibility placed upon my broad shoulders has been that of gunner for the BAR (Browning Automatic Rifle) with two men assisting. At the rate now commissioned officers are pouring into our outfit, ratings will be taken away rather than given for months to come. I sometimes wonder what I would or could do with a position of responsibility even if I had to. I have been "under thumb" for so long that I fear I have lost much of my old self-confidence. I care little for this life.

Forgive me, Darling! I should never allow myself to sink to such a depth of blackness. I have really gained much from my experience and I truly believe that I have a new understanding of human relationships. In humility I pray, "I believe, Help Thou my unbelief."

Yesterday we watched three women come into the field behind our bivouac area with sythes [scythes]. They began to work and in two and a half hours the fields had been mowed. I am amazed at the tenacity with which these women pursue their work. Seldom it is that the men display an industrious nature. However, the effects of word are quite apparent in the features of the women. All appear overly muscular and age begins to show at an early age. I think that G.I.'s all over the world are learning a new appreciation of the American female populace.

Our Love,
Bushy

Letter from Art to Dotty
Neuhofen, Austria
May 28, 1945 [105-111]

My Darling,

I am sitting in front of Beul's tent two and a half miles down stream from my own area. Thus the stationery. Beul finally admitted that this was the only way he knew to get his picture to you. (It is nice stationery don't you think?)

After lunch we had to come down here for sports and so I enjoyed five innings of soft ball—the first that I have played since Doudeville. After working up a good sweat, we quit for a good swim. The water was cold but very invigorating.

Chow came last night. Beul came up to our area afterward and we went to see "Mrs. Parkington."—the picture, you know. But in the meantime I received letters from you. One from the 16th and one from the 21st. Seven days for the latter was excellent time—4 ½ actually since it was postmarked five o'clock in the afternoon. I was certainly sorry to hear of the death of Uncle Sam and I know that it was a loss to Mom. I hope that the difficulties of the final arrangements were accomplished with the minimum of trouble for those concerned.

I am so glad that Dean, and David and Phyllis were able to be home at the same time. If only Carl could have been with them, but that too will come. Tanka for the picture of the trio. I enjoyed the first article on Anglo-Russian relations, and I look forward to the others in the series. My copies of <u>Time</u> indicate the rough water through which the S.F. Conference is travelling. I do hope that the situation will improve. It will truly be one of the greatest disasters of all time if a workable plan does not evolve. It appears to me that the present difficulties arise from two point—the U.S. and the Soviet Union. In the former case, we are just now emerging from our former isolation. The clothing of internationalizing is new. It is for this reason that we have difficulty in making agreements with those powers with whom we have had little contact. I do not believe that we understand the point of view nor the workings of the Russian mind. Now as to Russia herself, she suffers from the same self-centeredness although the cause for her isolation differs from ours. Since our early success against the French and the British we have had an overemphasized feeling of self-sufficiency and independence. We ruled the Western Hemisphere; to heck with the rest of the world. After World War I we continued to think that we could tell the rest of the world when and how we would play and it took another war to convince us otherwise. Now in regard to Russia, it has been her internal difficulties (growing pains) that have kept her isolated from world circles. Now she is on the stage for the first appearance. This explanation is my own coming merely from my observation, but I believe that it explains in part the difficulties that are being encountered at San Francisco. We simply do not understand the Russians reactions. And they do not understand our attitudes and feelings. If we are really in earnest, if they are seriously trying to find the real solution to world peace, then the Conference will find success. I believe that already it is evident that the cards are held by the United States and Russia. Great Britain has taken up second fiddle.

'Tis now Wed. morning. I seem to be having a terrible time writing this letter, but our days have been more fully occupied of late. The duties for the past few nights have been most pleasant. Sunday my guard duty was from six to seven in the morning; Monday from two to four; Tues. four to six and this morning three to four again. The early morning hours are very wonderful and I always enjoy them.

This morning even as I arose the clouds were pushed to show a moon just past the full. The clouds added a background of great beauty to the scene. I began my watch sitting before the fire which we keep burning all night. An almost perfect stillness prevail. It was broken only by the slow steady breathing of another G.I. curled up in his sleeping bag and lying near the fire. On the other side, "Kaputt." Our mascot (dog) dozed. (He actually snored before I left) There is something about a fire in the open which intrigues men. Be it a cold winters night or a warm night in June, a conversation is doomed when begun around a fire. Invariably eyes become fixed deep within the flames or perhaps within a dying amber. Thoughts are lost in faraway places. I gazed into the fire this morning as I stood my watch.

But soon I was drawn from the fire. The moon in full glory shown out upon the land. I walked out upon the bridge which we guard. A hundred yards down the road a G.I. truck stood in plain view before the "Gasthaus." The hillside beyond was also in clear view. Along the river bank to my left deep shadows engulfed the shore line, and the water merged into the trees. A few rays from the moon managed to filter through these trees and these reflected in shimmering patterns upon the water. The sounds of ripping water came to my ear and I thought of times and paces long since gone.

I turned where I stood and faced the eastern sky. A faint trace of dawn creeped with hesitating steps to the horizon and I saw that for a brief space of time I alone separated night and day. Behind me shown the moon in all nocturnal beauty. Before me the heralds of day snuffed out the candles of heaven and the "rosy tipped fingers of dawn" followed close behind.

Darling, I am very much ashamed of the way I am writing this letter. Perhaps if I would not try to write an entire book I could get my letters out on the same day on which they are begun. ('Tis now Wed.) [Little did Art know that he was actually writing a book.]

I shall say goodnight and go to dream of Our Love. Believe me when I say,

      I love you,
      Bushy

Dear Art,

Received a letter from you & Pratt just about the same time; his took as long to get from Salzburg to here as they do from home & Cordelia. Quite surprising—maybe they have trouble catching the mail when it's dumped off the cliff up there in the remote Alps. But Salzburg is a famous spot & would be a pretty good spot to be in a while. I know approximately where you are since you are quite near div. h.q. Maybe one of these days I'll get a chance to go to div & stop off & see you. Do you ever get into Steyr to go to the show or something like that? I see quite a lot of trucks from the 14th around the theater & thought maybe you get in here once in a while. We are across town from the theater but walk over there about every other evening.

Pratt is all wrapped up in the glory of the 3rd & he himself seems to be doing well enough as acting Co when the Co is on leave. I was glad enough when I had those letters from him after we got here & know that he was in the pink of condition, etc. Glad you got to go to Gmunden [town in Austria]—I haven't had the chance but have heard plenty of excellent reports on the beauty of it. Now the place is Canisse I understand which they say is excellent, but not quite as good as Gmunden. We had a chance to go tomorrow for 3 days, but the chance of going to Birtchesgaden [Berchtesgaden] seem even better, & I certainly want to get in on a trip there.

Did you hear of the death of Bunny McCartney? My mother is in Knoxville now. She wrote me of it. She was sick for a week with some unknown disease and the doctors couldn't do anything for her. She had just been married a week & I presume it was Bob Lord she married, I don't know. Do you know anything more about it? Had you heard Bill Sweeney was missing? Anyway, he showed up in Russia later safe & sound. Mother is in Knoxville because my grand folks got in such bad shape that one of the aunts there sent an S.O.S. & mother went down to help. She says she can't do much since it's just a matter of existence for grandfather, & grandmother is losing her strength rather fast.

I hear it rumored that you are going out on points! A good rumor, anyway. There are naturally all the rumors possible already cooked up, but I have a telegram straight from the horses mouth today which I like to believe as well as any & it said (very officially, of course) that we'd probably be here another three months! Well, you know how it is; as much as we'd like to see the dear wives, I believe I'd forego a trip to the

US right now if it was only a stopover. However, doesn't this outfit impress you as being C131 material! It does me & in this office they keep kidding me that I'm essential now & never will get out!

Hope you are not in for wishful thinking when you wish for little Oxford or Cambridge culture & education. Such a thing seems just a little too good for the army to offer. Are they throwing you all the C.S. stuff too now that the war is over? What a drain it is on one's self-respect and decency to have to take that stuff though right here at the office we get very little of it. You probably know what little I know on this education deal; next to nothing has come down about it in writing but if it does I'll let you know. Haven't heard about that volunteering for anything with linguistic ability the requirement. Can't think of anyway to get with the 5th, but I did see the other day where a fellow transferred from the 5th to 66th, because a chaplain over there asked for him for his assistant & this fellow put in his application! It happens to other guys—you know the story & so do I!

Scratch off the Munich rumors, Art; those big plans seem to have all been called off. This is a nice town; picturesque & I've covered it pretty thoroughly at different times on foot & otherwise. Have had 2 roll [rolls] of film developed & printed (both taken back in France) but have 4 more in town now. It's quite a job talking [to] this German speaking fellow into getting them down for us, & then the prints aren't so hot, but the negr look good & will make good prints back in the States. 3 of us just drew straws to see who got to fill the extra seat in the jeep tomorrow to Bertchesgaden [Berchtesgaden] & I won! So I'll load up with camera & film (looted!) & hope old jupe plavius stays at home.

Thanks lots for your letter, Art, & I still have hopes of getting out there while in some other mission of mercy if not otherwise. Give Dot my regards. Ted

Letter from Art to Dotty
Kematen, Austria
May 31, 1945 [112-123]

Dearest,

Outside a cold wind is blowing and a light rain comes down. The regular cycle continues—four or five days of sunny, warm even hot weather, and then three or four days of rain and clouds. Ah lockaday! At least I am inside at the moment. We are awaiting chow in the little day room which we take over when it rains, and meanwhile we are being entertained. Living in this Gasthaus is a tiny boy for his age, he is seventeen. He spent three months in the German Army before being discharged. Now he is working on a farm near here. The poor guy seems to be off just a bit, but he has terrific musical ability. His range goes higher than my falsetto and at one time that was rather high. I have heard him begin singing after supper at 5:30 or 6:00 o'clock and sing until 10. He sings German songs one after another—many of them with the same melody as there Am. counter part. He does a great deal of oompapah and adds all sorts of effects. The kid really has musical talent, but it is the comedy of his action and song that attract attention.

This fellow is not one in my kindergarten group, but it continues to grow on three occasions I have had the children bring eggs to me without my asking and without asking for anything in return. Of course, I frequently give them chewing gum, chocolate and crackers, but for them to bring me eggs was surprising. The little group of from four to six children come around every afternoon and often stay until nine o'clock. Often it is because of them that I am unable to finish a letter already begun. They will not sit by my tent tonight—the wind continues to blow and it looks like a winter's day outside.

I am glad that my new bed will keep me high off the wet ground. Don't think I told you about the bed, did I? When Beul and I went to the show "Mrs. Parkington" we were sitting on a hillside in the open. Before the show began, we scouted around to find a seat. In a nearby junk yard we found the back of a truck seat and carted it to the open air theatre. After the show I decided to carry it home with me. Now I have the next thing to an air flow mattress. It really isn't that good but it beats the ground.

By the way, I wrote a long eight page letter to Dr. Hunter this week, another of similar length to Dick Boyd today and a shorter one to Bob Hunter. Think I had better write Dr. Gates & Dr. Shrine soon. Wish I had the Glathe initials (think it is H.B.). I suppose my request for addresses came though.

For the second day in a row we have had no mail whatever. I have had but two letters from you now in more than a week and none from Mother and Dad. I shall be patient, but I cannot understand the hold up in the mail now.

Darling some time I would be interested in a financial report of our corporation. In addition to the regular allotment and the bond I have sent a total of sixty dollars in their allotments to you. The first was for $30, the second for $20, and the third for $10. I hope that these have come through. Beul and I were talking a few days ago about the experience that we will have as we return to set up a home. It is a bit staggering at times and yet you and I will spend with care. I have no feeling of apprehension about that, and I still believe that I can capture a PhD. at Yale without borrowing a penny. I will never [be] satisfied with anything less than a PhD., and I sometimes wonder if even that will make me completely happy. I really think that after ten years of teaching and study I will know my subjects well enough to feel that I am accomplishing something. We have heard nothing more at all concerning the educational program, of course, we will have no opportunity for it unless we remain as AO. That still hangs in the balance.

The last time that I went back to my combat story, I had reached the march to Bitche. This we began about two o'clock in the afternoon, marching back through the little town of Mizenthal [Meisenthal]. We were carrying all of our equipment and clothing which I think I have described in some detail before. We marched about four miles before we reached the point where the trucks were to pick us up. (This happened time and time again: we marched half the distance to be picked up by trucks for the remainder of the trip. The trucks could have picked us up at our original position just as well.) By truck we travelled a circuitous (sp ?) route. There was much evidence of recent fighting and destruction was on every hand. The ground which we now covered had been the scene of the fighting which we had observed from our rearward positions on the hills outside of Mizenthal [Meisenthal]. About dark (probably six o'clock) we de-trucked and began to march again. Hour after hour, mile after mile we marched. Ten minutes out of every sixty is supposed to be for rest, but we marched for two hours with no break. A few men fall out and many dropped behind. At last we reached a town which had been taken late that very afternoon. We climbed a nearby hill and at last reached a bivouac area. The hour was ten. Overhead the artillery whirred and I thought I distinguished a buzz bomb during my hour of guard. (If this was a buzz bomb, it was the only one which I heard during the entire period of combat.) At three-thirty we were awakened and told to move out in ten minutes. Of course, that was impossible. All of us disgusted and much equipment was either lost or thrown away. I left behind my tent pole and pegs, but carried everything else. (I had no use for these until the war ended.) Our platoon started out with one entire squad (there are three in a platoon) remaining behind. We started out on one of the roughest marches of the war—the "death march to Bitche." Packed in the dark, our packs were none too secure and more than one fell out to remake the pack. We marched on and on at a fast clip—too fast for marching under such conditions. Again we went for two and a half hours without a break. Lt. Moberg (my platoon leader) plopped down along side of me when we finally stopped in Bitche. He, like everyone else, was almost ready to throw in the sponge. (It was as we marched through Bitche that we saw the only Mark VI tank. It had been knocked out and stood with its 88 pointing limply toward the ground.) It was on this march that I learned to find strength by asking God to help me put one foot before the other. We continued on beyond the town for three quarters of a mile. And then, then to cap the experience we were told to drop everything but a light combat pack, (containing only a rain coat) gas mask, rifle and belt. We could have just as well left all of this stuff back on the hillside where we spent part of the night. However, that would have been too practical—not the Army way. We continued on to Laze – Bitche, (Camp Bitche) about a half—mile farther down the road. Our mission was to relieve the 104th Div. who had just finished a hard battle in taking the city. They had fought all night. Tired and weary faces marched passed us as we moved in. There were no smiles, no talking. Those boys were battle hardened fighters; they had seen their buddies die.

June 1st

They knew that this was no dress parade. We moved into their positions, with the few remaining men in our platoon who had made the march. Our platoon normally consists of forty men. Nine of us were there to go into a defensive position. (our Lt., two non-coms, and six Pfc's.) A counter attack by the Germans at this point would have been an unfortunate affair for us. Even before we found our places, two Germans ran toward us, with hands high. This was the first of a long flow of prisoners to come to us to surrender. Here is a rough picture of our situation: [The handwritten diagram is at letter's end.]

Our purpose was to hold in case the Germans attempted to break through here. (Bitche had been retaken at the time of the "Ardennes Bulge.") Our CP was a large concrete pill box and the location had been used by the Germans for some time. A great deal of equipment was scattered throughout the area and even women's clothing was found. (We later found that some infantrymen had had their wives with them for two years.) Our job was merely to wait and watch. The first shot was fired on our platoon that morning when the BAR man saw two figures approaching. These were never identified and they got away.

Late the same afternoon we had orders to move and so we packed up. The move was a short one and we moved into a position just east of

Laze-Bitche. The town of Camp Bitche contained many large barracks and must have been a large post. This time we were actually on the front lines—the woods to our front contained enemy! There was no temptation to sleep on guard that night. About nine o'clock two more Germans came down the road talking as hard as they could. We were certain they came to find our positions—others being probably behind them to check on our strength, etc. In addition to this, there was heavy artillery fire going both ways. I learned that night to judge the spot where the shells would land by the approximate place where the whine ceased in flight. As long as the whine continued passed the vertical, everything was safe. This night it was that I challenged a chipmunk that was playing around in a stump behind my fox hole. The following day we worked four or five hours fixing up our position. Just as we finished, orders came to pull out. We learned never to spend too much time on our fox hole homes because we never stayed in one place more than two nights—usually one.

We moved out across the plain in front of us as the sun sank low in the west. We were surrounded by low hills in the distance. We were glad to keep well separated. The ground that we covered had been used for training and many concrete emplacements were along the way. Mortars were firing at intervals ahead of us and we saw the bursts on the hillside ahead. A Piper Cub flew sailed overhead and we were glad to see it. Suddenly a couple of shots rang out. We had seen a few Germans on the hillside and were in a perfect position to be raked by machine gun fire. We stopped and waited. Darkness fell and we finally dug in defensively. It was this night that I fell into one of the concrete fox holes to be thoroughly soaked. We remained here two nights before moving out again. I must discontinue this tale and continue the fourth chapter in the next issue.

This morning (this now Fri.) I received your letter written on the 16th and 20th. Glad to get your reports on two trips to Maryville. Will say more about them in a later letter which I will probably begin this afternoon. Almost time to go on guard and I must say good bye. I love you with all of my heart.

Thine own,
Bushy

P.S. We are supposed to move to platoon C.P. today.

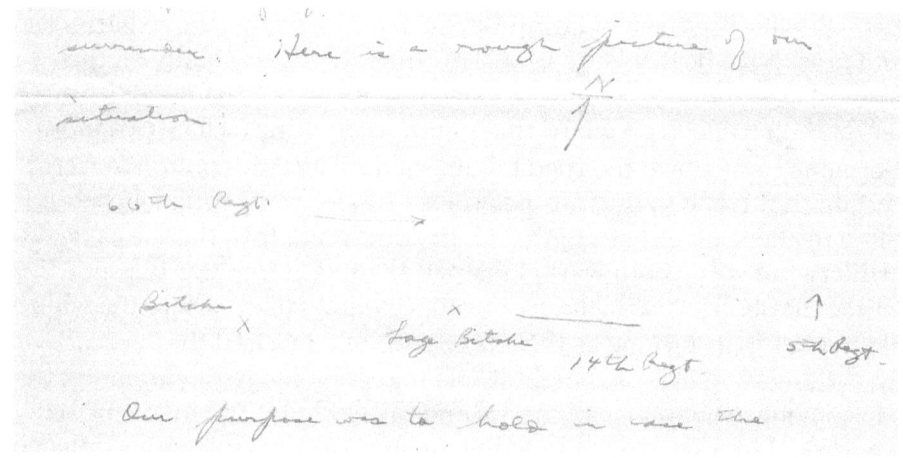

Diagram in letter dated June 1, 1945

Letter from Dotty to Art
Sunday, June 2, 1945
My Dearest Husband,

Move your book, please. I'd like to sit in your lap for a while, rest my head on your shoulder, kiss your neck and a few other choice spots, and just bask in bliss for a time. Then when we get around to talking I'll tell you of yesterday and today's activities.

June and I had a very nice visit yesterday. But I had better start with the beginning of the day. Mary Ruth and I both arose at six to get Dad's breakfast and get an early start on the day's work, by ten we had cleaned the entire house. I then changed my clothes in a jiffy and ran down to the church to register the kids for Bible school. That lasted for an hour, then off to town to pay the bills, do the banking, etc. before meeting June. She appeared at the appointed time, looking extremely English. She was wearing a lavender dress that encouraged her blond hair and violet eyes. June's mother really came from England—I don't know about her father. At any rate, June really looks like the typical English lady, who, according to tradition, has blond hair, violet eyes and a delicate complexion. It was nice to see June and talk about you, but the best part of the day was coming home to find two letters from you! Joy! Rapture!

Said letters were penned May 11 and 17-22 (started on 17 & finished 22). The latter letter was the first uncensored one to come through, and furthermore it came in about eight days (postmarked

5/24, received 6/2). It told of your trip to the mountains. Your freedom must have tasted wonderful to you, especially with such a beautiful setting. What with mountains, lakes, sunsets, rainbows, hikes, boat rides, and companionship with Beul you must have had a marvelous time. I'm so glad you got to go, Darling. I can hardly wait to see the pictures you took. Still unable to get any film here, so don't know when I can send you any pictures.

Wish I could write at length like you do. My letters must seem awfully short to you. Yours are so nice and long and wonderful. Teach me to write, Darling. And teach me to have thoughts, and after having them to express them. Will you teach me?

This morning was rather hectic (when I tried to do three jobs at once, but there wasn't any church tonight, so the afternoon and evening were restful. I took Mother's place in the Primary Dept. this morning, and at the same time saw to registration for Bible school, to distributing conference materials to young people, and a few other assorted duties—signing in choir, etc. The sermon this morning was excellent—"A Pattern for Living" was the theme, and he really bore down on it.

This afternoon was spent in study and deep (?) concentration on the opening session of Bible school. I need your prayers for this project, Darling. I know I can do it, but doing it affectively and inspiringly is another matter.

I miss you so—especially on Sundays. My thoughts continually creep around to the theme of
Our Love,
Dotty

Letters from Art to Dotty
Krematen, Austria
June 3, 1945 (5:00) [124-133]
My Darling,

'Tis an early hour this Sabbath morning. 'Tis early and all the attributes of late spring are in the air. I came on guard at four this morning: the moon still shown and the contrasts of color were black and white. Buildings were but outlines and trees appeared "en masse." Birds had begun to voice their approval of the day and the first one I heard was the cukoo.

In this rapidly changing light of advancing day, objects began to assume a gray tone. Down stream a bluish mist arose from the river. The bright green of the nearby field of wheat began to show more clearly. Overhead birds hastened this way and that, gathering the morning food. A couple of old crows disputed politics in a nearby tree and across the road a pigeon complained about breakfast—or the lack of it.

Ah Ha! The sun has just appeared above the horizon and its faint rays strike a new chord of color on the symphonic landscape. Smoke rises silently in the distance, more birds sing, the sun climbs quickly, dew drops reflect the morning sunlight as though there were thousands of tiny mirrors upon the ground. There goes a rooster with his harem. He stops, and with thumbs in his suspenders, leans back to declare himself supreme.

And so another day dawns in Springtime in Austria.

Noon

Yesterday I spent a most pleasant afternoon with a visit to the nearby town of Kresmunster. Two from my platoon were allowed to go on a sightseeing tour to visit the monastery there. We rode on trucks to our destination where we found Hungarian troops guarding the buildings and grounds. The monastery is located high on a hill overlooking the village of Kresmunster (pop. c 1200). Surrounding the entire grounds, which covered perhaps ten to twelve acres, was a high wall showing many signs of age. Within the second inner court (there were three) was an ancient moat built for the final line of protection in case of attack.

Our group of about thirty was met by a monk who was to show us through the cathedral. Speaking with the aid of an interpreter he gave us a bit of background material concerning the monastery. It was here that the Order of St. Benedict was founded in the year 1777. Prior to the advent of the Nazi Regime a college was conducted here, but this was finally closed entirely in Oct. of 1944 and many of the monks including the abbott were sent away in exile. Only seven monks remained, and the entire property was claimed by the invaders.

The lower portion of the cathedral which we now entered was built in about 1300; the upper portion three hundred years later. The predominate influence was Gothic but effects from the Near East were not entirely absent. A series of curves built into the front were intended to give the appearance of ocean waves.

Upon entering the first European cathedral of this size which I have seen from the inside, I was amazed at the elaboration of the decorations. Around the long pillars was stretched tapestry which dated from 1581. On the walls hung paintings ten to twelve feet in height. These were done about seventeen hundred and were very beautiful. The center ceiling contained a series of New Testament pictures and on either side were pictures from the Old Testament stories. Though smaller that those in the Stanford Chapel the effect was somewhat similar. These however seemed less ornate and more beautiful. In a glass casket on one side was the body of a martyr who died in the year 300 A.D.

We were taken down into the catacombs where the ashes of monks had been placed. Long rows of skulls stood watch and on one side was a large pile of bones.

We now moved out of the cathedral and across the grounds to the school building. This was the first skyscraper to be built in Europe and was constructed two hundred years ago. The building is 50 meters (162 ft.) high and required ten years to build. In each floor was a branch of the natural scenes. Among other things I saw what was claimed to be the earliest globe, made in 1056. There was a steam made in 1870 and a model of the first Air Pump. In the room containing astronomical instruments was an "Astronomy Table" with a glass top supposedly the only one of its kind in the world. One other at Ausberg was destroyed by bombs. Here too was a mummy 3,000 years old and the skeleton of a dinosaur 3 million years old. This building rather than being bombed had been used by our fliers as a point of reference in bombing Prague, Ling, Vienna, etc. Only in the latter days of the war were the grounds used by the Germans for supplies.

We spent about three hours in looking about, and I found the sights very interesting. It was certainly a diversion from the monotony of my daily routine. I may have very few other chances to see Europe and I want to take advantage of every opportunity I have.

Reports are that five day passes to Paris are beginning. Men going leave from the airport at Wels (only a few miles away) It seems that a large hotel has been taken over in the gay city and so food, housing and transportation would be G.I. It would be a wonderful trip, but I doubt that we will be here long enough for the openings to go around. Only two or three are allowed at a time.

> Our Love,
> Bushy

P.S. Mizpah

My Darling Wife,

This will probably be my last letter from this carefree spot on the Krems and there may be some delay before I am able to write again. Even this letter may be held up.

There is an old Bushing saying, "Never belief anything of what you see and only half of what you read." Approximately half of what I read does seem to have some basis for truth. However, the latest bit of information which I have gained from the newspapers seem to have a firm foundation. According to a clipping posted on a bulletin board near our post, the new Third Army under Patton is the largest in Am. history and contains eighteen divisions (12 inf. and 6 armed) for a total strength of 300,000 men. Further the clipping says that this Army was the first to learn that it was to go to the C.B.I (China Burma India) or more accurately to the Pacific. Patton is said to have made this statement on May 8, to his men. However, this was the first news that we had received other than innumerable rumors, as to our future.

The immediate prospects narrow down to two: we will go to the Pacific via the States or direct. I dare not become too hopeful and I think it better if we both prepare for the worst. After all, our division was one of the last to leave the States. Nevertheless, there remains the possibility that—! We shall hope and pray and remain patient.

In view of all this it is of course not advisable to mail any packages. I do hope we can continue to write regularly, but if there are delays I know you will understand. The one tremendous gain I have made in addition to my complete rest here has been to go a long way toward catching up on my correspondence. I am sure that I have written you more frequently and fully than ever before (possible exception—Camp Roberts Hosp.) and I have written Mother and Dad almost as much. To add to this I have written more than eighteen people since V-E Day. My latest letters were to Jean & Olson, John Hawkins, the Glathes, and Dr. Gates. Hope to write Dr. Shive and Joe Brown before leaving. Letters to Ken C. and Jim Garvin await receipt of their addresses. No letter as yet from either Ted, but I am sure that at our next stop will be able to see Ted K.

If I wander a bit please forgive me, Darling; there are several odds and ends that I wish to pick up. One is in regard to a few customs which I have noted here in Austria. The habit of shaking hands is a noticeable one and is practiced upon meeting and leaving (The Austrian appear to be a very friendly people). As I have mentioned before, the woman are very hard workers but I have yet to see men show any ambition. A third point of interest is the number of small shrines which are to be seen along every highway and byway. These vary from simple tin crosses to elaborate designs with two or three figures. These are found at crossroads, on bridges (there is one on ours), and many times at any convenient spot to be found. I wish I knew their full significance, but so far I have not been able to find out. I think that an opinion of the morals of these people would be one sided. The group with which some of the men "fraternize" is certainly not the highest type and another factor involved is that the general chaotic conditions which follow war always leads to a lowering of standards. Withal, free love does not appear to have the stigma placed upon it in the States.

To switch rapidly now to a totally unrelated subject, I want to say something concerning decorations given for combat services. At least in our outfit we have lost all faith in the awards which purportedly are given for varying degrees of outstanding service. The bronze stars which all of us received is merely for battle participation. As far as I know every man in the division received them whether he was twenty miles back or on the front lines. Now the silver star is more exclusive. It is given only upon proper recommendation by squad members, platoon leaders, etc. I shall cite but two examples of this award being given and you may draw your own conclusion as to how we feel. When our unit crossed the Danube near Regensburg we encountered the stiffest resistance that we met any where. Four or five in our company were killed and probably a dozen were wounded. During the advance, a twenty millimeter gun pinned our platoon down and to go farther was impossible. In the various attempts which were made to knock the gun out, a member of our squad (Pfc. Mornean) moved to a more advantageous position and fired one anti tank grenade from his rifle. The grenade failed to explode and thus did no damage. Nevertheless this man was awarded the silver star for "outstanding performance of duty" (or some such tommy rot) and was credited with silencing the 20mm.

A second example: During a three day period, our battalion advanced from Bayreuth to Amberg (a distance of about fifty miles), encountering varying degrees of resistance. From all reports we had expected to meet a determined stand before the city. However, we moved through the outskirts and into the heart of the city without finding more than a few scattered snipers. Yesterday I read a half a page of mimeographed tripe telling of the way in which our Bn. C.O.

"lead his troops for sixteen hours with complete disregard for his personal safety, applying pressure first here and then there, allowing the enemy no time to reorganize until the capture had taken place. There was much more even more disgusting. After we had entered the city the Bn. C.O. did march near the head of the columns, but the main gist of the citation was complete erroneous. He too wears the silver star, next medal to the Congressional.

No one can blame the men for having the star. They were given it at the recommendation of someone else, but the fact remains that the facts cited were not correct. It would be foolish to imply that every holder of the Silver Star did not earn it. Many deserve even more credit, and yet it is unfortunate that its value has been degraded to the point that G.I.'s in the line have no respect for it as an award.

It just occurred to me that you might look around for a couple of rolls of film just in case we have a chance to use them sometime in the next ten years or two months. I would be more than happy to get a few snaps of (not from) my lovely wife in case my direction is not U.S. 'ward.

This is being written a bit later,—in fact after supper is over and the evening mail in. Nothing from my wife but a letter from Mom dated May 27 (mailed 28th). Thus it arrived in 6 ½ days. Glad to get the wonderful news about the new baby girl. These lucky people! What I wouldn't give—! Along with all my losses I do not have Samarriet's address. Will try to write and include it in a letter to you. It's hard to realize that Mae is two years old. Just think what a start they have on us. Tsk! Tsk!

Also tonight came a letter from Ted K. He had just rated a trip to Bertchesgaden—lucky guy. Ted P. is having a gay time in Salzburg. It seems that the rumor which we have had for several days about moving tomorrow have blown over more swiftly than they came. Everything seems up in the air at the moment. Ted thinks that he may possibly get a chance to drop by and I certainly hope so. There is much to talk over with him.

At the rate I am writing letters, the squad supply of stationery is running dangerously low. We will have to hi-jack the Red Cross Director as he passes by. By the way, Ted sends his regards but said nothing about Cordy. Maybe she will spend some time with you this summer now that "Mom" is away. Say, you should get plenty of practice keeping house now. Don't try to do everything, since Mary Ruth must practice too. You have your man (did someone say "sucker"?) and she is still angling. Oh me.

All of this uncertainty must be hard for you to put up with, along with everything else. I long for the day when something of a stabilized order will return to this war torn world. Darling, no matter what comes,—separation for long months, days, and weeks of anxious waiting, perhaps suspense—in all of these things the great stabilizing force will come from our Faith in God and our complete trust in
Our Love,
Bushy
P.S. I. In separate envelope I send an issued statement of information—Austria. Very interesting.
C.S.II. "Mizpah"

Letter from Art to Dotty
Kematen Austria
June 6, 1945 (D. Day) [143-147]

My Dearest,

The sun sinks beyond the western hills; a few thin clouds are scattered, enough to make the fast falling even tide more beautiful. The birds sing a late song; laughter of children floats through the air, a watchful cat looks eagerly for a field mouse in the stubble where hay was cut today. My children play around my tent; three more are coming around the field.

A few minutes later.

It's no use, I must stop work when these folks come around. I cleaned up a great deal of odds and ends—coffee packets from C & F rations, sugar cubes, bread units (crackers), etc. These I divided among my kindergarten group. There faces shown in a way to make my heart sing. To return the gift they went away only to come back with eggs. Two of the boys try very hard to practice their English, and they say "Thank you" with perfect ennunciation.

We were told tonight to be prepared to move tomorrow morning at eight. We will leave any time after that. We will probably move only a short distance tomorrow, but this is the beginning. Our next stop for any length of time at all will be many miles from this spot I feel sure.

I shall miss the freedom of this spot. The Army has been very far away during these twenty-five days. On hot days I shall recall being able to strip down to my shorts, lie in the shade, or catch ball, write a letter or swim. I shall recall being able to bathe daily and keep clothes in good condition and clean.

I will enclose in this letter a two page article from April copy of Encore. There is little to add to its discussion except to say that I know of what he speaks. I believe that it "rarely happens in this world" that people find their own true loves, and yet I know that I have found the perfect compliment to my nature. The answer to my soul's deeper longing came when I found you and only as I live my life with you can I find happiness. As our love continues to grow day by day, so do we melt into one being, blessed by the perfect gift of His Love. Over and over again I am amazed and thrilled at the wonderous adventure of joining our lives together. We two have found Love.

According to all of the rules governing the separation of man and wife, I should not express feelings of loneliness or low spirits. However, I have broken these rules often before. I am lonely and I miss you, Darling. At times a wave of longing sweeps over me and the heart's desire becomes almost overpowering. I can but pray that God will hasten the day when our lives will be reunited, I love you.

Eternally thine,
Bushy

Letter from Dotty to Art
June 8, 1945 [typed]

Darling,

I am ashamed of me. Can you forgive me? I didn't write you yesterday or day before. Tsk. Tsk. Tsk. Oh, Tsk. I plead guilty on two excuses -- I've been very busy and last night I wasn't feeling well. Today I am quite O.K. and very much in love with a certain husband of mine, Last night I dreamed about him -- he had returned from distant lands, and was attempting to make love to me (delightful), but for some strange reason there were a great number of people around who just wouldn't vamoose and leave us alone. Can you imagine that?

Good news I have! At long last the bonds have starting coming in. I now have in my possession the two bonds for February and the two for March. As soon as I saw one of them, I knew how the mixup occurred. They have your name as the person to whom the bond should go, and my name as the co-owner or beneficiary. I say both co-owner and beneficiary because I am listed as co-owner on the ten dollar bonds and as beneficiary on the twenty five dollar bonds. Should I try to get them to reverse our names on that or let them keep on coming as they are? On the one hand trying to change it might only cause more confusion, and on the other hand leaving the present set-up like it is may cause the same mistake that has happened in the past to occur again. What to do? Your opinion, please.

Bible School continues apace. It rained all last night and was pouring down in a tropical sort of way this morning when it came time to go to the Church, so our attendance was a bit slim today. We had 18 Juniors, and it was the first time this week that attendance in our department had dropped below 20. Things didn't go so well today, for several reasons. Due to the rain they didn't get their outside play period, and so were restless before closing time. On account of not having enough helpers the handwork has dragged a bit, and some are losing interest in the projects they have started and do not want to finish them. I am certainly glad glad this is Friday, and I can have a breathing spell before Monday. Welllll, for a small breath, anyway.

Florence got a letter from Carl today dated May 30, in which he stated that he would be heading for a French port in a couple of days, from which he is to take off for the States. So, it looks as if we will be seeing Mr. Alette (pardon, Pfc. Alette) in a week or so! Which reminds me--no mail from you in three days, so I am expecting a stack in tomorrow's mail. This morning's paper carried an item about the homecoming of Gen. Patton, and I have been wondering whether that will mean anything at all with regard to your future. Probably not. Wish you were a general--for a while, anyway. All of them seem to be coming home. Doggonnit, they get all the breaks. Yeah? Who says they get all the breaks? I says. Wellll, they don't. They don't?? Well who does get them, then? I'll bite, who!

I am, obviously, at the office, and must get back to work, which I can tackle with vim now that I have written to my beloved. I am living for the day when spoken words will take the place of written, when actuality will replace unreality, when separation is a thing of the past and we may continue making true progress in

OUR LOVE,
Dotty

Letter from Art to Dotty
Near Bad Hall, Austria
June 11, 1945 (Mon. [153-162]

My Darling Wife,

The sun shines with gratifying warmth upon my face. I have just finished washing clothes and cleaning my rifle and have now a few moments of free time. A very good time I should say to write my dear wife.

If my memory serves me correctly, this will be chapter five in the adventuresome mishaps of one Jr. Bushing or "we won the war with walking." I believe that in my last account we were preparing to leave the area of Bitche. One important event I failed to mention. While on the outskirts of Laze-Bitche, the BAR man in my squad (William Giesking) was sent to the hospital with several bones broken in his foot. This had occurred during the "Death March." Now the weight of the M-1 Rifle is 9 lbs. plus 1lb. for the bayonet. Our belt of ammo amounts to another 10 lbs. As asst. BAR man, I carried about 6 magazines of BAR amo—wt. 15 lbs. When Giesking left, I was given the priviledge of carrying his weapon (wt. 22 lbs.) and the ammunition for it (wt. 30 lbs.). I bore new burdens! (As I think I have failed to mention previously, I am still the possessor of the Browning Automatic Rifle in our squad).

Before going on, allow me to insert a few dates which I have just found. Many of the later dates I will not have, but I shall peg the incidents whenever possible. We were in Doudeville, France, from Feb 8 to Mar. 10. At Tarquinpol March 12 & 13th. On the 14th we were in Miesenthal (Mizenthal) and we reached Bitche (also Bitch) on the 16th.

Leaving there again by foot we began another very long and very tiring march. Moving forward also was a convoy with the rear echelon commanders. We slogged along. On this march I saw Marvin Flowerman for the second time over here. The convoy was moving very slowly and I passed Marvin two or three times. We yelled back and forth but couldn't say much. Mile after mile we continued. I developed a pain in the arches of my feet which was to last for weeks. Sometimes after dark we took a break which lasted for two or three hours. We had no supper and lay on a damp hillside—cold, hungry, dog tired, while a bright moon shown down from a misty sky. We slept as best we could. About eleven o'clock our meal arrived and we ate hungarly. Artillery was bursting in the distance as we began climbing a long hill. I do not have the name of the town but it was very close to the German border. We passed through the town and on to a very high ridge. The moon was low; artillery was falling around the nose of the hill. We moved into positions occupied by the 5th. Here we remained for two days. In the second night five men from my squad went out on a reconnaissance patrol to found out the location of a German 88 which continued to give us trouble. They earned the combat Badge that night and accomplished their mission. On March 22, we moved down into the draw in front of our positions. As I jumped the small brook I passed from French soil into that which was German. Part of our march was across country and part was by road. We passed through our first German town. Clusters of children stared at us in curious silence. We moved on. In another town we stopped for a break, expecting to spend the night here. An elderly German respond to request for "wasser" by coming out with a large container. When one G.I. hesitated before drinking, the old man drank from the can. We crossed the border near the City of Piramasen which was taken by other units of the division (5th, I think). At last we stopped in the town of Vinnigen and filleted. This was our first experience in houses and was most gratifying. We remained here a second day and managed to work, shave and clean several bits of clothing. Looting began for the first time. Cows were cornered and milked (as we marched into the town, I saw men rush around a building during a ten minute break. They returned with canteen cups filled with milk fresh from the cow.) I was asked to accompany one of the lieutenants on a mission to check all houses for Nazi soldiers on the following day. I was to go along as interpreter. From a hillside on one side of town I caught a distant view of the famed Siegfried Line. Late in the afternoon we were issued ETU ribbons and about eleven o'clock that night we loaded on trucks and tanks. Six of us are atop of one truck loaded with cans of gasoline. We unrolled a canvas cover and made ourselves as comfortable as possible. As we rolled on, we began to pass the outer defense of the Siegfried Bastian. Heavy concrete pillboxes, row upon row of concrete teeth designed to halt armed advance, field fortification of every description. The moon shown clear and we rolled swiftly forward. I thought of the millions spent in time and labor to construct this great defense work. We rolled on. The country seemed ideal for defense. Massive ridges bordered deep ravines and the terrain seemed almost impossible, except as we moved along a highway. My sleep was restless as I tried to find a comfortable spot atop a gas truck riding into Germany on my twenty-third birthday. As the day dawned we found ourselves in a productive valley, with row upon row of grapevine on every hillside. Vineyards seemed to be every where and there was little evidence that fighting had taken place here. We had no food but managed to bum cans of ration from the truck drivers. Finally in the early afternoon we detrucked in a large field and drew a food ration. Along the entire route we had seen many abandoned fox holes and some German equipment. These holes were usually more elaborate than ours since they were dug by slave labor and dug long beforehand. The zig zag form (^^^) was most often seen. Later in the afternoon we again mounted trucks, and continued on our way. The city of London was visible but we missed it by about ten kilometers. During one of the many pauses along the way, we learned that a convoy like our own from the 5th Regt. had been fixed upon by civilians while passing through a town already surrendered. I should mention that in all of these towns through which we passed white flags were flown from almost every window. Or the roads over which we passed streamed long rows of civilians. They pushed carriages, carts, bicycles. They carried bundles, bags, and trunks. They cried and were sober. They were fleeing and I thought of a dozen different races who had been forced to flee in similar fashion. I recalled stories told by Meurous Heymann of her flight from Amsterdam when the Nazi power struck Holland. I wondered if these people saw the irony of tables turned.

We drove through the streets of Speyer, a large and beautiful town. As we passed on North we saw abandoned 88's left by the fleeing enemy. The body of one who had remained lay alongside the walls of a cemetery. His fox hole was now but a hole in the ground.

Our destination, Otterstadt, was reached long after darkness fell. Our position was along a dyke overlooking a branch of the Rhine. The River itself was only a few hundred yards away. My BAR and team were placed on an open flank; there was enemy reported in the woods two hundred yards away.

The story of the "Watch on the Rhine" is a chapter in itself and I will save it for a later time. It was here that we experienced some of the most exciting (I cannot say thrilling) events of combat.

Even as I wrote, two big letters came from you. Written on the 1st & 2nd of June they were postmarked on the 4th. Thus they arrived in just six and a half days. So glad that you had the conflab [discussion] with June Evans. I hope to look up her husband soon, but after all he is a Lt. Remember, I'm still a Pfc.

After writing last night, Beul and I took a long walk in an attempt to lift our morale. We reached "L" Co. and talked with MacIntosh for several minutes and then returned. Our spirits were lifted by merely getting away from camp and having a chance to brag to each other about our very wonderful wives. As the fog moved in from the creek, we retuned to our barn and to bed.

Our move has been delayed again. It will come shortly. Supposedly we will go into houses and training will begin soon after our arrival. Hmmm!

Darling, my prayers are for your complete success as the work of the Bible school goes on. I know that you will do a grand job. Poor Dad must be having a terrible time with his chow. Tsk! Tsk! With all your cooking

> I love you still
> Bushy

Letters from Dotty to Art

Friday, June 15
1945

My Dearest,

Afraid I can't finish this tonite for it is late, but I did want to tell you about what a nice birthday I had. Mary Ruth relented and gave me my presents at breakfast, because there wouldn't be much time at supper. And besides—who wants to wait till supper! A package from Jamestown arrived yesterday, and it contained the most beautiful white pocket book I've almost ever seen. The family presented me with an adorable table cloth to be embroidered. Mary Ruth has applied for the job of making it, and I may give it to her. Now don't get excited over this—Grandmother Parmelee gave me a pair of pink booties for the babe we will some day have. The choices present was one that came from you (according to Beulah), so naturally I liked that best. It was the cream and sugar to our china. Cute as a bug's ear and just so pretty. Thank you, Darling. You are so wonderful. And I love you—oh how I love you. Come here immediately—to collect some of the kisses I've been saving for you. I'd rather have you for my birthday than anything else in the wide world.

Never in all my life have I been wished happy birthday so many times by so many people. Word leaked and somehow to the kids that it was my birthday, and they sang "Happy Birthday" to me after we got assembled in the Junior Dept. this morning, and all day long they kept it up.

Saturday night.

Well, well. I am quite a few miles from yesterday. Around 50, to be exact. The familiar sights and sound of the cabin are music to my ears and delightful visions to my eyes. But it would be better to start the story of this day from the beginning. It has some good ones in it.

Mary Ruth and I arose at 6 as is our custom on Saturday. We got Dad's breakfast and ate with him, then read the paper and finally were ready for work. We got out the washing machine, hitched up the tubs, and filled them all with water. Unlike last Saturday the weather was perfect for washing. But the machine took a notion to go pluey, so we did the entire washing by hand. Well, that is , we got about 4/5 through when I had to quit & get ready to go on the Bible School picnic. During the morning Flo came in with a birthday present—it was a rose chenille bath mat which makes quite an addition to our hope chest.

The kids were all waiting impatiently at the church when we arrived, and soon we got packed into a bus and traveled quickly to the picnic grounds. There were swings and see-saws for the youngsters, and a creek with a concrete bottom, there were balls and things for the older ones to play with, so all had a big time. Lunch was varaciously consumed, and ice-cream for all made the occasion festive. We had a number of games and relays planned for after lunch, but before these got under way there was a tragic accident that put a stop to everything, more or less. One little girl fell out of a swing and broke her arm. After that all the other kids wanted to go home. Se we went, and that was the end of that picnic. I arrived home hot & thirsty and anxious so see if there was any mail. There were two birthday cards propped up against a gorgeous pot of flowers. The tag on the flowers said "Love, Bushy." Darling, how thoughtful of you! I dashed upstairs to pack with a light heart, thinking what a dear sweet husband I possessed, when the doorbell rang, and there was the florist with more flowers! Huge beautiful glads these were, of a warm glowing pinkish-orange color. Mary Ruth was about to blow up because the flowers didn't arrive yesterday—I knew there was something from you that hadn't come from the way M.R. acted and dropped hints all around. Such a lovely surprise they were, Darling. I am so excited and pleased. And so in love with The Most Wonderful Husband in the world! Alas I didn't have time to enjoy the beautiful posies, for we left for the mountains a few minutes after the flowers came. "We" includes Flo, Aunt Carol, Uncle West, Addison, and Aunt Lois (Mrs. Cain). Flo and I put on our bathing suits first thing and jumped (?) into the river, which was very cooling and pleasant to our hot sweaty bodies. I washed my hair in the river as part of my dip. The water was just cool enough to be decidedly refreshing and I enjoyed it thoroughly. It was the first time I had been swimming in two years!

Sunday morning.

Looks as if I'll never finish this, but it will be long for a change.

Flo and I sit by the river as we write our respective loved ones. The mountains rise in familiar, beloved tiers, very blue against the paler blue sky. The water attracts my eyes with its movement just as a campfire draws all glances to its core. And as I sit here I long for your presence at my side. The rugged beauty of this place would make such a lovely setting for

> Our Love,
> Dotty

Monday
June 18, 1945

Darling,

By shifting my eyes from this paper a little to the left, I see a vase of beautiful gladioli, and I can think of nothing but your sweet thoughtfulness.

Today came your letter of June 6, the first I've had in almost a week. In it was Plato's discussion. It was wonderful, and quite true in spots, for what he said holds just as much water today as in his day. Your remarks are even more wonderful than Plato's. I never cease to marvel that you found me and I found you and we realized we belonged. It was surely planned thus by a hand greater than ours. The infinite unity of our oneness continually amazes and thrills me. Your happiness is my happiness, your life my life. I now have a much clearer conception of the meaning of the verse "For me to live is Christ." I love you. My soul revels of our separation.

I suppose by now you are somewhere else than Kervatin, Austria. What did you mean by "our next stop for any length of time…will be many miles from this spot"? Would it be possible for you to tell me which direction you are moving in? And whether or not you are headed for home? The suspense is killing me!

I got back from the mountains this morning just 15 minutes before time to go to work, refreshed in body and spirit. Uncle West, Flo, and I came back this morning, the rest stayed a while longer. Wish I could have.

Did I tell you that the lady who had been acting as principal of our Bible School fell and broke her leg the day before the school closed? What a thing to happen.

Gen. "Ike" was given a royal reception in Washington today. Oh for the homecoming day of Pfc. Bushing! That will indeed be a happy day for

> Our Love,
> Dotty

Near Bad Hall, Austria
June 13, '45
My Dearest,

Rolls have been rolled; packs made. A big game of pinnacle (sp?) goes on in the room. A few men read and a few write. Outside the day is dark and dreary. Water stands in small and large puddles everywhere, a cool wind blows. In the next two hours we will load up our equipment and march to the "bahnhof" (RR station) in Bad Hall. There we will wait for at least an hour or two. I trust there will be no rain. We will load on box cars—thirty men in each small car. The floor will be covered with straw and there will be a few cracks. The wheels will seem square as we begin to roll out of the station. Slowly and painfully the pint sized engine will gather all of its steam together. As we pass through Keaten and Neuhofen some of the "Austrian friends" may wave to the Yanks who gave them chewing gum, chocolate, and other sweets. Our remaining stay in this country will be a matter of hours.

A flood of impressions and events crowd my mind as I think of Austria. I recall that our first in the country was spent in one of the most modern apartment houses which I have seen in all Europe. I recall those final days of the war when Nazi soldiers came to us literally in droves in an effort to escape the Russians. I recall highways lined with refugees from almost every country in Europe—shouting, waving throngs who saluted in varying degrees of proficiency and waited expectantly for cigarettes to be thrown to them. It is most difficult to speak of the Austrian people. (Aboard train awaiting departure) As we learned to know them during the Kematen interlude we found Romanian, Italian, Polish, Russian, Czech, German, and a few Austrian. Four of my kindergarten group were Romanian, two or three Austrian and probably one or two German. But the people for the most part were very friendly. These children represented the limit of my fraternizing but they did provide some of the most pleasant houses of my stay. Other lasting impressions of Austria are of mountains, snow-capped and remote, lakes, cold and colorful, resort towns, row boats, sailboats, racing streams, ancient monasteries. Yes, with all this, complete rest and general laxness of regimentation. My stay in Austria has been pleasant.

The news is semi official that we are heading for occupation. There will be training along with it, of course, and it is rumored that some of us will be taken for re-enforcements in the Pacific. This will likely be for

Art & Friends

men with low points. Whether or not I will be able to partake in the educational program and to what extent—all of this remains a mystery.

I have noticed a marked change in the reaction of men to good news. On Easter we were in Weiskirchen, near Frankfurt, in the barroom. We were all elated with the rumor that fighting for us was over and we were A.O. Now such news hardly causes a ripple of excitement. We know by experience that the changing situation in the tides of war can change our status. All of us are now from Missouri.

Since coming to the company assembly area where our platoon has been together again, Beul, Sod, Price, and I have gravitated together more and more. We attend church, band concerts, swim, etc. together. Yesterday we walked into Bad Hall just for the stroll. Since the theatre was almost the only place open to us, we went there. The place was empty except for a few women who were cleaning and a G.I. playing a piano behind the screen. We walked into a booth and enjoyed Debussy and a few other classical works. A performance of the 14th band was scheduled for the evening and "reserve" signs had been placed for officers on the doors of the best boxes. In a playful mood we placed them on the boxes with a poorer view.

A brief stop here. The boys are out on the platform stretching their legs and whistling at an occasional female passing through the station. There seems little evidence of the bombing here which was so apparent in Rosenheim. The station is a very large one, the largest I have seen in Germany.

Friday—Gungberg

I awoke this morning with a prayer on my lips for you on this your birthday. I shall write my birthday letter to you a bit later today. At the moment I shall hasten to prepare this letter for the mail which leaves in a few minutes.

Briefly, we arrived last night in our new home—a school building in Gungburg, not far from Ulm. We have nice mattresses to sleep on, running water, and electric lights. The set-up seems not too bad.

Our battalion will begin by training for a month while the two other battalions will occupy. After the first month, we will occupy for two. As I mention before, there will be a great deal of shifting of personnel. Where I stand as an individual I do not know. I have many things about which to write and I hope to bring my writing up to date this afternoon.

Throughout the day I shall be thinking in a very special way of you. I hope that my plans for your birthday were not delayed by slow mail. Perhaps one year from today I shall be able to celebrate the event in the proper manner.

I love you with all of my heart. Bushy

June 14, 1945
Rosenheim
[A LISTING OF OBSERVATIONS FROM TRAIN]

Box car overturned
[RR] Tracks in air
Giant craters
Houses blown apart
Engines shot to pieces
Engine cut in two with a direct bomb hit

Water main still broken
Laborers exerting their puny efforts in an effort to clear
Germany, which will never recover
    as a nation
[SO MUCH FOR MY PROPHETIC SKILL; MARSHALL PLAN
WAS STILL A DREAM]

Letter from Art to Dotty
Gunzburg, Germany
June 15, 1945 – 09:00 [170-173]

My Dearest Heart,

A beautiful sun is sinking low in the western sky and the insects of a summer evening play in its horizontal rays. Birds sing a vesper hymn; the strains of a violin are heard in the distance and a piano tinkles from a room in our barrack building. I write from a secluded corner in the little garden behind our new home.

I awoke this morning from a deep sleep with a prayer on my lips; a prayer for you on this very special day. My thoughts have been with you almost constantly as I have carried on the activity of the day.

The medium of a letter seems but a faint signal by which I tell you I am here, thinking of you alone. How I long to be with you, to hold you close to my heart, to wish you all of the happiness that you so justly deserve in the years that lie ahead. How I long to whisper my dreams of working for you,—no, it is far more than that. It is working <u>with</u> you, sharing life's joys and sorrows; building a home, Christ-led; rearing children, Christ-blessed; finding the satisfying joy that can come only as two find the perfect union.

The greatest gift in the world is the Love of our Savior. Deep within your heart is emplanted the Spirit of Him who revealed to us God's Love. I pray that your vision of His Face may continue clear and bright and that in the future years your reliance upon His power will be ever increasing and rewarding.

From the very depths of my heart I would offer my love to you; to provide the needs of every day living and a bit more, to be the father of your children, loving and caring for them with a love approaching that which I bear for you; to work with you, play with you, worship with you —to love you with all of the love of which I am capable.

I do not even know that my plans have been carried out today. More than six weeks ago I wrote Mary Ruth explaining my desire for you to have flowers and a present today and it was two months ago that I asked the First Sgt. to send the money to "Mom." I do hope that both arrived in time.

'Tis time for bed and I shall end my day as I began, with a prayer for you on this, the 15th of June. With all my heart

I love you,

Bushy

P.S. Mizpah

Letter from Art to Dotty

Gunzburg, Germany

June 16, 1945 [174-184]

Darling,

For the first time in what seems weeks I heard from you today. Actually it has been within the past week but it certainly seems far longer. Your letter of the 7th came along with Mary Ruth's letter of the 5th. In the news you tell of the progress of the Bible school, the pictures taken by Jack Mehoney and the questions concerning my adventures, I want to go back and recount in more detail our trip from Austria to Gunzburg.

We left Bad Hall on schedule, however there was no straw. With a bit of a break I found a lucky spot in our box car. Five of us took over a small room in which the brakemen must have ridden. There was a desk, a couple of mats, an ancient stove and even a small toilet. The room was much warmer than the outer box car and I slept better than on many pullmans. We traveled north to Linz and it was there that we went to bed. We awoke on Thursday morning on the outskirts of Rosenheim. (I presume that we passed through Salzburg during the night, and only about twelve miles from Berchtesgaden.)

Sunday Night

I have seen rail centers that have been badly bombed but Rosenheim was in the worst shape of any that I have been near. Long lines of box cars had been burned; some were lying on their tops. Tracks had been tossed like baling wire into the air, and giant craters spotted the yard. Along the row of houses, I saw buildings blown completely apart with naked walls standing precariously straight and tall. Many engines stood where they had been straffed with holes every where; one engine had been cut into by a bomb. Around the rail yard, laborers worked in small groups, exerting their puny efforts in an effort to clear the rubble. Their tools were picks and shovels.

Darling, from what I have seen I am convinced that Germany will never recover as a world power. The destruction has been too vast and too complete. In an integrated economic machine such as Hitler developed, certain links making up the chain were indispensable. Many, too many, of these indispensable links are gone. Entire cities have been wiped from the map. (I have seen such cities as Bayreuth and Darmstadt; there are dozens which I have not seen.) Problems of housing, transportation, distribution, medical care, education —these are but a few of the basic links which have been smashed. I do not believe that the unifying force will be found which would create the one gigantic effort necessary to rebuild the Germany Reich.

Well, I diverged slightly from the tale of my travel. Our long train of box cars was pulled from Rosenheim by an electric engine. The electrification of every village and hamlet seems to have been the successful aim of Hitler. With some speed we moved north through rolling farm country, Ostermuchen, Grafing, and finally Munchen (or Munich as we spell it). To my complete surprise the rail yards there were almost untouched. These yards extended for miles it seemed and I soon realized how true it has been stated that Munich is the rail hub of Southern Germany. In the station we saw two or three streamlined diesel trains which appeared unhurt and were certainly quite modern.

After a delay of two or three hours, we moved on again, this time passing through Olching, Mering, and into Augsburg. In the city of Olching we were but five miles from Dachau, the scene of the infamous prison camp. In Augsburg we detrained and loaded on trucks. For the first time since we have ridden in trucks over here, we had plenty of room. Augsburg appeared to have seen little of war, trolleys were in operation and activity seemed normal. G.I.'s dotted almost every corner. In the outskirts of town we pulled onto the superhighway (autobahn) leading farther west. The highway is as modern as any in the States being four lane with a center protection. In one section along the way we say plane after plane which had been partial destroyed in its parking place along the road. (Many of these were jet propulsion) Farther along we saw a stretch perhaps a mile and a half long, in which the center division in the road had been take out and the strip camouflaged. This had been used as a runway and the planes were able to taxi along the highway to their various parking places. Very practical and ingenious I would say.

We arrived in Gunzburg late in the evening, and we were overjoyed to find our new home in a school building. In other letters I have briefly described the general situation here. Already some of the advantages of garrison life have borne fruits. On Friday night I went to the theatre which Special Service has taken over to see "Brazil." Last night I returned again to see a show put on by a group of Russians who come from a nearby camp. The movie was fair, but the Russian show was most entertaining. The program began with three or four choral numbers which were various national songs. These were followed by a number of dances representing the various cultural groups present. There was a Serbian Dance with two other types from the East, a Gypsy number, a Spanish Dance, and the national dance of the Ukraine. One of the soloists possessed a voice far above average even by our standards, along with a pleasing personality. These qualities soon made her the hit of the evening.

The real pleasure of garrison life came today when I entered a civilian church for worship for the first time since I attended church with you in Columbus. We are blessed with a Lutheran Church here in town and this morning the pews were packed.

It was good to be in a regular service again. I feel that I have allowed a veiled curtain to separate me from God. Similes are often misleading but I think that the one comparing the individual to a radio set is particularly appropriate. In the old set which we have at home the stations tend to fade and others cut in unless the dial is adjusted constantly. I find that unless I maintain a constant alertness my receiving set tends to lose contact with God. Constant vigil in prayer, reading, and meditation are essential.

Yesterday showers were installed and I took my first shower since the latter part of April. That is another of the many advantages but tomorrow the disadvantages begin. We have a training schedule calling for "fast speed marches", and other items which have little appeal. After a month of this we occupy again if we are still here. I suppose that the rapid changes in status are reported in the papers there. One day the picture seems rosy; the next it is black. I have learned to be rather indifferent to these changing tides.

Here in the school building I have found a large number of Nazi magazines filled with pictures extolling various phases of the Third Reich. I hope to be able to send them home. The photography is excellent and the propaganda punch powerful. Each magazine is an entity dealing with any one of a wide variety of subjects. "Hitler in Italy," "Mussolini in German", "Hitler Youth," "Aus dem Schwarzwald," "Passions-spiele in Obermmergan," "1930 Olympics in Berlin," etc. I shall send these at the first opportunity.

"The Poop" Third Battalion 14th Infantry Newspaper
dated June 16, 1945 in Gunzburg, Germany

On the train from Austria I read that condensation of the book The
Road to Serfdom, dealing with the dangers of a "planned economy" in
our society. I hope you have read at least this condensation if not the
book. Just in case you can find it in the Pocket Book Ed. I wish you
would send it in a package some time. The use of such propaganda
instruments as these magazines which I described above is more
apparent as I couple them with the trends pointed out in this book.

I cannot speaking of fraternization without a mounting feeling of
disgust. The enjoyment I had as I played with my little Austrian friends
sinks into oblivion as I see the "double-standard' of morals being
practiced by an appalling number of men. For a single fellow to run
after these German women is bad enough but when married men with
children seek their pleasure and return to laugh and joke about it—my
respect for these individuals sinks to an all-time low. I am deeply
thankful for such friends as Beul, Sod, and a few others who share my
disgust.

241

From these base matters of my surroundings I turn to take renewed faith and comfort in the depth of our Love. It's basis is spiritual and its existence eternal.

Ever thine,
Bushy

Letter from Art to Dotty
Gunzburg, Germany
June 19, 1945 [185-190]

My Dearest Heart,

Again from my nook in the corner of our backyard, at the officer's private table, I write on a memorable occasion. Three years ago tonight at this very moment I sat with you at the picnic grounds while a half moon shed a quiet glow upon the scene. With no little confusion I expressed the inner-most feelings of my heart. Before we left that spot you had made the most wonderful promise that I could ever hope to hear. You had promised to share with me the adventure of living. The culmination of a long latent dream within me became reality, and the way was open for us to plan our future lives together. Day by day and hour by hour I continue to work and plan for our future. I continue to pray that I might be worthy of your love and worthy to be called your husband. I love you.

Today while standing in chow line I thumbed through a booklet "On Building Your Own Home." The subject is not new to my thinking but I gleaned a few bits of information from the pamphlet. Of course, it will be some years yet before we will face the problems of building for that indicates permanency. However, the day will come and we will be prepared for it. Prefabrication will have gone a long way by that time and the cost of houses with all of the modern conveniences should be within our reach.

Tuesday Night

Just returned from our first choir practice since France. Good crowd of twenty and this only from the Battalion here in town. The other two battalions will be brought in later—I hope. With an organ and a church the situation will be far better than formerly. A second incentive to bring up the numbers is the fact that we will be using our training time for practice.

We finished our second day of training with two inspections of weapons—one this morning and one after retreat. The schedule is very much like basic with exercise, close order drill, marches, etc. etc. So far everything is more or less half-hearted. I do not think that we will kill ourselves.

Tonight came your letter of June 4th along with the latest Hearth Log. Many laughs came from the squad as they read the account of my "improved" C rations. Am always glad to hear that the Bible school work is going well. Good practice, my Dear. Last night came your letter of the 8th, telling of the arrival of the bonds. Although I regret the mix up, I think that at least for the present we had best leave it. I shall enquire further into the matter.

* Wednesday Morning

'Twas time for lights out before I could finish last night and I will probably not be able to complete the letter even now. I just came up from noon chow. A shortage of salt has caused much consternation in the kitchen, but we still eat the stuff. An interesting situation has arisen in regard to our food which is worthy of note. The stage has been reached already where a crowd of perhaps a dozen small children mill around the side yard where we wash our mess kits. They carry buckets with the aim, of course, to get whatever scraps are available. They often get what is not an inconsiderable amount, particularly when the food is unpalatable. Today I walked toward the line with one swallow of cocoa left in my cup. Just as I brought it to my lips, half a dozen children cried out and held their cups before me. I didn't have the heart to drink it in front of them, so I merely walked on. I feel a bit brutal about giving these people food, etc. When it is in excess, all right; but I think that we are making beggars out of the younger generation. I think I mentioned before how we are often followed by small kids crying "chew gum," or "chocolade."

Another side light concerns the way in which the Germans, grown ups and children alike, go after American cigarettes. I came out of the first show a few nights ago and stood watching the G.I.'s file in for the second. As they flipped away their butts the surrounding group of kids did everything but fight for the tobacco. One or two grown ups were as guilty as the kids. Wherever G.I.'s stand around smoking, there is certain to be a furtive-eyed German watching for a chance to pick up a cigarette.

Our orientation programs are proving to be a bit above the average, and may improve. We discussed compulsory military training at some length yesterday. I regret to find that the general suppressive effect of Army regimentation has tend to make me more and more reticent about expressing myself. Nix goed!

In order to get this in the afternoon mail, I shall continue writing tonight in another letter. My love is always with you.

Thine own,
Bushy

P.S. Ted is in Augsburg

* Letter from Art to Dotty
Gunzburg, Germany
June 22, 1945 [191-196]

My Dearest Heart,

Yesterday I was the proud recipient of your letter written on the 11th . For some reason I seem to be getting very few letters this week, but I suppose that a stack will be forth coming. These delays only make me more anxious to hear from you and increase the excitement of seeing those now famous blue envelopes.

Let me hasten to assure you that the risk was slight as I played with my kindergarten in Austria. Ike himself has made the statement that the non-fraternization policy did not apply to "very small children." In the second place but of less direct importance, the general attitude even by the officers in regard to the enforcement of the rules has been an attitude of laziness. Even before we left Austria the trend seemed to indicate a gradual abandonment of the once strict policy. Probably for home consumption, the law will stand but it will be nominal. In Austria even our officers were guilty of fraternizing and to an extent beyond that of playing with the children. Price, "Sod", Beul & I claimed a new B.A. degree (Batchelers of Austria) since we were almost the only men in the platoon who did not have a "girl." The things that went on were disgusting. I think it needless to assure you, My Love, that your husband will never be guilty of any notion of which he would be ashamed to relate in full detail to you. After seeing some of the things that I have seen here, I little wonder that homes are broken and marriage goes on the rocks. For some of these men, love is nothing more than physical pleasure to be gratified when and how possible. They seem to have absolutely no concept of the deep and abiding love which can and does exist in holy union.

The financial report exceeded my fondest hope. Nice going, Bud! I hope that we can make it $2,000 by the time I leave the service. The $300 mustering out pay will go a long way toward that goal.

On Wednesday I received my duffel bag which had been left behind at Tarquimpol. It contained many small items which I was eager to get, not the least of which was my little note book. I shall endeavor to continue to fill its pages as I did before I had to leave it behind. I was also glad to get my Bible again. With my duffel bag on hand I will not have to carry everything I own on by back. I picked up a very nice locker in which to keep my equipment and clothing. As I write, I wiggle my toes in the freedom of a worn pair of cloth slippers which I had tucked away. They feel wonderful, after wearing combat boots for so long.

Last night I dreamed of coming home to you from a normal day's work as a civilian. There was an overflow of deep joy and happiness as I kissed you and set down with you at the evening table. How I long for that day to become reality. I love you, Darling.

The field of entertainment seems to be opening for us as never before. On Wednesday evening I heard the first real concert that I have enjoyed since the boat ride over. Beul and I went to hear a German string quartet render a group of classical pieces from Beethoven and Hayden (?sp). The program closed with a delightful Swedish folk song. It was a real thrill to hear good music once again. There is to be another concert on Sun., which I of course will attend. Our choir practice continues and we hope to attain some degree of proficiency. The number is still small but it will grow. Beginning next week we will practice two mornings per week (during a training period) and one evening. We had our first U.S.O. show today. Of course, it was geared to please the average G.I.'s taste. Just as in my Restoration Period the most common means of creating a funny situation is by innuendoes and plays on the subject of sex. It is interesting to see the similarity in the minds of the average G.I. and the average play goer in the time of Congreve & Wycherley.

Our food has improved a 100% in the past few days. We are beginning to get pastries again and yesterday I had my first Coco-Cola on this side. Tonight we had both ice cream & pie. Oh joy!

I remained in tonight to write you a very long letter but before I was well started MacIntosh dropped by. He is here in town but this is the first chance I have had to talk with him. We always enjoy catching up on politics, Far East, Stanford etc.

Tonight I had a long letter from Dick which I shall discuss in greater detail later. He is working in Martin's Ferry, Ohio, for the summer. There are still a few questions in his mind as to his future.

I have another Bn. paper which I shall send in totem since it has several good articles which I think you will enjoy. Also a couple of pictures. By the way, I do not intend to subscribe to the Inf. Journal. I have also a write up on the area around Doudeville where we were located for the first month of our stay in Europe. These papers I will send in a separate envelope rather than over load this one.

Today one of the fellows received films which he had sent out recently. From the entire roll, two pictures were printed: one of your husband and one of another dog. I enclose the former. I sent two to Mother & Dad so give the extra one to Sis or Mom if you like. I hope to have some better shots when the pictures which Beul and I took come back.

Sat. morning,

More pictures which I enclose next letter. Also SS collar insignia in other letter mail going out right now and I will try to make it. Dreamed again of you last night. Always I dream & pray for

Our Love,
Bushy

Letter from Art to Dotty
Gunzburg, Germany
24 June, 1945
Sunday Evening

Darling,

Yesterday came your letters of the 9th, 10th and 14th and tonight came your letter of the 12th. I am so glad to hear that Roland & Helen are in Knoxville and that you three will be able to have a few get togethers. What I wouldn't give to be in on that mountain trip. Mother writes today that on the 11th they received four letters from ranging from May 6th to June 1st. Oh this mail! As perhaps she has written you, their work is piling up again but they are able to handle it. Hope you will be able to visit with them again soon.

My luck continues good and I am reaping a few of the rewards in the entertainment world. Yesterday afternoon I just finished a rousing volleyball game when the C.Q. (Change of Quarters) came out to say that one man from the first platoon could go to a concert in Augsburg. My eyes began to sparkle and I spoke up before it was to late. (Actually Beul is perhaps the only other one in the platoon who would have wanted the trip and he was not present.) I immediately came inside to take a shower, shave, and dress up. There were only twelve from the entire battalion and we loaded on trucks to ride in the thirty five miles into the city. After getting lost among the ruins of that much-bombed town, we arrived at the concert two numbers late. None the less, we were (at least I was) thrilled to the core by the remainder of the

Volleyball court located in the square outside our quarters
in Gunzburg, (U.K.) June '45.
[Note the destroyed buildings in the distance.]

program. The concert hall was large, holding perhaps a thousand persons. It was comfortably filled with men in uniform (and a few women). In the rear to my surprise were a few civilians who had been allowed to attend. We had been told nothing of what was in store and so it was a surprise to see a large symphony orchestra, numbering perhaps thirty-five or forty pieces and in full dress. After the first thrill of again hearing a symphony orchestra had passed, I attempted to analyze the music and the conducting in an objective manner. It seemed to me that the orchestra itself was a bit above the S.F. Symphony Orchestra which we heard and the conducting on a par with that of Pierce so and so who conduct the S.F.S.O. The soloist were good, particularly the soprano. I must confess that it seemed a bit strange to be sitting in a German auditorium, listening to and applauding the efforts of the Augsburg Symphony Orchestra. Somehow I felt that here music was transcending the world of politics, rare hatred, and war to reach a higher level of human relationships and understanding. When, for the final encore, the orchestra played "The Stars and Stripes Forever," a deep emotional thrill filled me.

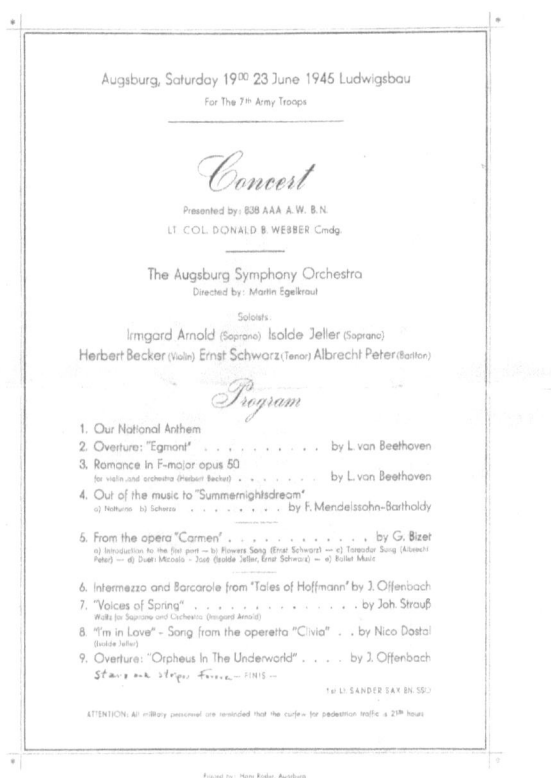

Augsburg, Saturday 19⁰⁰ 23 June 1945 Ludwigsbau
For The 7th Army Troops

Concert

Presented by: 838 AAA A. W. B. N.
LT. COL. DONALD B. WEBBER Cmdg.

The Augsburg Symphony Orchestra
Directed by: Martin Egelkraut

Soloists:
Irmgard Arnold (Soprano) Isolde Jeller (Soprano)
Herbert Becker (Violin) Ernst Schwarz (Tenor) Albrecht Peter (Bariton)

Program

1. Our National Anthem
2. Overture: "Egmont" . . . . by L. van Beethoven
3. Romance in F-major opus 50
   for violin and orchestra (Herbert Becker) . . . . by L. van Beethoven
4. Out of the music to "Summernightsdream"
   a) Nolturno b) Scherzo . . . . by F. Mendelssohn-Bartholdy

5. From the opera "Carmen" . . . . by G. Bizet
   a) Introduction to the first part — b) Flowers Song (Ernst Schwarz) — c) Toreador Song (Albrecht
   Peter) — d) Duett Micaela - José (Isolde Jeller, Ernst Schwarz) — e) Ballet Music
6. Intermezzo and Barcarole from "Tales of Hoffmann" by J. Offenbach
7. "Voices of Spring" . . . . by Joh. Strauß
   Waltz for Soprano and Orchestra (Irmgard Arnold)
8. "I'm in Love" – Song from the operetta "Clivia" . . by Nico Dostal
   (Isolde Jeller)
9. Overture: "Orpheus in The Underworld" . . . . by J. Offenbach
   Stamp and Alright Force — FINIS —

                                    1st Lt. SANDER SAY. BN. S5U

ATTENTION: All military personnel are reminded that the curfew for pedestrian traffic is 23ᵗʰ hours.

Printed by: Horn Fröter, Augsburg

Concert in Augsburg, June 23, 1945, Ludwigsbou, for the 7th Army Troops
The Augsburg Symphony Orchestra, Directed by Martin Egelkraut

I knew, of course, Ted would be present if it were at all possible. It was. During the first part of the program, I craned my neck in every direction, but met with no success. At the intermission I began a more detailed search and was properly rewarded. We had time for only a few brief words of greeting before the second half began, and then we resorted to shouting into each other's ear during the applause. He hopes to come to Gunzburg sometime and I certainly hope that he can do so. Little news from him, except that he thinks we will be here longer than I had supposed. The poor guy gets to visit some point of interest every two weeks, while I'm hoping for a least one furlough to

England before I leave. As you can well imagine, it was grand to see and talk with him again.

This morning I attended church in our Lutheran building. The crowd was again large (c. 165) and the choir came forth with an anthem. We still need more voices and the cohesiveness which comes only after much practice together. I think that we do have potential.

I like our chaplain very much and yet I must criticize one outstanding failure in my eyes. They do not attack the problems of our daily living in a way to show the practical applications of Christianity. There is a Christian approach to fraternizing, to drinking, to finding a way to get along with those who do not share our ideals. I hear nothing of these subjects. To me the great undeveloped theme of the Church is the underline practical in the teachings of Christ. Few things it seems to me are more pertinent.

I have a few more pictures which I enclose. Still await those which Beul and I took in the mountains. My guard duty tonight is from midnight until three o'clock. I shall whisper messages of love to a full moon—messages which you will hear as you too gaze into the heavens.

> Eternally thine,
> Bushy

P.S. We are told that Airmail is uncertain. Perhaps I should use a few V-Mails.

* Letter from Art to Dotty
Gunzburg, Germany
June 26, '45 (Tues. [201-206]

Dearest Heart,

How perfectly wonderful! Here is sit on a quiet evening with your picture before me—you're beautiful, My Love,—and with consecutive letters for six days. The last letter was written only a week ago. By the way, I now have your picture on a shelf in my locker where I can look at it every time I open the door. Often three or four times a day someone stops behind me to compliment me on such a lovely creature to claim as a wife. I just as often admit that I still do now know how I could be so fortunate. What is the secret of my—don't answer that! In all seriousness I receive many compliments on the picture which I carried in my pocket throughout combat. Among my worldly possessions on this side of the Atlantic, I value this picture of you most highly.

Let me hasten to clear myself in regard to the rumors with which Beul is building morale on the home front and at the same time tearing down my standing (?). He maintains that he put the label "rumor" on his report to Dorcas. True enough we have heard that we may be home in Sept, but we also heard that we would parade in New York on July 4th. There have been as many rumors to the contrary as to the affirmative and so I have refrained from repeating these pure rumors "latrinagrams", we used to call them. I do not believe that anyone at present knows exactly where or when we will move.

My mind was more than a little relieved when I found that my plans for your birthday had been completedly successfully. Though I had written concerning them almost two months in advance, I was afraid that in some way the whole thing would not materialize at the proper moment. I shall thank "kleine zuster" in a personal letter. Sounds to me as though Grandma Parmelee is "rushing the cadence" as we say in the Army. Why you're not quite middle age yet! (Ooh what a nasty crack that was! Slips!) But you know that I want a permanent job, social status, and an extended "fling" before I am back in the turbulent sea of fatherhood. Nevertheless at the insistence of such meddling-in-laws or Grandmother Parmelee we shall put her present to use at the earliest possible moment. (nicht wahr?)

I trust that this will have been the very last birthday that you have to enjoy in my absence, for I would ever be by your side in every joy and every sorrow. I love you!

Your description of the mountains brought me to your side in my dreams. How I long to be there in the flesh. Sunday night as I stood guard from 12 until 3 o'clock Monday morning, I watched a full moon play among the clouds and I sent you messages of love and I received your thrilling answer. God will surely continue to bless and guide the path of Our Love.

This morning I had opportunity to attend my second entertainment in Augsburg. This time it was fifty from the company who went. The show was held in a large hangar outside of the city and we were among the first to arrive. After exploring a Junker 88 (light bombers) which was nearby, we stood around in the hot sun while a slowly gathering crowd milled around. Four divisions were represented and 10,000 soldiers were supposed to fill the hangar when the show began.

Darling, I must be getting old. Even Jack Benny fails to arouse me for more than momentary pleasure. Jack did have a good show and Larry Adler, famed harmonica player, performed with remarkable talent. Martha Tilton (sp ?) also is supposed to be a top notcher, and sang several songs. Nevertheless one strain from the Augsburg Symphony is worth more than an entire program of jokes and songs to me. The long, hot ride must have been the reason for my lack of enthusiasm.

I am reading Maugham's <u>Razor's Edge</u>, and find it very enjoyable. Hope to finish it and read Beard's <u>Republic</u> soon. By the way, I wonder if you have had opportunity to read much of late and if so what. What conclusions have you reached in your thinking regarding the Church. Your particular work, the role of the pastor? I find certain comments in Dick's letter of especial interest and I shall send it to you a bit later. It seems that he has been making a detailed study of faith and his conclusions point in the same direction as mine—namely that complete abandonment to His Will is the answer. I shall send the letter to you.

At last we have the pictures taken at Gmunden and I enclose most of them. Beul is sending the negatives to Dorcas to get more pictures enlarged. She will send them to you. I send the entire group to you and you can send part of them to Mother and Dad. Better still, take them over some time.

As the sun sinks under the western rim of the sky, so will I soon sink into my nesting place for the night. There to dream of the wonder of

Our Love,
Bushy

P.S. Complete darkness does not come here until almost eleven o'clock and the first light of day appears shortly after three o'clock.

Letter from Art to Dotty
Gunzburg, Germany
June 29, 1945 [207-208, typed]

Dear Heart,

If I were only back in Kematen with hours and hours in which to write, I should spend half a dozen pages on things incidental and then at last spring the news. Since I am here, and endless hours are not mine to spend, I shall begin with an interesting event which happened this morning.

Last night I was on guard for four hours and thus was not required to fall out for duty today. This morning I slept! Shortly before lunch I was told that the First Sergeant wished to see me. Upon arriving in his office, I was told to pack my clothing and equipment and prepare to be transferred to Service Company. I was slightly shocked to say the least. Within the past two weeks, Chaplain Hail had told me that he still hoped to use me in the capacity of an assistant, but my hopes were not high. My hopes had sunk to a new low when Chaplain Hail met with an accident two days ago and was taken to the hospital. When told of the transfer, I hardly dared hope that I would be going to Service Company as a chaplain's assistant, and yet I hardly knew for what other reason. To make a delightfully long story short, I went to Service Co., and found that the First Sgt. there did not know why I had been transferred. However, at the evening meal I spoke to one of the assistants and he took me in tow. Again I packed my belongings, and loaded on to a jeep. This time I moved to my present location were the three chaplains, their assistants, and the Red Cross Director live. I am still a bit breathless. We have a large private home, entirely away from a GI atmosphere.

Before you become excited, my dear, let me sober you with a conversation which I just had with Chaplain Webb, the second Protestant Chaplain in the Regt. A few days ago, an order came through under which each chaplain may select a second assistant as some thing of an understudy. It seems that the arrangement is temporary at best, and no one knows just how long the period of trial will last. A second and more serious complication comes from the fact that Chaplain Hail will probably be away for some weeks. His two assistants are here, and now Ch.Webb has two. Whether or not higher hdq. will ask for the staff to be cut is a matter of conjecture. At the moment I am here. Where I will be tomorrow I cannot know.

There is also a brighter side to the conversation which I just finished. In recent days the announcement has been made that those who plan to go on into seminary work would be allowed to do special study under a chaplain. I explained to him tonight that while I am not likely to go into the minister [ministry], I would be interested in doing some study work in my spare time. The idea at once struck fire and he suggested a subject which he has wanted to study for some time, "Pastoral Psychiatry. There are two are [or] three books here on the subject, and I shall begin my study tomorrow. The idea at present is merely to outline the chapters and perhaps bring up questions that are pertinent. Ch. Webb thinks also that he may wish to use me to teach a Bible Study class. I intend to take piano or organ lessons from one of the other assistants to fill up my spare time. Oh joy! Real honest to goodness work again! If it only lasts a week, it will be very near heaven. If it lasts longer, well....

It was a real pleasure to turn in my BAR today and now I have an M1 (the regular rifle, you know.) We do not carry weapons nor are we burdened with the steel helmet which I had to wear all during duty hours in "K". Ch. Webb explained that the duties are not so time consuming, but that one is always on call and many pastimes must be foregone. Since the sports and shows to which he referred hold but a minor attraction to me, I shall not find it difficult to be on twenty-four hour call if that is what is called for. Darling, I hope so much that this will be something permanent. However, if it isn't I shall always know that I can go back to the line and know what the score is there. Since I was actually transferred to Service Company, I can only hope that if I do not remain here in this capacity, that I shall be able to fit into a clerical position perhaps in regiment. We shall see.

I must write Mother and Dad tonight to tell them the good news, and so will have to cut this letter short. Since there are three machines [typewriters] in the house, I should be able to use one for most of my writing. Your letters of the 19th and 20th received.

Join me in thanking our Father for his many blessings to us. May we be ever worthy of His care and protection, and may He continue to grant us the deep joy which comes from the depth of

Our Love,
Bushy

THE FOLLOWING NOTES WERE MADE [BY ART] AFTER VE-DAY.

ADDITIONAL NOTES

For security reasons, we were limited in what we could put in letters home. We were warned not to keep notes that would reveal vital information to the enemy should we be captured. Thus in my notes made in combat, I avoid mentioning specific locations. I was able to follow our progress to some extent with road maps that I had found. These were similar to maps which in those days were available at gasoline stations in the United states. Our officers often had small topographical maps of our area of operation but not maps of Germany. Often our lieutenant would ask to look at the maps I had.

I was further aided in keeping up with our progress and with world events by receiving weekly copies of TIME. The magazine was stripped of advertising and reduced in size so that an issue fitted into a long, business-size envelope. Arriving irregularly, these contained maps and articles on the progress of the war both in the ETO and in the Pacific.

MEMORIES OF COMBAT

When my unit moved forward to the front, we found ourselves at first in positions near the Rhine that had been occupied during winter months when that sector had remained rather static. I recall one night when we set up a defensive position in an area with foxholes already dug. Near my location, I found an abandoned bunker containing an old mattress. This I dragged to my location, thinking that at least once I would have a soft bed. Shortly before dark, we were ordered to sleep in our foxholes, an artillery bombardment begin expected. Not to lose the use of the mattress, I used my bayonet to cut the double mattress in half, stuffed it into the foxhole, and slept sitting up with considerable discomfort. We heard the bombardment, but fortunately the guns were aimed in other directions.

Shortly after the drive into Germany began, my unit was positioned west of the Siegfried Line, a German fortification built after WWI to prevent a direct invasion from France. Late one night when the moon was nearly full we were ordered to throw our packs on tanks, climb on, and ride through that famous defense. Although a narrow path had been cleared of mines, we were warned not to get off our perch. In the night hours when I see a full moon descending in the west, I can still see the white dragons' teeth through which we passed. These were pyramid-shaped concrete barriers intended to deter tanks and other vehicles.

Another less pleasant memory is one of crossing an open field with machine gun fire and mortars kicking up dirt all around me. We ran, of course, with our heavy packs on our backs. Mike, an older man in our company, was killed; I recall that he was married, with children, and had a very difficult time keeping up with the rigors of our training. When we reached a point of comparative safety, another member of our company realized that something warm was running down the back of his leg. Upon inspection, he discovered that his canteen of water, hanging from is ammunition belt on his right hip, had been opened up with a bullet. He had not been aware of the shot before.

At Regensburg on the Danube, we met the most resistance of any battle in which we were engaged. When the newest member of our squad raised up, a bullet centered his forehead, killing him instantly. Tony, another squad mate, had a bullet rip open the top of his helmet. Not a hair was touched, but the experience was a psychological blow from which he did not recover. He was unable to take his watch at night and was soon removed from the front.

Two vivid experiences were less traumatic. One night, after an exhausting march, we had no food, and I crawled into my sleeping bag. Shortly thereafter, the food truck arrived and I was told to go out on the perimeter of our position and call in a buddy who was standing guard. I put on my helmet and felt my way forward. Just as I saw the shadow of the guard and spoke, I found myself suddenly in water up to my waist. I had gone through a ground-level, narrow slit into a concrete pill box. Fortunately I had not buckled my helmet; otherwise, I could have snapped my neck. The helmet had come off and was lost in the water. I looked up, saw stars, floundered around, and found a ladder. But I was soaking wet. Fortunately, I was taken back in the food truck to the kitchen where I was able to dry out. The next morning we were not ordered to leave at the crack of dawn. I had time to go back to the pill box; and, with the aid of a long pole, retrieved my helmet. Had I not done so, I would have been out of luck because no extra helmets were available.

The second experience had to do with an assignment that turned unexpectedly pleasant. After getting settled in a position one rainy night, my squad was ordered to pack up and go to a new location. Such an order often meant a night patrol. We were trucked to a house that had a commanding position overlooking a road and ordered to maintain a watch from that point. While not on guard duty, we had the luxury of being inside and out of the rain.

Other memories provide some amusement in retrospect. As we were moving through a Bavarian town, my squad was spread out but our advance stopped on a bridge. An elderly German woman who spoke very good English came along and engaged us in conversation. She was naturally rather bitter about the events of the war, but she had a ready explanation as to why the Americans were winning. It was, she explained, because we had so many Germans in our ranks! I did not reveal my German name.

A more amusing incident involves my finding an egg for my supper. Shortly before nightfall, we came to a village that had been destroyed by a tank unit. Almost every building was burning. We set up our perimeter of defense and dug foxholes before we could eat. I had searched a nearby barn for straw, and in one corner I had spotted a hen's nest with a single egg in it. This I secured and began salivating in anticipation of a fresh egg—something I had not seen since I arrived in the ETO. We were not allowed to build fires, but there was no order saying we couldn't utilize the embers from a fire already burning. I opened my "C" rations, one can of which contained dry items. I emptied it, poured in water, put in the egg, and found a place in the coals where my delicacy could boil. After a suitable time, I removed the egg and let it cool, all the while imagining how good it would taste. My buddies looked on with some envy. When the egg was cool, I started to crack the shell on a rock. Clink, clink, clink. I had cooked a nest egg! In response to the ribbing I took, I could only say, "Well, if it was good enough to fool the old hen, don't be surprised that it fooled me." In partial defense, I must say that the German nest egg looked more natural than ones I had seen at home.

Sometimes we found abandoned German equipment that was lighter and better made than some of our issues. On one occasion, we came upon an abandoned mule-drawn wagon train with a considerable amount of equipment. I uncovered a new American Army field jacket that was lined and much warmer than what I had. I truly liberated that item and eventually shipped it home. "Liberated" was a term that GIs often used for stealing whatever they happened to find. One fellow in my squad found a set of bone-handled knives that he continued to carry with him until the war ended. The problem was that although we occasionally received packages from home, we had no way of mailing packages back. Thus, anything that one wished to keep became a part of the heavy load that we already carried.

I have mentioned elsewhere that when we were first committed to combat, we were loaded with excessive gear. Many of the men threw away their combat boots on the first forced march. By retaining my extra pair, I was able to put on dry ones each day, throwing the pair, usually wet, on my back to dry out. The boots became my pillow at night and likewise provided a safe place to put my glasses. Fortunately the especially strong lenses that the Army issued were never broken.

My extras were a pocket New Testament also containing the Psalms and a Pocket Book (the name of a series of paperbacks) of British and American Poetry. I often read from both of these.

After we crossed the Danube, I believe that we received only one hot meal from the kitchen unit until the war ended. The usual pattern was for us to be issued six cans of "C" rations each morning. After eating two of these for breakfast, we carried the other four in our packs. Three of the cans contained a monotonous diet—I believe only three variations (hash, pork and beans, and something else). The other three cans, appropriate for each meal of the day, contained instant coffee, instant chocolate, instant orange or lemonade drink mix. Each can contained five hard tack biscuits, cube sugar, and a piece of hard candy. Usually, but not always, our rations caught up with us.

My stomach finally rebelled to the point that I could hardly tolerate this diet. I found that I could make a kind of bread pudding by mixing the chocolate or the citrus mix with the biscuits, adding water, and, when possible, heating the concoction. Often my squad mates made fun of what I was doing, but when they tasted it, they asked for my recipe.

On Easter, we were provided white bread, and a couple of us found a hausfrau willing to exchange a generous piece of German black bread for our white. On another occasion when we thought we were settled into a location for the night, I found a hen's egg—this a good one. Just as I was preparing to cook it, the order came to move on. As we marched away, I broke the top and sucked it raw. I remembered my father telling me that when he was preparing for track meets at Sue Bennett College, he would eat nothing but a raw egg in preparation for the event. Neither of us were aware of salmonella poisoning.

Let me summarize a few points about our living conditions in combat. We did not have the heat that marked the North African campaign nor the prolonged rain and mud that our men endured in Italy and in the Pacific area. But we did have prolonged periods of rain and snow in those late months of the 1944-1945 winter, which has been identified as the coldest on record. We rarely had shelter at night, and we were not permitted to have fires except during daylight. A genuine luxury was to have a full canteen cup of hot morning coffee. The cup, by the way, fitted around the bottom of the canteen and held a pint. The canteen itself held a quart, when on occasion we were pulled back from the front line, we were usually assigned another area for mop-up operations, hardly R and R, i.e., rest and relaxation.

I don't recall a single shower after we moved forward into the fight zone. One experience illustrates the water shortage that we sometime faced. I was desperate to make myself a little cleaner, but I had only a single steel helmet of water. With that, I followed a shave with a full sponge bath; I then washed my winter underwear and finally my heavy woolen, double-soled combat socks—all in a single helmet of water. When I threw out what little was left, I was careful to contaminate neither plant nor animal.

After I was hospitalized briefly, I kept almost no notes until the war was over. We crossed into Austria, and the 71st Division met the Russians in Vienna. In those last days we had to deal with great numbers of German soldiers streaming from the East to surrender to the Americans rather than be captured by the Russians.

On one occasion we were guarding a large number of German soldiers in an open field. One officer came up to talk to me. He was a Viennese doctor with excellent command of English. Having seen the devastation through Bavaria, I asked why the Germans had not given up sooner. He replied that until the soldiers heard that Hitler had flown back to Berlin, they thought they had a chance of winning.

That seemed hard to believe except for two things: first, the German propaganda machine was highly efficient in convincing the Germans of things that were far from the truth. Second, later records revealed that there was a plan, never carried out, for the Germans to pull back into the Bavarian mountains and make a last attempt to defeat the Allies. Apparently part of the reason for my unit turning southwest from Fulda was in anticipation of this possibility.

Two unpleasant incidents have haunted me and have supported the theory I developed in combat that war is brutalizing and de-humanizing. I did not observe these events, but I have no doubt that they happened. They were openly discussed at the time.

The first occurred shortly after we were on the front line. Early one morning the popular first sergeant of our company sent into the bushes to relieve himself. As he started to rejoin us, he came upon a small group of German soldiers, some still sleeping. Apparently he was checking a sleeping man when he was shot and killed instantly. This was our first casualty; emotions ran high. The small group of German soldiers were immediately captured, and shortly thereafter, they were taken behind a hill and summarily shot. No rules of war would justify that.

The second incident happened near the end of the war when we had taken over a Bavarian farmhouse for the night. Five or six men discovered a young German girl, forced her into the hay, and raped her, one after the other. One of the culprits was a corporal who was immediately stripped of his rank. I was grateful that the event was not taken lightly by our officers. Although I don't recall that the privates were punished, they may have been reduced from Private First Class to Private, a minor change.

In the closing days of the war we were worn down with little sleep, poor food, and we were emotionally drained. I recall when the news finally came that Germany had surrendered, I was more saddened than overjoyed because of the brutal treatment of German Prisoners that I was observing. Many of these prisoners were very young boys and very old men.

On the first night after hostilities ended, some of the members of my squad were searching for something to drink. They came upon a German still in uniform and a civilian with a small truck. The back was loaded with German marks. Our men took a few bills to distribute as souvenirs and let the two go. Later we discovered that the old currency would continue to be used. Our men had passed up a fortune, but even so there was very little to be bought.

After six weeks in Austria, we returned to Southern Germany, where for a few weeks we were stationed in Gunzburg, a small town near Ulm and the Rhine.

[SOMETIME IN THE 1980'S, MY FRIEND TOM JONES RETURNED A V-MAIL LETTER WHICH I WROTE TO HIM ON MAY 7, 1945, FROM AUSTRIA. AT THAT TIME HE WAS IN A NAVAL TRAINING PROGRAM AT GEORGIA TECH. THE LETTER PASSED CENSORSHIP WITH THE SIGNATURE OF MY PLATOON LEADER, LT. DONALD R. MOBERG.]

Dear Tom,

"From an Austrian peasant home within sight of the snow-capped Bavarian Alps, greetings. Today the news is semi-official that all is over in this theatre. We rejoice, but even as we do, our thoughts turn to the Pacific and the war there. The next big news which I expect is the declaration of war on Japan by Russia. Much will be simplified if and when that happens. Certainly there are political difficulties to solve over here, but the top has been reached. I survived this job with little more than the Combat Infantry Badge and vivid memories to show for my labor. However, I have no reason to complain. At the moment, we are enjoying a much deserved rest. I attended church services yesterday for the first time since Easter, and our kitchen served the first chow since before Easter. Surely, I will have opportunity soon to read and write a bit at leisure. Perhaps I will be able to take a course or two by correspondence. One never knows. I may use my Stanford training yet. What do you think of Truman? Also give me a report on the SF [San Francisco] Conference [which was organizing the United Nations]. Our political news here is scant. Will

try to do better than a V-mail from now on. Meanwhile write when possible." As ever, Art

[I CLOSE THIS CHAPTER WITH THE FOLLOWING QUOTATION FROM STEPHEN AMBROSE'S _D-DAY, CHAPTER 22:

"As always in war, the infantry ... got stuck with war at its most cutting edge, where it is at its most shocking, dangerous, and decisive. The most extreme experience a human being can go through is being a combat infantryman...." (419). [I am glad I did not read that in 1945!]

[DURING APRIL, 1945, THE NEWS MEDIA CARRIED MANY STORIES CONCERNING THE DEATH OF PRESIDENT ROOSEVELT. I RECORDED MY MEMORIES, LATER PUBLISHED IN THE MARYVILLE DAILY TIMES.]

Dear Editor,

"Near midnight on April 12, 1945, a GI stood guard in heavy rain at an unprotected Bavarian outpost. Like hundreds of other infantrymen he had been marching ("trudging" is more descriptive) and fighting across southern Germany. The 71st Infantry Division had veered southeast, responding in part to the persistent rumor that Hitler planned a final stand in the Bavarian Alps.
"The soldier was tired and hungry, wondering how long the conflict could go on. Although the German Luftwaffe no longer threatened, the ground forces still had effective artillery and small weapons. Pockets of resistance remained.
"Shortly before time for a relief guard, a member of the GIs squad came out of the darkness. In an excited tone the new man whispered, "The President is dead." No details. Just the single fact. During the preceding weeks and months, front-line soldiers had no inkling that one of the towering leaders of the allied forces was failing in health.
"Some GIs were not politically conscious when President Roosevelt had been elected in 1932. Then came 1936, 1940, 1944—some had voted by then. For many he was the only

president they had known, and they were aware that his powerful radio voice had rallied the Americans even as he had inspired hope in the lives of people world-wide.

"The drenching rain, the hunger pangs, the aching muscles—all were forgotten while the implications of the loss of the President were being absorbed. A recent historian has commented that 'his [FDR's] contribution to the salvation of the West in incalculable.' On April 12, 1945, American soldiers around the world learned of the loss of their Commander-in-Chief.

"I shall never forget that isolated post, that cold rain, that darkness, those shocking four words: 'The President is dead.'"

(Signed) Arthur S. Bushing

[LATER I RECEIVED A VICIOUS, UNSIGNED LETTER DENOUNCING FDR.]

___

Letter from Art to Dotty
Gunzburg, Germany
1 July, 1945, Sunday
[209-212, typed]

Dearest Heart,

The past two days have passed in rapid succession and I have been busy almost every minute. Yesterday I began my work on the little research project and made good start. I had to make two trips to "K" Co. to collect my pay and find that I had no mail. Just before lunch I sent out with Bob Mulford, Chaplain Webb's first assistant, to find one of the companies which is pulling guard (occupation) duty in a nearby town. It was on this trip that I drove my first jeep, and I expect to get my driver's license in the early part of the week. In addition to taking care of the office during the absence of the others, I did various and sundry other small jobs around the place. Last night I enjoyed a movie after which I pumped the organ while Scotty (Harold Scott, another assistant) practiced "The Holy City". We do not have the music nor the words, and our memories are not the best. Not until almost ten did I get overto a "K" Co. party which was being held just across the street from our house in the large gym. After the party, a shower and to bed past midnight.

I would like to dwell a moment on the party merely to record it as a GI party in Germany. The gym is a large one, perhaps a third larger than the one at Maryville [College], and about half of it was taken with tables and chairs. The rest was bare for dancing. German fraus and frauleins were there as waitresses and DPs (Displaced Persons, Polish, Russian, etc.) were the theoretical feminine guests. From my observation it seemed that the females were 99 44/100 pure—German. Beer, wine, and French Fried potatoes seemed to be an abundance. I tasted a couple of bites of potatoes and manage to get a couple of very good doughnuts. Later in the evening we had delicious, creamy ice cream in plenty. Music was supplied by the regimental dance orchestra, and the floor was filled most of the time. All stages of ability took part, and the linguist barrier appeared to be no obstacle either on the floor or off. The popular style in evening gowns was a skirt which reached to within three or four inches of the knee—above, not below! I presume that the females were supposed to leave unescorted, but I am just as sure that few did. The non-fraternization policy is rapidly fading into a nominal existence. A couple of nights before I came here, some of the officers in my old company were supposed to have had women in their quarters, and I have no reason to doubt the story. I stayed about a half hour, watching the party progress, and then came home to prepare for bed. Our source of a shower is over at Service Company, about half a mile away. So every night we right over, take our shower, drive the jeeps to the motor pool, and walk the intervening distance to our quarters. My head touched the pillow about 12:30 and music still issued from the gym.

While I am in full accord with the attitude of higher headquarters on the subject of fraternization, I must admit that from my observations I believe it an impossible ruling to enforce. This outfit is fresh from the States by comparison with men here for two or three years, and yet the urge for female company is overpowering for some men. Since the war ended we have hardly had sufficient exercise to keep healthy much less do anything to take up time and interest. For myself I can turn to reading, writing, choir, etc., but some men simply do not know how to occupy themselves. Thus it is that many seek to fraternize in various degrees. I heartly [heartily] disagree with the general attitude but you can't ration passion and you can't buck Dame Nature.

As I watch the waitresses serve the beer, the wine, and the food, as I watched couples dance in each others arms or hold hands in a dark corner, as I saw them laugh together and make flirtatious passes, I thought of the same place a mere three months ago when perhaps German soldaaten had held a similar party with the same girls to serve them, laugh with them, flirt with them. Ugh!

Sunday dawned bright and clear, and we arose at 7:30 with a busy day ahead. Bob and Ted Livingston (the third assistant) rushed through breakfast in order to leave with Chaplain Webb for the nine o'clock service at 1st Bn. Scotty and I were more leisurely since we did not have to leave the house until 9:45. We went over to the Church at that time for the Bible Class which had its beginning today under the leadership of a Capt. Jacobs. Chaplain Webb and cohorts returned just in time to get everything set for the 10:30 service. We had a good crowd of about 150 and the service progressed in good order. With an hour out for lunch, Scotty left with the Chaplain for errands at the second Battalion. The rest of us left shortly thereafter to meet with them in Ulm for the third and last service. (I am reminded of the schedule which my dear wife keeps on Sunday!)

Oh, I forgot to mention that I had to take a couple of fellows back to their outfits after lunch when they were stuck without transportation. While passing through Burgau, I stopped with Ted long enough to take a look at a very beautiful but very ornate cathedral. I am but slowly becoming accustomed to the flashy and almost gaudy effects which some of these European churches process. In the foremost part of the sanctuary was a design of gold and silver which shone like one of the lesser suns. The walls on every side were filled with figures, designs, and pictures, and an unusual feature was a second-tier above the organ loft.

A second and more impressive cathedral was one which we visited in Ulm after the service this afternoon. This was a very large Lutheran Church which is supposed to have the highest tower in all of Europe. It is 161 meters our [and] about 500 feet tall. The magnificent structure was begun in 1377 and finished in 1890. We did not have time to go all of the way to the top, but we hope to return at some later time, perhaps next Sunday when we are in Ulm for another service. A startling thing about the building is the fact that it stands almost untouched among the rubble and wastes of a large section completely destroyed. I have seen a number of pictures in Life and other magazines showing towns flattened by bombs and artillery, but no pictures ever taken could show the stark naked ruin that follows in the wake of war. On every side of this beautiful "Ulmer Munster" (Cathedral of Ulm) for literally blocks, the buildings have been flattened. Of buildings which had stood only across the narrow street from the Church, nothing remained but a few sections of wall here and there. On four sides I counted less than a dozen buildings that had any roof whatsoever. The amazing thing part of the story is that the cathedral stood out among these ruins almost untouched. The tower stretched sky-ward for 500 feet without a visible scratch; the main roof was intact. Not until we descended from the tower and walked to the rear of the massive auditorium did we see that one bomb had landed arye and had destroyed a part of the sanctuary. The damage seemed infinitismal when compared with the surrounding ravage. This is but another evidence of the care which was taken in bombing only military objectives. It could not have been mere chance that saved the inspiring "Ulmer Munster".

Still much to say, but I have spent the entireevening on this and 'tis now past bed time. Chaplain Webb has just told me that he going to Nurnberg tomorrow and I am to go along. Hospital calls and sightseeing. Will try to make long report tomorrow. Letters from Mother, Dad, and Harriet today.

My Darling, with every fiber of my being,
      I love you,
      Bushy

Letter excerpt from Dotty to Art
Wed., July 4, 1945

Darling,
Tonight I am home, Angeles is spending the night with me. Last night I spent with flow. Mother dad and Bulah are in the mountains, and mother made me promise not to sleep in the house alone. I am not afraid, but perhaps it is best this way. I'm having fun, anyway. Just finished washing my hair & setting it, so I'm a bit damp in the noggin.

You spoken one letter a feeling as if you were slipping away from God. I don't think you should be alarmed for worried about that, darling. While you were in combat, god seemed very close, as indeed he was. But that was in mountain-top experience (insofar as being close to God was concerned). Now you are more or less in a valley. We can't expect to stay on the peek all the time. The disciples went way up to hear the sermon on the Mount, but they had to send to sea level to get to work and put it into practice. Another way of looking at it is this: "the nearness of God is not approved buy a cozy awareness that he is close to us, but by a constant adequacy to a critical situation." We must always guard against "soul-erosion" (quoting Graham, but erasion is not [letter ends]

Letter excerpt from Art to Dotty
Gunzburg, Germany
6 July, 1945
[217-218]

"From what you say about the newspaper report concerning our location. I judge that you had not heard at that time that I was in Gunzburg. Yes, as I have said before, the indications are that we will be here for some time to come. Whether it will [be] weeks or months, we do not know; but the latter seems most like. Bets are being made on Feb., but those are merely guesses. There does seem to be some possibility of openings for the educational program, but as yet the quotas are very low by the time the company units are reached.

"Our choir attendance has grown steadily worse, but Chaplain Webb saw the Regimental Colonel tonight and he gave the go-ahead signal for time off from training. Next week should show a marked improvement in our work. Last night we had a performance of the 66th Regt. Glee Club. They have a mere seventy voices with a nationally famous conductor, Harry Brown. They are [our] own Detached Service, have no duties except choir, and have at their disposal $3,500 worth of music. We in the 14th have a few hymn books from which to sing. There is a slight difference in situation."

Letter excerpts from Art to Dotty
Gunzburg on the Danube
July 9, 1945 (Mon.)
[19-22]

"Chaplain Webb had the address of a friend who was located near Munich and he wished very much to see him. Although the rain was pouring down, we decided to go. Scotty and I drove for the Chaplain, alternating throughout the day. To shorten a long story, we found that fellow had been transferred only a few days previous, and so we continued on into Munich. We saw a great deal. For place names, I nearly mention a few: Maxmillian University, City Hall, Konings Platz. which include Hitler's famous Brown House, a shrine where the first sixteen Nazi to be killed were placed, an Administration building where the Munich Pact of '39 was signed, an art museum, etc.; we were in the famous Beer Hall where the Nazi party had its origin, and in one or two of the cathedrals there. From Munchen (as the Germans call it), we made our return trip via the infamous camp of Dachau. Our guide was a Polish priest who had himself been in this camp for five years. His stories I hope to record in some detail in addition to the sights which I saw and my impressions.

"A second bit of news is that I purchased a wonderful collection of large photos of the famous cathedrals in Europe. Some one found these in one of the school buildings here in Gunzburg, and I felt that the collection was easily worth the price which I paid. (I was able to get a number of very good postal cards of places seen in Munich for a few cigarettes.) I am in the process of making my latest purchase which is a camera. I think you know how I felt in combat about looting; I simply refused to take things. Perhaps I was foolish, but I do not think so. At any rate, I found today that the Chaplain has a very fine camera for which he has no use. He was on the point of selling it to someone else when I told him that I would like to buy it. I am certain that it is not less than a $50 camera, and Beul says it would cost more then $100. I can buy it for $20, and I think that I will grab it. I have been able to get two or three rolls of film, and I hope to get more. By the way, the camera takes a 120 roll.

"I dislike so much to rush, but I must get on with the big news. First, I suppose you have long since seen the announcement that 71st is one of the divisions scheduled to remain in the [?] at least for the remainder of '45. This announcement was in the "Stars & Stripes" today....

"You see it must have been on Wednesday that I went to lunch at Service Co. to find that anyone wanting to find out about the GI Edu. in ETO should see a certain Lt. I went over to see him to make a casual inquiry. The Lt. was to have two men which he selected at Regt. Hdq. by one o'clock. It was then 12:45. One man was to have a college degree and another to have at least two years. Already one man has spoken to him who had his degree. However, the other man was dressed in fatigues and there was not time to change. I went along as the man with the degree. My first choice, naturally enough was English Lit. to be given at Cambridge. However, the quota for this was but four men for the entire corps, comprised of nine divisions. My second choice was for French Lang. and Civilization which has as a quota a much larger figure. This course is to be given at the Sorbonne in gay Pariee. Now, sadly enough, I did not get the appointment to Cambridge. Of course, I hardly dared hope for such good fortune. Chris told me tonight that he has seen my name on the list of fourteen names for the Fr. Course from the 71st Div. He thinks that I am to be in Munich by the night of the 12th, which is Thur. As I said before, I have nothing official as yet, but I can only hope that his report is correct and not subject to change. I regret very much that I should leave my new job so soon after taking it, but I feel that this is a wonderful opportunity not to be passed up. I shall endeavor to put everything that I have into my work, and hope to come away from Paris the better for my studies there. But more along that line tomorrow...."

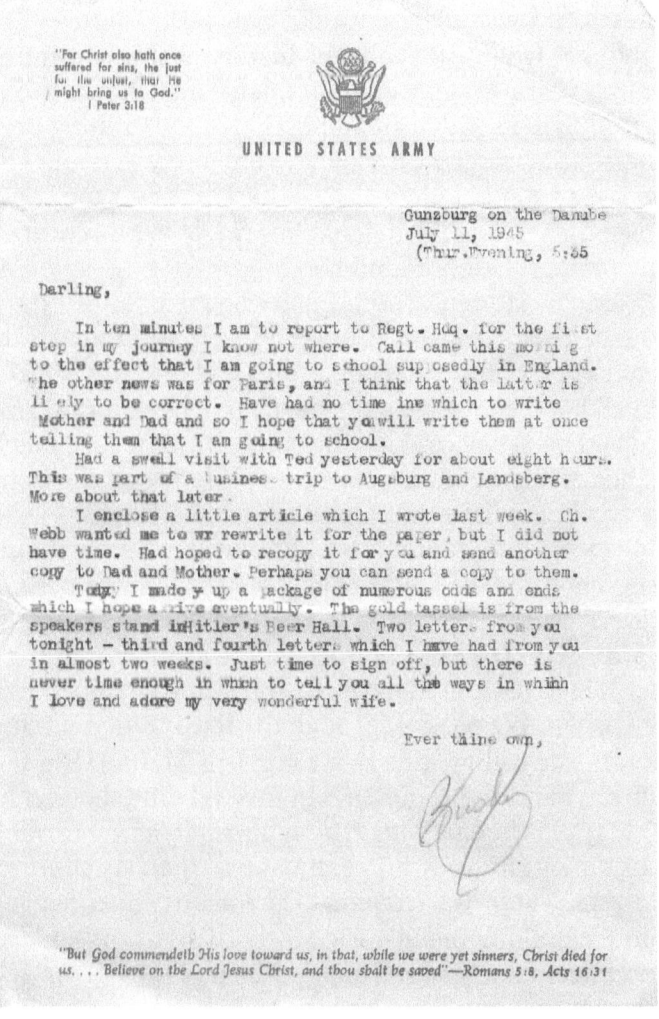

Letter from Art to Dotty on United States Army stationery,
July 11, 1945

My Darling,

The chimes outside have just announced to the winds that the eleventh hour has come and gone. Lights in the barracks (or better, our room) are out, and I have found seclusion in a musty classroom. I fancy this desk at which I write, these walls, these blackboards—all have stories to tell that would sidelight the history of this institution already seven hundred years young. I shall not delve into the past tonight, but rather attempt to deal with a small portion of the exciting present.

In a short note which I hurriedly wrote today at noon, I attempted to give you a very general idea of my situation. Allow me to go back just a bit and pick up a few of the details thus far. When I reported on Wednesday to Regt. Hdg: I found two others waiting—one Benny Goodman, a Malay student whom I had known at Stanford and a fellow by the name of Myers from "K" Co. We went to Augsburg by truck, and there joined the rest of the division group. I was to find that only fourteen in all had been chosen for the course here at the Sorbonne, and no one had been selected for the course in Eng. Lit., due I suppose to the absence of any quota for our unit. We left soon thereafter for Munich by truck. I believe that I mentioned in a previous letter that Marvin Flowerman, my roommate at Stanford for three months, was among those chosen. (We have begin [been] together since Camp Roberts days.)

We were put on trains in Munich where groups from the entire Third Army joined us, and at 4 o'clock the following morning, (Thur.) the journey began. We passed through the flat Daufion plain, through Ulm, Stuttgart, the rolling hills as far north as Mann Heim (although not into the city) and then south again through Strasbowry. About noon on Friday we were passing through the city of Luneville, near which we began our journey into combat less than six short months ago. On through Nancy we arrived at Chalon au Marie just at sunset. Thence into Paris along the historic Marne. The river seemed peaceful, almost motionless as we passed along. Much of the horror of Chateau Thierry is forgotten now. Time and the river have done their work well. The grass has covered the ground where those soldiers fell.

About three o'clock on Saturday morning, a train pulled into the station in Paris. Street dances were still in full swing as we ate in the Station dining hall. As the light began to break on the first Bastille Day since 1939, I stood in a long line of travel-worn GIs to register at the Sorbonne. We were then rushed to our new quarters at Lycee St. Louis

Services, Fireworks Open Celebration of Bastille Day

S. Y. S. July 15-45

The first Bastille Day celebration since 1939, and one of the most impressive since the revolution of 1789 which the day commemorates began at midnight last night in a blaze of fireworks and will continue throughout today with parades, street dances and municipal celebrations.

France's greatest traditional holiday was ushered in with a period of prayer at the Sacre-Cœur cathedral in Montmartre and special services for the French men and women who died in wars for liberty from 1789 to V-E Day.

At midnight, fireworks bloomed in the sky and buildings flared with illumination from the Etoile to Montmartre and Montparnasse. Crowds surged through the Champs-Elysées, some marchers holding aloft torches.

As churchbells pealed, throngs ranged about the illuminated Arc de Triomphe and sang the "Marseillaise," the national anthem.

Elaborate ceremonies are planned for today. At 0930, Gen. Charles de Gaulle is to mount the reviewing stand at the Place de la Bastille —site of the ancient political prison which became the symbol of despotism—and preside over the awarding of decorations to units of the new French Army.

The parade of tanks and infantry of the French First Army, the Foreign Legion and special metropolitan units such as the colorful Garde Républicaine, will move through Paris from the Place de la Nation via Faubourg Saint-Antoine, Boulevard Diderot, Boulevard Haussmann, Rue Tronchet, the Madeleine, Rue Royale, the Concorde and the Champs-Elysees.

The parade is to be preceded by a revue of the troops by De Gaulle.

(Continued on Page 8)

Bastille Day . . .
(Continued from Page 1)

He will be accompanied by the Bey of Tunis.

At 1430, resistance organizations will march from the Concorde to the Bastille by way of the Opera, the grands boulevards and the Place de la République.

Water sports will be held on the Seine between the Concorde and Alexander III bridges between 1500 and 1800 hours. Traditional free matinees will be given at three great Paris theaters, the Comédie Française, Châtelet and Gaité-Lyrique.

At Versailles, the great fountains will be turned on between 1630 and 1730.

Street dancing will follow in the evening and continue all night.

A ball will be held in the Place de la Concorde. Orchestras will play at the Hotel de Ville square, the Places of the Bastille, Nation, Armand-Carrel, Fêtes and the Porte d'Orléans.

Fireworks and light displays will be held on even a greater scale tonight.

Bastille Day, July 15, 1945

on Blvd. St. Michel (not "Rue"). I slept until breakfast and then went out to see a bit of the celebration. As people lined the streets, French, British, and American flags waned, and a parade of French armor passed through the streets. One of the first things which we did was to get tickets at the opera Comique for "Cavalliera Rusticana" and

"Paillarse" for last night and for "La Bobeme" today. Tickets for Richard III had already been sold out.

In the afternoon we had our first meeting of this student group. When I first saw Major (Air Corps) Fragier on the platform, I assumed that he was merely another Brass Hat. I was entirely wrong. Dean Fragier, for such he is, was asst. dean at Columbia before entering the service. One of his first statements was to say that he hoped to avoid the usual regimentation in every way possible. This was met by an ovation. The major has been at the head of this program since its origin just two months ago, and he states these two thoughts behind its planning. First, that this is to be something of a transition to civilian life, and, second it is to take advantage to the maximum of the great opportunity offered here by this institution.

Our language classes will be conducted by members of the staff of the Sorbonne and we will receive nine semester hours of credit upon successful completion of the work. Classes will meet for three hours each morning for six mornings per week, and a few of the afternoons will be devoted to conducted tours of the city.

Officers, nurses and wacs are here studying and all of us eat in one cafeteria about three blocks from our dormitory (across from the Luxem bourg Gardens). Time outside of classes is almost entirely our own, but of course we will have large assignments for home work. Tomorrow we have the first formal opening in the amphitheatre of the University. The U.S. Ambassador to Fr. will speak as well as the Fr. Minister of Edu. It is a solemn meeting which marks the first time in the history of the Sorbonne that such a group has been made a part of the university family.

Much to say tomorrow. I trust that these pages did not become too confused. I shall begin my study with a determination to make the utmost of my stay here.

I love you with all my heart. I shall be working for you
> Your husband,
> Bushy

Mizpah

7

PARIS I

July 15 [1945]

y pilgrimage to the gay city of Paris began when I reported
to Reg Hq. in Gunzburg. There I found that only two others
from the 14th Regiment were going to school at the Sorbonne; later I
discovered that there was but a total of four selected from the 5th and
66th Regiments [THESE THREE REGIMENTS MADE UP THE 71ST
DIVISION]. In Augsburg we joined the remainder of the group from
the 71st and continued our journey to Munich. We boarded the train
there about ten-thirty although we did not leave until four o'clock the
following morning. When I awoke we had just passed through the city
of Ulm [NEAR GUNZBURG WHERE I HAD STARTED] and were
continuing through the flat plains of the Danube. Our trip carried us
through Goppingen, Stuttgart, Kornwestheim, Ludwigsburg,
Heilbronn (where we found ice cream during a stop), Stetten,
Waldorf, and Buchsal. It was in the small town of Waldorf that John
Jacob Astor was born, I am told. Again darkness fell, and again we
slept as best we could on narrow wooden seats.

The following morning I awoke in Sarrbrucken, and next we
found ourselves on French soil again at Strasbourg. By noon we had
reached Luneville, but a short distance from the spot where we began
our trek to the front and combat. In contrast to the flat country of
southwestern Germany, we were now in the rolling countryside of
eastern France as we passed through Blainville, Luneville, and Nancy.

Sgt. Rbt. B Wilihite "Bob reads a letter from Sarah,
Gunzburg, Germany

In many of the places, the marks of war are passing into oblivion as
the sands of time and the river perform their duties. In Leroueville, a
small wayside station, we stopped for a G.I. supper in a mess hall
built for just such a purpose. We were served here by German POWs
[Prisoners of War]; our dishes were washed by them, and we took
advantage of the latrines and wash stands which they had built. I
somehow expected to be poisoned by the food, but I survived with no
ill effects. One of the things which displeased us a great deal was to
see a latrine "For Officers Only."

By sunset we were passing through Chalon-on-Marne, and then
began our journey along that famous river. The valley through which
it flows is a rather narrow one, with hills rising on either side. The
waters seemed without movement as we followed along the banks of
the stream. Now and then I saw a row boat floating along with a
couple as the shadows of evening fell. The scenes seemed so peaceful,
and yet I knew that along these very banks one of the famous battles

of the first world war was fought. I thought of Sandburg's poem, "Grass." We stopped briefly in Chateau Thiery and then moved on toward our destination.

We arrived in the outskirts of Paris about three o'clock [AM]. For many of us we were seeing lights of a city for the first time since leaving the states. I could see busy sidewalk cafes doing business, and I viewed for the first time something of the night life of Paris. Immediately upon arrival, we were shown to a dining hall and served a good meal. Officers and enlisted men ate together. I do not believe that they (the brass) were harmed to any appreciable degree. I ate across the table from three majors and a captain.

From the dining hall (which was in the station), we were taken by bus to the Sorbonne for registration. At 8:30 on the morning of Bastille Day [THE FIRST, OF COURSE, THAT THE FRENCH HAD BEEN ABLE TO CELEBRATE SINCE BEFORE THE GERMAN OCCUPATION]. While the eastern sky made ready for the path of Aurora, I stood in a long line among ancient walls of the University of Paris to register my name as a student. From here, we were taken by jeep to our quarters on Rue St. Michael and after washing a bit I slept until breakfast.

July 16
Luxembourg Gardens

After breakfast Myers (from "K" Co.) [my company], Ranger (a new fellow), and I set out to see a bit of the Bastille Day celebrations. We also wanted to obtain tickets for the Opera, and so we headed in that general direction. We took the metro (subway) and were pleasantly surprised to find it an efficient service. After a somewhat lengthy search we at last obtained tickets for "Cavalleria Rusticanna" and "Paillasse" for Sat. night and for "La Boheme" on Sunday. The holiday crowds were large, and we were jostled and pushed about as the parade of French armor passed through the streets.

When we came from the PXA, an unusual experience occurred on the streets immediately to our front. Ranger was eating a piece of candy when a lady stepped in front of him and grabbed his hand. Before he knew what had happened, she had taken a bite of the candy and moved on.

July 17

On Sat. afternoon we were to have an orientation program, and so at 1400 [2 p. m.] we were seated in the Salle de Fetes. The benches were packed with EM [enlisted men], officers, WACS, and nurses, and I was glad to see that there were a number of colored men in the crowd.

When Major Frazier (Air Corps) arose to speak, I thought that this was merely another brass hat who by some bit of luck happened to be in charge of our unit. I was very wrong. The Dean (as he would prefer to be called) was, before his entrance into the Army, Asst. Dean at Columbia U. He has been working on the plans for this program ever since the entire plan was merely an idea on paper, and from what I have seen thus far, he has created a smoothly working organization. Major Frazier is strictly non-GI [a high compliment]. At the outset, he asked that no one salute when entering his office. As many rules and regulations as possible will be lifted here. "The cut of my clothing does not effect the cut of my mind," he stated. Two thoughts have been behind the formation of the program. First, it is considered that this is a period of transition into civilian life. Our time outside of classroom will be ours to organize as we will. Second, it is a purpose of the program to assist and encourage us to profit to the maximum extent by the great opportunities offered by Europe, by Paris, and by the Sorbonne.

The officials of the university have cooperated in every way possible, and one example will suffice to indicate the truth of this. In order that the soldier group could come to Paris in time for Bastille Day, graduation exercises were moved up five days ahead of schedule. This enabled the dormitory facilities to be prepared for our coming so that we could arrive on the 14th of July.

Saturday morning Myers, Ranger, and I attended the "Opera Comique" to see "Cavalleria Rusticana" and "Paillasse." To my surprise, I learned that all operas are sung in French rather than the original tongue. Although I do not consider myself a competent of judge of music, I did feel that the operas were well done. The staging was excellent and the costumes very colorful.

The famed sidewalk cafes have a story all their own, and we sit down now and then to observe the life of Paris which passes by one of these centers of French life. Every type, size, color, and creed is to be seen on the streets of Paris. Uniforms from every corner are to be seen —Czech, Canadian, British, Australian, Polish, Russian, Sudanese.

Many GIs are here on pass, and many more are stationed in and around the city. They are to be seen at the bars, at the cafe tables, in the metro (subway), in the park, arm in arm with a young French lass on the street, and smoking with the elite at the opera. An interesting thing that I have noticed is the prevalence of G.I. clothing on non-GI.s. Sometimes it is only a shirt or a pair of pants; sometimes a field jacket or blouse; and sometimes it is a complete uniform where only the insignias give away the fact that the fellow is not a G.I. Whether these outfits come via lend-lease or via the black market, I do not know. I suspect the latter.

The famous Place de la opera and The Opera House
which I [Art] frequented, Paris Aug. 45

After the opera on Sat. night, we stopped before the main Opera house to see the milling masses. Just as we came up, lights were directed onto the front of the building, and its true grandeur was fully revealed. Search lights fingered the stars, planes dashed through the sky overhead, and fireworks broke out first in one spot and then in another. The crowd swayed aimlessly from one side of the street to another. We worked our way to the metro and thence home before the masses had thought of the same thing. Upon arrival at our quarters, we noted a street dance in heated progress across from our quarters and directly in front of the Sorbonne. We walked over. The dancing was fast and furious although hardly to be put in the jitterbug class. Recorded music was being used, and there was almost no intermission. Entire family groups sat along the sidewalk. I saw a father teaching his little ten-year old girl to dance. To my surprise, I find that although there is much drinking in Paris, the great majority

This is a typical house in Memmingen.
Note returned soldier.

are drinking orangeade, lemonade, mint, and unfermented fruit juices. We went to bed about 12:30 while the party continued at the same wild pace. There seemed to be no let up in the celebration of this, the first Bastille day since 1939.

Later
(Seated before the Palace of Luxembourg)

How lovely is the loneliness that one feels amid the throng! For the past two and a half hours, I have wandered amid the gardens here.

Now and then I have stopped to write or to study my French lesson or to observe life around me. I sit now overlooking the fountain and the Palace of Luxembourg. On the small lagoon, children sail their toy boats in a lively evening breeze; hundreds of couples are seated on the benches and chairs which are placed at every convenient spot. Frequently, a G.I. is seen with his latest feminine friend. Elderly couples, middle-aged couples—all are to be seen.

Within me there is a longing which comes from the deep heart's core. I long for the soul-satisfying companionship, which comes only from being in the presence of my wife. I long to walk with her hand in hand in these gardens. I long to sit with her and watch the children play. I long to whisper to her words of love.

Letter excerpts from Art to Dotty
Paris
17 July '45 (Tues.)

"Today began our first classes and I can see that my work will be plentiful. We began at a terrific rate. Twelve in my class and I think that I will learn a great deal—I'll have to.

"After supper tonight I walked through the Gardens of Luxembourg which are located just a block away from my dorm. I take the following from my 'little black book:

"'How lovely is the loveliness that one feels amid the throng! For the past two and a half hours I have wandered amid the Gardens here. Now and then I have stopped to write, to study my French lesson, or to observe the life around me. I sit now overlooking the fountain and the Palace of Luxembourg. On the small lagoon children soil their toy boats in a lively evening breeze; hundreds of couples are seated on the benches and chairs which are placed at every convenience spot. Frequently a GI is seen with his latest female friend. Elderly couples, young couples, middle-aged couples—all are to be seen.

"'Within me there is a longing which comes from the deep hearts core. I long for the soul-satisfying companionship which comes only from being in the presence of my wife. I long to walk with her hand in hand in these gardens. I long to sit with her and watch the children play. I long to whisper to her words of love.'

"I miss you here, my Darling, more acutely than ever before, for at every turn I am reminded of things that we could share together. I miss you very much.

"A report in Stars & Stripes today tells us that a great deal of the airmail will go by boat due to shortage of shipping space. I begin again to write V-Mail just in case some of the letters come the long way. Mail from the states will continue to come by air, by the way."

July 18

On Monday evening, I had the pleasure of seeing Shaw's Saint Joan in its first performance of the season here. This is the first play by Shaw that I have seen, and I found it very fine. The biting satire, which comes to the front from time to time, was in sharp contrast to the towering faith of Joan. The humorous comedy and the serious thought were well-balanced. With very few points of exception, the part of Joan was performed in an excellent fashion. One or two speeches bordered on the rhetorical, and the diction varied somewhat from that of the poor country lass, but nonetheless her part was played with great feeling and understanding. The part of the Archbishop of Rheims seemed to be the second best performance.

Tonight I have just returned from my first ballet in Paris, and also my first view of the Opera House. The first, "Impressions of Music Hall," was only fair, but the second, "L'Appel de la Montagne" ("The Call of the Mountain") was excellent. This piece is new, the performance tonight being only the third. The music by Arthur Honegger was expressive and descriptive, with references to Swiss folklore. The principal role was done by the choreographer Serge Peretti, who received warm applause. Staging, costumes, and supporting cast were all in keeping with the fine performance. The classical story of "Daphne and Chloe" completed the evening of entertainment.

I was much impressed with the Opera House itself. The seating capacity must be at least 1,000, as there are six tiers above the ground floor. The inlays and the carvings are very beautiful, and the chandelier is one of the largest I have ever seen. The lounge contains ten somewhat smaller chandeliers, and many paintings adorn the ceiling and walls. Spacious but not ornate, the entire building both inside and out is a credit to Paris. (The building was begun in 1669, I believe.)

Tonight we sat in a box just to the left of the stage. On the second balcony, our seats seemed to be in the section for royalty. As someone remarked, we almost seemed a part of the show where we were. Our seats cost a mere 75 francs, but, of course, there were 10 more for the program, 10 for the usher, and so on. The ushers are usually elderly ladies, and if no tip is offered they generally ask for something.

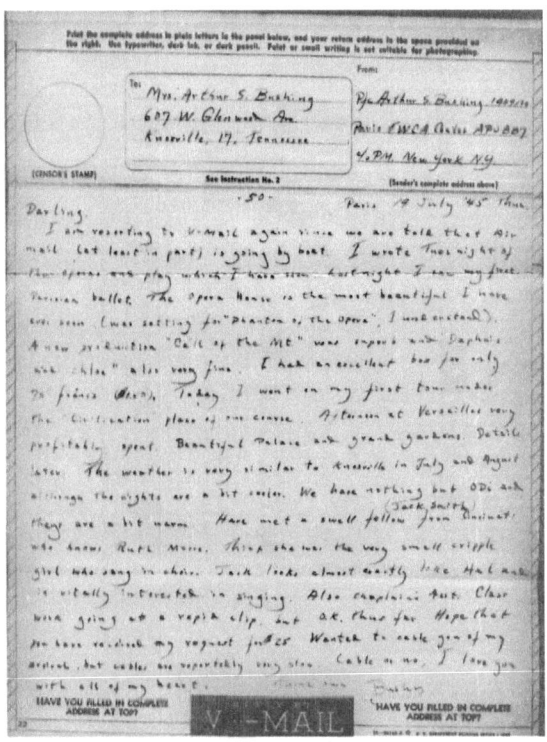

V-Mail from Art to Dotty, July 19, 1945

19 July

I talked with our guide today who took us to Versailles concerning French wines. There is very little wine in Paris today. Before the war, it was used as we use water. With every meal, it was drunk. Our guide does not like water and cannot see how we drink it. She told us that the French never mix sugar and salt in a meal. Therefore, they take neither coffee nor sweet wines with their food.

She told me a joke which was popular here during the German Occupation. The story was that the war was to be decided by the man who could catch a certain gold fish. At the appointed time Hitler, Mussolini, and Churchill met at the fish bowl to see who could catch the fish. With sleeves rolled high, Hitler blustered and ranted around the bowl but was unable to capture the slippery quarry. Mussolini stepped up with much pomp, but he too was unable to capture the elusive fish. With a well-worn cigar in his mouth, Churchill walked up and with a spoon calmly dipped the water from the bowl. The fish remained.

20th July

Classes continue apace and what a pace! In the beginners course we have nothing but French spoken by the instructor. So far I have had not a great deal of difficulty, but some in the class have had no French whatsoever. For them it is very hard. Our teacher is a funny little Frenchman with a long nose, and he uses his hands constantly for speaking. In addition to a fine sense of humor, he has effective methods of teaching, and I think that I can surely learn French under his supervision.

I must force myself to like the French language, for I have never cared for it. I wonder if the root of my negative feeling springs for the decision I made at Maryville of taking French as my language rather than German. I wanted the German but felt that it was not as practical because of the war situation. And yet, my entire life might have been changed if I had taken German, for my ASTP (Army Specialized Training Program) status would certainly have been different. How little we realize the difference a small decision can make. ("The Road Not Taken"—Frost: "Two roads diverged in a yellow wood....") At the same time, how useless it is to harbor regret in one's mind.

Our instructor took a volunteer group to the Colonial Museum today. There were only four of us, and we enjoyed a fine collection of interesting things from the various French colonies around the world. I was particularly impressed by certain of the Roman statues from N. Africa, the small gods from India, and some exquisite ivory inlay work from Indochina, I believe.

Weather much cooler this morning and not unpleasant throughout the day. Cigarettes are selling for 70 to 100 francs ($1.40 to $2.00) per pack.

A blackout of news from the Potsdam Conference by the Big Three. Unopposed shelling by American fleet lying just off coast of Japan. Raids of B-29s have reached 600 in number of bombers taking part. Devastating blows are being delivered daily. A great deal of interest being given to definition of "unconditional surrender" terms. Trial of Marshall Petain to begin shortly. Franco in Spain is attempting to gain recognition by promising the return of the monarchy. Non-fraternization policy lifted in Germany a few days ago even though the preponderance of opinion in the states favors the continuance. Of course, 99 44/100% of the G. Is. think that the non-frat rule was "nix gut" to begin with.

Letter from Art to Dotty
Paris - 22 July, '45
[251-258]

My Darling,

Sunday evening, my lesson for Monday prepared, time for writing. I am positive of one paramount factor: I must arrange my time to include more writing, both to you and in my little black notebook. I am sadly behind in both. My last letter was a V-Mail on the 19th. Of course, when I look back over the things which I have done during the past nine days I can see why I have had little time for writing. Four operas ("Manon," this afternoon), a ballet, a play, the Concert, two conducted tours, a number of individual tours, church (Am Church this morning). —all this in addition to the three hours of classes per day and big assignments of homework.

Of course, the tours are a part of our scheduled here and every time I hear an opera I am listening to French. I understand a great deal more of the opera than any previous one, simply because my ear is growing more accustomed to the sounds of the language. I shall have to set aside certain nights when I shall do nothing but write, I guess.

No mail has come through as yet for me, but I hope that in the next few days it will begin to arrive. Some of it by now will be going to Service Co. and some to "K", but I sent my new address to both places.

I fear that as a result of not being able to sit down and write at length every day I will skip some important events, but I shall to [do] my best to prevent this. Lengthy descriptions of places such as Versailles I shall try to get into my notebook even though I may not write it to you. I also must attempt to complete my detailed account of combat before the vivid events fade.

But to get on with my story tonight. On Friday afternoon I went with a small group from the class, accompanied by our delightful professor to the Colonial Museum on the outskirts of town. The trip proved to be rather interesting for there were unusual items from all parts of the world in which France has possessions. On Saturday afternoon, I hurried across town to the PX for my rations and thence to Versailles for the second time this week for "le Concert de Musique Classique. Versailles is located about 20 millimeters (c. 12 miles) out of town and is reached by electric train. We were a bit late, but we did hear most of the find program. It was held [in] the chapel, one of the most beautiful of all the spots in Versailles. The chapel was completed in 1710 and used, of course, by the current Louis (XIV, I think). The chiselled marble and gilt bronze give effects of beauty and yet a simplicity that I have seen but seldom in the chapels and cathedrals in Europe.

This morning I wandered down Boulevard St. Germain toward the Am. Church. I had plenty of time, and so I enjoy the sights of several large churches, the Chamber of Deputies, Seine, etc. I found the American Church to be very beautiful. The program which I shall send gives many of the details. The sermon was good, but I found the organist a bit too loud. The choir was small and the plan is to use soldiers if a group can be gathered together. I rushed back for noon meal and then off again for L'Opera Comique and "Manon." I knew little of the opera but I found it to be the finest that I have seen thus far in Paris. The leads were done exceptionally well, and the music was good.

Next week we have tickets for a ballet on Wed. and I hope to see "M. Butterfly" on Fri. but tickets are hard to get. I could not get one for "Carmen" at all. Another thing which I hope to work into my schedule next week will be a tennis game. Courts, balls, raquets, and shoes are provided free, but the courts are out of town.

I have yet to see the inside of Notre Dame, but I did see it last night by the light of a half moon. I was struck by the towering size of the beautiful Cathedral which was begun in the year 1163. In the dim light of the moon the massive structure stood beside of the River Seine as a monument to those who strove to express the deep inner feeling of the soul. I wish so much that you could be here with me to see these beautiful buildings of ancient Europe!

I have been able to get a few rolls of film, but as yet have found no place to have them developed. To get a portrait done requires a very long time but I still hope to find a suitable place. There are a couple of good shops with quick service back near Gunzburg, and I may have to wait my return there. I have the enclosed shots taken tonight, and I think they are not too terrible. Am sending others to Mother & Dad.

By the way Fontainebleau is just outside of the city, so try to send me Dr. Shine's Address and mine to him.

Darling, I miss you; I love you with my entire being; I dream constantly of the future which shall enlarge the wonders of

ı Our Love,

Bushy

P.S. The box which I sent from Gunzburg contains a large collection of Nazi insignia from Dachau. However, they are very dirty and perhaps contain lice. I would like to keep them, but they will have to be cleaned in some way.

July 23

The trial of Marshall Petain began today in the Court of Justice at La Cite [ISLAND IN SEINE A FEW BLOCKS FROM MY HOUSING].

At four this afternoon we met in an assembly in La Salle de Fetes. Major Frazier spoke of general business matters, but also made a very fine statement of the purpose of the course here in "French Language and Civilization." He himself was here in school many years ago, and from his own experience, he found that the lasting lessons he gained came not from the class work, although that was important, but rather the lasting lessons came from the experiences outside of class, on the streets, in the subway (metro), in the Gardens, at the Opera.

Thus it is that we have three hours of class work per day while the reminder of our time is largely our own. It is for us to choose what we shall learn. The class work will provide that door, but we must step into the room alone. We have the keys to the heart of France; the door is open to us! As we attend the opera, as we walk in the Garden of Luxembourg [LOCATED NEXT DOOR TO THE LYCEE LOUIS LE GRANDE, WHERE WE HAVE BARRACKS-LIKE QUARTERS] or go along the streets, we will pick up, absorb as it were, something of the life as lived by the Parisians. In two months, we will delve beneath the surface to know something of the lives of the people here. This is the *purpose of the school program, and everything is planned accordingly.*

One hour each week will be devoted to a general assembly which will offer movies and concerts of leading artists. Another afternoon hour will be for special lectures to smaller groups on the subjects of current interest to young Parisians – international affairs, current social problems, etc. A third afternoon will be spent in the conducted tours which we began last week.

I have great hope for the general broadening and the very wonderful experiences which I shall have here. Tonight I saw "The Corn is Green" with the actress Betty Davis in the leading role. She is superb. I am thoroughly convinced that I need a year in Great Britain before I [will] consider myself well started on my road to being an educated man. (I am reminded that I stated as my ambition at the end of high school that I wished to become well educated. I have only begun to realize the deep set ambition.)

I think that it will be wise to secure my PhD at Yale and perhaps teach a couple of years. However, I could not consider myself equipped to teach English Lit, had I never been in England.

Now and then I feel within me the stirrings of things yet to come – something that the mother must feel when the new creation is yet in embryo. "There are rivers to cross and mountains to climb," as I once wrote. The path ahead is long and weary, and obstacles which seem unsurmountable will present themselves. There will be times when I shall throw up my hands in despair. Then is when the Rock of Faith which the love that my wife and I share will come to my rescue. I once called her a goddess who "gave me new light," and again and again she will come to me to give new light, to caress my troubled brow, to soothe my seething brain, and to urge me on to do the impossible. The subconscious instincts which told me how wonderful she was when I first met her are still only hazily aware of the full wonder of her love. But with her devoted watchfulness and care, with the aid of a God who answers those who faithfully seek his help, by prayer and faith and work (much work), I believe that I shall achieve ends of which I will in no wise be ashamed.

July 24

Today I attended the trial of Marshall Petain in the Palais de Justice at the Cite. I knew that passes were required, and so I had little hope of even entering the building. However, when I arrived I found that by assuming a business-like air, a wrinkled brow, and a notebook in hand, I was able to go almost anywhere. Six hundred police guarded the court and its environs, but I could surely have tossed a grenade in the courtroom had I so desired. I wandered into many blind alleys before at last I found the door to the courtroom. At first, I was stopped there and turned away. I waited outside the door until another G.I. appeared on the scene (the only one I saw in the building). We made a fruitless search for a back entrance and returned to the front again. Here we managed to talk to a robed lady (I presume a student of law) who spoke to the guard for us. We finally managed to gain admittance. At the rear of the courtroom where we entered, the crowd was packed to solid mass. By straining on tiptoe, I managed to catch a glimpse of the Marshall.

The courtroom is very small for such an important trial. High walls with a beautiful central painting on the ceiling and elaborate engravings are broken on one side by a balcony which was also crowded with the invited guests of the court. The judges sat at one end of the central oblong while the lawyers and the defendant sat at the other [end]. Newsmen sat between along the sides. My limited knowledge of French allowed me to follow only the general trend of the proceedings, but without a shred of knowledge of the language, the tenseness of the situation could be felt. Today the crowd was orderly; yesterday there had been demonstrations and outbursts. I hope to return for more visits to the trial. I feel sure that a few cigarettes will provide the necessary pass.

Yesterday seven prisoners escaped from the Palace of Justice, though 600 police are placed around the Palace in seven cordons, down a drain pipe to make good their escape. The Paris police are everywhere around the Palace with their pistols, their rifles, and their "tommy guns." However, I found it not at all difficult to work my way to the very threshold of the courtroom without a question.

The papers today carry the story of "perhaps the greatest mass raid in history." During a 48-hr. period over the weekend, 500,000 Am. troops searched every house in the Am. Zone for weapons and loot. More than 80,000 persons were taken into custody in addition to guns, ammunition , Am. uniforms, Army rations, gasoline, and vehicles. However, no sign of an underground movement was found, and many of the arrests were for minor infringements. The raid was in conjunction with a British decree that all Germans turn in contraband materials within the week ending July 20th.

"This buying of eats is getting to be somewhat of a problem. Meat, butter, sugar and seasoning can only be bought on rare occasions and then one must stand in line. I only have 5 lbs of sugar for canning but hope to get 7 lbs more. I'll use that for peaches, and don't need to make any jam or jelly. So far the peaches brought in here are rather poor, but I think there will be better ones later....

"Our work isn't any less, and this being the mid year our work has been real heavy. We always survive, so I guess things will work out O.K. Our call for men is 50 this month and same number for August—that many when we thought the war would soon be over.... Mother B"

July 25

First exam in the Sorbonne today. Rather go on tour with my instructor, I begged off to see the Petain trial again. First to the PX for my rations and then down to the Palace of Justice. On my way home, I did the thing one always jokes about but hopes never to do. At the Madelaine, a crowd boarded the train, and I had never seen the metro packed so tightly. I had my PX rations – candy, cigarettes, soap, chewing gum, etc.—wrapped up in paper to keep away prospective bargainers. In some strange way, the bottom fell out, and everything fell to the floor. Somehow, I managed to find it all before the train stopped at the next station; I still wonder how.

Managed to buy one roll of film this morning for 35 francs ($0.70), not bad for Paris, I should say.

The WAC in my class has spoken of desiring very much to attend the trial of Marshall Petain, and so I asked her today if she would care to go. She still wanted to go, and at about 4 o'clock we approached the gates. I expected more trouble than yesterday, and in fact I was asked for my pass three times.

Back in Germany and Austria, I found that soldiers who check the pass of a foreigner will accept almost anything produced. Playing on this hunch, I brought my Sorbonne card as though it had the signature of the Chief Justice. At all three stops, it was accepted without question, and we passed quickly into the Courtroom. I had cigarettes in my pocket to offer as a bribe, but this had been a needless precaution. Although not so packed as yesterday, there seemed to be much more movement. A long speech by Leon Blum was in progress, and I understood but little of the procedure. I managed to work through the mass far enough to make a couple of pictures with the camera held high over my head. I trust that they will turn our well. Many of the former high government officials were making strong testimonies against Petain. Reynaud began yesterday by citing many instances of Petain's attempts to discontinue the war, make terms with Germany apart from Great Britain, and to collaborate with the Nazis.

July 26

Last night I attended the ballet at "Theatre National de L' Opera" to see one of the finest performances I have yet witnessed. The first was "Suite de Dances" with music from Chopin's famous pieces in the form of mazurkas, waltzes, and polonaises. The sole object was to present a series of dances. Mlle. Chaunire, whom I have seen before, was the leading ballerina, and her performance was outstanding. A few of the dancers seemed uncertain, but the effect as a whole was pleasing.

My box was perhaps the best in the house, being on the second level and in full view of the orchestra and stage. These boxes (there are two on each side at each level) are very elaborate with two doors leading to them (both of which lock automatically). There are two couches in the rear with large mirrors, and still another room leading off from the box which I suppose was used as a powder room for the ladies. In these boxes sat the royalty to see, but more perhaps to be seen. Much of the glory is gone when three G. Is. take the front seats, but we nevertheless get a thrill from occupying the boxes.

The second ballet was "La Pere" with music by Paul Dukas. The story is based on the search of King Iskender for the flower of immortality. With the use of two persons in only one scene, the expression was most clear, and the dancing (by Mlle. Lorcia and M. Serge Peretti) without flaw. These two danced in "L' appele Montagne." As a humorous sidelight, we glanced down at the music scores in the orchestra, and one joker in good French style had made an addition to the title: "La Peri (tif)." An aperitif is a popular light drink very much like a wine. I find over and over a striking similarity between the French humor and our own.

In the last ballet of the evening, "Coppelia," the topic is drawn from the "Tales of Hoffmann," with music by Delibes. Mlle. Darsonval presented a brilliant performance, and I think I have never seen finer.

She was beautiful, graceful, and very expressive. The supporting cast was also beyond criticism. The stage sets were far better than the others, and the lighting was well done. As a whole, the entire performance was most pleasing.

Tonight I visited a little music shop on the Blvd. St. Michel, where for a few francs one can listen to an entire symphony. A large directory contains a list of more than 6,000 records, and these are dialed on a small machine. With earphones one may hear records from Chopin to Am. jazz. The place is very popular, and the 30 machines are usually kept busy.

Earlier in the afternoon, I returned to the courtroom to hear and view a bit more of the trial of Petain. This is my third day, and I found that several other GI's have caught on to the trick of using our mess card as a pass.

Paul Valery, French poet and philosopher, who ranked among the greatest French writers and thinkers between the two wars, died a few days ago at his home here in Paris. He began as a poet in the nineties to follow the symbolist school which was built around Verlaine and Mallarme, but his early work attracted little attention. Delving into philosophy and scientific studies, M. Valery strove to attain the universal mind of Leonardo da Vince and Goethe, whom he took as his guides. His prose and poetry produced between 1917 and 1942 resulted. He had been a member of the French Academy since 1925, when he succeeded to the chair of Anatole France.

V-Mail from Art to Dotty
July 26, 1945
Paris

Darling

Still no mail! Today I attended for the third time the trial of Marshal Petain. French courts, unlike ours, are notable for their long discussion. The intense heat and crowded courtroom hardly encouraged attendees, but the proceedings are extremely interesting. Last night I attended The ballet "Suite de Danses" (Chopin), "La Peri" and Coppelia (Delibes). The total affect was the most pleasing I have yet witnessed in ballet. Had wonderful box. Flash!!! Have just heard peace rumors from Japan. How wonderful if..... I dare not think! Certainly the tremendous preponderance of power will flatten Island Japan if she does not surrender now. Watch Russian influence in the Asiatic sphere. In the near future <u>Time</u>, <u>Life</u> and perhaps other news

Sgt. Robt B. Wilihite, Lt. James H. McAllister,
and Art Bushing in Memmingen, Germany.

magazines will carry stories and pictures of our class at The Sorbonne.
Also Pathe Nem. (RKS) will release a short entitled "Americans in
Paris" about Aug 15th. Hope you will tell Dr. Hunter a little about my
recent activities. Work goes on with little that is new, except that we are
making progress. Hope to get my first pictures back on Sat. Will send
them to you soon. Love to all and all of my love to my most adorable
wife.

       I love you
        Bushy
Fri. morning: Am taken completely by surprise at the results of British
election.

July 28

*The news came yesterday that Winston Churchill has been defeated in
an election which swept Labor into unprecedented power in Great
Britain. My first reaction was one of complete surprise, for I had not*

followed the campaign. After a little thought and bit of reading, the defeat of the conservative Party seemed only to be expected, but the degree of the defeat remains the surprising factor. During the campaign for reelection, Mr. Churchill offered little in terms of a positive program for reconstruction when compared to the sweeping reforms which Labor put forth. That England has suffered much is a well-known fact, but the amount of her discontent and restlessness was only now made apparent. The masses are not satisfied with the present conditions and seek new leadership. Furthermore, the uncertainty offered by Britain's precarious trade position after the war is a factor which the British have not overlooked. Mr. Churchill will go down in history as one of the great coalition leaders of England, as the man who saved England from destruction, and yet even more, as one of the first world leaders to emerge in our "One World."

Churchill left the Potsdam Conference to await the election returns. Clement Attlee will now return as the new member of the proverbial "Big Three." And now only Stalin remains of the original group of world leaders.

With the announcement of the defeat of the Conservative Party came news of Tokyo peace bids. The gist of this report seems to be that the military leaders announced that they would gladly stop the war right now if the U.S. would ease the unconditional surrender terms. However, a short time later an ultimatum demanding complete surrender was issued from the Potsdam conference, and this was rejected by Tokyo. Nevertheless, a collapse seems imminent in the Pacific War. I do not believe that the Japanese will allow their homeland to be completely destroyed, and I do not think that even an invasion will be necessary. Of course, plans are for invasion and destruction if the surrender terms are not met.

Letter from Art to Dotty
Paris
July 30 '45 (Sun.
[270-277]

My Dearest Heart,

Oh day of days! Certainly today had been the happiest one for me since I arrived here two weeks ago, for it was today I received my first mail. Eleven (11), Eleven fat letters from my wonderful wife and seven others from various and sundry people (along with a copy of Time).

The first of your letters was written on Jun 29, and the second on July 5. The remainder were for July 6-14 inclusive. Gee, it was so wonderful to hear from you again! I have only read the letters through twice this afternoon but just give me a little time.

I took a few notes as I read through the second time and I shall comment on several small items with little order or arrangement. Thanks so much for your lengthy comments on the Trinity. I shall study them more closely, but it did throw a great deal of light on the subject for me. Thanks too for the lock of hair which I received and the stationary which is on its way. I need the latter very badly and even here in Paris it is not easy to find.

You gave some broad hints concerning your attitude toward my upper lip. I have every respect for your feelings, my Love, and promise not to kiss you with said disturbing factor. I promised in Palo Alto never to grow one in the states, and I didn't. I waited until the boat sailed. I shall remove sad cause for trouble before you are forced to live with my upper lip again. However, over here I like it and would like to leave it. (It helps keep the pretty Parisians from attacking en masse.)

I am glad that you and Hal have had a chance now and then to talk. 'Tis interesting I think that I should have consoled Muriel before and now you are able to offer some little comfort to Hal. I still hope to write him again soon, but you can give him my best regards and let him know something of my activities.

The letter telling of the trip to the mountain makes my mouth water and increases my longing to see them with you again. I envision for us a second wonderful honeymoon at the cabin which will be even more wonderful than those which we have already known. May that happy day come soon again.

In another place you speak of coming over if I am to be here for long. I have gone over the matter very seriously in my mind, and talked with others about it. There are many factors involved not the least of which is my overpowering desire to be with you as much as possible and as soon as possible. On the other hand, the reality of what would be involved must be considered. Both you and Mother write of the shortage of food at home. Can you imagine the conditions that prevail here? While some prices are low, others are beyond all reason. Many of the necessities are not here it all. In Gunzburg the civilians could hardly buy soap for instance. Travel is for all practically purposes impossible unless one has Govt. transportation. Housing conditions are still terribly crowded and the living standards are far below normal. I would give a very great deal for you to be able to see Europe now if it were not for the conditions, the hardships, the privations. I am thinking not only of you, My Love, but also of the hungry children, the shivering aged, who would be sharing their meager bit of bread and piece of coal that we might enjoy the companionship of being together. As far ahead as I can see now, the situation does not seem too practical or possible for you to come to Europe in the near future.

The situation regarding trucks for the UNRRA is typical. I think of the bungling going on now, and that which will continue. I say this not entirely in condemnation for a great deal has been done. However, much red tape remains.

You ask of the Red Cross over here. At present I can go across the street to a Red Cross Club and get Coca-Cola, coffee, doughnuts, and colored boys on pass eat three meals a day there. Sightseeing tours, theatre tickets, and much entertainment is carried on by the eight ARC. During combat we saw the Red Cross Clubmobile with its coffee and doughnuts now and then—once or twice, I think. A field director is with our regt. (in the bldg where Chaplains office is located), and he handles problems of money, establishes contact with member of the family, gets through messages of death, sickness, etc. While there has been criticism of the Red Cross, I think that the organization has done a tremendous job, and I am deeply grateful. There are many fields of its activity (bandages, etc.,) with which I am not familiar and so say nothing about. For their workers to volunteer to come overseas and do their welfare job is a contribution which many GIs appreciate very much.

Since my paper supply is gone and since it is time for supper, I shall adjourn to the cafeteria. However, I shall talk more with you tonight. For the present, I shall mere say, my love for you grows day by day and I feel constantly the need of your companionship and understanding. God will surely bless
   Our Love,
   Bushy
Mizpah

P.S. Were you able to get my watch fixed? Could you get a rubber stamp made for marking clothing? The number should be B-9120. I need a permanent mark for my clothing. If you can get it done please send stamp and pad.

July 29
Blvd. Saint Michel, Paris
Sunday afternoon 6:45

One only learns to know a city by living in it, by watching its populace live from day to day, and by learning to feel the atmosphere, the spirit, the thoughts.

I have just come from "a' Chanteclair" at 61 Blvd St. M., where I listened to choice bits of classical records, 1 ½ francs per record the charge, and tomorrow the shop like hundreds of others will be closed. It will open again on Sept. 1st after the holidays. The place was teeming with people who sought to hear a few of the 6,000 records of which the establishment boasts. I walked down the street past the Red Cross Club for colored soldiers. They too are leaving the city, their pass or furlough ended. Along the street in front of Lycee St. Louis, are a series of art displays on sale. The work is little more than mediocre, but it shows a bit of the taste of the people here. They have artistic tastes, and they know something of that which is good and that which is bad.

The street cafes—Dupon, La Sourse, Le Palais des Café—all are filled with people. The presence of G.I. color seems only a part of the cosmopolitan group. Bicycles are in abundance, but there are few civilian cars. The Parisians are a gay lot, and they seem to get away from realities of daily living as they promenade. Couples young and old make love in the street, and now and then one sees "la fille," the woman of the street ready to give a passerby the eye at the slightest provocation. The portable ice cream bar is at the corner with its sherbet; the sidewalk concessions are doing things farther down the street; and Paris is learning to be gay again. Just now, I see a bicycle built for two with a family of three sail down the street. Children never seem to keep these people at home.

Later: Entrance of Jardin de Tuileries overlooking Place de la Concorde

One of the most interesting things about this amazing city is that one can hardly stop and look around without seeing something of historic interest. As I sit overlooking the Place de la Concorde some of its history comes to mind. Its story begins as far back as 1763 when it was called Place Louis XV. In 1792 the spot was named Place de la Revolution, and directly in front of where I stand, Louis XVI was guillotined on Jan. 21st 1793. On Oct. 15th Marie Antoinette faced the guillotine directly across the Place de la Concorde near the entrance of the Champs Elysee. Danton, Corday, Robespierre, and others met a similar fate here. In the middle stands the Obelisque de Louxor, brought from the temple built by Ramses II, 2100 B.C. in Thebes, upper Egypt. It is a pink syenite monolithic stone, 76 ft. high, weighing 5,000,000 kilograms and having on its four faces hieroglyphs depicting the deeds of Ramses II. Fronting the obelisk on two sides have been erected graceful fountains, imitations of those on the St. Peter's square in Rome. At Basin Octagonal Jardin des Tuileries, probably a hundred people sit around the pool here watching the fountain in the center. The small boats that sail in the light breeze, the sun that sinks low too soon go below the Arc de Triomphe. Some of the plots of grass nearby are dying for want of water, but the trees in the garden are green and cool. Fish come to the surface of water at my feet. The small boats come to shore and go out again. The afternoon fades slowly and quietly and shades of evening are near. I am lonely.

Farther along in the garden I find the inevitable artist. This time he is doing a general view of the Grande Allee in this garden with the small Arc de Triomphe in the background. The usual crowd of curious and interested spectators grows and dwindles, dwindles more and grows again.
Eastern Bassin

As a bit of a side trip, I wandered into the Place Vendome a block away from the Jardin. In the center of the Place stands the Colomne Vendome (142 ft.), "the most beautiful and famous column in Paris, erected in 1806-10 by Napoleon I in memory of the Grand Armee and its victories." It is a reproduction of Trajan's column in Rome. On the spire are described the memorable events of the 1805 campaign into Austerlitz by Bergeret; and the monument is surmounted by the reproduction (by Dumont) of a statue of Napoleon as Caesar by Chaudet.

July 30

I ended my walk last night behind the smaller Arc de Triomphe at the Palais of the Louvre. Through the archway, down the Grande Allee of the Jardin de Tuileries, past the Obelisque in the Place de la Concorde, along the Champs Elysees to the large Arc de Triomphe, I watched the sun sink behind these objects as they stood in perfect alignment. The *sight was impressive and very beautiful as the colors waxed and waned in the western sky.*

Letter from Art to Dotty
Paris
31 July '45 [278-281]

Dearest Heart,

Today I received six wonderful letters from you and one from Dr. Gates. It would seem that my long delay is at least being rewarded, since that makes a total of 17 from you in three days. Not bad n'est ce pas? The wonderful thing (or one of the wonderful things) about the mail is that two letters came direct to Paris. The last was mailed on the 25th (1:30 PM) and arrived yesterday. However, I will get all of my mail a day late due to the mail system here at school.

Haven't time for a long letter tonight but will comment briefly on some of your questions. Others have been answered in previous letters I believe. So glad you were able to visit the Evauls, and give them my regards. Hope you get to see them often for they were wonderful to us in Calif. I envy Carl a bit and yet I know that from the practical side of the question, I am better off then he. Don't get me wrong, My Love. Our separation is almost unbearable, but long months in the Pacific would be even worse. If I remain here (ETD) until the first of the year, I am sure that I will never see combat again.

You asked many questions about school, and I have answered a few. As you know by now, the course is for but two months, after which I return to the 14th. I hope to go back as chaplain's assistant. In case the 71st were to be alerted, I would leave here immediately and rejoin the outfit. TWCA is merely the short way to say "Training Within Civilian Agency." Forgive me for not explaining it before. Our dormitory is rather nice, and for the most part the facilities are adequate.

The pictures are wonderful, Darling. Thank you very much. I have been looking at them all day and it surely makes me homesicker and homesicker. You know how it affects me, affects me, affects me when you look at me in such a way. Oh me, Oh my! I love you, in case I forgot to mention it before. Saw three swell ballets last night which I haven't time to describe. Concert yesterday afternoon planned by the University which was good. Found the Am. Library today and browsed through its shelves. Began a list of France, and hope to read exteminely in that field. If and when I find that Dr. Shrive is here now will try to see him. Can you get his address?

To Petain trial for a short time this afternoon to hear Gen. Weyand give his report. The trial is of course of wide interest here, and yet there is not the intense feeling that I had expected. Signs "Vine Petain" are to be seen chalked on buildings, and some current of feeling in his favor is being expressed.

Have two rolls of films developed and a few prints from negatives which I borrowed. Will send a few at a time. Will try to get prints for Ted here. If not you can get them & send to Cordy. I have only one set so take them to Jamestown when next you go—I hope soon!

I am getting a bit of writing done in my journal each day—impressions, incidents etc. Better send another package of paper 6 ¾ x 3 ¾ —two ring. I think you have a packet at home.

What is the trend of opinion concerning Britains new Labor Sort. It seems to me that it indicates the same trend shown in Roosevelts election. The PAC (C.I.O.) was probably the largest bloc behind him. Labor is coming into a position of power which it has been heading toward since the first gilds were established in the Middle Ages. We will live to see what it does with its new power.

Must close but not before I say
> I love you
> Bushy

Aug. 1
Luxemburg Gardens

I have been reading The Story of France *by Paul Van Dyke, and the story reads rather well. However, I struck a road block when I came upon a reference to Charlemagne cutting off the heads of four thousand "rebels." The sentence means little in a history filled with war and killing, but it did lead to another thought in my mind. What would have happened in the course of combat (or what might happen again) if I had been ordered to kill even a small number of prisoners. Actually we were told by our platoon leader more than once not to take prisoners. Actually the story was circulated freely that another platoon "disposed" of several prisoners shortly after the death of Sgt. Utrup. What would I have done had a direct order been given me in a specific situation? At a moment's thought and particularly since I am almost three months away from combat, it seems only logical to say I* would have steadfastly refused to obey the order. I seriously think that I would have [DONE] just that, and yet I would point out my position in such an event. I could have been court martialed and convicted of disobeying an order. I could have been sentenced severely. The underlying reason for my disobedience would have submerged completely. The intense and irrational feelings (animal emotions, if you will) which are aroused in combat have strange effects.

Later

Before I entered the Garden tonight, I watched an escorted car drive past with two distinguished looking gentlemen riding within. Since they were escorted by motorcycles, I assumed them to be high dignitaries and was later told that it was Gen. de Gaulle on his way to the Genet, which is within the limits of the Luxembourg Gardens.

Laval, long considered the arch traitor to France, gave himself up to the Am. authorities near Linz, Austria [WHERE I HAD BEEN STATIONED FOR A FEW WEEKS IMMEDIATELY AFTER VE DAY]. He will be brought here for trial. Both yesterday and today I heard Gen. Wegand testify in court. He is an impressive man with a quick retort, a live wit, and is extremely active for a man of his age. His testimony was to the effect that Petain was in a hopeless position and that France could do nothing but surrender in 1940. Today the court was very crowded, and one woman had fainted just as I came in. My mess card pass was questioned, but the guard supposed that I was a reporter and allowed me to pass. My authoritative camera helped, I suppose. [I CARRIED AN INEXPENSIVE VOIGLANDER WHICH LOOKED LIKE SOME OF THE EXPENSIVE CAMERAS THAT REPORTERS USED.]

Found the American Library yesterday on Rue de Teheran and was interested in several good reference works which I found. Began Van Dyke's Story of France.

My Dearest Hubby,

Tsk, Tsk. Prayer meeting night and I have no urge to go. What's the matter with me? Perhaps it is because I am in the church so much that I don't feel the need of going back for prayer meeting. Shame on me.

I was very interested to note, in a letter from you which arrived today, that you had been selected to join the group of those who would attend the Univ. of Paris. Now that is indeed interesting. Too bad you made such a pretense in the letter of delaying the news just to tease me, because the letter itself has been on the way for 3 ½ weeks, whereas I have been aware of the news for about 2 ½ weeks already. Yaaaanhh!

I do hope you are filling that little black book, because you mention several events and visits that you haven't written me about. [Dotty is referring to Art's Diaries, which are included in these two volumes.] By the way—do you need any more paper for said black book? I'll be glad to send you some filler at any time.

If you care for a resume of today's exciting activities, here they are. Even if you don't care for them, here they are anyway: ironed all morning, ate lunch, went to work; got off some letters and business, talked to the Reverend, and typed the bulletin; ate supper, washed dishes, listened to radio, and knitted. Now I am writing my beloved husband, about whom I have been thinking all day, in addition to all the other (?) activities. Flo and Carl are due to arrive on the 8:30 train. Got a letter from Dorcas today. She has her piano now, but little time to play it—she works 9 hours a day, six ½ days per week! She says Buel misses you, but is glad for your good luck.

I wonder why the Potsdam Conference of the big Four has been so shrouded in secrecy? What good can come from that, unless they are making military plans that Japan doesn't need to know about? Or perhaps it was some whim of Stalin's. He has a lot of those, you know.

Tonight, in a borrowed "Life" magazine, I read an article on Chicago Univ. Things are really progressing there, in an educational sort of way. If I can gain permission to keep the magazine, I'll clip the article and send it to you. I think you'd be very interesting. 'Scuse. Of course you'd be very interesting – I mean interested, at this point. I love you with all my heart.

Dotty

P.S. I think I'd better start numbering pages. This is probably around 400, so I'll start there.

Paris
2 August, 1945

Dearest,

Today came your letter of the 25th with the Money order for $30. Thanks loads. You have no idea how money goes in this city and it would be three times as bad if I were spending for drinks (what few that there are!). I still have not been able to find presents within reasonable prices, but I hope to find some soon. As I think I have mentioned, most of the shops close for the month of August or a part of it.

Yesterday I heard Wegand testify for the second time. Today I had a tour to Notre Dame & the Clung Museum, but managed to get the trial in time to learn that Lovel will be questioned tomorrow. I shall forego a trip to the Curie Institute and try to attend the trial again. The guards think that I am a reporter and continue to accept my student card. "Rigoletto" tomorrow night and three other operas (including "The Enchanted Flute," "Fidelio", and "Boris Godunov") during the next ten days. We have tickets for the best box (I think) in the house, for all four performances. The same seats, mind you!

My study tonight for exams tomorrow was some what interrupted by an upset stomach. Nothing serious but enough to interfere a bit with my work. I am going to bed very early (11:00) and hope to get up early and study in the morning.

Trip to Notre Dame was very wonderful today. I shall describe it in more detail later. For now I must say goodnight & sweetest dreams. May you dream tonight of the wonder of
Our Love,
Bushy

Aug. 3

Today was my fourth in succession at the Petain trials. On Tues. and Wed. I heard Wegand give his testimony, and yesterday I was present when the news was dramatically announced that Laval (who gave himself up to the Americans by flying from Spain to Linz, Austria a couple of days ago) would be brought before the court. Today I just managed to get in as he began to testify and remained in the crowded, sweaty courtroom for three hours. Laval must have been a powerful speaker for his voice is forceful, his manner convincing (if we did not know his history). Although the crowd pushed and elbowed, there was little demonstration. However, a number of times when Laval spoke of his patriotic spirit and his service to "La Ile de France" there were subdued "ahs" and even titters of disbelief. I took more pictures, but was not able to get enough exposure. I am accepted now by the guards as a member of the press, although I continue to use my TWCA student card to gain admittance. Some of the pressmen were unable to get in today, and many of the civilians usually present were turned away.

The Potsdam Conference has ended. Truman sails for America after meeting King George VI. The Conference announced the following decisions:

1. *Establishment of a council of Foreign Ministers to draw up treaties and settle territorial disputes.*
2. *Destruction of Germany as a military power (immediate trial of war criminals).*
3. *Compel Germany to compensate to the greatest extent possible for losses and suffering of United Nations [since the UN had not been formed, I assume I refer to Western Allies].*
4. *Russia to be given Koenigsberg and adjacent territory.*
5. *Disposal of German fleet and merchant ships among allies.*
6. *Poland to get territory to the Oder (including Danzig) until final settlement made.*
7. *"Big Three" to accept applications for membership in the United Nations from neutral countries.*

V-Mail from Dotty to Art
August 3, 1945   Friday

Dearest,

Perhaps this will reach you faster than the other letters have, at least I hope so. I have been writing to your Paris address for almost two weeks, now, yet is a V-Mail from you which came today, written on the 26 July, you said you had no mail. At any rate you will have a stack of mail when it finally comes, for I have been writing daily almost. Isn't that something to look forward to? Don't answer that!

I went to work at eleven this morning, refrained from coming home for lunch, and worked right straight through till 2:30, at which time I knocked off and went home. I was so hot and sticky that I had a time changing my clothes—they didn't want to come off or go on—then

I hurriedly read your letter when an impatient honk sounded outside. I dashed outside to discover I was holding up the party. They were anxious to be off. However, we made it to the dock before the boat pulled out. No, Darling, not the boat to Paris, much as I wanted it to be —merely a small cruiser which plied the muddy Tennessee. Some friend of Uncle West's owns it, and they jointly invited people for the cruise. There were 17 in all, most of them us (Barbers) and we had a peck of fun. We cooled off in a hurry, then we climbed all over the boat, settled on the top like like a flock of birds, then we started singing (like birds). We sang and sang and cut up foolish, Carl took a picture, and then it was time for supper. Thus it was that we stuffed ourselves, fried chicken, egg salad, slaw, sandwiches, tomatoes, punch, etc. I really stuffed on account of such a slim lunch. They laughed at me for stuffing, in fact. But it she tasted good, and now we are back in our snug little cottage (?). I did miss my wonderful husband all this time, though.

You say that you may be in the movies soon? My, my. Now I will HAVE to attend the cinema at least once a week so as to be sure not to miss your debut. You won't be debuttin, though, will you—it will be a repeat performance for you. I almost forgot that you crashed the screen in Washington D.C. I'm gonna git jealous now. Just think of all the girls that will swoon when they see your handsome profile, and how they are going to run after you and chase you upon viewing the dashing figure you will inevitably cut on the screen. How can I stand a chance? I who do not make it a habit to run after movie idols. Oh, wee, oh lamentations, oh grief! This cruel, cruel world, to snatch you from me when I am not there to defend you from the she-wolves.

White Coral bells, upon a slender stalk,
Lilies of the Valley deck my garden wall,
Oh, don't you wish
That you could hear them ring?
But you will not hear them
Till the fairies sing.

This charming little verse has just as charming a tune, which can be sung as a round, with very beautiful effect. Remind me to teach it to you sometime. I learned it years ago in Scouts, but had forgotten it till we sang it tonight, and now it runs through my head constantly. You know how things will do. One thing that runs through my head more constantly than any song is the theme of

Our Love,
Dotty

Aug. 4

Saw English play "June Mad" tonight—a light comedy and well done. After the play, Ranger and I were to meet Myers in the Montparnasse section. We were a bit late from the play and so looked around when Myers was not found at the appointed place. A night club (Venus) was going full blast, and so we glanced in to see if perchance our friend were inside. As we approached we noticed a couple of girls looking at us, but we passed by without a second glance. As we stood at the door we saw a typical French night club of the so-called "swankier" type. There was a piano, and accordion, probably other instruments. There was a small and very crowded dance floor—a crowded bar. A French blonde was fondling a poor G.I., and their bucket of ice melted on the table. Nudes and pinups adorned shelves behind the bar, and the lights were shaded. As we craned our necks to search for Myers, I felt hands on my shoulders, and some one brushed very close to me in passing. I withdrew into the facing of the door, and the spider moved on to repeat the procedure with Ranger. We decided that a quick exit was advisable, and so we left for home. I am sure that many suckers do not find the door so quickly.

The stories of exorbitant prices are legend in Paris, but one usually doubts the written word until actual experience replaces the doubt. Well, I take the word of others to replace the sad experience that would otherwise be necessary. The first one I heard was told by one of the fellows in my class who had to pay 400 francs ($8.00) for a round of drinks for four people. Today I heard a better one, 500 francs ($10) for three drinks. And then there is the classmate of mine who took a friend to dinner in a café near the Opera. He had a good meal of fish, a salad, potatoes, etc. with one bottle of white wine. The cost was a mere 1080 francs or almost $22. Tonight I received my monthly pay—498 francs!

Letter from Dotty to Art
Sunday
Aug. 5, 1945

My Darling,

Sunday afternoon, and quite the time for writing my wonderful husband. The usual Sunday afternoon music strikes chords of pleasure in my being, and I am reminded of some of the wonderful (excruciatingly so) Sunday afternoons we have spent together while listening to just such music; what a pleasant accompaniment it made for our love—two harmonies well blended. I miss you terribly, my Love.

The lesson in Sunday School this morning concerned the beautiful love story of Isaac and Rebekah. The teacher got off on marriage in general, and the importance of choosing the proper mate. I sat there agreeing with her all over the place. The first year of marriage is supposed to be the hardest, the fullest of peril, the most difficult to "weather." If so, I can hardly wait for the other years of our marriage—the first was so wonderful I didn't think it could be any better, but apparently they will be. Now I knew that already. Why tell you? You know it too. We both know how steadfast and eternal and a bit unusual our love is. May God continue to bless our union and fulfill our dreams. May He speed the day of our reunion. I am fully aware that the happy day may be months, possibly a year from now, but I dream of little else. Even keeping busy fails to divert my mind from its constant thought—you. Oh you can't stop me from dreaming!

What do you think will be the ultimate results of England's new political set-up? Or should I say shake-up? Frankly, I don't think much good will come of it, or maybe I'm just sorry for Churchill.

Have you heard this one?—After giving the private a dressing down for being so late in returning with the supplies, the sergeant demanded, "Okay, let's hear how it happened, Miller."

"Well, I picked up a chaplain along the road," explained the woebegone rookie,—"and from then on the mules couldn't understand a word I said!"

I shall write to Dr. Hunter tonight and tell him of your adventures, also try to find Dr. Shine's address.

Mary Ruth, Flo, and I sang a trio in church this morning.
Bye' now.
>   Your Loving Wife –
>   Dotty

Letter from Art to Dotty
Paris, Aug. 5, '45 [84-89]

My Dearest Heart,

Your letter of the 17th arrived from Germany and I believe that I have now received every single letter through and including the 25th of July. I received three letters last week which came direct and two of them arrived in five days. Not bad at all! As I mentioned in a previous letter, I received the money order and thanks very much. I shall not use it until the situation becomes critical. Yesterday I was paid, but only received 498 francs or about $10.

I have a few first hand figures on the black market which may be of interest. A fellow in my class had to pay 400 francs ($8) per four drinks for a party a few nights ago. Another fellow told me of paying 500 francs when three had a round of drinks. Still another fellow took a friend out to dinner. The meal was well prepared, with fish, salad, potatoes, one bottle of white wine. The change 1080 francs ($22). You see, the authorities are taking no active measures against the black market and we are suffering. Of course one can sell cigarettes on any street corner for 70 francs ($1.40) per pack and a bar of soap is worth 40 francs. One fellow brought a portable typewriter from Germany and sold it for $120. Cameras still bring a big price here. I understand that the exchange value of the franc in the States is 1¢; we are paid at an exchange rate of 2¢. Thus if one takes the exchange value in N.Y., we should receive twice as much per month for our pay.

Sat. night I attended the opening of the Nat. Opera with the showing of Rigoletto (the other operas which I have seen have been at the Opera Comique). The staging was the best that I have yet seen. The music was very fine (Verdi) and the singing was good. In the last act the clouds looked absolutely real—I suppose they were done by projection as was the snow scene in "La Boheme." How I long for you at these operas, for I know that you would thrill far more than I at the wonderful music.

Sat. afternoon I had a lecture on the "Reconstruction of France". The Frenchman who gave it spoke perfect English and had a thorough knowledge of his subject matter. He covered the Physical Reconstruction, Economic & Financial, Political, Social, Moral, and Colonial. He emphasized that the "moral" problem was probably the greatest. During the occupation of France, the civilian population were taught by the underground that lying, stealing, murdering were duties that were to be performed against the Germans. During war this was necessary, but five years of this practice and training is hard to abandon overnight. (One interesting point he mentioned was that the Protestant Church in France openly sided with the Jews during the Occupation). This is merely one of the many sides to the problems of reconstructing France, Europe—the World!

As a bit of diversion, I attended a play last night—again by an English company. "June Mad" it was called and the story was a light comedy dealing with the life and love of a sixteen year old. It brought to my mind a vivid foretaste of the problems which we will face 17 ½ years from now.

This morning I enjoyed the luxury of sleeping until ten o'clock. After a couple of doughnuts and coffee at the Red Cross, I dashed to church with a very nice fellow from Cincinnati—Jack Smith by name. He is a voice student and hopes to study at the Conservatory here while carrying on his French. Knows Ruth Moore—the small crippled girl a year ahead of you at M.C. I believe—who writes to him often. I joined you in prayer and thought at the Communion table this day and prayed for His blessing upon our divine Love.

This afternoon I went out to Cité Universitaire for a group of pictures of France. The first dealt with various places in Paris: the second was a wonderful film on mountains; the third a work of art called "Rain upon the City", had some delightful shots of Paris in the rain, reflections, drops of water, etc.; and the third was called "Mornings of France." I was duly impressed with the skill and art that some of the shots displayed.

I hope I mentioned that I attended the Petain trial for four days last week. On Friday, Laral was to testify for the first time. The courtroom and halls were crowded with the people trying to get in—one fellow told me that he had waited from 8 in the morning until 4:30 in the afternoon to get in, but to no avail. I managed to get into the back of the room just as Laral began, and I sweated and struggled with the rest for three and a half hours. We were packed in so tightly that when one person moved, the entire crowd would sway. I have seen more than one person faint from heat and exhaustion and why women insist on remaining in such a crowded place is difficult to understand. However, I find that the French are politically minded. They gather in the gardens (parks), on the street, are at the cafés to discuss politics and the discussion is not always calm.

Think I mentioned hearing from Dr. Gates last week. Sorry to hear that he is leaving Maryville. Also had a note from Harriet. Darling, I want to write Mary Ruth, and Mom, and Daddy and everybody; but I can't write even to you half so much as I would like. There is so much to do and see here, and I can't possible see it all. I hope that they understand. I haven't written Pratt since Austria and for that I am very much ashamed. Have you heard from the Glathes? I wrote but no answer—yet.

The course here is not intended to develop study habits and I am beginning to wonder if I should take a refresher course for a quarter before going to Yale. Perhaps a quarter at U.T. would be good. It would keep us at home longer and give me a chance to revive my study habits as well as review my English Lit. Well, we shall see. Meanwhile, I love you with all of my heart.

Thine own,

Bushy

P.S. Invitation to Versailles, Cité Universitaire etc. may be interesting souvenirs for scrap book.

Aug. 6

Saw "Fidelio" (Beethoven) at the Opera last night. It should have remained in German, for the translation is never so good as the original tongue. Yesterday afternoon [SAW] an old French silent movie, one of the last, from about 1928. Very funny and most enjoyable.

The news of the atomic bomb was announced today. This new bomb is based on the principle of smashing the atom, and it is claimed to be as powerful (one bomb) as 20,000 tons of TNT. Another comparison is that it would take 2,000 Superforts to carry the destruction equal to that of one bomb. Of course, the immediate end of the war against Japan is being played up in the paper. The city of Hiroshima is reported to have been wiped out by the bomb. However, the long range use of such power is not hidden from view. Such tremendous [POWER] diverted to peacetime utility can revolutionize the world just as its discovery will revolutionize the world of science. What hath man wrought? What hath man brought against man?

---

* Letter from Dotty to Art
Monday
August 6, 1945

Darlingcal,

I am so relieved to know that your mail finally caught up with you. Mail from you in Paris continues to come speedily, averaging from six to eight days in transit. I am amazed! Your letter written July 30 arrived today, for example. It makes you seem much nearer, which indeed you are.

Oak Ridge sky-rocketed to fame today when the president announced the well-kept secret of what they are making. At last we know! But the knowledge is a bit fearful. Almost two billion dollars has been spent in building up the 'The Project" for research in and production of the deadliest weapon yet devised by man—the Atomic Bomb! Here I am within easy traveling distance of the mushroom city that is destined to take its place on the pages of history, and I've never seen it. The project has been called the "greatest scientific gamble" ever made—but we won. The possibilities of this atomic bomb are fearful in the extreme. Just one of these bombs is equal to 20,000 tons of explosives, and it takes only one to demolish an entire city! Today's headlines carry the report of a Japanese town thus destroyed, with the threat that there is more to follow. I shudder to think how easily entire civilizations could easily be wiped out with just a few of these bombs. The great discovery carries with it great moral responsibility which we must maintain, or else ----! The gov't is to exercise strict control of Oak Ridge till all threat of war has ceased, then the startling discoveries in electronics will be used for the benefit rather than destruction of mankind. WE HOPE! Yes, it looks as if Oak Ridge in on the map to stay.

I suppose you are right about my coming to Europe—besides, Truman has flatly put his foot down about it—he says NO. My only hope would be to join the Red Cross, and even that might not work out so well—by the time I got to Paris (provided I could select where I was to go) you would probably be gone, and then I would be stuck. I guess I'd better resign myself to looking for you when I see your coming, and not before!

Naturally I like to tease you about your fluffy upper lip—don't take everything I say too seriously, Darling. Many have been the comments on your latest pictures (Which I proudly display to anyone the least bit interested) taken in Paris July 22nd. All the men unanimously agree that the mustache "does something' for your face and betters your looks; the women either make disparaging remarks about mustaches in general, or say that it makes you look much older than you should. And I say—ah—those wonderful eyes! [regarding photo below]

Thanks for the comments on Red Cross. The drive for a new Chapter House here is coming nicely, no thanks to my fruitless efforts in its behalf.

I was unable to get your watch fixed—it still takes a part that no one seems to have or can get right now. As for the rubber stamp, I can probably get that in time. Will try, at any rate.

It is late, and I must to bed, to pray for and dream of
   Our Love,
   Dotty

Art Bushing in Paris, July 22, '45
[Referenced in Dotty's letter of August 6, 1945.]

* Letter from Dotty to Art
[on Gertrude Stein]
Tuesday
August 7, 1945

Dearest,

The papers this morning were full of pictures and articles about Oak Ridge, full of speculation about the new "atomic age" that is being ushered in. Everyone is waiting breathlessly to hear what Japan has to say, but so far Japan ain't talking. Let's hope she talks peace when she does start talking!

Are you familiar with the poetry of Gertrude Stein? She wrote "Pigeons on the Grass, Alas." Seems like you once showed me something she wrote, and neither of us could make heads nor tails of it. She (is now in Paris, by the way), recently made a trip to Germany, wrote it up for Life magazine. Her style is crazy as all get-out, but cute;

I chuckled constantly while reading it. I'd like to quote part of it you here:

> *"You see it is natural that I see many more enlisted men than officers, that is natural enough. Anybody interested in art or literature almost automatically does not become an officer, he is either a private or a non-commissioned officer, they are mostly now commissioned officer, It is natural quite natural that I quantitate naturally to the society of the enlisted men."*

And again:

> *"We drove around & around, everybody had told me that the Germans looked well fed, well yes in a way, but, and eyes trained by 4 years of occupation, I noticed that the men's clothes did not quite fit them, they were beginning to hang, the women did not yet show anything, the children a little, but as I found out in France it is men grow 30 on, who give you the 1st indication that they are undernourished. Was I pleased to see it, well a little yes."*

Isn't she wonderful? Keep your eyes peeled—you may see her sometime. She is an old lady, with her hair cut in a very boyish bob, and a twinkle in her eye.

Flo, Carl, & Aunt Carol are in the mountains, so Uncle West is alone. We invited him to supper tonite. Later he had to go out Washington Pike way on business, and invited us to go along just for the ride. The sky was clearing off after a rainy spell, and all the clouds therein were tinged pink by the setting sun. Smells were fresh and tantalizing, and the landscape & blue of the sky appeared quite clear, sparkling, and freshly washed.

Hey! Guess what? Mail from you in <u>five</u> (5) days! But alas 'twas not a letter, just a map of Paris. A very interesting map, by the way. The little pictures on it greatly enhance it, and give me a much clearer idea of your surroundings. I was a little confused by some of the markings on the lower (unpictorial) portion, but perhaps you will explain in a letter.

I am making a blouse of the most enchanting material—I seem to sniff a faint fragrance every time I look at it. Enclosed is a sample for your inspection. Hawdya like it, huh?

I love you, Darling. I love you with all my heart.

> Your affectionate wife –
> Dotty

My Dearest,

The world shaking news of the discovery and gruesomely practical application of atom smashing was announced today. Rather than being thrilled by the prospects as many seem to be, I am chilled to the very marrow of my bone. Not "what hath God wrought?" but what hath man brought against man? Of course, there cannot and will not be a question raised as to the application of this new mode of destruction until Japan falls. War leads inevitably to an acceptance of the Machievillian (sp?) principle that the end justifies the means. And yet I am lead to wonder at the inhumanity of warfare. Of course, when I recall the things I saw at Dachan, the things that are proven facts from Bataan and hundreds of other places, I realize that there is suffering worse than death. But it does seem ironic that we should have questioned the use of gas.

Well, Darling, we are on the threshold of a new world, whether for better or for worse. The discovery of the secret of atom smashing will truly revolutionize our modern science as much as did the discovery of the elements or the invention of the microscope. The fields that immediately open with this revolutionary power are unlimited. I wonder how we will use them. I am convinced that unless we progress in moral, ethical, and religious fields as well, civilization as we know it is doomed. I think that these are not words of a pessimist but rather these words are merely a summation of an inevitable conclusion.

You see, the difficulty is this: a few scientists can discovery [discover] how to smash the atom and a few thousand people can perform the mechanical jobs connected with producing the bombs, engines (later) etc. which use this power. The entire world is effected. However, in the field of moral and ethical values, such results are not so easily obtained. The wisdom of Truth is compared to the yeast which works slowly. But it does work!

My thoughts race one upon the other. They are not entirely clear, concise, or coherent. Yet allow me to take the subject one step further. With all the despondency that comes from reading of the fruits of men's labor, one must also see the small glimmer of light which burns steadily. I have just read tonight that in the 13th cent. the Jews in France were robbed of all that they owned and the Church approved. At least today, the great majority of people in the world shudder at similar atrocity. There has been a growth from city organization, through state, groups of states and at long last a body called the United Nations. I see in this growth the fruition of the work of a certain fisherman who taught the Golden Rule and preached of the divine spark within each human soul. Withal, we progress and only tomorrow can tell what mankind holds in store for man.

I would write more but there is no time. Saw "Fidelio" (Beethoven) last night. First act very disappointing but the second made up for it. Tried to look up a Capt. Brock (MPs) who married my cousin, to find that he left for the States last Monday. Miss Burkhart is on leave for seven days (Have a full letter to write about your suggestion) Thank you, My Love, for suggestion that I see her. Visited Eiffel Tower and Air Corps Exposition also today. Met four soldiers from Holland & talked Dutch with them.

Darling, amid all the rush of these passing days, I have time to think and dream of the abiding wonder of
> Our Love,
> Bushy

P.S. Your letters of the 27 and 31 arrived today.

Aug. 8

Saw "Boris Gudounov" tonight. Furthered Franco-American relations by not asking for front row seats which we had bought. We arrived late and three civilians occupied [THEM]. They did not seem to know that the seats were ours. Music very fine, but often covered up the singing.

Rumors fly tonight that Russia has declared war on Japan. This is of very great significance along with continued reports of the atomic bomb. (One bombing mission by 25 bombers loaded with atomic bombs could have done the same damage which the Air Force accomplished during the entire ETO operation – or so the story goes.) All rejoice that Russia had declared war (except Nippon), but there have been rumors that Washington would have been just as happy if it had not occurred. (These rumors were current six weeks ago). Russia will now have all the more to say in the Asiatic peace settlement.

I visited an old bookstore along the Quai this afternoon prior to going to the Louvre. Many paintings have still not been replaced [i.e., PUT BACK IN PLACE AFTER BEING HIDDEN DURING GERMAN OCCUPATION], but many are. Saw the "Mona Lisa," "Whistler's Mother," "Venus de Milo," "Winged Victory," etc.

Letters from Dotty to Art
Wednesday, Aug. 8 [1945]

Darling,

Wow! Of all the pictures! Today came two wonderful letters from you, each containing snapshots, plus an envelope from Dorcas containing the enlargements of Austrian Lake scenes. I am very pleased with the pictures, Darling. There are several excellent ones of you (thrill, thrill), good ones of Ted, and nice character shots of Austrian gentlemen. Were those taken with your camera? If so you made a good buy. If not, you still made a good buy. I am anxious to see that fancy camera. Carl brought home about three liberated (?) cameras. Goodness. I was so busy looking at the pictures and reading all the mail I was nearly late to work. Tsk, tsk.

More big news—Russia has declared war on Japan—not only declared it but has already commenced military activity against them. Japan will be very foolish if she doesn't surrender in short order, what with atomic bombs and Russians and such.

Daddy led prayer meeting tonight (Peyton is vacationing), and I don't think it is altogether filial pride which prompts me to say he did a dandy job. He did yes he did.

Friday, Aug. 9, 1945

Just finished listening to Truman for a half hour. He apparently had a bad head cold, and he doesn't have a particularly good speaking voice, yet what he says means a lot, is always well put, and seems very sincere. He spoke of the Potsdam events and developments, of the atomic bomb and its peacetime significance, of how much in accord the allies were, etc. In all it was a very fine speech not so well rendered.

Today I got your letter of July 24, containing the picture of Buel—it was really swell—I can see why Dorcas was so happy about it. Could you maybe have one made of the same place when you get back to Gunzburg, huh?

Had lunch with Hope Pleyl today in town, and enjoyed it very much. We chatted of church work, of you, of this and that. She told me some very interesting things about her parents, both of whom are Austrian-born.

I love you so terribly much
    Your Own
    Dotty

[Editor's Note: The following notes from an interview with Gertrude Stein are so fragmented and abbreviated that I have made no effort to change what the author copied from his original diary.]

*Aug. 9

Very informal. Asked for questions. Seated in front with dog.
Q. "What about the statement that French are frivolous and immoral people"?
A. Studied science in America until 29 years old, then decided that what doesn't change is human nature. Only what we see with our eyes changes; the composition for our eyes. Science important in changing the composition. Funny war we have just been through. During the War years, there were middle-aged people who lived their lives within the village, dependent upon the war. 10 Kilo. for four years. This was not very bad. Not impossible. Army life narrow horizon. Food a mere accident. Soldiers came to conclusion that life too was worthwhile. Amazing the no. of visitors in [TO SEE] Miss Stein during her war years.

Humanity isn't so changed. The human being leads his normal life in all of the changes. We express our emotions the same way as BC "or any other damn time."

Sat. afternoon party to read Shakespeare during [GERMAN] occupation. Read the Kings. How similar today. 60,000 men crossing channel in Shakespeare's day. Thus from standpoint of history, the invasion not so much. Romans landed 20, 000.

"You [AMERICANS] must get rid of the idea that you are peculiar."

No one in France thought that the Germans would stay. "We talked perfectly comfortably of when the Germans would leave." French have a general opinion that the Germans are unsuccessful. "They always get kicked out." They don't count very much. The French don't take the Germans seriously. Very unsatisfying.

"When Russia came into the war, my whole village got drunk." When Moscow wasn't taken, "everyone said, isn't it just like the Germans. We on our feet walked into Moscow; Germans with her motorized troops didn't."

No one so reasonable as a French farmer. Tremendous production under French farming system. Usually about five people in a family. Germans took ½ to ¾ of production. Produced enough to supply country around. Quietly and without the usual American efficiency. American farmers do not produce like the French. No organization and no orientation.

We Americans want to be told what to do. We lack spiritual courage.

_____boy. "you don't understand, Miss Stein. We know we will sooner or later get the better of the Germans, but we are not so sure of the English."

The French are individuals and have 37 parties. French want to know all points of view. 60 views of Petain. That makes it interesting.

Germans tried extremely hard to win the French. Extremely polite for first six months. Then they were discouraged when they realized the lack of French interest. Dinner party with Germans and French. Germans asked why they were not liked.

"You are not 'Rigoletto'; you are dull."

"What can we do"?

"Nothing. You are Germans."

Passive resistance. Blind spot developed by French. FRATERNIZATION. No German had to make a law about Fraternization. No French woman ever looked at a German man except the most base. Morale of Germans broken by French ignoring them.

In 1943, no gas for German cars. So German officers sat in cars in [RAILROAD] flat cars riding to Italy. Germans were wilted; "became disagreeable ghosts." German soldiers demoralized in France so that they had no background for fighting later.

Ten soldiers in her village wanted to surrender. 380 wanted to surrender. No one would accept their surrender. Macca [?] came in and shot them like partridges [?] when they went down into the swamp. They came to the French to tell them how scared they were. The French defeated the organization of the Germans. They would have been defeated even if America had not entered the war.

* * * *

*There is something besides efficiency. Easy to be efficient when you have a preponderance
of manpower and material. Do we have the spiritual courage to defend ourselves?*

Fraternization [IS] disgraceful.

Prisoners gave them the same listless impression as when in Wehrmacht. The same nothing!

What do the French think? Never lost faith that we [AMERICANS] were coming. Everyone celebrated finally when [AMERICANS CAME]. Not like Americans of 1917-18. They [CURRENT AMERICANS] don't drink; they are not happy. Why so sad? Why not like in '17 – '18? Like people expecting a Christmas tree and get a tooth brush. General impression of sadness. Been away from home a long time and don't like anyone. Don't like Italians, French, etc. "And someone says they don't even like Texans!"

Parting of the ways now. World has shrunk. Life is dangerous. No longer away [?]. This is at the bottom of the seriousness. The spiritual courage lacking. Plenty of efficiency. Like science it isn't humanity. Humanity is what everybody had to live. In this war if you were but liked, one got along with difficulty.

"I am well liked. In all modesty, but I am. I talked life with the peasants and got a little extra butter. Be friends for humanity's sake."

Try to understand Latins. They have spiritual courage that the Anglo-Saxons [LACK]. Don't forget that half of America is Latin. America must understand the Latins. French can't understand. Don't expect you to be contemptible but don't admire them. French use them but they are merely conquered property.

Caste system—white man's burden—all out of date. The Asiatic will come into its own and we can't stop them. Russia half Asiatic. Looked to Americans for spiritual guidance. What did we do?—nothing. We fraternize with the Germans.

"I am not trying to frighten you. I am trying to humanize you! Americans have innocent and kind hearts—the Germans have neither."

"My work isn't incomprehensible if you read me quietly. I don't repeat. Stars and Stripes says same thing they said 20 years ago."

Americans swallow one idea over and over—usually a false week [?].

"Have you ever tried to read my work? Those who are accustomed to reading good poetry can read my poetry, and those who read good prose can read my prose."

"We have lost the spiritual courage of Emerson and Lincoln during the lush years. Go back to America where a single point of view and orientation will engulf you."

Is it sadness or cynicism? You are disillusioned. But you don't know about what. If you want something more than another, it is confusion. The Germans had hard emotions and that is our tendency.

315

"Wake up! Life got too easy. Efficiency became god. We had efficiency to come to Europe. All right. Let's forget it."

Spiritual courage: "That which makes you able to live alone with yourself and not be afraid."

It is neither an end or a means to an end. It is humanity.

The only reward on earth is that you will never be bored.

We have gotten into the habit of learning in large groups. Mental habits all alike—the same old repetition.

What forces are at work in the U.S. to contribute to spiritual causes? People in South most alive—N.C. and GA. Negroes have made the South think. The problem is constantly changing and thus requires thought.

Letter from Art to Dotty
Paris
9 Aug. '45 (Thurs.

Darling,

How exciting, eventful, and withal, thought-provoking are these days in which we live. Atomic bomb announced on one day, Russia declares war the next, Truman makes speech tonight which may reveal important facts. While the world rocks madly with one news flash after another, I have enough things going on here to keep two occupied—or perhaps a third as my busier days. Yesterday afternoon I snooped around ancient bookstores along the Seine [river] on my way to the Louvre. At the Louvre, we found the home of some of the more famous paintings and pieces of sculpture. All (3,000) of the paintings were removed during the war and only a few (about 80 to 100) have been replaced. I saw the "Mona Lisa", "Whistler's Mother", a few Rembrandt, Reuben, Van Dyke, etc. Also saw the Winged Victory and the famous Little Lady, "Venus de Milo." The latter certainly doesn't fill my bill for the "perfect woman" for my ideal is still a certain little girl very far from the Louvre. Don't' be bashful, Darling. Of Course, I mean you!

I tore myself away after only beginning to look at he pictures in order to get ready for the opera. Saw "Boris Godunov" and found the music enjoyable indeed. Due to a mix up in the time schedule, I was half an hour late and so missed the coronation scene. Also lost my good seat and missed much of the staging.

Today I had a regular weekly tour through "Invalid" (Napoleon's Tomb, etc.) and the Rodin Museum. The latter is located in a former palace of some grandeur with a spacious court and garden. Almost everything done by Rodin was intended to be a part of his life work —"The Gates of Hell". Of course, his "Thinker" is one of his most famous. Was also very favorably impressed by other pieces of his work.

As if all of this was not enough for one day, I went tonight to hear Gertrude Stein in an informed talk at the Foyer (small hall ajoining the cafeteria where we eat). I took nine pages of notes and found her talk stimulating. One of her major themes was that we in America suffer from repetition of thought, too much organized efficiency, and not enough spiritual courage. I could write pages on her observations, but I will merely comment on her personality. Extremely forceful and dogmatic, she was as someone aptly put it, a mild irritant. She aroused thought which is an accomplishment for any one. She shows signs of having done some thinking for herself which is also an accomplishment. She does think that the South (particularly N.C., and Ga.) are more alive than any other section. The negro question, she says, has keep us on our toes.

Heard from Beul yesterday and Ted K. today. Nothing much new. Patton reviewed the troops (14th Reg.) I think and told them that we were going to the States Pacific bound, or we were going to the States period. When, he didn't say. Of course, this was nothing particularly new. Ted sent a couple of pictures which I shall enclose. (Have two of the single shots & will send one to Mother & Dad.).

Took census of twelve people in class today on length of war. The guesses ranged from 15 to 188 days. Average 59 7/12 – Oct 9, 0400. My guess is that with Russia in for the kill the surrender will be within a matter of days or, if not that, perhaps three to four months. What I mean is, that if they do not surrender now, they will attempt to hold off to the last. Japan will be demolished if they resist. It isn't pleasant—it's war!

Darling, I will ever appreciate your suggestion that I look up Miss Burkhart. She isn't here now and I probably will not see her until Tues, but you don't know how much it will do for my morale to speak to a woman again. Since I have avoid fraternizing either here or in Germany. I have hardly spoken to a female since leaving the States. I shall enjoy meeting an East Tennessean and talking with a woman. From the time of your letter, I take it that you would give your permission to my taking her to an opera or a show. To me it seems socially proper, but please tell me exactly how you feel. I would prefer not to see a woman until I return home rather than have you feel that I was doing the wrong thing. I think you trust my judgement, and I certain believe in it whole hardly, (for after all it was my judgement (accompanied by divine guidance) which led me to you, My love.

I will be very glad to get Chicago Il. article. Am having a difficult time reading Fr. history, but manage to get a little done each day. I tried to look up Dr. Cain but no civilian instructors are here. Was also told that the same is true at Fontainebleau. Guess Dr. Shine is somewhere else.

"The Enchanted Flute" (Mozart). Tomorrow night. Then I will have seen all of the operas save "L'Roi dyre". Hope to get in a few plays, both Fr. and Am then, along with more Fr. Movies.

The hands of the clock point nigh to midnight, and it is time for sleep. Sweetest dreams, my Lovely, and always know

I love you,

Bushy

P.S. Picked up Julius Caesar in French today. But I really do not intend to buy many books here.

8

PARIS II

Aug. 10 [1945]

*T*he day dawned in an unusual manner for we had had almost no rain since we came to Paris. During the entire morning, heavy clouds piled one on one, and a strong wind blew cold rain into the face of hapless Parisians who hurried down Blvd. St. Michael. I had always thought of walking the streets of Paris as a romantic and picturesque sort of thing. The long days and miles in combat during the March and April rains took away the glamour of walking in the rain for me. But there were other reasons why Paris did not seem romantic in the rain. It was a very early forerunner of the fall rain, of early wintery November days, of winter. Paris does not look forward to the coming of winter. Fuel will be very short, and there will not be enough food. The prices will go up still higher, and the government will probably do not more than it has already done to halt the black market activities. Clothing will be thin, and new clothing is not to be had. The rains will come, and the cold finger of the North wind will penetrate. No, the people of Paris do not look forward to winter or even the cold November days when leaves gather in the gutter and cold rain beats against the face.

After lunch Ranger and I went to the American Library to study and read. A G.I. told us that peace rumors were in the air, but we merely laughed. After we had finished, we started to walk down Haussmann Blvd. to the metro. A young boy passed us with a newspaper announcing that Japan offered to surrender. The boy's words were, "Japan kaput!" Suddenly I seemed to be walking on very light air. I seemed to hear birds singing, and I wanted to dance and shout. I thought seriously of dashing up to a few of the mademoiselles but decided to refrain. We saw more headlines as we continued down the street, and in a brotherly fashion I inquired of a major on the corner if he knew any details. Since we thought the latest news would be found at the "Rainbow Corner" (Red Cross), we decided to continue on there. In front of the Madeline we saw a jeep loaded with G.Is. and WACS bearing a sign "Japan Licked." We let off a little steam with a healthy yell. The French smiled at our outburst. The soldiers standing around the Red Cross seemed to hardly know what was going on. There was little sign of rejoicing. A few began a parade in the direction of the Opera House, but the large majority merely watched in silence. I was forced to agree that the Am. Soldier is a bit glum.

Ranger and I decided to hurry to the foyer, eat, and return to celebrate in the evening. We had tickets to the opera, but we were in no mood to hear "The Magic Flute." After dinner when we returned, the streets were no more crowded than usual. Everything seemed to be on at normal. We walked over to Champs Elysees but found the same situation prevailing. We went through an international exposition of wartime industry which was very uninteresting and decided as a final resort to go to the Eiffel Tower Club, which we had not seen. Stopping briefly at the Trocadero, we heard the large Air Corps band which is playing there and continued on to Eiffel. We reached the first level of the tower (where the GI Club is located) just as the sun was sinking in the western sky. There were a few clouds – enough to make a beautiful effect. The last rays of the sun faded on the golden Dome of "Des Invalides," and the Paris panorama caught our eye spell bound. We walked around the gigantic floor and looked at the famous landmarks standing out among the roofs – Notre Dame, Sacre Coeur, Arc de Triomphe, Pantheon, the Louvre, etc., etc. The slow moving Seine wandered in lazy fashion down its chosen course and seemed to ignore completely the history of the hour. For the Seine, what was another war? Merely another war! The club was, of course, crowded, and the dancing seemed to be literally bump-idy-bump. We stayed but a few moments inside, not even long enough to celebrate with a glass of orangeade. This is one of the cheapest places for GIs to buy drinks. (Cognac 350 francs per bottle or $7.00); 25 francs per glass).

We walked down the stairs (we had ridden up on the elevator) and spent a few minutes looking at the Air Force display of bombers and fighters. At 10 o'clock we heard the latest news. There was really nothing new. The note from Japan accepting the Potsdam Ultimatum (but asking for retention of the Emperor) has been relayed from Sweden to Switzerland to the Allied countries. (The first news of the note came from our intercepted radio broadcast from Domei, Tokyo). No word of acceptance has yet been given.

The second atomic bomb struck Nagasaki yesterday. The Russians have been rolling through northern Manchuria since their drive began 10 minutes past midnight last night.

The war is all but over! Of course, return of troops to the States will be speeded. I should be in the States by Christmas now. [WHAT OPTIMISM!] Perhaps I will be out of the Army in time to take a summer course at UT in '46 or at least by fall quarter.

Letter from Art to Dotty
Paris
10 Aug '45

My Dearest Heart,

The news that Japan has offered to surrender came like a bolt of lightening today. I had been studying in the Am. Lib. all afternoon. As I started to walk to the metro, a small French boy passed with a paper announcing the news, "Japan Keputt," he said. I suddenly felt as tho I were walking on air. I wanted to shout & sing. I even sold my opera ticket to the "Magic Flute" for I felt in no mood to see an opera.

However, there was little celebration in Paris tonight. The news of the acceptance has not yet been announced. The Japanese wish to retain the emperor, and I think that it will be a grave mistake if we refuse. I think that the acceptance of her surrender will come tomorrow.

I almost go wild with the thought of what this means for all of us. I should be in the States by Christmas. Perhaps I will be able to enroll at UT for the summer quarter. Darling, it will be so wonderful!

The fact remains, nevertheless, that I have a French test tomorrow and it is 12:30 P.M. I still have studying to do. So I must say again, goodnight. May God hasten the day when we'll be completely united again in the wonder and terminal joy of
Our Love,
Bushy
P.S. Pictures are a letter late.

Aug. 11

Reports have been confusing today as we eagerly awaited the latest news of peace. Reports in the early afternoon were that the Allied nations had rejected the peace offer of the Japanese. Tonight it seems that they have accepted it, although fighting has not ceased. The whole affair has developed into a series of accepting the acceptances. The Japanese accepted our ultimatum (Potsdam); we accepted their acceptance: and now we await their acceptance of our acceptance of their acceptance. Meanwhile the average G.I. in Paris seems to be noncommittal. I cannot understand the general attitude here. It will certainly mean that all of us will get home far quicker. Perhaps the full implication of victory has not yet dawned on the soldiers. I don't know. I still think that I may be able to enter UT for a summer quarter in '46. [AS MATTERS TURNED OUT, I WAS ASKED TO TEACH IN UT SUMMER SCHOOL, 1946.]

This afternoon I heard a rather interesting lecture on "Paris in French Literature" by Mr. Graves. Many of those present dozed, but I found the lecture of interest. After all, few soldiers care to know that Moliere wrote early satire on the French court and its manners.

Tonight Ranger and I went to the Marigny Theatre (Champs Elysees) to see another English play, "The Case of the Frightened Lady" by Edgar Wallace. Rather interesting murder play.

Aug. 12

Attended High Mass in Notre Dame this morning. Music and choir very fine. Ted Kidder arrived today on a three day pass. Decided to show him the town, and we certainly made a start. This afternoon we saw Notre Dame, Palace of Justice (and chapel there), Tower of St. Jaques, Chatelet, Louvre, Tuileries Gardens, Place de la Concorde. After supper we visited Arc de Triomphe, Eiffel Tower and night club, Trocadero (and Air Force Band Concert).

Letter from Art to Dotty
Paris
Aug 12 '45 (Sun.)

Darling,

Last night I saw my usual Sat. night play. This time it was "The Case of the Frightened Lady," by Edgar Wallace. Just a good comic

Ted Kidder at Notre Dame [diary Aug. 12]

murder mystery a la Scotland Yard. This morning I arose late but in plenty of time for church. Decided to attend High Mass at Notre Dame. The choir and the organ were very wonderful and the beauty, the grandeur, and yet the simplicity of the cathedral were truly inspiring.

After lunch the real surprise came when I met Ted K. He arrived this morning from Germany for a three day pass. I immediately decided to show him the town. We started in at Notre Dame. Palace of Justice (and chapel which is located there,) Tower de St Jacques, Chatlet (Theatre), Louvre, Tuileries Garden, Place de la Concorde. After supper we returned to see the Arc de Triumphe, Tomb of the Unknown Soldier, the Trocadero, the Air Corps Band & Concert there and finally the Eiffel Tower and the G.I. Night Club there. We didn't even get a drink of orangeade there! Poor Ted was tired, but I think happy. I was terribly happy to see him, and we still have three more days to see Paris.

News is still hanging concerning the final peace. We are becoming slightly indifferent to the many acceptances of acceptances. However, that is not the proper attitude.

No mail for three days but will probably get a lot tomorrow. Will try to write again then although have a big schedule with Ted planned.

In all the rush and hurry, I still think of you and talk of you, dream of you, long for the day when I can be with you again. A wonderful future will be ours, My Love.

Eternally thine,

Bushy

P.S. Your V-Mail of 3rd & Air Mail of the 5th just arrived (Mon. morning.)

Letters from Dotty to Art

The Sabbath

August 12, 1945

Darling,

It is a typical sunny Sunday afternoon—peaceful, quiet, and a trifle on the drowsy side—the radio yields Rachmaninoff's exquisite Piano Concerto in C Minor. Mother is asleep in a back room, Daddy snoozes in his chair, the dog (yes, dog) makes a white fur collar for the rug, Mary Ruth and I are writing. The atmosphere as a whole seems quite peaceful, but beneath the quiet surface of our calm lies a tenseness. We are really sitting on the edges of our chairs waiting for someone to say that we are no longer at war. We await the big announcement which may very well come today, at any moment.

The excitement of yesterday and day before has died down somewhat, but it won't take much to start it up again. This has been an extremely exciting and historic week, what with atomic bombs, Russia's joining war, and the war drawing to a close—all in one short week! I keep wondering where and how and how much of the big news you are getting in these days. I long to hear your remarks about it and its possible consequences.

I like that "17 ½ yrs. From now." Yes, I like it very much, and hope with all my heart it will be quite, quite true. Not only, but also— 17 ½, 19 ½, 21 ½, etc. As many as we want!! However, if we do work well in the first years, Darling, we won't be having much trouble when they get to be sixteen.

Have you definitely decided that it is to be Yale, my Love? I still want to send you that article on Chicago Univ. that I saw in Life. Your going to U.T. for a while to brush up on your study habits seems an excellent suggestion. I could continue with my work and save that much more money, besides which we would be close to "homes."

The dog I mentioned a while back is Dr. Peyton's—he left it with us while he is away. It is a lively, affectionate dog, with long silky

324

white hair (completely white) and big beautiful brown eyes. She is just the kind of dog we have always wanted—even Mother has taken a shine to her, and Mom doesn't care for dogs as a rule. Dad & dog seem to have the same affinity as Dad and children. Mary Ruth & I have been wanting a dog for some time. Thus we all enjoying the dog.

At the news reel the other nite there were pictures of the Petain trial, so I sat on the edge of my seat, attempting to pick your face from among the mass of faces during occasional shots of the audience. But alas, I could not find it. However, I still believe that you were among those present that day.

Perhaps within some months I will see your face without having to look in the newsreels for it. Oh, happy day. How glorious are the wonders of

Our Love!

Dotty

P.S. I think I'm mixed up on my page numbers. Please forgive, please.

* August 14, 1945

V – J DAY

(ALMOST)

My Darling!!

I am pinching myself! The great day has came!!! (We hope) It is still diplomatically unofficial, but by now almost the entire world knows that peace is happening. After three days of tense waiting, it looks as if our hopes are to be fulfilled. The radio has taken me twice to Paris this morning, describing how you are celebrating. It has also taken us to London, Guam, Times Square, Chicago, Washington, and San Francisco, telling of whoopee there. I have heard no unusual sounds in this neighborhood at all—things are very quiet. If anyone around here is celebrating, they are keeping it mighty quiet. As for me —I thank almighty God that peace has come.

I awoke at 6:30 this morning, and the first sounds to greet my ear were from the radio which was already on and full of the big news which had flashed in during the night.

Oh, Darling, is it really true? Can we definitely look toward our wonderful future? Comeer. I wanta hug you and kiss you and kiss you and kiss you and dance a jig with you and oh my. Oh my indeed.

I keep trying not to hope that you will be home any sooner, but fail utterly. So far I have seen or heard <u>nothing</u> about any changes in redeployment in Europe—but I keep listening for it. In other word, Darling. I can hardly wait till we are reunited for good in
     Our Love,
     Dotty

Aug. 13

Our class became officially an elementary class, progressing from "beginners." Very good instruction. Went with Ted to the famous Eglise de la St. Etienne du Mont., and then to Sacre-Coeur. Attempted to see Invalides and Rodin Museum, but they were closed on Monday. Strolled through Luxembourg Gardens. Tonight we attended the opera, "Le roi d'Ys." Very fine staging of ocean and clouds.

Aug. 14

Today, at long last, came the news for which we have waited so long. Finally, Japan has agreed to the surrender terms. After fighting since 1931 against the Chinese, since 1941 against the British and the Americans, for a week against Russia (and thus the entire world, Japan surrendered today.

A party planned for more than a week came at an appropriate time, and our class visited Professor Menard at his home a few miles out of the city at the small town of Champigny. [Champigny-sur-Marne is in the southeastern suburbs of Paris, France. It is located 7.8 miles from the centre of Paris.]

I met Ted for lunch just as I heard the big news, and so we began the war together and ended it in the same way. After lunch we hurried through the Pantheon and then rushed to the Bastille, where I was to catch the train. I almost missed it but managed finally to find the rest of the group [MY CLASS]. Our cars were double decked affairs—the lower part having separate compartments with doors on the outside and the top having the conventional aisle.

The apartment was a lovely little place, and the furniture was of good quality. M. Menard plays the piano with much vivacity, and he entertained us with everything from "Home Sweet Home" and "Boogy-Woogie" to the "Carmen" overture, Liszt, and Chopin. There was much to drink, and I managed to sip a drop of cognac. It was not pleasant but it would have been an insult to have refused it. I also had

My Sorbonne Classmates, August 14, 1945

"My Sorbonne Classmates" [Back side of the above photo.]

Prof. Pierre Menard Paris 45.
My French Prof. z la Sorbonna

a taste of a weak French beer which tasted like very poor cider t'hat had just begun to turn. We had sandwiches in abundance and some delicious pastry—the best that I have yet tasted. A great deal of fruit (grapes, peaches, and pears) were on the table, and so we did not go hungry. There were many bottles of white wine, but I cared little for it.

Had much difficulty in getting away, but returned an hour late to the "Folies Bergere." Ted had brought the tickets and had gone in. Some of the staging was very good, but for the most part I thought the show was second rate. Almost the only thing not shown was modesty.

And so the War of the World is over. It hardly seems real. It is difficult to realize that for the first time in many long years man is not pitted against man in a death struggle tonight. It is with a humble heart that I turn to God to give thanks. May the blessing of peace be a lasting one, one which we will prove equal to accepting.

———

VICTORY NIGHT
!!!

Darling!

This is it! This is the happy hour we've been waiting for far so long! Now that it is here, it is hard to believe that it is really true. However, I have only to listen to the bedlam pervading the city, and I am reassured. At about 6:00 the great news flash came over the radio, and this time it was <u>official</u>! (It must have been about midnite in Paris) We tearfully hugged each other and went into conniptions, then went out on the porch to just listen. Factory whistles were blowing, horns were to be heard honking all over the place, and me without a horn of any description. All I could do was to jump up and down and holler. Flo and Carl and the rest of the family came down for supper, which we had in the back yard, picnic style. Flo & Carl had a couple of tonettes, and they were tooting away for dear life.

Later in the evening most of us piled in Uncle West's car and headed for town, with Flo & Carl tooting tonettes, also we finally dug up two bells, which we kept ringing in approved Salvation Army style. We had to go by back streets, park, and walk a few blocks to get to Gay Street. [downtown Knoxville] On the way we stopped for a few moments in Scrand Presby. Ch. and bowed ourselves in prayer. Following that we went to Gay Street, where noisy celebration was in progress. There were no cars or street cars on the street—it was filled a gay, milling crowd of people. People mostly just stood on the sidewalks, but in the street they were walking up and down. Some marched along beating dishpans, garbage lids, etc., forming impromptu and rag toggle hands.(?) Paper and confetti covered the street, 'til it resembled an inch of snowfall. Younger ones made improvised paddles of paper or

anything available and went about swatting unsuspecting suckers in the place where you sit down—I was among those so afflicted. One clownish fellow went up and down the street with an old broom, pretending to clear the path for any soldiers who might be following in his wake! Oh, it was gay, mad, exciting, delirious. After we returned home Flo, Carl, M.R. & I played games till midnite. It is extremely late, and I go to bed happy, filled with thoughts of the now clearer future of
Our Love,
Dotty

August 15

This morning we had a very small class, as everyone seemed to suffer from the celebration of the victory news. Ted came after lunch, and we rushed out to Versailles. I showed him the places I had seen, and we took a few pictures. ["Chapel at Versailles with Ted"] We ate together at the Foyer and then dashed madly to his hotel for his baggage, which was gone. We found it at the train with his other friends and managed to get a good seat.

I must give a great deal of credit to the Transportation Corps and the MPs [MILITARY POLICE] for the way they handle the thousands of GIs coming and going on pass to Paris. They have certainly worked out an efficient system.

Tonight I am very tired form the three and a half days of showing Ted the sights of Paris. I shall revert to normal speed as soon as possible.

We saw the Statue of Liberty which is here in Paris on the Pont de Grenelle. How wonderful it would be to see the sister Lady! The one here is a smaller model of the one in New York harbor.

MacArthur was announced to be in charge of the occupation of Japan. High point men are to go out first. The question on every GI's lips is "When do I go home?" Marshall Petain judged guilty but jury asked for mercy.

Letter from Art to Dotty
Paris
Aug 15, 45

My Dearest Heart,
Just put Ted on the train for Germany. What a three and half days! Monday it was the "Pantheon," "Sacre-Coeur," and Luxembourg

Chapel at Versailles with Ted, Aug. 15, 1945

Gardens. We tried to see "Invalades" and Rodin Museum (Hotel Biron) but they were closed. In the evening we saw a fine production of "L 'Roi D'y's." "Sacre Coeur" is one of the more famous churches here and is located on a high hill overlooking the entire city. It has usual architecture and is very beautiful. One of the outstanding things about the opera apart from the music itself was the staging of the last scene in which the ocean waves are seen dashing against a lone rock in the sea. The mad clouds and angry waves were very realistic, (being projected).

Yesterday I was obliged to go into the country for a party given by my professor but I left early to go to the chow with Ted. Had a taste of white wine which is not to be compared with a glass of water.

The news of Japans acceptance I heard just as I was meeting Ted yesterday for lunch (He ate three or four meals with me.) We, of course, we overjoyed, but the celebrations have been going on here for several days so it was merely a continuation.

Your letter today came concerning G. Stein. Interesting that I should have heard her just two day after you wrote. As I entered the Lycee tonight she was standing in front with her dog, talking to three or four G.I.'s.

Glad to see the beautiful material for the blouse, but would rather see the blouse with a certain wonderful girl in it. Must to bed to dream

I love you,

Bushy

P.S. Tanks for "Hearth Log", but who is supposed to censor jokes? Wow!

Ted says we were originally scheduled to return to States in Feb. should be speeded up.

Aug. 16

Went quite a distance out of town today with some classmates for a tennis game, my first since the day I played at Stanford and was stricken with appendicitis. Had a good game at a small recreation center....

Letter from Dotty to Art
Aug. 16, 1945
Record Breakers

Darling,

Forgive me, but I was too tired to write last nite. In the morning (of yesterday) we washed. In the afternoon I worked only long enough to type up the bulletin, then dashed through the pouring rain (unprotected) to catch a bus for town, where I met Ruth Lane. Nothing was open save the shows, and we went to the Strand just for the heck of it. I am still looking for you in the news reel, but no luck so far. Ruth came home with me, ate supper & spent the night. We had a very special prayer meeting at the church last nite, too—held in main auditorium, organ, special music, and a number of very special prayers were offered from full hearts. After we got home from that we sang and talked till midnite. Looks like I never am gonna catch up on my sleep! Oh, well—there will never be another time quite like this, so I may as well make the most of it. Oh—Carl left last nite, too.

Guess who showed up at Record Breakers tonite? None other than Jan Naberhiers! Remember her? She was in my class at Maryville, but turned traitor (?) and graduated at U.T. She was an athletic sort of girl —has returned to Knoxville to teach Retail, Merchandizing at Knoxville Hi. She will probably become one of our gang here.

Two letters from you today! One written the 7th, one the 9th. As usual I love reading your mail. How I wish I could browse into all that culture with you! Thanks for the compliment about my figger, but after all I could hardly compare with Venus! Wow!

How odd that you should write me of an encounter with Gertrude Stein just before you got my letter telling you to do that very thing! Tell me—does she talk like she writes? Truly, she intrigues me.

When I told you to look up Miss Burkhart, I didn't fully realize how much it would mean to you. Of course you may feel free to take her places, Darling. I have no idea how old she is—possibly old enough to be your mother, but I have a hunch she is nice, and would also welcome some Tennessee companionship.

I am so glad your classmates all guessed wrong about the end of the war! It was sooner than any of them guessed. Pardon the pencil— my ink ran out, and I know not if I can get any more here. Please pretend you don't mind. Thanks, Darling—you always were an understanding soul. And furthermore,
                    I love you,
                    Dotty.
P.S. The family say they are looking for you home on the next boat! Wish it were so.

Aug. 17

Today was declared a holiday in the ETO. Went to the American Library this morning. Returned by way of the Red Cross Hdq. to look up a Knoxville girl who is a sec'y there—Miss Burkhart. Had only a few minutes to talk, but she invited me to dinner tomorrow evening. Dotty had asked me to look her up some time ago. Rushed over to "L'Etoile" (Arc de Triomphe) to see Gen. Patton place a wreath on the Tomb of the Unknown Soldier, but arrived in time to see the wreath only. Patton had just left.

This afternoon Ranger and I took a boat trip on the Seine. Good view of "Statue of Liberty." Also saw the Renault Automobile Plant on an island in the river. Saw evidence of bombing and fighting in that

Arc de Triamphe del 'Etraile, 162 ft. high, 147 ft. wide, 75 ft thick. Begun 1806 erected to commemorate the Grandde Armee Napoleon, Contains beneath The Tomb of the Unknown Soldier

area. Went over to the Champs Elysees to see a movie, but the line was almost three blocks long. "Pas bon!"

Ted heard a typical conversation, or rather remark, from one of the fellows from the 71st. One fellow said, "We must get out and go see the Eiffel Tower." Like many other GIs, this fellow had seen only the inside of a few rooms in Paris.

* Letter from Art to Dotty
Paris
17 August, '45

My Dearest Heart,

Today was declared a holiday for us and so no classes—no mail either, but there should be a stack tomorrow. This morning I arose a half hour later than usual (8:30) and went to breakfast. Afterward I went to the Am. Library, which is located near Parc Monceau, D-6, on your map. In my return I stopped by to see Miss Burkhart who had been away when I was down two weeks ago. Only had about ten minutes to talk but she invited me to dinner tomorrow evening at her R.C. Hotel.

She has a pleasing personality, as you mentioned, but also is not eighteen, as you also mentioned. Knows Dr. Lloyd quite well and also Dr. Barbour. We should have an interesting conversation concerning East Tennessee tomorrow night.

After leaving her office (near the Madeleine—7 ½-E), I went to "L Etoile" where Gen Patton was to place a wreath upon the tomb of the Unknown Soldier at 12:00. Just as I arrived I met the crowd leaving, but I did see the wreath. After lunch I hurried back across town and thence to the Seine for a boat trip. We went up almost to Pont D'Austerlitz and thence down the stream for three or four miles. Saw a few places I had not seen before. The view of the Statue of Liberty at the end of "Allie de Cygnes" (2 ½-H) made all of think of the sister statue in New York Harbor. How I long to see that one!

Oh I forgot to mention that yesterday I played my first tennis since that memorable day last August at Stanford when I was stricken with appendicitis. Went out with a few of the fellows in my class to play at a swell recreation center. Balls, racquets (new ones) and shoes were provided and the courts were swell. It felt good to be back on a court.

To go from sport to things more serious, I have been thinking recently a great deal of a plan for a filing system. I will have a real need for an efficient system of putting away poems, articles, notes, comments, etc. Perhaps you will have some good ideas from your office experience and perhaps you have found a system far better than mine. However, here is a rough idea of what I think would serve my purpose. First, I would have a series of files with such titles as "Poetry," "Criticisms and comments on Books & Poetry," "Authors," "History," "Philosophy," "Politics," "Esthetics," "Education" etc. etc. The articles and notes which I put in these files from time to time would be pasted on a sheet of paper of uniform size, with space for comments, notations, or appropriate title, and a number. A second file would be a cross index of 3" x 5" cards—one for each item placed in the main file. The cards would contain the title of the item (and would be filed according to their title), the file name ("Poetry" or some such), and the number. This number would show the order in which the individual article or notation would be found within its file. The third component of my system would be an alphabetical listing of my files for handy reference. Perhaps another section in my filing cabinet could be used for filing class notes in "totem"—"East India," "China," "Japan," "Shakespeare," "Ethics," etc. What do you think of this system and what suggestions could you make? As you may suspect, My Dear, I envision you as my private secretary to help in some of this. I want to begin with a system which will be as efficient after twenty years of teaching as it will be by my first year. [Now, the reader might understand how two people could have ever kept, well-maintained, all these letters, photos, and diaries after all these years!]

You ask in a recent letter what I think of the British shake up in politics. In the first place, I think the election shows a definitive trend to the left. It is as useless to attempt to halt that trend as it is to try to halt the tides of the seas. I think the same trend to the left will be seen here in France in the Oct. election. Mr. Atler has a tremendous advantage in that many of his cabinet members served in the coalition government under Churchill. England's political future is changing just as it is changing for every world power. Perhaps, the labor party will be able to adjust to the new situations. I hope so. I wonder just how we are going to adjust our politics to internationalism. The question is an important one.

By the way, as I wrote Mother and Dad, I think it would be wise for you to begin writing to Service Co. after about Aug., 28th or 30th. We finish here on Sept. 7th, and I expect to return at once to Gunzburg. Also hold all Xmas packages. I know nothing new, but I do know that a lot of men will be in the States by Jan 1st.

It was grand to have had three and a half days with Ted here in Paris. We spent a lot of time talking about you and Cordy and about our plans. I asked Ted how he would like to spend a few days with us at the cabin & he said he would love it. They do not have access to a mountain cabin. Wish we could invite them over when that wonderful day arrives. Of course, we want part of our time at the cabin to be absolutely our own. Do you suppose we could find a nice little apartment in Knoxville for that quarter at U.T.?

By the way, again, in regard to film and my camera: I can use either 620 or 120 so buy either. At present I have a good supply on hand, so if you have not sent any yet, just hold on to any that you find. We can always use them later on, and my supply could always run out. Have three rolls now waiting to be developed, and I take more all the time.

I must say goodnight, my Darling, but not before repeating.
        I love you, Bushy

P.S. No mail this morning and I can't get stamps. Will mail this as soon as I can get the postage.

Letter from Dotty to Art
Friday Nite
Aug. 17, 1945

Dearest One,

Any new rumors as to when you will be coming home? I homep? [Dotty often used this type of play on words.] Of course I want you to stay until you finish your course at the Sarbonne, but after that I see no reason for you to hang around Europe any longer. I am now beginning to hope you will be home by Christmas—please dash me if said hopes are utterly in vain, as I am a bundle of hopes—therefore quite dashing—er—dashable.

I just figured out why a virgin birth is absolutely necessary to our Christian faith. Before I had accepted it fully, but still it seemed mysterious, and I saw no good reason why it should have been that way. Most explanations of it say that the virgin birth was necessary so that Christ could be born "without taint of sin." It seems to me that that implies that the most joyous act of a man and a woman in holy union is sinful. The reason I have figure out for the virgin birth implies no such thing. Here's what I think: if Christ had been conceived by man and woman, he would have been completely mortal. As it was, he was sired by the Holy Spirit, and God is indeed Christ's true father, in every sense of the word. Only by such a unique birth could Christ contain elements of both God & man in his personality. You probably figured all this out long ago, if so I am sorry to bore you. I think I've known it for a long time, but just hadn't put it to myself very clearly.

Japan is certainly in no hurry to sign the surrender documents. She acts as if the situation were reversed, and that she had conquered us. Mc Arthur has a short temper—if Japs don't comply soon he will do something drastic, methinks. It seems to me that Japan's future will be good or bad in proportion to the activity of Christians there. They are few, but they are powerful.

What a beautiful dream I had last nite. You were kissing me the most beautiful kiss—really it was quite realistic. I should have said we were kissing each other, because my response was really terrific! And so with continued fervor I send you my utmost
Love,
Dotty

Aug. 18

Went to a rather interesting lecture on "Social and Political Conditions in France" by a former Lt. in the Maquis [FRENCH RESISTANCE GROUP]. My ideas concerning the black market are gradually being changed by what I see and what I hear. The gov't. is doing nothing to stop it, because everyone is taking part. Some say that the reason the gov't. does nothing is because too many in high gov't. positions are involved. Perhaps so. One thing seems paramount to me; the French are not yet unified. For five years they fought the Germans in small bands of resistance, oftentimes not knowing whether or not their neighbor was friend or foe. They thus reverted to the primitive type of relying solely on one's immediate circle. They learned to seek the necessities of life at all cost, whether by thievery, by illegal selling and buying , or in any other way which was expedient. Today they still cling to their habits formed by five years of hardship and resisting. There is still no group trust nor willingness to submit to the greatest good for the greatest number. As long as this attitude exists, so will the black market. Much remains ahead before France will be on her feet again. De Gaulle will meet with Pres. Truman in Washington next week, and perhaps essential needs will be worked out.

It is announced today that De Gaulle has commuted the death sentence for Marshall Petain to life imprisonment. I am glad.

Tonight I had dinner with Miss Gladys Burkhart, a Knoxville girl and now a Red Cross sec'y here in Paris. We had a wonderful steak smothered in French fried potatoes and carrots. It was the most tasty meal I have yet had in Europe. After the meal, we attended Somerset Maughm's "The Circle," put on by an English cast. The play was the best I have yet seen here, and I enjoyed it immensely. We talked Knoxville and East Tenn. all evening, and amazingly enough I met a Goddard girl from Knoxville who is also here in the Red Cross. Such a small world. It was pleasant to find that Miss Burkhart neither smokes nor drinks. Women always cheapen their feminine attractiveness when they hold a cigarette so unnaturally.

My Darling,

Today (Sunday) has been the first day of rest which I have had in a very long time. I arose at the luxurious hour of 11:45 A.M., went to lunch, prepared my lesson for Monday, read a bit, and slept again for an hour and a half until supper time. Whata way to spend a rainy Sunday in Paris!

Well, I must tell of my first date as a married man. Did I feel guilty? Well, yes. But after all I had instructions from you to look her up. One must be obedient to one's wife. Mustn't one? It all began at six-thirty when I was scheduled to meet Miss Burkhart for supper. From the hotel where we met (near Place de la Concorde) we trudged through a torrent of rain to another Red Cross dining hall near the Madeleine. Here we found a string quartet playing dinner music, and a very neat tables. Waiters served us and it was like eating in a deluxe hotel back home. We had a wonderful steak (rare) smothered in delicious french fried potatoes and creamed carrots. The meal was by far the best I have tasted since eat the last meal which my dear wife prepared. Before we had started on our soup, another Red Cross girl came over to speak to Miss Burkhart. Who should it be but another Knoxvillian—a Miss Goddard—can't think of her first name. Both of them worked in the TVA. What a small world!

We talked Maryville, Knoxville, and the Smokies, and after dinner went again through the rain to a theater on Champs Elysees to see "The Circle," by Somerset Maugham. The acting was superb and I recall that the same play was given at M.C. while we were there.

I received several pleasant surprises in the course of the evening, but let me first assure you, My Love. Miss Burkhart is at least thirty five, so you have no cause for worry. I found that she is one of those rare women over here who neither smokes nor drinks nor uses profanity. From her conversation I gather that she was activity [active] in the Sec. Presbyterian Church work. She has been over here for eighteen months now and hardly expects to get away for another six months. Almost as tall as I, she has a pleasing personality and appears to be extremely fond of music.

As Miss Burkhart remarked, it was like old home week, to meet someone from Knoxville, and I enjoyed the experience very much. Darling, I hope you realize the desire one has for wholesome female company. By no means will it become a habit, but I know that you will have no objection to such an evening as the last one. If you have the slightest feeling that I should not see or talk to someone under these circumstances, please do not hesitate to say so.

I spent the day in bed in an effort to throw off a slight cold before it gets a start. I think that I succeeded. The weather here of late has fluctuated between extremely hot and extremely cool, and it hardly helps sinus.

I trust that the shifting of units in the ETO will not leave the 71st in a position for prolonged occupation. Of course, many changes in personnel will take place, and I fear that my point score is rather low. I shall keep my fingers crossed and hope for the best. Let's try to hold our hopes within bounds and not be too disappointed in case something unexpected comes up. I am not trying to see the black side, but this is still the Army you know, even though the war is over.

Am not sure that I mentioned it before, but I had a good letter from Phil & Peggy last week. Hope I can write them sometime. Say have you heard anything from Hargrave? I wrote a V-Mail from Austria but have heard nothing in months. Also should write Tom soon.

Did I tell you that Dad sold my old '28 Chevrolet? The price was only $112 ½ cash but with new cars soon to be on the market I think he was wise to get rid of it. He put the money in bonds for me so that adds a bit more to our little nest egg. I talked with Ted about furniture etc. and he agrees with me that we would hardly be wise in buying very much right away. I fear that Cordy too will wonder when she will be able to settle down! Every now and then I jot down ideas I have for a house plan, but the day when we will build seems far away.

Darling, I miss you, and long for you. I long to talk with you of our plans, I long to hold you close and tell you how much I love you. I am thankful that at least in my dreams I can hold you close and kiss your sweet lips. May God richly bless
Our Love,
Bushy

Letter from Dotty to Art
August 19
1945

My Dearest,

Still haven't seen your news reel, and I went to two theaters yesterday. I'm <u>so</u> afraid I'll miss it, yet can't possibly cover all the theaters in town adequately. We just have seventeen theaters in Knoxville, and none of them seem to be able to tell me over the phone just exactly "what's playin'" in the newsreel. It gives me the awfullest feeling to know that I can't attend every show at every theater and make sure about the thing, to think that the newsreel might come to town and I might miss it. And <u>that</u> is too horrible to contemplate!

Also got a new winter coat yesterday. It is a dark brown Chesterfield with velvet collar. Very plain, but warm as everything. It has two linings, one of which is detachable—suited for very cold weather, made of a leather like substance, ends in knitted cuffs that fit the wrist snugly. The coat looks very nice from the outside, but I think 'twas the lining that sold me the coat. Cost—$35. Hope you approve.

Do you remember hearing of John Magill? He was a Maryvillite in Harriet's class, married Louise Wells of Maryville. Has been out of Seminary several years, has a small church in Chicago. He filled our pulpit this morning, but eloquently, came here for dinner. He was here several times during his college days. He has a beautiful speaking as well as singing voice, which makes for a fine delivery. He has something vital to say, too. His sermon theme was "Earth Might be Fair" <u>if</u> we recognize the infinitude of God, practice the practical realty of Christ's teachings and (pt. 3)—shucks. Can't remember it. You make it up.

Only 40,000 people out of the 150-200,000 people in Knoxville have registered for voting. How in the world can we hope to do anything about the present (deplorable) city administration at that rate? Politics here are pretty bad; why is it people will gripe and gripe about it, but fail to do anything about it when they have the opportunity. Furthermore, the good, solid, upstanding citizens refuse to run for offices for fear of getting their names besmirched. Discouraging, ain't it?

Enclosed is an excellent editorial from today's paper.

I am ever strengthened and sustained by the power of
>Our Love,
>Dotty

P.S. The Lord bless you and keep you, and make His face to shine upon you, and give you peace.

Aug. 21

Spent most of the Sabbath in bed but did wander down by the art sales on Blvd. St. Michel after supper. [The boulevard Saint-Michel is a tree-lined boulevard in the Latin Quarter of Paris.] Picked up a beautiful autumn landscape for 450 francs—very reasonable price. Mailed to Dotty today.

Weather continues cold and rainy, and my cold has made life rather miserable. Went to the library this afternoon. Found Ludwig's Napoleon *and was very much taken by its beginning.*

The keeping of a mistress is an age-old custom in Paris and is as much a part of city life as the Seine itself, I suppose. However, it seems a bit strange for the average G.I. Some take up the custom in an attempt to "follow the style." I heard a typical story yesterday of an officer who was describing the very comfortable quarters which he deeps across town. However, he was bewailing the fact that the young lady insisted that he pay the monthly rental of 3,000 francs!

Letter from Art to Dotty
Paris
21 Aug, '45

My Darling,

Yesterday came your letter of the 10th, and today came two more written on the 12th and 14th. Your description of the tense moments of waiting were good and I enjoyed them. What a blessed relief it is for all of us—now that the war is really over.

I shall attempt to answer your questions before going into more discussion of affairs here. In regard to the lack of ribbons, patches, etc., I must confess that only today was I able to get my full set of ribbons. Frankly, I take little pride in them but I suppose I should. I shall try to get a picture with all the battle array shining. Those pictures were taken in Augsburg, where Ted was located—not Gunzburg. (Ted has since moved to another location in the same city.) As to my room in Gunzburg, it was very small and there were five of us therein. Nevertheless, it was quite nice. (Perhaps my letter describing the house did not arrive!)

Your question concerning Yale is more difficult to answer. One day I am decided, the next uncertain. There would be definite advantages to going Chapel Hillward for my M.A. Yet, if I attended Yale for everything, I could possible swing part of my PhD. in England under some exchange system. I shall continue to weigh the questions, seek competent advise and reserve my final decision until a later time. Would like to discuss it with Sam sometime.

Don't take too seriously my optimistic hopes for a speedy return to the States. I fear that the excitement of the moment held sway. Unless we are thrown into occupation, I do think that my return will be within five or six months, but even then I will not be out.

By the way, I have made a good contact here. Met a very nice T/4 (Technical Sgt.) on the train coming to Paris who is also from 71st. He is in the IT E. (Information & Edu.) Office at Division. (Hdq.) We eat together quite often and find many things in common. He is probably about thirty, from Boston, and something of a philosopher. Should I find my position with Chaplain Webb precarious, I think my friend could do something for me in Division. The Chaplain has done much for me and I do not want to run out on him, but, nevertheless, a secondary plan of attack is always a safe precaution.

I bought a small present for you Sun. and mailed it (First Class) today. I trust that it arrives in good condition. As I have mentioned before, there are few things here which are within reason for presents. Today came the news that the French Gov't will increase our purchasing power with 850 francs per month. That will surely help. I had wished to hear Lily Pons Sat. night at the Opera in a program commemorating the liberation of Paris. The prices range from 700 francs to 2,000. I shall not attend!

My cold has improved none at all and the weather has been beastly. Rain, cold, with alternating warm intervals to make one all the more susceptible to cold. I have slept more in the past three nights than in any previous week in Paris. Have likewise seen little. Visited the Library this afternoon to browse and to read a few notes on Paris in my old friend the Encyclopedia Britannica. Found Emil Ludwig's Napoleon and came home tonight to be set on fire by the style of writing and perhaps more by the man Buonaparte himself. If I could only read for four hours every day, write for four hours every day, exercise for two hours, study for six hours, tour Paris for four hours, sleep eight solid hours—well I can't!

Letter from Mother & Dad today. They hope so much that you will be able to visit them soon. Take the pictures with you for I have been able to get only one set of most of them. Try to stay longer than last time if you can, Darling. They love to have you. (So would I!)

I got a bunch of pictures back tonight which I will begin to send shortly. I thought I had completely ruined one roll taken at the Petain trial, but I saved about half a them. Two pictures of the trial came out. Am very much pleased with my camera and hope to get a filter here. This will bring out cloud effects much more clearly. Have a tripod which a friend gave me and this enables me to get slow shots and time exposures. Remember I can use 620 or 120 and get 12 shots to the roll. The lens has an opening from 4.5>16 and the shutter speed is from 1 sec to 1/300. The make is "Voiglander" on a Rolla Flex model.

Heard from Mary Ruth today. Seems impossible that she should be a junior already. My, my! I do hope to write her soon and also must write "Mom". What are the prospects for Carl now? What do they plan to do? Have you heard from the Roblene? Had nice letter from Hal yesterday from Chicago.

As my experience broadens day by day. I only realize the more the deep significance attached to the meaning of the perfect gift of
Our Love,
Bushy

Aug. 22

I noted the following quotation while reading in Ludwig's Napoleon: "'It is but a step from victory to defeat. In affairs of magnitude, I have learned that in the last resort, everything turns on a trifle'" Napoleon (p. 57)

"'A famished soldier perpetrates excesses which make one ashamed of being a man,'" said Napoleon when speaking of looting. How well I know this to be true from my meager experience in Germany and Austria.

"With the pen, Bonaparte rounds off the Victories he has won with the sword."

Ludwig seeks to explain Napoleon's early successes: (p. 59)

"First of all, he owes his success to youth and health. A body that can endure interminable riding without fatigue; the power to sleep at any moment and to wake whenever he pleases; a stomach which can digest anything and make no complaint at being put on short rations; eyes that see and arrange everything."

These words have a very special application to the infantryman of this war. We too learned to drive our bodies, to sleep at any moment (and at every opportunity), to wake at a moment's notice, to go for days with no variety in diet. We too were successful.

Ludwig emphasized Napoleon's intense love for Josephine and the indifference to his passionate expression of feeling. Not only a lover but an artful diplomat was the man, and he is given credit for having the first publicity agent in history. The Louvre is stocked with works of art which he demanded during his conquest of Italy (today we call it loot) as well as the Conservatoire de Paris which received many manuscripts of music sent from Italy by Napoleon.

After lunch today, I borrowed a bicycle at the Left Bank Club (Trion Hotel across the street) and made my way to the Bois de Boulogne. Stopped along the way to view Eglise St. Leon, a modern church of brick near Parc du Champs de Mars.

Entering the Bois at Place de la Pt. De Passy, I rode between Lac Superieur and Lac Inferieur toward the Cascades, meanwhile passing by Champs de Course d'Auteuil (Steeplechase). The Cascades are artificially formed by two small lagoons and are very beautiful. Passing by the Hippodromede Longchamp (the race course) I continued on to the Palais de Bagatelle. The Palais is famous for the oil paintings exhibited there in the spring and for the rose garden. To me the spot was more like an American estate than anything I have yet seen in Europe. Broad lawns, shady nooks, winding streams, grottos, beds of flowers, a multitude of shrubs, two or three planned gardens, semi-formal—all these things made me feel perfectly at home. Mother would love it, as would Dotty. I rode on past the Jardin d'Acclimation and out by way of Porte Dauphine. The entire woods (containing 2,180 acres) is most picturesque and reminiscent in many ways of the College Woods at Maryville. Many parts are completely untended, although footpaths and riding trails are everywhere. I encountered very few people in the lower part of the Bois, but as I neared the Jardin d'A the number increased. My cycle ride was a bit long but thoroughly enjoyable.

The following passage is from a letter which Mother wrote on the 10th of Aug.: "We fully realize what will happen to us, but if we can stay on until Oct. 19 (the date on which their work in the Jamestown Draft Office began in 1940), I'll be perfectly satisfied to go back home to stay. Five years with one 12-day vacation is quite a record, and I'm ready to quit. However, I'm just as ready to work on if our work is needed. To date we've had about 65 calls for men for induction, and I've made up the list for every call and been here on the date of departure of every call...." [IN FACT, THE WORK CONTINUED UNTIL MY FATHER RETIRED IN 1959 AT AGE 83. DURING THE ENTIRE PERIOD IN WHICH HE SERVED AS CLERK OF THE LOCAL DRAFT BOARD, MOTHER WORKED WITHOUT PAY. HE COULD NOT HAVE HELD THE JOB AS LONG AS HE DID HAD MOTHER NOT ASSISTED HIM.]

In the same letter, Dad speaks of the termination of the work, of plans to make improvements and repairs at home, and of getting a physical checkup: "After a few months for these matters, we'll see about some interesting salaried occupation. *[AT THIS POINT IN 1945, HE WAS NEARING HIS SIXTY-NINTH BIRTHDAY!]* We have saved up a nice comfortable amount toward our future security ... we'll try to live carefully and happily in the home we made together—but to Mother goes all the credit of the hard work and planning which was largely hers and hers alone...."

Another quote from Mother's letter on the 15th of Aug.: "Today is a great occasion for the people the world over, but only those who have someone in faraway places really know just what the ending of the war means. We are eternally grateful that you had some part in the affair and came through without injury...."

Aug. 23rd

Napoleon said, " 'Do you know what amazes me more than all else? The importance of force to organize anything. There are only two powers in the world: the spirit and the sword. In the long run, the sword will always be conquered by the spirit' " (p. 167).

"'Looting enriches very few, dishonors all,'" Ludwig calls him the "champion of order, an anti-revolutionist."

"'He will not go far who knows whither he is going'" (p. 210). "Napoleon ... used both honors and money to attach peoples to his cause, making not friends but dependents."

Visited Louvre today on regular tour. Two more rooms have opened up as more pictures are being returned all of the time. I find that some of the pictures "grow" on me as I return from time to time.

The average American soldier lacks the tact of gentile breeding which the French culture gives. G.I. Joe takes no pains to hide his feelings, complimentary or otherwise. One fellow in class is a decided sour grape who has no interest in French, the language or people, and is highly insulting by reading or writing while the class is in progress. I oft-times want to punch a fellow's head when he shows no respect nor courtesy in such a way. After all, we are guests of the French here. I certainly do not agree with all that they say or do, but I feel very appreciative of my opportunities here.

Grand letter from Dotty today describing in detail the Victory celebration in Knoxville. How I would like to have been there.

Dearest Heart,

Your very excellent description of "VICTORY NIGHT" came today and it brought the celebration very close to me. We rejoiced here, but for most I think a note of restraint came as we also thought of the months and miles which separate us from those most dear. Our real celebration will come when time and space have surrendered to put us in the arms of our loved ones. Your description glowed with the excitement of the grand occasion and I read it over and over again.

Also today came your letter of the 16th (mailed the 17th) which arrived in five days. I like to see old records broken on this mail schedule.

Yesterday I borrowed a bicycle from the Red Cross which is across the street from us, and rode out to the Bois de Bologne. It was an interesting—if somewhat long—ride, and the Bois itself is wonderful. The entire woods (containing 2,180 acres) is most picturesque and reminisent in many ways of the College Woods.

Many parts are completely untended, although foot pathes and riding pathes abound. A steeplechase and a racing course are contained within the Bois, and there are a number of lakes and lagoons. I was most impressed by the beautiful Palais de Bagatelle with its enclosed grounds. Broad lawns, shady nooks, winding streams, grottos, bridges, beds of flowers, a multitude of shrubs, two or three planned gardens, (semi-formal)—all of these things gave the impression of an American estate. It was wonderful!

A full moon tonight! I am alone and very lonely for you. Darling, I love you very much. Be it repetition or no, I love you with every fiber of my being, and I miss your tender charms, your flirting eye, your winning smile, your puns, your laughter! I miss the passion of your kiss and the pressure of your arms holding me to you. Again, my Dear, I can only say, I love you.

Visited the Louvre again today (my third time). A couple of more rooms opened and some very fine work therein. Just to show how, my hands are tied here, I will report two incidents which occurred today. First, on my way from lunch I spied a window filled with miniatures. Ah, thought I, a lovely gift mayhaps for my lovely wife! I soon noted a beautiful landscape scene with mountains, a lake, etc. Exactly right, thought I, I glanced at the price. Gasping for breath I turned quickly and walked away. 1580 francs the tag had read $31.60.

Walking back from the Louvre today, I wandered, as is very custom through all the back alleys and streets which I could find. In one shop filled with ancient relics I spied two beautiful candlestick holders. What a lovely gift mayhaps for my lovely wife, thought I. An elderly lady had just latched the front door and waddled to the rear, but she returned when I indicated my desire to enter. "Com bien pour les deux —? I asked as I pointed with an admiring eye to the two candlestick holders. "Alors, tres chere!" says she—"4,000 francs" ($80). I smiled a little weakly and turned a few degrees whiter in color. They belonged to Louis XIV, she explained, and they were pure silver as I could see. I managed to reach the door and she closed it behind me. Perhaps I should buy the "Mona Lisa" and give up trying for anything else.

Letter from Ted P. today along with M.C. bulletin. Wrote three other letters tonight—a record. "The Magic Flute," Mozart, tomorrow tonight. Wish you were here with me to enjoy it. My whole being cries out

I love you,
Bushy

P.S. Enthralled by Ludwig's Napoleon.

Letter from Dotty to Art
Thursday
Aug. 23, 1945

My Dearest,

Precisely why I am heah! I have written a poem:

Night
Was numbed in sleep
I too
Rested in slumber deep
When lo
A wondrous dream arose
Your arms
They circled me close
Your body
Was tangible upon me
It seemed
Here was true reality
Suddenly
I no longer dreamed
Half awake
Yet still it seemed
I felt your presence with me

Still
Your touch remained reality
Your face
I could no longer see
But yet
Your touch remained reality.

That isn't a very poetic poem, but that was the way the dream was
—you were holding me close, very close, in a dream, when suddenly I
wasn't dreaming—I was half awake—but I still felt the pressure of your
arms around me, your body against mine. It was the most peculiar
sensation! Peculiar, but oh, so nice.

The pictures you send me are so comforting—just can't get enough
of looking at them. ('Tis the pictures of you I'm talking about—those of
Paris are nice too.)

Your letter of the 12th arrived today—only two days preceding
victory. So glad to hear that you and Ted had some time together. And
what a time! If my calculations are correct, you and Ted were together
when Victory broke loose. How wonderful that you had someone to
celebrate with whom you cared a little bit about. Badly put. What I
mean is, it must have meant more to have someone who meant
something to you around at a time like that. Oh oh. That sounds even
worser. Oh well—I am shore glad you all wuz together.

Darling, we shall always be together in the joy of our eternal
            Love,
                Dotty
P.S. I understand that our friend Miss Burkhart is smart as whiz, loves
to write—especially poetry.

Aug. 24
(23:45)

*As I returned from the Opera tonight, I heard the sound of bells
ringing over on the right Bank, and search lights flirted among the
clouds. I ascended the seven flights of stairs to the topmost floor to
view the city. Gazing out over the roofs I was delighted to see Notre
Dame aglow as though under a single spot on a gigantic stage. Every
detail seemed to be magnified, and it seemed as though I could reach
out and touch the towers, the spires, the Rose Window. The roof top of
the Hotel de Ville was also visible from my vantage point, and across
the blur of a Parisian night, Sacre-Coeur stood bold against a clearing*

sky. The effect of the lights again was to bring the magnificent structure closer and its paramount position overlooking the city gave it the appearance of holding supreme above all else. The lights from the Opera, the Madeleine, and others were visible; and the bells continued to peal. Paris has begun to celebrate the first anniversary of liberation. And so ended a busy day!

April 25

I left class early today in order to get to the Opera in time for a tour at one o'clock. I just made it, but the hour was well worth the effort. I have attended the opera many times in the past six weeks, but I did not know that the beautiful chandelier in the auditorium (which never fell as MGM said—"Phantom of the Opera") has a weight of five tons and contains 400 lights. Nor did I know that there are only 2,200 seats in the building. The low cost for seats is made possible by the subsidy by the State (30,000 francs I think).

We were shown the stage which is said to be the largest in the world. The figures which I recorded are that the stage is 90 feet deep and 120 feet high, but I am not certain of these. I am sure that a softball game could be played on the stage, and at least two tennis courts could be placed up it. The fire curtain weighs 30 tons (I was told.), and the screen behind 24 tons. I saw the control room which has a mere 4,000 buttons for controlling the lights. 80 men work on these lights, and there are 800 men on the state crew. We visited a beautiful practice room for ballet in the rear, and then went down the five levels below ground into the cellar. I certainly have a new appreciation for the opera.

After the tour, I went to the Am. Library to read a bit. Read a complete book on Paris and glanced thorough part of another. Found a fellow (civilian) studying the geog. of Calif. and immediately felt a bit homesick.

On my way home, I walked through the very beautiful Parc Monceau and on to the Russian Orthodox Church near the Etoile. Found it very interesting to look around inside and see where Czar Nicholas worshipped. The altar is hidden by a screen. Only a few chairs are to be seen within. A beautiful crown of the Czar is on display with the pearls and other jewels shining brightly. The total effect is one far less ornate than that which usually one receives in a Catholic church.

Tonight the Opera was "The Magic Flute," Mozart. The music was wonderful, the staging good, the singing fair. Still find the greatest fault lies with the very dim lighting for some scenes.

Aug. 26
Sun. Morning

The celebration of the liberation of Paris continues throughout the city. The grand fete de fete was last night at the Opera where Lily Pons snag. Prices of seats ranged from 700 to 2,000 francs. On my way to town [I SUPPOSE I MEANT OVER TO THE RIGHT BANK] to watch the celebration last evening, I stopped by to see Miss Burkhart, who had been in bed all week with sinus trouble. We had a long talk about everything in general and Knoxville in particular. Ended up discussing religion. Met Marguerite something or other, a nurse who seems rather jolly.

I was interested to note my own reaction to this latter introduction. The nurse had evidently been drinking and was a bit verbose. Six months ago I suppose I would have been something less than horrified at the sight. Last night I was rather disgusted, and yet ___. The girl has been overseas at least 30 months. Extended time over here can do strange things. I still can in no way condone drinking, but neither can I condemn it in every case.

Aug. 26
Cont.

After leaving Miss Burkhart last evening, I continued on down St. Germain to Place de la Concorde. A steady stream of passers by moved up and down the thoroughfare. I stared up the Pont de las Concorde and watched the faces pass. Old women, young women, women in love, women seeking love, children tired, children gay, elderly men, happy men, sad, tired forgotten, forgetting. All pass beneath the lights of the bridge—pass into the darkness beyond. I watched a moon just past the full find a tiny slit in the bank of clouds and peep through for a brief glance reflecting herself on the quiet and peaceful river. I continued to the Rivier Droite and walked down the steps to a walkway along the water's level. I turned toward La Cite and began to stroll in the shadows. The night air was pleasant and the cooling breeze came from the river. There were many shadows, many benches, many lovers. A dance was in progress on the Quai near Pont

Royal. The lilting dance music came across the water to my ears, and I caught something of the spirit of gaiety and celebration. I finally reached Pont Neuf and decided to cross there. Lights from either bank played on the water, and the wind made small ripples as I leaned over the railing of the bridge. Near Chatelet I could see and hear a street dance in progress.

Upon crossing Pont Neuf I saw another street dance in the Rue Dauphine. Standing in the shadows, I looked on at the gay festivity. The music was swing, and a few were dancing. The great number of the crowd however were going round and round in an elongated circle (the street is very narrow), where three or four "victims" stood inside with a square piece of cloth about two feet across. If the person holding the cloth were a man, he would select a pretty girl from the circle, and she would have to kneel with him on the cloth. They would then kiss twice, and she would take the cloth and search for a handsome male. The process seemed to go on indefinitely and seemed to be a much more interesting game than our version of "Postoffice." Young and old played alike, and all seem to have a gay evening. (This dance is called "Le Dance de Topis," or Rug Dance.)

I moved in the general direction of Lycee St. Louis [MY LIVING QUARTERS]. The same chance was being conducted near the corner of St. Michel and St. Germain beneath brightly colored Chinese lanterns—or the French version of the same. The Parisians are truly a gay people, and they enjoy themselves on festival days as we seldom do. For two days and nights, these celebrations have gone on. Tonight at the Champ de Courses de Auteuil, a dance is being held which will last until daybreak. I went to bed about 1:30 and arose again at 7:45. It took willpower, for I wanted most intensely to remain in bed. However, I also wanted to visit Fontainebleau. I found that I could get the bus here at the Left Bank Club, and so at 10 o'clock I boarded a chartered bus for the Red Cross Tour to Fontainebleau (Charge 170 francs). The bus was a charcoal burner with a large tank in the rear, two feet in diameter, and about seven feet high. On top of the bus were several bags of small chips which were put into the burner from time to time to provide the means of locomotion. [THE GERMANS HAD MADE EXTENSIVE USE OF THIS SOURCE FOR ENERGY DURING AND AFTER THE WAR.] We stalled on a hill once, but finally made the pull. There was a rattle with every screw, but we reached our destination and returned without mishap. My seat was beside two English girls who took the trip, and their naivete provided diversion *and interest on the trip. They feel sure that the English people will realize what a mistake they have made in electing Labor.*

I knew little of what I should expect at Fontainebleau and was pleasantly surprised by the beauty and the grandeur of the Chateau there. I shall go into greater detail at a later time.

Letter from Art to Dotty
Paris
26 Aug '45

My Darling,

Just returned at supper time from a big day—spent all day at Fontainebleau—about 30 miles outside of Paris. The Chateau there is the most beautiful that I have yet seen and has a great deal of furniture which Napoleon used. Took copious notes and many pictures, but tonight, after doing my home work, I am a rag.

One reason for my washed out feeling is that I went out to watch Paris celebrate liberation last night, and didn't get home until very late. Then I got up early for the tour this morning. What a life! Stopped by to see Miss Burkhart on my way to town. She has been in bed since we attended the play last week,—sinus trouble. We started in talking Knoxville and ended up discussing religion. She belongs to the Minnite (sp?) Church but has been attending Sec. Pres. a great deal. Has some interesting views.

After I left there I wandered on down Blvd. St. Germain to Place de la Concorde. Crowds thronged the bridge as I stood at the rail and watched them pass. I walked along the river bank all the way up to Pont Neuf on the Cite. There were many shadows, many benches, many lovers. I missed you intensely. The moon peeped through the bank of clouds to reflect in the water. I was very lonely, Darling.

I crossed back to the Left Bank over Pont Neuf (oldest bridge over the Seine) and watched the street dancing going on. The music was light and the people gay. At a late hour I reached my bed.

I must go now to make up for sleep lost, for my eyes will hardly remain open. Much more tomorrow. Until then, I love you with all my heart.

Thine Own,
Bushy

Aug 27

Shortly after our arrival here, one of the fellows obtained permission to journey to Belgium to get his wife. She is here with him now eating in our mess. For her it is only the beginning of the long adjustment she will be forced to make when she goes to the States. She is an attractive girl with large brown eyes, full red lips, black hair, and slender figure. She is the type that makes a GI look twice and turn his mind to thoughts of his own American wife or sweetheart. The details of this girl's appearance are merely incidental—the story of her marriage and her new and very different future appeals to my imagination. What adjustments, what disillusionment, what infinite happiness and joy will be hers for having gone through what she has and will for Love.

Saw a good French movie (attendance required) at the Cite University today. The old Restoration drama theme of the husband betrayed was retold. No one seemed to get the significance when a pair of horns were handed the poor husband. As a whole, the film was done well, but in the slow, easy manner which seems characteristic of the European movies.

A friend gave me a .32 pistol, western model, yesterday. Today I traded it for a smaller .25 and a trip [CORD] for my camera. Gave a couple of film to boot.

Dotty sent a very fine editorial by David Lawrence today. (_Knoxville Journal_, Aug. 19). In it he speaks of the excitement of VJ Day:

"... There can be no happiness either if we are honest with ourselves and recognize our own responsibility for bringing on these wars. The same superficiality, the same careless or uninformed thinking which only a few days ago wanted more blood spilled, to eliminate the Jap emperor and carry on an invasion with high losses, the same man-in-the-street ignorance that is content to blame it all on Fascism or Nazisim alone and cares nothing about the economic conditions that bring on such extremes is going to be responsible for more wars in the future unless the peoples of the world change their attitude toward truth."

And again, "The indifference of the American People to truth, materialistic things, the mind that scoffs at spiritual force as a means of compelling us to meet fully our responsibilities—this is the background of our guilt."

Lawrence goes on to cry out against an uneducated public—he begs for the free flow of information and for an acceptance of spiritual responsibility. It is a good indication to see such writing in an editorial column.

Letter from Art to Dotty
Paris
Aug 27, '45

My Dearest Heart,
    Your letter of the 19th arrived this morning to make bright my day. What a lift your letters are, for they always bring us a bit closer. How much we are a part of each other now, and yet how much more so after twenty years of married life together! I fear that far too often I fail to tell you how lucky I really am to have found you, my Dear. I can dwell apart from the crowd as I can mix in the lighter vein, but with few do my real thoughts come to the fore. You have the power to bring out the best in me (however little that "best" may be.) As a rule we see that the wife of a man can mould him as she wishes. She is an unseen force which weakens him, if she is weak; strengthens him, if she is strong. Your understanding, your faith, your total strength will always be a challenge for me to strive for higher levels of attainment.
    Where our strivings will lead I know not. Napoleon is quoted as having remarked, "'He will not go far who knows from the first whither he is going.'" The meaning, of course, is that one must not be blind to changing circumstance and sudden opportunity. I recall a case in point. When I first applied for school over here, my first choice was naturally enough Cambridge. I knew the quota was extremely small, and that the quota for the Sorbonne was very large. I had only a few days before entered Service Co. as Chaplain's assistant and I did not want to lose my position. I was almost blinded by the proximity to my new work, and I hesitated before putting the Sorbonne down as a second choice. What a horrible mistake I would have made had I not decided to try for the course. As we climb higher the mountain so does our vista become broader. Let us always look to the farther range before becoming satisfied with the first ridge.
    Sorry that I put you to so much trouble searching for the newsreel. It really isn't worth it as perhaps you have already found.
    Am very happy that you bought the new coat. You needed a new one last year. Wished I could have sent you one from Paris. By the way, not until today did I cash the money order which you sent. I had hoped

to be able to return it to you, but necessity forced me to give in. I intend to buy some prints here which you can frame and give as Xmas presents. Will get some for us and others for you to give as you see fit. Will try to send one package this week. Mentioned before sending one last week.

Magill's sermon sounds Orrish, and being such I can be sure that it was good. I have not heard the Maryville quality of sermon since I left the States.

The editorial which you sent is very fine and I wish that I had a hundred copies to distribute to my friends. We Americans are so childish in our way of thought about so many things. And yet the young man is virile and strong of body, the ancient sage is weak.

I long for the time when I can express without the inadequate use of words the depth and meaning of my love for you. Until that time comes I resort to the words

I love you,

Bushy

P.S. We have been told to use our old address again. Send notebook paper if you can.

Aug. 28

After lunch today I sneaked in a short cat nap and then off on another personally conducted tour. Borrowed a bike from the Red Cross Club and began my trek to Bois de Vincennes. Stopped in the Jardin de Plantes which I had not seen and also glimpsed the Mosquee de Paris. Across the Seine at Pont de Bercy and on passed Eglise N.D. de Bercy. At last reached the Bois and rode around a bit. Saw the zoo and lost myself on a couple of islands. Came out by way of the Chateau and Fort. Part of the old fort (XVI C) is over 200 feet high and it was in this prison that Louis XVI was confined. The old chapel appears to have been hit, and there is little left inside. However the front (XVI C) is still quite beautiful. The Bois itself contains over 2.300 acres and has existed since the XII C. Louis XV had it cut down and replanted in 1731.

Hurried back by way of the Place de la Nation and the Bastille, crossing the Seine this time over the Ile St. Louis. Rushed through a shower and then down town for dinner with Miss Burkhart and Lt. Margurite Peters (Nurse).

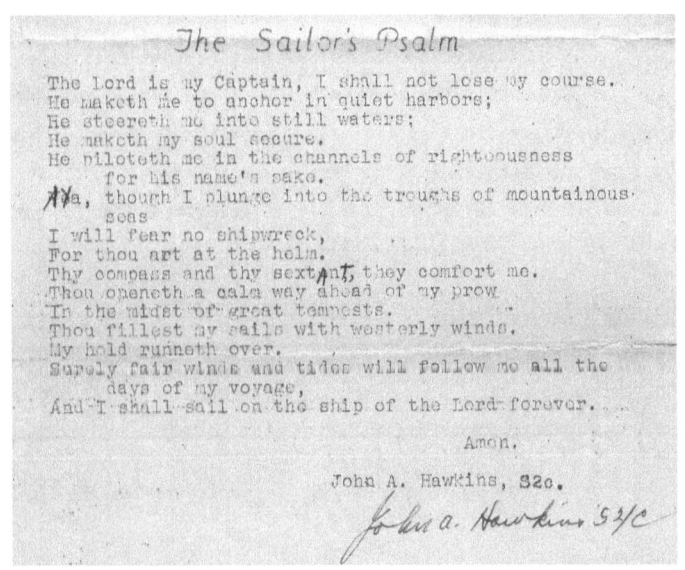

"The Sailor's Psalm" by John A. Hawkins [good friend of Art's]

Dotty sent copy of article from Life on U. of Chicago. I must investigate the possibilities before deciding where I shall work for my degree.

Very long letter from John Hawkins today. He was married on the 30th of June & seems very happy.

Letter from Dotty to Art
Tuesday
Aug. 28, 1945

My Dearest,

Whee! Big job done. Got energetic this morning and cleaned out the closet. Wanta buy any coat hangers, Mister? I'll sell 'em cheap—dime a dozen. The woodwork & shelf got washed, the walls got cleaned, the woolens got sunned, the clothes got rearranged, the trash got swept out, and I got dirty. But it was worth it, for the closet is really clean now. We hope. Wonder how long it will stay clean in this atmosphere?

The street is a mess. It's new dress was not packed properly, and it seems more tar & gravel than smooth pavement—in fact—it seems to me to be worse than before they started. Ain't that awful?

Dr. Peyton is back home. He says I may have Labor Day off, so I plan to go to Jamestown for a nice long weekend. This time I'll go in the daytime, get there Saturday afternoon, return sometime Monday.

Mother & Dad went to the show tonite, so I am here alone, writing letters. Yes, Darling—the doors are locked.

Ted's visit must be keeping you pretty busy—or perhaps you celebrated too much. Nope. I'd rather blame it on the postman. No mail from you in five days. Perhaps there will be a stack from you tomorrow. Some postman is holding them somewhere.

May God bless and enrich
    Our Love,
    Dotty

Letters from Dotty to Art
Wednesday
Aug. 29, 1945

Darling!

Your package came today—the one you mailed before leaving Germany. I have spent an enchanted evening poring over the contents. Everything is extremely interesting. Where did the sword come from, and the pipe? That pipe is an odd object, pretty in a way; the money pouch must have been thru a great deal! And the pictorial newspapers. Darling, many of those pictures are utterly beautiful. As to the journal— I'm not sure. I've discovered that the entries are dated 1917-1918, and that the whole bulky thing covers a period of but about two weeks. Whoever made it must have spent their entire time doing so. The written part is almost impossible to read (for me), and the clippings I can translate laboriously with the aid of a German dictionary. Do you suppose it is valuable? (The journal, not the dictionary?) As for the sword, it is a nasty (or Nazti) specimen. Everyone admires it immediately, for it is easily the most striking (!) object of the group.

Thursday
Aug. 30

Dearest One,

I got sleepy last night before I finished. Got a letter from your folks yesterday, but none from you, and none from you today. It has been eight days since I had a letter from you, and I don't understand such a delay, but there is undoubtedly a good reason for it somewhere along the line. Maybe I'll get five letters tomorrow, and then think how foolish I will feel for having talked like this!

Tonight was Record Breakers, at which I was hostess. The group was small—only twelve, mostly Barbers)—and I think that they got more out of my German newspaper pictures than the music. There were two present who could translate German in pretty good shape. My program consisted of assorted rhapsodies. I classed Brahm's "Hungarian Dances" 5 & 6 with them, also played Lizt's "Rhapsodies" 1 & 2, Weinberger's "Czech Rhapsody," and Enesco's "Roumanian Rhapsodies" 1 & 2. Then Flo played a piece called "Rhapsody" by Dananzi that goes bang bang—bang Bang! Bang, bang—bang BANG! Da, da, dee, dee, da-de-ah-ta-ta-tah ta, etc. Always did like that piece.

Enclosed are several good clipping and your Dad's letter, which was so cute I wanted you to see it. The objections were called for by some of those pictures like I sent you.

I go now to sleep, sheathed in the peaceful serenity of
      Our Love,
      Dotty

Aug. 30

Yesterday morning witnessed a rare thunder storm in Paris. Clouds rolled up from behind Eiffel, and the darkness was as night. One could not read without artificial light. A regular cloud burst accompanied the storm.

In afternoon visited the famous sewers of Paris. [THIS WAS ONE OF THE WEEKLY TOURS AS PART OF OUR REGULAR SCHEDULE.] The large tunnels permit a man to walk upright. Water mains, telephone lines, and pneumatic tubes are in these tunnels also. System very efficient with automatic flushing, etc. Brought copy of Venus de M[ilo] for Dotty on the Cite.

Last night saw "Le Tour de Feu" with Miss Burkhart. Staging was again superb. Wonderful fire effect in the last act. Lighthouse lamp looked most realistic. Appeared to have been a light cloth (perhaps silk) but in a cylinder and billowed by a steady blast of air. Yellow lights on this gave a very realistic effect of dancing flames.

Today on regular tour visited Palais Royal, Place de la Victoire, Norte Dame de Victoires, and Bibliotheque National.

Aug. 31

This evening I spent my most pleasant hours in Paris. Ranger had been asked to bring "his friend from Tenn." with him for dinner with a

French family living on Blvd. Berthier north of L'Etoile. We arrived about 6:30 finding the elevator very convenient in order to reach the seventh and top floor. Mme. Wolf greeted us and I was introduced to the two boys Jacque (c. 19) and Patrick (c. 16). A short time later a neighbor came in and still later M. Wolf. He is a textile merchant who works about half way between Le Havre and Paris. We had a well-prepared meal with a wonderful salmon and tomato salade, excellent beef with a sauce, fried potatoes and cake. I tasted my first red wine and found that it was pleasant with the meal. My hostess was kind enough to offer us ice water both before and during the meal. After the meal we had a "fin" so called, which consists of brandy and cognac. I did not care for it particularly.

These people I think are representative of the upper middle class in Paris. The Germans took all of their household furniture during the war, but they now have a nice apartment (though small) and are wealthy enough to own a car. The latter is of course for business, but nevertheless very rare in France now. Both mother and father speak English with some degree of proficiency and the children have studied English. They read Sinclair Lewis and other Am. Writers (Bromfield, etc.). Mme. Wolf has visited India & England, and I am sure that M. wolf has travelled a great deal. Jacque attends the Lycee St. Louis (where I am staying) where he studies math, physics & philosophy. Tomorrow the family goes to the country where they will spend their vacation.

I spoke a great deal of French by comparison with what I have been speaking. It is a pity that I did not meet such a family long ago. However, it is not so easy as it would seem. My study of French would have been far more effective had I known a French Family with whom I could talk and visit.

Letters from Dotty to Art
Friday
Ten Mile Creek
August 31, 1945

My Darling,

In Case you are wondering where Ten Mile Creek is I'll tell you. That is where I am now. Now you know! Here is another clue—I am spending the night with Uncle "R" & Aunt Kap, whose home is about ten miles out of town on the Nashville highway—I've pointed out to you when we were coming in from Jamestown.

This is the life! Soon after arriving we changed our clothes (I put on a pair of Aunt Kap's pants and took off my shoes), then went to feed the chickens & pigs & cows and horse and turkeys, and to milk the cows. I tried milking, but with no success!

We had ham for supper, and all sorts of other stuff. I ate till I popped nearly. If you look closely you may see it oozing out my ears!

Whee! A letter today! The 1st in over a week, and I _was_ glad to see it. I can tell by reading it (didn't have time to compare page no.'s) that there are several letters missing in between this one and the last one from you. So glad that Miss Burkhart is like she is and that you all had such a nice time, even if it did rain. Go ahead & see her all you like—I understand how you feel about desiring female companionship. I'm a little starved for male "   " myself—you see, Daddy, Dr. Peyton and Uncle West are about the only males I see or talk to much—and they don't keep me from being lonesome a bit.

Jamestown
Sunday afternoon
Sept. 2, 1945

Dearest,

Your Dad slumbers on the couch on the back porch, Mother sleeps on the couch in the front room, and I sit in the familiar front bedroom to write you a letter. The last trip I made to Jamestown I almost missed the bus, and the same thing happened again this time. Yesterday morning I went out to Kingston Pike in front of Aunt Kap's house to catch the bus (she said it nearly always stopped there). Aunt Kap waited with me, and it was a blessing that she did; for when the busses (both sections) finally arrived they both passed me up and went on as if they hadn't seen me grab my suitcase and start waving my arms at them the minute they came in sight. Unfortunately a huge red farm machine of some sort was passing by at the same time the busses did, and both busses seemed so intent on passing the lumbering, slow-moving machine that I was ignored. So—to make a long story short, we jumped into Aunt Kap's car which was at hand, and chased the bus down doing seventy or more, and narrowly escaping another car which refused to move over for passing despite our honks. At length we overtook the bus, and thus I breathlessly started another trip to Jamestown. The rest of the trip was uneventful, and I arrived here about 4:30 yesterday afternoon. We had supper, then sat out in the swing and talked. Before supper tho, we exchanged pictures—they had a few I hadn't seen, and I had a number they had not seen. I proudly displayed some of the stuff you sent me from Germany—they took a great interest in everything.

This morning we went to church—that is, Mother & I went—Dad stayed home. I met Chesterlyn & Jessie Reb at Church—Chesterlyn sang a solo—she sings nicely.

Your folks get tomorrow off too, so we shall have a nice holiday. Am having a wonderful time, and am constantly reminded here of

Our Love,

Dotty

Sept. 1

Examination in verbs and a dictation this morning as part of the final. Spent an hour singing preparatory to the graduation exercises next week. I dashed to the PX for my rations and learned a few odd bits concerning the 71st. Latest rumor has it that men with points between 45 – 70 will be left in the outfit and will go home by Xmas. Heard a very uninteresting lecture on "Paris, Center of Government." The only worthwhile thing I gained was to note the importance of introducing wit when possible in discussing a dry subject. A lecturer should never take himself or his subject too seriously. Particularly is this true when he is talking to a group from another country (or even section).

After supper tonight, Ranger and I took the metro to the Bassin de la Villette. There we saw the canal which extends c.125 kilometers (we were told) into the country. The canal goes underground at the point from which we observed, and it continues most of the way underground to the Seine. We watched a barge go through the locks on its way down the river. From there we walked along the Avenue Secretan to La Parc des Buttes Chaumont. It consists of sixty acres of lakes, lawn, grottos, and hills. Rising from the lake is an island 160 ft. high. It is very picturesque, and we climbed over a fence to mount the staircase in the rock leading to the miniature "Temple," as exact replica of the Temple of the Sibyl at Tivoli (Italy). Very fine view of Sacre Coeur and the industrial area of Paris to the NE. (Found a nice collar [FOR DOTTY] in one of the side streets near here [IN A SIDEWALK MARKET]. Passing Eglise St. Jean Baptiste and Notre Dame de La Croix we wandered through back streets, fish markets, and ancient swellings until we reached "La Cimetiere du Pere Lachaise." We could not enter, but behind the tall ivy covered walls lie the bodies of Daudet, Chopin, Corot, La Fontaine, Moliere, Balzac,

Sarah Bernhardt (who was born in a modest house just a block away from my Lycee – Rue de l'Ecole de Medecine) and others of renown. We walked down the long hill (Rue Roquette) which these people travelled on their last journey. It was a quiet street as the dusk fell. A small boy passed and grabbed the hand of my friend to say, "Bon Soir." We smiled and replied. From Place Voltaire we took our metro home.

Sept. 3

Last night the lights went out all over Paris and my writing was interrupted. Tonight I tried to make up for it. Yesterday morning to church (on Quai). Communion service. Ranger and I met Miss Burkhart & her nurse friend M. Peters after church and we were invited to lunch. After lunch we took a boat ride on the Seine again and then visited a Moslem Mosque beside Jardin des Plantes.

Today to Am. Lib. to give back with reluctance Napoleon. Then Parc Monceau again w Ranger. To Sacre Coeur and dome. Afterward through the rain to Flea Market.

Letter from Art to Dotty
Paris
Sept. 2, 1945

My Darling,

Last night I had good intentions so I remained home to study and to write my lovely wife. I studied (for finals) and began a letter to Mother and Dad, whom I had not written in a week, when lo out went the lights. I waited but nothing happened. I found that the lights were out all over Paris and so I went to bed at the very unusual hour of 9:45

Well, I should begin where I last left off. I think that I told you of my invitation to dinner on Fri evening with a French family. The apartment house proved to be on Blvd. Berthier (B-5½) in a very nice section of town. We ascended in the elevator to the seventh floor where Mr. & Mrs. Wolf have their penthouse home. Both Mr. & Mrs. speak a little English but we talked French most of the time. How wonderful it would have been for me had I been able to visit in such a home throughout my stay here. I have had very little contact with Parisians outside of class, and my French is certainly the poorer for it. Mr. Wolf is a textile merchant working between Paris and Le Horne. Seems to be of the upper middle class. We had a wonderful meal (my first real home cooked meal since I ate with you in Philadelphia on Jan 22nd.) Red wine with the meal which isn't too bad when taken as a beverage accompanying the food. The evening was very enjoyable.

Sat. afternoon I had my usual lecture; and, after an early supper, Ranger and I took the metro to Basin de la Villette (B-C-13). Here beings the Canal St. Martin which goes underground from a point just below, and continues underground to the Seine. We watched one of the long barges enter a lock and be lowered to a level below the ground surface. We walked over to "Parc des Buttes Chaumont, thru this park and on toward Cimetiere du Pere Lachaise" passing by "Eglise St Jean Baptist" and "Notre Dame de la Croix." These streets are very old and the section poor. Old shops, fish markets, one horse theaters, slums, dirt, stench. In this cemetery are buried Chopin, Alphonse Daudet, Sarah Bernhardt, Moliere, Balzac, and other French notables. We walked down the famed "Rue de la Roquette which is the long hill ending at the cemetery door. How many have taken their last ride up that hill!

The walk was a very long one and took us about three hours to cover (Ranger had bought the sheet music to a "Song of Liberation" and learned the words and music as we strolled along). I came home too tired to write and so to bed.

Sunday morning I wanted to hear the organ in St. Sulpice and so left for church early enough to stop by. No service was in progress so Ranger and I continued on to the A. Church (Quai Branly F-51/2). It was a communion service "sans" sermon. I like a sermon.

Miss Burkhart & her nurse friend were there and invited Ranger and me to lunch. Knowing the Red Cross meals we accepted and by way of the Petit & Grand Palaises to the club near the Am. Embassy. After lunch we took the A.C. boat trip on the Seine. I had been before but found out a few new things. The trip is rather nice. We stopped by the Moslem Mosque located beside the Jardin des Plants (I-11). The mosque is very beautiful and some of the architectural designing is very delicate. Heard one of the priests calling his prayer.

You know, I always feel as though I am intruding in such a place even when it is just a regular cathedral or place of interest. When possible I usually wander about without insignia of any kind and at such times I look like many Frenchmen who have acquired G.I. clothing.

Today I returned a book to the Library and showed Ranger Parc Monceaur (C D-6). We then went over to Sacre Coeur where I wanted

Paris "Union Sportative" Aug. 45
Frank Dana (NY), Abe Chanin (Arizona), "After the Game."

to pick up a souvenir for Dad. Found that and then climbed the high tower which over looks the city. The Church itself is built on a very high hill and there is a wonderful view of panoramic Paris from its dome.

After leaving Sacre Coeur, where a movie scene was being shot, we took the metro to Pt. De Cignancourt (off the map) to the famous "Marche au Puce" or "Flee Market." The market is a long boulevard and the market itself must run for at least a half mile. On either side of the side walk and on both sides of the streets are multitudes of stands and small shops filled with every thing that one can imagine. Furniture, combs, old pictures (brush attached), thread, stoves, shoe laces, radios, handkerchiefs, cheap jewelry, hairpins—literally everything that any five and dime has in the States. There is very little worth buying, but it was a new side of life in Paris to see.

The wonderful poem arrived, Darling. Thank you very much. It is very nice and very expressive. I hope that I have not forgotten how to be so expressive when that glorious day does come.

Rumors fly concerning the future of the 71st. I know now that organization means nothing now—points everything. My arrival in the States will depend upon my point-standing. Can't be sure but things may happen. I have hope!

As usual it is very late. I enclose a shot taken after my tennis game. The boys are in my class. The big picture is a poor enlargement of one of the small shots I sent. I hope that in my eyes you see the depth of my love for you.

Eternally thine,
Bushy

P.S. Tues. morning—New point score Bushing should have 55—going up!

Sept. 5

To Malmaison yesterday afternoon. The house itself is simple in design (outside) and I like the modern lines of its architecture. "Lakme" last night. Music good, singing poor, scenery good.

To Fontainebleau today with class. Sorry I spent the day there again although I enjoyed the picnic, etc. Visited home of Millet at Barbizon. With Ranger tonight to see "Une Femme Dans Un Lit." Very Amusing and in the Restoration style of Wycherely and Congreve.

Sept. 6
Pont St. Michel

Heavy clouds seem to remain motionless above my head. Above the buildings, I see the Eiffel spot lights opening a hole in the sky. The evening is a bit cool and the air is damp. A cool breeze on my back makes my jacket feel very comfortable. Four young Parisian boys pass by—perhaps they have been discussing French politics, philosophy, or perhaps some subject on the weightier side concerning a certain "jeune fille." A G.I. is wrapped up with his French feminine friend as they stroll down the Quai. A middle aged couple stop to dream on the Bridge Saint Michel. Street lights point fingers at me in the water, and the breeze ruffles the water of the river to give a dim shimmering appearance. People in groups of two and three and four drift from side to side in Place St. Michel. The clocks throughout the city begin to announce the half hour. Ten-thirty it is and these small groups will wander and drift far into the night.

Over one shoulder the towers of the Palais de Justice lurk in the dim and misty darkness. Over the other, the towers of Notre Dame offer dim evidence of the presence of the Cathedral there.

I see many types of light here. There is the light in the sky over Eiffel—a bluish gray against the misty clouds. There is the golden yellow lights of the street lamps reflecting upon the waters of the Seine. There is also the lights of the lamps themselves as I see them dim and dimmer along the banks of the River. And then there is small flickering light of the bicycles which race regularly by. They dart from side to side, and yet in all they seem so fragile and frail. The lights from the automobiles come and go, and one sees them reflected upon the streets from the distance. There is the curtained light that comes from the apartment houses along the Quai, and the light of the cafes where the customers drink inside tonight. And last of all I see the light of the young lovers who pass by arm in arm and who now and then steal kisses as one plucks daises along the meadowed path. 'Tis Paris and Pont St. Michel.

Later

Dined with Miss Burkhart tonight. After leaving her, [I] wandered through a number of back alley ways. Missed tour of Gobelin Tapestry Works today to mail packages. Thought I was leaving Fri. night but it is Sat.

Aboard Train

A slow drizzle, which has attempted to fall since noon, began shortly before we boarded our train at Gare l'Est. With the usual amount of confusion in the loading, six of us from the 71st managed to find a plush apartment, which is far different from the wooden benches on which we rode coming into Paris. We ride smoothly along, and lights blink with uncertainty thru the blackness. As we left the city, the streets threw out to us a last reflections of the street lamps.

My longest stop in Europe has been Paris. The most eventful period perhaps has also been Paris. I gained much.

Sept. 9
En Route

Friday afternoon I spent a couple of hours waiting to collect my supplementary pay (850 francs) from the French Government. (This has been given to the GIs in France in an attempt to equalize our buying power). Attended the graduation program at the Cite University. The musical selections and skits (Moliere, etc.) were put on by the soldiers. Entertaining but very long.

I left early in order to return for dinner with Ranger and Meyers. We had intended to eat in a French restaurant and ended up in a Chinese Café on a side street near St. Michael.

I had intended to see "Murder in the Cathedral," T. S. Eliot, but was persuaded to go with Ranger to see "Montmartre Memories" at Marigny. The program, a variety show, was only fair, but I did get to see something of a cross section of French entertainment. A couple of the "stars of the French Cancan from the Bal Tabarin" performed, and we heard the Band of the Paris Polise and an athletic show (wrestling, tumbling by the Police). Returned through the Latin Quarter near the Seine. As we passed within half a block of a dimly lit hotel, we heard the familiar call, "Hey, Baby, over here, Come over here." We passed on through the narrow streets, past the small cafes. Laughter, song, an accordion here, a stringed instrument there. The half drunken laughter of a blonde as she strokes the cheek of a drunken soldier.

Sat. Morning Ranger and I checked out, and packed most of our belongings. Frenchmen who clean the Lycee were coming into the rooms to buy anything that the GIs might wish to sell. We left about 10:30 for Sever to see the China Factory. The plant is noted for making the finest quality China in the world. We could not see the men at work (since it is closed on Sat.), but we did see an exposition of some of the beautiful work. I returned to the Trocadero. Went through the Maine Museum, the Museum of Man, and the Museum containing the reproduction of the famous cathedrals of France (also stained glass windows and Roman paintings). Continued on to Palais de Tokyo (closed). Went to the Greek Church near Ave. Marceau and arrived at St. Pierre de Chaillot just in time to hear the bells peal out announcing the happy union of a young French soldier and his bride. The Church is very modern in design but very beautiful inside. Visited the Eglise Am. on Ave. George V and then to the Louvre for my farewell to Venus and Mona Lisa (home by Rue De Seine).

Later in the afternoon I visited Notre Dame for a final meditation. Then to St. Julien le Pauvre on Rue de la Harpe. The foundation of this church is purported to be the oldest in Paris, dating from before the 6th Century. Across the street is the "Cabaret des Oubliettes" a musee in the caves of a prison which formerly were part of the "Petit Chatelet." Here I saw many of the old methods of punishment—spike wheels, spiked chairs, the stretching table, etc. These instruments seemed far worse than anything I saw at Dachau.

Sept. 10
Gunzburg

Saturday evening as the rain began to seep down through the mist, I stood with all of my European possessions outside the Gare d'Est. A crippled boy hobbled through the line of GIs selling long French loaves of bread. A number of people sought to interest soldiers in cheap souvenirs—handkerchiefs, bracelets, etc. One lady made money by selling tomato and onion sandwiches for twenty francs each. I gave the crippled boy a real bargain by trading him a partially used pack of Marvel cigarettes for a loaf of bread. [IN PARIS AT THIS TIME, CIGARETTES CONTINUED TO BE A MUCH SOUGHT AFTER ITEM JUST AS THEY CONTINUED TO BE IN GERMANY.]
We loaded on the long train and left on schedule at 9:15. By a bit of forceful planning, six of us from the 71st Division managed to get a compartment with plush seats. We watched the dim street lamps reflect their dimmer rays from the wet pavement as we rolled swiftly into the night. For us, Paris was a pleasant memory.
I awoke on Sunday morning as we passed Luneville [THE STATION FROM WHICH WE DETRAINED EN ROUTE TO THE FRONT A FEW MONTHS BEFORE]. We were making fast time. About ten in the morning we stopped to eat at one of the transient mess camps. Clouds hung low and rain poured down as we passed through Eastern France and thence into Germany. Obtained a somewhat distant view of the cathedral at Strasburg as we continued on our way. To our amazement, we arrived in Augsburg by 8:30—just twenty-three hours after leaving Paris. We spent almost 48 hours going [to Paris] from Munich.
We ate in the mess at the station, and having no transportation at hand, made ourselves at home in the baggage room. We arose about eight o'clock this morning and after breakfast were taken to Division Headquarters. There I waited until six o'clock tonight to get a ride to

369

Gunzburg. Looked up Ted [Kidder] in the meantime and had a brief talk.

Letter from Art to Dotty
Augsburg, Germany
Sept. 10, '45 [48-49]

Dearest,

While the rain seeped through the mist in a steady drizzle we waited outside of the Gare d'Est. We loaded on the train about 8:45 and promptly at 9:15 (on schedule) we watched the dim street lamps reflect their dimer rays from the wet pavements. We rolled swiftly into the night and gay Paris for us was a memory.

By a stroke of real luck, six of us from the 71st managed to secure seats (plush seats, at that) in a swell compartment. As some indication of transportation improvements we arrived in Augsburg just 23 hours after leaving Paris (It took us almost 48 the first time.

We spent last night with some old bags (in a baggage room, my Dear!) and this morning we managed to get a truck to bring us to Div. Hdq. We should get down to Gunzburg some time this afternoon. What we will find there I do not know. I have overheard here that men with less than 37 points will leave the Division on Thursday. That will take Beul, Fred Price, and a few other friends of mine in "K" Co. This 37 point score does not include the 8 points for the V-J count. As time goes on I have a growing fear in [letter ends]

GUNZBURG, GERMANY
Monday night

Dearest Heart,

The fear which I was about to voice this morning was never fully realized. I waited all day at division, and not until six o'clock tonight did I manage to find a truck coming down to Gunzburg. When I arrived here, no one was at home and so I proceeded to shave and clean up.

All is not cleared up by any means, but here is the general situation as it looks after having talked with Scotty and Bob Mulford. Chaplain Webb and Ted L. have gone to attend a chaplain's retreat. They return Friday. Scotty leaves Wednesday for home and discharge. He is thirty-eight. Bob has but thirty-six points and may leave Thursday for another division. Bob has been assisting the new chaplain, although a great deal of friction seems to have developed in that quarter. Bob is the only qualified organist that we have in the regiment, and so it will be a real loss should he have to leave. Doubly so since he will have to handle the choir when Scotty leaves. As to my position, I shall continue to consider it uncertain until I have talked with Chaplain Webb. I did learn again today that personnel is changing rapidly, and I am sure of a job as clerk somewhere. UNLESS—there always remains the possibility that I would be shifted out of the division in some sudden change of point value. I don't think so, but I always include that in my thinking.

Letters from Dotty to Art
Monday
Sept. 10, 1945

Darling,

A letter from you today. That's what I call starting the week off right! The news about recounting your point score sounds encouraging —will that not bring your score up to at least 50 or so? I hope? Or more? Well anyway goody.

So Squawky is married. I hope he is happy, etc., and that he picked a "goodern." A lot depends on a minister's wife.

Things are perking up in the church. Activities that were more or less suspended for the summer are resuming their programs, and there is quite a bit for me to do in the office. I was pretty busy all day. I couldn't find anyone to go to show with me, so went immediately after work to see "The Story of G.I. Joe," starring Burgess Meredith as Ernie Pyle, got home and ate a very late supper. I think everyone should see "The Story of G.I. Joe". Meredith did a splendid characterization of Ernie Pyle. It is considered to be a much truer picture of actual combat conditions for infantry than any picture yet released (Carl vouches for this fact.). It was the story not of one man but of all men in infantry. Heroics was entirely absent, making this unusual among war pictures— it merely showed men plugging along, doing what they had to do, many of them getting killed in the process.

Tuesday
Sept. 11, 1945

Whee! Another letter today. This is more like it. It was written 18 days ago—it must have sailed across. There are still some back numbers I haven't received yet, and according to my calculations they were written (by you) about a month ago, and should have contained news of Ted's visit and V-J Day in Paris. I refuse to worry about them, but would hate to miss the big news items they must have contained. Perhaps you could repeat it for me in some future letter.

In a few days it will be time to mail Christmas packages. At one time you wrote not to send any to you, but later you sounded more pessimistic, as if you wouldn't get home till the 1st of the year. Please let me know post haste what to do (if you know yourself).

Congress is trying to do something to see that more men are discharged from the Army and Navy faster. They are not satisfied with present situation. For once I'm for 'em!

I miss you, I want you,
    I Love You,
        Dotty

Letter from Art to Dotty
Gunzburg, Germany
Sept. 11, 1945

My Dearest Heart,

My first day in this other world. Truly it is far different from the world in which I have lived during the past two months, but it is good to be back. This morning I was introduced to Chaplain Bowman. I trust that I will be able to remain with Ch. Webb.

Beul came this afternoon and we talked for several hours. I returned with him to Co. K, for supper and saw a number of the old gang. However, many will be leaving within the next few days for 9th Div. and occupation duties. Others are on their way home on points or age. Beul is to go to Pilsen, Czechoslovakia, for a Post Office job of some sort. Looks like a swell deal since he has a low score. Sod is almost the only one of my former close friends that will be left. Price, Sod, and Beul came back into town with me tonight and we went to see "Wilson". It occurs to me that just about one year ago we were seeing the picture together in Palo Alto. I thought of you a great deal as I watched the story unfold. It was interesting to see some of the shots of Paris, or Versailles, and others with which I am now familiar.

Scotty leaves tomorrow morning and I will be left with the office alone until Friday. Have a few small jobs to clean up, but will spend most of my time writing—I hope. One of the greatest advantages of this job if I stay will be the opportunity to think now and then. It is to be regretted that we find so little time for contemplation and real honest-to-goodness thinking.

My reaction to the change in language setting is interesting to me. When I first entered the French Class at the Sorbonne I was almost tongue-tied because my French words came out in German. Now the reverse is true and I find that instead of saying "Ya", I want to say "Oui". Instead of "good", I want to say "tres bien". Ah me, lackaday, it will be nice to return where everyone speaks some form of the English tongue. I think that we should have a short wave radio to listen to French and German broadcasts. Good for the ear. Also good for the kids. I think that we should start the kids in with French at the age of seven or eight. German at ten. It is a great handicap to begin a study of language after passing the age of sixteen. Perhaps we can afford a private tutor by that time. Hmm!

By the way, what do you think of the names Cordelia Marie or Helen Jeanette, Anieta Marie or Marion? Of course, I don't mean that we should use all of them, but a name should be given due consideration. The poor baby has absolutely nothing to say in the matter, and after all he or she will be directly affected by the choice. Well, there will be plenty of time for discussing these matters, but it never hurts to look to the future.

I constantly look to the future; for you, My Darling, are my future. I share with Wilson the need for the kindness and affection which only an understanding wife can give. I need you and shall go on needing you while life shall last. Behind the veil of years which is called eternity, I shall continue to share with you the completeness and unity of our Love. And thus I am

Eternally thine,
Bushy

Letter from Art to Dotty
Gunzberg, Germany
Sept. 12, 1945

Dearest Heart,

Scotty left about eight thirty this morning for the USA and I spent most of the day alone in the office. I finished a few odd bits of work to be done, and spent most of the day and night writing letters. Tom and Ted P. today, and will try to write Hawkins and Hargrave tomorrow. My greatest joy came when I received three big letters from you, a letter from Mother and Dad, the notebook paper, poem and my _Time_. The latter was date-lined Sept. 10, although it was mailed on the 6th, which means that it came all the way to Gunzburg in exactly six days. Not bad at all.

I am so glad that you had the long (?) visit with Mother and Dad. Their accounts are glowing, and they enjoyed it very much. Wish you could go more often, but I know how the job ties you down. Try to get Mother over to Knoxville if you can, for it would do her good to get away from Jamestown now and then. Your descriptive account of all the difficulties involved in travel help me to realize a bit more the situation at home.

Thanks, Darling, for the poem. You know me! And "it is colder now..." and ... "we are drifing". How far I am drifting I do not know. It seems that the big shift of low pointers has been called off. There are confused and confusing reports about the division being kept at a "holding force", or some such. One report is that all men below sixty points will be held for a prolonged period. I think that someone is a bit cuckoo.

I have 55 points with the new count, and that was just swell for the situation which I found upon my return. The division was to be filled with 45 to 65 pointers and return to the States before the first of the year. Now it seems that everything will be changed. Ah me! Whata life (withouta wife!!) Still think that you should hold all packages until further notice. We may perchance find out something definitive sometime, but I am not at all hopeful on that score. Glad to see that Carl is not headed for the Pacific. I'm afraid that to be stuck out there is a bit worse that ETOwed.

It is interesting to note some of the differences here and in Paris. Parisian women have no stockings whatsoever, except for very special occasions. Here, stockings are worn all the time. There is more food here than in France and I think that as a whole the people have better clothing. I think that I told you that Mr. and Mrs. Wolff (with whom Ranger and I had dinner) had everything they owned taken by the Germans. Much of the stuff was brought back to Germany and sold. The conditions that I see do not make me happy. How far we are behind the simple teachings of Brotherly Love!

I enclose a letter which Ted. P wrote to us some time ago. I answered tonight, although I wrote him from Paris just before getting this letter.

I go to bed to dream to be with you. May God hasten the day when our lives will again be joined completely in the eternal joy of
Our Love,
Bushy

Letter excerpts from Art to Dotty
Gunzburg, Germany
Sept. 14, 1945 [58-60]

"I was a bit flattered to find that my position with Chaplain Webb is secure, as far as he is concerned. What the latest dope will be in regard to points we do not know. As it stands now, I have more points than

374

anyone else in the Chaplain's section. Perhaps all of us will be shipped out for occupation, or someother duty. We do not know...!

"All of us are standing on quicksand, and until we know more of what is going to happen, any decision involves many unknown factors. My former choices in important matters have always seemed to have been guided, and I have every reason to believe that it will continue to be so. 'Two roads diverged in a yellow wood, And sorrow I could not travel both, And be one traveller, long I stood, And gazed down one as far as I could, To where it bent in the undergrowth; Then took the other as just as fair, thought as for that the traveling there had worn them both about the same....' [Robert Frost poem]

"Tomorrow may prove eventful and even decisive. I must go to bed and to sleep. My prayer will continue to be that God will guide us in our decisions, great and small, and that He will bless our feeble efforts to follow in the path of our Savior."

Letter excerpt from Art to Dotty
Gunzburg, Germany
September 16, 1945 [61-62]

"A week ago it was reported in the papers that men below 45 points would make up the Army of Occupation. In the middle of the week the figure went up to 60, back to 57, then 56—latest rumor says 45 again. Whata life! As of VJ, I have 54, since a straight eight points was not given. So far I still have my ERC credit, but I hardly hope that I can keep those points. If I lose them, my score would drop back to 44. That isn't good! Whata mess!"

Letter from Art to Dotty
Gunzburg, Germany
17 Sept. 1945

My Darling,
The scene is a usual one: The Chaplain is sitting at his desking pounding away on a typewriter to his wife and boy. I sit at my desk pounding way to my wife. What a boy wouldn't mean to me right now (in addition to the twelve points!) Ch. Webb and Ted were away all day and I had a chance to clear up several odd jobs. Made out my first regular Sunday program for next Sun. Also wrote a couple of letters which the boss dictated before he left. Fixed a flat this afternoon. "Sod" came in with some very sad news concerning his family. His father is seriously ill, or was eight days ago when the letter was written. He is

trying to get the Red Cross to confirm the information and try for a furlough. I doubt very much that he can get one.

By the way, in case anything of great importance happened at home, you can send a cablegram to my regular mailing address. Previously it has been necessary to use a special code number, but now the regular mailing address is sufficient. Remember this in case of sickness or other difficulty. Also, the Red Cross must confirm any reports of illness. If their confirmation is sent immediately, far more speed is made than if a letter or cablegram is sent to the GI. He goes to the ARC, and they have to wire back to the States for the information which should have come in the first place. I want to send this dope on to Mother and Dad just to be sure that they know the procedure.

As I go to meals at Service Co., I pass the high flag pole which bears the Stars and Stripes. Today has been very beautiful: the sun has shone, the temperature has been high, and a light breeze has been blowing part of the time. As I pass and see Old Glory waving, I feel a real thrill. All that I went through in combat seems insignificant when I watch my flag fly against the blue of a German sky. In the middle of the afternoon a group of small Ger. boys between the ages of five and eight were brought by their teacher into the field where the flag pole stands. On one side the GIs played softball; on the other, the small boys played their games. The Stars and Stripes fluttered in the breeze overhead. A deep sense of pride and inner happiness filled me.

By the way, some of the boys up at Division have had a good deal of publicity with their baseball clinic for German boys who are eagerly coming each day to learn something about the great Am. sport. I think that it is a wonderful idea, and should be carried on by every outfit in the ETO.

Today came your letters of the 8th and the 9th, telling of your cabin Retreat and enclosing the very descriptive piece by Daddy. I enjoyed very much hearing from you, since I had no letters for several days. I mean, especially because I had received no letters for several days. I always love to get your letters, My Darling.

In a small way I can understand how you feel with all of the fellows returning home to their wives and sweetheart. Men are leaving here every day for the States. We must recall that we were together a full nine months while other men were overseas. In fact, we must even think of all of our four years at college, for remember that we started to Maryville just as the war broke out over here. Some of these men who are returning have been away for four and five years. I have not yet been overseas for a full year. The separation is very, very hard, and I can not prevent moments of brooding. However, patience is still a virtue.

Mother's newsy letter came today, and I shall try to write her very soon. Had planned to write this week anyway. Started a letter to Hargrave, but was interrupted and not able to finish.

Rumors continue to fly, and I grow indifferent to them. Part of the regiment has already moved to a new location, so I am sure that we will move soon. Our new area is south of Augsburg and not far from the Brenner Pass I think. Our facilities could hardly be better than here, but a change of scenery will be interesting. However, the regiment will take over the area formerly occupied by the entire 80th Div. That will mean we cover a great deal of territory.

I shall try to include a few pictures each time I write, although often I forget. Nevertheless, I can never forget how close you are when I look out at a clear moon, almost full. I hear you whispering through space and time the words of
Our Love,
Bushy

GI's at play Summer '45 "Strike!"

My Dearest Heart,

What a day! I began this morning as a chaplain's assistant. At 8:30 I was told that I was no longer a chaplain's assistant. Chaplain Webb had hoped to hold me as a third man, but that is impossible. He must have an organist, so I can't qualify. He was good enough to speak to the Personnel Officer, and I will be able to do some temporary work there for a few days. However, there is little possibility that I will get anything permanent out of it. Henry Fairbanks, my friend in I and E, called today and told of an opening there. I am not at all sure that I will be ask for, since the division is still assuming that all men below 56 will be leaving shortly. Late this afternoon another possibility opened up in Service Company. So here I am in somewhat of a quandry. Which to pursue? I have a great deal of faith in Providence, but I must exercise choice also.

Wrote a big letter to Hargrave today with a note to his parents. Sent it to his home address, since I am sure that his Navy address has changed since I last heard from him. Also wrote Mom and Mother and Dad. Hope to write Mary Ruth in a couple of days. I had planned to write her tonight, and I was urged to first go to the movies with Bob and Ted. Saw a Jack Benny fantasy "The Horn Blows at Midnight". Crazy and more than the average number of good laughs. Upon our return at eight o'clock, Ch. Webb had the monopoly set lying out on the desk, and he prevailed upon us to sit down and play. We placed a time limit of nine o'clock, but it was too interesting then. I finally won after putting up five hotels.

By the way, I learned from Mom that Mary Ruth is working for Ma Snyder. Glad to hear about it, although I hope she doesn't allow it to interfere with her social activities (no dig intended—ed—well, not much of one!) I wonder if you had a chance to see "GI Joe". Mom wrote of seeing it, and I understand that it is a very fine picture. It is supposed to be the most realistic of any of the war pictures produced so far. I hope I can get a chance to see it.

Today came the news that MacArthur is asking for only 200,000 men for the occupation of Japan. That is good news for us, for that will mean that the Army will need to hold only a minimum of men. It may directly effect the point score which will be decided upon as the demarcation line for AO troops here in Europe. This uncertainty reminds me of the latter days of combat when we knew that victory

378

could not be far off, and yet the waiting was hard to bear. One's senses are so dulled by long delays and changes in plans that when the big news does come a great deal of the meaning is lost. This was particularly true on VE Day. I think I described to you before that it was more or less a let down, and VJ also to a certain extent. When I first heard the VJ news I was walking on air, but I never rose to such a height of rejoicing again. I don't mean to imply that I will not be excited when I board the boat for home, but I may listen to the results of the point decision with little emotion. The Army and war effect one that way.

I think that I have mentioned two or three times that I think you should hold all packages. I shall repeat it here, for I fear that some of my letters may be delayed or lost. How do the numbers agree on my pages? I am not optimistic about getting home by Christmas, but I think that there is so much shifting around of addresses etc. that I would be likely to get half of the boxes you sent. If I have to wait for my presents, it would be better than to miss them altogether.

What is new with Samarriet and family? Haven't answered Phil's letter since he moved to Maryville, but I hope that you keep in contact with them. I shall try to write them also within a few days. Hope to write Sam and Harriet too. By the way, where are Art and Marianna these days?

I will probably continue to sleep here at the house until something definite is settled as to my job. The Catholic Chaplain just brought in a radio, and I guess that I am leaving at the wrong time. Well, my associations here have been very pleasant, and I of course regret leaving. However, there would be absolutely no future as for a rating. In I and E or in Service Co. I might have a chance for something more than a Pufk stripe (As Jean Kaelber called it).

I shall attempt to keep you abreast of the developments. I do hope these letters are coming through in some sort of sequence, because if not they will certainly cause even more confusion. Of one thing there can be no confusion, My Love: You are mine, and I am yours, and the future belongs to
Our Love,
Bushy

My Dearest,

My day was made brighter by the arrival of a long letter from you which was written on the 10th and 11th. I am always able to face the day with a brighter smile and a more optimistic outlook if I get your cheery words. Glad that my letters are beginning to come through, and hope that they continue to do the same. You answered a question which I asked last night concerning the movie, "GI Joe", and I am certainly glad that you were able to see it. Hope it comes my way soon. I think that it was also last night that I answered a question which you asked today concerning Xmas packages. I still think it wise to hold them even though my trip to the States continues to seem very far away. I am sure that my ERC points will be taken away eventually and that will leave me with only 44. That isn't particularly good. Say, I think that we should send Squawky and wife a present. If I didn't send his letter all ready, I shall do so.

I went down to Personnel today, and I must admit that I worked harder and longer than any full day since combat. It is all too true that I do not work in the same way to which I was accustomed as a student. I will have to learn a great deal about concentrating and study when I return. We are working on a complete list of all the men in the regiment, along with their VJ score. Should be able to finish up tomorrow. I found out from Div. today that my points are not sufficient to warrant pulling me out for the work there. This is as I had expected. However, I did talk with the CO in Service Co. and he wants me to come into his office. The job may prove both interesting and valuable background if and when I ship out of the division. If I stay, I will be able to hold the job I think. We shall see!

Tonight I talked for two hours with a middle aged German business man who lived behind our house. We discussed war, past, present, and future; politics, past present, and future. I think I gave him a few of our democratic conceptions, and I certainly gained a better slant on the German attitude and thought. His wife does my laundry, and when I took my clothing to them tonight he invited me in and we talked. In regard to the Church he told me that Hitler never dared close it. However, he did require a period of recreation for all children which came just at the hours for Sunday School and Church on Sunday. He also closed the convent schools. Crosses were taken from the school room; but public opinion was so strong, particularly among the people in the smaller towns, that they were brought back.

Well, the Chaplain is just leaving. He came in a short time ago and began talking about his wife and my wife, etc. We discussed Calif. and railroad trips etc. I listened mostly, always trying to get back to my letter. Now as I try to write, Bob wants to tell me about his new set-up in a new location. I guess I may as well give up for the night. More tomorrow. Meanwhile, I love you with all of my heart.

> Thine own,
> Bushy

Letter from Dotty to Art
Thursday
Sept. 20, 1945

My Dearest One,

Sounds good to me! So good that I get all excited whenever I think of it! And Brother—excuse me—Husband—it looks pretty definitive now! All right, all right, I'll explain. News came over the radio today (wonderful thing, radio) that critical point score for discharge is cut to 70 by October, and to 60 by November, and shortly thereafter they will discard the point system altogether and a fellow will be automatically eligible for discharge when he has seen <u>two years</u> service in Army! Thus spake Gen. Marshall to Congress today. Darling, do you realize what that means for us? Say I, as if you didn't. It means that we will be together again <u>for keeps</u> within a few months, and the Army shall no longer order our lives. It means, to tell the cart after the horse, that you will <u>soon</u> be eligible for a discharge in way or another! While I am getting excited I might as well wish for the moon and hope you will be in the States before you become eligible for discharge—before Christmas to be exact! Darling, I refuse to be weighed down by pessimism any longer—I'm gonna hope for your return <u>so hard</u> that it will take place in short order. But better than hoping I shall pray as never before that God may guide each step we take; that His power may be used in our lives to His glory; that He shall provide the strength and grace with which to accomplish the tasks of His choosing; and that His fullest blessing may rest eternally on

> Our Love,
> Dotty

P.S. It is summer again.

Dotty Lehman & Ralph Paruim have broke up.

Joined the Nut Club today—five days late! Dunno why.

Sang myself out of choir practice tonite.
If you want to read a book
with real spiritual meat
in it, try a Careful
Perusal of Romans.

Letter from Dotty to Art
Friday
Sept. 21, 1945

My Dearest,

Say, when is your Dad's birthday? I can't seem to find a record of it, you haven't mentioned it, and neither has your Mom, but I seem to remember sending him something last year in September. On the strength of that I got him a necktie & birthday card and will mail them. If I am wrong it'll just be too bad!

Strikes are rocking the nation. Thousands are idle. Output is already noticeably affected. Most workers (or rather their unions) are demanding a substantial wage increase to compensate for shorter working hours now going into effect. What they are asking for is more pay for less work, a great deal more pay for the same amount of work they were doing before the war. Unions have many advantages and do numbers of good things for its member, but sometimes their demands seem outrageous to me. The power of unions can sometimes be a dangerous thing, both in the things it <u>requires</u> of its members, and the things it forces employers to do. Surprisingly enough, they, for the most part, seem to operate in a very undemocratic fashion, despite the fact that they are supposed to be of the essence of democracy itself. Ah, me. Wotta mixed up world we live in!

Mother has arthritis, she has just discovered. About a month ago she realized something was the matter—her ankles were swelling, her knees stiff, etc. So she called her doctor to get an appointment to find out what was the matter and was told it would be <u>three weeks</u> before she could see the doctor! In the meantime the condition of Mother's legs & arms grew a lot worse. Grrrrr. The doctor situation in this town makes me mad. Sometimes even in a critical emergency you can't get a doctor to save yourself. Not long ago a woman in this neighborhood had a stroke; the family called nearly every doctor in town in an effort to get one that would attend to her, but failed to secure one till a whole day or more later. I hope as how soon a lot of doctors are released from the Army to relieve what is becoming a critical situation.

My, what a gloomy letter I've written! Cheer up—the worst is yet to come! I wonder why I keep repeating that ugly proverb—it sounds so awful. At least the fact that I love you with all my heart, soul, & body should sound good to your heart. Each day I become more engrossed in turning over new pages in the story of

Our Love,

Dotty

P.S. So glad to hear of Ted's impending promotion. It is about time they promoted you also. You tell I said so. Way past time, in fact.

Letter from Art to Dotty
Guzburg, Germany
22 September, 1945 [76-78]

My Dearest Heart,

A day such as this one could only happen in the Army, and in such changing times as these. When I finished up a letter to you and mailed it this morning, Yung, the company clerk, was still undecided about going home. For weeks now he has been letting the situation ride, and has passed up several shipments to the States. About eight-thirty we received a phone call that today was his last chance to wait. He must either decided to stay as long as the division stays (which is still a mystery), or go on a shipment next week. It looked as though he would go rather than take a chance on being stuck over here for several months until Wilhite, the First Sgt., brought back the news that Personnel would try to hold him a few more weeks.

Now for the big news: We had a quota of three men for passes to Switzerland and could only find one man who wished to go and who had the proper point score—only those between 55 and 69 are eligible. I casually mentioned the fact that if it were not for the fact that I am being broken in here I would like to go. Both Wilhite and Capt. Jacobs spoke up immediately to say that if I wanted to go I should not allow this job to hold me back. So, my Dearest Darling, your little hubby leaves for Switzerland on Tuesday morning at three o'clock. That is, I am supposed to go. I am certain of nothing in this Army, and I will not be certain that I am going until I am well on my way. I have the required 55 with the new blanket count of eight points, but that has not come through channels yet.

Here is the situation I faced in deciding to go: I am catching on to the job here, and it will be mine when Yung leaves—if I am here to take it. Even if I am away on furlough, I think that it will be held for me for the few days that I will be away. If the job is taken by someone else, I have not lost a great deal. I could possibly get a rating out of the job later on, but it would only be for the matter of a few months at the very best. I would rather have the trip than another stripe. One thing I learned long ago in the Army: take what you can when you can. If I had not gone to Paris when I did I might never have had another chance. So I chose to go to Switzerland.

As I mentioned, I leave here at three o'clock on Tuesday morning unless something unforeseen occurs. The trip will cost thirty-five dollars plus anything that I spend. I regret very much that I find it necessary to ask you to send me another twenty-five dollars. I will be away when this month's payroll comes in and so I will be red-lined for the month. That merely means that I will get twice as much on the first of next month. I came back from Paris with a little for [more] than twenty dollars in my pocket, and so I had to go to the Red Cross today to borrow the money for my trip. The lady was not in and so I asked Ch. Webb how much I would be able to get from the ARC. We ended up by him lending me seventy bucks. I gave him a thirty day note to cover the bill, just in case. The reason for the large amount is that he wants me to buy a watch for him if possible.

Darling, I think I know how you really feel about this money. Six months ago I would never dreamed of spending so much money as I did in Paris or of paying thirty-five dollars for a tour through Switzerland. However, I truly believe that this is my chance of a life-time to see Europe. A tour of Switzerland before the war would have cost an American several hundred dollars. As Scotch as I really am, I do not begrudge the money which I spend. My only regret is that you are not with me to share these experiences.

* 10 O'Clock Sat. Evening

Since I wrote the preceding pages much has happened—again. Capt. Jacobs received orders this afternoon late to leave tomorrow morning. Yung will have to leave Monday if he leaves. If he does I will have to forgo my trip. Ah me!

I went to the show tonight to get away from the office and the general situation. Saw "The Keys of the Kingdom" for the second time, and I was impressed with even more than the first time, I think. Anything that arouses thought is good for me here, for there is so little that is stimulating. That is one of the reasons that morals are so often completely forgotten by the GIs: there are so many things that are

The American Church in Paris, July 22, 1945
Letter postmarked to Dotty on Sept. 22, 1945

degrading and so few things that are uplifting. I would rather forget than record some of the depths to which I have seen men sink as they cast aside all sense of moral value. There is one thing which is paramount in my thinking: real values are eternal; are as true here in the Army in German as they are in Maryville College or Knoxville, Tennessee.

I found out this afternoon that Wilhite, the First Sgt., is from Monticello, Ky., only about fifty miles from Jamestown. He is a very nice fellow, and one that I would be glad to look up when I return to the States.

I shall mail this tonight, and it will go to Augsburg tomorrow morning. I know full well that even before it leaves the news which is contained herein will probably be outdated. Tonight: Flash: all men with 60 points out of ETO by Dec. 31—with 45 out by June 1. Well, well, well!!!

385

Constant and abiding is the reality of Our Love. One of my greatest desires is to spend my life attempting to prove myself worthy of the love which you have given me. I can but say,

I love you, Bushy

P.S. Hold money until I write that I am sure of going. If Yung goes, I will have to stay.

Letters from Art to Dotty

Gunzburg, Germany
Sept. 23, 1945

My Darling,

The hour is late as I have just returned from a long trip with the Chaplain. He invited me to go to 1st Battalion with him after lunch. We had a two o'clock service in a little town about twenty miles from here, and then continued on from there for a distance of about forty miles. We visited with Bob Mulford and Ch. Bowman, and speaking of real set-ups they have it. The office and sleeping quarters for the chaplain was formerly the quarters of a colonel from another division. All kinds of swell furniture including radio, record player and lots of records in the classical vein. Hq. Co. of 1st Bn where Bob stays occupies a sumptuous hotel building, and most of the fellows have either private rooms or two in a room. In their dining hotel they are served by German girls and eat on white table linen. What a deal! It was rainy and very cold in the open jeep, but I had a blanket and didn't suffer. Enjoyed the outing.

By now you know that the 71st is slated to remain as a part of the clean out force. The news looks rather good on the whole, and I am glad that at last there is some hope of —————

Gunzburg, Germany
September 24, 1945

My Dearest,

It is far in the night, and I have but a few minutes in which to write of many things. I received three wonderful letters today from you. One contained your excellent description of the trip to Maryville, and I shall discuss it at some length at a later time. Another brought the article by Dorothy Thompson.

I was very much impressed by the article, and throughout the evening my mind has been consciously and unconsciously planning a letter to write Miss Thompson. In the first place, I think that her views are very sound, and her observations unusually correct. I have observed the same situation in Austria, in Germany, and in France. My ideas are just beginning to congeal, but here are three suggestions which I would make in this regard. First I believe that I & E Section (Information—not "intelligence"—and Education) of the Army should be revised. I think that a concerted effort should be made by the department to secure the advice and help of national educators to the end that a well defined program of instructions would be presented to the GIs who are performing the duties of occupation. This group would have complete control of plans and instructions which eventually reach the individual soldier. On the next level would be schools in which I&E Officers would received detailed instructions as to methods and approaches to be used in presenting the program to the soldiers. The I&E Officer should not always be the one to present the material, since far too few are qualified teachers. There job would be to supervise and see that the spirit and purpose of the program were accomplished. A part of their job would be to prepare and present lectures and discussion periods on various phases of occupation duty, foreign relations on an individual basis, etc. The third level would be just this— the classes and discussion periods led by teachers who know something about teaching. That is a rough a summation of a plan which has evolved itself in my mind this evening. I shall smooth over the rough spots, revise, and write it then to Miss Thompson.

I had to give up my Switzerland trip because of the shortage of help and the tremendous turn over of personnel this week. Lots of work to be done. Saw "A Tree Grows in Brooklyn", and found it to be far beyond my expectation. It is truly a fine picture, well directed and well played. More about it later.

By this time you know out [our] situation in the 71st. I am glad to know something definite for a change.

I must say goodnight, for tomorrow is another day. I love you very much. May God bless the wonder of
Our Love,
Bushy

Letters from Art to Dotty
Gunzburg, Germany
September 25, 1945 – Tues. [81-82]

My Dearest Heart,
This is the first time in several days that I have had a chance to sit down and plan a long letter. I hope that nothing comes up to interfere with its completion. It is just seven O'clock and things are quiet around the orderly room. Most of the men are out "visiting" or attending the

show. The CQ (Charge of Quarters) huddles over an electric heater which we were just now fortunate enough to borrow for the evening. I sit at my desk with my field jacket on, and it feels very comfortable. Today has been one of the first days that has had the real fall nip; the kind of day when it feels good to stand in the warm sunshine at high noon; the kind of day when one checks the stove to see if it is in working order, and thinks with dread of the long winter weeks and months ahead. The prospects for even the GIs are not pleasant this winter, and heaven only knows how much suffering the millions of civilians will experience again during the long months. The fall here has been little different from the ones which we know in Tennessee. In the early days of September the weather was warm and summer was paying its lasts respects. During the past week the nights have become increasingly cooler and the days are no longer noticeably warm. It is fall and winter is not far away.

I cannot complain about the mail in recent days for I have had three letters since Sunday. Yesterday I received a letter which had been mailed at five o'clock last Wed. Your letter describing the Maryville visit and the walk in the woods was all too realistic. A flood of memories sweep in upon me, and I am frightfully conscious of the loneliness of a winter's eve in Bavaria. Wish I could see the Evaul babes, along with another cute babe I know. I fear that I am missing a great deal when I miss all of these solo numbers, but I certainly intend to make up for it someday.

Oh yes, I wanted to comment concerning your failure to receive letters from a number of people. It really takes a great deal of time, My Love. During the month after combat in Austria, I wrote about twenty people in addition to my letters to you and the folks. I am still getting letters now and then in answer to those. Be patient and do not judge too harshly. People are so terribly human just as we are.

Another thing which I had intended to mention concerning my grades in Paris. They were not of the best, for there were several in the class who out-did me by a great deal. I did little outside of class to contact French people and talk with them—in French. As a result my conversation did not improve so rapidly as others. I shall enclose the only credit card which I received. Please keep it for I may need it for later credit. I should be able to use some of the nine semester hours which earned. What I gained in understanding the French thought and the French way of life cannot be measured in term of grades. I was satisfied with the results of the "civilization" part of the course, and for me that was the most important.

Yesterday we had the busiest day that we have had thus far. There is still a great deal of shifting around, and much more to come. To get away from it all I went to the show with Livingston last night. We saw "A Tree Grows in Brooklyn" and a very good picture it was as I mentioned in my hurried note last night. The book is reported to very risqué, but there is hardly a touch of that in the movie. I am worrying my head off trying to think of the play of which I was reminded. It too has the setting in New York, and I think that the author is Rice. The movie attempts and succeeds in presenting everyday life in the home of a struggling family in the slums. The acting is excellent. I hope that you can see it.

And now to get on with the exciting story of the life of a 55 pointer in the ETO. "Lafayette, we are here," and it would appear that we will be here for another five or six months at least. Perhaps there is a fifty-fifty chance of getting away by March. I shall not go into detail, because I am sure that you have read and heard more news already than we have. Although most of the regiment has moved away from this immediate area, it seems that we may stay in Gunzburg. There was even a rumor today that the other battalions would return to the area. At least Service Company is taking over better sleeping quarters for the men. That would seem to indicate that the company would be here for sometime.

Yung, the company clerk, was supposed to go again this week, and the only way that he could be kept was to put him on furlough. So, officially he is on a two week furlough. I suppose that it is the first time that a GI ever took his furlough in his own office. Wilhite will also be leaving soon, and I will certainly have my hands full then. Since things seemed so uncertain, I was asked to forego [letter ends here]

Letter from Dotty to Art
Wednesday
Sept. 26, 1945

My Dearest,

Tsk, tsk. I should be at prayer meeting tonite, but stayed home to wash a big stack of dishes and be with Mom. She had a tooth pulled today and so isn't feeling so well—not that she is in much pain, but it is still "sluggin." The tooth was abscessed—perhaps it has been causing the arthritis—we shall see. I have an appointment with a dentist to have my teeth cleaned and checked soon. I shall show him what happened a year ago, and see what he has to say about it.

Well, well. Frances (Lane) Edwards has a baby girl, born today. Due to the fact that they wanted it in Sunday's bulletin (which I prepare today) I got the news pretty fast. Frances lives in Schenectady, you know. There was so much to go into the bulletin this week I could hardly squeeze it all in. I was in the office til almost six o'clock this evening.

Darling—I've been thinking—if you plan to attend summer school (you might even be here in time for the Spring Quarter) here, is there any reason why I shouldn't continue working here as long as you are (here)? Of course I mean to knock off as long as you are on furlough or until you get out, or for at least a month after you get back. I have had no vacation at all since the week in Phila. seeing you off, so I think I am due a little time off. Tell me what you think about these snatches of ideas. And remember that the main idea is

> Our Love,
> Dotty

Letter from Art to Dotty

Gunszurg, Germany
September 26, '45
Wednesday Night

My Dearest,

I have difficulty writing in the evening now for Yung sleeps in the Orderly Room where I must write. Actually there is almost no other place, for the lights are almost non-existent in the room where I sleep. Yung usually comes in just about the time I get ready to start, and he prepares for bed. I can't go ahead and pound the typewriter while he tries to sleep, and so.... At any rate, I shall take time tonight to dash off a quick note, and try to write more tomorrow.

Work continues enough to keep us busy, and I have no time during the day for anything more than the newspaper. Saw still another show tonight—"The Affairs of Susan". Many good laughs, and a thoroughly enjoyable show. However, not to be compared with the others that I have seen recently. I do not feel that I am getting settled down very well to my new schedule. I am keeping busy, but I am more or less running away from myself with shows, etc. I must settle down to a schedule of regular reading and writing if I am to get anything accomplished.

Yung is now in bed and I must get out. It seems early at ten o'clock but I suppose that I should get to sleep. After all this business of standing reveille every morning at six-thirty is something new. I shall finish this letter tomorrow morning, but for tonight I must say goodnight and very pleasant dreams. I love you with allof my heart.

Thursday morning

'Tis morning and almost time to go to work. We are expecting a big shipment of 65 pointers early next week, and then the 60 pointers will follow shortly thereafter. My work will be much simplified when at last the shifting and moving settles down, and we are merely carrying on the regular routine.

By the way, I have never received a box of stationery which you mentioned sending before I went to Paris I think. It just shows how packages can get lost, although I do not need the stationery at the moment. I think that I mentioned sending a box of books from Paris, as well as another big package. I have three or four rolls of film which I must get developed soon before they deteriorate.

I will have to continue this letter tonight or perhaps this afternoon. I love you.

> Thine Own,
> Bushy

Letter to Art from Dotty
Thursday
Sept. 27, 1945

My Poor Confused Darling,

Your letter of the 18th arrived today. If the Army has to work so hard to find a place for you to fit in, they might as well just send you home! But just try to get them to see it that way. Ha. Just think how far toward home you would be if you added up all the distance covered in shuffling about between Chaplaincy, I & E, & Serv. Co. and converted it into a homeward bound journey.

Thanks for the pictures—I love getting them always, and they mean so much to me—I wonder if you know how much.

Glad you are getting caught up on your correspondence. However, it doesn't always pay to get caught up, as I am finding out. You and Dorcas, and occasionally Beulah, are my only regular correspondents. Everybody else ignores me when it comes to writing. It is the same with Mary Ruth—she writes cute letters (as you know) to a number of people, but gets very little mail in return. It really grieves her not to get mail, especially when her roomates have always received lots—yet they don't spend much time answering their letters which still continue to come whether they answer them or not. 'Scuse me. Didn't mean to gripe.

Practiced at choir for two solid hours tonite, so don't have much voice left at this point. We have started work on our Christmas music already. Ruth Lane is going to sing with us then, so she was at choir practice tonite. How I wish I knew whether or not you would be with us then. How I wish I knew. Patience, patience, patience. Always patience we must have. The cords which bind us closely together have been stretched so taut by your continued absence that they are beginning cut. In other words, I miss you so it hurts. It grows more consuming all the time—what grows, why

> Our Love,
> Dotty

Letter from Art to Dotty

Gunzburg, Germany
28, Sept. 45 (Fri.) [86]

Darling,

This is somewhat of a new experience for me: I am writing shortly before reveille this morning, since I will have little time during the day to write. I am getting in the habit of hearing the six o'clock bell strike every morning and we do not have our first formation until six-thirty. I write with one eye closed—slmost.

Big shipment of men with more than 66 points leaving on Saturday, and there is a strong rumor that men with less than 45 will leave next week. That will surely clean us out completely. I think that we will have only about one-third of our company left when both high and low pointers leave. Passes are wide open, and we get a quota for three or four every four or five days. It goes against my good Scotch nature to see them go to waste, but there is nothing that I can do about it just now.

I intended to write a long letter last night, and so went down to the Chaplain's office to do a bit of reading. Well, I read for about an hour and a half, and then C. Webb insisted upon a game a chess. We had the best game that we have played so, a game which lasted another hour and a half. I still intended to write when he brought a bunch of pictures which he decided that Ted and I could divide. We sat in one corner of the office and there picked pictures one by one. The process had all the excitement of a game of chance, and we had a great kick out of it. Also got some wonderful pictures of typical scenes in Germany and Austria. I shall begin at once to send them to you.

Reveille is over and I must get to chow, wash, shave, and settle down to another day's work. Working, sleeping, playing, or dreaming, I think of you and of

> Our Love
> Bushy

Dearest Dotty,

This is my second letter today, but I hope you have no serious objection. You see, I really love to write often, but there are times when extenuating circumstances, etc... The day has been a hectic one, and tonight I am in the sort of mood when only your soothing presence could drive away the wrinkles in my brow and cause me to separate myself entirely from the worries and troubles of the daily routine. My life is very empty apart from you, my Love; with you my horizon seems boundless. In simple words, I love you.

One of the joys of this little job just at present is the fact that the CO is in charge of Service Co., Regimental Motor Pool (which handles all transportation in the regiment), and the regimental repair shop. Normally three men should be handle [handling] the work that one has to perform now. The various battalions have moved out over a wide area, and we have to keep supplies of gasoline, food, etc. moving. Key men are leaving every day and inexperienced substitutes are replacing them. As a consequence, a bad situation is made worse. Yung is the only man in the office who knows what the score is on most of the things that come up, and without him we would surely be lost.

We know that all men about 60 points will be leaving within the next two or three weeks, and the latest rumor is that men below 45 points will leave next week. Two-thirds of our company strength will then be gone, and I suppose replaced by new ones. We are losing men every day, and at the same time many new ones are being brought in on DS (detached service). That is they come temporarily to work, draw rations, sleep, etc. All of these things must be accounted for on our morning reports, etc. Sum fun!

In addition to our GI strength, we have about twenty-five DPs and German civilians who are working for the company. Most of these eat with us, and all get paid by the military government. Some are on KP duty, others clean the quarters, and others are firemen. As I described after my visit to 2nd Bn. with the Chaplain last Sunday, some of the companies have waitresses who are in this category. These are not forced laborers, for in many cases they come to us looking for work. The advantages are many for in addition to small items which they can pick up or are given to them by the GIs, they get good food, usually light work, and some clothing.

I note that there is much discussion at present in the States concerning the atomic bomb and its future. Without thinking the question through thoroughly, I believe that the only wise thing is to place it in international hands. We are a young people even with the maturing influence of two far flung wars, and we possess the same human traits of other humans. I do not believe it wise for any people to gain too much power, even ourselves. As I look at the home front from my peanut gallery seat over here, it appears that the ensuing years are even more challenging than those through which we have just passed. Many GIs have lost the rosy optimism with which they entered the service, and they look upon they look upon the industrial and political situations with sober realism.

Had a note from Miss Burkhart tonight, and she says that she will be returning to the States in November. Lucky girl. Also says that she is writing you. I have had but one letter from Mother and Dad since I came to Service Co., but the mail from the States has been a bit scattered. I suppose that it will get through by and by. Your letter of the 19th came yesterday, telling of the suspense and confusion of the constant stream of rumors. I suppose that I should never have set down almost every rumor that came along, but I did want you to get something of a picture of the chaos which was reigning (also spelled, raining).

Speaking of pictures, I am enclosing five of the thirty-five which I bought from Ch. Webb last night—only 7½ marks (75 cents) for the lot. I have them grouped in some semblance of sets, and I shall send them together as much as it is possible to do so. With the exception of a special group such as this one of scenes at Berchtesgaden, the pictures are typical scenic shots that are seen throughout the Bavarian region. I was with Chaplain Webb when some of these were taken, but for many I was not. I think that it is a swell collection, and I am certainly lucky to get it. With a job such as the one which I now have, there is really little chance of getting out to get many pictures. I still have some of my Paris shots to send, but eventually I will get them to you. I was able to get a wooden box the other day and I shall ship my field glasses home in it. Also, want to include a few other items one of which will be the set of German Cathedrals which is very fine. Am still anxious about the box which I shipped from Paris just before leaving.

Wish I could take you in my arms and whisper the wonders of
        Our Love,
        Bushy

My Dearest Heart,

Yesterday came your letter of the 20th in which your optimism broke all bounds with the news contained in Gen. Marshall's speech concerning the points and length of service. Your optimistic view-point constantly displays a faith and hope greater than mine, and I certainly hope that once again your are correct. At the time of your writing, I believe that the news concerning a "close-out force" had not yet been released. As far as we are concerned over here, that news put a damper on our spirits to the extent that few feel we will be home before April or May. Others think that we may move in a hurry. One thing is definite in all of this confusion, we are losing all men with more than 60 points, and probably all with less than 45 (perhaps 40). My most optimistic hopes offer nothing better than February or even March, and anything sooner will be nothing short of wonderful. Your faith is ever wonderful, and indeed it does make me strong.

Another portion of your letter was very meaningful for me yesterday, and that was the latter portion in which you say "...I shall pray as never before that God may guide each step we take;".... Yesterday I came very unexpectedly upon another one of those forks in the road, and I certainly needed help outside of myself to aid in my decision.

In other letters I have described something of the situation here with Yung, his desire to go home with the outfit, the passing up of six shipments to go home, etc. Yesterday morning came a call from Personnel saying that he could no longer stay with the 71st. He must either go to an AO outfit, or leave immediately for the States. In all events, he could not stay with the division. Well, that was that. We had been expecting such news for sometime, and so we were not taken entirely by surprise. However, within a half hour, I received a call from my friend Fairbanks in the I & E Office in Div. Last week, they wanted high pointers; now they must have medium pointers. Would I come up Monday morning for an interview? I ask for a short time to consider the matter. The question was a difficult one for there were many variables on both sides.

On the positive side for going to the I & E Office there was the matter of interest in the work. Frankly, the job which I am now doing is little more than a job. It has great variety, some little responsibility, a few compensations. However, I have found little thus far that provides real interest. The I & E work would be a regular eight hour a day job, whereas this may run twelve and fourteen hours per day. Generally speaking, the I & E work should be interesting. Second, while there is no ratings open in the office at division now, Fairbanks and some of the others will be leaving soon and I would have a chance for a T/5 or T/4 (Technical Corporal or Technical Sgt.). Third, if I went to division, I would be within a few hundred yards of Ted's office, and we would be able to spend much of our spare time together.

On the other side of the ledger, and one of the most important factors was the general situation in the office. I have been trained in this job for almost two weeks now, and, while there is much that I do not know about the various things to be done, I do think that I know [more than] that anyone else around. Capt. Garner, the new CO, is handling three jobs and has only had charge of the company for a week. Wilhite has been in here for about three weeks, but he has spent little time with the various reports, etc. There is such a shortage of help that I do not know where a clerk could have been found had I decided to leave. I don't mean that I am indispensable by any means, for in the office with Yung gone it will be the blind leading the blind. However, the fact is that all of us are struggling together. Another thing involved is the fact that I will be in line for Yung's old rating eventually. However, I will probably have to wait a long time to get it. The last factor involved in staying is the promise which Capt. Garner made when he learned of the situation. When he found that I would be passing up a shot at a T/4 rating by staying with him, he promised to train a man for this job as soon as we get settled again. He will then put me in the RSO (Regt. Supply Office) where there is more chance of getting a rating than here.

Well, I swayed back and forth for a couple of hours trying to decide what course was best. I finally decided that perhaps the only thing to do was to stay. I couldn't forget that there was a responsibility to the job for which I had been trained and particularly so since Yung leaves at 8:30 tomorrow morning. I decided to stay. Perhaps time will decide whether or not I chose wisely; perhaps not. In an objectively a manner as possible, I chose the thing which I thought was best.

Yung, of course, has busied himself with saying goodbye to his girl friend, and packing to leave. Thus it was that yesterday I went to The Regt. Px to draw our rations. This morning I spent three hours of my Sunday selling the weekly ration of candy and cigarettes to the fellows. That is just another one of my jobs.

Last night we had a company party which proved to be a rather gala affair as such things go. I had worked to do and so spent very little time at the party. I did show up for a few minutes, but only for a Coca-Cola. Wine and beer flowed freely, and there were a surprising number of women present. The Regt. Dance Band provided music and there were sandwiches, cake, etc. Actually the problem of entertainment is terrific for the large number of men that there are in the ETO. Wilhite did a good job of planning and putting on the party.

71st won a big football game today to the tune of about 90-0 against the 83rd Div. I had an invitation to go up with Ted and Ch. Webb, but I had worked to do and I was very tired. I slept for a couple of hours this afternoon, and that was much better for me.

The mail has been very slow during the last week, and I have had nothing from Mother and Dad in many days. I must write them a long letter tonight and bring them up to date with the recent turn of events. I shall include the second group of pictures which I bought from Ch. Webb.

With a humble heart, I thank our Father for the wonderful wife which I have. I am truly undeserving of her love for me, but I shall ever strive to prove myself worthy.

Thine Own, Bushy

Letter from Art to Dotty
Gunzberg, Germany
2 October, 1945 [95-96]

My Dearest Heart,

Again and again, what a difference a day makes. Yesterday morning Yung left the company. An hour later, we received another clerk to help me handle the load. My assistant, by the way, is a T/5—a most unusual situation in the Army. Today we took over an extra room where the regimental mail room operated, and tonight I have my desk in this room, my typewriter, my own telephone, my bed. This afternoon I set up a small PX in here and sold most of the rations to fellows who had not received them before and also sold almost all of the extra luxury items which we have this week. I don't know what will happen tomorrow, but I'm sure that it will.

My day begins at six o'clock and ends by eight in the evening if I am lucky. If I am not lucky, it is later. As I wrote Mother and Dad tonight, I suppose that his [this] is partial payment for my two month vacation in Paris. There are two compensations which I have along with this job: One is that the First Sergeant, my immediate superior, is a wonderful guy to work with, and is co-operative in every way. The CO is also easy to work with, and so far he has appeared to be satisfied with my work. The second compensation is that the days speed past in a terrific hurry. Every day that passes brings me closer to that glorious moment when I shall be with you, My wonderful Wife. I love you, very, very much, in case I had forgotten to mention it in the last three lines.

Again no mail today, but I keep hoping. There is really a good excuse, for no first class mail has been coming through in any great amounts. I do love to get letters from you, however, and I miss them so when they do not come.

By the way, when we get back to school I want you to see that I get proper exercise. An office job such as this is very confining, and I feel twice as good if I can get out and get a bit of air and exercise. There is no chance now, but in school I must work a bit of swimming, tennis, tumbling, etc. into my regular routine of work.

Although the paper came about three o'clock this afternoon, it was nine tonight before I had a chance to read it. I am sorry to see that there is a great deal of unrest in the Far East. I am still afraid that there will be difficulty in China and (or) India before a peaceful settlement is made. The horrors of war seem to be taken so lightly in the minds of men—particularly those who had no contact with real battle conditions.

They seem to forget the horror of the uselessness of destroying a single individual personality, not to mention the thousands of lives that are affected in one way or another and the millions of dollars of property which is damaged.

I see that my mind is inclined to wander and that my sentences are inclined to become incoherent. My mind is very tired and I must to bed to sleep. I shall join you in my dreams. Goodnight, Darling,

I love you,
Bushy

Letter from Dotty to Art
Tuesday
Oct. 2, 1945

My Dearest Co. Clerk,

So they finally found something for you to do! Amazing. By the way—isn't a company clerk supposed to be a sergeant or something? Seems like it is. By the way—according to Mary Agnes D., Ted was promoted to Corporal rather than T/4. Is that true, or was she confused? Something tells me that if you are being trained for Co. Clerk that you will stay with Div. and something tells me that if you stay with

Div. you will get home sooner. I hope. Pardon me for wishful thinking—in case you are wondering why, I am in receipt of your letter of Sept. 20.

Got a letter from Helen today. She is a busy woman. Busy woman. And Roland is a busy man. Seminary is absorbing to them, also fixing up their place to live. They weren't very satisfied with it at first, but like it better the more they are in it. From her description it sounds like our two (?) rooms in Palo Alto. Roland is taking only 15 hours, and Helen is auditing several courses. They are both in the choir and enjoying it a great deal. They send their regards to you, and their address is 66 Mariposa Ave., San Anselmo.

Ruth Lane & Flo and I have joined a women's chorus directed by Mrs. Leslie (the woman who referred me to Gladys B.) There are several other girls in it that I know, and it should prove to be a lot of fun. We are gonna put on a program in December!

Our love is wonderful no matter [where] you are, but it would be so infinitely more wonderful if you were here, where you were meant to be. I miss you so much, my Darling. So extremely much, because I so deeply

Love you,
Dotty

P.S. Would it do any good to harp on the fact that your education was interrupted, etc., etc., etc.?

Letter from Dotty to Art
October 3, 1945
Wednesday
Oct. 3, 1945

My Darling,

Your two packages from Paris came today (books & souvenirs) and I am entranced by the contents. Almost like Christmas it was. Everything came through fine except Venus, whose lonely neck was broken alas. Head completely severed from body. Horrible murder. Indescribably horrible. Such mutilation. Tsk, tsk. Parts of her base were broken off, too, but I think perhaps she can be put back together again, unlike Humpty Dumpty. Mother thinks the scarf is lovely, and Daddy is intrigued with his busts. By the way—who is the block one? We couldn't make out what is faintly scratched on the name plate, and—er—we don't recognize the gentleman right off-hand.

Darling, those black & white crocheted gloves are out of this world! I can hardly wait to wear them, but suppose I must since they are not suitable for winter. The pictures you sent are very interesting, and part or all of them shall go into the scrapbook. I shall have to learn French in self defense, looks like. Perhaps I can with the aid of the book you sent—"French Without Toil." Then at least I would know what it says about the pictures. And some of the things you may blow in into my innocent, unsuspecting ears!

No mail today, other than the packages. Perhaps tomorrow—(That aught to make a good movie title.) I am still hoping against hope that you will be home by Christmas. The hope grows a bit fainter with each passing day, but it is still there, and still glowing brightly. Only a definite statement to the contrary can put it out.

Despite the war's end, the world is still in great confusion and unrest. Peace cannot come overnight. In this country the labor situation is red hot & boiling over in many places, and there is political unrest. Many islands & small countries, many of them former colonies, are demanding freedom—but the pleas fall on deaf ears, for the mother countries refuse to even consider such things. Cold, hunger, and inflation will bring great "stress & strain" on all by their unavoidable presence in conquered & war-torn countries. The big powers are now finding it extremely difficult to agree on anything (now that they don't have to). Only the peace of God, the peace that passeth all understanding, can heal the wounds and soothe the feverish unrest now felt in all parts of the world. A sense of peace like that just mentioned I can always find in

Our Love,
Dotty

* Letter from Art to Dotty
Gunzberg, Germany
4 October, 1945 [97-100 (500)]

My Dearest Heart,

The hour is late, but I had a most enjoyable evening away from the office. Tonight I went to the show to leave the company area for the first evening in almost a week. It was so good to get away!

In recent days I have thought how much the little things mean to us in life. It really isn't the big things that matter so much. In combat it meant everything to have an extra blanket in a fox hole, to have thick pine boughs to lie on, to have a few old boards to assist in making the tent more roomy. I can think of times when it was almost heavenly to be able to sit down on a cold, wet roadside and rest my pack and weapon. To go to a far more interesting subject, there are millions of people in this world who are married, and yet how few there are who know the wonder of one look of love, one little kiss filled with so much meaning, one little act of thoughtfulness such as my lovely wife has performed for me so many, many times. A friendly smile or a kind remark can mean a great deal in the affairs of business, and work seems lighter. Thus it is a show tonight, a friendly talk concerning politics with Wilhite today, a long letter from you tonight—all of these things brightened my day.

The picture was "Valley of Decision" with Greer Garson and Gregory Peck. A few years ago if I had seen Greer Garson in pictures I would have been inclined to say to myself that it was all very nice in the movies, but the stories of girls such as Miss Garson portrays are hardly true to life. I like her acting very much, and I can now appreciate her roles much better. She is usually cast in the part of a noble, true, and beautiful personality. In her small way she approaches something of the wonder of the character of the girl that I married, and so I like her pictures very much.

Darling, that is a crude way of trying to say what I mean. I do love you so very much, and I try to put my feelings on paper and it is so hard to do. I want to tell you how much it means to be in your presence, to gaze in your eyes, to have your cooling fingers press the wrinkles from my forehead. Sure 'n I'm tellin' ye, Lass, I luv' ye truly, I do.

Ted Livingston applied last week for a theological school in Scotland. There was a quota of one for the entire Corps (seven or eight divisions), and he has received that one. I think that it is wonderful news for him, and I rejoice with him at his good fortune. Usually I like to wait for the arrival of good fortune before I tell you, but this time I shall let you know of my plans aforehand. The new man in the office is catching on very quickly, and I think that within a week or two he will know as much or more about the office than I. We are reorganizing the files, etc, and I think that within a couple of weeks everything will be running smoothly. I may pass up the next chance for another strip, but I think that when and if I am offered a chance to go into the RSo Office I shall ask to be released for school. I feel that two months in school in England would mean far more to me than another strip and the small amount of increase in salary which it would bring. Of course, the chance may never come, but it seems far more likely right now than every before. Only men with certain point scores are eligible for school. I am in that category. If I were alone in the office, I would have difficulty getting someone worked in. Everything seems to be going swell to the end that I might be able to get away. I shall not hesitate if the opportunity presents itself.

The Radio City Music Hall Rockettes are playing in Augsburg for a few days, and I may get up to see them. I also think that there is some chance of spending next week-end with Ted, but we shall see. At long last today I was able to get two rolls of film into a photo shop. These are some of the last I took in Paris.

By the way, today we learned that our Commander, Gen. Patton has been relieved of his command. There is a great variety of opinion concerning Patton among the GIs. Many have no use for him whatever, and think that he is nothing more than a fiend for show and pomp. Some consider him a good man in combat, with many minor faults. Others think that he is completed justified. For myself I think it [he] did a good job in the field, but I think that he lacks a great deal in diplomacy.

Chaplain Webb and Ted heard him speak at a Chaplain's Retreat during the week in which I returned from Paris. He began by saying that the newspapers greatly exaggerated his language. He went on to say that really he was a very devout Christian. I have heard few Christians say that.

There have been a number of incidents wherein gangs of German boys and men have attacked GIs at night. I wonder if any such news has reached the States. I do not intend to take any more long moonlight strolls alone, and I may begin to carry one of my small pistols—I have a very tiny .25 which would offer some protection.

The hour is long past my bedtime, and I have rattle on a great rate. It is perfectly all right about the packages, Darling, I really can't think of anything that you could send me at present. Just keep writing, and I can ask for little more under the circumstances.

I love you, I need you, I am
Eternally thine,
Bushy

Letter from Art to Dotty
Gunzburg, Germany
4 October, 1945 [501-503]

My Dearest,

It just occurs to me that It was a year ago tonight that we stood in the Oakland Station for three and a half hours in an attempt to get good seats on the Train east. Our efforts were to no avail. How much has happened since that day just twelve short months ago! How much I hope that by the time another twelve months have passed the tumult and uncertainty which has marked our lives will have passed!

Darling, I fell like kicking myself! I wonder if I will always be as soft as I am now. This afternoon I stopped down at the I & E office to check up on the possibilities of getting in on another school. (I wrote you about this in my letter last night.) Many of the schools are just beginning, but there was one possibility of getting a Liberal Arts Course at the U. of Aberdeen, Scotland. I would have only two days to get my application in, and I was told that in all likelihood, the quotas are in. Still it was a chance. I brought the papers back to fill out tonight, but the Capt. came in about eight o'clock. The application required his signature, and so I talked to him about the matter. He was reluctant to release me, and ask me to remain until the quotas come out again in a couple of weeks. Again he promised to give me a rating as soon as the freezing order is released—that may be next Spring! Well, I let him talk me into waiting, but I think that perhaps I should have insisted. Of course, Wilhite will be leaving very soon, and I suppose Capt Garner wants to hold on to every one he can. Well, I shall try again in a couple of weeks, and then I shall try for Oxford or Cambridge. Who know? If perhaps I can get a rating and also the school, well so much the better.

Had a chance to go to Augsburg tonight to see the Rocketts, but I decided to stick around. I am rather tired, and I would like to get a good night's sleep for a change. I sleep like a baby, but my hours have been rather short of late. The second game of the World's Series is in progress, and some of the fellows have come into the office to listen. I am hardly a fan, and I wish I could hear some nice music. It really does liven things up during the day to have a radio playing, and the programs from AFN Munich are surprisingly good.

Of late I have written little in my black book, but I have tried to include most of my trends and threads of thought in my letters to you. Since I am writing almost every day, it is not difficult to do. Still no letters from you or from Mother and Dad.

I talked to Myers today, and found that Ranger is going back to Paris. However, his outfit is going back to the States in a few weeks, and so he is preferring to remain over here a bit longer. Bill M. is working in the PX for the Regt. and so I do business with him each week as I purchase the rations. An Old K Co. Officer is the PX Officer for Regt. and he has all K Co. men working for him. Tomorrow we have the first shipment of low pointers, and I notice on my Special Orders that Fred Price is leaving for the 9th Div. (AO). There but for the grace of a few points would go I.

My reading has gone down to almost nothing of late. In such a job as this where I am working right in the room in which I sleep my work is always with me. I go to sleep at night planning files or work for the morrow. I awake in the morning thinking of the day ahead. I almost wish that I were sleeping about a half a mile away from the Office where the rest of the company is quartered. However, I can hardly get away now. I shall attempt to visit with Ch. Webb more during the long winter evenings. Found out this afternoon that Ted will be leaving in the morning at seven o'clock. He thought that he would be here for several more days and does not know that he must leave tomorrow.

Guess that I will go up to Augsburg on Saturday unless some thing unusual (or rather something "usual") comes up, I shall try. It will be nice to get away and spend a little time with Ted. I made an attempt to call him today, but was unsuccessful.

With two or three interruptions the evening has passed, and it is time for bed. I have been listening to some good music for the past hour, and it is very pleasant. I long to be able to kiss you goodnight and say,

       I love you,
       Bushy

Letter from Dotty to Art
Tuesday
Oct. 9, 1945

My Darling,

My, what a long circle meeting. It lasted almost three hours, most of which time was spent in just gabbing. Some of it was very constructive, though. I was called upon to make a few comments on the returning soldiers probable views on social issues & ethical standards. Your excellent comments along that line were a great deal of help, although, as I brought out, you by no means represent the masses! I think the trend will be toward broader views on social issues and more liberal views on ethical questions. Nicht wahr?

A girl next door had her tonsils out today, despite the very imminent arrival of her husband from overseas. You couldn't persuade me to do that unless it were a case of dire emergency.

In a letter or two you have mentioned playing chess. I hope you learn how well, because I would like for you to teach me. We could play beautiful chess together, don't you think?

Wednesday

What a thrill I got today when the postman brought four letters from you! Of course two of them were almost a month old, and the most recent was fifteen days old, but your letters are wonderful as usual. The past 2 weeks had brought me only about four or five letters from you all told, and I was beginning to wonder what the heck, but having promised not to gripe about the mail situation anymore I had said nothing to you. However, I still claim it will be O.K. for me to wonder what the hold-up is, especially since you get my mail so fast. It really shouldn't take airmail 25 days to get from you to me no it shouldn't.

Alack and alas. You stun me with the news that you may remain in Europe until March, and apparently assume that I knew all about it long before you, but I don't. So give with gory details. I scour each day's paper for just such news as that, but have seen absolutely nothing to that effect. How can they keep you in Europe till March when you will have enough points for a discharge in December? But then I suppose I should expect that from the Army---they have [been] so nice to you so far! AND besides, by March any soldier with two years of service will automatically be out. Why gracious---by March you will have been in almost three years, active service. It ain't fair, that's what it ain't.

If such is the case, I had better get busy on the Christmas presents to send you, since I have but five more days in which to mail Xmas packages without a request. I shall send them though, but I want you to know that I still haven't given up hope that you will be home in December or January.

We are having a church supper tonight. I sincerely hope more come than have indicated they were coming, and I think they will. It is hard on the cooks not to know how many to prepare for, though.

I must on with my work. Today is also bulletin day. As will always be true,
        I love you,
        Dotty

Letter from Art to Dotty
Gunzburg, Germany
10 October, 1945 [514-516]

My Dearest Heart,

I failed to write last night for the first time in many days now. After a very rushing day, I accepted Ch. Webb's invitation to come over and play Monopoly. I finally went broke about ten o'clock, and came home. I was too tired to think coherently, and so I went to bed without delay.

I am beginning to be just a bit disturbed by the lack of mail, but I think that it is due entirely to the strike situation in the States. I believe that the latest letter that I have received from you was written about the 25th of Sept. That means that the latest news I have is almost three weeks old, and I only hope that the same is not true of the letters coming to you. While in Paris I wrote about four letters a week, but since I returned to Germany I have written almost daily. I hope that the letters recently have reached you in particularly for I have been sending the pictures which I secured from Chaplain Webb. So far I think that I have sent thirty-two of these pictures, and I have three more in that series. Today I was able to get two rolls back which were taken in Paris during my last days there. These are not too bad and I will begin to send them a few at a time.

Today came very encouraging news in the S & S. It is announced that all men with two years of service will be eligible for discharge by March. That means me you know. If the men with 60 points are eligible for release Nov. 1st, there is always the possibility that we may leave shortly after the New Year. I am more hopeful.

One of the best moral boosters during the past few days has been the decided change in the weather. Yesterday the sky cleared and today was actually warm. I went outside without a jacket and found the experience pleasant. Never-the less we did draw our winter issue of clothing today—overcoat, long underwear, seater, etc. All the more that we will have to carry when we leave. I have a box of things which I will try to get off in a couple of days. There are a number of odds and ends that should have been mailed some time ago.

By the way, Mother wrote in a recent letter that her pen is wearing out. She had a nice new one when she began work in the office, but of course it has had constant wear since that time. I was wondering if perhaps we could pick up a nice one for her for Christmas. I will have little chance for presents of that sort, but I would be very glad if you could find a nice one for her. Buy a good one if and when you do. Anything that I can get over here for the folks I will buy, but the opportunities are few and far between. I am hopeful that I can find some thing nice for my very lovely little bundle of charm—my wife.

Work in the office continues at the mad pace mentioned before, but we are getting things done. I am regaining a bit of my old confidence I think for this is a job with at least some responsibility. It is interesting to note the change in attitude of men as they approach me in my position of company clerk. I take no pride in the new respect or rather attention for I know that it is the job that is receiving the attention and that I myself have nothing to do with it. Yesterday some one offered to bring me a bottle of wine if I would sell them a few extra cigarettes. That sort of thing is not at all unusual, but I still find it very easy to say no. One thing that I am trying to cut to the minimum is the general habit of the officers of getting in on the first cut of PX rations, etc. A system cannot be changed overnight, but little by little I intend to place the officers on the same basis as the men. We are lucky in the respect that we have a bunch of men in charge who are regular guys.

Mary Ruth mentioned in a letter which came last week that a movie is being shot on the MC campus. I would be happy to hear more details of this, but I suppose that you have discussed it at length in one of the letters which I have not yet received. I am getting behind in my letters again, but I just don't feel like writing anyone else after I have written to you. Perhaps I have mentioned that I do not have an abundance of spare time in my new job. How is Samarriet progressing, and what is the status of Carl now? He should be getting out any time now. Do you know anything about Bob Hunter? I have written him a couple of times over here, but have had no answer. Nothing from Ted P. but Ted K showed me a letter in which Pratt mentioned that he had turned down a job leading to a captaincy. Since as an officer he will probably be over here for a while, I think that perhaps he would have been wise to take it, and yet circumstance can alter situations greatly.

The last game of the World Series is in the final stage and my bedroom, office, dayroom, is filled with listeners. I shall try to get rid of them, and go to bed to dream of
Our Love,
Bushy

Letter from Dotty to Art
October 11, 1945
Friday Afternoon

My Dearest Bushy,

Heavens above! What a busy week this has been. Just like last week. Something on every night in the week, mornings too for the most part. The week has included giving blood, attending a chorus rehearsal, going to circle meeting, attending Church night supper and program, choir practice, company last night, skating with Intermediates tonite, and the Intermediage Rally for all kids in Presbytery tomorrow afternoon at this church. I miss you woefully when I am busy---how would it be if I were not busy I hate to contemplate.

Vivian Creech Purdy is back in town for a little while (while her husband gets discharged from the Navy). And came out last night for supper to spend the night. That gal can really talk your right ear off, left one too. After we went to bed we kept on talking, and jabbered away to 4:00 this morning! I'll confess I did my share of it, too. At 8:00 I awoke and couldn't go back to sleep again, so I got about four hours sleep in all.

Santa and I are busy working on your Christmas things, and the boxes will probably go out tomorrow, if all goes well. I am not sending anything of very great value---they will keep until your return—but things that you can consume or have fun with and then throw away, etc. I <u>sincerely</u> [hope] that the boxes reach you in good time and in good shape. If the boxes reach you long before Christmas just keep them unopened until Christmas day <u>unless</u> you should happen to head this way before that date---in that event open them before you leave. The greatest gift I could possibly dream up or ask for would be to have you home, my Love. I can but pray to God for this favor.

We are having beautiful weather, by the way. The leaves are just barely beginning to run, and do not seem nearly so colorful as last year at this time. We have had our first frost already, though, and it is nippy enough for fires - - we have had the furnace on for two days at our house. Luckily we have, little by little, been able to lay in a goodly supply of coal before the cool weather began. If we had not done this we might have found ourselves shivering for lack of fuel ere many months had passed. Strikes have done severe damage to the coal industry, and an acute shortage is expected in this country in addition to the nations still suffering from effects of war. It is becoming increasingly obvious that strikers think only of themselves---if they think at all---and if union members are brazen enough to to think they rapidly lose both union and job. Most of the strikes are for higher wages, and if granted it will not help to lower prices one bit, yet not granting it only makes the strikers more insistent and snarls up industry the more. Battle, travel-weary soldiers have been longing for a return to normal living, but they are out of luck, for normal living doesn't seem to exist any more. Do you think we can find it, Darling? (Just give us a chance!)

No letter today, and none yesterday. I miss you letters a great deal, and find it hard to be patient with whatever unknown force seems to be fouling up proper mail delivery. My concern over this matter is due to the wondrous, glorious, delightful, simple fact of
    Our Love, Dotty

Darling,

Things are beginning to happen again, and so for the next few letters I suppose that I will keep you in a state of suspense again. Now don't get excited, it isn't that good; but we are going to move. The news came about ten o'clock this morning, just as I was getting that self-satisfied feeling that everything is under control. The entire regiment is being shifted around, and in the next two or three days we willmove to a town called Memmingen, which is almost due south of Ulm. There we will be far more centrally located that we are here in Gunzburg in regard to the battalions, but I fear that we will not have the facilities there that we have here. One difficulty in regard to Ser. Co. is that we must be located where a large garage or shop is at hand, a large parking lot for our trucks, as well as the usual requirements for a kitchen, mess hall, billets for the men, etc. Usually the set-up is rather poor for these reasons.

A second beg event of the day was the receipt of two letters from you today. There were really three for one contained the "Hearth Log". Your letter mailed the 1st of Oct. arrived this morning, and the one mailed on the 29th of Sept. came tonight. Vat a systemm, I!m telink you! I enjoyed the description of the home movies which you saw, and also the article concerning the NEI. The latter brought back memories of my Stanford days. I actually wish that I could have done some work in the Indies, but I should be satisfied for one war. Maybe we will be able to take the Indies on a summer vacation sometime.

This guy Devers with whom I am working is a very interesting character. He just came down to talk for a few minutes. He is not afraid of work, and has adjusted rapidly to the job. Of course, he is still a T/5, and is still my assistant. So far I think that he does not resent the queer set-up, but he would have every right to do so. I try to make the situation as easy for both of us as possible. He is beginning to wonder just who will stay for the job, and so do I. Between the two of us, I feel almost sure that I could work myself into Wilhite's job when he leaves. I am wondering if I should do so in preference to going to school in England (if that is still possible). If I choice [choose] to ask for the job, it would mean, of course, that I would remain with Ser. Co. and not go to school should the opportunity present itself. However, my status in regard to coming home would not be affected. Frankly I do not know what I would do, although the appeal of school in England is very strong. We shall see what develops.

In the two letters which I received today you make mention of letters from me, but I assume that mine are being held up also. I do hope to hear that all thirty five of the Webb pictures come through all right. Let me know if and when all are received.

I am terribly sorry that I overlooked Daddy's birthday, and I also passed up Dad's (which you remembered). I will write to both and beg forgiveness, but I can only excuse myself by saying that all of my spare time is spent in thinking of you. I shall try to make up for the error in some way.

I am terribly glad that you like your work, and that it keeps you occupied. It is so much better for both of us that we are very busy, for so the time flies. I see that a new moon is just beginning to make its brief entrance upon the stage of the evening sky, and I know that soon again it will be full. The news looks good concerning 135,000 replacements that are being sent over here, and also the news about two year service men getting out in March appeals to me. If the two year men get out in Mar. the three year men should make it before May or June, nicht wahr?

Got a date with a dream!—and I do mean you!! I love you with all my heart, my Dear. May God continue to bless

> Our Love,
> Bushy

Letter from Art to Dotty
Gunzburg, Germany
October 12, 1945 [520-521]

Darling,

I have a great deal of sleeping to get out of the way, but I must dash off a note to you—though I do not like to dash. A long day's work was made infinitely brighter by the receipt of six letters:—one from Mother, one from Daddy, my <u>TIME</u>, and THREE wonderful letters from you (3, 4, 5, Oct.) Gee, it was so good to get some recent mail, and hear all of the news.

One bit of news which Mother wrote concerns us very directly. She has checked on this GI Bill for Edu., and finds that I will not lose my ASTP time. Thus I should be able to get about four years in under it. Ooh la la! PhD, here we come!

I was also very happy to learn that the packages finally arrived, although it is regretable that Venus suffered during the trip. I do hope she can be repaired. Let me know about the possibilities, for if not I can get Ranger or Miss Burkhart to get another and send it to you with a better wrapping system being utilized. Glad you like the gloves, my Darling. I should have told you a long time ago, "stick with me and you'll be wearing diamonds—well at least, gloves from Paris. I have at least one more Paris item to send, and some other things which I have acquired.

The Captain and Wilhite were again gone all day long, making arrangements for our new location. They returned late tonight, and the reports are good as to our new billets. I hope we have a good place for the office. The CP (Command Post, or office) will not move until Sunday, but most of the company will move tomorrow.

I was just this moment interrupted by a good talk with Wilhite. We straightened out several points that we [were] causing some some difficulty. He assures me that my work is satisfactory, and that the Capt. is also satisfied. They are still willing to do all that they can for me in the way of advancements, etc. Yes, Ted only made Cpl. Instead of T/4, but I hope that he will get another promotion soon.

I gotta sleep, but I will try to write again before I leave Gunzburg. Don't worry if my mail is held up for a couple of days. Know always that I love you with all of my heart.

Thine own,
Bushy

I failed to number the pages of the letter for the 10th. I think that there were three (17,18, 19) It also contained pictures of Paris.

Letter from Dotty to Art
Saturday
Oct. 13, 1945

Dearest,

It seems as if I have not written my full quota of letters this week, so I shall depart from my usual custom and write tonite.

Flo is spending the night with me because her folks are gone and she sits over there in the big chair by the radio, writing to Carl.

We (me & the Inter.) had great fun skating last night, but how much more fun it would have been to have had you to skate with. I skated by myself some, and with the kids some. During one of the "couples only" periods a soldier came up and asked me if I cared to "learn how to fall," so I skated with him; but far from falling—he skated rather well.

This afternoon's weiner roast & Rally at the church completed my busy week, and now I don't want to do nuthin' but just sit here. Sit here and write you.

I certainly am glad you are not on Okinawa—the Typhoon which raged there has done almost as much damage as an atomic bomb.

No mail again today. There has been no mail since Wednesday, the day on which I received four older back numbers from you. My morale will certainly improve when your letters come through as they should. If I thought you were on your way home, I wouldn't gripe a bit about the mail, but your coming home doesn't seem at all probable at this points, so I wish whatever mysterious force is tying up the mail would spend itself. I can hardly wait to get your letters, because

I Love you,
Dotty

Letter from Art to Dotty
Memmingen, Germany
October 14, 1945 [522-524]

My Dearest Heart,

I write my first letter to you from our new location in the town of Memmingen. My light is a candle, and I am reminded of days and nights in combat, when I scribbled brief notes to tell you that I was all right. I spent most of last evening packing office equipment and my own personal things. Rather than write, as I should have done, I went to bed in an effort to sleep a bit. The attempt was hardly successful until about an hour later.

This morning we finished the job of packing, and finally found ourselves loaded on the truck. We arrived here about one o'clock, and by three we had the situation well in hand. Our CP is located on the third floor of a Ger. hotel. I said Ger. to emphasize the difference. For the present the company supply room and the regt. post office is also located in this building, and there are a number of drivers sleeping here. Before I found out that there are civilians living in the hotel, I opened the wrong door a couple of times. I do not like the idea of sleeping next door to a German family, but I shall have to put up with it. Devers and I have a very nice room, with lovely beds of finished oak, a cabinet and dresser to match. There is also a stove in the room, which will be a very important item this winter. We are away from our work enough that we will not have to sleep with it, and yet we are close enough to be handy if anything important comes up. We have two rooms for our office, with a bath tub and wash basin adjoining. Our kitchen set-up is very nice, but it is terribly small. I am glad that it is about two blocks away for that will probably be my only exercise. We have tables for about eight or ten men each, table cloths, and waitresses.

I missed church today, but it was actually a good day for the move. The sun began to shine before we had gone far, and the countryside was beautiful. The trees are just beginning to turn over here, and I was constantly reminded of the Smokies just about one year ago. Splotches of color spread out through the flat valley, here a yellow, there a red, there the dark of green of the balsm and pine. A trip up LeConte would be so beautiful just at this time of year.

We had a great deal of mail come in tonight, but I received none at all. Some of the letters had been postmarked in NY on the 10th, and that is about the best time that I have heard.

O by the way. Yung came into the office last night. His shipment has been delayed a great deal, and I suppose that he will be in the ETO for several for weeks now. The strikes in New York certainly through a monkey wrench in the redeployment program.

Regt. hdq. is located here in Memmingen along with another company or so. There are movies every night I understand, as well as a dance. I may see a couple of movies now and then. What I do intend to do is to cut out this night work. No [Now] that I do not sleep right in the CP I will try to get away in the evenings for some quiet reading and writing. It is not yet eight o'clock, but I intend to get to bed and to sleep. I will go back to the regular routine of work tomorrow, with the added problem of setting up my PX and selling the new supply of rations. At least, here I will have a separate room for PX and mail. That will help a great deal.

I will write more at leisure tomorrow, when my thoughts will be more coherent. Three words are always coherent in my mind—three words guide my thought and action—three words make the world a different place in which I live—those three words are these—I love you!
Ever thine own,
Bushy

Letter from Dotty to Art
Sunday Night
Oct. 14, 1945

My Dearest,

I put in a full day's work at the church today, almost—seven hours, at any rate—3 this morning, and 4 tonite. And all the time in between dinner & time for evening session was occupied with company. Ralph

Batey (remember?) came over this afternoon to see all the stuff you have sent from Germany and France. I showed him every little thing, all the postcards you have sent, etc. He looked at every little thing, and seemed quite interested in all of it.

We had four "new" civilians at church today. It looks _so_ good to see them back, but not half as good as it will look when I get mine back! There are times when I must struggle to keep patient and serene about your return. One of the new civilians has been back only a week or so, has fewer points than you (and is a Lt., at that), and has been overseas less time than you, was in the Air Corps. Yet here he is already, and discharged already. And when I think that you may be kept in Europe three months _after_ you are eligible for a discharge, my soul rebels. Yes, I must struggle to keep patient and serene about your return.

We had a very nice service at church tonite. The organist went to some lengths to "do it up brown" as it were. The entire service centered around the hymns of Isaac Watts, and performed by the choir for the most part. Dr. Peyton gave a short sketch of Watts' Life. As we sang "When I Survey the Wondrous Cross," candles were lighted on a small cross tilted toward the audience. We sang eleven numbers in all, including responses and hymns sung by the audience too. All were by Watts, even the responses—and the Hymnal contains eleven more that we didn't use. The audience was pitifully small, and part of that was composed of strangers. The bulk of our church members will not come out to church on Sunday nite. It is rather discouraging to those who spend a lot of time and effort working up such a program as the one tonite. It had plenty of publicity, too. The Journal took a picture of the choir Thursday, but it failed to get in the paper, naturally. Something happened to the film, of course. Something always happens to the pictures that are taken of me because I want so badly to send you one occasionally. There seems to be a jinx on the thing. I still can't buy film, and if I am in a picture someone else takes, something invariably happens to it. It's a great life!

I have to get the pictures you send me and wish with all my heart that I could return the compliment.

'Tis late and I must say Good Night,
    My Love,
    Dotty

Darlingest,

Whee,—mail today—three letters! Naturally the day is much brighter. Also the night and the next day. These letters made pretty good time, too—Sept. 27 & Oct. 7 & 8. And I can see by the page numbers that there are about twenty pages in letters that I have not yet received, so that is certainly something to look forward to. Hmmm—I wonder where those six or seven letters can be hiding?

I was especially glad to hear the news about Tally and Van. Wonder how they reconciled their religious differences? Is Van a Catholic, or Tally a protestant, or have they both made a change? I still greatly favor the solution. I read about once—that of both making a change to a new church rather than either having to give in all the way. The Episcopalian Church would make an excellent choice in such a case, because it combines many elements of both faiths.

I admire you for being so diligent about your job, but please don't become too essential—just in case. By the way—will you ever get rating if Yung does not leave? That's what I thought. It's always the way.

I really enjoy this chorus we've joined. It revives memories of the good old days, and provide a long desired opportunity to sing with a large group. Three part music for female voices has a beauty all its own. Our first concert will be Dec. 10—wish you could be here for it.

I have mailed three Christmas boxes to you—please let me know if & when you get them.

How often I wish I could put into words the deep meaning of
Our Love,
Dotty

My Darling,

Again last night we had no lights in our quarters or in the office. Again I was in bed before nine o'clock, and what a difference two good nights' sleep make!

Yesterday we suffered the throes of getting settled, with Capt. Garner gone all day and Wilhite out most of the time. The fact that our CP is on the third floor of the hotel makes things a bit difficult, but I think that we are going to move down stairs to the first floor.

Everything is unsettled, and we are trying to leave things packed as much as possible and get out merely the essential part of the work. Yesterday I had to pick up two weeks supply of Px rations, and so if we do move very far I will have a big job with all of that junk.

I am expecting something to break in regard to school in the next few days. I talked to one of the fellows in the I&E Office yesterday and he told me that they were trying to find men to fill quotas for one of the French Schools. Perhaps in a few days they will be trying to find men for schools in Eng. Keep your fingers crossed. Redeployment seems to be slowed down here for another three months or more anyway.

Yesterday the papers carried the story that Java is declaring war on Holland. I just thought that had I been shipped to the S. Pacific to utilize my Stanford training, I might have found myself involved in another war.

It is passed time for breakfast, and I must rush over and eat.

At breakfast time, supper time, spring time, winter time, sun time, war time, any time, all the time, Gruen time, Bulova time,

I love you,
Bushy

Letter from Art to Dotty
Memmingen, Germany
October 16, 1945 [527-528]

My Dearest,

My letters during the past few days have been rather rushed, but I hope that I can begin to settle back to normal (or is it abnormal?). Just as we are about to get settled here in our new quarters we are ready for another move, but this time it is only down stairs to the first floor. As far as we know now we will be here in this location for sometime to come. At last today we were able to get our lights fixed up, and now our room seems more livable. It really is a very nice room, and almost as large as both of our rooms in Palo Alto. Devers has a big radio, which I think I have mentioned before, and the short time that we are in the room seems almost like being at home. There are, of course, several outstanding things lacking; not the least of which is my lovely wife.

We are tp have plates in our mess hall with waitresses and tomorrow we begin a regular cleaning and pressing service. Also, Special Service is handling film for us, and I will be able to get prints made in a couple of days time. I have a good PX set-up even though it is located on the third floor, and I did a big business today. More luxury items tomorrow, and I will spend another afternoon selling. I think I mentioned that there are movies in town every night, but as yet I have not seen one.

My mail is far behind, but I suppose that I will receive a stack of it sometime soon. I am wondering if you have received the pictures which I bought from Chaplain Webb. There are thirty-five in all, and I sent them home in groups of five or six at a time. If there is plenty of photo paper in town, I may be able to get more pictures from Chaplain. He has a new assistant now who is an organist, and it will be of tremendous advantage.

I am glad that I am so busy that the redeployment mix-up passes over my head. I think that I would be very much disgusted if I stopped to really get mad about the way things are going. The S&S carries the headline today that shipping has been turned back a month by the strikes, etc. That isn't good.

I shall enclose tonight the last of present group of Paris pictures, but I believe that I have a few on another roll which remains undeveloped. I hope to get it fixed up shortly. I am getting a money order made out for thirty-five dollars which I hope to put in the letter tomorrow night. Since I was paid for three months last time, I shall try to send most of it to you as I see that I have enough to keep me running in case of an emergency.

The moon is passed the full tonight and I shall ask her to carry a message of my deep and abiding love to you. I miss you and need you, my Dearest. May God continue to bless

Our Love,
Bushy

Letter from Art to Dotty
Memmingen, Germany
October 17, 1945 [529-530]

My Darling,

Ah, and at last we have moved into a place that is supposed to be at least semi-permanent. This morning in about half an hour, we moved our belongings downstairs and set up our new office. It is right on the street, and is large enough to accommodate all the facilities that we need. We have three phones in the one large room, and five desks, including the typing table. We [have] good lights and a stove we are about ready to "sweat out" a long winter.

After moving I dashed off a quick report, and then went after extra PX rations to put on sale. This took two hours, and the rest of the day and part of the night was spent in sorting this stuff out and selling it. By the way, at long last I have a watch. When I began working here, I was able to get a regular GI issued by the supply room. However, I will have to turn that back in as soon as I leave. When I first returned from Paris, and still working with Ch. Webb, I placed my name on the waiting list for watches. At long last my name stood second on the list and today we received two watches. Ironically enough, the watch is exactly what I had hoped to get when I first came into the Army. It is water proof, antimagnetic, sweept second hand, luminous dial, Swiss make, etc. It would cost twenty-five or thirty dollars at least in the States, and I bought it for nine dollars here. Not bad!

I was happy to get a long newsy letter from Mom this morning, along with a wonderful five page one from you. Why don't we do this more often? I am terribly sorry to hear that Mom is having so much trouble with her arthritis, and I only hope that she can be relived of the trouble. By the way, how is Aunt Mary getting along? You have not mentioned her in along time.

Tomorrow I will not have to worry about PX until late in the afternoon, and I hope to be able to get a few things fixed up here in the office. Devers is doing good work, but on some things he wants to be told exactly how a job is to be done. He is readdressing almost all of the mail now, which relieves me of a time consuming task. Wilhite said the other day that he wanted both of us to get a chance at a pass right away, but I am going to hold out for school even if I have to give up that Switzerland trip. At least, I appreciate Wilhite thinking of us and planning to release one of us for a furlough.

Days are cooler now, and nights are cold. A fire feels very good, and I am thankful that I can work inside. I long for a fireplace, soft lights, sweet music, and the wonderful presence of you, My Love. I do love you with all of my heart. I marvel at the future which is ours in the years that lie ahead. Goodnight and sweetest dreams.

Eternally thine,
Bushy

Letter from Art to Dotty
Memmingen, Germany
October 18, 1945 [531-534]

My Dearest Heart,

Today came your letter of the 9th in which I find that your mail has been coming though as poorly as mine. I do hope that it all gets there sometime, for as I have mentioned before I have written almost every day since I returned from Paris. A number of the letters have contained pictures which I hope come through, and there are many thing which I will probably forget to mention should my original letters fail to arrive.

I hope that the number system which I continue to use is of some help in determining how much has been lost or delayed. I was also the lucky receiver of a long letter from Mother and another long letter from Sis. I hope to write the latter tonight, along with a note to Ranger. I am sometimes almost certain of the fact that I shall never catch up with all the writing that I would like to do—other times I know it to be true. Ooh la la! Whata life withouta wife!

I appreciate your kind remarks concerning the help which some of my comments have been in reviewing certain topics. However, I am sometimes frightened to think how much weight is given to viewpoints that are highly individual. If Joe Louis or Commando Kelly express a preference for this this fountain pen or that brand of corn flakes, thousands will reject their own tastes and try the other. The same will be true of many views expressed by returning service men. Nevertheless, I am flattered that my remarks were of some value, although I still think that always such views should be considered as strictly those of your own perverted husband.

I must explain myself further on the question of being in the ETO until March. I believe that I wrote that in connection with the announcement that the 71st would be in a group of outfits to be known as a clearing out force, and that these outfits would leave Europe between the first of the year and the first of June. There were twelve of these divisions listed, and so that means two would probably be leaving each month. At that rate we would have a fifty-fifty chance of leaving by March. Of course, since I wrote that and even since you wrote, the strikes and the loss of the Quenn ships have changed the picture a great deal, and everything is being set back. Where that will place me, I do not know. Of course, if this two year business goes into effect, I should get home a bit quicker, or if they continue to lower the point-scores a bit at a time. The general situation grew black in a great hurry, and I have found that it can clear just as quickly (although it does not often do so.). As Mother suggested today, even though I may have to remain over here through most of the winter, it is not half so bad as if I had been over here either last winter or the winter before. We still have much to be thankful for.

By the way, speaking of Christmas, I bought a little present for you the other day. It isn't very much, and I suppose that it will take a very long time to arrive, but I hope that it gets there before the 25th of December.

The mixed feelings that one has in a German city are very difficult to describe in words, and yet I would like to record at least a few of these. It is just as it was in combat, although not quite so bad: I want to give you a complete picture of my feelings and my impressions, and yet that is impossible. We have German women cleaning our rooms, making our fires, working in our kitchen and serving our food. How little did we imagine ten months ago that such would be the case in such a short period of time. It is difficult to realize that less than a year ago these same women were waiting on Hitler's soldiers, and perhaps in these very rooms plans were being laid for a stiffening of resistance, a counter-offensive, or a secret weapon. Today I went into a barber shop to have my hair cut. Perhaps it was the barber who cut my hair who fired artillery shells at me on the Rhine. An example which I know to be fact was the case of one of the German nationals who worked for our company in Gunzburg. The fellow spoke English with fair command, and he seemed to be a very intelligent fellow. Less than a year ago he was captured near Frankfurt, not far from the town in which I spent Easter. Last week he was wearing GI clothing, eating GI chow, sleeping on a GI cot, and cutting wood for Service Company. Such is the irony of war.

Another difficult feeling to describe is the one which I have in regard to our food, clothing, fuel, transportation, etc. I suppose that I am soft hearted, in fact I know that I am in many respects; but there is such a tremendous gap between the standard of living which the soldiers know over here and that which many of the civilians endure. Half a block away from our office today I saw a crowd begin to gather early this morning. Late this afternoon the crowd was still there. They came and went all day getting their small ration of wood. I always feel guilty if I have food left over in my plate for the German children, and even the adults, gather around our messkit line. At Gunzburg it became so bad that they would pick bread or small scrapes out of our messkits as we passed, and almost always there is one or two with a bucket begging for any coffee that is left in our cup. I understand that cigarettes are selling here at the rate of twenty-eight dollars a cartoon—that is worse than Paris! They still grab every butt that is tossed aside by the GIs, and in our former location we had a fellow who came around regularly. He was always well-dressed and spoke excellent English. Very politely he would come in and ask if he could pick up the butts that were in the ash trays. He would then proceed to carefully pick out any butts or any tobacco that was lying around.

Well, I have carried on at some length. I still want to dash off a note to Mary Ruth. I have not read my Time for the past three weeks,

but there is plenty of time. There is not enough time to tell you one thing. I love you very dearly. I long for the future of
Our Love,
Bushy

Letter from Dotty to Art
Thursday
Oct. 18, 1945

My Darling,

Whee—a letter today to make me happy. Question—Where are the ten (?) letters written between Sept. 26—Oct. 6? I have already letters you wrote Oct. 6, 7, 8, but the others are still missing. If its kissing you've been missing—oh, Brother!

Grandfather Parmelee died yesterday (Flo's grandpa). He was 93 years old, and a wonderful guy. Grandmother P., who is 94 is taking it like a veteran, a veritable rock. I was in this noon—paying my respects, helping in the kitchen, etc.—and went to see her. She heard I was there & asked for me. She was in the process of eating her lunch, but stopped to talk to me. She talked & even laughed at something Aunt Carol said, and asked me several questions about you, when were you coming home, where you were, etc. She is truly a remarkable old lady. Do you suppose I'll be that alert & interested in people when I am 90? I doubt seriously if I attain such a ripe old age. [As I type this, April 24, 2020, Dotty Bushing is 99 years old, and she is everything she hoped to be with regard to maintaining a caring disposition and youthful exuberance.]

Ran into Margaret Messer McClure in town today, and lunched with her. You know her husband, don't you? Scott McClure? Well, anyway he phoned her the other night—from London! He was there on furlough only, as he doesn't have many points. His Army life has been very much like yours—ASTP, etc, back to Inf. also he is going on to school when he gets back, as he was just a sophomore when [We are missing a page here.]

Flo & Ruth are both spending the night here. I invited Ruth, & Flo invited herself—her relatives here for the funeral fill up her house!

Good night, my Dear. May the beautiful bright moon I see in the sky carry the message to you of
Our Love,
Dotty

My Darling,

Tonight I have had a very enjoyable evening which began with a good show after supper. I saw "Our Vines have Tender Leaves" with Edward G. Robinson in a very unusual caste. The story was of simple life ona farm in Wis. among the Norse stock. It was well done, and was my type of a picture through and through. After I returned I called Ted and spent the last twenty minutes talking with him. I received a letter from him today, in which he told me that he was on duty tonight in the Orderly Room up there. He called while I was at the show, but I called back after I returned and we discussed everything under the sun. Unless something comes up tomorrow, I hope to get a pass and go up to visit with him. Next week he will be leaving for England on furlough, and will probably be gone for three weeks. These furloughs are for seven days plus travel time. The trip to England by rail is terribly long. By the time he returns, I hope that I can be on my way to the same place for school. Who knows?

Today I received your wonderful long letter of the 8th—six whole pages is very, very, very good. I love it! I think that most of the questions have been answered in previous letters, but I must dash your hopes in regard to the stripe. All promotions are frozen now, and we have no idea of when they will open again. I frankly have little hope of getting it. Ted will probably get another if and when things open up again.

When I hear some of the stories such as the one you tell concerning Carl, I am actually glad that I am over here instead of sweating out a discharge over there. When I get home I want to discard my uniform for good, and I certainly do not want to see any type of training again. Today it was announced that the point score would possibly be lowered to 50 points come Dec. 1st. That sounds good, but it still does not mean that I will be home for some time to come. We still have all men with points above 65, and there are many left in the theater with 70 and more. Just to show you how pessimistic Ted is, he said tonight that he hoped to be home by May. Now I think that that is too much, but I still fear that I will be lucky to be out of the ETO before the 1st of Feb. We shall see.

The hour is late and I lost sleep last night as a result of writing a bit later than usual. I shall say goodnight, My Love, sweetest dreams, and may you know always that I am   Eternally thine, Bushy

Darling,

Yes, I have to admit that the mail situation has been better now for about three days, but there is still a peck of mail from you that is still missing. I have received every letter you have written since Oct. 6, or rather all letters written since that date have been coming through swell, but letters written previous to that date back to Sept. 27 are still on their way. (I hope). Two letter arrived today (Oct. 10 and 11), both containing pictures. In them you mentioned sending 32 pictures taken by Webb, but to date I have received but six of that number, so the rest of them must be in the ten missing letters.

Just one year ago today we made a memorable trip to the mountains. Remember? We climbed among the rocks and trees and streams, and looked out upon the flaming hills, and we rejoiced to see God's handiwork. Today too is a clear, warm, sunny day, and I hear the call of the wild. My rebellious soul yearns for the hills and high mountains, for wild beautiful places, for the invigoration of cool, pure, air. But there is work to do at home, and my friends cannot get away. So I must either forget my wild urge or attempt to sneak off by myself to hit the high spots. O would that you were here dere, would that you were here.

I had intended getting a sweater for your Mother for Christmas, but perhaps a pen would be better. Last time I was there she asked me to send her that old sweater of yours, but looked in all your stuff at our house, and it was not in any of it, so I thought perhaps Mother needed a sweater and we could give her one for Christmas. Perhaps we could manage both, but I doubt it, the way good pens cost these days.

Glad you are now receiving the attention and respect you so richly deserve. Could the army not go even farther, and add a bit of rank as well? Also richly deserved?

I've forgotten how much I told you about the movie shot on the campus at Maryville. M.R probably told you about as much as I know. She was in some of the shots. The movie was all about church related colleges, apparently quite a big thing, shot by ex-Hollywood man, etc. The historical phase as shot at MC. Hunter and Orr and others had a big time acting as founding fathers, I hear.

Latest rumor is that points will be lowered to fifty in December—they say they will have to to keep up the present discharge rate. Thus my hopes start rising again that you will be here the first of the year at the latest. I am indescribably eager that we soon be reunited in

Our Love,
Dotty

P.S. Grandaddy P's funeral this afternoon, skating tonite. I'd rather not go tonite, but anything for my kids!

Letter from Art to Dotty
Augsburg, Germany
October 20, 1945 [534-536]

My Dearest,

Well, I made it! At eleven thirty this morning I found that a jeep was coming to Augsburg at twelve-thirty. I rushed around to shave, wash up, change clothing, sort mail, finish a report, and do half a dozen other things. My lunch consisted of a hamburger between two pieces of bread, but I made my connections, and in an hour and a half I was in Augsburg.

It was again a beautiful day for the ride. The air was just a bit nippy, but the sun shone brightly, and the countryside reflected all of the beauty of its Fall dress. The colors were brighter than last week, and more leaves had fallen beneath the trees. Many of the country roads in Germany are lined with trees, and as one looks across the countryside the ribbon of roadway is outlined by the these trees dressed in the their fall colors. In many fields the cattle grazed peacefully, tended by a small child or a women. Here and there and farmer followed his plow as the ground he prepared for the next Spring. Often I saw the "honey-wagon" spreading its richness on the ground. Often a horse and and ox pulled side by side. At one point in the ride I was able to count nine church steeples within a 180° arc. The German countryside is truly beautiful, and I wish so much that you could ride with me as I enjoy its colorful scenery.

My jeep brought me to Ted's very door, and I found him in the process of sending his clothing for their weekly wash. We took a spin over to his washer woman's location, stopping on our return for coffee and doughnuts at the ARC Club. Ted has a nice place to stay in the building where he works, even though his room is in the basement. There is of course a radio, and in one end of the room there is an underfed pingpong table. We went down town tonight to see an all girl orchestra. The music was largely jive, and so we were both disappointed. However, the program was for only an hour, and it was a diversion. We retuned to more pingpong and to write our dear wives. Good boy, nicht wahr? Ja, ja!

Nothing much new with Ted that I did not mention last night in the letter which followed our phone conversation. He leaves next week for England as I mentioned before. We have a quota for the same trip, and I think that I could swing a deal to go at the same time. However, I would lose my chance to go to school, and so I shall refrain from doing that which I would like to do for the moment.

There was some news tonight concerning men who are not slated for occupation being home by Feb. Under the present shipping conditions, that seems a bit fantastic, but who knows. Sometimes it seems so futile to get excited about news concerning redeployment. The situation changes so often, and so radically that I sometimes want to hear nothing until the real news does come.

I forgot to mention an incident which occurred last week in the office that represents the fantastic extreme to which Army GIness goes sometimes. It must have been Tuesday or Wednesday when we were in the middle of getting settled in our new location in Memmingen. The Capt. was away and the First Sgt. had gone out to take care of a few small jobs. A phone call came for the Capt. and when his absence was announced the person at the other end asked for Wilhite. Devers told the party that Wilhite was out also. Then he was questioned as to where Wilhite had gone, and Devers answered that he had gone to the MG (Military Gov't). Well, then the party asked that Wilhite call upon his return. Devers was curious and so he asked who the party might be. The answer was, Col. Halter, Regt. Commander. When Wilhite did call, he was questioned as to why he was at MG. He stated his business. "Well, I just wanted to know", stated the Col. and hung up. What a lot of trouble to get an answer to such a petty question! That sort of thing is thoroughly disgusting. And yet, we won the war!

I happen to be using a swell little German portable which one of the fellows here acquired in the trip through Germany. You know, I think that I will have to get a good portable before I go very far in my graduate work. You know my affinity for a typewriter anyway. I think that Dad may be able to get one for me wholesale through some of his connections. Goedzo! I long with an intense longing to get back to real intellectual atmosphere and study. It will take a bit of time to get back into the habits that I once had, but I think that they will come. When they do, I think that I will be able to eat up a lot of work.

Ted goes on duty as CQ again tomorrow at noon, and so we will not be able to go to Church in the morning. I will probably stick around most of the afternoon and try to get a ride back to Memmingen about four. I have no idea how the hitchhiking would be, but I think that I had better try to get a ride all the way from here if possible. I have a great deal of work to get started on on Monday, but as usual we will get through it one way or another. Today Wilhite managed to get a good desk for Devers, and also a couple of cabinets for filing. We are still finding ways to improve our office system, and I think that progress is begin made.

For tonight I shall say again, goodnight, and sweetest dreams, to the most wonderful little wife in the whole wide world.

Luv ya,
Bushy

Letter from Dotty to Art
Monday
Oct. 22, 1945

My Darling,

A solid, steady rain is pouring down from the skies, making it sound very damp outside, as indeed it is. I just got in from the show. "Wilson" is here for the first (!?) time, so I went to see it again. I was mortified to see that the great picture was being shown to many empty seats. Perhaps the rain had something to do with it, but usually the Tenn. Theater is full no matter what the weather or the picture. On the way out of the theater I listened to comments about the picture, and they were none too complimentary! They were bored, or the picture was too long, or there was too much speaking, etc. I still consider it one of the greatest pictures I have ever seen. Knoxville should not have waited till the picture was two years old before bringing it here, methinks.

The Evauls & I are trying to arrange a trip to the mountains for Friday of this week. I rearranged a dental appointment and fixed things up with Dr. Peyton so I could go, so—it had better work out! However, if the weather remains like this it won't be too much fun. Phil's parents are here (at his house, natch), and they too will enjoy the trip. We would have chosen Saturday for the trip, but that is Homecoming Day at the college, & we all want to be there for that. A justice of the Supreme Court who was once a Maryville student will be the figure of the day. (Hope you can read this scribbling).

Two letters from you today, an "old" one & a "new" one. Both contained pictures—five more of the "Webb" pictures came, making eleven of them so far received. The letters were dated Sept. 27 & Oct. 12. I am very happy to hear that Wilhite & the Captain are satisfied with your work—after all, how could they help it, you being you. Darlingcal, Am anxious to hear about your new location, living quarters, working quarters, etc. Ted hasn't moved, has he? Still in Augsburg? You'll be farther apart now, too bad. Your new envelopes with return address printed on is quite the stuff!

I am endeavoring to get your folks to my house for Thanksgiving. Do you think I can get them to come? Perhaps if you wrote & urged them them to come it would help. I know it would.

'Tis way past time to sleep now, and dream sweet dreams of
Our Love,
Dotty

Letter from Art to Dotty
Memmingen, Germany
October, 23, 1945

My Darling,

For a welcomed change I am not writing tonight from my desk in the office. We have a newly opened beer hall next door to the Orderly Room and the place is a bit noisy at night now, and there are always interruptions. So, we have a nice fire in our room, and the radio is playing softly. I brought the typewriter up from below, pulled off my shoes, and decided to enjoy a quiet and peaceful evening. That is I did all of this after I finally finished up a few odds and ends. That is one thing about my job, it can be at least an eighteen hour a day affair,—if I allow it to be. I am gradually changing my attitude concerning the work. As is always true, I find that one can become a work horse who is constantly called up on to do things merely because merely because I do not know how to say no. I do not mean to imply that I want to slack in my work but there are certainly lines that I shall draw.

I donot mean to begin my letter in a blue vein. The work is going along, and we continue to keep it under control. Devers is the type who constantly gripes at the work, but he is always willing to work overtime to see that it is done. Actually the two of us make a happy combination, for he takes care of the regular routine jobs such as readdressing mail, etc. and I make some attempt at coordinating the dozen and one things that we must handle. PX takes too much of my time, but this is because of the fact that so many of the fellows are drivers and come in at all sorts of odd hours to get their rations. I have a lot of money tied up in that store, but I think that I can manage without using up all of our reserve to pay my way out.

Tonight came two long letters mailed on the 15th in which you tell of your latest skatecapades with strange soldiers and the poorly attended Sunday evening special service. Wish that I could have attended both of them. Sure, I'm a tinsy winsy bit jealous, because I envy anyone who was priviledged to skate with your, My Love. Don't get me wrong, I don't object, but I am still jealous. Too bad about the program, but at least you had the satisfaction of doing a good job.

Ted and I were speaking the other night of the type of fellow with which we have come in contact in the Army in comparison with those we knew at Maryville. There is certainly a wide chasm separating the two types. I suppose that these men with who I associate from day to day represent the average American, but they are influenced by the fact that they are pulled down the scale. I mean by that that I have observed that men are prone to do things they would never have done as civilians merely because they are soldiers and away from home. Nevertheless, I am shocked by the actions of men who seem to have no control over their emotions, and no sense of ethical values. I wish that I could confine my remarks to the men at least who are are single, but the married men seem to be as guilty as the others. Not only men who are married, but married men with children seem not in the least ashamed of telling about "shacking up" with some German "babe". I could not even sit down to write a letter to you had I been unfaithful to my vows or to your faith. How these men can carry on as they do I cannot understand.

But to go from a sordid subject to a more pleasant one: The latest news on the radio announced all mail will be carried by air which is so intended. Some day soon you should be getting a large stack of mail which was slowed down by boat. I have averaged about six letters per week for the past six or eight weeks. I think that I repeat myself too much in regard to this mail situation, but I am always afraid that some of my letters will be lost amid all of the confusion.

I forgot to mention a little sidelight to our moving which is interesting—at least to me. After everything was packed, and kitchen moved out, I found a couple of cases of grapefruit juice in the basement of one of the buildings. I rather imagine that some of the DPs had made off with the cans either to sell or give away. Well, you know me! I am a confirmed sot when juices are in question. Devers and I loaded these two cases on the truck in which we rode. At the present moment they are hidden among our cloths in the closet. Strangely enough, only about half of one of the cases in gone. Devers doesn't drink. At my present rate of consumption (a can almost every night), I should have

This is the house in Memmingen where I lived and worked.
Note the horse at the corner. Oct. 1945.

Repairs had begun in Memmingen by Oct. 1945.

enough to last for at least six more weeks. By that time I do not think that I will be around to enjoy the juice anyway. Since I am dealing with candy all of the time, I suppose that I am eating more than I should even though I doubt that I eat more than my regular ration. I have a sneaking suspicion that my teeth are in very bad shape, and I hope to find time to have them checked soon. I hope that our children inherit your beautiful hard teeth.

I am glad to see in the paper today that France is voting for retention of De Gaulle. That seemed to be the trend in Paris while I was there, and I believe that he is the man to solidify his torn and bleeding nation. I wonder if you have noticed that the 71st football team is leading the 3rd Army again. I take a bit of pride in that, although I contribue nothing more than moral support.

If I go to bed now I shall be able to catch up a bit on delinquent sleep, as well as a bit of dreaming. My constant dream is the dream of
Our Love,
Bushy

Letter from Dotty to Art
Wednesday
October 24, 1945

My Darling,

This letter is really for last night. I'll write another tonite and come out even. Slowly but surely that back mail is catching up with me. It seems queer that it never comes all at once, but in two's and three's, almost as if it were rationed. Perhaps that is a good thing. Three letters came in today's mail, all of them wonderful letters, just like you. I am so fortunate in having you for a husband in the first place, and in the second place that you like to write, and write regularly. I could carry it on to the thousandth place, but I think you know that I love you that much and more. My point is that I have heard tales of men who did not feel compelled to write to their wives but about every two or three weeks. I would go nuts in short order without your sweet letters to give me a boost. It has been so much nicer for the past week on account of your mail has been coming in much better for a while.

Darling, may I be frank? I really think that you would stand a chance of getting home quicker if you stayed where you are than if you applied for and got another whack at some schooling. School in England or some other place would be wonderful, a golden opportunity, and all that, but your coming home at the earliest possible moment would be even more wonderful. After all, you still have a lot of school to look forward to after you return! I am not influenced in the least in what I say here by the possibility of your getting another stripe - - that has nothing to do with my feeling. I really cannot explain why I feel so strongly that you should remain with the outfit; it is more of a hunch than anything else, perhaps - - certainly I have nothing definite or factual to base it on - - just a feeling. I had no such feeling at all about your going to France. And then, too, I may be all wet about this whole thing; if so, forgive me. I hate to think you might turn down some swell opportunity just on account of some silly "feeling" of mine.

Phil came by the house this morning to straighten out details of our trip Friday. It looks as if we are all set for a swell time. We are to leave about 9:00 p.m., and get back in time for Phil to make a 7:00 meeting at one of his churches. His mother is going, and an aunt of his may arrive in time to go. The weather has been bad so far this week, but I think it will clear before Friday.

Gotta get a few things done around this here office, so will sign off by swearing

> Our Eternal Love,
> Dotty

Letter from Dotty to Art
Letter No. II
Oct. 24, 1945

My Own,

Say! What have I done to deserve this!? Three letters from you this morning and one this afternoon. What is this world coming to? It is uncommon enough for us to receive afternoon mail at all, much less getting four letters from you on the same day. Swonderful!

I have just recounted the "Webb" pictures, and find that I now have 24 of the 35. There must be about two more batches on the way. It is extremely interesting to have pictures drop out of almost every letter. They tell me, better than any words you could use to describe it, what your surroundings and companions look like, you are are already quite familiar with me (fresh!) and my surroundings, so perhaps it is not so essential that I send you many pictures, although I wish I could.

Too bad you were not in Paris long enough to attend the Laval trial. [Pierre Laval] It must have been a riot, literally speaking!

I'm sleepy, Honeybunch, but not too sleepy to tell you that

> I Love You,
> Dotty

P.S. I wouldn't write you sick puny letters if I wuz me.

Memmingen, Germany
October 24, 1945 [545-546]
Darling,

Had a call from Ted tonight. Our quota for the furlough to England was cancelled today, but for him it was only delayed a couple of days. I am certainly gald that he will be able to make it. He had a letter from Pratt today, and no wonder he has not been writing. He is in Shrivenham, England, in the GI University there, studying contemporary philosophy, the English novel, and something else. Poor Ted was trying terrible hard to get to school, and I am happly that he made the quota. It seems that he ran into Dr. Shine in London recently and found that the good Doctor is teaching in France—but not at Fontainbleau. I shall write both of these gentlemen in the near future—I hope.

Work continues as per usual with little let up in the pace. I have a swell map of Germany which I shall send to you in the next couple of days. I wanted to mark out a few of my travels on it before I send it along. I wonder if you received the two maps showing the route of march of the 71st and the second one of the 14th. Hope you did for they gave a fairly clear picture of our activity.

I took a few minutes of my lunch hour to snap a few pictures of the buildings which are kaput around town today. Hope that I can get a few more while the nice weather which we have been having holds out. Today was almost like summer again, and tonight the room is comfortable without a fire.

Bill Myers, my buddy in Paris who was also from Co. K, is leaving Saturday on a shipment of low pointers. He has been working in the PX (Regt) since our return, but now will go to the 9th Div. A sort of exchange is being made between the 71st and the 9th of men in order that we may fill up with those between 45 and 59. I am very happy that I am not doomed for the 9th.

I talked with Chaplain Webb today and he is going to get more pictures printed for me. We took some in Munich which I was never able to get, and also shots of the castle near Gunzburg of which I wrote. Will send these along to you as soon as I can get the work done.

I regret very much that I am doing very little writing in my notebook since my return from Paris. By the time I shave and bathe at night, finish up a few odds and ends in the orderly room, and write to my lovely wife, I find little inclination for either reading or writing more. I have a bad habit of allowing a job to consume too much of my time. It is really a habit which I wish I could avoid. During the past months, Ted has done a great deal of work with regard to architecture, much of it being done on duty hours. I never allow myself time on the job to do things for myself, and I wish that I did. If I could write a letter or two each day in the office, I could soon catch up on my correspondence. As it is, I always seem to find something to do.

I wonder if you can ever realize just how much I miss you in every little thing that I do. Your smile, your cheering remark, your calming and relaxing presence, you! I miss you, My Love. God was truly kind when he gave me the wonderful blessing of
Our Love,
Bushy

Letter from Dotty to Art
Thursday
October 25, 1945

My Darling,

This is too good to be true, and it can't last, because I think all the missing letters finally made it—at least all the 35 pictures are all accounted for. Three more letters from you today, and one from Helen. The letters are postmarked Oct. 1, 2, & 17th, and the news in all of them is a bit stale, except the part that never gets stale about I love you & you love me ad infinitum. Really.

That silly girl! That screwy Helen. She answered my letter (the same one) twice. That is the second time she has pulled that stunt. Not that I mind, of course—I always love to get mail. She informs me that Ted is where you would give your eyeteeth to be—in England for 8 weeks of study.

By the way—I think those blouses with no tail flaps, which ends at the waist, are very attractive. Most of the guys from overseas seem to be wearing them, and I noticed in some of the pictures of Ted that he has one. Do you? I hope?

Sunday

I am just now finding time to finish this and get it ready for mailing. I'll explain in later letter. Meanwhile may you rest content in
Our Love,
Dotty

Memmingen, Germany
October 26, 1945 [47]

My Dearest Heart,

Today I was overjoyed to receive four letters from you and I had fully intended to spend my evening answering them. However, we had a meeting of the company until about eight; and then, rather than spending my evening in writing, I went to the show. I would not have gone had it been any show, but this was "GI Joe", and I could not afford to miss it.

As much as I love to write to you and as much as I love to talk with you each night, I am glad that I went to see the picture. I shall go back now and find your letter describing your reaction to the picture, but tonight I do not have time. It is very late. I must get to bed, but not until I have written a few thoughts concerning the movie, "GI Joe". Darling, I suppose that little money will be made on that picture. It has none of the flash and show which make for big box office returns. Nevertheless, to me, and to thousands like me, the picture is one of the truly great films. The scenes that I saw, the emotions written into the faces of the men, the stark realism which was in every foot of the movie —these things made it a picture which is a record of war.

I wondered why I could not write more realistically of the experiences of combat, but those things cannot be recorded even by such a writer as Ernie Pyle. He indicated them and did a grand job of that, but his was only an indication. To my mind tonight came vivid memories of long marches through driving rain, through deep mud; of fox hole homes half filled with water; of dugouts—if one was lucky— where men piled almost on top of one another to get out of the rain and get a couple of hours of sleep. I recalled moments when death rained from the sky, when around me men were dead and dying. I recalled the tenseness of the advance when any moment bullets may come from some hidden spot. I recalled the crack of a German "Burp" gun as the bullets passed close above my head, and the dirt was kicked up a few feet away from me. I thought of those breaks when one dropped in his tracks and slept for nine of the ten minutes because exhaustion was in every muscle. We still use the expression, "my poor aching back!", but the expression comes from an honest-to-goodness ache. I take off my hat to the producers of such a memorial to one cog in the wheel which one the war.

Goodnight, My Love, and I shall write much more come the morrow.　　　　　　　　I love you, Bushy

Sunday Nite
Oct. 28, 1945

My Darling,

This is the first chance I've had to write since Thursday nite! So I have much to tell you, and hope you'll forgive the lull in letters. I'll go chronologically and bring you up to date on "my days."

Friday morning dawned clear and beautiful, after a week of nasty weather. It was as if God answered my prayer for a nice day. I arose early, dressed, cleaned my room, and took the bus to Graystone Church to await Phil & Peggy. They were just an hour & a half late, and I promptly forgave them. The day was just perfect for a trip to the mountains, and we were off. The leaves seemed a little past their prime —but sufficiently beautiful to bring forth from us many oh's and ah's all day long. As I always say every time I see them, the Evaul kids get cuter and cuter. Phyllis took a fancy to me (for some strange reason) and followed me around most of the day, chattering constantly the while. You can understand at least half of what she says! She is so much fun to play with, to hold & love, etc. Darling, I wonder how soon it will be before we have one of our own? I shan't get off on that subject now, but it seems so senseless to spend some of the best years of my life, our lives, just waiting.

We got to the cabin about noon, and started getting lunch immediately. In this process (of eating) we stuffed ourselves silly. As soon thereafter as we could move we took a short trip upstream, and Phil took several color shots. The river was clearer than I have ever seen it—you could see the bottom all the way across the river, even at the swimming hole. Still later we hiked part way up the road to Addison's cabin. The views from that road never fail to inspire me, and always they are different.

We would up the afternoon playing horseshoes. Phil beat Peggy, then I took on the winner and I beat Phil! Didn't know I had it in me— even made a ringer, which is something I haven't done in years. Phil must have been off the beam, or something—I don't believe I can beat you, but that will not keep me from trying sometime!

Starting back came hard, as it invariably does, but we managed to get away by 4:30, and were in Maryville by 7:00. The leaves seemed much more colorful than in the morning—the afternoon sun seems to bring out more color—much more. What is the explanation for such a phenomenon?

Much to my surprise and extreme consternation I discovered that the bulletin, which should have been turned in to mimeographers Thursday was still in my purse. Oh, me. All I could see to do was to get a thing, cut the stencil myself and take it to them Sat. afternoon. They could then run it off in short order. (Out of ink.) [Dotty now writes in pencil.] Phil kindly saw to it that I got a stencil sheet, and Ann cut it for me.

Mary Ruth was not as surprised to see me as I thought she would be—Mother had written her that I was coming. She is in the throes of hard study, still no dates poor gal. I wish some of them boys would come to their senses and discover what a cute kid she is.

Chapel was set for 10:45, the first item on Founders-Homecoming program, so I was all set to write you a letter between breakfast & chapel. However, Beulah had not finished her interior dec. notebook due the day before, so I worked on that for her until the very last minute.

The Chapel service was long & drawn out, but good. Yes, and impressive, too. Dr. Lloyd got his mords wixed several times, but once it was extremely funny, and the audience just howled. Several times in one speech he spoke of something that took place "on the platform of this chapel"—he went to say it again and it came out so: "on the chapel of this platform." Contrary to his usual custom he made no attempt to rectify this misstatement, but just stood there and grinned. An honorary degree was given to Wiley Rutledge—once a student at Maryville, now a member of supreme court. He made a splendid speech, stating that justice must strive to remain unadulterated, and that it must become internationally standard to be truly effective. He warned that America must not turn isolationist as she did after last war & could easily do again. The alternative is apt to be pretty horrible. Enclosed is the program.

I had to rush off to catch my bus, and so had no time to see people or attend the barbecue. This disappointed me greatly, but was the price I had to pay for my forgetfulness about the bulletin. Once I got the stencil to them they mimeographed it in record time, so that was that and also a load off my mind.

This must be continued later. There is still news to tell you, but I can never finish telling about

      Our Love,
      Dotty

My Dearest Heart,

Tonight I hope that I can write without saying that "it is very late, and I have but a few moments to dash off a note to you". I am sure that your are tired of reading that same sentence so many times, and I am certainly tired of writing it. I hope that I can arrange my time in such a way that I can write you in a leaisurely manner.

The day has been a pleasant one for me. I arose at the unusual hour of ten this morning to find the sun shining brightly. After getting out a couple of reports which must be submitted daily, I went to church for the first time in three weeks. After lunch there were a couple of things that I had to type, but by two o'clock I was able to grab my camera and wend my way through the streets of the city. I walked for a couple of hours and saw part of the very nice residential district of the town. One stop that I made was in a very modern church which must have been built within the past twenty years. Some of the architecture over here is very modern, and shows sign of individuality. I stopped for a while to meditate, to get away from the world outside, to think. I shall practice this habit more often. Later I stopped in at the new DoughnutDugout which was opened last night. I find that the restaurant for coffee, doughnuts, cookies, etc, is very nice and includes ping-pong tables and a small library. I shall go there again.

Tonight I began the evening by writing Ranger (my Paris friend) a long overdue letter. I then began to sort out a few pictures and negatives which I had in half a dozen different places. I find that I have a number of Paris pictures which I have yet to send, and I also have a few which I have taken since I returned to Germany. These I shall begin to send in each letter.

No letters for two days, but the four which I received on Friday compensate for the delay. I am so glad that your are getting a chance to do a bit of singing among your thousand and one activities. I would give a lot to hear you sing again for I know that all of these months of singing in the choir have made your already beautiful voice more so. I love you, too, in case anyone should ask. Say, why can't you get DRE status? I suppose for the same reason that I can't get full company clerk status! I can truly sympathize with you for doing a job which calls for a higher rating.

Now and then I realize with a renewed sense of guilt the many things which we are missing as a couple. When you speak of buying the last piece in our china set, I realize that I hardly know how our china looks. I am terribly happy that your are going ahead and buying things for we can't buy everything at once. Gee, I wish I were there to help.

By the way, I just took a ten minute break to go down stairs and tell the CQ his duties for tomorrow morning. The dance next door was going full blast and I stepped inside to see it. There must be twenty-five or more girls with their dates, there is a small German band, and everyone seems to be having a grand time. We get the band about two nights each week, and it does provide a bit of entertainment for the men. So far it has been keep in a very orderly fashion, and I hope that it will continue to be so.

This afternoon I happened to be in the Orderly Room when one of the fellows called me. He said that he had someone that wanted to speak to me. I almost fell over when I found myself talking on the telephone with a N. Carolina girl. The boys too had been surprised and they put her up to calling someone and talking. I thought that it was a Red Cross girl—there are a few around town, but I found at dinner tonight that she came over in '39 just before the war broke out. She could not get back, and of course has been here sine that time. It sounded very strange to hear that NC drawl here in S. Bavaria. I can imagine that she has a real story to tell of her experiences.

I fear that you misunderstood my remarks concerning Cordy and Ted. Darling, I hope that we can be utterly alone for a couple of weeks, and I want nothing to interfere with the real honeymoon that we will enjoy. I hope that we can have an even more wonderful time than the one we had in the mountains near Santa Cruz. Cordy and Ted have no such mountain retreat to which to retreat, and I merely thought that it would be nice if they could spend a couple of days with us while we are at the cabin. I had no idea of a prolonged stay for them. Because of the difference in our point scores, Ted and I may not get out at the same time anyway.

Unless you have found a pen for Mother, why not go ahead and get the sweater which you spoke about getting? I think that I will be able to get a pen in the PX here, and when I do I will send it right along to her. In regard to other presents, I am sending a box of Parisian perfume to you for Mary Ruth. Perhaps you can fix it up in a fancy paper etc. So far I haven't been able to get a thing for Mom and Daddy. Perhaps I can find something before Christmas comes. I am not satisfied with anything I have found for my lovely wife, but I shall continue the search. As I have said before, my choice here is not wide. I must take what I can find.

Last night I broke away from work and went out for a visit with Chaplain Webb. He has a nice house in the residential district for his office. We talked and played an interesting game of chess during the evening. He gave me more pictures, and has a large group which I will be able to get next week. We should be able to work up quite an album of ETO shots by the time I get through sending photos home.

I heard an interesting story today which illustrates the way in which things are run over here. It seems that while we were in Gunzburg, a few Russians who were working for one of the units in the Regt. did not wish to return to Russia (there are many that I have found like this). At any rate, Col. Lundequest who was our Regt. CO at that time decided that he would solve their problem by declaring them "stateless". So he gave the order to the Adujant that he should declare these people stateless. Hq. Co. began making out these slips signed by an officer that this particular individual declared himself stateless. The impression was that about twenty people were involved. The first day about thirty papers were given out. About forty came the second day. By the time the third day dawned, DPs were coming from miles around on bicycles, wagons, on foot. Any means at hand in order to get one of these slips of paper. It was finally realized that a halt must be called but not before more than three hundred papers had been issued. Now it is very evident that the mere order of a Regt. CO, even though he be a full Colonel, cannot make a person stateless. To even attempt such a thing is to play with international dynamite. The point is that such things do occur here all too frequently, and it is no wonder that a confused situation remains confused.

As I see the GIs at the show, on the street, at the dance with their German girlfriends, I have not the slightest desire to associate with a fraulein myself; but it most certainly increases the intense longing which is constantly with me for my own petit chere. Darling, I love you with all of my heart. God grant that we may soon be reunited in the wonderous joy of

Our Love,
Bushy

Letter from Dotty to Art
Monday Morn
October 29, 1945

Darling,
To continue with my belated story of this weekend...Your mail is coming through swell now. There were three letters awaiting when I got home Saturday night, and one from Dorcas. I really don't know

what I would do without her to tell me the things you never get around to telling me. After all, I'm your wife. I should know these things, because I am prouder of you than anyone else. But perhaps I'd better explain before bawling you out—-maybe you did send it and it never got here or something. WHY DIDN'T YOU TELL ME YOU WROTE AN ARTICLE FOR STARS AND STRIPES? Also, WHY DIDN'T YOU SEND ME A COPY OF THAT ISSUE? Was it that thing you wrote about the visit to the Schloss? If so, you did send it to me (your ms.), and you did tell me that Chaplain "wanted" you to write it up for "the" paper, but you never said what paper nor that it definitely was in any paper. Perhaps you wanted to wait and surprise me with it, so you could <u>see</u> the buttons pop off my blouse. Please straighten me out on the matter, Darling. I'm confused. Or maybe Dorcas had it all wrong.

It is plumb mean of them to freeze the ratings just when you are in line for one. Fate shore has been agin you in Army life, in some things. Yea, in most things.

Yesterday afternoon I was all set to sit down and enjoy the symphony and write a flock of letters when the phone rang. It was Mrs. Peyton asking me if I would substitute for the Reverend at the evening service. She said he practically collapsed after the morning service, and seemed to be coming down with a terrific case of Flu. Were there any notes? No, nothing. I would be entirely on my own. Fortunately there was a topic, and one to my liking. The talk was to be on the life of Handel, and all the music on the program by Handel. In the space of two hours I had to pick out hymns and scripture and arrange the program to include all the music that had been planned, and work out a ten or more minute talk on the life of Handel from about three books plus my general knowledge. By the grace of God I did it, but without His help would never have made it. The Sunday evening crowd was quite slim, as usual, so I didn't get at all nervous- -it was just like talking to home folks almost. The Lord was indeed with me, and with all those who did so well on the musical end of the program. It included several hymns from the hymnal by Handel, "He Shall Feed His Flock" from the <u>Messiah</u>, and a violin and organ arrangement of "Largo". And also the prelude and postlude were from the <u>Messiah</u>.

Enclosed is an editorial and an item from a veteran's affairs column. It sounds from it as if you ASTP would count against your school time that you will be eligible for, but I hope your folks are right with their information to the contrary.

"When You're away, dear, how weary the
    lonesome hours!

Sunshine seems gray, dear, the frangrance
   has left the flowers—-
Ever I hear you in seeming whisp'ring
   soft love words to me!
Hold me again to your heart!
I love you alone!"
       Ever Thine Own,
         Dotty

Letter from Art to Dotty
Memmingen, Germany
October 30, 1945 [551-552]

Dearest Heart,

Tonight my spirit was lightened by the arrival of your letters of the 21st and 22nd. I was especially glad to get the picture of the "six leading figures". That broad smile did my heart good, and I wish that I could see it in person. Can't tell exactly what sort of hair do at the particular moment, but it brings back wonderful memories. Darling, the pangs of our separation are acute, very acute at times.

I do hope that you were able to make the trip to the mountains with Evaul as you planned. I still have not written Phil, but I hope he can understand how busy I am at the moment. The mountains are surely beautiful just now! I shall certainly write to Mother and Dad and urge that they join with you for Thanksgiving, and I do hope that they can come over. A trip away from Jamestown would be very good for both of them. I also received a long letter from Mother tonight, and she tells me that they will have a total of ten days off during the month of November, and perhaps they will be able to get away for Thanksgiving Season.

Mother also writes that we are getting a new minister in the Church at Jamestown, a young fellow recently discharged from the Chaplaincy. That does not guarantee that he will be a grand success, but a man with a real spark could do a lot for the church there.

Speaking of chaplains, I had to send a man in our company to Ch. Webb today. Last night the poor fellow received news of the death of both his father and mother. The news itself was bad enough, but the most horrible part was that his father had died in the early part of Sept. and his mother early in Oct. Only last night he received word of these losses. The fellow came into the 71st from another Div. and the news was returned to the States from there because they had no record of where he had gone. Such is another of the sad tales of warfare and its chaotic effects.

441

Well, My Love, yesterday I did something which I thought I would never do. I turned down a T/4 rating as flatly as though it had been an offer to join the Army for thirty years. As you know, Capt Garner promised to advance me as rapidly as possible after I remained with him when I&E called for me. A few days ago an opening came in the RSO section of the company which called for a T/4 rating. The good captain called me to his desk and told me that he would put me in this vacancy if I so desired. I asked for a little time to think it over, and then on the following day I gave a negative answer.

Two questions were involved in my refusal. The foremost reason was that the job had already been promised to a fellow that I have come to know rather well, although the promise was made by another officer. Capt Garner could have gone over the other man's head to give me the rating, but I do not care to get a rating by pushing another man out of the way. Another reason is that I would hardly want to take the rating for the work, hold the rating, and then leave for school. While I was away someone would have to do the work, and then could not get the rating which I would hold. So, I passed up my first opportunity to get out of the "private" class. Perhaps something else will come up—perhaps not. If not, I will have done the thing which I thought was only right to do. I still have to live with myself.

The thing which I feared is happening in China as the news comes that Communist forces are waging battle against the Government. I fear that the worst may come and a real revolution will be fought again. How horrible it would be if other nations were drawn into the fight as well they may be.

I think that we are taking the wrong attitude by withholding the secret of the atomic bomb, which, after all, cannot be kept. The mere attitude of saying that we hold it as a sacred trust indicates a feeling of superiority which we should not hold.

I was interested in an incident which occurred today in the office. We received a number of posters which were intended to increase the sense of responsibility of the individual soldier as an occupying force. Most of the remarks were good, but one was entirely un-American. Remember, the poster said, that you are to impress the German people with the superiority of our ways and "conduct". I sometimes wonder! An hour after we received these, we were instructed to return them. I suppose someone with a bit of common sense saw the implications of the poster.

I shall include a few more pictures of Paris which I believe I had not sent before. Any duplicates you might send to Mother and Dad for I have been sending them far too few of these pictures.

Goodnight, and sweetest dreams.

I love you,
Bushy

Letter from Art to Dotty
Memmingen, Germany
October 31, 1945 [553-555]

My Dearest Heart,

You say such nice things about my letters that I can't afford not to write very often. I do not mean to imply that I do not want to write as often as possible anyway, but all of the flattering remarks that you make are added incentives. Darling, I would do anything to make you happy, even to writing every day. (As perhaps you can see, I am using an American typewriter once again, and I am having the old difficulty with mz "z" and "y", I mean mz "y" and "Z". Oh me!) Your two letters of the 24th came tonight, and that means that I am answering letters which you wrote just one week ago tonight. Not bad, not bad at all. Wish all of our mail would travel as fast.

I am very glad that you speak frankly about school, My Love. I always want you to tell me exactly what you think about such things. It may well be that I will never have my chance to go to school in England, for most of the schools are closing as I have pointed out before. I know that I will get a good promotion if I remain here, and that would be some compensation for staying. However, I am still certainin my mind that two months in England would be invaluable to me, to us, later on as I settle down to my literature again. There are two reasons why I think that my chances of getting home would in no wise [way] be affected by going to school. In the first place, the paper yesterday carried the news that 70 pointers will be out of the ETO by Nov. 31. Yung passed up five or six shipments and thought that when he did go he would sail immediately. He is still waiting in one of the poorest camps in Europe, and the shipping date has been postponed again and again. The redeployment program is falling far behind the schedule, and the papers reveal very little of the true situation. The date that I might be leaving seems farther away every day. In the second place, if I did get to school, and shipping reached a point that I would be eligible for release, I would be able to leave school immediately.

The last thing that I want to do is to go against your wishes in anything, My Love. School in England is entirely secondary to our

443

reunion; but under the circumstances I think that I shall be forced to accept the opportunity if and when it comes. It would mean a very great deal to have Oxford or Cambridge behind me in addition to Maryville, Stanford, the Sorbonne, UT, Yale, Chicago, etc. More than the name alone, the experience of traveling and living in England for two months would be of immense value in making more alive for me the scenes and characters which will occupy my mind in the years ahead. Whether under the GI program or on our own, or both, I think that England is a "must" on our list before we are ready to settle down for a more or less permanent situation. (Think of all the pictures, too!)

I see more and more evidence here of the effect of the Nazi regime on the minds and characters of the German people. One evidence that is particularly apparent as one works among GIs is the effect of the loose morals which Hitler encouraged. France has long been known for her attitude toward sex, but from my observation I think that Germany has gone her one better. The women, and particularly the younger ones, seem to have no sense of moral question being involved in relation to sex. In Paris I was told that the women were out for all the money they could get; here they seem to be our [out] for all the sex they can get. Of course, there are probably decent ones, but the GIs don't see them. I have lost much respect for the morals of these people, and I have lost even more respect for the morals of my so-called "buddies". I am embittered but I am very much disgusted.

Pardon me, Darling, for ranting at such frequent intervals, but I have to express my views to someone. You are the only one I feel like to talking to, and after all you can't do very much about stopping me when I get started.

By the way, here is another one of the ideas I have had which I shall probably never carry out. I think that I might find a real story connected with this North Carolina girl who has been stuck over here since1939. I told you about her in my letter Sun. I would like to interview her and attempt to write up the article in such a way that Sat Evening Post, or some such magazine could use it. We shall see!

Wilhite is a regular fellow. I have been trying to get out a new roster of the company for almost a week now. Every day something came up to interfere with my work and I have not been able to get it typed out. This morning he sat down to the typewriter and before he was through he had finished a complete roster. Of course, by tomorrow three more men will have joined the Reg. Army, and our roster will be outdated. Nevertheless, we have to make them out again and again. Wilhite told me yesterday that I could have any pass that I wanted, but so far I have waited for some definite word concerning school. If that does come in the negative, I shall go ahead to take a pass to England or Switzerland.

It hardly seems possible that another month has rolled around, but that one month means one month less in the ETO. Today I received a letter from Carl. He says that he expects to get out sometime in Dec. Wish I could be at Maryville when his symphony is played. He says that he probably has more points than I, but actually both of us have 55.

I had expected to write three or four le ters tonight, but here it is half an hour passed bedtime, and I still have to write out some explanations of pictures. In case there was a question in your mind, I love you with all of my heart. May God continue to bless most abundantly

Our Love,
Bushy

Letter from Art to Dotty
Memmingen, Germany
Nov. 1, 1945 [556-557]

My Darling,

The band next door plays the strains of "Lili Marlene", and the walls sway with the crowd. The party is going full blast as it does about three or four nights a week now. The room next door is filled with girls, German, of course, and I am glad that there is at least a wall between the orderly room and the beer hall. A couple of us are sitting in the orderly room writing our respective wives, and wishing that we too could enjoy the caress of a women—not any women, but our own loved ones. I miss you, My Love!

Today Service Co. followed the order which came down a couple of weeks ago and took a half day off. That is we were authorized a half day off, but as usual my time was hardly my own. I had to sell PX rations for an hour after lunch, and then I had to find an empty bed for a guy returning from England. Capt. Garner was in Augsburg, and Sgt. Wilhite was sick in bed. I did get a chance to sleep for about an hour and a half before someone called up to inquire about some papers. I had to get up and so that was my half day off.

Wilhite is under the weather from shots which we took a couple of nights ago, and all of us are under a bit from the after effects. We sat around the table after supper discussing politics for awhile, and then he suggested that we go to the show. It was a musical variety with Jack Oakie, but it was at least relaxing. I enjoyed the change.

No mail today, but I did received the most recent "Hearth Log", along with my "Time". Read every word in the former and enjoyed it very much. I think that I will really feel very much at home when I return to the Fourth Church.

Going back for a minute to the business of a half a dy holiday each week, it will provide a nice break in the middle of the week. Of course, I suppose that it will be seldom that we in the orderly room can take advantage of the break, but if we can we most certainly will.

I find that in old "K" Co. one Staff-Sgt. is in charge of the PX and nothing else. They also have one man who handles nothing but the mail, and another fellow handles the company paper work. Even he has an assistant. That means that Devers and I are doing work that four do in other units. Well, we enjoy it, I guess. I am not complaining, exactly, Darlin; would be nice to be something more than a Pfc. for a change.

By the way, I received a note in my Time tonight that I can get a subscription to Fortune for $6.00 per year for a gift to someone. It is a very fine magazine, and I thought that I would send a subscription to Mom and Daddy as being inaddition to any that you are planning to get for them. I also have a nice bottle of Paris perfume for Mary Ruth which I am sending in a box to you. I have found a nice Schaeffer pencil which I shall send Dad, and I think I mentioned that I had already sent a box of Swiss handkerchiefs to Mother. Even though some of the things are late, I do hope that I can get everything home that I want to send before too very long.

Nothing new in regard to ratings, but so far everything is closed up tight. I could not have been made a T/4 had I taken the RSO job which Capt. Garner offered. Perhaps I was destined to remain a Pfc. all of my army life; but as mother so aptly put it, "it is extremely difficult to tell the difference between a Sgt. and a Pfc. in civilian clothing."

Gotta go up stairs and write a few more explanations on pictures. I hope you do not tire of the pictures I send; and I pray that you may never tire of hearing me say
I love you,
Bushy

Letter from Art to Dotty
Memmingen,
Nov. 2, 1945 [558]

Morning, Glory,
I have about ten or fifteen minutes before breakfast in which to tell you how beautiful you are this morning, so here goes. You are— beautiful, I mean. Even if your eyes are still closed in sleep, your hair

more or less uncombed. I always did like that hidden smile which plays around the corner of your mouth just as it did the very first morning I awoke to gaze into your closed eyelids and hold your hand. That was up at the cabin, remember? From an hour before dawn, I watched you, and then you awoke to gaze back and whisper of our Love. That was a wonderful morning for me, and yet every morning was wonderful when I awoke to find you near. Well, good morning, My Dear!

I have been wondering in recent weeks if it would be practical for us to meet somewhere when I get home. That is, would it be better for us to meet perhaps in Chattanooga or Bristol, or some other town close by. We will naturally want to be alone for a little while together, and the problem will be greatly increased if were were at home. After all, it will be a very wonderful honeymoon, Darling. We could meet in some nearby town, spend three or four days catching up on all that we have missed so much, and then come home together. What do you think of the idea?

Well, my time is almost up, and I must collect the mail, eat breakfast, and begin the routine duties of the day. I shall write again tonight and every night, and every night I shall say

I love you,
Bushy

Letter from Art to Dotty
November 4, 1945
Memmingen, Germany
November 3, 1945 [559-560]

Darling,

Last night I went to bed with a guilty conscience. I went to bed without writing you, which in itself is unusual. Yesterday afternoon I had a call from Ch. Webb inviting me up for the evening, and so after shaving and cleaning up I walked up to his place. We had our usual game of chess and followed it by a couple of games of checkers. Chaplain had suggested once before that I should teach him a bit about checkers, and he would teach me a bit about chess. I have never been able to beat him in chess, and he ended up last night by beating me two out of three in checkers.

Yesterday I managed to get another filter for my camera. About a week a go I was able to buy a yellow filter in one of the photo shops here in Memmingen, and yesterday I bought a red one. I also have been able to get a good light meter, and so my photographic equipment is almost complete. The prices here are almost nothing, and so my expenses about to little. If I can only get home with all of these items, I should have equipment which would last us a long time.

We have more big rumors via the <u>Red Circle news</u>, the Div. paper. It seems that our category is soon to be changed either for permanent occupation or for redeployment. If the former occurs, I will come home on points are length of service—eventually. If the latter, I shall come home with the division in all likelihood. All ratings are frozen tighter than ever until our status is clarified, and I received some discouraging news from I & E yesterday. I called from friend, Fairbanks, and he told me that there was little possibility of getting a shot at TWCA in England now. If not, I intend to take a pass to Eng. on the 24th unless something unforeseen occurs.

By the way, I forgot to say that this is another before-breakfast letter. The CQ has just returned and I must go down to breakfast, but not before I say

I love you
Bushy

Letter from Art to Dotty
Memmingen, Germany
November 3, 1945 [561-562]
Saturday night

Darling,

This is my second letter today—the first having been writing before breakfast while I waited for the CQ to return to relieve me. I like very much the habit of beginning and ending the day with a letter to you. It is the nearest I can come to the far nicer of habit of being with you at the beginning and ending of day, to talk with you, laugh with you, and merely be with you. Is it needless repetition to say, Darling, I love you?

Very little happened today that was unusual except I was able to get a bit of time off. That in itself was not only news but was also a welcomed change. We had an orientation period this afternoon which lasted for a couple of hours—I spent the time sleeping, although I had intended to attend. I came up after lunch to rest for a few minutes, and I wok e up two hours later. Did a little work after I got up, but after supper I slipped off to the Doughnutdugout for a bit of reading and a few games of pingpong. Came back about eight to take a nice hot bath, a shave, clean up a few odds and ends, and write.

Received a nice long letter from Pratt today. As I mentioned before, he is in Shrivenham, England, in school. Having a wonderful time, he says, but finds the classes a bit erudite. Did I tell you that Donald (Hoppy) Hopkins is married? Think you told me that Parvin and Dorothy Lehman have broken their engagement. Pratt seems to be settling down on one girl, and I suppose he will end up the way of all flesh. No, I didn'tsay "sucker".

I do not know how much you have seen in the paper concerning the change in policy over here in regard to money orders, but a drastic system will be introduced on Nov. 10th. As of that date we will declare the amount of money which we have on hand, and this will be entered in an individual account book. All payments made to the soldier will be entered in this book, and any money sent home will also be entered. If at any time money is converted from one type to another, i.e. marks to francs or pounds, then this conversion will also be entered. No one will be allowed to send home more money than he has legally gained from official sources. Of course, the idea is to curb the very active black market (marche noir), which is flourishing all over Europe. Although I think that many GIs will find ways to evade the system, I do believe that to a large extent the system will work. Ifa fellow cannot send the money home, there is little point in selling large quantities of cigarettes etc. Of course, it will be hard on the poker players who send three or four hundred dollars home after each pay day.

I brought a little money from Paris, and I have received two payments since then. The only reason that I have not sent home money ere now was that I thought I might get away to England and miss a payroll. As soon as I found out a little more definitely what I can expect in the next few days and weeks, I shall send you a couple of money orders.

I think that I failed to tell you a good rumor that has been passed among the German civilians lately. The story is that the United States is trying to ship home the GIs as fast as possible in order that the birth rate in German will not increase so sharply! All that I want to do is to help increase the rate in the USA by about three or four during the next eight years, n'est pas? Mais oui!

I am hoping that the Chaplain will invite me to go along with him for the afternoon service for the third Bn. tomorrow. They are located down rather near the Alps, and scenery is reported to be very beautiful. He is going all the way to Garmish next week, and I am keeping my fingers crossed that I will be able to get away and go along. It would be a full day's trip and would be through some of the most beautiful of the Bavarian Alpine regions. It would in a small way make up for the Switzerland trip which I missed. As I mentioned last night, I intend to go to Eng. during the latter part of Nov. unless I get away to school, or unless the quota of one which we have is cancelled. Wish I could get to

Eng. in time to see Pratt. I understand that the time for a furlough inEng. has been increased to ten days. With only seven the trip takes at least three weeks. Our quota for one is for Nov. 24, and if I get to go I shall try very hard to be in England for Christmas. Although nothing to compare with Christmas with you, My Love, Christmas in Eng. would be far merrier than Christmas in the Bavarian Alps.

I shall enclose three pictures which I was able to get from Ch. Webb last week. Two are of a historic event in the annals of the 14th. I must spend a few nights in giving a hasty sketch of my combat experiences. I began these back in Austria, and somehow I was never able to get started on them again. But I promise that I will continue them in some detail.

Tis late and I should sleep. I long so much for you, to hold you close and whisper

> I love you,
> Bushy

Letter from Art to Dotty
Memmingen, Germany
November 7, 1945 [564-565]

My Dearest Heart,

After almost ten months over here I have at last found someone with whom I can speak Dutch! This afternoon I was in the PX when a strange face appeared and asked for rations. I did not know him, and so I asked for his name. Although he spoke very good English, I found that he was a Hollander, and that he is working for us. I spoke a few joyful words of Dutch and happily sold him his rations. I told him that I would like to speak more with him, and he told me that he would be in the recreation room next door to the office tonight.

After selling rations tonight and cleaning up, I came down to the room. The first person I bumped into was my little Dutch friend with one of the nicest looking girls that I have yet seen around. No, Darling, I do not go around making note of the good looking girls. However, I learned to appreciate real beauty when I first me [met] you! I find that his girl friend is Dutch, or I suppose that is is his wife. Anyway, she came here two weeks ago to be with him. The fellow has been with the American Army for more than a year now, having worked with the 103rd Div. through combat as an interpreter and driver. When the 103rd left for the States, he almost succeeded in going with them for he could easily pass for a GI. He failed however, and then returned to Holland for a furlough. His "mooi mesije" followed him down here, and both hope to come to the United States as soon as it is possible to do so.

I sat with them for two and a half hours and talked Dutch as hard as ever I knew how. We had a grand time and I enjoyed every minute of the evening. I talked so long however, that I am having to finish up this letter on Wed. morning. They complimented my Dutch, and the fellow said that he had found only two fellows before who spoke the language. These had learned the tongue at home from their parents. I hope to see more of these two and to talk more with them.

There has been little that is new during the past few days. I have had a bit of kidney trouble, but nothing that amounts to anything. On Thursday we are losing the sixty-five pointers who were alerted to ship back in Gunzburg almost six weeks ago. I think that we will lose all of the men with sixty points and above during the month of November. If so, that will take Wilhite for he has sixty-two points. We will also lose three other men in Service Co.—all of whom are heads of various sections of work.

The weather here is just beginning to give us a foretaste of what winter will be. For the most part we have had low clouds with some mist falling and increasing cold for the past week. I am ever and again thankful that I am working inside during these days that are to come.

The CQ just returned andI must dash to breakfast. More tonight

    I love you,

      Bushy

Letter excerpts from Art to Tom
Memmingen, German
November 8, 1945

...One of my regrets at the moment is that I have found very little time for writing or for reading during the past few months. I write Dotty almost every night, Mother and Dad every three or four. However, I have hardly found time to read my Time with close attention. It is thus that I have not been able to keep in close touch with events of world-shaking importance. From my observation here I would like to comment briefly.

In the first place, I think that the Army has failed miserably in its meager attempts to train the GI for occupation duty. I seriously believe that 95% of the men and officers would go home tomorrow if they could with no thought for their responsibility as an Army of Occupation. We are not told why we are occupying, how we should act, why the job is necessary. In the second place, I think that the personnel in military government is not the type that can best carry on the work for which their office is set up. I understand that the entire organization is to be put on a civilian status, and I think that perhaps that will improve the situation. I certainly hope so. Going on to a third point, I think that our foreign policy represents the same type of wishy-washy reaction as I have already noted; and of course that in itself is the reason for these other things being as they are. I feel a growing discontent with our new President because he seems hardly capable of fulfilling his responsibilities to the what is perhaps the most important post of power and influence that the world has ever known. I realize full well that my view point may be incorrect since I have access to little news other than that which is carried in the Stars and Stripes and my Time. We as a people have not matured to the point that we are able to shoulder the full burden of our position. History will record the tragedy of this single fact.

The Dutch are having their hands full in Java, and perhaps it is as well that I was never sent to that area. As I had feared for a long time, China is still undergoing the birth pangs of the modern age. I fear that much more bloodshed will come before her internal questions are settled. It will be a strong test for the United Nations to settle this dispute, and I shall watch the drama unfold with much interest. Glad to see the results of the election in France for certainly DeGaulle is the only one who can put his beloved country on her feet again. Unless we improve our policy I fear that Germany will have a long rode to travel before she is able to set up a progressive and recuperative government.

... You are always more than welcomed at the Barber-(Bushing) home in Knoxville, and naturally in Jamestown, I hope that you can see both Dotty and the folks before you head for the Pacific. Wish I could make it also, but that is out of the question now.

As always, my heartiest good wishes are with you. God bless you.

As ever,

Bushy

Letter from Art to Dotty
Memmingen, Germany
November 10, 1945 [571-572]

My Dearest Heart,

Day of days! Today for the first time in six we had first class mail come into the company. Yesterday we received two truck loads of packages for the regiment, but no letters. Today came four big bags of first class. The boys in the post office are "snowed under", to use the current GI slang. There is much to be sorted yet, and I am sure that I will have more letters to read tomorrow. However, tonight I did rather well when three of your letters came. Two were postmarked the 29th and one was from the 30th. Gee it was good to have long letters to read again!

In one of the letters you described the week-end at Maryville and in the mountains. I always like to read your descriptions of the mountain trips because I always feel that I am there with you in spirit at least. Every time that I see the leaves of autumn browning and falling over here, I think of the leaves in the Smokies and the splendor of their color during the past weeks. I knew that winter was really here last night when a cold rain turned into snow. There was little evidence except in some of the eves this morning, but pure white snow was there. About four o'clock this afternoon a real snow fall began, and tonight it continues unabated...

The snow brings back vivid memories of the last snow which I saw over here. I do not remember how much I was able to write about it at the time, but about May 1st, we made a river crossing south of Regensburg. Late in the afternoon there was a very heavy rain, and shortly after we crossed the river we had to dig in on the reverse slope of a hill. About seven or eight o'clock in the evening snow began to mix with the rain. We had no shelter save a heavy woods which was just to the rear of our positions. I pulled the BAR team back from the hill and into the woods. There was not much protection, but the heavy foliage did serve to hold back the driving wind and rain. Company headquarters was of course located back in a building, but we had no such comfort. Sometime during the night our platoon leader did find a dugout nearby which offered space for about a dozen men to find room. During the two hour intervals which we had off from guard, we piled on top of one another in order to rest a bit. All of this was against orders and especially the fact that we had a small fire in the opening of the dugout. Pardon me from reminiscing, Darling, but there are certain memories which are very vivid.

I wish very much that I could have joined you at Maryville for the Founders Day program. I can imagine that it must have been a gala occasion. And dear little Phyllis! By the time I see her again, she will be flirting with my uniform, I suppose. I think I shall always remember her as she was when I first met her, age six months. But really, My Love, we are not missing the best years of our lives. Those years will always be ahead of us for each year will always be more wonderful, than the one which it follows. I know what you have in mind, but remember that Mother was thirty-two when I was born. We have plenty of time left for our children. There are many men and women who have been separated far longer than we who are far older than we. Think what it would have meant had I been in my thirties.

I shall try to send you a picture showing off my "Ike" jacket, as we call our combat jackets. I too like them far better than the old blouse with tails. A short time ago I ordered a leather jacket on the same order as the Ike model, but I fear that I will never be able to pick it up. The factory was near Augsburg, and I can only rely on Ch. Webb to be passing by there sometime.

Yes, the 71st is again making a record with its driving power. This time in the field of football. On Sunday we play the 1st Div. for the 3rd Army title, and the winner will play the championship team from the 7th. I have been unable to see any of the games because of the long distance to go, but I would like to see them before the season ends.

Nothing new on our status, but we did ship out the 65ers today. There is a strong rumor that men down to sixty will be leaving within the next few weeks. I certainly hope that this will be true, because, well, just because! There is only one phase of the homeward trip to which I do not look forward. I know that when we leave here, I will probably go to at least one other outfit, perhaps several. Some men have been in as many as six outfits within a period of six weeks. I do not care for that sort of moving about. Even when I move from here I may get stuck somewhere and stay for weeks. All of that comes in the confusion of the redeployment problem. (See I cannot even talk about it without getting my letters confused.) Today's paper carries the story that all men with fifty points will be discharged, that is, of those who are in the States. Glad that Carl will be able to get out now. Perhaps he will be home for Thanksgiving. Lucky man! I must admit that I am slightly envious.

We had a big party in the company tonight, but I only went for a few minutes. I enjoyed watching the others have a good time. The little Dutch girl quickly took the eye of almost every GI in the house, and many of the fellows avowed that they intend to visit Holland.

Saturday Morning

Joy of Joys! While the party was going on, Devers went over to the postoffice and by himself sorted two and a halfbags of letters. He did not return until after eleven, and to my happy surprise I had three more letters from you. That makes six in all from you in one single day —a record I think since I had eigthteen in three days. The letters were from 29th, 30th, and 31st. I just spent the last few minutes giving out most of the mail to the sections, and I hardly have time to do more than promise another long letter tonight, and to say from the very depth of my heart

I love you,
Bushy

Letter from Art to Dotty
Memminget, Germany
November 12, 1945 [573-575]

My Dearest,

I did something yesterday that I should never do: I wrote a couple of letters which were long over due at the expense of writing you. I had planned to spend the afternoon in writing notes which were long overdue, and then spend the evening writing you and the folks. Well, as it happened, I caught up a bit on my correspondence, but the evening was too short for me to write the important letters. Last week, Bill Myers called me up and asked me if I cared to attend a concert on Sunday night. You, of course, know the answer.

I met Bill at his quarters and we made our way to the city theater. The crowd was just gathering and I think that we were the only GIs attending. The hall was not large, but every seat was taken. The stage was plainly set with panelled drops and a few potted plants for decoration. I had no idea what the program, but found that it was a group of folk songs sung by an accomplished ministrel singer. Myers thought of Burl Ives, and I suppose that he would be a good comparision. My Dutch-founded German was not without use, and I was able to follow a number of the songs. It seems a bit strange that, although I have never studied German, I feel more at home when hearing it than I do French. The evening was enjoyable and I hope to go again to hear a Mozart program tomorrow night.

About eleven fifteen on Saturday night, Devers came in fromthe Post Office. He had spent the entire evening sorting mail, and he made me the happier with three big letters from you. These were of the 30th, 31st, and 1st, and so I am catching up again. Before I go further, I must clarify a bit of confusion concerning a certain article. Dorcas was slightly mistaken, Darling, for I have never written an article for the S&S. As you know, I took some notes at the time Ch. Webb and I visited the Schloss near Gunzburg. For my own amusement, I wrote up these notes and sent you a copy of the result. The Chaplain asked for a copy, and Scotty copied the article prior to my trip to Paris. The Chaplain had said something about my re-writing the script for the Regimental Newspaper, but I did not have time before I left. Now, it must have been that the paper was desperate for filler. At any rate, it seems that they obtained a copy of the article; and, without my knowledge or consent, cut the thing to ribbons. They reproduced a few of the pictures which we took, and recounted a bit of the story. Actually I could only recognize a sentence now and then, and I was completely disgusted with the result. Someone sent it to me in Paris, and I never thought to send it on to you. I am sure that you would have been greatly disappointed in it. That is the entire story, and I must assure Dorcas that there is a great difference between the Reg.t Paper and the S&S.

'Tis later now and I have had a chance to get a few more pictures from the Chaplain—67 in all. Some of this group includes pictures which we took at the Schloss. I shall send this on to you as fast as I can, but 67 pictures will take a long time at the rate of four or five pictures per letter.

I wish that I could have been around to hear that Sunday Evening Program, My Love. I can imagine that it was very much worth while, and I would certainly have enjoyed it a great deal. I am really proud that you are taking such an active part in the work, and I really wish that I were there to do something also. I look forward to the future years when perhaps I can get back into Boy Scout work again. The letter describing the Halloween Party was interesting, and I enjoyed reading about the group.

In recent days I have noticed that things are being done to release more doctors all the time, and fromthe story which you relate I can see the need for it. Surely some of the investigations that are going on will reveal at least some of the bottlenecks that are holding up redeployment. I can never be sure when to expect a sudden change, but the trend at present seems encouraging. Yes, Darling, I think that I can definitely count onbeing on my way to the States by the time February rolls around.

By the way, wonder of wonders! Your Christmas package arrived today, and it took all of my resistance to leave it closed. I could see nothing on the outside which said not to open until Christmas. Perhaps I may as well open. Well, now you did say something about refraining from......but how do I know that this is the one.....I may be on the move ere Christmas comes....but how nice it will be even if I am on the move to have a Christmas package to open. Guess I had better leave it closed.

I sent a box to Mom first class, so it too should travel in a hurry. I sent it to her in order that she could wrap certain items for certain people, etc. Let her open it while you're away. I shall write these instructions to her also, but I tell you too. There is a box of perfume for Mary Ruth which you can wrap for me, si'l vous plait. With the exceptions of certain item Mom may as well give you the rest of the junk. The bit of red cloth came from a very large Nazi flag which we captured in Bayreuth. I was short of handkerchiefs and used this piece as such for a long time. It needs washing up, but I would like to keep it as a souvenir. The spoon was the only eating utensil that I had through combat save my pocket knife. I carried it wrapped in paper in my shirt pocket. (Most of the fellows stuck their spoon in the top of the boot after each meal.) The little hat was from the prison camp at Dachau. These hats were special for the Moslem SS Troops who were supposed to be the most ferocious of them all. The field glasses are those which Beul gave to me on the day we fought for the last time. It was on this day that the first rumors of surrender came. I used them at the opera in Paris a great deal, and I think that we will find use for them in the Smokies and elsewhere. I do hope that everything arrives without being broken up. How is my gal, Venus, getting along? I do hope that her head is much better now. If you cannot get her fixed let me know so that I can attempt to get another.

I shall send in this letter a money order which I have been holding for some time.. Perhaps you will want to use it for Christmas, or perhaps for the bank account. I have been holding my money for some time, hoping that a pass would soon come. However, it seems that I may lose out on the pass deal. Wilhite may leave sooner than we had expected and that will leave us with more work involved in getting organized again.

As usual I could talk far into the night, but tomorrow is another day and there will be much to do. Today was a legal holiday, but it made little difference. I did take most of the afternoon off, but there are always odd bits to attend to.

Separation is one of the hardest things that I have to bear, but the reunion of Our Love will be a glorious experience. My heart is filled with the wonder of our love for each other. May God continue to bless it as he has in the past.

I love you,
Bushy

Letter from Art to Dotty
Memmingen, Germany
November 13, 1945 [576-577]

My Dearest Heart,

As I read the paper from day to day, I feel with a growing certainty that much remains to be settled inAsia before peace is really secure.

There is no question but that a more liberal system of government must be set up by the colonial powers, and never again will empires exercise the same control which they have wielded in the past. India, Indo-China, the East Indies,—all of these offer their individual problems, and yet basically the problem is the same. All seek the fundamental right of a free and independent government. I believe that the colonial powers see the futility of their former policies, but the question of "when" these peoples are to be granted independence is the real issue. The problem in China is somewhat different, for there it is a clash of ideologies. Cooperation was never complete even when both sides fought a common enemy. How can they cooperate when the enemy is defeated and each side is trying to establish its own form of thought and government?

I have spoken before of the problem which the atomic bomb presents to us, and yet how can there be a problem for us to decide? We can only sow distrust if we insist on withholding the so-called secret. Why should we consider ourselves worthy of keeping a "divine trust"? Only as we put our faith and our efforts into the working possibility of the world government, which does exist in little more than name, can we lead the world into a era when world peace is not only possible but probable.

I wish that I were not so far removed from the events which are taking place with each new day. I so much miss variety in my newspaper and magazine reading.

Christmas packages are coming through in record time at the expense of our first class mail. I suppose that it is good for morale to get all of the packages which are coming but the lack of letters certainly helps little. I finally managed to get a letter off to Miss Burkhart, but I am sure that she has long since left Paris. She expected to head for home in November. Still must write Beul and Carl.

I shall enclose herein the rest of the pictures of the Schloss Reisenburg. I sent the first of these last night, and these are a part of the group of 67 which I bought from Chaplain Webb. Today I got a couple of swell enlargements of Venus and Notre Dame and these I will have to wrap carefully and send later.

I have time to say from the depths of my heart,
I love you,
Bushy

Nov. 14
Fore breakfast

In regard to the pictures of the Schloss which I included in these
last two letters, I put nothing on the back because I thought that the
notes which I took and sent to you describe the pictures in some detail.
In one of the shots of the river, a bridge can be made out on the
Autobahn. This bridge was blown up by the Germans, and I have other
pictures of it at closer range.

I think I forgot to say that I am still a Pfc, My Love. The Captain
sent in a list for promotions last week, and my name was on it.
However, since the regiment is over in strength in the number of
corporals, no corporals could be made. I am still a Pfc. And so it goes!

Yesterday I cleared the red tape for my furlough to England, but I
have little hope of being able to make the trip. Although I would far
prefer to go to school than to get stripes, I would prefer the stripes right
not to the furlough. And so, if I find that I would lose my chance for
stripes by going to England I shall probably stay here. At any rate,
Wilhite will be leaving soon, and I am not sure that the Captain would
let me get a way. The date of leaving is for the 23rd of Nov, in case I do
get away, but I have little hope.

I wish that I could tell you inadequate words just how much I miss
you, My Darling. There is so much I would like to tell, so much time I
would like to spend with you, so many things for us to do together. My
whole present is reduced to existence by your absence; my future is
taken to new heights by the happy prospect of a life time of happiness
in
Our Love,
Bushy
In yesterday's letter I sent a money order for $35

Letter from Art to Dotty
Memmingen, Germany
November 14, 1945 [578-579]
My Dearest Heart,

How can you every forgive me, My Love? Before doing anything
else I must sit down and confess that which I have so recently done. For
months long I have ranted frequently in my letters concerning the
actions of the GIs with who I work, and yet I have at last broken down
and committed a crime myself. I wonder if you can ever forgive me!

Before you seek divorce measures, let me continue with my story. I spent a little time tonight talking Dutch with Rina and Leo, the Dutch couple, and I found that they were planning to go to the late show (8:30-10:30). They invited me to go along, and so I accepted their invitation. I had planned to stay home, write a couple of letters, shave, bathe, and read. Well, I decided to go along and spend the time at the show. Leo understands the moview without difficulty, but he does not like to take time to explain everything to Reni who does not follow so well. I enjoy attempting to keep her posted on the trend of events, and it is good for my morale to be in the company of a nice girl—as long as we are properly chaperoned! Well, perhaps you can forgive me, and I will assure you that the incident may be repeated but always under the proper conditions—namely her husband accompanying.

Although I heard from Beul some time ago, I have not answered him as yet. I just happened to read his letter over tonight and I find that he is in Munich. Perhaps I will be able to visit him sometime, and I certainly must write. I have been looking over my pictures, and I think that I will get an enlargement made of his picture which I sent you and send it to Dorcas. I think that she might like to have it. May just send it with other to you, and let you send it on to her for Christmas.

Well, I didn't get to shave, bathe, or read tonight, but at least I did get to write my lovely wife. I love you, Darling, in case you wonder. I love you with all of my heart. I have had no affirmation of the fact by letter from you in almost six days, but my heart tells me. No first class mail is coming through, but sometime I hope that it will catch up. I haven't heard from Mother and Dad in almost two weeks.

One bit of good news is that we are bringing another man into the office. He will eventually take over the PX from me, and also the mail. Devers has been handling most of the readdressing of late, and this will relieve him of the Christmas rush so that he can work more with the reports etc. All of which means that perhaps I will have a bit more time in which to write, and read, and think—primarily of you.

Luv ya,
Bushy

Thursday Morning

Chaplain Webb and his two assistants are leaving today for Switzerland together. They managed to get furloughs together, and I am certainly happy that they could do so. As I mentioned before, my furlough to England has been approved but I am not sure that I will be able to take it. If I do, I will leave on the 23rd of the month, which is on

Friday next. It will take more than three weeks for the complete trip, and I stop in Paris both ways I think. I intend to write Pratt that I may be coming, and also Ranger. Would be nice to spend a little time with Pratt. I will receive no mail while I am away, but I shall attempt to write as often as possible.

I do not think that I have mentioned an interesting habit which the Germans seem to have over here. Last spring on our way through, I sometimes crawled beneath the feather mattress on the bed for greater warmth. Almost every house had these feather mattresses on top of the sheets. I thought that the Germans usually slept on top of them as we sometimes do. However, every morning when the maid makes up my bed she places the one sheet which I have beneath the mattress. I finally gave up change the two each night, and so I conform to the custom and sleep beneath the feathers. Of course, it is far warmer that manner!

I trust that I will be able to take half a day off as I am supposed to have on Thursdays, although I will have to sell rations part of the time. The weather is much colder now, and some of the snow from last week remains in shaded spots. Winter will not be pleasant here as I have mentioned before. Wilhite's thoughts are so much of home that he thinks little of any thing else, however, I could not blame him if I were so close to seeing the one I love more than anything else in the world.

Again the CQ has returned and I must eat breakfast, sort the mail, and begin the work of the day,

I love you,
Bushy

Letter from Art to Dotty
Memmingen, Germany
November 15, 1945 [580-581]

Darling,

This morning we had this office looking like the personnel section of the regiment. We had three typewriters in the room and all of them we going hard. The new man which we have working here is a good worker, and I think that he will fit into the routine rather well. He has worked two days with me in PX now, and I will be happy to turn it over to him next week. As I mentioned before, he will take over the mail and relieve Devers. We will be able to use him as a messenger for our running around, and thus both of us (Devers and I) can spend our full time here. It will make everything far easier for all.

We have a big rest camp which was organized last week. I tis [It is] about sixty miles away and is in the heart of the resort section.

Supposedly the facilities are second only to those found at Garmisch. Just in case that I am unable to go to England next week I shall try to take a vacation down there for a few days before Wilhite leaves. He is talking of going down there next week and leaving me to act in his position.

Rumors are picking up again, and one of the worst ones that I have heard so far is that the 97th Div is being deactivated; that the men will come to the 71st. That would probably mean that all stripes would again be frozen. If I do not get something before this happens, if it does, I may as well forget about any thing more than what I have. Ah me!

I hardly know what to do about this furlough to England. If I thought that it would mean a loss of the stripes which may come my way, I would delay it. I hope to get an assurance from Capt. Garner that he will put me in for the promotion if the opportunity comes while I am away. That will help some. I believe that if I do go, the trip will take up almost a month. By that time I will surely know something definite concerning my point status in relation to shipping home. Ted should be back in the next few days and he can give me a few pointers concerning the trip. It will be very cold for travel, but well worth the discomfort I think.

The repertoire of the German band which we have in the beer hall next door three or four nights per week is rather broad, and especially since almost without exception the songs are American. From my observation I have noted that Europe in general is very familiar with the songs and popular music of America.

In my group of pictures for tonight, I shall include a group which I have taken here in Memmingen of the houses disemboweled by war. I think that I had some in the first group of pictures which I bought from Chaplain Webb. There is little need for taking more of this type of thing, for all are so terribly alike in the horror of what they represent. How can we be so terribly ignorant of the horrors of such a tragedy? And yet I see far to few of the signs which would indicate that we will be able to prevent further war. I hope that I am unduly pessimistic!

More tomorrow morning, but for tonight I must to sleep. Ik ben zo moo ik wiet niet wat te doen! Darling, you are ever in my dreams, in my waking thoughts. I am ever alone when you are away, and the only completeness that I can know is the completeness of
Our Love,
Bushy

November 16
Friday morning

Mawning, Glory!

At least inmy dreams last night I came home to you! My dream was most vivid as we met and I held you close in my arms. There was another portion of my dream in which we were visiting in the Church at Jamestown. I felt a new pride in my uniform which many of us often forget over here. In even another portion of the dream, I recall that someone made a remark concerning the fact that I must have been inside during my entire time overseas. I was also proud to be able to inform them that I had been a foot-slogger in the infantry. I dream often but seldom in such a vivid way as I did last night. You were even more beautiful than before (don't try to tell me that dreams are not realistic!), and it was truly a joyful meeting. Surely the day is not so far away for us, My Love.

At present we have plenty of coal and wood, and with a number of stoves we are keeping warm. However, we have only 25 watt bulbs in many of our lights, and that is no good. Hope to get some bulbs in soon.

I must go and eat now.

I love you,
Bushy

Letter from Art to Dotty
Memmingen, Germany
November 17, 1945 [582-583]

My Dearest Heart,

Another week has flown past, and how happy I am that they do go by so swiftly. Tonight is Saturday and I am relieving the CQ at a late hour in order that he may take his girl friend home. She came earlier in the evening and so they celebrated their part of the party in the orderly room. Again we had our party tonight. Again I went over late and returned early. Everyone was enjoying themselves and so I suppose that the party was a success.

I do not care for the sort of thing which we have, but I do realize that it is very good to have these parties. These men must have some sort of relaxation and enjoyment, and a well conducted party is better than leaving them to their own de-vices. Last week an order came out which prohibits women from going to the show with the GIs. Now, as far as I am concerned, it makes no difference what so ever; however, I am well aware of the fact that if they are not permitted to take their girls to the show, the GIs themselves will not go. They will get in more trouble of two sorts or another, and it would be far better to allow them the dubious pleasure of taking the girls to the show. This is especially true since there is plenty of room for all that come. I understand that a dance which is held two or three nights per week here in town will also be cut out. I think that the officials are making a mistake, and many of the officers are against the new moves.

We have the regimental band for our parties, and it is not bad. The music made me want to dance a bit tonight, but I nevertheless refrained. The little Dutch girl, Rina, dances quite well, and she would be the only one with whom I would dance even if I considered it. However, I can wait a few more months for the dancing that I want to do, and that will be with my own lovely little ballerina. Miss ya, Daalin! How much I miss you I can never say for my words are not adequate.

Tonight I sent you a copy of the Red Circle news which contains a partial explanation of why we are still receiving no mail. I quote, "... Although packages and other mail have been coming through, letters are apparently being held up either in New York or Paris, perhaps under the mistaken impression that the Division is moving or slated to move shortly." At all events, the mail is not coming through. What a pile we will have when it does arrive! Oh joy!

I think that I have mentioned beforethe name of a good friend that I have made in Sv. Co.-Wallace, from LA. Calif. He has his Masters from Harvard in business and was an executive officer in his own business in Calif., before coming into the Army. As was true in so many cases, however, he was placed in the infantry; and, like me, carried a BAR in combat. He is now working as records clerk in the Regt. Supply Office. It was his job that I was offered at the RSO. If I had taken it I would be wearing T/4 stripes for Wallace received orders on his last week. I am glad that he did get the break for he certainly deserves it, and I could never have been happy wearing stripes which had been promised another man.

Sunday Afternoon

I arose at the delightful hour of ten o'clock this morning. Last night I made out my reports and so all that I had to do was to get up this morning and go to church. There was supposed to be a Bible Class at 10:15, and I made it by 10:20. No one was on hand, not even the fellow who has been conducting the classes. I went on to the Doughnut Dugout and had a cup of coffee and doughnuts before returning for the regular services. The room was very cold, the service short, and only a few were present. I think that I enjoy the songs about as much as anything else, and I certainly long to return to the regular services in a real church. Chaplain Bowman was substituting for Ch. Webb, who is in Switzerland as you know.

After lunch I went over to the Dugout again to play a bit of pingpong and read. It is always a tonic to get away from the office, and I am shifting more of the responsibility over to Devers and the new man, Grimwood. I will help Grimwood in the PX this week for the last time, and he will begin to take over the mail.

The big news came when I returned to the office. Captain Garner is leaving tomorrow! We have been expecting orders for Sgt. Wilhite almost everyday, but Captain Garner expected to be here for another month. The Capt. is down at the rest center and we had to callhim up and get him back as soon as possible. I was glad to find out soon after that Lt. McAllister will take over the position as CO. If another man had been brought in, many changes could have been expected. As it is, Lt. McAllister is already here, and knows the workings of the company. I expect few changes to be made. Whether or not my situation will remain the same I do not know. I shall insist on knowing exactly how things stand before I go to England.

There is one bit of information about which I never need to check. Without asking or wondering, I know that I love you and that you love me. I know that the solid foundation of our Love will be a basis for any undertaking which we launch upon.

Eternally thine own,
Bushy

Letter from Art to Dotty
Memmingen, Germany
November 18, 1945 [584-585]
(Sunday Night)

My Dearest Heart,

Tonight came more news which actually may mean very little, but it certainly does help morale around here. At eight o'clock came the news on the radio that as of Dec 1st, men with 55 points will be eligible for discharge. It was also announced that as of Dec. 1st, we will receive a new point rating with credit sine [since] Sept. This would give me a total of 61 points. Upon a giving this a bit of thought it is not difficult to see that this does more for the morale than for the process of getting us home faster. Actually, or I should say supposedly, we are being shipped out as fast as it is possible to ship us with the number of ships available. Every man in the ETO who is near the discharge score will receive the same six points, and so what difference to the point makes to him? At any rate, it is some index as to how the shipping is coming along. Our 60 pointers are supposed to leave within the next ten days. Perhaps they will be in the States bz the first of the year or mid-Jan.

That brings me to another little minor point which I have been holding out for some time. Itwas and remains a mere possibility and I have hesitated a long time in telling you. Perhaps it is unwise now, but I shall go ahead anyway. As you know, Sgt. Wilhite has 63 points and will be leaving very soon. About two weeks ago, Captain Garner called me over to his desk one day and informed me that he would like to make me First Sgt. when Wilhite leaves. If it were as simple as all that, everything would be fine and dandy. As I mentioned before, we are expecting to get a number of men from a division which is being de-activated. If this happens, it is very likely that we will get a First Sgt. who would of course take Wilhite's job when he leaves. Another thing which causes me to be constrained is the fact that very seldom is a man jumped from Pfc to First Sgt. The latter is the highest pay bracket in the enlisted ranks, and a staff or tech sgt. usually receives the promotion. That is the GI way but Capt. Garner was not at all GI. He believes that the man who is qualified for the job should have it. I do not mean to imply that I am qualified to handle the work, but at least I am familiar with the various phases of the work. Frankly I think I could handle it, and I would of course like to try. Now that Capt. Garner is leaving, I know what attitude the new CO will take. He may wish to carry on as Garner had planned, or he may have his own ideas concerning the job.

The whole situation puts a new wrinkle in my position as far as the furlough is concerned. If I go and Wilhite ships, will I get the job or will I lose out? If I stay and Lt. McAllister decides to use someone else, or if some other First Sgt. is brought in to the unit, I will have lost my furlough to England and my chance for advancement. What a situation! Perhaps you can see just what sort of a decision I may be forced to make in a few days. As far as my discharge is concerned, it will make no difference whether or not I am a First Sgt. or a Pfc. The money would make some difference, but not much.

I do not like to contemplate another war, but if at any time I were recalled into the service a First Sgt. background would be of infinitely more value than a Pfc. or Cpl. Rating. A minor item, and yet one to be weighed along with everything else is the experience gained in handling a group of almost 175 men. Well, I shall worry little about my bridges until I reach them. I may never be called upon to make such a decision: it may be made for me. I have had a great deal of faith in a Guiding

Hand in former decisions which I have made. I shall trust in His guidance again.

I would not have written of these things until later, had it not been for the fact that the next few days may be decisive. I had no intention of holding out on you, but I did hope to be able to have a big surprise for you when and if the good news finally came. Now it may never come, but I have the questionable satisfaction of having been proposed as a First Sgt.

I have a few pictures to send to you which are in addition to the group of 67. These three were of concentration camps or rather a camp located near Gemunden in Austria. The one of men under the shower is a picture to be censored, and I leave it to your discretion as to whom it is shown. It is certainly not a nice thing to look at, and yet it is horribly true to the facts as we found them at places like this, at Dachau, and other places.

How can I tell you how much your picture means to me as I look at it on my table a dozen times every day. I love you, My Dearest. May God hasten that day when we will be reunited in the wonder and glory of our Love, Bushy

P.S. Three pictures are of 67 group.

Dachau Liberation, taking showers after being liberated
by our forces near Gemunden, Austria. May 1945.
[Mentioned in letter of November 18, 1945.]

Liberating Camp in Austria.

Letter from Art to Dotty
Memmingen, Germany
November 20, 1945 [586-587]

Darling,

And then there was the sad story of the little boy who missed a few things in life. Later in the Army he missed a few more things; and, late in his Army career, there arose the possibility that he might soon attain a certain status. But then again, he missed this particular chance, and like thousands of others resigned himself to the fact that he was still in the Army.

I shall not become despondent over the affair, and neither shall I wax sentimental. However, I can look back and say that I missed the rating of First Sgt. by a matter of thirty hours. I wrote you at some length a couple of nights ago concerning the plans which Capt. Garner had made and the possibilities when Sgt. Wilhite leaves. I also pointed out that, since the Captain was leaving, the new CO would decide his own course as to who he would have for First Sgt. Captain Garner left this morning about 11:30. Sgt. Wilhite leaves tomorrow at 10:00, and the letter for promotion will go in for a new First Sgt. tomorrow

A crematory in one of the prison camps near Gemunden, Austria.
The ashes in the can have been pulled from the furnace.

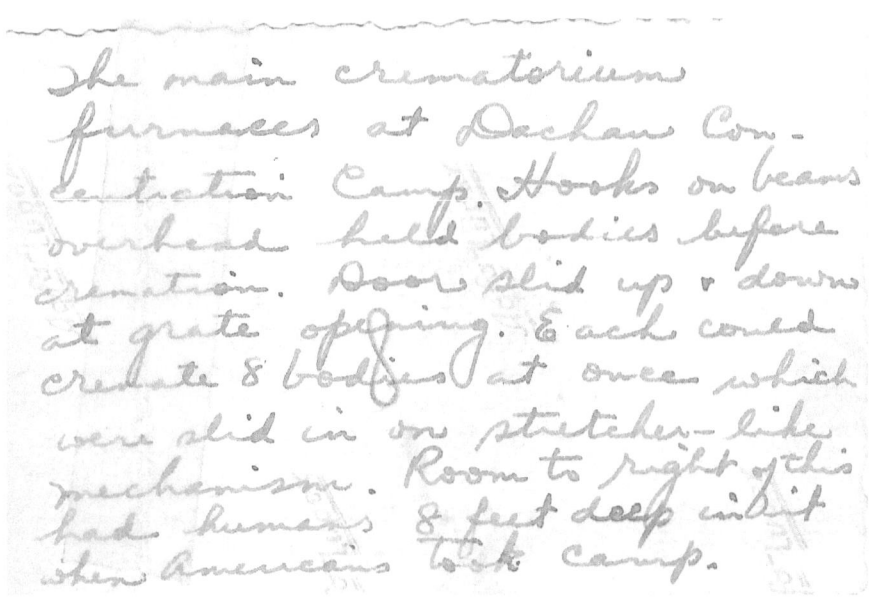

The main crematorium
furnaces at Dachau Con-
centration Camp. Hooks on beams
overhead held bodies before
cremation. Door slid up & down
at grate opening. Each could
cremate 8 bodies at once which
were slid in on stretcher-like
mechanism. Room to right of this
had humans 8 feet deep in it
when Americans took camp.

[Art's notes on back of above photo.]

"Escape was not easy, as these electrical wires show.
This is the camp near Gemundon."

afternoon. However, My Dear, the name of Bushing will not be
attached thereon. Lt. McAllister, our new CO, picked a very capable
fellow from the RSO to take Sgt. Wilhite's place. I think that Findlay,
the new man, will be a swell guy with whom to work, and I think that
he can handle the job without difficulty though it will of course require
a bit of time in which to become familiar with the routine matters.

I received another set-back today when I was called to be informed
that the furlough to England had been cancelled. Well, it turned out to
be all right for it is merely postponed until the 26th. That is, I will leave
here on the evening of the 25th, go to Augsburg for the night, and leave
there early Sunday, or rather, Monday morning.

I called Ted last night and found that he had just returned from
England. We had a long talk lasting almost half and [an] hour, and I
learned the entire story of his trip. He had a swell time, but was only
able to see Pratt for a short time. He spent a couple of days in Scotland,
and three or four days in and around London, seeing the king and
queen and many of the sights. I am hoping to see him in Augsburg

before I leave, and he will try to write up a few pointers for me to follow when I make my trip. He tells me that I will have one day each way in Paris. Ted was delayed for five days before he crossed the channel, but the time was pleasantly spent at shows, etc. Ted by the way is a Sgt. now, or to be technically correct, a T/4.

I shall include a few more pictures—this time typical scenes along the autobahn in Germany. This autobahn, running East and West, was carrying heavy traffic during the past summer when many troops were being moved via convoy toward France. The pictures of the bridge show in some detail the results of the destruction left in the wake of the German retreat. Rather than being destroyed by Allied bombing, this bridge was probably blown up to slow down the advance by Germans themselves.

I must write a long letter to Mother and Dad today and tell them of the latest turn of events. More and more frequently do I dream of the wonderful reunion which is in store for us in the early months ahead. I long for that day with an ever increasing longing. May God continue to grant his abundant blessing upon
> Our Love,
> Bushy

Letter from Art to Dotty
Memmingen, Germany
November 22, 1945 [588-591]
Thanksgiving - 8:30

My Dearest Heart,

Less than an hour ago I returned from Augsburg over fog filled roads. 'Tis the end of the day and another Thanksgiving has passed. It did not occur to me that this makes a total of seven Thanksgivings which I have spent with Ted—not bad, I think. The idea suddenly came to me yesterday when the new First Sgt. told me that he wanted Devers and my self to enjoy oursleves and stay away fromthe office today. I called the dispatch office to if any trucks would be returning from Augsburg in the late afternoon or evening. No, I was told, but perhaps a jeep could be sent for me. I called the MTO (Motor Transportation Officer), the CO, and finally cleared the pass. Late in the evening I called Ted and told him to expect me this morning.

It was one morning that I could have slept until a late hour, but I arose at the early hour of seven to dress and catch the mail truck to division. With my big overcoat on, my scarf, etc. I was warm even riding in the back. My journey was hardly made more pleasant by the presence of a German lady and her daughter who rode up. For a very long time, this was strictly verboden for civilizations to be carried by GI transportation. However, the rule has been relaxed and many Germans ride back and forth. I had a wonderful meal with Ted, and we enjoyed a haircut together this afternoon. The rest of the time, we sat around and discussed our situation past and present. He gave me a number of tips on my trip next week to England. As usual, it was swell just to get away from here and to be able to talk with Ted for a few hours. My driver, Grimwood, came up about four o'clock and brought Devers along for the ride. We left immediately but it was already dark. We had doughnuts and coffee in the Red Cross Club, and returned here.

But, Darling, far more important than Thanksgiving Day, my trip to Augsburg, my visit with Ted, etc., was the mail which came in last night. As of Wed. we were fourteen days behind with first class mail. Letters for seven days came in, and I scored with about twelve. Ten wonderful letters were from my very wonderful wife dating from the 1st of Nov. through the 11th. It was wonderful to sit back in a chair and read them through and through. I spent most of my evening doing just that and in writing a letter, already too long delayed, to Mother and Dad. During the rest of my time, up until 11:45, I arranged for my trip today, prepared my routine reports for today, shaved, and cleaned up.

I have an envelope filled with notations which I want to cover in answer to various questions and discussions brought up in all of these letters. Perhaps I will not be able to get to all of them tonight, but I shall try to cover as many as possible.

Before I go on with those things, however, I did want to mention that Wilhite left yesterday. I certainly regretted very much his leaving, for we became very close during our work together here in Service Company. Bob had more interest in the Army, and I do not believe that he did anything that he did not think was the thing to do. He has promised to call Mother and Dad when he returns to Monticello, Ky., for it is only about forty or fifty miles north of Jamestown. Before he left, he gave me a swell portable typewriter which I am now using. He did not want to bother with bringing it home, and so he passed it on to me. I only hope that I will be able to get it home either by mail or by carrying it myself. If I can only get it home, it will be invaluable at school. I have been trying to figure out how to buy one after I get back.

Your little story of "Dependable Dora" is all too true, My Love, and I am glad that you are aware of the situation. I only hope that, realizing it, you will proceed to do something about it. I began to realize a long time ago that it is very impractical for anyone to become indispensable. Particularly if he or she does not intend to remain at the task indefinitely. Why not attempt to shift some of the responsibility of your work to the shoulders of someone else? After all, Darling, you will not be working in that capacity for many more months. If some one else can begin to learn some of the duties, you can slip from under the job without the confusion that would otherwise result. I am breaking in this fellow Grimwood for the PX and mail, and Devers is familiar with the various reports etc, connected with the rest of my work. It is not fair that you should have so much to do, even though you are willing to do it. In a certain sense it is not fair to the Church to ask you to do so much, for you cannot give your full attention to any one phase of it.

I fear that I have not received a letter telling me of Mom's condition, or that you have not told me all that there is to tell. I did not realize that she would have to have extensive treatments. I do hope that her condition has improved since you last wrote, and that she will be on the road to complete recovery long ere now. Please tell me more about her illness. I shall try to write her again before I leave for England.

In connection with sickness, I am glad that you were able to help someone with your pint of blood. It was certainly very nice of the lady to send you the check for the contribution. I am glad that you are giving it to Mom for her treatment. That reminds me of another thing. What do you think of giving Mary Ruth a little gift as we did last year. You are more closely connected with our bank account than I, and you know her needs in regard to school. I shall leave it to your discretion as to the gift, and I will be perfectly happy with any decision that you may make.

I shall include in this letter a money order for 30.00 dollars which perhaps you can use in relation to Christmas. If every thing has been arranged, it will always help in the bank account. The additional twelve dollars per month will help that much more, although I hope the addition will not [be] held for many more months.

I am not at all clear as to what Phil wants me to find over here for him, but I presume that it is an enlarger for a 35mm camera. I shall see what I can find, but I doubt seriously if it would be possible to find that sort of thing now. A great deal of photographic equipment was looted during the war, and there is very little on sale just now. I shall be on the lookout, and perhaps can find a GI with somethingalong that order to sell. If you can get a better description of what he wants,, it would be nice to get it to Dorcas by Christmas if possible. I will try to get these off tomorrow.

Darling, I have been writing for an hour and a half, and I have covered only ten of the twenty-two subjects I had hoped to cover in this letter. I need to get a good sleep tonight, and so I shall try to wind this letter up on the next couple of pages. I did want to say something concerning Thanksgiving, for truly it is a day when we should stop to think a bit of the blessings which we have received and to thank our Father for his goodness and protection.

It was just a year ago that we were together in Columbus. How much has happened since that day! We had exactly two more months together, for it was on the 22nd of Jan. that we said goodbye on the ice covered sidewalk outside the city of Philadelphia. We had the long period without communication as I left the port of New York and sailed, destination Le Harve. We landed, letters began to come through, there was the month of toughening up as we waded through the mud and rain that we found in Doudeville. Then we moved up. The big push was just beginning around the area of Bitche. Perhaps there were many far luckier than we, but there were far more who knew much more of the horror of war than I. During all of it, your wonderful letters came to tell that our love grew as the days of separation lengthened. My morale, low at times, was always lifted high by the reading of even a short note from you. And then, one fine day, the war ended, I recuperated from the experience in Austria, returned to Germany, went to Paris for a two month stay at the Sorbonne. I was constantly aware that you were working far harder than you should, but I also knew that the work would divert you mind. Your letters continued to strengthen me and help me carry on during a separation that seemed (and still seems) unending. War left us unscathed, and for that we can be thankful. The past year brought an end to the most horrible stuggle [struggle] which mankind has yet known, and it also brought a glimmer of hope for a world united against aggression and war.

Let us thank God this day for the gifts which He has given unto us, for the gifts which he has given to mankind everywhere. Though separated, our Love stands as a bulwark against thw world. In the coming year, we will be able to join more completely than ever before in finding our work, our Love, and our God together. Let us be thankful this day.

I shall go to bed now, to attempt to compete if possible with the dreams of another who would seem to take advantage of the thousands of miles which separates me from my lovely wife. If by thinking of her, I can bring myself a wee bit closer, I shall be with her tonight. I love you, Darling, with all of my heart.

Thine own,
Bushy

My Dearest,

I still retain my former conviction that everything which happens to us can be for the best. However, at times this conviction is difficult to maintain. In the early days of this very week, I missed a promotion to First Sgt. by about thirty hours. Today, I find that I have missed my furlough to England by a mere sixty hours. As I mentioned before, I was originally scheduled to leave tonight at six-thirty. Then the time was postponed until Sunday evening. Today, as I say the entire furlough was cancelled. A friend of mine up at regiment has promised to do what he can on a furlough to Switzerland, but I am very much afraid that he will not be able to help in this manner. If that fails, I shall attempt to go down to our rest center next week, but I wonder a bit if even that would be worth the effort if I could go. Actually, I suppose it would for as I have said, the place is in the heart of the resort section. I am not even sure that I will be able to go down there. Ah me, what a life wit outa wife!

By the way, only day before yesterday I received the second Christmas package, and today came the square flat one of which you spoke. The letter announcing it came only two days ago, and both came in just about three weeks. That is the fastest time for any package yet. Thank you very much, Darling, I appreciate your thoughtfulness, and I know that my Christmas will be made brighter by the nice things which you sent.

Sat. morning

Back at my desk for the work of the morning, but not before I have said, "Mawning, Glory"! Instead of writing as much as I wanted to write last night, I went to the late show. The picture was a Sherlock Holmes (Lady in Green); and , since I enjoy a good mystery, I spent an enjoyable evening. Today is Sat. and so I should be able to have the afternoon to myself. Hope to sleep, read, write, and wrap a couple of packages. I am told that I can send my type writer home without difficulty, and so I will try to get a box made within a few days.

By the way, there is more shifting coming up shortly, and I think it wise for you to send no more packages to me. Also, better not send anything of too much importance in the letters—now, Darling, don't get me wrong. What I mean is, don't send such things as thousand dollar bills, diamond rings, pictures, etc. The most important thing in the world you must continue to send at every opportunity, and that is your love. I hope that you will send that ad infinitum—if I stay away that long!

I must to breakfast. By the way, yesterday I sent a money order for $30.00 which I hope arrives. Let me know when you receive it. Let me know also when you receive word that

I'm yours eternally,
Bushy

Letter from Art to Dotty
Memmingen, Germany
November 24, 1945 [593-595]

My Dearest Heart,

I shall make an attempt tonight to continue with some of the points brought out in the stack of mail which I received a few days ago. As I mentioned before, I wrote for two and a half hours and covered less than half the points which I had noted. Perhaps tonight I can do better. The girl friend of the CQ came to visit him today, and so I offered to stay in the CP while he went away.

As you know, my furlough has been cancelled again, and so I suppose that I shall give up all hope of seeing my "beloved England". You were right I guess concerning school, and I am better off here than in England in school. The near miss will remain in the category with the apple pie long ago and far away. I shall always think of the GI schools in England with a bit of regret. Your alternate suggestion concerning coming back during the summer is very excellent. I had in mind spending a year in study in England with you (and the kids) after I take my PhD. However, we may find that it will be more practical to spend a couple of summers there instead.

I am very glad that you spoke up about our meeting when I return. Never worry, My Love, about differing with me on such minor points— or even on major points. After all, it is far better that we always speak up rather than agreeing only on the surface. I suppose that you are right, and that we should get to Jamestown at the earliest possible moment. I find it hard to imagine how I can give much attention to any one else when I see you. I think that your idea of my picking you up inKnoxville and then continuing to Jamestown is perhaps the best. However, if I found it necessary to be around such place as Oglethorpe for a few days before my discharge was complete, it seems that it would be nice for you to be in Chattanooga. I could probably get passes without difficulty, and then we could come home from there. Really,

Darling, I think it would be rather wonderful as well as practical for us to have a couple of days together before we see anyone else. I suppose that we will have plenty of time to discuss it again, but let me know what you think about these angles.

(After all, I must spend a little time conter-acting the influence of a certain popular bobby socks star!)

I am sending the latest Red Circle News which has more information concerning the situation at the present moment. You are a bit confused concerning our role as a close out force. So are we. The only difference that our change of status has made has been on paper. The battalions are still pulling guard territory. We shipped out a number of low point men, and now this week a number of these same men are returning. It would appear that the division is destined to remain for a time as definite occupation. There is a rumor that the score for occupation will be lowered to 35. That would be a good deal for the large number of fellows that are in the lower brackets. It is also rumored that the point score will be dropped to 45 before the entire system is completely abandoned. There are certain indications that shipping will continue. Menwith 60, 61, and 62 points shipped out during the last two days. If that sort of thing continues for a few weeks longer....I am sweating more than ever before concerning those ten extra points which I may or may not get. Perhaps in a short time we will know. As I suggested in my letter last night, I think thatyou had best send no more packages. We are again ten days behind in the mail, and I do not know when the system will return to normal.

So far I have sent nothing for Harriet, but I will try to find something and get it off immediately. Perhaps there will be something in the PX ration next week which I can buy. I sent another little package to Mother tonight. It is something for you for Christmas—not to be opened until then. I have the three packages which you have mentioned, and if I start to move I may find it necessary to open at least part of them. However sad we may feel come Christmas Eve, we will know that our separation will not be for a long period. I have almost reached the point that I am counting on being home by February, but I hesitate to build up my hopes to have them dashed again.

I failed to mention an incident which occurred on Thanksgiving. We invited a group of DP children to our mess hall to eat with us. Of course, I was away, eating with Ted, but I understand that about seventeen or eighteen kids ranging in age from six to twelve were present. Different fellows took kids approximately the age of their own at home, and everyone had a wonderful time. The kids saw perhaps more food than they had ever seen in their life, and the [they] stuffed themselves in a way that only hungery children can. I am glad that we were able to have them, and I wish that it could be arranged more often.

I am glad to see the problem of the atomic bomb is being discussed from many angles in the States. I hope that we look at the problem in a sensible light before any action is finally decided upon. How can we do anything but put the discovery in the hands of the UNO. I fully believe that this single action would be forceful enough to solidify the United Nations' Organization and make it workable. To hold it as a secret from the world is as though the largest stockholder in a bank were to say that he preferred to keep his money elsewhere, not trusting his own bank.

Wallace has just entered the office and turned on the radio at AFN, Munich. Ted Husing is calling the Pen-Cornell game direct from the States. It sounds just as though we were sitting somewhere in the States listening to the news, or the football game.

An interesting experience came to me tonight when I had the first drink of water which I have had since we came here to Memmingen in the middle of Oct. No, I haven't been drinking beer or wine. I have been drinking a great deal of fruit juice, coffee, etc. The water in the papers is not supposed to be potable, although most of the fellows drink it all the time. I have never taken any, except one time to wash down an aspirin. Tonight I found some of the halazone tablets which we used all of the time in combat to purify river water, water from mud holes, or any other source of the precious fluid. I fixed up a cup of water, put the tablets in, waited the required t wenty minutes, and drank great drafts of water.

Later [handwritten]

Devers is asleep and it is long past bedtime. Again I spent another full evening talking with you. What a pleasant experience! Had a card from Bob Schwartzwalden. He is still over here and I will write him soon. I must to bed. More tomorrow. Goodnight, my Darling, I would that I could press you to my heart and say
    I love you
    Bushy

My Dearest Heart,

I guess that I am learning how to become a civilian a bit quickly, but it was so wonderful to sleep until 10:30 this morning. I just did make it in time to get to Church. Chaplain Bowman again conducted the service, and I am glad that I did not go to work for him when I came to the Orderly Room. Myers had invited me to go to a Marionette show at the Stadt Theatre, and so I met himshortly before two. We reached the door and turned away. It seemed that the place was filled with very small children, and we decided that it was no place for us. We did go to the movie this afternoon which was rather good. Perhaps you have seen "The Bell for Adano" with Wm. Bendix.

I still do not know whether or not I am to go down to Obersdorf to the Rest Center tomorrow or not. Perhaps I shall find out tomorrow. The order which cancelled my furlough stated that no man with 55 points could go on "pass or furlough", and if they stick to this I shall not be able to get away even to the Rest Center.

By the way, Darling, I wonder if you received the letter which contained two magazine subscriptions. I hope that you sent those in for I do think that the magazines would be nice for our folks to get during the coming year. Mary Ruth sent me a program from the opera Rigoletto. I see a number of things which we may be able to see, just in case I get home sometime in the next six or eight months. I would certainly like to see a ballet again. What say?

I had completely given up hope of getting a leather jacket for which I was measured in early October. I ordered it while driving for Chaplain Webb at a leather factory near Augsburg. He had checked on it a couple of times for me, but it had not been completed. When the Chaplain left for Switzerland, I gave my ticket to Chaplain Bowman and asked him to get it for me sometime when he was up that way. Today he brought it over for me. It is made on the style of an "Eisenhower" or combat jacket, and fits rather well. Since the cost was only six and a half dollars, I thought that I could afford the present for myself. I will try to pack it and send it on its merry way next week.

I had thought that I would save all news of shipments and hold out for a surprise, but perhaps it is better that I keep you informed as to the changing situation. The order which stopped my furlough the other day was to the effect that no men with 55 or more points could leave on pass or furlough. The meaning of this order is left to our own interpretation, but it is reasonable to believe that the Division expects to lose us within a short time. In one ten day period we lost all men with point scores between 65 and 60. However, we cannot hope to see the others go as fast as that. It is encouraging to hear that enough ships have been converted to afford a surplus of 34,000 beds over the number of men who are expected to ship home in the month of December. If there is actually a surplus of shipping, the tremendous backlog of men will soon disappear, and we should be able to get home not so long after we become eligible for discharge.

Darling, I do not dare build up your hopes too high, and I do not dare allow my own hopes to soar. Nevertheless, it seems within the realm of possibility that I might be leaving the ETO by the early days of Jan. I always try to remember that my points could be cut in the twinkling of an eye to 45 rather than the present 55. That would set me back a great deal. We will be very, very lucky if only we can be united again before a full year of separationhas elapsed on Jan 22. Let us hope and pray that we will see each other long ere then.

I have spent the entire evening writing Mother and Dad, Mary Ruth, and you. I must write a bit in my diary tonight, for I have wrote nothing in weeks.

Before I say goodnight, may I tell you Darling, that at times our separation causes and [an] unconsolable loneliness to well up within me. I love you with a love that grows with each passing day. I need you, and can know no joy in life that is apart from you. May the Lord bless you and keep you.

> Eternally thine,
> Bushy

> Mon. Morning

Good morning, My Dear,

Another twelve hours has passed bringing us twelve hours closer to the time when I can awaken you with the touch of my lips, saying, I love you.

Letter from Art to Dotty
Memmingen, Germany
November 26, 1945 [598-599]

Darling,

I am waiting around the office as I have been doing for the entire afternoon. I cleared everything this morning for my leave to the Rest

Center, and now I await the jeep which will take me down. Today the weather cleared for the first time in many days, and perhaps I will have a good week. I have plenty of film and I will be able to take some good pictures. There are plenty of skiis down there, and the instructors are supposed to be some of the best found anywhere in Germany. Of course, I do not expect to learn how to do the figure eight in three or four days, but I do hope to learn a few things about the slippery art.

Obersdorf [handwritten]

As I wrote the last line, the jeep came and I hurriedly threw my things in. The sky was marvelous as we rode into the foothills of the Alps, and multicolored clouds peeped over every peak. When I came to Sonthofen with Chaplain Webb, heavy fog shrouded the countryside and I could not enjoy the landscape. Today, there were only a few clouds, and these made reflections for the setting sun. I could almost imagine myself riding through the Chilhowees, but there are many more white birtches [birches] here.

We arrived in time for me to shave before supper, and I had a good appetite for the food which we had.

I had hoped to do a great [deal] of reading and writing, but I shall have to find more lighting than I have in my room. I can hardly see the letter which I write. Other than the lighting, my room is very nice with nice curtains, hot & cold water, and a nice bed. There is to be a dance tonight, and a show is in town. I understand that skiing is almost the only recreation, but that will be enough for me. The quiet and rest away from the office will be most refreshing.

Still Later

Spent the evening writing in my long abandoned journal and reading a bit. It occurs to me that one important thing for us to do during our period of readjustment will be to work on some sort of budget. Will discuss this more at a later time.

How I wish you were here to enjoy with me this vacation. I miss you always,
            I love you
            Bushy

My Darling,

The orchestra opens with a fast tango that would put rhythm in the eurythmic stone of my beautiful Venus de Milo. I care not so much for the tango, but there are certain waltzes which make me want to hold you in my arms and dance far into the night.

The shaded lights of the dancing room cast empty shadows for there are only eight GI's on leave here. Only four or five of this number are in the room now. It seems a pity that more of the fellows cannot enjoy the rest and comfort of this place.

I arose this morning at the delightful hour of 9:30, washed, and dressed for breakfast. By ten I had finished and then began a little tour of the town. Took a couple of pictures and before I knew it the time was for lunch again.

After I had finished this uninteresting process, I hastened to prepare myself for my first experience on skies. So few are here that I had an instructor for myself. We secured our skiis and boarded the cable car for the mountains.

I was surprised how easy the process is—until I began to try a few turns. Balance is the primary objective and much of it is like ice or roller skating. In straight down hill runs I felt like a bird. When I attempted to turn. I felt like a flop.—I was! Of course, the principle that "what goes up, must come down," is reversed. What goes down must climb laboriously back up if the fun is to continue. I did have a great deal of fun, and I shall return tomorrow and the next day.

I returned in time to shave and dress for a far more interesting supper. Today I exercised strenuously for the first time in weeks and I had a real appetite.

I forgot to tell you last night that I am the proud possessor of a pair of skiis as of yesterday. I really should say, owner, for I do not yet possess them.

Some time ago Ch. Webb and his boys told me of getting skiis for only $5 a pair. I made some remark that I would like to get a pair. I never thought that anything would result from the remark, but yesterday, Chaplain Webb told me that he had secured a pair for me. When I return I shall ship them home immediately. Perhaps I will be able to use them in the Smokies or near in Conn. when we go to Yale.

I think I have mentioned it before, but I am ever and again amazed by the repertoire of Am. numbers which these German orchestras possess. I never knew that our popular music was so popular in Europe.

You know, I think that we should develop our dancing to the point that we could present at least an average showing at social functions where dancing is going on. I do not always think that comprise is a good thing, but there are certain harmless things often expected which we might be prone to avoid otherwise.

I shall try to find a good book or article and read for the remainder of the evening. I think that a nice hot bath and to bed by about nine will suit my purpose in an excellent fashion. I am ever lonely while I am away from you, and yet our separation can only strengthen
          Our Love,
          Bushy

Letter from Art to Dotty
Obersdorf, Germany
Nov. 28, '45 [606-611]
[handwritten]

Darling,

The day dawned clear and cool, and the blue sky beckoned me as I finished breakfast (again at 10 o'clock). I could hardly pass up such a chance to take pictures and so I began a long walk to the nearby foot hills in order to get shots of the mountains. I tried my new filters and can only hope that I used them properly. Some of the houses, in fact, most of the houses here are quaint and very nice from the outside. Now and then I see murals on the outside of the houses—something which I have seen only here in Bavaria. Large windows are popular and the eves (?) of the roof extend two and a half or three feet beyond the edge of the house.

After lunch I met my individual instructor and we headed for the hills. We crossed the valley on our skiis and reached the foothills on the other side. The cable car to the Nebelhorn—the popular skii spot,—is broken and so we had to be satisfied with the foothills. At my stage of learning it makes little difference!

You know, Darling, the claim is that these instructors are some of the best in Germany. I would pay dearly for the hours of individual instruction which I am getting were I to pay for it as a civilian. I have had two full afternoons of instruction and tomorrow will make the third.

Wendell, my instructor and I spend a great deal of time skiing but we also talk a great deal. I can understand his German without too much difficulty, and I can express a few of my own ideas.

Later

The party waxed and I waned. I sat in my corner for a couple of hours observing and taking a few notes in my little black book. (Oh, I guess I had forgotten to say that I was writing at first in the dancing room downstairs) There are two GI's in charge of the entire Rest Center, one of whom is from So. Co. He came over to talk and express surprise that I was all alone. I told him that I enjoyed watching the crowd very much.

The only explanation that I can find for the actions of the majority of the GIs over [here] is that they are trying to get away from their surroundings, from themselves. Wine and women are usually at hand and they drift into the habit of finding diversion of losing themselves in this way. All of us are lonely—it is inescapable. All of us have certain basic drives. Some cannot or do not want to resist the temptations which arise. Rather than face their situation, many fellows find escape in one way or another.

I think that this vacation is just what I have been needing. The fresh mountain air, the outdoor exercise, good food, plenty of sleep, freedom from worry concerning the office,—all of these things provide a tonic that I find delightful. I shall return on Friday feeling that I can endure anything until that big moment arrives when I shall begin the long journey home.

Until that day arrives, I must continue the feeble repetition of the thought which I would fain express without words.

I love you always, My Darling
Bushy

P.S. I wonder if the song "Lili Marlene" has become popular in the States, of course, it is a German "lied" [a German term to describe something poetic set to music], but it is very popular with the GI's. The tune is rather easy to learn and it flows smoothly. I like it.

Darling,

I am told that as carefree and as happy as one can become with "le petit vin blanc" or a mug of ripe old ale, there is always the morning after. My vacation draws to an end and I already suffer the pangs of the hangover. Rather than resulting from what has gone before, I suppose that this feeling comes as a foreboding of the future. Truly I have little desire to go back to the routine of the office.

I thought of arising at eight this morning to eat, and then wander around town. I arose at nine instead. When I started to roam about town, I walked for half a block, turned around, and retreated into the four walls of my room.

Guess it boils down to one very evident fact: I'm more than a bit lonely for a certain little wonderful girl. When I have time on my hands, my loneliness grows acute; I miss you intensely, My Darling. May our kind Father hasten the day of our most joyous reunion. I love you!

I have been interested to find that there are in this town a large group of Russians from the Ukrain. Many of these are soldiers or rather were soldiers in the Russian Army. I have asked three or four if they intended to return to the Ukrain. Without hesitation they hasten to give a negative answer and to ask me if I am not aware of the fact that Stalin is "nix gut"! This is a small town, remote from any large cities. I am sure that many of these are deserters from the Russian Army although some may have been brought here as forced laborers. In a recent issue of Time I read that soldiers in large numbers are coming into the Am. Zone of Occupation in an attempt to get avoid returning to their home land.

There are many sides to the Russian question and I wonder just what answers we will find.

Amid all of the failures, all of the disappointments which we have seen in a world struggling to find a common basis for cooperation, there is much cause for pessimism. However, one flicker of light denoting progress shines from the little courtroom in Nuremburg where the individuals who led Germany to destruction are being tried for their actions. Never before in world history have men been tried before an international court for international crimes. Perhaps our efforts will be crowned with success, and perhaps a lasting peace will come. I am sure that the issues at stake are far more apparent than ever before to the average man on the street.

Memmingen

Spent most of the day waiting and finally arrived here late tonight in time to get paid, bathe, and read a stack of mail. The small flat package also arrived.

'Tis late and I shall not attempt to answer your letters tonight. Will try to do so tomorrow afternoon. Glad to get a couple of letters from Mother. The last which I had received was written on Nov. 1st.

There is some indication that I may go to RSO, but nothing definite. More tomorrow. Sorry to write this in pencil, but still no ink in my pen. I wrote every day from Oberstdorf (except yesterday) and hope the letters not too long delayed from there.

Goodnight and most pleasant dreams (even Van J. if you like) [Dirty dig!].

I still love you
Bushy

Letter from Art to Dotty
Memmingen Germay
December 1, 1945 [618-619]
[typed]

My Dearest Heart,

And a very happy December the First to you, and may another thirty days find me much nearer home than I am at this particular moment. Bill Myers came over after lunch and spent the entire afternoon—almost. I did enjoy talking with him, but I had planned to do a lot of writing this afternoon. As he left I picked up a copy of the Red Circle News which has just arrived. The paper says that a mass shipment of men with points between 56 and 60 was expected by the 1st of Dec. (today), but that it has been postponed until next week. At that time all men between 56 and 60 points are to go to the 80th Div. which will sail in Dec. Men with exactly 55 points (that's me) are expected to ship out in Dec. Something of a blow to be just one point short of the required amount, but it will be nice to be high point man awaiting the very next shipment. Of course, often enough, the news in the RCNEWS has been completely outmoded by the time the issue reaches us. Ah me! This uncertainty; this waiting; this constantly longing for one so far and yet so near. Luv' ya!

I had a rather strange experience yesterday after writing you in the morning fromOberstdorf. As perhaps I did not mention, I had called up on Thursday requesting that I be allowed to remain over the week-end at the Rest Center. My reason was that the ski-tow had not been working, and I had been unable to get up the mountain (with exception of the first day.) Findlay had said OK, but Lt. McAllister revoked the permission. Thus it was that I packed yesterday morning, and spent most of the day waiting around to get a ride coming back. About three o'clock in the afternoon, Jones, the fellow in charge told me that the Special Service Officer had called to say that I was to remain. There would be no transportation. He called McAllister to tell him this, and so everything was set for me to stay. The SS Officer knew that his jeep was coming down, and so did Jones. On the basis of their kindness, I could have missed the jeep which did come, and remain until Sunday. However, I was all packed, I had wasted almost the entire day waiting to return, I was a bit tired of inactivity, I was anxious to get the letters which I knew awaited me, and on time [top] of everything else, I had a hunch that I should come back. As far as I know there was no imperative reason that I should be back, and it is seldom that I have such a strong hunch. However, I did come back and perhaps I will be able to return again to Oberstdorf for a week-end sometime.

I was fully rewarded in my return to find four big letters from you and just a couple of minutes ago, Devers walked in with another. To show how screwy the mail service is, the letters last night were dated Nov. 6th, 12th, 13th, 14th. The one which just came in was dated Nov. 19th. I am sorry to learn that the mail to the States is also being thrown around in a thoroughly disorderly fashion. I had hoped that it was at least come through with some degree of regularity.

Later

I had to take time out to shave and eat supper. After supper I met Myers for the show. Saw "Junior Miss" and consider it an outstanding show. The human side to the comedy was so real that I kept reminding myself that we night find ourselves in very similar circumstances in a short twenty years. I hope that you have seen the picture or will see it for it is hilarious. Bill tells me that the stage version was even better, but I think that I would have to see it to believe.

We had our usual party tonight, and I merely showed up to duck in and duck out. I returned here with the good excuse that I wanted to relieve the CQ and give him a chance to see the party. I returned to find the Army-Navy game in full swing, and I had to listen to a bit of it. Gee, it sounds good to hear a game again. I also heard that UT won from Vandy 27-0, or some such. 'Swonderful.

Doggone it though! It is late, and I cannot write the six or eight pages that I had hoped to write tonight. I will not even be able to write Mother and Dad, Bob. S., Van, Ted P., and a few others that I had hoped to write.

I am glad that you finally persuaded David to take you to the square dance, Darling. Too bad that you had to use "Daisy Mae" tactics, but it is good practice. Perhaps I should play hard to get when I return. Huh! Just watch me! I do envy Dad being able to take you to hear the Pittsburg Symphony, but I am terribly happy that you can go. There will be other symphonies.

Your description of the bus stoppage reminds me of some of the transportation over here. It really sounds more like Augsburg than Knoxville, but I suppose that the old buses have really seen a great deal of service during the past few years. Speaking of Augsburg, I talked to Ted this morning. I had hoped that he would be able to come down for the week-end, but perhaps I can get him to come down next week-end. If I am around on Christmas, we will certainly spend the day together; but I have a feeling that I may be somewhere between here and the port. If I am on my way, I suppose that I can eat K rations for a week anywhere—if that is necessary.

Wherever I am and whatever may be my status, I will know and you will know that with God's help we will never be separated at this Yuletide season again. Though separated, the day will be a merry one for we will know that within a short time thereafter we will surely be reunited in the wonder and happiness of
>   Our Love,
>   Bushy

Letter from Art to Dotty
Memmingen, Germany
December 2, 1945 [620-622]

My Dearest Heart,

I had planned to write Bob Schwarzwalder tonight, but I decided that my wonderful wife comes first. If I finish this in time to write another letter, I will, of course, do so. Otherwise, my long delayed letter to Bob will have to wait. After I went to bed last night, I got up again to put down concerning a few points of which I will speak later. In the first place I must repeat an oft-repeated warning. We both know that any day the decision might come which would cut my points from 55 to 45 (due to the 10 months of ERC credit which I now have). If this happened, my homeward trip would be postponed for at least a couple of months. However, we must be realistic. There is a possibility that I will retain my 55 points, since I have held them this long; and that I will be on my way to the States sometime in Jan.

It was with the latter inmind that I put down a few notes last night. In the first place, I think that we are fully agreed that if possible it will be far better for us to find a little apartment in Knoxville for the quarter during which I hope to take refresher work. If we need to discuss this we can, but I believe that we are already in agreement and that the point does not need discussion now. If so, we can go on to the second point which is this. You probably know far better than I the housing shortage which exists all over the country at this time. I am wondering if it would not be wise for you to begin the lengthy process of finding out just what the possibilities will be for us to find a little apartment, preferable near the University, which we would hope to take by February the 1st, or shortly thereafter.

Now, I am not sure that I will be able to make that Spring Quarter at UT. If, for the sake of the discussion, I could be in civilian attire by the 20th of Jan., and the Quarter begins on or about the 10th of Feb., I think that the intervening time would be enough for us to vacation. I am absolutely against rushing the cadence. I want you to have a good vacation and I want to have a chance of you becoming my own boss again (or vice-versa)! If there is not enough time for us to enjoy our second honeymoon, we shall wait until the summer quarter. I am debating whether or not that would be best anyway, for I think that I should begin at Yale in the Fall rather than in the Summer. We may find it wise to kill time in one way or another until the Summer Quarter at UT. If that were the case, I would try to find some sort of a short time job to make up the interim.

No matter what we decide about school, we may be looking for an apartment about the 1st of Feb. Perhaps you could do a bit of research to determine just about how much it will take for us to live for a month in Knoxville. We did extremely well in Palo Alto, and I think that perhaps prices are more reasonable in Knoxville. At any rate, we will not plan to live on noodle soup, dehydrated at that! Probably from your own buying at home or from the cost of living for some of the other couples around you can figure just about what it will take for us to live. I feel sure that the new allowance of $90.00 subsistence per month under the GI-Bill, we can manage without too much difficulty.

You spoke once of working in your present job while I am in school at UT. That too will call for a bit of discussion. I would much prefer that you take a couple of courses also, or that you took special music perhaps. I am absolutely against any sort of schedule resembling the one which you now have. If you wish to keep up with the Young People, that will be one thing. If you wish to continue working with Dr. Peyton, that will be something else. Both, along with the choir etc. will be by far too much. We hope that within a few months, we will have our own young people to worry about. Our time together as merely a couple will be all to short, for after the first child is born we will not for a long time know the freedom of action which will be ours as a couple. Therefore, we will not have a skating party or a picnic interfering with the time which is rightfully ours. Your story of "dependable Dora" is very true. Remember it!

As I wrote Mother and Dad this afternoon, I hope that I can kill two birds with one stone in regard to my courses at UT. I will have credit for Stanford and for the Sorbonne. At least some of each of this should apply to credit for my MA. Insofar as possible, I want to take refresher courses which will also help toward my degree. I think that you have a Yale catalog, but if you haven't perhaps you could send for one—specifying, of course, that the catelog be for the graduate school. I will want to study the requirements for an MA in deciding upon my courses at UT.

It seems to me that between 16 and 18 hours of work should be quite sufficient for a refresher. I would like to select about three English courses, designed to survey the field so much as possible. These would make from ten to twelve hours of my work. I would also like to take a course in English History for another two or three hours, and last an elective. The elective would probably be in the field of philosophy, esthetics, or even economics. At least for the present, I think that I shall steer clear of the scientific and mathematical courses which I minored in at Maryville.

I do not mean to burden you with all of this at once, but I would appreciate it very much, My Love, if you could investigate some of these things for me during the next few weeks. I must find out if a certain number of hours work will be required under the GI Bill. Also, in regard to the courses, you perhaps could find out something regarding the teaches. Since I do not know whether or not I will be able to make the Spring Quarter, you might also investigate the courses which will be offered during the summer term.

"My aching back", to use the GI vernacular. I didn't realize how many things I was piling on you to do, My Darling. I do not mean for you to drop everything and start in on these little odd jobs, but perhaps in your spare time (what's that?) you can check on a few of these things. Oh by the way, I just thought of something else. From now on, we could think of buying those items which we will be using in Knoxville and later in our apartment in Yale. That is, items which we can carry with us from place to place.

I was glad to get the picture of Francis Sisk and the announcement of her marriage. I am very glad that at last they will be able to go ahead with their plans. At the same time, I am terribly happy that we did not wait to get married. By the way, I wonder if you remember that I once dated Francis at Maryville. Mother wrote that little Chersterlyne, another old flame of mine, has jumped the gun and married. Her parents were very much opposed to her marriage and so she walked in one evening to in announce her husband. I understand that there is a great deal of concern caused by this little event in Jamestown.

Well, the hour is late, and I guess that Bob's letter will have to wait until tomorrow. Devers is in bed trying to sleep, and I will have to end this clatter.

In all of my planning, the paramount thing is the importance of the greatest thing in my life, which of course is
>Our Love
>Bushy

* Letter from Art to Dotty
Memmingen, Germany
December 3, 1945 [623-624]

My Dearest,

I am in one of those moods tonight when I want to be with you, and yet I do not feel like talking. I just want to stretch out on the couch with my head in your lap. I want to turn the lights down low and listen [to] the quiet, soothing music. I want to look into the depths of your eyes and tell you, with out words, how beautiful you are and how much I love you. I want to experience once again the soothing peace and inner strength that comes as I bask in the warmth of your smile and feel the soft tough [touch] of your hand on my brow. Miss ya! luv' ya! want ya! need ya!

Perhaps my depression is the result of what I did today. Go ahead and call me names and reprimand me. Perhaps I deserve it, although I really don't think I do or I would not have done it.

You see, in all of my unhappiness (the unhappiness caused by my failing to get to go to England), I forget one little item—yes, perhaps one little loophole. I forgot that there were also a group of five day courses offered in England during the month of December. One of these was a five day course being given at Stratford-on-Avon. I happened to notice the bulletin announcing these courses yesterday, and noted that one of them was a group of lectures on English Lit. Now, you know full well that a group of lectures on English Literature given at Stratford-on-Avon would be of no particular interest to your scientifically minded husband. However, it would provide a trip to England.

Another fact came to my mind this morning: some of the 60 pointers are still in the Division, and Sgt. Fairbanks, my I&E friend, might perhaps be among that number left behind. It was worth a try. I called I&E and who should answer the phone but Henry Fairbanks himself. He is now a Staff Sgt. by the way. By a mere coincidence, I called just ten minutes before the deadline for the names to be sent to Corps. Since there is a quota of but one for the entire Corps, I have a slender chance of getting the school. Henry promised to all that was possible for me, and I am sure that he will. Tomorrow I will probably know. The course begins on Dec. 10th and ends on the 15th, so probably before you get this I will be either in England or here. I think that I can safely assure you, Darling, that this will be my last attempt to get to England on this trip to Europe.

I heard more rumors today that [than] I have heard in a long, long time. As I think I have noted before concerning Army rumors, none of those we hear may be entirely correct, but it is extremely likely that something will happen very soon. I am sure that the 56-59 pointers will leave shortly. And lo, Abu Ben Bushing's name will lead all the rest on the point roster then.

Last week while I was away, we had twelve replacements from the States come in and tonight we received seven more. I shall not try to describe their reactions as rookies over here—there is such a satisfaction one feels at being an oldtimer! I cracked a rather poor joke when I remarked that at least some of them have six or eight points. When we came over, we had none.

Today we received orders from the Medics to place another man under a 21 day restriction. This is restriction placed on men who are VD contacts. This fellow is in his early thirties, is married and has at least one child. He has 56 points and would probably have left for home this week. Now he will be delayed at least a month and perhaps longer. My blood boils when this sort of thing comes up, and I can have no sympathy for those involved. How men can run the risks involved is beyond my comprehension.

While I am in a black mood, perhaps I may as well go on to relate another sad reflection on Army life. Today one of our boys walked into the Regimental CP. After reaching the inner hall, he began to unbutton his mackinaw. Now, of course, there are stringent rules concerning outer garments being buttoned outside. I have never seen rules that one should be muffled for the arctic in a building. This fellow began to unbutton his mackinaw when the Regt. Commander walked up to him. The remark was something to this effect, "Well, soldier, since I see that you don't know how to wear your clothes, you can leave that coat here." The GI could do nothing but remove his coat and leave it with the Colonel. Devers was so burned up by the incident that he sat down and wrote a letter to B-bag, which is a gripe column in <u>Stars and Stripes</u>. I hope that the letter will be published.

I should say something about this particular column for it has been of invaluable service to the enlisted man. Any man may write in to the paper and air his personnel gripe. Many times incidents and situations have been uncovered in this was and definite improvements made. Viva la <u>Stars and Gripes</u>, as it is sometimes called.

I must go from the the sordid to the sublime and tell you in three little words that the dominating factor in my life is merely this,

I love you,

Bushy

All of these pictures are unfortunately light struck.

Letter from Art to Dotty
Memmingen, Germany
December 4, 1945 [625-626]

Darling,

I was the joyful receipent today of five big letters from you. First, in the late afternoon came three mailed the 19th—those Mon.—but-it-should-be-Sat.. Mon.-but-it-should-be-Sun, etc. etc. About supper time I received your letter mailed on the 21st and late tonight came another mailed on the 23rd. Not bad for one day. Rather than write tonight, I had to pack a big box and get a couple of pictures ready for the mail. It is now past bedtime, and I must hasten.

Before I discuss your letters in detail, I shall recount the events of the day—events that seem to change hourly in an old familiar way. This morning we found ourselves with another clerk in the office—that makes a total of five clerks for a job which was handled by one man. Grimwood has 57 points and will soon leave and so we had to have another man to take over the mail and the PX. I may leave shortly and Devers has 51 points. The latest rumor (for the last two days) is that 50 and above will be out of the Div. by the 15th of Dec. If so Devers will also leave. The new fellow is one of the men who just arrived from the States—he landed on the 24th of Nov. From N. Carolina he has had typing before, but is sadly out of practice. I think that he will take over without too much difficulty.

The other bit of news today was that which I received from Fairbanks concerning the school which I told you about last night. The quota is already filled, and so I suppose that I can forget all about England—doggone it!

As I described last night, the rumors are flying thick and fast. Today more came, and from another source I heard that 50 pointers and up will probably leave within the next two weeks. Let us not base too much hope on these rumors, but it may be an indication that things are on the move. Of course, fellows have shipped out of here and hung around in another outfit for six weeks and two months. However, if I can ship out of here by the 20th of December, I think that I have a fair chance of reaching home waters by the latter part of Jan.

I can hardly share your excitement concerning the announcement that the 71st is to be alerted in Dec. We have had all sorts of wild tales come back from the States via newspapers, radio reports, etc, concerning our activities. We are still receiving men with three and four points and Friday we have a big shipment of 59 pointers. Of course, radical changes can take place very quickly in the army, but your news is as of the 17th of Nov. and on the 4th of Dec. we have these orders which I mentioned.

By the way, I must describe the packages which I made up tonight. I do hope that it gets home in good shape, for it contains the nice leather jacket which I was finally able to get. (It cost only six dollars and a half.) I also sent a set of pictures which I bought before I left for Paris. These are the ones of the various beautiful cathedrals in Germany. I also included a pair of opera glasses which I bought from Devers, and a tripod which Myers gave me. I included also a few maps, a few odds and ends of civilian clothing. The latter was put in mainly to fill up space. Am anxious to hear if my Christmas boxes to Mom arrived OK.

It is very, very late. I must to bed to dream of the wonder of
        Our Love,
        Bushy

Letter from Art to Dotty
Memmingen, Germany
December 6, 1945 [627-628]

Darling,

I must blame this short note on the fact that I am becoming more and more restless and unsettled. I seriously wonder if I will settle down again until I regain that delightful status commonly known as civilian life. Yes, the rumors continue good, and the prospects seem bright. As the time approaches when my orders seem about to appear, I think more and more of how horrible it would be should I suddenly be cut to 45 points. The more I think of it the more probably it seems that such an error will never go unchecked. However, it has gone this far, and why couldn't it continue? Don!t answer that!

If, by a mere freak of chance, I am able to retain my present point score of 55, it seems very likely that I will leave the 71st next week. For the last couple of days we have had the rumor that 55 (or 56) and up would ship to the 94th Div. As I think I have mentioned before, the 94th moved into our occupation area with the purported intention of being de-activated. Now it seems that the division is supposed to be filling up with high pointers and preparing to sail shortly. Ooh la la!!!

I talked to Ted today by phone, and I am hoping that he will be able to come down for the week-end. It may be the last chance that we will have to be together for sometime. Travel is extremely bad now, for all of the roads are sheets of ice. We have had intermittent snow for the past week. Now and then the temperature goes up to the point where a little of the snow melts and then it immediately freezes again. The result is that trucks are cracking up all of the time. The poor mechanics in the shop are being driven mad with all the work that is piling up, and they are terribly short handed on top of everything else.

Today I got my skiis from Chaplain Webb. And tomorrow I shall try to get a box made for them. The limit for shipping is 100 inches combined girth and length. It is a very narrow squeeze to get skiis in a box of such specification. My typewriter box is already finished and I shall have it all ready to ship when I leave. I certainly hope that it makes the trip. As I have not heard of any of the boxes arriving, but I hope that they do so before Christmas. I described in a letter a couple of days ago the last big box which I sent, containing my leather jacket and other items. I have it insured and so if it doesn't arrive I will collect. Within the last week, I have also sent two large envelopes with items for you. I suppose that two recent money orders for thirty five and thirty dollars respectively have reached you ere now.

Beginning this morning, the new man has begun to relieve the CQ before reveille. This morning I slept until almost seven-thirty and I should be able to sleep late every morning now—until some change occurs. I have been wasting a terrific amount of time in the evenings during the past week. I have intended since Sunday to write Bob S., and I just can't settle down to writing. I guess I have what is known as the "short-time shakes".

Why shouldn't I be excited at the prospects of heading for home? The past year has been an interim; life will begin again for me when we are together. The only happiness for me in this life will be as I seek the Christian Way of living with you. May God continue to bless

Our Love,

Bushy

PS   I am reading the world-wide Bible readings as we read them together during the pre-Christmas season. I join with you each evening as we think on these things.

Letter from Art to Dotty
Memmingen, Germany
December 7, 1945 [631-632]

My Dearest Heart,

Strangely enough the rumors continue, and, in fact, the news is almost past the rumor stage. <u>Stars and Stripes</u> today carried the story that the 94th Div. is alerted and will consist of men with point scores ranging from 55 to 59. How much confusion, changing, and disappointment will occur between now and then—time along [alone] can tell. At the moment it seems that we will leave here sometime next week. I do not like to tell you to stop writing for there can always be delays. If you do continue to write, the mail will always be forwarded to me either here or home, so don't stop writing unless I tell you later to do so.

Tonight I made something of a farewell trip to visit with Chaplain Webb. His new chess set has been completed and I enjoyed the first game with it. He of course won, but we had a great deal of fun. It is a thrill just to play with the swell set of chessmen. In a half joking manner I offered him one hundred dollars for the men and the chess board (inlay leather). I could not have bought the set for a hundred and fifty, but I seriously would have been foolish enough to give him the hundred. I believe that he could sell the set in a minute in the States for two hundred dollars. The workmanship is excellent and the detail simply marvelous.

I talked with Ted by phone again tonight, and hope that I succeeded in persuading him to come down for the week-end. If he is unable to come tomorrow, he hopes to come Sunday. It is terrible weather for travel but I do hope that he can come.

The work in the office during the past week has gone down to almost snail's pace. Sgt. Findlay, the new First Sgt., is doing a great deal to help out with small details. Three of us are on hand to take care of the clerical work, in addition to the fellow handing the mail and PX. It is certainly an over supply, but when Grimwood (the mail man) and I leave the force settle back to a more normal number. I spent a little time today doing a very unusual thing—writing a letter during duty hours. I have at least started a letter to Bob, but I only hope I can get it finished tomorrow.

I think I forgot to describe the manner in which I found a very important little piece of paper a few days ago. The service records of one of our men were missing, and I went to Personnel in an attempt to locate these papers. I ended up going through the files of every man in the Regt. As I passed through Co "K", I noticed that an old envelope with my name was still in the file. Looking inside I found, believe it or not, the travel orders sending me from Stanford to Ft. Benning. As you well remember, I had a hectic time while at Benning, trying to get the travel money which was due. I tried again in Gunzburg and was told that I would have to have a copy of my orders. This I have at last found, and it is in my pocket. I shall have to wait now until I return to the States to present it to finance, but I believe that the money will finally be forth coming. It will all help as we launch out into the briny deep.

There was a long article in the <u>Start and Stripes</u> a couple of days ago concerning the housing units which have been installed at Yale to take care of the couples who are turning up. Apartment dormitories are being set up which will cost between thirty and fifty dollars per month. It was stated that students are finding it extremely difficult to live on the ninety dollars per month—or rather the seventy-five, which they now receive. I think that we can manage, Darling, and we most certainly shall try. It seems to me that with the three hundred dollars which I will receive as mustering out pay, we should be able to boost our total savings to a figure approaching twelve hundred—I hope a bit higher. Fact of the matter is,—no, I have put aside all thoughts of buying one! Of course, we will need one—would be swell to have one, wouldn't it? Perhaps we could see the way clear to invest three hundred dollars in one. Oh, but by the way, how much do babies cost? That is a good question to weigh heavily. Maybe, if we are very careful, we can have a car too!

I am hoping that you will be able to make a trip to Jamestown again either before Christmas, or shortly thereafter. The folks, as always, would love to have you come. Perhaps it would be wise for you to take one of my suits or perhaps two of my suits back with you. I certainly hope that I can wear my old clothes, for that in itself will save a lot of money if I can. I am [have] gained perhaps a bit of weight, but I think a few alterations should fix that. I had one good blue suit and a couple of others that were not too bad.

The hour is again late; my mind is filled with the thoughts of home. Our faith in a kind and loving God has been justified in a hundred ways. May we continue to place utter trust in Him and in His plan for our lives. God bless

Our Love,
Bushy

PS. I muster have forgotten to number my letters for the 5th & 6th. "Short time jitters" it is sometimes called. Love ya

Letter from Art to Dotty
Memmingen, Germany
December 8, 1945 (Sat. [633-634]

My Dearest Heart,

'Tis Saturday night, I have taken my bath, and shaved. I sit crossed-legged on my bed, my shoes off, my typewriter sitting on top of its own box. Devers and I are eating, or trying to eat, a few of the extra large grains of Morton's Iodized Salt which I found the other day. The grains have a faint resemblance to a nut of some sort, and I feel like one after patiently extracting the individual grains one by one. Devers comments that my wife must have a great deal of patience, and I agree. (After all, she worked four long years to get me! Who said that? Take that man's name, rank, and serial number!!!)

As usual there was a great deal of nothing to do today, but I managed to occupy my time in one way or another. I had a couple of reports to make up this afternoon, but I managed to finish up a long letter to Bob which I started yesterday. Tonight I played ping pong at the Red Cross Club and did a bit of reading. I had hoped that Ted would be down, but he said last night that there was too much work in his office, perhaps will come down tomorrow.

I intended to explain above about the peanuts. I believe you told me that if I started moving before Christmas to go into the Christmas boxes. Since it seems evident that I will be leaving next week, I made bold to open them and begin to eat the food. Unless it proves otherwise impossible, I shall hold the items which seem to be something other than food until Christmas Day. The closer I amto you, My Darling, on Christmas Day, the more bearable will be the separation.

I failed to mention last night an encouraging event which took place yesterday. I had long planned to visit the dentist for a check up since I had not been in a dentist chair since Menlo Park days in Calif. I expected to find that I needed at least six or eight fillings for in combat it was not easy to take proper care of my teeth. I had put the matter off as one can so easily do, but finally I went down yesterday morning. After an examination, the doctor could find but one small cavity and proceeded to fill that. Teeth in good shape he reported. "Well, good for me," to use an old Bushing expression.

It is hardly encouraging to hear that the boys who went to the 80th Div. yesterday are living in tents. I suppose that a fellow can put up with anything if he is on his way home, but I see no reason for this sort of condition to exist. Winter has begun and winter is no time for men to be sleeping in tents. I am glad to say that the 94th (where I am supposed to go) is located in good billets at the moment.

By the way, I wonder if you could write to Time and request a change of address for me. May as well have them sent to 607, for we can get them there throughout most of the year. I shall ask Dad to write to Encore. By the time you can write and the change go into effect, I am sure that I will be well on my way—I hope! Gee, it's hard to realize that I may be coming home soon. As I think I described ina precious letter, during the past few months I have been suspended in a seemingly everlasting "now", between a dimming past and a clouded future.

I wish that I could describe in detail the changes that have takenplace in my attitudes and thoughts during the years-long months which have separated us. I cannot put them down, for I do not know. I do not think that the changes have been unusual or tremendous in any way. Once or twice I have realized with a start that small things which I thought funny before no longer strike a humorous chord. I think I have broaden my viewpoint, generally speaking; have become more liberal without becoming radical. Through lack of use I have lost some of my habits of concentration. My hair line has receded a bit more, and my feet sometimes remind me that they fell nobily, while serving their country. I still read Time with avid interest, although I have given up taking Time with my meals. I still feel pangs from the "Lonely Heart" at times when you are so near and yet so far. I will return to you, My Love, without reservation, knowing that I have nothing to withhold, have done nothing of which I am ashamed. I will have no fears of letters, ghosts, or memories coming to haunt me and disrupt me and disrupt our perfect union.

I will come to you with on paramount thought in mind—that we will continue to climb to higher heavens as we continue to find the wondorous joy of

Our Love,

Bushy

Letter from Art to Dotty
Memmingen, Germany
December 10, 1945 [635-636]

My Dearest Heart,

Tonight you are singing at the First Christian Church, and my heart is also singing. Darling, imagine! The big news came tonight—about seven-thirty we received orders which will start me on my way. All men with 55 points and above will leave here on Wed. morning (Dec. 12), and go to the 302nd Inf. Regt. which is located at Sonthofen. There is a very fine rumor out which says that we are to be processed for shipping right here in this area and then ship direct to the port. Now, of course, I expect to encounter the unusual 'Snafu", and the usual postponements. We will probably have two or three shipping dates when one after another is canceled. However, the big thing is that I am on orders and will ship out to the 94th Div. I still remember, and you must also, that I could still lose ten of my points. I do not like to repeat this so often, but it remains a shadowing possibility which must be taken into account.

Ted called yesterday and again tonight. He tried for several hours to hitch-hike down here yesterday (Sun.) but was unsuccessful. The roads are solid sheets of ice, and there is little unnecessary travel. I wish that I could have seen him before leaving, but I suppose that there is little help for it. Perhaps I will be able to get a pass from the new outfit and go back to Augsburg.

Your letter of the 26 Nov. arrived today, my first in about a week. It seems that the mail is terrible going both ways, and I can see no reason for it. Even if it is coming by boat, it should by now be coming with some regularity. However, we are getting mail about twice a week now, and very little even then.

I think that your idea about the car is excellent, and I think that it would be very fine if we could rent one for some of our "gadding about", as you say. I spoke in a letter a couple of night ago of buying a car, and I am still thinking seriously about it. We could not buy a new one, even if they were available, but I would consider buying a used car if we could get some reasonable price. A car is an investment, and like everything else should not be bought unless there is a sufficient need. That need is something which we will have to discuss further.

I also wrote in a previous letter concerning an apartment for us. Unless something unexpected happens, it would seem to me that perhaps we could hope to make use of one soon after the 1st of Feb. Keep your eyes peeled. Darling.

I wish that I had saved an article on housing units which are being set up at Yale for couples coming back to school. It sounds good, and perhaps the price will be within range of out pocket book. (By the way, I repeat again that I have sent two money orders to you in recent weeks —one was for thirty-five dollars and one for thirty.)

Last night I spent something of a farewell evening with Chaplain Webb and the boys. We played Monopoly and had an enjoyable evening. The evening proved profitable when I was able to trade Ch. Webb the French Francs I had bought from Ted when I though [thought] I was going to England. Sometimes the exchange of the various kinds of money involves difficulty, and especially when one is on the move. I also was able to get a few more pictures from the Chaplain. What a pile we are going to have! I do hope that we can work up an ETO album with all of these, or rather with a selection from the pictures which I have sent home. Many are not worth much, but others will be nice to look at at a later time. [We wish that Art could have seen his collection in this two volume set of books. He might have enjoyed that.]

By the way, I was at last able to get a rather nice fountain pen in the PX. I signed the list for pens before I took the PX and my name took a long time to reach the top. We usually draw only four or five pens a month, but my name finally arrived. I am now the proud possessor of a Shaeffer Lifetime for about four dollars. Not bad, eh what!

The hour is very late, and I must read my Bible lesson for today and go to sleep. Will spend most of the day tomorrow in sorting through my "junk", ridding myself of unnecessary items, and perhaps packing another box or two. I want to travel with as little as possible. Glad that I have plenty of film, and hope to be able to get some good pictures on the way back.

Until I get my new address, you may as well continue writing to my old address. I hope to be able to tell you very shortly to stop writing altogether. However, I am always mindful of the fact that we could be delayed for a few weeks as many others have been.

My heart leaps high with the thought that soon I will be on my way to you, My Lovely. There is a deep and lasting joy in the knowledge or

Our Love,
Bushy

Letter from Art to Dotty
Sonthofen, Germany
Dec 12 1945 [637-640]

My Dearest,

At 6:05 this morning I opened my eyes when the CQ ascended the stairs to awaken the company. As sometimes happened, he missed my room. I stretched my arms and smiled inwardly. I had much to do, but my last day in Sv. Co. was no time to arise for reveille. I thought of the comfort of my bed. Before I sleep in such a bed again I will probably be in the States—home! Even though I was then fully packed, I could hardly realize that this was really the day. As I listened to the company falling out, I thought of the things left to do, the trip ahead, the possible and probably delays, home! I thought of many things.

At 08:30 I said goodbye to the boys in the Orderly Rm. and carried my bags to Personnel. Although I had sent almost all of my extra junk and carry little more that [than] my GI equipment, I still have two bags of stuff to carry.

We stood in front of Personnel, about four hundred of us, while the snow drifted down. Farewells were being said, the Chaplain joked with first one and then another, everyone was happy and no one objected to the cold. This was the Day.

We rode for two hours over a beautiful Bavarian countryside. I was dressed in my woolens, coat, jacket, overcoat. The cold gave me no trouble. To make a long, boring, story short, I found myself in Service Co, 302 Inf. along with twelve others from the 14th.

We hardly know that the score is here. We have been told that the outfit is to be shipped directly to the port about the first of the year. We have swell quarters—that is—we have army cots in a hallway. However, the building is very warm and when a few low pointers leave we will have rooms for two or three. I shall describe the post here in greater detail at a later time.

I must write Mother and Dad, for I have not written them in two days. Will try to write a long letter tomorrow. Do not write any more after receiving this for it will never reach me—unless I am pulled back. Darling I'm on my way to tell you

I love you,
Bushy
PS. I have sent my skiis, and typewriter. Devers is sending two smaller packages for me containing odds and ends—including a chess set.

Letter from Art to Dotty
Sonthofen, Germany
December 14, 1945 [641-643]

My Dearest Heart,

From behind my new desk at the hour when I should be beginning my morning work, I begin a letter. Perhaps no one will bother me for the next two hours, and perhaps someone will come up in the next ten minutes with a job on which I will work all day.

But to start where I left off with my last letter. Yesterday morning I arose about eight o'clock. When I heard a call for the truck drivers, and another for one of the fellows who worked in RSO, I decided that my turn might be next. Having been in the army too long, I did what every veteran would do, I disappeared. I went over to O'Connell's room in Co. "K", and spent the morning in talking and writing a long letter to Mother and Dad. At noon I found that a clerk was needed in the RSO; and, knowing full well that sooner or later I would be roped in for work of one sort or another, I decided that I would try to get into the Regt. Supply Off. I really had no desire to begin before this morning, but one of the fellows turned in my name and I was called immediately. It really made little difference for there was almost nothing to do. I read "War of the Worlds", by H. G. Wells, most of the afternoon.

As perhaps I should expect, everything is thoroughly confused here. The old personnel has either left or is leaving, and no one seems to know that [what] is going on. Honest, I sometimes wonder just how the Army ever won the war in the first place. Actually there is not too much left to do to clear the Div. Most of the Ordance items (rifles, machine guns, etc.) have been turned in, and in the next couple of days a complete check of clothing will be made. This will be about the last job to requisition the clothing needed to bring home and to issue it to the companies. As far as I can see so far, I am merely excess equipment here in the office. However, it does provide a typewriter for me to use, and I will not be shoved here and there on this detail and that.

Last night I visited the EM Club here on the post which has become famous for its ritzy-ness. It is really a swanky place and I have seen few night clubs that were nicer. (Of course, I have seen few night clubs period.) The movie is on a 16mm projector and I have not been able to work up enough interest to attend as yet. I played a bit of ping pong and read. Strangely enough, I am getting to bed by nine-thirty or ten every evening now and getting up about seven-thirty.

Some of the fellows are doing a great deal of skiing, but I have not participated. I really do not feel like taking the slightest chance on this deal. A broken leg could hold me up for weeks around here, and I intend to do nothing which could perchance cause delay.

Friday afternoon

It is difficult to describe the prevailing attitude of the men in this outfit, but I suppose that it is best reflected by the phrase "light-heartedness". Such an attitude builds morale, but the efficiency of the work done is certainly not improved. As I said before, the old persnonnel has either left or is leaving, and those of us who just came in hardlz know what the score is. The most important thing for all of us that we are on our way home, and everyone wants to get the minor details out of theway as fast as possible. This afternoon we had our clothing check and shortage list will come in to us in the RSO in the next couple of days. We will requisition these from QM (Quartermaster), and issue them to the companies. When this is done we will be just about ready to ship. Oh happy day!

Darling, I must admit that even now I find it difficult to realize that I am on my way home. So many weeks and months were spent in going on through one twenty-four hour period after another. The shipping orders from the 14th came much sooner than I had dared hope, and now we are in the process of preparing to board the boat. It is all too wonderful and too dream-like to be real.

I hope that my letter concerning the search for an apartment has long since reached you. It looks as though we could possibly be ready to take one over shortly after the first of Feb. I hardly know how long it will take to get out of the Army after I get home, but I really don't think now that I will be a free man before the latter days of Jan. We will certainly want to spend a couple of weeks at Jamestown. As the time approaches, I am wondering if perhaps it would be wise to wait until the summer session to attend UT. It would perhaps be better to begin at Yale in the fall rather than in the summer, I hope that I can find some sort of a job for the intervening time which will build up our little reserve and keep the wolf from the door. If I collect the long-due travel money which should be able to bring home a sizable little sum in addition to my $300.00 mustering out pay. I have a couple of money orders in my pocket now, but I may as well carry them home rather than send them. I still have not heard that you received two money orders which I sent during the past six weeks.

I think that it would be wise for us to work on a little budget as soon as we get settled down, and try to follow it as closely as possible. In regard to a car which I suggested once before, there is another point in its favor: With a fluctuation in money values, a bank account will not always represent the same amount it does at the moment. Investments are sometimes wiser than large amounts of cash on hand. A car is an investment which we can always cash in. I think it likely that we will want and need one for some time, and the original purchase can always be turned in on the new one. I think that it is too bad that Dad sold the second house which he owned in Jamestown, along with a valuable lot in town. Both of these would have been worth far more at present, and the money which he received for them is doing little good in the bank. Of course, he put a great deal of it in to government bonds, which are drawing interest. I hope that we can hold on to our bonds, and collect on them at as late a time as possible. Probably our investment there will bring as much in returns as anything else that we could have. Perhaps in ten years we can use the money as a down payment on a new house of our own. (But really, Darling, I do not mean to imply that we will wait that long to have a home of our own.)

Well, it is almost time to close shop for the day. I have spent the day writing you, reading, and going through a clothing check. The day has passed quickly, and I can complain little. I do hope that this news reaches you before Christmas, for perhaps it will in a small way make Christmas Day the merrier for you.

Wherever I am on Christmas Day, I will be thinking of you, praying that once together again we will never no separation. Our joy should be full on the Day of our Lord's Birth, for He has surely blessed us in a multitude of ways. God bless you and keep you, My Dear.

I love you,
Bushy

Letter from Art to Dotty
Sonthofen, Germany
December 16, 1945 [644-645]
Sunday afternoon

My Dearest,

The sun sinks slowly into a crevice of the Alps to find a hiding place unto the morrow. The snow-capped peaks of the surrounding hills reflect the rays, and a moon almost full gazes casually from the

Eastern horizon. It is Sunday afternoon, but I find myself stuck in the RSO. There is nothing for me to do, but everything is in mass confusion. I am supposed to be here, and so here I am.

Yesterday my weekly stack of mail came in, and I was lucky enough to find three big letters from you. How lucky I am that I have a wife who writes both frequently and interestingly! These letters were written on the 28th and 29th of Nov., and the 1st of Dec. I must admit that I am slightly jealous of the Air Corps, especially when fellows like Dean are kicked out while on a furlough. Of course, I am very happy for Dean's sake. I think that I mentioned a long letter from Hargrave the other day. Heis in San Diego, and expects a discharge around the first of the year. I still can't figure out where he acquired the necessary points, but good for him. Bill intends to go back to school in either chemistry or electronics, and will probably get married to the Oregon gal along about the same time. Hope I can see him sometime after I return.

I agree with your optimism concerning readjustment for us, but I think we should consider nothing amiss should we find ourselves changed in one degree or another. I believe that there are no differences which frank and intelligent approaches cannot solve. I do believe that a minimum of church responsibilities for you will be of great help at least during our first month. By that time, we will better know just what our plans will be, and we can adjust our church program accordingly. I realize full well how difficult a break from all of your jobs will be, but I do think it will be necessary. (Remember "Dependable Dora")

It is too bad that you must relay upon dreams in my absence, but dreams can be pleasant. I hope to be able in a small way to make your dreams come true, my Darling, when I do return. When I see all of the confusion that goes on around here, I wonder just how long this process will take, but we are on ourway.

I think that in another letter I indicated that all of your Christmas packages had arrived. I received the four while still at Memmingen. I disposed of the food before leaving, because it was not convenient to carry all of it with me. I am holding on to the square, flat package which will be opened along with the other packages on Christmas morning. I do hope that all of my packages reached you before Christmas. I hope also that all of my letters eventually get there, for at least two contained money orders and others contained pictures.

In the stack of mail which came yesterday was a long letter from Dad—my first in many weeks. He admits now that he has been rather ill with kidney trouble, and is still not exactly well. The work with Selective Service seems to be winding up, and for that I am very glad. However, I hardly know what he will be able to do now, and I think that some sort of activity will be rather necessary for him. He and Mother have accumulated something of a nest egg, but we will nevertheless need to consider them in our plans, just as we must consider "Mom" and Daddy.

My mail also included a long letter from Tom Jones. He was supposed to have finished up onLong Island on the 15th—that was yesterday. Probably you have seen him—(hope Mary Ruth was there to meet him, and that he was properly impressed. I'll never be happy until I make a match out of those two. It seems to me that the match would be just about an ideal one.) I can't think that he is really serious about joining the regular navy, andremaining in the Service. I shall write him and tell him just what I think of anyone who decides to remain in the Service. As you know, his parents are located at 107 Aspen Lane, Oak Ridge, and we must visit them when I get home.

There is little that is new here, except that the confusion continues and that is old news. MacIntosh returned from England a couple ofdays ago, and I visited with him for a couple ofhours last night. He had a wonderful time at school, and I turned all shades of green as I listened to his stories of life there. He is seriously considering continued study in Far Eastern History with a professorship in mind. I think that the idea is an excellent one for him, and the field is certainly wide open. He has a good background for it with the nine months at Stanford. I have often thought of the subject as a sideline myself.

Almost my only recreation is ping pong, and Grimwood (PX and mail assistant from the 14th) and I play a little ever day. We went to church this morning. The sermon expounded the lessons in the first psalm, verse by verse. Today was very warm, and for the first time the sun shone most of the day. An acute water shortage in this area should be relieved by all of this snow which is melting rapidly. For the first time in two or three weeks the roads are clear of ice. The remaining snow is wonderful for skiing, but I refuse to be tempted.

Most ofthe fellows spend the time doing "bunk fatigue", interrupted only by two or perhaps three meals per day. These days are spent as though time was a vacuum: it is a process of waiting, waiting, waiting. There is no library, and few books. One cannot read all of the time, and few men feel like writing very much now.

Much later

Had to work late and I do mean late. Just time to wish you a fond good night and to say, with all of my heart,
I love you
Bushy

Letter from Art to Dotty
Sonthofen, Germany
December 18, 1945 [646-648]

Dearest,
Our trucking express came through late last night, and I was happy to find that I had two healthy letters written on the 2nd and 4th of Dec. Rather than going through the devious routes of Army channels, Devers is holding our mail and sending down as often as he can find the means. Usually some of the drivers can stop in Memmingen on their way to Augsburg. I take the mail on their return and see that it gets to the men in the 302nd.

The first letter brought the article and pictures of the Choral Group. Darling, of the fact of your wonderful voice there is no question, but I must admit that I never knew you were in possession of such a broad smile. Glad to note that your teeth are in perfect shape as usual. Seriously, I was happy to see such a good picture, and you so happy. I can only surmise that your dreams must have been of Van Johnson on the night before. Speaking further of music, I must admit that I am slightly envious when I read of the concerts at Maryville, but I hope that soon we will share them together. I really am not envious; I am terribly glad that you can attend.

So you really thought I went to England. Well, that is one of the reasons I do not like to tell you of things that are coming until they come. Everything was all set for that trip until forty-eight hours before I was scheduled to leave. Here the latest rumor this morning is that further delays have pushed our shipping date up again. According to this rumor we are not supposed to leave here until Jan. 2, whereas originally we were scheduled to sail on that date. Knowing the Army, I can hardly hope to leave even on this new date. As I mentioned before, I expect three or four delays at least.

No, I guess that I forgot to mention the promotion, which really doesn't amount to very much. The increase of about $15.00 per month will help out, although not for long. This, by the way, was one of the last things that Capt. Garner did for me. For some reason, the rating was made in one of the first groups that went in. He kept riding the S-1

Office even as he was getting ready to leave. If the rating had not been made at that time, I would probably never have received anything. I am still lucky.

Among all of the other stories which pass around, one has continued long enough to indicate some degree of authenticity. It seems that Personnel discovered that some of the men reporting here had been given an extra point or two by their old outfit. That is, if a man had 53 or 54 points, he was given the extra boost needed to get him into the 94th Div. Now it seems that all records will be carefully checked. Some of us received only 7 points after VJ Day, until the revised score gave everyone a flat 8. When this point-change is noted by Personnel, a few questions may begin to fly. Whether or not my ten points will be removed at this time remains to be seen. If they to decide to take them off..... Another little encouraging note to add to the news: Three hundred men in the regiment are reported to have a skin infection, called "scabies". If this number cannot be cured quickly, our shipment could possibly be postponed. Can you understand why I expect delays? Darling, I do not mean to discourage you; but I do want you to realize that, while there is reason to rejoice at the recent turn of events, there is also reason to expect discouragement and delay.

I was glad to get your slant on strikes. I think you know the general view which we over here have taken toward strikes, especially during combat. I have tried to follow the general trend and the events leading up the [to] these strikes, but it is hard to do this with the inadequate news coverage which we have over here. A few of these are certainly due to the convulsive pangs of a nation attempting to adjust to peace-time living. Others are caused by basic differences between labor and management. We still have a great deal to learn.

I should like to clarify the boxes which I have sent home if it is possible to do so. I fear that I may have forgotten one or two. I sent one wooden box to Mother which contained my field glasses and presents for you and for Mary Ruth. I sent another package direct to you with a Christmas present enclosed. Shortly before I left Memmingen, I sent my portable typewriter in a wooden box and my skiis in another. I also left two packages for Devers to mail containing for the most part odds and ends, letters, etc. I left the letters too long and did not get to sort them as I want to do later. Gee, I forgot another big package which I sent insured about two weeks before I left. This included my leather jacket, a pair of opera glasses for you, and other items, including my cathedral prints of Germany. I believe that that takes care of all the packages, and I only hope now that they arrive.

Well, now I recall two other things which I sent. One was an envelope containing some enlargements of Paris pictures, and the other was a much larger envelope with ....well, I let you find out when it comes. Both of these came first class, and should not take too many weeks to get there.

Sunday was a beautiful day, as I think I described in my letter on Sunday. Yesterday the sun continued to shine, and all night long I could hear the snow melting on the roof. Now and then a great hunk of snow would begin to slide down the roof and pour down on the ground. There is still a great deal of snow on the ground, but it is melting fast. The mountains are still covered, and they reflect the bright rays of the sun.

Tuesday night

We are very busy working on requisitions for clothing, and I had to come back after supper for a little. Outside, the full moon shines on the surrounding snow-capped peaks. The sight is awe-inspiring and a deep sense of longing overwhelms me as I guess at the wondorous night. I do not dare allow myself to enjoy the full beauty of this night, for my morale could not stand it. Need I say that I miss you terribly, and long with an intense longing to be with you.

Forgive me if I do not write with as much regularity as formerly. Last night I was expecting the two letters which I knew were on their way. I did not get them until about ten o'clock, and I hardly had time to start writing then. I really prefer to write on the typewriter if and when I can, even though it does take all day to write one letter to you. I began this early this morning, and was only able to write a little at a time. Perhaps it would be wise for you to write a couple of letters a week just to let me know that everything is all right. If by chance I did not leave on schedule I would have your mail to boost my morale. Better use my old address at Sv. Co. 14th, for I will be able to let them know when I move from here.

I say goodnight with the prayer on my lips that before many moons come again we will [be] watching them together. I would say again and again

I love you,
Bushy

Darling,

On Tuesday I thought that I was on my way to Augsburg, when I found that one of the fellows from the 14th was making a run by truck. Rather than leaving without permission, which I could easily have done, I went to the First Sgt. and asked for a pass. There were many details and the Sgt. told me that he could not spare anyone. That was that! However, on Wednesday I found that someone had to go to Augsburg on official business to take the requisitions over which we had labored. No one wanted to go the hundred miles and stay overnight, and so I volunteered, and thereby hangs a tale.

We left in a convoy about two in the afternoon. Before we were well on our way, the convoy had scattered like a group of children turned loose from school. After passing through Kempten, we took the wrong road; and during the remainder of the afternoon we wandered over most of the back roads in Bavaria. We ended up in the French territory, and it was not until five o'clock that we reached Memmingen. (The run usually requires less than an hour and a half.) I stopped in the Orderly Room just long enough to say a hurried hello, and call Ted to tell him that I was on my way. I wish that you could have seen the moon which was shinning down. The country side was covered with snow, and the full moon was so bright that it actually glared in our eyes. We arrived about eight o'clock in Augsburg, and I was soon in the 5th Inf. CP.

As usual, Ted and I brought our books up to date on all of the old Maryville gossip. Before we realized the time, it was midnight and time to get some sleep. I was able to return Ted's fountain pen which I had inadvertently slipped in my pocket when I was there on Thanksgiving.

One thing which I did learn concerns the DP camp at Landsberg, which is being guarded by the 5th Inf. GI's. The Camp contains a number of Jewish people, and has received a great deal of publicity during the past few weeks. According to the <u>Stars and Stripes</u>, the conditions there have been "worse than a German concentration camp". A number of investigations have been made, and the picture painted has been very black. Ted has been handling a number of the papers and reports on the camp, and he avows that the <u>Stars and Stripes</u> version has been utterly false in many cases. He says that the camp receives milk for everyone and rations just about as good as those which the GIs receive. Ted says that the people there have made one complaint after another, and have received all sorts of concessions. They have all of the fuel that they can use, and their quarters are as good as those which the soldiers have. The major in charge of the camp was Jewish, as was the UNRRA director and the chief of the Military Gov't there. It seems that people can take advantage of a good thing and cause a great deal of trouble. Ted is not inclined to be anti-semetic, but he certainly thinks that the Jews in this instance are at fault.

Thursday morning I took my papers to 94th Div. Hqs. There I found that other sets of papers had to go to scattered points all over town. An officer asked if I could drive a jeep, and when I said yes he turned his over to me to finish up the work. I spent the morning dashing all over the city, and held up the ration convoy a half hour before I could finish up everything. We had a long trip back, but I returned to find a big stack of mail, and my morale was boosted again.

Before I begin with that I must tell you about a little incident which occurred in Memmingen. I rushed in the Orderly Room and hurriedly called Ted before he left for chow. While I was waiting on the phone, Chaplain Webb walked in. By the happiest turn of events, he had just returned from Ulm where he had been able to get for me.......you'll never guess. That's right, a chess set!!!!! It is a handcarved set which is really very, very nice. He could not give it to me yet for the shop in Ulm wants to use if for a model for another set. However, as soon as the second set is made, the lady there will make a box for it, along with a leather board, and send it to me. I was thrilled just to see the set, and I know that you will be when you see it. We will have to learn to play chess with some degree of proficiency now.

Darling, the pictures are wonderful! I received the letter with the five pictures and I have been showing them to almost everyone. One of my friends saw the two of you just a few minutes ago, and told me that you look like one of the movie stars. I suppose he intended the remark as a compliment, but I could hardly agree. I STILL HAVEN'T SEEN A MOVIE STAR THAT COMPARES WITH YOU, MY LOVE! So there too now! I love you, just in case you had wondered during the last few paragraphs. I will be very happy to receive any other pictures which you have, but thanks a million for those which you did send.

Friday Night

Ted tells me of a new pass which is opening up next week. This one will be to Rome, Italy. Crossing Switzerland, the party stops for about two and a half days in southern Switzerland, and then goes on for a day in Milan. From there south to Rome for four or five days. The trips has the advantage of covering both Switzerland and Rome, and should be thoroughly worth while. Ted says that he intends to hold out for that when his turn comes up again. At the present he is holding down two men's work, and is doing a great deal. It is certainly too bad that he took so long to work up in that office for I am sure that he is an efficient worker. I believe that both he and I lack a certain aggressive drive which helps tremendously in the Army.

Oh joy! I received a pile of letters from you. Two separate groups seem to have arrived for the first three were written on the 23, 25th, and the 27th, of Nov., and the next three were written on the 5th, 6th, and 7th of Dec. In two of them you told me much more about Mom's situation, and I must hasten to write her again. I had not realized before just how serious the situation was, and I am terribly sorry. Do insist that she continue the treatments. I certainly hope that by the time you receive this she will be much improved.

I enjoyed hearing about your Sunday School experience, and wish that I could have been behind a curtain listening to your answers. How I miss the discussions which we used to have, and which we shall have again. I need the stimulation which those discussions brought to my mind, for heaven knows I have little enough that is stimulating to real thought here. I never realized just how much my Bible reading could mean under such circumstances, and yet I fear that I do not read so much or so often as I should. I long for the time when we will be able to read and discuss our reading with regularity.

Since hearing about Flo's trailer, I have tried to do a bit of speculating. To buy a trailer we would naturally have to have a car. The two would cost about $1500.00. We could perhaps count on using the trailer for two years at any rate, perhaps longer. Depreciation on the trailer would amount to about ten percent per annum. Therefore at the end of two years, the trailer would probably be worth about $800.00, based on an initial price of $1,000.00. Parking space would probably amount to about $10.00 per month, or roughly $250.00 during the two year period. Electricity and water would probably amount to about $10.00 per month or another $250.00. Adding to this $150.00 for upkeep, minor repairs, etc. we have a total of about $850.00 for two years use of a trailer, and this does not figure in the depreciation on the car, which we might own anyway.

On the other side of the picture, rent during that period would amount to roughly $1,000.00, based on a monthly average of about $40.00. Travel back and forth would amount to about $300.00 based on an estimation of at least four trips from Conn. to Tenn. Very likely there would be more than this. (I was counting that as two round trips.) Actually, I think that at least $500.00 should be allowed for travel as against about $150.00 for the same trips by auto.

These estimates are based on hurried thought, and are probably off by a good bit. However, they indicate to me that the monetary margin in favor of a trailer amounts to something like $400.00 to $500.00. The questions of convenience, practicality, etc. are entirely different. Until the terrific housing shortage is alleviated, a trailer would certainly save many headaches brought about by searching for apartments. Living space would, of course, be very small; and we would perhaps be able to count on certain additions to our family during that two year period. Nicht wahr? Wahr! We shall discuss this more at length, for the idea certainly is worth considering.

Had one of those fast letters from Harriet this week. She speaks of other letters, but I am afraid that they never arrived. She also accuses you of telling her nothing about my activities, and so I guess that I will have to write a long letter bringing her up to date on my general situation. Will try to do that right away. She asks about signs of a <u>Sat. Revue of Lit.</u>, but this is the first that I have heard of it. I will certainly be happy to get this subscription, for it is a swell magazine. Gee, I never did get around to sending that gal a Christmas present. Will try to find something, and get it to her even though it be late.

A number of fellows with whom I have talked in the last few days were fighting for their lives in the Battle of the Bulge just one year ago tonight, and I realize just how lucky we were, My Love. To think that we had been in the war for a year and a half before I went into uniform, and that I did not come over seas until the war was almost won. The fifty or sixty days during which I saw combat were nothing in comparison to the long, weary, soul-searing months in Africa, Sicly, Italy, France, and the Low Countries. As hard as these months of separation have been, we must realize that actually we have many things for which to be a thankful.

By the way, I had a long letter from Mother in which she tells of receiving three letters from me within a twenty-four hour period. Their mail has been held up a great deal; and, since I do not write to them more than two or perhaps three times per week, delays effect them even more than you. I hope that you can make up for this, Darling, but [by] dropping them a note now and then. Mother also heard about the 71st coming home in Dec., but that is still an incorrect report. Three fellows who had just reported in to the office with their discharge papers had been in German prison camps for three, eight, and ten months. What an ordeal that must have been!

More delays are on the horizon for me here as I had expected. No one knows when we will leave this area, and so do not be surprised at anything which may come. During the past couple of days there have been confused reports concerning the checking of our service records. Some of the fellows are losing a point for the three week furlough which they received after being sworn into the Army. I think that that is the limit! Some outfits have been very lenient at this point in the game, and yet others are just the opposite. One fellow that came down with me was cut from 59 to 54 due to a miscount in battle stars. What a mess this Army can make of things at times. At any rate, Darling, do not be surprised or too disappointed at anything which may come during the next few days. I do hope the news of my transfer to the 94th came before Christmas.

Christmas will not be Christmas for me this year, My Love. I will celebrate it as the birthday of our Lord, but the added meaning which comes from the presence of those most dear will be lost. We will know deep, down within our hearts that for us this will be our last Christmas apart. May God continue to bless and strengthen the eternal bond of
Our Love,
Bushy
PS. Enclosed is MO for $40.00

Letter from Art to Dotty
Sonthofen, Germany
December 22, 1945 (Sat) [655-656]

My Darling,

What a wonderful time to write my lovely wife! I just walked into the RSO to find no one here. The very large room is filled with the Christmas Rations for theRegiment, and I cannot understand why it should be left open as it is. I see cases of turkey, beef, fruits, vegetables, cases of juice, great bags of bread, etc. etc. etc. Rather than sending the usual four or five trucks for rations this time, we sent eleven. I am sure that we will not go hungry on Christmas Day.

Darling, you are wonderful, and I love you a very great deal. I was swept off my feet with the news of your music lessons, and I am thrilled to think that you had your chance for a solo at the concert. Would that I could have been there to have heard unobserved. I am terribly happy to think that you have gone ahead to do that which you have wanted to do for so long, and I can hardly wait to hear your voice again. However, I feel that you will hardly be able to put up with an unmusical body like me. You'll probably be doing light opera next and then....well, who knows? Dearest, I am only kidding a bit, but I am so happy that you are able to develop your musical ability. I can hardly wait to open that one certain package now, and hear for myself your lovely voice.

Tonight I attended a Bible class conducted by the chaplain here (who happens to be from Jackson, Tenn.), and I enjoyed the discussion. In the past couple of days I have had much pleasure from reading an introduction to the works of Plato, and I hope to continue with my reading into the works themselves. For a very long time I have felt a serious gap in my studies since I have never made any study whatsoever of the classics. I hope that I can rectify this situation at the earliest opportunity.

Such quotations as the following excite me as though I were on the threshold of a fascinating adventure—which, indeed, I am: In reference to Plato, the following, "Himself professing no knowledge at all, he yet was profoundly convinced that knowledge was possible, a knowledge at least of one's own soul, one's own mind, and genuine good and evil." And again, "Knowledge of good and evil, knowledge of that part of one's self, the soul, which alone can measure, estimate, choose, is the central wisdom, and wisdom is the essential virtue of which all the virtues turn out to be simply special instances of parts."

My mind has been inclined to wander during the past months, and I have failed to stimulate it with good reading. I have gone little further than Time, and H. G. Wells, and actually these are not sufficient to exercise the mind properly. I quaver with anticipation when I think of burrowing deep into my literature again and meeting the minds of such figures as Emerson, Shakespeare, Wordsworth, and all of the others. I must soak myself in many a literary bath before I absorb even a few of the facts and principles so long removed from my thinking.

There is no news that is particularly good here. Points are still being tossed in and out with little regard for the confusion and uncertainty that this process can cause. Many a fellow tonight is wondering whether or not one point will mean the difference of staying or leaving in the next few days. I wonder how and when this uncertainty, this confusion will end. Darling, I hope that we can fortify ourselves against any delays that may arise, and that we may rest in faith that "even the weariest river winds somewhere safe to sea".

Your letter written on the 9th came today to tell me of the wonderful news of your voice lessons and singing. All of the mail seems to be coming through with a bit more regularity, and I certainly hope that mine is doing the same. I sent two or three enlargements to Ted at the same time I sent a few to you. That was two weeks ago and he has not yet received them. All they had to do was to go from Memmingen to the APO in Augsburg, and then across the street to Ted's office. What a system!

I must go over and take a shower tonight, but will try to write a longer letter tomorrow. Last night I wrote five pages like this and also sent a money order for $40.00. This is the third money order in recent weeks and I have not heard that any were received.

Whether you hear me say so or not, My Love, know that every day I love you with a deeper and more eternal love. I long to be with you for I am

Thine own,
Bushy

P.S. Continue to write to Sv. Co. 14th for Devers can always forward my mail from there.

* Letter from Art to Dotty
Memmingen, Germany
December 25, 1945 [656-657]
Christmas Day

My Dearest Darling,

As I came out of the dining hall today, the snow began to fall, and now, an hour later, the ground is white. The snow falls steadily; across the street I see the face of a small baby pressed against the window pane. The atmosphere is truly that of Christmas in Bavaria, and I sit by the radiator in Baker Wallace's room, alone.

Christmas Eve began for me in circumstances which were hardly in keeping with the season. As darkness rolled in across the landscape, I stood at a crossroad twenty miles outside of Memmingen. The cold creeped through the protective covering of my overcoat, a flight of crows circled in a great circle over my head, traffic seemed to have ceased altogether. I smiled ironically at myself that I should be spending Christmas Eve in the heart of Bavaria, alone, cold, at the crossroads of no where, wondering if and when a car would come my way.

By seven o'clock I was in Memmingen, and had eaten a bit of supper. In order to break into the true spirit of the season, I went around to wish a few of the fellows Merry Christmas. I had spent Monday night with Baker Wallace, and now I asked again if I might sleep in the empty bed in his room. In friendly fashion he invited me to help him open his Christmas packages. We had great fun opening one after another, and I began to feel a bit more that it was really Christmas Eve after all.

A short time later I called Chaplain Webb to wish him a Merry Christmas, and he kindly invited me over to his office. I did not know the situation, but I joined Alsup and Graham (assistants), and we rode over in the jeep. A happy surprise awaited me for we were invited to join with a German family in celebrating their Christmas Eve. Father Fahy (the Catholic Chaplain) and Chaplain Webb have their offices in a private home, and it was here that we were invited. A beautiful tree stood in the corner of the room, and small candles provided a soft glow. When we arrived the presents had been opened and were placed on the table for everyone to see. (I believe that it is the custom in Germany to open the Christmas gifts on Christmas Eve rather than on Christmas Morning. In fact, we used to do this at home sometimes.) I was happily surprised to find the wide variety of gifts which were at hand, even though conditions are certainly not favorable for obtaining nice gifts this year. The two small girls had their little dolls, little pocket books; the older boy, of about fourteen, had a new razor, which as yet was of no practical use, and a toilet kit which even had a zipper. Father too had received a toilet kit; the older girls, leather belts; grandmother, a large shipping bag (which would probably stand in many a long line). For Chaplain Webb there was a lovely set of handcarved bookends; and for Alsup, a book of music. Of course, they had not expected Graham and myself and so there was nothing for us. In return, Alsup and Chaplain Webb had brought a box of candy, chewing gum, soap, and a pack of cigarettes; and these were passed out in an appropriate manner. Two or three in the family understood a little English, and we understood a little German. We sang a few Christmas songs, ate Christmas cookies, and spent the remainder of the evening admiring the array of gifts before us. For me it was a most unexpected pleasure to be spending Christmas Eve, which had begun in a desolate spot on the highway, amid the warm and friendly surroundings of a German home and a German family.

Chaplain Webb had learned that one of the Red Cross girls in town was ill, and so we gallantly rode around to their quarters and favored them with a couple of carols. The evening was really beginning to feel like Christmas. From there we rode on to Chaplain Webb's quarters and attempted to find a recorder. I wanted so much to hear the wonderful records which I found in my stocking, but no recorder could we find. I had a chance to look again at my chess set, and I felt like a little boy with a new toy. Chaplain Webb suggested that we play a short game, but I countered with the suggestion that he read to us the Christmas story. This he did, followed by a prayer. After this we broke into discussion of various religious points of prayer view, and soon it was eleven o'clock. I had remarked earlier in the evening that I missed so much at least selections from the Messiah. I had not been in my room ten minutes when a choral group from Heidleberg began to sing a group of numbersfrom the Messiah. I sat on the edge of my bed, in prayerful silence that my Christmas Eve had been so pleasant under such adverse conditions. Across the abyss of time and space, I joined with you in thankful prayer for Christmas, 1945.

I have much, much more to say, My Love. The letter which I had planned is a very long one, but time slips apace and even now Alsup should be here to take me back to Sonthofen. Rather than finish this tonight down there, I shall attempt to get it in the mail here, for it will go out at least two days faster. I shall finish the second portion of the letter tonight, when I will no doubt have many more things to tell you.

I have tried to picture only the brighter side of this Christmas Season here in Bavaria. I think it not wise to attempt to describe the intense longing which I feel deep down in my heart for you at this time. With all my heart I hope and pray that your Christmas has been a very marry one, knowing as you do that this interminable separation will be our last. The years ahead will be the dearer to us that we have spent these months, these seeming years, apart. May God give us patience and understanding; may He continue to bless the eternal holiness of
Our Love,
Bushy

Letter from Art to Dotty
Sonthofen, Germany
December 26, 1945 [658-660]

Darling,
I devoted my letter yesterday to the topic of Christmas Eve and Christmas Day, but I shall go back now and attempt to recount the events which led up to my spending the early hours of Christmas Eve on the open road, waiting and hoping that a car would come along to pick me up.

Late Sunday afternoon I found that passes were being given, and without further ado I wrote out a pass for myself and secured the proper signature. With a bit of luck I found that ne [one] of the fellows was going to Memmingen by truck, and I loaded on. By eight o'clock we were in Service Co. and I spent the evening talking with the boys. I was

Christmas Service, Memmingen, December 25, 1945

able to sleep in an empty bed in Baker Wallace's room, and on Monday morning I arose early in order to catch the same truck on which I rode the night before on to Augsburg. The eastern sky had been splashed with color as the forward rays of aurora announced the fact that dawn was near. We had a load of men with us heading in all directions, and I suppose that by nightfall these GIs were scattered throughout southern Bavaria.

My plan had been to spend the reminder of the day with Ted, eat Christmas dinner with him, and then return to Sonthofen Tuesday afternoon. However, these plans were turned awry when I found that Ted had secured a jeep a couple of days before and had gone to Patton's funeral. No one knew when he would be back, and I suspected that he might be spending Christmas with Pratt up north near Kasel. After dinner I decided that it would be of no use to wait and expect his early

Taken on the way back from Heidelberg
when we went to Patton's funeral. [Dec. 26, 1945 letter]

return, and so I began the trip back to Memmingen. I left Augsburg
about 1:30 and I did not arrive in Memmingen until 6:30. The
beginning of this Christmas Eve I described in my letter yesterday.

I arose at a late hour on Christmas morning, but in time to get to
Church Services at 11:00. The Services were very nice as conducted by
Chaplain Webb, and I shall enclose a program. After a big dinner, I
retired to the room to write you until time came for me to leave. Alsup,
the Chaplain's assistant, brought me back in the jeep; and I was back in
Sonthofen Manor by six last night. Up until that time I had been unable
to take full advantage of one of the most important presents which I
have ever received. Darling, the record of your voice was the nicest and
most thoughtful gift that you could have sent to me. You will never
know what a thrill it was last night when I found a machine in the
Public Address room, and played the record. I was pleasantly shocked
to find such an improvement in your voice, for I truthfully could hardly
recognize it at first. The deep quality, the tone, the range,—all, My
Dear, have improved remarkably. I was thrilled beyond words, and I
can hardly wait to return to hear you sing to me. I shall carry the record

with me, and treasure it, and play it at every opportunity. Thank you, Darling, from the bottom of my heart. I love you.

Wednesday Night

I think that you are well aware, My Love, of the uncertainty which one finds in the Army. I suppose that our first real experience came to us as we tried to plan for our wedding and the confusion of ASTP helped not at all. It has followed me, as it has followed every individual, and it will continue to follow me throughout my Army career. There are errors—human and in human—which come along, and we can do nothing whatsoever about them. The redeployment problem has brought delays and disappointments in increasing numbers, and so it is not surprising that we should encounter some of these. I have tried to prepare both of our minds for any eventuality, and I hope that I have succeeded in at least some small way. The fateful news which has been pending for so long has at last come, and I have delayed the final word until the final ray of hope flickered and died. The final word came tonight concerning my ERC points, and I am to leave the 94th on Friday.

One of the most difficult jobs that I have ever done in my life was to write this news, Darling. I have [been] suspect for several days that this would be the outcome, but I have delayed writing until I knew that there was no alternative. The consoling element for me is that you, My Love, have a depth of faith and understanding that can bridge such disappointments. I rely upon that fact as I write in order that I may feel the stronger. I think that the delay will not be long, and will actually amount to only a few weeks. We have waited for low these many months, and we can surely be patient for a very few weeks longer.

I found tonight while attending the Bible class that all men with 54 points and below (of which there are about 200 now with the newcount) are to ship to the 66th Regt. (which is the third Regt. in the 71st Div.) on Friday. I also found that I could probably have my orders changed to send me to the 14th if I could get on the ball and put a request in thru the proper channels. I called Devers at Sv. Co. and talked also with Baker Wallace in a three way conversation. They promised to do what they could tomorrow for me, and suggested that I call Capt. Grace tonight. Capt. Grace is the S-4 or Regt. Supply Officer for the 14th and has wanted to get me in the RSO for a long time. I did get to talk with him after some delay and he seemed delighted to do whatever he could for me. He will call the Personnel Officer here tomorrow morning, and I will also go over to see what I can do about the situation. Many things will be better if I can get back into the 14th in Sv. Co.

In the first place, I will be entitled to the ten points back should I return to the 14th. Now whether or not I would be able to ship to another outfit and come home with the 55 points on my record again remains the $64 question. However, there are definite possibilities along that line. In the second place, I shall insist on taking a pass either to England or to Rome when I return. I believe that I can surely swing one this time, for goodness knows I have been knocked out of two before. The third prospect is that I feel sure that I can obtain a rating in the RSO, and though that means very little it will be some small consolation. To be with old friends such as Chaplain Webb, Bill Myers, Devers, Wallace, etc. will help boost my morale, and it is ironical to note that again Ted and I will be in the same outfit. I am almost beginning to feel superstitious about our connection.

Well, Darling, the hour is late and I must leave the office and retire shortly. I have delayed this letter as long as possible, but I do know that you will be brave in the face of this new disappointment. Our deep and abiding love has roots so deeply embedded that nothing can shake the foundations of our faith and affection. No matter what delays or disappointments we know, we will also know that God has blessed us in a multitude of ways and he will surely continue to bless the glory and wonder of

Our Love,
Bushy

Letter from Art to Dotty
Sonthofen, Germany
December 27, 1945 [661-662]

Dearest,

The snow which made the world so white on Christmas day is fast melting under the steady beat of a downpour of rain. The night is altogether miserable and depressing and I am glad that I am not on the move tonight. Tomorrow morning at eight o'clock about two hundred of us leave Sonthofen and to go to the 66th Regt. at Garmisch. I look forward to seeing the famous resort center, and hope that I will be able to visit Oberammergau which is located nearby. A large sport center has been developed at Garmisch as a GI Rest Center, and I think that one of the Red Circle papers which I sent had pictures of the location there.

As I wrote last night, I had hoped to be able to go directly from here to the 14th. However, this morning I found that I would have to go on to the 66th, and then sweat out a transfer from there. I think that it can be arranged, but it may take time. I called Sv. Co. today and talked with Findlay. He told me that both he and the company commander had gone to the Personnel Officer in an attempt to get me back. If they work on it, in addition to the Regimental Supply Officer, perhaps something can be done. I must admit that I am a bit flattered that I should be "wanted" for a change, but I should not be proud. After all, there is a desperate need for anyone who can punch a typewriter, and I should take no credit for that. We shall see what we shall see, but I hope it will not be too long before something definite is known.

Again tonight I attended the Bible Study Class and enjoyed the discussion. I hope that I can find another group wherever I land that will provide such stimulation, for I feel the definite need for it. Harriet wrote a few days ago of <u>Sat. Revue of Lit.</u> which is supposedly on the way to me. I suppose that it is a subscription, and if so I certainly appreciate it a great deal. My magazines are my constant companions, and I read them avidly. The <u>Sat. Revue</u> is a very excellent magazine, and I shall find much of interest between its covers.

By the way, I answered Harriet's letter today, and I also wrote Mary Ruth. Not bad for one day to get letters written to three sisters. What wonderful sisters they are too—especially one that I know rather well. Love you, Honey! I wrote Pratt, Schwarzwalder, Root, and perhaps one or two others to address future letters to 607. However, I shall try to drop them a card explaining my new situation. As I think that I have indicated in other letters, you may as well continue to write to Sv. Co. 14th until I find out definitely where I will be. There seems to be as good a chance as any that I will get back there, and if I do not the boys will be glad to forward my mail until the whole affair is cleared up.

Later

I just spent the last forty-five minutes talking to Devers and then to Ted. Nothing new with Devers concerning the progress of S-4 (Supply Officer) in getting me transferred. Of course, it is a bit early to expect anything. I shall see what I can do when I get to the 66th tomorrow. Nothing much new with Ted either. He had a four hundred mile trip to Heidleberg, and commented that it was hardly worth it. He did return to Augsburg on Christmas Eve, but I suppose it is just as well that I did not wait. By the way, the first rumor that I have heard that in any way

Sonthofen Manor in Bavaria, Germany.
The Flag is at half mast in honor of Gen. Patton
whose funeral was held at Heidelburg a few days before.

indicates the announcement in the States concerning the 71st, was one which Ted has heard that the 71st would be coming home in March. That seems a long time away. Devers tells me that I have two or three letters, one from you postmarked about the 14th and one from Mom postmarked about the 13th. I will be unable to get these however until I either return to Memmingen or he sends them to me. I hope that I can pick them up personally. I find that a couple of days delay in the mail help not at all to boost my morale, but it is at least nice to know that I have letters waiting somewhere.

The hour is late, and I must take a bath and sleep a little. Both sleeping and waking I think of you, My Dear. May God grant us patience that we may await that happy day when we will be re-united in
Our Love,
Bushy
P.S. I enclose a couple of pictures which one of my old squad mates in "K" Co gave me today.

Darling,

For the same reason that I am stuck here until Wednesday, this letter will not go out, but I must at least begin to recount the events of the past three days or I will never catch up.

As I wrote on Thursday, I was scheduled to leave Sonthofen eight o'clock Friday morning. However, there was the usual delay and our trucks began to move at two o'clock in the afternoon. The trip to Garmisch was long and for the most part seemed up hill. We moved north to Kempten and thence to Fussen and finally Garmisch. The landscape was increasingly beautiful as we penetrated deeper and into the Alps. We passed more than one vast mountain lake tucked between high ridges and peaks, and outside Fussen we passed one of the famous castles built by "Mad King Ludwig" of Bavaria.

Later

When we finally arrived at the Regt. Hdq. of the 66th in Garmisch we were assigned to various companies for the night. My name was the first of the two hundred called, and I was told that the order was a mistake and that I should have gone to the 14th (What a time to tell me!) I was told further that I would return to Memmingen on Sat. I spent the night with Cannon Co. (where Wiche, Oelbaum & Okarski— Stanford boys had been. They have all shipped out to other outfits over here.) Sat. morning I spent most of the day waiting to be sent back to the 14th. Finally, at long last, I was told that there would be no transportation over the holidays. I could find a room at the Leone Center Hotel and remain in Garmisch until Wednesday. Since I had long wanted to visit here, I made no serious objection to this plan. First of all, I took in my first hockey game at the Olympic Ice Stadium. The game was exciting and often a bit thrilling.

In the evening I saw "Paris Under-Ground" and spent the remainder of the evening in a small library which is located here.

I find that Garmisch has been untouched by the physical wreckage of war and it seems to exist here in the Alps in a world apart. In 1936 the Olympics were held here and there was an Americanized influence even before the GIs came. I have seen no town in Europe with so many facilities for entertainment (excepting, of course, Paris).

Sunday morning I attended a comfortably filled Lutheran Church house where GI's and a few civilians were led in worship by an Army

Chaplain. My Sunday afternoon was spent in reading at the library—reading <u>Best Plays of 1943-44</u>, and I attempted to jot down short reviews for those which I read. Sunday evening I attended the Olympic Stadium again—this time to see a very excellent skating exhibition featuring a couple of World's Champion skaters along with other skating artists both civilian and GI.

Memmingen, Germany

Jan. 2, 1946

My Dearest Heart,

I put this paper in the machine almost two hours ago, and just now am I able to go ahead with the letter. Our lights went out as I was beginning and I was unable to do anything. Since it is so late, and since I have already fallen asleep once, I must ofnecessity make this letter short. I shall leave until tomorrow a continuation of the description of my vacation at Garmisch. Sufficient to say at the moment, that I left there this morning, rode the 90 or so miles to Augsburg, saw Ted for five minutes, and returned the 60 mile trip to Memmingen.

One of the principle reasons that I did not stay in Augsburg for the night was the fact that I had had no letter from you in a week and a half, and I knew that letters awaited me. I was very anxious to get the latest news from you. Darling, I do love to get your letters! The two that awaited me were written on the 7th and 14th, afull week apart. Glad to hear that you were able to see the two Parisian girls and to know that they came through for the bribe which I gave them to build me up with my wife.

There are other things which I shall discuss in your letter, but too these things must wait. Regarding my situation here, I can only say that I live in a state of suspended animation. I shall go to Personnel tomorrow and discuss my point situation with the Pers. Officer. I seriously wonder if it would be wise to even try to regain the ten points for I would in all likelihood be tossed around in another outfit and probably not get back to the 14th the next time. We shall see. There seems to be some confusion at the moment as to what I shall do, whether Orderly Room (since Devers will soon leave with 52 points) or RSO. I do not wish to return again to the work in the Orderly Room unless I have some definite promises beforehand. Of course, I may have very little to say about the matter, since I am still in theArmy.

Our mail is still far behind as attested by the fact that I have received only two letters from you in ten days. A letter from Mother, or rather a note on a Christmas Card, mailed on the 17th says that have received my letter concerning shipment to the 94th. I still dread to think of the way in which the later news of my shipment out again was received.

I have four rolls of film (48 pictures) which I must try to get developed as soon as possible. Some of these were taken at Oberstdorf when I was there, and the last were taken inOberammagau of the Passion Play House today. I have other snaps still which I bought from Chaplain Webb, and these too I will try to send along in my letters. I sent a couple of enlargements to Ted almost a month ago, and these he has never received. I trust that the large pictures which I sent you met with better luck.

I have a very great deal to write, My Love, but I must wash up, shave, and sleep. My eyes droop even now, but I am aware, whether sleeping or awake, that I love you with all of my heart. God grant us patience that we may better endure the separation which impairs the complete fulfillment of

Our Love,
Bushy

14 degrees below ZERO on top of the Zugspitz, Dec. 31, 1945

Valley of Garmisch, Obevamuzgan begone near edge of mountains, taken
from atop Zugspitz, highest park in Germany 1.1.46

Morning Dawns in Garmisch Parterkirchen

Garmisch, a street cleaner.

Mountain around Garmisch early morning, 12.28.45

1945 BNatalenky, Oberstdorf Germany

1946

Dear Dorothy:

I began the new year by first going to the Dentist to get some much needed work done, and second by trying to get some delayed writing done. I fully intended to write you last week, but just after the holidays we were crowded with fellows coming in to report, I didn't have any time in the office which I could call my own, and there is always so much work when I get home.

We received your good letter and today came the card telling the best news of all. How long those 3 or possibly 4 weeks will seem, but one by one they will go by. It seems like a dream too good to be true that after five long years, the one GI we're most interested in will have done his part and will be home to stay. Can you believe it?

The Suit will be put in mail tomorrow and we hope it will arrive O.K. You didn't say which one to send, and I am sending the heaviest one which seems most suitable for the kind of weather we are having here at present. We have had the coldest weather that we've had in a long time—also the deepest snow. The cars just slip and slide all over the highway. There have been two wrecks between here (home) and the church.

Your Xmas program at the church sounded awfully interesting, and I can imagine what a job it was to put it over. You must have worked real hard.

We had special Xmas music and a Xmas sermon on Sunday morning, and a pageant Sun. evening with music of course. The church was never so impressive so far as decorations go and was really very pretty.

On Xmas day we stayed home enjoyed the nice gifts, and were grateful for the time away from the office. We surely appreciate the nice sweater & scarf you sent, and when we opened the "notice of a gift" and found that we are to get "Fortune" magazine we just couldn't hardly believe it. In fact its been a long time since I've received so many nice things all at one time. I, too, got a box of Swiss handkerchiefs, and I got a lovely slip from New York. A peach colored rayon all trimmed with lace and embroidered.

Am glad you think the umbrella we sent will be useful. I know I use mine an awful lot. I have one, not so good, which I keep at the office so as not to have to come home through a rain which I didn't expect.

We've had no letter from Junior since the one of Dec. 9 in which he said he was leaving there 12th or 13th. The New York Times of Sunday last again listed the 94th as having been alerted for sailing. Our boys are reaching the states in 6 to 14 days from date of sailing—depending on the kind of ship and route. Most of the ETO veterans go to Camp Atterbury, Ind. for discharge; and, as a rule, are discharged in three days after landing.

With you we'll be counting the days until the ship lands, and the long days of waiting will be over.

With all good wishes for a happy new year we send lots of love.
Mother B.

Tues. AM

Dear Dorothy:

We are back on the job. Lovely day here. We had a very nice lonesome—some Xmas. Your gifts were appreciated as also the remembrances from son Art. We missed you about the tree, but our thoughts were on you. So thankful that the long wait for the return of the prodigal, will soon be over. Enjoy your good letter. Your card note was received yesterday a.m. Well, we will be seeing you soon. Kind regards to the folks & with "lotions" of love, I am
Daddy
ASB

9

OCCUPATION

New Year's Eve
Garmisch, Germany

$\mathcal{O}$ ne hour left in the year 1945. One hour left in a year filled with world-shaking events. The German collapse and defeat, the discovery [DEVELOPMENT] of the atomic bomb, the defeat of Japan, the formation of the UNO—all of these things have headlined the news. In world politics the late President Roosevelt passed away; Mr. Churchill's party was defeated by Labor; Stalin was left to go carry on as the only original member of the famed "Big Three." Harry Truman came on the world scene as an unpretentious man—a man who brings to the White House a down-to-earth friendliness recalling the simplicity and directness of Lincoln. His degree of efficiency and effectiveness as our nation's leader remains for the future to decide.

As the year ends, the world is nominally at peace; the great war ended. However, unrest and festering sores continue to reveal that all is not well and all is not right with the world. Japan is undergoing the transition from war and control by a military clique to some form of democratic rule under the control and direction of Gen. MacArthur. China is backing away from the brink of revolution with the old friction between Communists & Nationalists. India is restless. Trouble brews in Iran with a possible clash between Anglo-British and Russian policy. Palestine is boiling. Reports are current that Tito's gov't in Yugoslavia will face civil war in the spring. Germany is *suffering from a lack of unified control by the four occupying powers. France has only begun a new regime under the leadership of Gen. de Gaulle and the Fourth Republic, and England is learning a new mode of thought under the socializing Labor Gov't. Both Britain and the Netherlands are involved in the quilling of a strong nationalist movement in Java. The United States on this eve of a new year finds itself launched upon the sea of international politics in the role of senior partner. The course is plotted for the Lagoon of World Unity; but the barometer indicates storms ahead, and a long, rough course is expected for the entire voyage. On the home front, pent up unions have unleashed their powers, and thousands upon thousands of workers are striking.*

In my own little world, I have found the year of 1945 filled with events and incidents affecting my entire life. One year ago tonight I was on my way home [to Jamestown, Tennessee] with Dotty. In late Jan. I came overseas to enter into the final phase of the war as an automatic rifleman. The war ended; I worked a short time with the Chaplain in my unit; went to the Sorbonne for two months of study (attended the Petain trial and explored the sewers of Paris); returned to Germany to take over the duties of a company clerk. I missed several things in the latter months of the year, including a trip to Switzerland, a trip to England, first sergeant's stripes, the shipment home, my wife. I missed particularly the latter.

As the year draws to a close, I await return to my outfit and a job in RSO [regimental supply office]. I await also my trip home with my revised point score of 45.

One of the biggest events at home was Dotty's well-kept secret that she had been taking voice lessons since March. Her voice has improved remarkably, and I am happy that she has been able to fulfill her dream.

Today I spent my daylight hours taking a trip to the Zugspitze – the highest peak (9,700) in Germany. I shall describe the trip in greater detail later. Tonight I saw the first of "A Thousand and One Nights" and later watched a skating exhibition at the Olympic Rink. After the exhibition I went to the crowded Red Cross Club to drink coffee and eat doughnuts & to observe my fellow GIs. After walking to my hotel, I continued to the Lutheran Church up the street. In the stillness of the night, I knelt on the door step to seek the quietness and calm of prayer on this New Year's Eve.

Jan. 1, 1946
Garmisch, Germany

Yesterday I pulled my body out of bed most unwillingly to eat breakfast and hasten to the Zugspitzbahn or Zugspitze railroad. The sky was overcast, but I optimistically hoped that I would have clear sky atop the Zugspitze—which is the highest peak (9,767 feet) in Germany. Though fog-bound most of the way up, we were able to see a bit of the beautiful scenic landscape around us. The railroad itself was completed about 1930 and features a cog wheel track for most of the climb. An added feature is the tunnel, which is three miles long through the solid rock of the Zugspitze. A great crowd came along to ski but this was out of the question, as a new blizzard swept across the barren rocks surrounding the hotel. During the entire day the crowd, which came up for the view and skiing, sat in the dining hall of the hotel, talked , played cards, read, waited for the train to begin the homeward trip at 03:15. A few minutes before leaving I went up on the observation platform. There, faintly through the fog and mist, I could see the mystical outline of the surrounding Alps in a sort of Disney fantasy.

I had to leave, and half an hour later we emerged from the tunnel. The clouds which had hung on the mountain top for the entire day had broken. Floods of sunlight poured down from the mountain top, and the surrounding peaks rose heavenward in a magnificent display of grandeur. I promised myself that should the morrow be fair, I would return.

I rode up the mountain with a friendly Lt., and later I joined him, along with a Capt. friend of his, at a table for lunch where we ate our K rations and the German soup. The two were cordial, and we whiled away our time in discussion of the Occupation Army, GIs, officers, politics, etc. Later on the way down, a second Capt. joined the party, and my heart was further warmed to their species when the captain began to recite poetry—good poetry too!

I arrived at the Leave Center Hotel just in time for supper after which I cleaned up and dashed off again to the show. I later attended the "Ice Revue" in the Olympic Stadium. The show repeated much of that which I had seen on the previous night; nevertheless I enjoyed it as did the hundreds of civilians & Army [personnel]. Two of the featured stars were former Olympic champions, Max and Irma Bair, I believe. Their waltzes and other dances were marvelous for the perfection of coordination and gracefulness of their movement on ice.

Fred Bennett, former director of the Nuremberg Stadium, former co-star with Sonja Heine and now GI director of the Olympic Stadium, performed in a barrel jumping exhibition. First, nine barrels in a row, [then] three decks of barrels, and various other combinations.

This morning I again pulled myself out of the bed but only after being told that the sky was clear. I could hardly decide just what I should do since there was to be an exhibition of ski jumping, and I had thought of hitchhiking to Oberammergau, which is only a few miles away. However, as I ate my breakfast, I saw the sun kissing the snow-covered peaks surrounding the valley. I could not resist the appeal of returning to the Zugspitze.

I found that two English fellows who had made the trip yesterday were also returning today. We began to talk and did not stop until after dinner tonight. The two are from Stuttgart and are working in some phase of censorship. We found much to discuss, and I enjoyed my conversation with young Beck. Our thoughts were similar along many lines, and I would like to carry on some sort of correspondence with him. In some ways, he reminded me of Tom Jones [a high school friend].

I think that I have never seen a sky so blue as the sky which hung above the Zugspitze today. Range after range of Alpine hills stretched out in glistening white. We rode immediately the cable car to the top-

Art Skiing Near Oberstdorf

most peak of the Zugspitze. From there the city of Munich is visible at times. Garmisch-Partenkirchen and Oberammergau were plainly visible to the north, while the valley leading to the Brenner Pass was only over the next range. Austria, Tyrol, Italy, Switzerland, Germany – all are visible from the Zugspitze, and of course the city of Innsbruck is only a few kilometers away.

After lunch we (the two English fellows and I) obtained skis and went skiing on the snow-covered glacier. The snow was deep, but the skiers soon had regular trails worn [OF COURSE, WE HAD NOT SHAIR LIFTS]. The lack of oxygen at that altitude had no serious effect, but I was none the less noticeable. The views on every hand were breathtaking, and they were constantly changing. On the way down, the sinking sun seemed to delight in spreading light yellow and green tints on the mountain sides, and the heart of an artist would surely bubble in rapture. The trip could hardly be called a repetition of yesterday, for it was utterly different. My one wish would have been that Dotty could have shared the day with me. I miss her on the first day of the New Year, 1946.

In discussing the British Foreign Service tonight, Beck remarked, "... and it (the Diplomatic Service) is called 'Diplomatic' for the very reason that there is nothing diplomatic about it."

Art Falling Near Oberstdorf

[AN INCIDENT I DID NOT RECORD OCCURRED ON THE RETURN TRIP. I WAS SEATED WITH MY ENGLISH FRIENDS IN A COMPARTMENT FOR FOUR. MY SEAT MATE HAPPENED TO BE A VERY ATTRACTIVE YOUNG LADY WITH WHOM WE DID NOT CONVERSE, ASSUMING THAT SHE DID NOT SPEAK ENGLISH. THE CONVERSATION TURNED TO THE TOPIC OF FRATERNIZATION, AND I REMARKED THAT I WISH I COULD HAVE CASUAL CONVERSATIONS WITH GERMAN WOMEN WITHOUT IT BEING ASSUMED THAT I HAD THE INTENTIONS OF MOST GIs. WITHOUT LOOKING AT MY SEAT MATE, I CITED HER AS A CASE IN POINT. THE CONVERSATION TURNED TO OTHER TOPICS, BUT WHEN WE REACHED THE STATION SHE WAS MET BY SOMEONE WITH WHOM SHE SPOKE IN PERFECT ENGLISH. MY FACE TURNED A BELATED RED.]

Letter from Art to Dotty
Memmingen, Germany
Jan. 3, 1946 [669-670]

My Dearest,

Speaking of mass confusions with the mail, you should see me. When I arrived yesterday, I found two letters from you—7th and 14th. This afternoon I received two written on the 12th and the 23rd, and just a few minutes ago Devers comes back from the Postoffice with one written on the 11th. Confused or otherwise, I love to hear from you. I feel very much at home tonight, for I moved back into my old room tonight and my old bed. The fellow who came into my room, left today for a furlough in Switzerland, and he kindly allowed me to come back in while he was away—after I requested it. The past four weeks seem like a bad dream during the time that I spent in the 94th. As much as I dislike the move, I am glad to be back here and especially back in my own room—which is really a very nice room.

I am glad that you were able to attend the Messiah, but I think it terrible that you could not stay and see some of the folks who were there. I think that I would have stayed anyway. But I envy even more those who were lucky enough to hear The Women's Choral Ensemble of Knoxville, and more especially those who heard the extraordinary solist, one Dorothy Bushing, by name. Thanks for the program, Darling, and I could only repeat that it is with intense anticipation that I look forward to hearing you sing for me. Will ya, huh?

I am glad that the news of my journey home came before Christmas and I trust that you did not hear the anti-climax until after

542

the holidays. I feel all the more terrible now as I read the letters telling me that you are justlearning of the shipment to the 94th. I hardly dare think how you will react when you learn the worst, and yet I have perfect faith in your faith and trust to bear up the extended delay. I trust with all of my heart that it will not be for long.

Glad to learn both from Mom's note and from your letters tonight that the wooden box came through in good shape. I trust that nothing was broken. You do not say, but I presume that the binoculars were intact. Gee, I hope that the other things came through without mishap, as I have said many times before I guess.

I found this morning, that there was some movement afoot to get me back in the Orderly Room as I mentioned last night. I went directly to Capt. Grace after reporting to Personnel, and he sent me to the RSO. It is rather ironical that I am to take over the job which Capt. Garner offered me when my rating first went in for approval. I refused it then, and Wallace received it (as well he should). He made Staff Sgt. about a month ago, and will step on up to Master Sgt. in a couple of weeks when the 50-54 pointers leave. I will take over his old job, which calls for a T/4 while the fellow ho [who] has been doing it goes to England on furlough. However, there will be no rating for me, for the fellow holds the rating that is going on furlough. What a situation!

Tonight I received a second announcement from Time that I have a subscription—this time the name on the card is Daddy. Another which I received about a week ago listed Mom and Daddy together. I hope that they did not make a mistake and send two. By the way, I wrote Mother and Dad that they were to get a subscription to Fortune. I havenever received word that you received this subscription card or sent it in. I hope that you were able to get in before Christmas.

I spent the early part of the even [evening] until seven-thirty, and I spent most of the restof the time moving in and settling down in my room. It is very late, and I must get up for reveille—for the first time in many months. I shall try to begin earlier in the evening tomorrow, and write much more concerning the joy and strength which comes to me from

Our Love,
Bushy

Am sending Garmisch postcards via free mail.
Will probably arrive same time as this.

Jan. 3
Memmingen

Wednesday I returned to Augsburg from Garmisch in a jeep crowded with six men (the authorized load is five). We stopped briefly in Oberammergau for doughnuts and coffee, and I was at least able to see the famous Passion Playhouse. This town seemed to be a typically small Bavarian village, and I wish that I could have spent more time there. Took a couple of pictures.

Letter excerpts from Art to Dotty
Memmingen, Germany
January 4, 1946

Darling,

I am seated in my old chair, at my old desk with my old typewriter before me. As I have done many times before, I am writing you while I relieve the CQ who wishes to go shave and clean up. It all feels rather natural, you know. Since I left here I have not used a German machine, and so I am again having trouble with the "y" and "z" and the back space.

Since I failed to keep up with my writing as I should have done while at Garmisch, I should like to catch up a bit by going back and writing up a few notes which I took in my little black book. The first set were jotted down on New Year's Eve and merely review a few of the events which marked the passing year....

I have more notes written after spending the day at the top of the mountain near Garmisch, but I shall have to write this at a later time. Work in the RSO is going well, but my hopes are fading for a furlough. Chaplain Webb is going to school next week in Scotland, and I shall soon be very much alone even here. In my old company. How I long to be with you, to think with you, play with you, work with you, love with you.

  I love you,
  Bushy

Jan. 4

To continue: I arrived in Augsburg in the early afternoon and found a couple of Service Co. boys coming back to Augsburg. Saw Ted for only a few minutes. I could have stayed overnight with Ted, but felt that I should return [to Memmingen] as soon as possible.

Yesterday I landed a job in RSO [regimental supply office] although there was some effort to get me back in the Orderly Room. I am taking over the job of Stock Records Clerk, which ironically enough is the job (and the T/4) rating which Garner offered me in Nov. I did not take it then because I knew that Wallace had been promised the job. Now the man holding the rating has gone to England on furlough, and I will get no rating out of it. I shall again try very hard to attend school in England, but I am doubtful of the success that I will encounter.

Letter from Art to Dotty
Memmingen, Germany
January 5, 1946 [673-675]

Darling,

Rather than stop inthe middle of the description, I finished it up tonight, as I had failed to do it last night. After supper I went with Alsup up to Ch. Webb's quarters where I played chess and pingpong with the Preacher most of the evening—all evening in fact. This morning I slept until ten and arose just in time to get to church. The sermon was about "mountains", and you would have been inspired as was I by the three points concerning mountains and God. I ate lunch with Alsup, and he decided that he would like to run up to the Ninth Div. area near Munich to see a couple of friends. I suggested coming back by the way of Augsburg and seeing Ted. This we did, and had a swell trip—though a bit long.

One thing which I saw which lead to a rather disconcerting feeling was a field containing about a thousand planes of our own air force. These planes, some new, some old, are in the process of being destroyed. An air corps boy that we picked up told us that GIs were not permitted to take radios, hearters, or anything else fromthese planes before they are blown up. I sometimes wonder about this Army!

More disconcerting news was contained in the Stars and Stripes today concerning redeployment. I have nothad time to analyze the contradictory statements, but the general idea seems to be that everything is going to be thrown behind schedule. Whata mess. Even though I can get a staff rating here, I think that the wisest thing would be to go to school if at all possible. I shall write more about this tomorrow.

Four big letters awaited me tonight—17, 18, 19, and 21. I shall have to wait until tomorrow to discuss these also. By the way, in the past two days I have received the announcements concerning the subscriptions for the two families (<u>Life</u> and <u>Fortune</u>). Am so glad that those were cleared up. I have time but to tell you that with all my being

     I love you

     Bushy

Letter from Art to Dotty
Memmingen, Germany
January 7, 1946 [676-677]

Darling,

I shall begin a letter at the office this afternoon, for this is ration day and we will have to work late tonight. Two or rather three days each week the trucks go to Augsburg to pick up the food ration for the succeeding days, and they return in the latter part of the afternoon. Here the rations for the regiment are broken down and issued out to the separate units. In order to get them out in the quickest possible time, all of us in the office go out in the shed and help to break them down. It is rather interesting work in a way. Last Friday for instances, we drew 5,000 pounds of potatoes for the regiment for three days, and about 3,000 pounds of bread for the same period. Remember too that the regiment is far below regular strength at the present time.

Last night I was most happy to receive four letters—17th, 19th, 20th, and 21st. I can well understand what you have to say concerning the housing situation in Knoxville, but according to the latest reports in the S&S we will hardly have need for an apartment very soon, My Dear. It would seem now that even to enter UT in March will be under a cloud. The news as you no doubt have heard is not in the least encouraging. This on top of the 94th incident has done little to put me on top of the world. The boys down at Sonthofen, by the way, are still waiting to pull out. Time after time the date has been set only to be postponed again, and the latest date for them to leave there is the 10th. It may be moved back again, for the 80th Div. is still in Camp Philip Morris.

The entire set-up here is up-set by the recent change of events. I found out on Saturday that I could be in line for a rating around here, if I decide that the present point score of 45 which I have is to stick. By using enough persuasion, I could possibly have my score put back to 55, but there is little chance that I could retain it. I would go to another outfit, but bounced again, and end up in a much worst situation than now. As it is, I have a much better chance of getting a rating here in R.S.O. or going to school. We're back to that again!

From what I can find out, the quickest way for me to get home now would be to get to England to school. That sounds like a paradox, but this is the situation. If one becomes eligible for discharge while at school, he is shipped to a port in England at the end of the term. There, he is put in a pool. As divisions load on the boats, there is almost always empty berthes left. These are filled with men from the pool reserve. Ted Livingston was to have finished up his school term in the middle of Dec., but he has not returned. I am sure that he went directly to a port and from there home. This would eliminate all of the confusion which goes on the processing of a large unit such as the 94th.

In the last couple of days new information has been received at the I&E office concerning quotas for schools in England. I am putting in my application for Oxford and a couple of other places, and will keep my fingers crossed from here on. If this does not come through, I think that I will resign myself to my fate. The work here in the RSO will be interesting, and I think that I can keep busy enough. However, I will consider my trip to Europe a partial failure if I do not get to England. I think that I have tried everything new except shooting my leg off. But even that would not help now, for no longer are patients evacuated to the UK. Perhaps we can hope that my efforts will meet with eventual success.

Later

Got out of work tonight in time to see "Johnny Angel"—rather good picture. Late now but I will write more tomorrow. Should not have too much to do at the office. Look forward to hearing about your Christmas & still hope that most of the boxes come thru. With a deep and abiding faith, I place utter confidence in
Our Love,
Bushy

Jan. 8
Memmingen

Yesterday I decided to wait no longer to apply for school and turned in my application for school at Oxford. There was little question in my mind as to what to do when the news came Sun. of a further slash in redeployment quotas. The 94th Division has been delayed three or four times already and is now scheduled to leave Sonthofen on the 10th. The 80th Div. is still at Camp Philip Morris [one of the redeployment centers near the coast of France]. Claiming that the Draft is not sufficient to provide the replacements necessary, officials say that redeployment will be delayed from one to three months for 50-55 pointers. The morale has dropped to a new low.

On Sun. after lunch Newton Alsup and I left for the 9th Div. Area & Furstenfeldbruck near Munich to see a few of his friends. On the way we passed a couple of air fields filled with light and medium bombers. We learned that these planes are to be destroyed in toto. One field contains about a thousand planes, and some of these were already blown up. From one of the Air Corps fellows riding with us, [we were told that] GIs are not allowed to take radios or heaters from the planes.

Later. Phoned Lee Grimwood tonight and found that he is leaving Sonthofen (with 9th) on Thursday. Also, found that either USFET or Corps IG called the 302nd after our shipment of 200 pulled out and raised the roof about the points being cut. What a fine time to find this out!

Letter from Art's parents to Dotty
Jamestown 1 - 8 - 46

Dear Dorothy:

You can imagine what a jolt we got upon receipt of a letter from Germany saying that those ten questionable points had finally been taken, and that there's going to be a delay in that boat we're so eagerly awaiting.

I'm sure you have had a similar message and realize that there isn't a thing one can do about it. I'm enclosing an article from the New York Times, which seems rather encouraging and the time may not be so long after all. [Article posted below.] After all they can't keep him over there forever, and personally I feel that he is awfully lucky. The boys

548

who are reporting now have been over there a lot longer than he (2 1/2 yrs. for some) and have from 60 to 108 points.

I was very much pleased with the information in the last paragraph of the enclosed, for in spite of the ten lost points every month from Sept on is piling up two points per mo.

Hope you are well and that your work is going nicely. I suppose you are kept busy most of the time.

Our work goes on round & round without much change, but enough to keep us from getting sleepy. Two mornings next week we get up at 4:30 to get off two bunches of boys, and on those two days we will be sleepy. For the past two days and nights we had a continuous rain, and the ground is just covered with water. When it isn't cold and snowy its rainy and sloppy, and that's another thing we can't do anything about.

We had a lovely day Sunday; and I could hardly believe my eyes, when I saw the crocus and daffodils just poking their heads up to the top of the ground to find out how soon they could announce that the Spring weather would not be forever getting here. You see not even the winter days, nor the occupation of Germany can last forever.

By the way, I got a most wonderful surprise yesterday when the mail brought me a battle of perfume straight from Paris I could hardly believe it, for it smelled heavenly, and I never expected to own anything so good. It was mailed in early Dec. and should have gotten here long ago.

Hope your Mother is well and that we will all have a good New Year.

Love from us both.

[From Art's father] Howdy! Sweet child—Mother has just gotten off a long letter to Jr., and I'm taking time off to do likewise. We are disappointed at demobilization delay. Loving & best wishes to you & the folks

Daddy—short legs.

M'NARNEY SPEEDS SOLDIERS' RETURN

Says Only 300,000 Men Will Be Required in Occupation of Germany by July 1

DENIES SHIPPING SHORTAGE

Expects to Send Home Every Man Within Three Months of Date of Eligibility

By KATHLEEN McLAUGHLIN
By Wireless to THE NEW YORK TIMES.

FRANKFORT ON THE MAIN, Germany, Jan. 5—Gen. Joseph T. McNarney, Commander of the United States Forces in the European Theatre, disclosed today no more than 300,000 American soldiers would be required to occupy Germany by July 1, 1946, and that he hoped to ship home every man within three months after his record made him eligible for discharge.

He said that none would be retained overseas longer than was absolutely necessary for the efficient handling of mopping-up operations still in progress. He added that the essential nature of the duties each individual was performing, and not the lack of shipping, was the reason for retaining some of the men now in the occupation force.

Special Board Created

To the end that each soldier be sent into the redeployment "pipeline" at the earliest possible moment, General McNarney has created a "Liquidation and Manpower Board," whose assignments check into every activity in the theatre to determine the minimum personnel required to carry out the functions of each one through the elimination of tasks or speeding their completion.

General McNarney said that while guarantees could not be given that all men would be shipped home within three months of the date of their eligibility, it was not impossible that such redeployment might be surpassed, at least for a large proportion. Developments depend to a considerable extent on replacements through re-enlistments, he pointed out.

"Today we estimate the occupation task will require 300,000 American soldiers through 1946," he said. "This represents a cut of 70,000 from the previous estimates. The close-out force of approximately 316,000 as of Jan. 1 is a reduction of 65,000 from the earlier estimates.

"This close-out force will be redeployed in six equal monthly increments, beginning with this month. The entire American troop strength in the American theatre at present is 616,000 (and it will be reduced gradually to an occupation force of 300,000 by July 1, 1946.

"No transportation required for the return of military personnel will be used for other purposes."

Incidents, such as the reported fund raised by 4,060 soldiers in Burtonwood, England, for cable tolls home, protesting the transportation of GI brides, are good examples of the misunderstanding of the actual situation, General McNarney declared. Therefore, he is anxious to have each man comprehend the factors governing his personal status and realize that considerations governing redeployment this time stem, "not from a non-existent shipping bottleneck, but from the necessity of maintaining an adequate organization to fulfill our nation's responsibilities in Germany."

Low Point Men Benefit

FRANKFORT ON THE MAIN, Germany, Jan. 5 (AP)—General McNarney's statement was good news for men with low points. Men with ten to fifteen points, who had thought they might be in Germany for years under the point system, could be home by July 1 if replacements arrived.

The general said that it had not been decided what divisions would compose the newly planned occupation force but that all would be infantry. There will be no armored divisions as such, but the constabulary will be entirely armored.

Infantry divisions will be composed of about 15,000 men each. The armored constabulary will have 38,000 men and the Air Force 62,000. The rest of the occupation force will be made up of headquarters, supply, engineers and other supporting troops, he explained.

In discussions later at Frankfort's Red Cross Nickel Bar American soldiers, both high and low pointers, voiced comments, some asserting that the Army was using men inefficiently.

Says Most Men Are Idle

"McNarney said 300,000 men were needed efficiently to control Germany, but most soldiers still here are doing unnecessary work," said T/4 Bernard Tepper of Pittsburgh, who has fifty-three points. "I wouldn't mind staying another year if I felt I were doing a worthwhile job."

T/Sgt. Jack Raquet of Los Angeles, Calif., had no protest at the order. With twenty-six points he said he intended to stay in Germany a year longer than he would have to.

"I want to counteract the disgusting behavior I have seen among GIs in Germany and to improve German opinion of the United States and her democracy," Sergeant Raquet said.

Corp. William L. Sharp of Chicago said American military authorities could not pursue an effective policy "when the four powers do not have an effective policy for governing Germany."

Corp. James T. Haight, a forty-seven-pointer, of Racine, Wisc., said he was unable to see why it was necessary to maintain an occupation army of 300,000 "when it would be possible with 30,000 men, aided by capable, efficient civilians."

Corp. James C. Woffold of Spartansburg, S. C., who has forty-eight points, criticized professional soldiers and officers, declaring that the general staff was "carving out an officers' empire in Germany."

PATTERSON SEES A CUT

Puts Overseas Forces at 795,000 by July 1 Despite Shortages

TOKYO, Jan. 5 (UP)—Secretary of War Robert P. Patterson said today that a "critical" situation existed in some United States Army overseas territories because of over rapid releases of men from service.

Mr. Patterson said that the War Department was preparing a release stating overseas garrison requirements that "may govern the rate of discharge for the next few months." He said that the discharge requirements gradually would be changed to reach a minimum overseas requirement of 795,000 men by July 1.

He added that men in some cases, however, might be kept at overseas posts until their replacements arrived "to prevent crippling of the occupational force."

"Already a critical condition exists in some areas due to disintegration following too rapid discharge of personnel without essential replacement," Mr. Patterson said.

He denied that the War Department was studying a plan to fix a March 20 deadline for the release of Army men with two years' service, and said that the point system had not been changed nor had the method by which points were piled up.

Jan. 9

Blacker news concerning Redeployment today when a two to three month delay was announced. Supposedly this is due to a change in policy whereby men will go home only as they are replaced. Everyone is going up in arms, and I foresee a reaction never before known. The figures presented are not convincing, and I wonder if political implications in Europe may not be involved. The change came suddenly without warning.

A British report concerning Russian discovery of a new atomic bomb making ours obsolete assumed minor significance in the eyes of the GIs. If this be true, our lives may be more profoundly affected by the latter news than by the former.

———

* Letter from Art to Dotty
Memmingen, Germany
January 9, 1946 [678-679]

My Darling,

THE STARS AND STRIPS

Volume 2, Number 8   (etc)   Wednesday, Jan. 9, 46
"54 - 59s May Ship out in February, 3 ½ Year Men,
50 - 54s in Mid – April. USFET Sees 2 to 4 Month
Sailing Delay
"USFET redeployment officials said today that men in the 55 to 59-point group were expected to begin moving toward home in February and that 50 to 54 pointers probably would start leaving in Mid-April.
"But they emphasized that, since shipments to the U.S. now depended upon the arrival of replacements, these dates were tentative and their statements must not be considered promises......"
And so the long, long story goes: statements, counter-statements; admissions, denials; hopes, disappointments. I suppose that very few GIs read the second lead article in the S&S today headed "Briton Reports Soviet Discovery of Most Fearsome Atomic Bomb". It seems most likely, upon examination of the paper and this article in particular, that all of our lives will be affected infinitely more by this second story, and yet how few will spend thought or effort on this report. I must admit that I spent little time in thought concerning a

new atomic bomb. Since early this morning we had heard in the office some of the portent of the newspaper today, but nevertheless the rude shock came upon looking at the details, the rude shock and something of the import of the news contained there.

I cannot describe, and would not if I could, my feelings today. This, of course, is hardly my first disappointment over here. Applications for two schools were cancelled for me in the Fall; two furloughs slipped from my grasp; I missed a few extra stripes by a small margin; I missed the boat with the 94th by a smaller margin. These things I bore with a smiling face though at times my heart hung heavy—never for long, however. Today, I could no longer smile and within is an emptiness that only your presence could fill. Today I realize all too well that our separation, unbearable as it already is, has been extended by weeks and even months.

Darling, it is not cricket for me to write such a letter at this time. I should not, according to the books, reveal my downcast spirit in my letters, but rather should smile and say, "Oh, 'tis nothing, this delay: a few weeks perhaps, but what will a few weeks be by comparison with the long months we have already spent apart." However, I cannot say that and be true to myself and to you. I freely admit that my spirits are not high, and that I miss you more each passing moment of this interminable existence apart from you. I love you, My Dear.

Again at a late hour last night, Devers brought in a letter for me. This time is [it] was the wonderful letter describing your Christmas. I am so glad that you had nothing but good news during the Christmas holidays for I think that they were the merrier for a' that. Your descriptive ability improves all of the time, Darling, and your description of Christmas at the Barber house was very realistic. I enjoyed the letter tremendously and I have read it over and over again. I hope that you will not wait until next Christmas to write one just as long (and as wonderful). Glad to learn that at least most of the packages with presents arrived, but I note that there is at least one other present which I had hoped would arrive for the gala season. It is not a package exactly, and perhaps it has arrived long ere now. Only tonight I was able to find a little gift for Harriet (a box of Swiss handkerchiefs) and I shall try to send them to her tomorrow.

By the way, the deal for my chess men is just about completed. The lady from who Chaplain Webb got them is going to make a nice box for the men and also a leather board. I have a larger box for both of these, and then a shipping box for the whole thing. I do not know how soon everything will be completed, but I think that it will be mailed without difficulty should I be so lucky as to suddenly leave for school. Nevertheless, I will never breath with ease until the chess set is at home and in good condition. By the way, Chaplain Webb leaves on Friday for school in Scotland. I am very happy for him, for it will be a grand opportunity. Also learned today that Ted Livingston is in a port in England awaiting shipment, just as I expected. He has 50 points.

There is nothing new concerning my application for Oxford. However, I should know definitely one way or the other in a few days since the schools begin their next term about the 20th of January. I think that I shall cable my new address in case I do get away. School seems to be my last ray of hope for my stay over here, although I could possible get a furlough in the long delay which lies ahead.

I like my work in the RSO, and find that now and then I can find time for personal work there. Half day off tomorrow and I shall try to clear up a few odds and ends around the room. Devers is trying to sleep, and I must give up typing for the evening. More and more I dream of being with you and always I dream of trying to tell you

I love you,
Bushy
PS. How does bank acct & other finances stand?

* Letter from Art to Dotty
Memingen, Germany
January 10, 1946 [680-681]

My Dearest Heart,

If all of this confusion concerning redeployment was not such a terribly serious matter to so many of us, it would [be] rather amusing I think. When I can detach myself from the implications which the news brings, I can smile ironically at theactions and reactions of the War Dept., Congress, and GIs overseas. We are a strange lot indeed!

Last night I quoted the headlines from the S&S, headlines which brought an immediate reaction throughout the world where American soldiers are stationed. I shall not quote very much in today's paper, but the headline is "4,000 Demonstrate at Frankfurt....." On Guam 3,500 officers and men go on hunger strike. A "near mutiny: is quelled at Yokohama. 1,000 men march down the Champs Elysees in Paris, and telegrams are pouring into Congress from points throughout the world. A news flash tonight announces that "Ike" has ordered all men sent home who are not essential. I suppose that this will quell the rising tide of unrest and discontent, but a close examination of this shows that it remains an empty phrase until clarified. The new plan of redeployment merely stated that men would be sent home as fast as fast as replacements can be had. This was another way of saying that all the men in the theater held essential jobs, and could not be sent home until another man came to take his place. What Eisenhower will do to explain his order remains for time to say. Meanwhile, we bit our nails and wait.

We get our half day off on Thursday, and so I came home after lunch and flopped in bed. After sleeping a couple of hours I felt much better, and managed to accomplish a bit during the remainder of the afternoon. Tonight I wrapped a couple of packages and these will go out tomorrow. One is to Harriet as a sort of belated Christmas Gift. I was able to find a box of Swiss handkerchiefs, not so nice as yours, and I hope she did not receive so many as you. Also sent a little something for you, a square, flat package. Hope it comes through without too much delay.

Work goes well as I mentioned last night, and I am catching on to my job without difficulty. As I have described it before, I merely handle the books and carry on a simple bookkeeping account of equipment in the Regt. For instances, if we receive a truck from Div. Ordnance, I put the record down as a debit to the Regt. and then debit the truck to the company within the Regt. The same thing takes place in reverse if the item of equipment is turned in, salvaged, or lost. Of course, since everything from a firing pin on an automatic pistol to trucks and 155s are handled on the books, there are numerous transactions each day and I manage to keep occupied most of the time.

I think that I mentioned also last night that I have been copying some of the notes which I took in combat to put in my little black book. I am also trying to put in something of a running account of my movements and experiences. The latter was a job which I once began in my letters to you but unfortunately never completed. As I look back over some of the things that I have in my book, I feel sure that I have a wealth of background material which I hope to use at sometime in the future. Over and over again I feel that some day I will sit down and begin to produce a bit of writing worth while. I know that there are words inside that seek and outlet, and I am sure that the outlet will be found. I find that when I can separate myself from my Army surroundings, I become far more fluent in thought and word.

I must write an apology to Mom and Dad for my delay in writing them, but the past days and weeks have hardly been conducive to writing anyone but you, My Darling. I hope to write Van, Tom, and all the rest soon. Still nothing about school and Ch. Webb leaves tomorrow.

      Goodnight and most pleasant dreams of
          Our Love,
          Bushy

Jan. 11

My first copy of Sat. Review of Lit. (which Harriet & Sam [Blizzard] sent me) contains a review of Harry Brown's "A Sound of Hunting." The play is currently being produced on Broadway and is given a favorable review. However, a minor criticism of Brown's book A walk in the Sun, brings to question a particular reference. Speaking of the book, the critic says, "It seemed written from a dislike of men, not an affection for them. I looked in vain for indications of that strange binding fellowship which I am convinced unite men who have faced death in each other's company. In avoiding the sentimentalities of war, I felt Mr. Brown had omitted one of its most sustaining sentiments."

Now from my own experience and my own observation, I seriously wonder if the critic has not seen too many Hollywood plays. I believe that my squad and my platoon were made up of average men. Many soldiers saw far more combat than we, and yet we faced the same death together as did others. We faced cold and hunger and long marches and disappointments and death. In all of this there were minor frictions and differences. We lived, worked, and fought together, and yet I question that there was an automatic "binding fellowship." Common ideals, ideas, standards, likes and dislikes are still the basis for real fellowship whether in war or peace. Certainly a book or a play goes over better if a touch of sentimentality is added, but the realism of such a sentimental touch is not thereby established.

My Darling,

Someone wrote a song, "Saturday night is the loneliest night..." For me this is true not only on Saturday night, but every night while I am away. The hotel is very much deserted, and Devers works down in the orderly room. Wallace writes letters in his room, and almost every one else is at the show or the club. Chaplain Webb left yesterday for England and School; Alsup leaves tomorrow for Cambridge! You smile at me from the picture on the dresser, but still, "Saturday is the loneliest night......!"

After a half day of routine work at the office, I came back, ate chow, and soon found myself at the Doughnut Dugout reading Emily Post, no less. Yes, I have reached that level in my reading for the unconscious hope, I suppose, that I will eventually return to that well-mannered existence known as civilian life. Rather interesting too, the book, and one worth adding to our library sometime soon. To my surprise the clouds had rolled up while I read, and continues tonight, and the stream of water falling outside my window from the roof enhances the coziness of my room.

This morning we had our first meal in our new mess-hall, which by the way is the nicest one which I have seen over here. Formerly the dining room must have been one of the swankier cafes in town, but one of the other companies used it for a club during the past months. Our Regt. Commander during combat has just returned from a leave in the United States, and he began to change things around immediately. At first we thought that we would have to move from our quarters, but he finally decided to allow us to remain and move only the mess hall. The room is quite large, and the tables seat from four to six. One the walls are small statues and the lighting is indirect. White table clothes are on the tables and waitresses bring the filled plates to us. Not bad!

Rina and Leo came around to see me tonight, and we talked for the first time in several days. She has been working at the theater as check-girl since I returned, and so I have had little opportunity to see and talk with them. They are planning to return to Holland as soon as possible since they will be proud parents in a few months. Leo is in the process of becoming a member of the USArmy and he hopes to take the thirty day furlough to which he is entitled now. If so he can take Rina home, and then return here. Of course, I think that the main reason that he wishes to join us in order to get to the States, and he will only have to serve eighteen months.

The news concerning Alsup came rather suddenly and unexpectedly. As we rode up to the 9th Div. and later to Augsburg last Sunday, we talked about going to school; and I urged him to apply. My application went in on Monday, but it was not until Wednesday that he finally decided (when the bad news concerning redeployment came in greater detail.). About noon today he found that he is to leave tomorrow morning for Cambridge to study music. As yet I have heard absolutely nothing concerning my own application, and I am losing hope a bit. I fear that the fact I attended the Sorbonne over here already may count against me, and too there were only two openings in the XX Corps quota. That means two men from three or four divisions. Hope springs eternal, and I shall never give up hope of seeing England —one way or another. Do I bore you, Darling, with the recurrent theme of England and my desire to go? I suppose but it is almost a phobia with me now, I have been frustrated so many times.

I am very happy that both the Chaplain and Alsup were able to go to school, and yet it is with a feeling of personal regret. I shall miss them both very much. Now and then I realize with a start that with few exceptions the men with whom I associate in the Army are not the ones with whom I would normally associate in civilian life. Part of this is due I think to the exceptional group which we knew at Maryville, the type with whom we will seldom be privileged to associate again. I do not mean to take a superior attitude, and I must take into account the fact that many of these men are entirely different in civilian surroundings. However, the caliber of manhood which Ted, Tom, Phil and the others represent is hard to find anywhere—except a place like Maryville.

Yesterday, just one day after I mailed the handkerchiefs to Harriet, I received my first copy of Sat. Review (dated, Dec. 8th) I am most happy to get the subscription and I shall try to write Samarriet tomorrow and thank them properly (although I did thank them in a previous letter).

For the past hour and a half I have been in lengthy discussion with Wallace on the subject of Christian Science. He is, I find, a close follower of that sect; and it has been most interesting to exchange viewpoints with him. He describes the Science point of view as a religion of the mind, and intellectual experience. There are small differences of thought which I find, but my interest is aroused to the point that I would like for us to study the writings of Mrs. Eddy at some future time. I think I have mentioned before that it would perhaps prove highly profitable for us to make a series of studies of various doctrines and beliefs. I wish that we could devote an hour each evening to some sort of study, using wide variety of subject matter to hold our interest.

Although I start early in the evening, I can never seem to finish all that I wish to say. Devers is now in bed and trying to sleep, so as usual I must stop in the middle of my letter to say Goodnight. I hope to spend a quiet day tomorrow, reading and writing and longing to hold you in my arms and say

I love you,
Bushy

Letter from Art to Dotty
Memmingen, Germany
January 13, 1946 [685-687]

Darling,

A long and dreary day was made bright by two big letters from you (one written on the 28th and the second on the 30th). However, when I read of your anticipation and even your guesses as to when I will be home this month, I immediately drop into the depths of despondency. Dotty Darling, please forgive me for not sending a cable as soon as I found that I would not remain with the 94th. It would probably would have taken as long as the letter which I wrote to reach you, for I could not have sent it from Sonthofen and the holiday delays would have held it back. However, I fear that each day during which you thought that I was on my way and anticipation grew, and the longer the worse. It is heartbreaking to realize how near you thought I was when I know now I far I am.

Like you, I have gone over and over in my mind the details of our reunion, and yet I suppose that it will [be] entirely different than we can imagine. The essential elements of the heartfilled joy which will be ours will be different for us only as it will be far more wonderful that I could ever imagine. Just to be within the smile of your presence will be as though I were stepping from the utter depths of darkness into the balmy spring of sunlight. I love you, My Dear.

Glad to hear the details of the Johnson party, and I certainly long to take part in one of those. You must feel something like an old maid with all of the other husbands around, but we can always recall the ten months which we had together while many of these same husbands were on Guadacanal Anzzio. The details concern a degree are interesting, but I wonder if Johnny Fuzek is working on a degree in Liberal Arts, English for example. I may be wrong, but I still think that an degree in English, even a Masters, will require a reading knowledge of one language. Of course, I think that a brush up on my French would be sufficient for this, but I will have to take German before I get my PhD I think. My Dutch and my stay in Germany will be of help, but the rudiments will only come by careful study. I think that my interest in German will be far greater than it ever was in French, even when studying the latter at the Sorbonne.

The current news concerning redeployment has thrown me for a complete loss as to my plans for school. The situation is so completely confused now that I dare not count on any particular date. If I could get to England to school I could be fairly safe in planning to be home in about two and a half to three months. (Alsup was told yesterday before leaving that he will not be likely to return to Germany.) However, if I stay here, I cannot plan anything at the moment. Perhaps some logical announcement will come out of this mass confusion. We can only hope.

Along with your letters came a note from Muriel—my first since coming overseas. I was happy to hear from her, and more happy to deduce from her letter that she is extremely happy in her marriage. I suppose that it will take me a long time to overcome the slight feeling of resentment which I feel. I should not, I know full well, but I cannot help the feeling which I have. She mentiones that Marian Avakian is engaged to a fellow at Princeton and that Mary Metcalf (somebody) and husband are beginning work at Moody with plans for the mission field. By the way, we have an invitationto spend part of our "second honeymoon" with Muriel and Larry, but I doubt that we will be able to get that far north in our travels.

As usual on Saturday night I slept my ten hours, awakening at the luxurious hour of ten this morning. After shaving and cleaning up I attended the church service conducted by Chaplain Bowman. After dinner I spent part of the afternoon writing Mother and Dad and afterward to the RCLibrary to read. During the last few days it has been with great difficulty that I sit down and really concentrate. Even when writing letters I write for a few paragraphs and wander about, write more, walk more. I continue to nurture a faint hope that I will get a sudden call to attend school at the very last minute, but it is only a faint hope.

By the way, I am not in the habit of doing business on Sunday, but a fellow came over to see me today to buy a camera. I have a small one which I bought for four English pounds or sixteen dollars. This fellow almost insisted on buying this camera at a price of fifty dollars—which by the way is comparatively cheap for a good camera over here. This one is a very good one, but I am satisfied with the one which I have been using. I shall try to send the money to you by money order if possible.

The letter was interrupted by a call from Ted about an hour ago, and we spent almost a full hour talking. He is on CQ and so was in the orderly room up there anyway. Sam Pemberton is now in Japan and stationed near Hiroshima. He was in Persia you remember for a year, came back to the States, was commissioned inthe Medical Corps, and shipped overseas again. Nothing else that is particularly new I guess with Ted although he has a terrible time with the Colonel under whom he works. Personnel can certainly make a job a pleasant task or a horrible ordeal. The latter seems to be wthe case with Ted.

One bit of encouragement comes from Ted concerning redeployment. It seems that rumors are still current around Division that the 71st may come home sometime in March with 45-52 pointers. This would probably be our best bet and probably our quickest way home if something like that did occur. March is not far away, My Love, and we will have a life time for

Our Love,
Bushy

Jan. 14

A sad commentary on the average intellect of the officers and leaders in our army is the rapt attention with which some of them peruse certain types of literature. Lt. McAllister, my former CO, sits at the desk in the RSO at the moment reading with avid interest a stack of comic books.

When I worked in the Orderly Rm., he used to read these books more than he read bulletins and orders concerning the company. He has just taken over the job of acting S-4 Regimental Supply Officer. Mr. Haden, the Warrant Officer in charge of RSO, and Asst. S-4, spends most of his time in the office reading comic books. What intellect; what breadth of interest!

My Darling,

Each one if the office yawns in turn as we settle down at eight
o'clock on Monday morning for a week of work. As would be naturally
expected, a couple of the fellows are late, including the boss; two of the
fellows are reading from the generous supply of comic magazines on
hand; a couple others are ambitions enough to begin their work
already; I begin a letter.

Stories concerning cigarette butts and the German populace are
legend in the ETO, and here is merely another to add to the collection—
no better, no worse. This one does happen to be true and I see it
repeated every morning. As you know, we stand reveille in front of the
CP every morning. About a week ago I began to notice that GIs were
not the only one standing reveille. Directly behind us I see standing a
couple of middle aged German men. As soon as the formation is
dismissed, they dash into the crowd and look (even though it is very
dark at 6:30) for cigarette butts. We go from reveille to the dining hall
and breakfast, and this morning I followed one of the Germans as he
scurried after the GIs. He stayed as close as possible to those who had
cigarettes glowing in their hand and picked them up as the fellows
tossed them away. A few of the men like to trample the butts into the
snow, but the Germans do get a large number. When I came out of the
dining hall this morning, I saw that one of them was still scurrying after
a man with a butt, and followed him all the way to the hotel where we
live. It is difficult to understand just how much these people value
cigarettes, but it has taken over as a primary item of exchange. I think I
have told you how Germans come into the various offices with great
regularity and ask permission to take butts from ash trays. Waiters and
waitresses will invariably clean out the trays and children still gather
around the doors of the theater hoping to catch an occasional stub.

In a somewhat similar vein is the situation concerning food. I think
that I have mentioned before themanner in which Germans, both old
and young, used to gather around the door where we left the mess hall
with our eating utensils. Most of the time they looked for coffee, but
small pails were also brought to fill with scraps of food. A far larger
source of food for the Germans is the individual GI. A very large
majority of the men gave more than a humanitarian interest in the
fraulein, and great quantities of food, candy, soap, etc. are diverted into

civilian channels. (The fuel shortage has also been alleviated by the warmth provided by the individual soldier for individual Germans.)

Monday Evening

A hectic day finally ended at the office, hectic because the rations came in late from Augsburg. We finished about seven-thirty and camein for a late supper. By the time I shaved and did a couple of odd jobs around the room, the clock had swung around to nine o'clock. A couple ofletters came through today, one from Phil&Peggy and one from John and Lorna Hawkins. Both were Christmas Cards, and both contained notes. By the way, you had better inform Phil sometime that I have left Paris. I have owed the Evauls a letter for a long time, but I have been in no mood for thelast few weeks to write letters, except to you, My Dear. Nothing particularly new from either of the Christmas Cards, but I was most happy to hear from both.

I think that I have mentioned a fellow by thename ofTony Baratta who came into the orderly room shortly before I left. He is a very nice fellow but has the curse of low points (37). The day after I returned from Garmisch Tony left on a furlough for Switzerland. Three or four days after he left, word came to the orderly room that he was to leave on that very day on an emergency furlough home. No oneknew of any sickness in his family and so we presumed that the furlough had gone through before the letter telling him of the sickness or emergency. Tony returned today from the furlough and we found that our assumption had been correct. By this time the letter had come tellinghim the details. According to the letter his father is slightly sick, but not serious. He leaves again tomorrow morning and may fly home. Needless to say, all of us are jealous, but I am certainly glad that he is able to go. Itmeans that he will get home and nothave to return overseas. He would probably have been over here for some time to come with 37 points. I am not trying to give you ideas; but, just in case any difficulties arose which would warrant a request for an emergency leave, do not hesitate to apply. It would seem that the stringent rules which formerly governed such leaves have been lifted.

Speaking of ways of getting home, Ted told me a new angle last night which I thought I would suggest. He tells me that should divorce proceedings begin against a soldier, he would be granted leave to go home. He thought that I should suggest this to you, but I am afraid. Of course, the idea is that the proceedings would be dropped immediately. However, if someone decided to go ahead, the poor soldier would be out of luck. No Darling, I do not think that I want to get home on those pretenses.

The snow which began yesterday afternoon has not let up, and part of the time itwirls down in regular blizzard fashion. As I have mentioned before, the RSO is located almost a mile and a half away from the office; I often walk just for the exercise. I have a swell hood for my field jacket which is lined with part of a heavy wool scarf. When I began to work on rations and walk now and then out to work, I began to wear my woolen underwear. It scratches, and I do not like to wear it, but it is certainly warm. During combat, I certainly had no objection to having it.

By the way, I suddenly realized to day that it was a year ago yesterday that I left Fort Benning for Camp Kilmer. What a difference a year makes! A very great deal has happened to us during that time. I wonder just where we will be twelve months from today. There is certainly much to look forward to for us. How I long to be with you, to hold you close in my arms, to press your lips to mine, to tell you in a song without words

I love you,
Bushy

* Letter from Dotty to Art
Wednesday
January 16, 1946 [typed]

My Darling,

Your mail is coming much better now, for which I am very grateful. Very. Your letter of Jan. 7 came in today's mail, your down in the dumps letter. I am inclined to feel the same way about the situation but we can't both feel that way, 'cause then neither one of us could cheer the other one up. So cheer up, Darling, assume that famous Bushing grin, and the world is yours for the asking. (Ed. Note; Don't overdo it— you might get a few jolts.) It seems that the Army has frustrated you at every turn, but in reality you have gained some valuable experience and even more valuable schooling during your Army life. Perhaps, as a last benefit, you are intended to receive even more schooling, in your beloved England or somp'n. while your wife spends her days in lonely solitude, pretending all the while that she is supremely happy and doesn't mind a bit. (Dotty! How do you think you are going to cheer him up when you talk like that?.........Answer comes there none.)

Also in the mail was letter from T.L., which I enclose. Afraid I shall have to disillusion him about your paying him a visit in the near future. And he could get you free quarters, too. Tsk, tsk. I took the liberty of opening it and reading it. As you see. He writes well—extremely well. Sounds as if he had a girl in Atlanta.

The reservations for the banquet (Westminster Fellowship of Presbytery) tomorrow night have been pouring in from all sides. It is as if someone had waved a magic wand, for it has been a long time since the churches of this Presbytery have showed much of a response to anything. Hope and I have spent much time on the phone, trying to get everything all arranged. The affair will be at her church (Graystone), but the reservations have been coming in to me. No sooner do I call Hope to give her the latest figure than someone else sends in more reservations, and I must needs call her again. More fun! 144 reservations so far!

Also enclosed in this letter are the rest of the pictures which go with that last bunch I sent you. These three were not printed at all when the other were, so I had to take the negatives elsewhere and ask that the entire roll be printed, no matter what they looked like, before I could get them done. Even then the photographer was reluctant to do it. I really don't think the pictures are that bad—a bit dark, but fairly clear. Please read comments on the backs.

I am at the church. It is after working hours, but I will be here for supper, so am using these few minutes to write to my honyeah.

[handwritten] There'll be a busy day tomorrow, so I had best turn in now, but not before whispering

I Love You,
Dotty

P.S. According to the latest on demobilization, you are eligible now—this minute—for discharge, and will be home sometime between now and April 30, an account of you have 45 points & more than 2½ years service. So there. If you have gone & gotten yourself into school already and have to complete your term, I shall be slightly (?) disappointed.

Tuesday

Just as I thought—this didn't get finished last night. I was too sleepy. You'll be able to read this a lot better, anyway.

The box containing the typewriter came yesterday, also. It arrived in good shape, and you won't have to worry about that any more. But Darling, please tell me how to unlock the keys and carriage! I pulled and punched every lever I could find and a few more things besides, and all to no avail. The carriage won't budge nor the keys space. Mary

Ruth ingeneously discovered that it worked fine if you tipped the whole machine at a 45 degree angle, but that seems a dopey way to have to type.

I think that nearly all if not all of the boxes you mentioned sending have arrived. The skis came and the box mentioned above, and the box with the leather jacket, etc., and of course the boxes that came before Christmas. Are there any others? I am having a big time stacking up all this junk(?) in my room, there being no other place that I can think of. Some day of course it can be spread out through several rooms or a whole house, depending on what we can find when.

Your vacation at Garmisch sounds delightful. How I wish I might have been there to see and do all those things with you!

Latest news on demobilization is that it will proceed at a slower rate but that all of you not in occupation will definitely get here by April 25. That is all men with 45 points or 30 months of service. I wonder if I am too bold in hoping that you will be here in time for our anniversary!?

No matter how I dish it out to myself that even though we have had several disappointments that you are really very lucky and are well off and have been overseas only a comparatively short time, etc., etc., -----now matter how much of that I tell me, my longing for you grows constantly stronger and more acute, and I yearn for YOU. Even though I am busy and reasonably happy, I miss you more with each passing day, because the biggest thing in my life is

> Our Love,
> Dotty

* Letter from Art to Dotty
Memmingen, Germany
January 17, 1946 [691-692]

Darling,

The moon outside tonight is full but I dare not look at it for long. My morale couldn't take it! And you know I believe that we are going to have some winter weather in Bavaria before the winter ends. Of course, last night was relatively warm—it was only 10° below zero (F).

Funny thing happened to me yesterday morning, and I would never have believed it possible had I not seen it with my own eyes. For some reason entirely beyond my comprehension, I began to whistle as I rode to work on the back of a truck. The tune I remember was "Dixie"; and, as I began, to my utter amazement I saw that the moisture from my breath was being frozen a fraction of a second after coming in contact with the air. I knew that the morning was cold, but I had no idea just how cold it was. The most curious thing was that the moisture was frozen in a long irregular line projecting out from my mouth, and would break off when it reached a length of about eighteen inches. I was so amazed that I put out my hands to catch these frozen pieces and kept right on whistling "Dixie". There I was, riding along to work in the heart of Bavaria, my nose rosy red and freezing fast, my toes already numb, holding in my arms bars from the frozen "Dixie". For the sake of curiosity I continued to carry them when I de-trucked and carried them right in to the office. I put them down on my desk, and it was a second miracle when I put them down with the first bars nearest the fire. As the frozen bits of moisture slowly melted, the notes which had been encased within the crystal came out, and there was the tune (flat notes and all) which I had whistled on my way to work. I could hardly believe my eyes or my ears, but the entire office force can vouch for the truth of these statements.

I must admit that I did not write to you last night, and the night before I numbered a page incorrectly. I think I put down 94 when it should have been 91, but you can check it by the date. Last night I spent the latter part of my evening working on an article which has been in the making for more than a week. Tonight I completed a second draft, but I think that it is in for more revision. The article has been brewing in my mind for some time and was augumented by a very fine editorial by Dorothy Thompson which you sent to me weeks ago, and another along the same line which Mother sent. The final push came about as a result of the demonstrations and mass meetings held by GIs throughout the world last week. I shall send you a copy of course, but I should like to revise a bit more first.

Tomorrow men with 54 points ship out to an engineer unit located in dear old Gunzburg. I managed to call the Personnel Section there and inquired concerning their policy in dealing with ERC points. They do not consider them. That settled that! April seems far away, and yet in eight short weeks I will probably be on my way, eight weeks at the latest.

The early part of my evening yesterday was spent at the movie where I saw "The Strange Affair of Uncle Harry". The picture was far different from the ordinary type which we get over here, and had an interesting psychological angle. Tonight I accepted an invitation long standing from Bill Myers to eat with him at Hdq. Co. I suddenly found out that Bill plays bridge and will gladly make up the absent fourth for Wallace, myself, and another fellow.

There is almost a total absence of mail these days, and I eagerly await each letter which is on its way. Remind me to spend a lifetime telling you in every way that is at my command that
I love you,
Bushy

Letter from Art to Dotty
Memmingen, Germany
18 January, 1946 [694-695]

Darling,

Last night just as I was selecting the pictures for your letter, I had a call from Ted. We had talked early this week in regard to the week-end, and he called last night to tell me that he probably would be unable to come down. The road between Memmingen and Augsburg is a solid sheet of ice, and I cannot blame him for not wishing to travel under such conditions. I will have to go to Division sometime soon to collect my travel money from Stanford and perhaps I can arrange to spend a night with Ted. An interesting bit of news is that at long last Ted received the enlargements which I sent to him long before I left for the 94th interlude. The pictures were postmarked, of course, at the APO in Division (just across the street from the 5th Inf. CP.) Ted received them on the 17th Dec., or forty three days later. If he can get away in the early part of February, Ted and I will try to go to Rome together. However, I cannot afford to wait too long, and if I can't go with him I shall take the trip to England I think. One reason that I want to take the Switzerland-Italy trip is that it will probably be my only chance to see the two countries, whereas I will undoubtly see much of England before I am through.

Ted gave me further information concerning news which has long existed in the rumor stage. It seems now at least semi-official that the 66th Regt. will be detached from the 71st and come home in the near future. According to the inside dope which Ted has, the 5th and 14th will come home later. Since these two regiments are supposed to be filled with 45 to 49 pointers, it would seem safe to assume that we would begin the homeward trek in the latter part of March. I have heard better news in the distant past, but this is certainly something to look forward to.

The cold weather which I described last night has abated somewhat and the sun is shining brightly this morning. It is warmer now, but snow still covers everything and the ice has not yet begun to melt. Friday is always the hardest day which we have since we have to handle three days rations tonight rather than two. The roads are so bad that trucks cannot make the trip to Augsburg and return with as much speed as before. However, when Friday comes, the week-end is only one day away. The week-end brings plenty of time for sleep, reading, and writing. I always feel a wee bit closer to you and I am talking to you or reading your wonderful letters (which I hope to get some of today!)

I had intended to mention before that Devers told me that he sent you a Christmas Card which I hope you received. Let me know if you did for it will make him feel good. He enjoyed hearing about the receipt of the Special Order making me a corporal. [Interesting how little Art talks of this.]

Friday Evening

I worked steadily all day but to my surprise the Sgt. in charge of the RSO told me that I could leave at four o'clock. The trucks had good luck and came back very early. I was back in my room five four thirty and had a fire made. I shaved, cleaned up, all before supper. After supper I went to the library to read a bit and then to the show. The picture was a Agatha Christie mystery, "And Then There Were None". The suspense element was outstanding and the acting above average. I enjoyed the evening a bit—well, anyway a movie does pass a couple of quick hours. Any hours that I can spend quickly over here is definitely to my advantage, My Love, as long as I am spending them away from you. When I am with you again, time will stop.

I had hoped to work a bit more on my article today, but there was plenty of work to keep me occupied. I shall try to finish it over the week-end and send you a copy early next week. I cannot describe the stifling influence of the Army, but I think it an understatement to say that the atmosphere is deadening. The article upon which I am working is one of the first creative bit of writing which I have done overseas. I have made plans many times for short stories and skits, but some how I have never been able to produce anything worth while. I hope that this is a definite break, and that I will be able to produce other things. I have a plan forming for a short story or play, and perhaps this time I can make progress. We shall see.

One thing which I am doing is to keep scattered notes on various subjects in my little book. My letters to you often contain reflections of my observations and thoughts concerning my surroundings. I hope that as I settle down to a more normal perspective at home; I can review these thoughts and observations, notes and letters.

I must address my box for shipping my chess set. It has not been gathered together as yet, but Bob Mulford is to take it to Neu Ulm where the other parts will be collected and readied for mailing. I hope that no slip-up occurs.

The moon shines fair tonight and as its beams circle the globe, may they carry the message which my heart would fain whisper:

I love you,

Bushy

PS. These are the las of the Garmisch, Oberstdorf set of pictures—about 43 or 44 in all.

Letter from Art to Dotty
Memmingen, Germany
January 19, 1946 [696-697]

My Dearest,

The first mail to reach the regiment since last Sunday contained your letter postmarked on the 4th. Two weeks seems to be the usual time, when we are lucky, and indicates that everything is coming by boat now. I suppose that mine is doing the same, although I continue to mail each via Air Mail in the faint hope that some of them may come by air to you. I cannot understand why my letters should be so far behind since, with the exception of about three or four days over New Years, I have written daily. I think that one thing which held up some of my letters was the great distance between the 302nd Regt. APO and 94th Div. At any rate, I hope that my letters eventually reach you and the numbered pages should be some help in indicating this.

Today I saw a fourth man who was formerly in Service Co., shipped to the 94th, and now back in the 14th. He like the two others spent some time in the hospital, just long enough to miss the boat. Of course, these fellows retain their high points and will ship out quickly. In all likelihood they will loose only a matter of a few days as a result of their delay. As I mentioned last night, 54 pointers left yesterday; and the Division Red Circle today rumors that the 53 pointers will leave next week. I like to see these shipments come and go for everyone brings closer the time when I will go without question. What a difference ten points makes!

I again spent most of the afternoon sleeping, just for the pure joy of sleeping. The weather continues unabated only more so. You should see how these people in Bavaria are adapted to winter. Children appear to learn to skii before they learn to walk very well. As soon as the snow comes and the roads are thoroughly covered, farmers bring out runners which they put on the wheels of their wagons. It seems so unusual to look out the window and see a wagon glide by, the wheels stationery.

Even baby carriages can be seen on the street with the wheels placed on runners. Of course, there are great numbers of sleighs running up and down the highways and byways.

In connection with the snow and ice on the roads, one of the silliest orders that I have heard yet has been sent down from the Regt. Commander. Of course, there has been a sharp increase in traffic accidents by the hazardous road conditions; and the new order states that any man involved in an accident, regardless of whose fault the accident is, will be shipped out of the company and his driver's license revoked. Such an order is perfectly senseless, but the army is the army.

Another example of what I mean came to my attention today in the form of statement of charges. When a man is found responsible for the lost or destruction of Government property through neglect, he may be charged for the value of the item on a statement of charges. The cost is then deducted by the payroll section and the item dropped from the company books and the regimental books. Few items are handled in this way, and usually it is something like a wrist watch which the individual wishes to buy anyway (since the GI watches are very good and relatively cheap). Much red tape is involved for such a settlement since all forms must be made out in five copies and many statements are required to ascertain the exact nature of the loss or destruction. All of these papers must pass through the payroll section, over the desk of the Personnel Officer, and finally to my desk where I take the item from the books. Today I saw a statement of charges made out against one man for a muzzle cover for an M1 rifle, price $0.99. To me that is the height of something, or should I say depth?

I am on the trail of a bit of leather for a pair of skii boots, and I have some hope of finding it. Leather is hard to get of late since the MG clamped down on all sale of it to soldiers. A good pair of skii shoes in the States costs forty or fifty dollars and I can get them made over here (providing I can get the leather) for almost nothing. Of course, I may never use my skiis and boots very much; but if and when I do have the chance, I will have the equipment if I am lucky enough to get all of it home. I think I told you that one of the boxes which I sent just as I was leaving for the 94th contained a couple of small pieces belonging to the skii sticks which in turn are in the box containing the skiis. What complications.

I think that tonight I put my article in its final form. I shall try to copy it tomorrow and send it to you. Tomorrow I shall also send you something else which I shall also send tonight. Each day I think of you

more and tonight I think of you as tomorrow. With all of my heart I send a reassertion of
> Our Love,
> Bushy

Letter from Art to Dotty
Memmingen, Germany
20 Jan. 1946

My Darling,

Joy of joys! Not only did I receive two letters fromyou today, but both were written within the past ten days and were postmarked only eight days ago, Jan 12th. I do hope that letters will begin to come by air for a change. This business of waiting six weeks for a letter to go and then reply to return is too much.

My first reaction to your question concerning voice lessons for me was an immediate and decided "yes". However, after thinking the matter over, I think that perhaps it would be unwise. I am sure that it would be the wrong thing for me to take half of your time with Mrs. Leslie. You waited for more than twenty years to take voice, and now that you have a chance I want you to make the most of it and not be hampered by me cutting in on your time. In the second place, with all the credit that I give you for your musical talent, I do think that you are biased in your opinion concerning my voice. Of course, you flatter me to say such a thing—you always were nice about making compliments. You know as well as I that I would love to take the lessons and it is possible that my speaking voice would improve. I am sure that you could help me a great deal with my voice, and that would be far more pleasant anyway. (I just mentioned to Devers that you wanted me to take the voice lessons. His comment, "I think that your wife is losing her reasoning power!") This of course was meant as a slam at me rather than at you, My Dear.)

In your letter of the 10th you speak of my picture, and I wonder if the water color finally arrived. The great gap which exists between your letters makes it a bit difficult to know just what has gone on in between. I sent a water color which was done in Oberstdorf, and I do hope that it arrived without mishap. In that regard, the small Red Cross Record which is on its way is nothing more than some poetry readings. The recording is very poor, and you will probably have great difficulty in hearing it. The large record was made under better conditions. In the haste in which this larger recording was made, a repetition of two or three adjectives is an element of great detraction. Shortly before making the record I found out that I was definitely to ship from the 94th, and my spirits were certainly not at their highest peak.

I accomplished two little jobs today which I was happy to have done. One was a letter long over due to Mom and Dad. The second was the completition and recopying of my article. Under separate cover I am sending you a copy of this article and I am also sending a copy to Mother and Dad. I have no objection to you showing the article to anyone who might be interested in the subject—not because it is my article but because I think that it represents a trend of thought at least current among a certain group of men overseas. As always I would like to hear your criticism on the paper. Evaluate it for the ideas present, the manner in which they are presented, and the conclusions drawn.

In the <u>Stars and Stripes</u> today there is a request for men to write their opinons concerning certain topics pertinent to the UNO. These are to be digested by a board of EM in the UK (United Kingdom) and presented to the US delegates in London. I intend to write up my ideas on two or three of the topics and send them along.

Began an interesting reading of Hemmingway today and find his style interesting. Many of his short stories are mere sketches, but I would do well to study such a style. It would be a very effective medium for some of the ideas which I have for portraying the mind of the American soldier in Europe. I feel new stirrings within me and I feel that all that has gone on during the past year will merely be a background for things yet to come. I believe deep down that I have something to say, and that I will someday begin to say it.

I do not need to wait until tomorrow to begin to say one thing. My love for you is no idle fancy, but rather is an integral part of my life and thought. May God grant us strength and patience to endure the separation of

Our Love,
Bushy

Letter from Art to Dotty
Memmingen, Germany
January 22, 1946 [700-702]

Darling,

The hands of the clock approach in swift stealth the hour of seven o'clock; the RSO crew sits in the office. A few read, a few write letters, others listen to the radio. All of us are waiting for extra ration trucks which are coming from Sonthofen. Pardon me while I gripe but we worked on rations last night until eight, and tonight it will probably be at least eight-thirty or nine. Actually, those of us in the office are not supposed to work on ration breakdown, but those in charge say that we will work all day at our desk and then at night help out with the other job. In addition to all of the other troubles, the colonel has decided that he wants us to use a new system which will take even longer to accomplish.

Glad that I am leaving on Thursday. Yes, that's right, Thursday. On Monday I told Devers to put my name in for a furlough to England which I thought was to be on the 29th. Telling Mr. Haden (Ass't S-4 and my boss) this [that] I received permission to go, since Sgt. Smith is supposed to be back by that time. However, now I find that I am supposed to leave here on Thursday afternoon, leaving Augsburg on Friday, the 25th. Devers is also going, and it will certainly be nicer to have company.

If I do leave, I shall try to send a cable gram to you; and it should get there long before this letter. I will have difficulty writing you very much en route, but I should be able to get off a few notes to let you know something of what is going on. I hope to take copious notes to write up in greater detail after I return. The actual furlough time is ten days in England plus the travel time to and from. I shall probably be gone at least twenty-five days from Memmingen, and you can be sure that I will not hasten any more than necessary. I will have two days in Paris, I think, one each way. Three or four days in Scotland would be very nice, and the other six or seven days in and around London. I think that it would take at least three days to cover London in any sort of decent fashion. I certainly want to see Stratford-on-Avon, Oxford, Cambridge. There will certainly be other spots that will be "must" on my list.

Later (At Room)

We finally gave up our vigil and must return early tomorrow to break down the rations. We will have ten trucks of food tomorrow whereas we normally have three. (Last night I worked with Devers & Findlay in the office until eleven trying to find out the number of men actually in Service Co., but as a result I slept through reveille.)

Sad news came to many today as a result of an IS. inspection at Personnel yesterday. ERC points were discredited and so all of us will resign ourselves to the now certain fate. Findlay dropped from 51 to 44 —rather big jump!

On the table beside me I have a list of thirteen things which I must do tomorrow in addition to working early and late. Correction please, that should be fifteen, I just added two more things. One of these things is to write you again before leaving, and another is to prepare a cablegram to send. Wish you would write Mother & Dad when this comes for I shall not send two.

We are just beginning to hear "Kiss me Once..." also "Biddin' My Time." Radio helps a great deal in the office and the AFN (Am. Forces Network) has a fair selection of musical programs. The only music which I really want to hear is the music & words when you sing "Indian Love Call", and a couple of other choices numbers. Darling, I can hardly wait to hear you again. I can hardly wait to see you again, be with you again, love you again, for you see, My Dear, I am

Eternally Thine
Bushy

Letter from Art to Dotty
Memmingen, Germany
January 23, 1946 [703]

Darling,

The sands pass swiftly through and I must get to bed but quick. I do want to dash off a short note tonight. Devers and I are leaving here tomorrow afternoon for Ausgburg, and from there on Friday morning in the direction of England. An interesting note is that I was away from the company for 22 days in the 94th, back in the company for 22 days, could possibly be away on furlough for 22 days, and then perhaps I will leave for a home bound unit twenty-two days thereafter.

I spent most of the evening doing very little, as one usually does before leaving for somewhere. Stillhave most of my packing to do tomorrow morning. Did write out a radiogram which I will send tomorrow before leaving. Hope it arrives within a reasonable length of time. Expect to see Ted in Augsburg. By the way, I was able to get a bunch of enlargements back from the Photoshop before leaving. These I will send to you as soon as I return. They are mostly of the Garmisch mountain pictures, and turned out better than I had expected.

Was able to put in an order for a pair of skii boots which will be ready about the time I get back. My chess set is still scattered but I think I can be sure of getting it together shortly. That, I want most of all. I intend to leave all of my clothing and personal things locked up, but packed so that they could easily be moved if necessary. I do not know what I would have done without the combination lock which you sent to me during combat. I received it in Bitsch, but carried it all of the way through.

Gotta get some sleep now, but will try to write some where along the route. We will probably have to wait a few days to get transportation across the Channel. I go on this trip expecting to fall in love with England. That is really not a good attitude with which to begin a trip, but I do not think that I will be disappointed. My happiness at being able to make the trip is only clouded by the fact that I am going without you. I miss you deeply, and especially when I am enjoying something with meaning. May God hasten the day when we are united again in

Our Love,
Bushy

RCA Radiogram, from Nuernberg, from Art to Dotty
January 24, 1946

Jan. 25
Karlsruhe
Furlough to England

Chow stop—our first today at 1530 [3:30 p.m.]. Henry A. Lewis brought Devers and me to Augsburg last evening, and we arrived in time to get a room in a transient hotel and get out to the 5th [REGT.] for supper with Ted. Afterward to a show. Dave Kidder [Ted's

brother] reports that as a civilian he cannot find a school which will take him, an apartment to rent, or a job. Sounds bad on the home front. After returning to the hotel, I was amazed to find that Bob Liddy had a room across the hall from me. He formerly worked with Chaplain Fahy and was in school in France for the past two months. Up at seven and caught the train at 8:35. Whereas when I made the trip to Paris in July almost no civilians were traveling, now the stations are filled with civilians. Snow covered the ground much of the way, but it thinned as we rolled westward. Here in Karlsruhe there is no snow whatever. Our car was cold this morning, but the heat has been turned on and we are very warm now. The transient mess here is in a former hotel and seems to be operating with a fair degree of efficiency. The usual crowd of children gathered outside to beg for cigarettes or chewing gum, and an old hawker tried to see antique medals and trinkets.

Letter from Art to Dotty
En Route- Karlsbuhr – Scarburg
Jan 25, 1946 [704-706, handwritten]

Darling,

The paper is hardly visible and the train moves with many starts and stops. However, I shall try to finish a note telling you of our trip— The train has just just stopped—a fellow in GI clothing dashes up to our compartment.. "Schocolade? Joe? You do business; yes, no?! The train moves on now and he is gone with a dozen candy bars which some of the fellows gave him. They have his 300 francs—about $3.00 with the lowered rate of exchange. This is just another indication of how the Black Market works.

To get back to my story—Devers and I left at 2:30 yesterday and came to Augsburg in a jeep. We arrived in time to get a room at the transient hotel. We continued on to the 5th Inf in time for supper with Ted and then a show. Nothing much new with him except that Dana (Kidden) cannot get in a school, find an apartment, or get a job. That is not encouraging.

We had a fairly nice room and I slept well. Up at seven and breakfast in time to get our train at 8:35. We arrive in Paris tomorrow morning, spend the day there and continue on to the coast tomorrow night. Will try to add a note to this tomorrow when I will again tell you

I love you, Bushy.

P.S. Thinking as I have been about the trip, I failed to mention the important news. 71st to be alerted on Feb. 10th. The Div Hq., Artillery, Sig; Units, etc. will be detached and out on a carrier unit for 50, 51, 52, 53 pointers. Approximately a month later the 66 Regt will be alerted to take home 45-49 pointers, 5th & 14th to remain as permanent occupation.. Ted thinks that we will go to 66th in late Feb. Looks as though I may be on my way by my birthday.

> Still luvya,
> Bushy

> Paris
> Jan 26

Arrived here about 9:00 o'clock breakfast & shave. No time for anything else. We leave here at one o'clock for the coast. Hope to have more time here on my return.

Wonderful to breathe the air in Paris again.

> Sill luv ya,
> Bushy

Jan. 26
Near Paris

River Marne winds lazily along through the countryside. Boats are frequently tied along its banks, and in late evening or early morning the French are seen rowing up and down. On either side of the valley the ridges rise in saucer fashion. Today low clouds cut visibility, but tall buildings appear through the haze as we speed by. The eaves are narrow in contrast to the wide Bavarian eaves. The tall buildings seem anemic, and the garden plots are unusually small. Sometimes brick fences surround the latter.

Leaving Paris

Arrived Gare de L'Est about 09:30 and wasted a great deal of time getting a good breakfast and checking our baggage at Gare St. Lazare. Devers and I dashed down to the Rainbow Corner (near Madeline Church) for a much needed shave and a welcomed Coca-Cola. Out fatal mistake was to pick up PX rations, for we were hounded continually by people trying to buy cigarettes. The sky was heavily overcast, and the dismal weather seemed to be reflected in the faces of the Parisians. The serious political crisis through which the French Gov't is passing seemed to be reflected in the attitudes of the man on the street. Nevertheless, it was good to walk in Paris again. I like the people, their natural warmth and gaiety. Again there was a long wait for baggage and finally boarded a train at one o'clock. Due in Camp Wing tonight.

One of the saddest mistakes that we generally make is the mistake of placing such a premium on the amount of money we have. The amount means nothing, but in the use we make of it lies the importance.

Letter from Art to Dotty
Camp Wings (Near Le Harve)
Jan 27, 46 [708-711]

Darling,

The little library here in camp is crowded and Jack Benny's program comes from the radio in the corner. The library is one of the several spots where we can spend our time while awaiting the channel boat. After an uneventful trip, we arrived in Le Harve about nine last night. The trip here—about five miles—was made in an open truck, and the misty cold penetrated our bundled clothing. We were quickly given tents, blankets, and a light supper.

I had wanted to go to Church today but we spent the morning processing. Most of this was the process of waiting and more of the same this afternoon when we converted our marks to English pound sterling.

It seems that the channel boat runs bi-weekly and we should be able to cross tomorrow or Tuesday. I care little for the prospects of arising at three or four o'clock in the morning, but the tides are beyond the control of man.

It is interesting that I arrived yesterday in the POE of Le Harve on the very date that I boarded in POE New York to come to France one year ago. We are not far from Doudeville where I spent my first month of training and so this damp cold weather is familiar to me.

A delightful program of music is on now—our well loved All-Girl Orchestra—and I separate myself from my surroundings to join you within the bounds of the music. You are very near to my, My Love.

Four movies per day entertain here on the post and I shall perhaps see a show tomorrow. This camp, by the way, is a tent city—that is, pyramidal tents have been set up as barracks and its purpose at the moment seem to be largely that of a funnel for troops moving to and from the UK (United Kingdom). PWs seem to do almost all the work, and they move about in complete freedom. I trust that the weeks will not be many until I am again passing through one of these camps and in the same direction as now—destination, "the hills of home."

By the way, the UNO Conference in London is getting into full swing. Well!! Yes, think I will. Would like to express a couple of view points to Mrs. Roosevelt or others of the U.S. delegation. Would of course want to hear some of the sessions. Hmmm! We shall see, and I shall most certainly try.

Second only to the shores of my native land, the sights of England, the Unknown Isle, will excite me to a new height. I wish you were standing by my side as I stand on the bow and look out toward the mighty cliffs of Dover. I shall think of you and whisper

I love you,
Bushy

Jan 28
Camp Wings, near Le Havre

We traveled from Paris to Le Havre in English-style coaches, which were quite warm and comfortable. Leaving Gare St. Lazare about one o'clock in the afternoon, we reached Le Havre at nine. With only a short delay, we boarded large semi-trailers and rode through the cold, misty night air to Camp Wings. An interesting sidelight is that I entered P.O.E. [PORT OF EMBARKATION] Le Havre [ALMOST] exactly one year after I entered P.O.E. New York, for it was on Jan. 26th, '45 that I boarded the boat in New York.

Upon reaching Wings, we were given beds, blankets, and a light supper. The camp is a tent city, and it seems that it is used for the most part as a funnel for GIs going to and from the UK. PWs do most of the work and move about in apparent freedom. The weather is reminiscent of Deauville, where I spent a month last spring.

We spent most of the day Sunday learning that our shipping number is 202-J, converting our money to English pound sterling, and taking a perfunctory "short arm" [A GI EUPHEMISM FOR A VISUAL INSPECTION FOR VD].

"THIS FORTRESS BUILT BY NATURE FOR HERSELF"

This royal throne of Kings, this sceptered isle,
This earth of majesty, this seat of Mars,
This other Eden, demi-Paradise;
This fortress built by Nature for herself
Against infection and the hand of war;
This happy breed of men, this little world;
This precious stone set in a silver sea
Which serves it in the office of a wall,
Or as a moat defensive to a house
Against the envy of less happier lands;
This blessed plot, this earth, this realm, this England.
This nurse, this teeming womb of royal kings
Feared by their breed and famous by their birth,
Renowned for their deeds as far from home
For Christian service and true chivalry
As is the sepulcher in stubborn Jewry
Of the world's ransom, blessed Mary's Son
This land of such dear souls, this dear, dear land,
Dear for her reputation thru the world,
Is now leased out – I die pronouncing it –
Like to a tenement or petty farm,
England, found in with the triumphant sea,
Whose rocky shore beats back the envious siege
Of Watery Neptune, is now bound in with shame,
With inky blots and rotten parchment bonds,
That England that was wont to conquer others,
Hath made a shameful conquest of itself.
(King Richard II)

Letter from Art to Dotty
Camp Wings (Le Harve)
Jan 28, 46 [712-715]

Dearest Heart,
        News came this afternoon that we arise tomorrow morning at
three o'clock (what a frightful hour)—to eat breakfast and leave at four.
We go, of course, to Le Harve to load on a Victory ship. Should arrive in
South Hampton late tomorrow afternoon. I learned today that it is

possible to secure tickets for the UNO Conference. I shall certainly try to attend.

This morning we slept until ten. I did little during the day but shave and shower and think of you. Wrote Pratt & Kidder tonight. I do miss you, you know—Love you, too, in case you are interested!

In a couple of notes which I jotted down on the trip, I commented that interior decoration should strive for simplicity. I was thinking particularly of our living room (to be). It seems to me that a few well chosen pieces (furniture, paintings, tapestry, bric-a-brac) can be improved upon by being limited to the very minimum. Variety can be obtained by rearranging the furniture from time to time and by replacing pictures with new and different ones. Since we will have three or four years at least before we settle down, we should be able to buy our furniture with care and discretion—buying only pieces of quality.

In another note which I wrote down the other day, I made mention of the mistake so often made concerning the value of money itself. So very often we are inclined to measure our desire in terms of the amount of money which we have.

Money is only of value insofar as as it is spent wisely. We may have amassed only a small nest egg during the past months, but if spent with care and discretion it can have a value far beyond that which a larger fortune may have. The small things still count most toward happiness.

Tomorrow I shall attain my dreams of stepping upon the soil of England. Tonight may I attain my dream (if only in dreams) of holding you in my arms, of pressing your lips to mine, of singing a song without words—all in an attempt to express in some small way the wonder and exceeding joy of

Our Love,
Bushy

***

Jan. 29
South Hampton Roads

As was true one year ago, I am on board a ship tonight – this time anchored off South Hampton. We arose this morning at the frightful hour of 0220. After breakfast we loaded on trucks and rode again into the port. I was happy to see an outlying district of Le Havre which apparently had been touched but little by the bombing and shelling of the city. Other sections however showed the utter destruction which the war wrought there. We stood in a driving rain for almost an hour but finally loaded aboard. We were given bunks, and very soon the entire ship was quiet. I slept most of the day but arose at noon to make the mistake of eating a "C" ration. Could only consume a small part of it and felt a bit woozy. "C" ration again tonight. For some unknown reason we stay aboard ship tonight and disembark tomorrow.

Dice games are going on all around, and pounds are being tossed down as though they were ten-franc notes. The fellows spread a blanket on the floor or on a table and get excited as though it were a horse race or a football game.

We were told that the channel waters are still infested with mines, and the men in one of the other compartments were warned to stay out of it as much as possible during the crossing.

Letter from Art to Dotty
Columbia Club
Jan 30, '46 [716-723]

Darling,

I have just returned from my first activity here in London. Tonight the London Symphony Orchestra played at Royal Albert Hall. I had two tickets and how I acquired them is rather amusing. As I mentioned before, my first interest here is to get to the UNO Conference. As soon as I settled down a bit this afternoon, I began to ask questions about the possibilities. As I waited at one of the information desks, I overheard the reference to tickets to Albert Hall. My nose shot into the air like a pointer on a hot scent and my ears stood up. Well, the GI in front of me happened to be interested in going and so he took what appeared to be the last ticket. My ears drooped, and, with my tail between my legs I began to walk away. However, the gallant Red Cross Lady was equal to the situation. She grabbed my hand and told me that she had two tickets—one was for one of the RC girls working in the Club and the other was for some "nice young man" to escort the young girl. Before I knew what had happened, I was talking with the girl and arranging to meet her in front of Albert Hall at 6:45.

I really had no intentions, Darling, really I didn't. But that's what happens when a Red Cross Lady picks me out as a "nice young man." Tch! Tch!

The girl was a pleasant, in fact, jolly type, but terribly plump (with a capital "P"). She has been in RC work since the war began, father's in

Am., and also her fiancée who is attending Johns Hopkins. She gave me a couple of good ideas as to places to go and see while here.

Throughout the concert I was just a tiny bit worried as to what she would expect at the end of the concert. I had no intention of taking her to a club for dancing and drinking, nor did I think that I could say goodbye at the foot of the steps and hurry away. I decided to compromise and offer to take her to a restaurant for a bit to eat. Well with a great deal of tact for which I gave her credit, she suggested that she had a great deal of work to do and that she would put me on the right track home and then go on herself. It worked with no complications and I appreciated her apparent understanding of my feelings. The concert was excellent though the hall was a bit drafty. Tchaikovsky's 5th highlighted the program and the eighty piece orchestra responded beautifully to the conductor.

But I must get back to the story of how I got here. I wrote from Camp Wings the night before leaving. We were awakened at 0220 Tuesday morning and loaded on the boat at Le Harve about 0730. Most of the day was spent in the bunk, since I had slept little before leaving. We had nothing but "C" rations to eat, and I found that I still can't eat those things. Although we arrived in Southampton Roads last evening, we spent the night aboard. My feet touched English soul at 0920 this morning.

I am a great believer in signs, particularly in good ones. Now we have hardly seen the sun in the past two weeks and when I left the boat rain was sprinkling down. However, as the train pulled from the the shed at the dock, the sun shone bright and clear and the sky was a deep blue. I day-dreamed of the time when I will be bringing you from Southampton to London.

Thursday 31st

Darling,

Have just returned from Drury Lane and Ibsen's "Doll House". I want to describe my day in much greater detail but I will have to do that in another letter. This one is becoming a bit bulky.

No UNO meeting today and so I paid a couple of visits to Westminister Abbey. Much to describe there. Also walked over Westminister Bridge just because my old friend Coleridge wrote a poem there. We simply must spend a year over here, My Love, before I can hope to teach anyone anything about English Literature.

Ran into one of my old students from Maryville High Sch.—John Crawford, I think. He's a buck sgt. in SHAE Hdq.
Will write more tonight telling you of
Our Love, Bushy

Jan. 31
Columbia club
London, England

My activities have occupied my time so much that I have been unable to take proper notes during the last two or three days. After many long months of waiting and hoping, my foot finally touched English soil on Wed., the 29th at 0920. It was misty and some rain was falling. We stood in a very long line for our London tickets and then boarded a special troop train. We cleared the giant shed, the sun shown clear and bright, and the sky was a delightful blue. I like to believe in signs – particularly good ones, and I wanted to believe that this was a sign for good weather. As we rode through the southern part of England north to London, I observed that the terrain is very similar to that of E. Tenn., though somewhat less pronounced. The hills seem to roll in the same fashion, the farms were cut up in the same fashion, the trees gave the same appearance. As we rode into London, many of the features of terrain were familiar from the pictures I have seen. I had no difficulty recognizing the Tower of London, Big Ben, St. Paul's, etc. With the usual amount of confusion, I hesitated after getting off the train. Finally I took a taxi to the Columbia, where we were to report. The English taxi is a rare combination of an elegant coach and an A model Ford, but we arrived. Before I had a chance to get inside the door, I was accosted by a hawker who wanted to know if I had anything to sell. My first concern was a room, and I brushed hurriedly past. I was to find that only a very few Englishmen appear to be dealing in the Black Market, but I am sure that the GIs have encouraged a few to deal in such activities. Watches, cameras, and fountain pens seem to be the principal items of exchange. I had not eaten a regular meal in 36 hours, but I wanted to get my bag settled and a room cleared. I was told immediately to leave nothing in the room, for thieving is reportedly very bad. As I was getting ready to inquire concerning tickets to the UNO [UNITED NATIONS ORGANIZATION; LATER SIMPLY THE UN] conference, I overheard "Albert Hall" mentioned.

My ears stood up and my nose went into the air. It was the last ticket. My chin fell down a couple of stories, and my ears drooped. The lady at the desk saw my despair and quickly rose to the occasion. She grabbed my hand and led me over to another Red Cross girl. She had two tickets, one of which belonged to the RC girl; the other to "some nice young man." I was the lucky fellow. What could I do but accept? It proved to be a most enjoyable evening with the London symphony with Edna Iles at the piano (for Medtner's Piano Concerto No. 2 in C Minor). Highlight of the evening was Tchaikovsky's 5th Symphony. The girl's father is in America and her fiance is also, and she has worked at the RC Club since the Yanks came. I was slightly worried about the moment after the concert when she might expect a club or a drink. I tried to avoid that situation by suggesting a bite to eat. With a great deal of tact, she thanked me but was sure that she had a great deal of work to do. Since I was completely lost, she started me home, and so ended a most enjoyable evening.

This morning I arose at eight for breakfast and a long line to book my room again. Dashed down to the UNO to find no conference, but enjoyed a visit to Westminster Abbey. Many, many of my old friends have residence at Westminster. The first one that I saw was Wm. Congreve. Beneath his bust was an inscription which I thought was worth taking down:

> "Mr. William Congreve Dyed jany (e) 19th 1728. Aged
> 56. And was buried near this place. To whose most
> Valueable Memory this Monument is Sett up by
> Henriette Duchess of Marlborough as mark how
> dearly She remembered the happiness and Honour
> She enjoyed in the Sincere Friendship of so worthy
> and Honest a Man, Whose Virtue Candour and Witt
> gained him the love and Esteem of the present age
> and whose Writings will be the Admiration of the
> future."

Another interesting note was to Wm. Tyndale:

> "This tablet was placed here in the year of our Lord
> 1939 in Thankful Commemoration of Wm. Tyndale
> B 1490 – D 1536 Translator of the holy Scripture into
> the Language of the English People"

Many others are buried beneath the floor of the abbey, and dear old Ben Johnson was place upright in his tomb. (I presume because he was as thick as he was tall). Westminster is, of course, French in style and architecture and seems very much like Notre Dame. The guide spoke with much wit and with a real background knowledge. Later this afternoon I visited Westminster again. Walked all the way to Lambert Bridge in misty rain after receiving the wrong directions, but I finally found Westminster Bridge. I wanted to walk across it, of course, because of Wordsworth's "Lines...," and it was well worth the trouble. [HAD A COPY OF THE POEM TO READ WHILE STANDING ON THE BRIDGE.] On my way back I browsed through a bookstore on Oxford St. and couldn't resist a couple of small copies of Shakespeare for spare reading. Tonight to Drury Lane and Winter Garden for a performance of Ibsen's Doll's House. Very well done.

"Composed upon Westminster Bridge, September 3, 1802" by William Wordsworth

Earth has not anything to show more fair:
Dull would he be of soul who could pass by
A sight so touching in its majesty:
This City now doth, like a garment, wear
The beauty of the morning; silent, bare,
Ships, towers, domes, theatres, and temples lie
Open unto the fields, and to the sky;
All bright and glittering in the smokeless air.
Never did sun more beautifully steep
In his first splendour, valley, rock, or hill;
Ne'er saw I, never felt, a calm so deep!
The river glideth at his own sweet will:
Dear God! the very houses seem asleep;
And all that mighty heart is lying still!

[Editor chose to include poem.]

Feb. 2, 1946
2320 hours
London, Columbia Club

When I visited Drury Lane on Thursday night, the London mist was falling, the street lamps cast grotesque shadows. I thought that the name should have been "Dreary Lane." I passed a group of corner buildings [?] which had been bombed, and this added to the somberness of the setting.

Friday morning I arose with the intention of attending the UNO, and so I hurried to White Hall only to find that the only meetings scheduled were for the evening. Walking up Whitehall, I couldn't resist Downing St., and so I strolled down the narrow way. The street is no more than thirty feet wide and ends in [a] staircase leading off toward St. James Park. I found the famed No. 10 in a most unpretentious two-story building of dark, discolored brick. After passing the full short length of the street, I turned and retraced my steps. As I passed the Prime Minister's door, Mr. Bevin himself, or a most reasonable facsimile of the same, hurried out and drove away. On up Whitehall to Trafalgar Square, stopping by the mall and a Malay Office. No, they had no Malaysian books. [I HAD STUDIED THE MALAY LANGUAGE FOR A BRIEF TIME AT STANFORD, SHORTENED BY A MONTH'S HOSPITAL CONFINEMENT FOR AN EMERGENCY APPENDECTOMY.]

I spent the remainder of my short morning in the National Art Gallery. Was interested to discover "The annunciation" by Fra Lippo Lippi (1406-69) – Florentine Sch., not for the work but for the fact that Browning deals with the painter. I was struck by Van Eyck's "Giovanni Arnolfini and His Wife." The colors were delightful to the eye, and the minute detail was well-nigh perfect. Many fine landscapes by Constable as well as other famous artists, Titian and the rest.

Friday afternoon was very mild, and I did little but shower, visit the PX, and search for a much needed comb. The last brought me to one of the larger department stores in town, and I was pleased at the great variety of goods which I saw. There was certainly far more than I had expected, even though coupons are still necessary.

In the evening, I was invited to a play with Edw. Swartz (a friend of Ted Kidder's in the 5th Inf. [REGIMENT]. We visited the Granville Theater out in the West End to see a mystery thriller, The Third Visitor. Actors were convincing and the plot exciting. Ran into an Irish fellow who tried to be very helpful in giving us information concerning the city. After the play, we went directly to the Westminster Station and the UNO meeting of the Gen. Assembly. It was a thrilling experience, and I shall try to go again. The meetings are held in White Hall in a room somewhat small for such a gathering. The new Sec. Gen., [TRYGVE] Lie from Norway presided in *front of the great golden emblem and the blue and tan drapes. Swartz and I entered as Sol Blum (U.S. representative) spoke for a second donation for UNRRA. Others spoke in turn – each speech being given in both English and French. Stenographers appeared to be taking down two sets of notes—one on a shorthand machine and the other by hand. We were happy to observe Mrs. Roosevelt, Mr. [AMBASSADOR] Stettinius, Mr. Dulles, Tom Connelly, and the other members of our delegation. The entire proceedings were interesting though terribly slow. We left about 11:30, and I didn't get to bed until one o'clock.*

Later

I wonder if anyone had ever known the longing, the heart-tearing ache, the desperate loneliness which I know for my wife. With tidal force there sweeps over me at times an acute emptiness which only her presence can fill. I need her. I must be with her to make my life full. May God hasten the day of our reunion, and may we never again be separated on this earth.

Feb. 3, '46 (Sun.)
Columbia Club

I have attempted to make Sunday a real day of rest by sleeping until 11:30 and planning to spend the remainder of the day in writing and reading. Yesterday was a full day, and I felt the need of a sort of break in my schedule.

Saturday began with a walking tour under the expert guidance and lecturing of our Red Cross guide. We stopped at Buckingham Palace to see the changing of the guard. It was not as spectacular as I had expected, although the drill precision was excellent. The old guard stood on the right side of the gate while the new guard came from the barracks marching behind the Grenadiers Band. We walked down past Green Park and along Birdcage Walk beside St. James Park (where a large bomb had just been discovered in a lake there).

A tour of Parliament was our main objective, and we thronged through. The first stop was in the new House of Lords (formerly the Kings' Gown Room). It was here that Wm. Joyce (Lord Haw Haw [A BRITISH SUBJECT WHO GAVE RADIO BROADCASTS FOR THE GERMANS DURING THE WAR] was brought only a few weeks ago for his final appeal for life. We continued into the present House of

Commons, formerly the House of Lords. The British have the tremendous advantage of dividing the members of each house into two groups—the government and the opposition. This eliminates some of the difficulty the French have of so many factions and combinations. We visited the 11th century Parliament Hall and the beautiful little chapel in the basement reminiscent of St. Chapelle in Paris.

After lunch I hastened out to Mme. Tussaud's Wax works, on Marylebone Road near Baker's Street Station. I was amazed at the life-life quality of the figures ranging down the line from Chaucer and Shakespeare to Truman and Eisenhower. This museum is certainly a "must" for a tour of London. From Mme. Tussaud's to St. Paul's for a short service being held. There is a simple grandeur about St. Paul's, which made an outstanding impression on me. The dome is of course magnificent. I wanted very much to see Henry IV by the "Old Vic" players, but tickets are very difficult to secure. I had been told that perhaps I could obtain a ticket turned in at the last minute.

From St. Paul's I took an omnibus to Charring Cross, thinking that the theater was nearby. After a long wait and no bus to my destination, I decided to walk. This I did from Trafalgar Square down the Strand to Waterloo Bridge, across and on past Waterloo Station. I found the "Old Vic" all right, but I also found that it had been closed for several years. After a number of inquiries, I found that I was really searching for the New Theatre where the Old Vic players was performing. When I finally arrived on Leicester Sq., just as the curtain was going up—not even standing room! The only ticket that I could secure for next week was a matinee Saturday. Rather disappointed in my fruitless search, I returned to Marble Arch [my hotel] for a cup of tea and a sandwich. Since it was still early, I bought a ticket for Arthur Rank's $5 million "flop" Caesar and Cleopatra. In my humble opinion, the critics have been far too severe in their reviews. It is supposed to be technically perfect and the most expensive film ever made. The acting is well-nigh flawless with roses to Claude Rains and Vivien Leigh. Shaw's keen wit is carried into the scenarios, which he himself wrote; and the cracks at the British are well received, especially by the British (if the crowd last night is to be considered typical). The Technicolor made for many lovely scenes, but for me the almost intangible psychology employed by Caesar pervades every scene and action and was paramount to every other single feature of the picture.

It is interesting to hear GI's blandly (and blindly) remark that here is nothing to do in London!

Had planned to leave for Scotland tonight. However, in deference to my cold I decided to wait until the morrow. Spent the evening writing to Dotty and the folks.

Letter from Art to Dotty
Columbia Club
Feb. 3, 1946 [724-729]

Darling,

An hour and a half ago I sat down to write. For that length of time I have been engaged in conversation with a sergeant sitting across the table from me, who happens to be from Mississippi. We have discussed everything from the racial question in the South to <u>Caesar and Cleopatra</u>. Sorry, My Love, I should have been talking to you. You know how I dislike conversation anyway!

This afternoon I planned to leave for Scotland tonight at ten— (thirty minutes from now). However, A bad cold—helped me decide to await the morning. I shall leave early in the morning and reach Edinburg about seven tomorrow night. I have much here in London to see and do, and so I hope to return here by Wednesday. Still must go to Stratford, Oxford, & Cambridge and I only have seven more days for all of this.

Because of my cold, I spent most of the day inside resting from the rat race of the past four days. In addition to the concert which I wrote about already, I have seen two plays and a very excellent movie. The movie was Arthur Rank's $5 million production of Shaw's <u>Caesar & Cleopatra</u>. I enjoyed the play a very great deal.

It was also yesterday that I saw the changing of the guard at Buckingham Palace, toured the House of Parliament, spent a couple of hours at Mm. Tussauds famous museum of wax figures (most lifelike), attended a service at St Paul's, and walked almost two miles in a vain attempt to see <u>Henry IV</u> by the "Old Vic" players. On previous days I have done other things like visiting the National Gallery, No. 10 Downing St. (where Mr. Bevin kindly made a curtain call), and the UNO.

The latter was an evening meeting on Friday. Saw most of the US. delegation including Eleanor, Stettinius, Dulles, Sol Blum, Tom Connally, etc. The business before the house was a proposal for additional aid to UNRRA. The proceedings were very interesting, but also slow due to the language problem—every speech is given in both English and French. I hope to go again if time permits.

By the way, I intend to try to call you before leaving, but the telephone strike in the States has created some difficulties along this line. I do hope that I can make it tho.

It is interesting how much variety of attitudes exist under varying conditions. Devers and I have done little more than eat meals together here. For the most part I have not gone to the movies since I can see the same ones elsewhere. However, I can't see the sights of London elsewhere. Thus he has been interested not a bit in the tours which I have taken.

Think I mentioned before that we are eating British rations—which I find to be very good—though of course, not so much variety as in our GI. ration. The people are really wonderful to us, even after so many years that the Am. soldier has been here.

I continue to run into one or two guys each day that I have known elsewhere. Today, it was a fellow I knew for a month at Santa Rosa before going to Stanford.

I must get to bed now, but will try to write from Scotland. In all of my activity here, I miss you acutely.

> Love ya,
> Bushy

Feb. 4
London

Morning spent at the Tower of London—a tower reeking with history. Interesting collections in the museum, including armor used by Henry VIII. Many people executed in the courtyard of the fort including Anne Boleyn, Lady Jane Gray, etc. Missed 11:00 train for Cambridge and had interesting dinner in a small restaurant near the Liverpool St. Late train but arrived Cambridge about 1500. Newton Alsup was the first GI I saw. Chaplain Webb also attending.

Feb. 5
Edinburgh, Scotland

What a setting! I am seated in a small dining room at a table just outside a circle of Scotsmen who are ranting over their teacups and the tax, the income tax, the cost of war, etc. They are seated around a

Edinburg Castle, Edinburg Scotland

Edinburg Castle

fireplace—four or five British soldiers, three middle-aged Scotch gentlemen. Another GI (Richard Middleton) writes on the table with me. The elderly lady in charge just came in to talk to us. She is extremely friendly, and everyone that I have met tonight has been more than nice to us. This is a "Hostel" for Service men, and seems to have been converted from a private dwelling. Old clocks, old pictures, old books—a lovely ancient atmosphere. Tea and sweet cakes are served between 9 [p.m.] and midnight, and we shall partake.

[UPON OUR ARRIVAL, THE LADY SHOWED US AROUND THE ROOMS. WHEN WE CAME TO THE KITCHEN, SHE POINTED TO A DISH WITH COOKIES AND ALONG SIDE IT A SMALLER DISH WITH A FEW COINS. "REMEMBER THE WEE SAUCER," SHE SAID.]

Arriving at 7 o'clock tonight, Middleton and I were given this address after inquiring at a British Club. [ALL SPACES THERE WERE RESERVED FOR BRITISH SOLDIERS.] It was a bit late for anything to eat here, and so we made a trek down town to a very nice café. For 2/3 (2 shillings, 3 pence) I had a four-course meal that tasted almost like home cooking. We have seen only one [OTHER] American Soldier here, and I think that there will be few to see later. There is no American Club here anymore, and far fewer GI's are to be seen anywhere in the Isles.

We had a very [GOOD] trip up on the train, leaving King's Cross station at ten. Shortly out of London the sun burst through the mist. The countryside was lovely—small fields, large haystacks, fat cattle. The hedgerows must be very attractive dressed in green in Springtime. Old castles are always in evidence far away, lost in great clumps of trees. We had a very good meal on the train (though I always feel a bit guilty when I eat the British rations). Between York and Newcastle, we began to see the factories and mining districts, and the flat country began to roll a bit. Beyond Newcastle we ran along the coast, sometimes being able to look over the edge of the barren rocks to the sea. The coast is very irregular here, and many good harbors are found.

Feb. 8
London

It was in Newcastle that the lady at the microphone in the station began each announcement with the cheery greeting of "Hello, Hello!" I had no difficulty in deciding the moment that we reached the Scottish border, for the conductor came around immediately thereafter for our tickets. (Rarely in England are tickets collected before the completion of the trip.) One other thing seemed to prove our presence in Scotland: the moon was a very thin silver, and it descended early in the evening. Sure, and it must a bin a Scotch moon.

My first night at the Margaret Tudor Hostel (1 Merchant St.) I met a couple of Polish boys who are attending school, a Dutch boy on furlough and a very nice Canadian fellow. Over our teacups and rolls we talked.

Feb. 9
London

I have just reached here from *The New Theatre* where the Old Vic Players have just presented *Oedipus* by Sophocles and *The Critic* by Sheridan. The first was in the translation by W. B. Yates and made effective use of the choral background. Laurence Olivier turned in a very fine performance as Oedipus and again as Mr. Puff in *The Critic*.

At the moment, I await a transatlantic call to Dotty which I booked two days ago. I had wanted very much to call Mother on her birthday, but due to radio interference, it was impossible to get the call through. Needless to say, I am rather excited at the prospect of hearing Dotty's voice again.

My day began at noon today when I arose to eat lunch with Devers. My lateness in arising was occasioned by a late return from Stratford last night. I left there at 7:37 last evening to arrive at Paddington at 11:55. The night was very wet, and the rain came down steadily. As I walked toward Columbia Club I was approached by a young fellow with a hard luck story. I began to suspect immediately that there was some scheme afoot, and the tales are legend concerning the many ways in which money is extracted from the gullible soldiers. I felt that my chances were about 9 to 1 that the story was a hoax, but I felt like a bit of adventure, and I wanted to see what would happen. His story was that he was a Br. Merchant Seaman who had been attached to the USMS in Galveston [TX]. He needed a few pounds to get his baggage from the customs building. I professed to have no money, & then he thought of my watch. His story was somewhat plausible, and I really wanted to believe him. To make an extended story short, he got an old watch which Devers had given me. I found

Oedius by Sophocles, starring Laurence Olivier, Feb. 9, 1946

that the fellow had given the same story to the Mgr. at the Columbia Club, and he may return.

Later
Columbia Club

My call came through about seven o'clock, and I think I have not been more excited since I came overseas. The reception was rather good, and it was a thrill to hear Dotty's voice.

I must go back to my Scotland trip and pick up a few of the incidents there. On Wednesday I spent my morning in the Edinburgh Castle. There, too, is much of historical interest. I was able to see the crown jewels of Scotland and snapped a couple of pictures of them. Also of interest was a War Memorial to those who died in the First World War. It is by far the nicest of its kind that I have seen. During my wanderings around town, I found a lovely little miniature. It is an 18th Cent. oil in a small gold case. I shall make it a wedding present for our second anniversary.

595

In the afternoon I visited Holyrood Palace—the home of Mary Queen of Scots, and later took a tour around town atop an omnibus. I found the Scotch most pleasant and inclined to be as helpful as possible. Both Canadian boys and American GIs seem to prefer a furlough in Scotland to that in England—because, I think, the people seem more like the folks at home. The stores seem to be filled with plenty, and I saw no evidence of food shortages, though of course the rationing of all commodities continues. I found that the people like to make jokes about themselves. They still claim that Aberdeen is the only place in Europe where the Jew cannot make a living. Another story concerning Aberdeen was told me by a Scotsman. The people say that when Neville Chamberlain was in Munich for his appeasement trip, he offered to give Aberdeen to Hitler. The proposal was so startling that Adolph withdrew for hasty consultation. After a brief time he returned. "No," said Hitler, "we would rather have the Jews back!"

[I WAS TOLD THESE STORIES AT THE HOSTEL WHEN I INQUIRED ABOUT THE POSSIBILITY OF GOING ON NORTH TO VISIT ABERDEEN. THEY ILLUSTRATE THE HABIT THE SCOTISH PEOPLE HAVE OF TURNING HUMOR ON THEMSELVES.]

—————

Letter from Art to Dotty
London, England
Feb. 9, '46 [730-737]

My Dearest Darling,

I am still a bit excited tho it was all of two hours ago that I talked to you. You know, I have had a few exciting moments since I landed on this side of the Atlantic, but at no time have I been more excited than tonight as I waited in nervous expectation in the telephone booth.

I arose this morning at the early hour of eleven (I went to bed at 1:30 this morning!), and shortly after lunch, went directly to Leicester Square and the New Theatre. I was lucky enough to have a ticket to see the famed Old Vic Players perform "Oedipus" by Sophocles and "The Critic" by Sheridan. (These players are best known for their Shakespearian plays, but this season they are also doing these others) Sheridan's play is very much in the style of the Restoration Drama which I studied under Dr. Shive. (Honor's Work) Oedipus, of course, is one of the best of the old Greek tragedies and the players did full justice to it.

From the theater I came directly to the Overseas Telephone Office to await my call. I went to the office on Thursday and tried to call Mother since it was her birthday. However, the connections have been very poor due to sun spots and radio interference. Thus I had to abandon my hope to talk to Mother on her birthday but I did book the call to you for tonight.

Darling, it was a thrill to hear your voice again. It's been a long time, you know. I hope that you had no difficulty hearing me (I understand that the reception over there is usually far better than it is over here.) I understood that you have received no money orders from me. I hope that I misunderstood this for as I have repeated before, I sent three in a two month period before going to the 94th.

It seems so strange—I have had no letter from you since one written on Jan 4th, and at that time you had not learned of the loss of points. I have not heard from Mother & Dad since their letter of Dec. 17. Of course, these letters are all waiting for me back in Germany, and that is why I am rather anxious to get back.

I am very much ashamed of the fact that I have not written to you this week, but when I go into greater detail concerning my activities, I think that you will understand what has happened to my time.

In my letter on Sunday, I told of my plans to leave for Scotland on Monday. However, I had a rather bad cold and really didn't feel like making the long trip. Thus it was that I visited the old Tower of London Monday morning. Parts of this were begun by William, the Conqueror in 1066 and there is much history connected with it. After a bite to eat in one of the down town cafes, I caught a one o'clock train for Cambridge. The ride took two hours and a half, but when I arrived the sun was shining. Since my old friend Alsup is there, I immediately went to the barracks where the Am. soldiers stay. With a bit of lucky coincidence, he was the first GI I saw. Wonder of wonders, Chaplain Webb is also there. He was sent to Birmingham and later transferred to Cambridge.

I must admit that I am slightly envious of their set-up. They sit in on the courses which they want, and are supposed to do a great deal of outside reading. No examinations, no tests, plenty of leisure time for entertainment and social contacts. The opportunity would have been of inestimatable value for me.

Newton took me around town and showed me a number of points of interest. We saw the chapel at King's College, the library and Chapel at Trinity. The lazy river Cam runs just behind these two colleges and the grass on the banks seems to be green the year round.

I find that the schools over here are quite as full as they evidently are at home. I forsee many difficulties but I am still determined that we shall spend a few months in the Isles for study and travel.

I returned to London Monday night only to leave Tuesday morning for Scotland. This trip and the ensuing days will come in the following letter which I shall write tomorrow. Happiness for me lies afar off. I cannot be happy until I hear your voice again and there is not the separation of these thousand miles.

I love you
Bushy

Feb. 10
London
UNO Conference

Under the dome of this room, I wonder how many members of this assembly are thinking primarily of the world good as they carry on various discussions and arguments. I wonder how many are still thinking primarily in terms of power politics.

One of the amazing points of this conference is the way in which the two languages used are translated. Many speeches are impromptu, of course, and whether given in English or French, [IT] is immediately given in the second tongue. Clerks take each speech down both in shorthand and on a shorthand machine. The length of time involved for repeating long speeches seems to be the most boring for the members of the assembly.

I have just observed a roll call vote in the Gen. Assembly concerning a proposal of procedure (whether or not those members elected in the September election should take office in Sept. or in Jan.). A roll call vote resulted in a close 21-22. Now it is being questioned whether or not this should have been a 2/3 majority for passage or rejection or merely a majority. It is clear that parliamentary procedure here is not settled on many technical points. This merely illustrates again the many, many minor problems with which the Assembly is confronted in addition to the major problems on its agenda.

I think that many questions will be voted on in the Assembly by delegates who do not have a clear understanding of the questions involved. A well-nigh perfect understanding of either English or

French would be necessary, and even then it is to be questioned whether or not all will understand clearly some of the questions which arise.

With due respect to President Lei, to me he gives the impression of lacking the decisive qualities which one in such a position should possess. I have heard him but twice however, and perhaps the judgment is a hasty one.

Later
London

Attended Presbyterian Service today. Somewhat more formal than our own, though order of service the same. [I RECALL THAT NO ONE SPOKE TO ME AS I ENTERED OR AS I LEFT THE SERVICE.] Channel conditions bad and leave extended until Tuesday.

Letter from Art to Dotty
London
Feb 10, 1946 [738-745]

My Darling,

Today, being Sunday, was a day of rest for me, and I enjoyed it thoroughly. Arising late, I was able to get to church on time. The Presbyterian Church is close by the Club, and I found the interior to be very nice indeed. The order of service was very similar to ours although the hymnal is very much like the Episcopal book. Many of the songs are psalms set to music and there is no music written in the books. I was glad to see an entire row of colored men seated in front of me and I could over hear a Dutch conversation behind me before the service began. The crowd was very small but the sermon was thoughtful and well presented. This afternoon I wrote Mother & Dad, received a two day extension on my leave (channel boat crossing delayed), and slept. When I awoke, I found tickets available at the desk to the UNO conference and so rushed down to the meeting. I missed my supper as a result but I am accustomed to that. (I can always get a snack in the snack bar open 22 hours per day.)

Took a number of notes on the proceedings, but nothing of special interest. A lengthy discussion resulted from an elementary question of parliamentary procedure, indicating many minor difficulties must be overcome in addition to their major problems. I am sure that many of the smaller countries vote on subjects which arise when the issue is still cloudy. A well nigh perfect understanding of either French or English is essential to complete understanding, and even then one wonders. I must get back to my story of events of the past week. Last night I covered everything except my Scotland & Stratford trips. Luckily, I ran into a nice fellow from Washington (State) who accompanied me to Cambridge, and then decided to go to Scotland with me. We left on Tuesday morning and arrived about seven PM in Edinburgh. I wanted to see the English countryside and I was rewarded by travelling during the daylight hours. Until we reached York, the landscape was slightly rolling, and afterward hills began. We passed through the mining and industrial area; and, beyond Newcastle, we rode along the coast.

With a minimum of difficulty we found a place to stay upon our arrival. The "Hostel" as it was called was carried on by an elderly Scotch lady who proved to be very lonely to us. The place was filled with Canadian & English boys, two there were Polish fellows as well as a Dutch soldier.

Wednesday was spent in visiting Edinburgh Castle and Holyrood Palace (where Mary Queen of Scots lived.)

Since our time was so limited we took a tour of the town by tram. I was impressed with the plenty which seemed to be in all of the stores and the food situation seemed to be anything but desperate. However, everything is still rationed, of course. The people were most kind and I heard a number of Scotch jokes all upon themselves. I longed to stay longer among them friendly people, but we left Wednesday night. As I think I described last night, I reached London early Thursday morning and slept the remainder of the morning.

My furlough time was up at noon today. However, the channel conditions are still very bad. We will not leave until Tuesday, perhaps Wednesday. I am getting a bit anxious to get back to Memmingen to get my mail. I do miss your letters terribly, My Love.

Big dance in the Club tonight so I write to you. I long to dance, but only with you in my arms. Until that day when I can press you close to me and dance to the harmony of Our Love, I shall wait.... In case I have forgotten to say so before
I love you,
Bushy

P.S. Will save until later the Stratford story.

Feb 11
London

I have delayed writing of my trip to Stratford too long. It was on Friday last (Feb. 8th) that I caught a 11:05 from Paddington [STATION]. I managed to get a seat in a compartment with another G. I. (the only other one on the train, I believe). Although the usual silence reigned in our compartment (one almost never becomes involved in conversation with a stranger on a train in England), the two of us managed to find out that both were going to Stratford. Our train was late, and we missed our connection, which made us arrive in the mid-afternoon. (We ran into another Am. soldier who was going out to be stationed in the town—the only one there! Our first objective was Shakespeare's birthplace, which we found very quickly. The notes which follow were taken as we went through the museum at the birthplace and show anything but order.

We were told that Chas. Dickens bought the old home place of Shakespeare in 1847, when he found it being used as a second class inn. Now thousands of people from every country and clime come as on a pilgrimage to see the room where the Stratford bard was born. The house contains the original beams, stones, etc., although a new stairway had to be rebuilt when the original stairs were worn away. No lights are allowed because of the fire hazard, and so we had to hurry to see everything before dark.

Shakespeare married Anne Hathaway when he was 17 (she being 25), but [HE] continued to work for his father until he was 21. At this time he came to London where he probably taught school. When he returned to Stratford he bought New Place – the best house in town.

When he died (April 23, 1616) he left the bulk of his fortune of 75,000 [POUNDS] to Susanna, including the house. According to the laws of the time, his wife would automatically receive 1/3 of the property and money, and he included in his will that Anne should get "the second best bed." (This is accounted for by the fact that the best bed was usually built in and was the guest bed). Sixteen ways have been found of spelling Shakespeare's name, and he is known to have used seven different ways. It seems that the seal was the important thing in those days—not the signature.

The bulk of Shakespeare's fortune came from the Globe Theatre. He began with 1/7 interest and at the end had about a ½ interest. His plays were sold immediately upon writing and were not published [UNTIL AFTER HIS DEATH. FIRST COLLECTION PUBLISHED IN

1623]. Some of the actors memorized the plays and wrote them down to sell, but these were usually incomplete. The last original portfolio was sold to an American for 21,000 guineas ($60,250).

In one of the lower rooms in the museum is a 14th century sword which is traditionally carried by the mayor of Stratford in an annual procession. In 1945, the 8th AF (Am.) Band came to lead the procession, and the sword was carried by a G.I.—the first time not carried by a British subject. This sword is referred to in "The Taming of the Shrew."

The room where Shakespeare was born is almost bare save for a fireplace, an English version of our "hope chest" (called a "Bridal Box"), and the bust of Shakespeare taken from Westminster. The ceiling and window pane are covered with signatures of people who have visited the room, including most of the figures in English literary history (Byron, Carlyle, Browning, Thackeray, Isaac Watt). Browning's poem was penciled in this room.

[May 4, Jamestown, TN]

Further note on Stratford and Shakespeare's Memorial:

Both "Stratford-Upon-Avon" and "Stratford-on-Avon" seen about town. Train station, "on" "Upon" seems to be old form.

Shakespeare's "curse" [ENGRAVED ON THE STONE IN STRATFORD CHURCH] accounts for his body being left in church rather than taken to Westminster. Body said to be 17 ft. in the ground to cause as much difficulty as possible in moving.

Letter from Art to Dotty
London England
Feb 11, 1946 [746-751]

Darling,

My week has begun in quite a different fashion today. Perhaps I'm not as young as I once was—I certainly can't keep up the pace which I once kept. Yesterday I spent most of my day resting, as I described last night, and I slept most of the morning today. In the afternoon I went after my PX rations, looked for paper for my notebook, and wrote a bit in my diary. (By the way, I can't seem to find any paper over here. Perhaps you had best send a few sheets in your letters as before. The size, you know, is 6 ¾ x 3 ¾). Tonight I was waiting for supper when the Information Desk announced that they had a free ticket to "Gay Rosalinda". I had tried several times during the day to get a ticket to this performances but with no success. After turning over my table, chair, two or three elderly ladies, and a couple of GI's, I slide into the desk to grab the ticket. I won! The music by Johann Strauss, was good and the singing fair. I enjoyed the ballet more than anything else.

The 5th & 14th Regts. are now officially AO according to a recent edition of S&S. The latest rumor here is that the Artillery is already in France on their merry way, and I presume that the division is officially disbanded. I think that my stay will be of short duration in the 14th when I return to Memmingen.

Devers and I plan to leave on the boat train to Paris Wednesday. This will eliminate the stop over in Camp Wings, as we will go across to Dieppe and directly from there to Paris. I hope to spend a short time there, that is a day if possible. Would like to get to the opera for one more performance but I doubt that I will be able to get a ticket for that.

Strangely enough I have become rather restless here during the past two days. As much [as] I have enjoyed my furlough, I am very ready to leave now. Of course, the real reason is that I know that ere long I shall be on my way again, and this time there shall be no turning me back. I expect the usual number of delays, shipping dates, cancellations, etc, but I will finally sail. My journey will soon begin, and this journey will surely end in lover's meeting.

I have not yet attended Parliament and this I would like to do tomorrow if possible. There is a great hue and cry here at the moment concerning the food situation. I am sometimes inclined to think that the question is overplayed a bit, but these people have suffered a great deal during the past few years. The general opinion seems to be that bungling and red tape are responsible for the shortage of food now. The Labor Gov't is not very popular among those with whom I have talked. However, I think the British are far more aware than we of the importance of the economic competition between the States and the British Empire. I think that she is well aware that she is fighting for her life. It will be a pity if the two countries fail to find a workable solution suitable to both sides.

It is late and I must sleep, perchance to dream, to kiss you and reaffirm

My Love,
Bushy

Feb. 12, 47
Grosvenor Sq., London
[AMERICAN EMBASSY?] Lichfield Trials

The room is very small with seating space for not more than fifty spectators. A few plain desks serve the courtroom, and the fireplace seems out of place.

Col. Kilian was brought in shortly after the trial called to order. The first question refers to treatment of men brought into the Lichfield. Gen. Court Martial if AWOL for 30 days, first offense. Three or four repetitions of AWOL warranted Gen. Court Martial. Questions concerning missing shipments, etc. These questions seem to be a long way from the original trial of Sgt. Judson Smith, on trial for mistreatment of prisoners.

The Captain who is questioning Col. Kilian is certainly asking leading questions in an attempt to get the answer which he wishes. The Captain who questions the Col. Is trying to bring out the point that Col. Kilian gave a Gen. Court Martial to men who missed a final roll call even tho they were present for the shipment. Kilian admits that investigations were made & then charges written up. Smith is certainly the forgotten man here. Personal inspections & inspections of the staff were made to insure that physical mistreatment was not permitted.

Afternoon Session

Long before the afternoon session is to convene, the limited space for visitors is filled. A few civilians are present, but of course the majority present is the G.I.

Kilian says that he was aware of an AR (600-375) [ARMY REGULATION] prohibiting prisoners from doing KP when he assigned men to this duty. Carroll crosses Kilian up rather well, getting him to deny something which he formerly affirmed. Kilian formerly testified that he inspected the guard house "very frequently," some times daily. He says that he saw Sgt. Smith very frequently. Now he says that he saw Sgt. Smith not more than 2 or 3 times between Aug. 1, '44, and Jan. 18, '45 (the latter being the date when Kilian left Lichfield). Carroll continues to bring up statements formerly made by Kilian which he has forgotten now. Kilian says that he has no recollection of visiting the solitary confinement cell between 1 Aug. '44 & 18 Jan. '45. He continually falls back on the stock answer,

"I don't recall!" He refuses to declare a statement of another witness true or false. However, he has just stated that any man could become a trainee. Kilian admits that he may have issued direct orders as to the running of the guard house without going thru channels.

Kilian refuses to recall having said that prisoners causing special trouble should be taken out of sight and only see that not too many bones were broken. Kilian recalls that he suggested to Gen. Thatcher [sp.?] that packets going across the channel should be accompanied by guards from the 10th Depot. Col Kilian attempts to withhold papers in Lt. Cubage's handwriting. However he is told by the court that they must be turned over to the D.A. (Kilian has a sheepish & silly grin on his face). These notes are quotations which Kilian had from conversations with Carroll; had heard Carroll saying; and conversations with other members of the court. The quotations seem largely irrelevant, but the Judge Advocate (D.A.) is trying to prove that these were to be used to cause a mistrial. A letter was later sent by Lt. Col. Hummel to the Command General of the area which included these conversations and rumors. Kilian says that he did not request a complaint. (3,500 pages of testimony).

Feb. 12, '46
UNO Conference [LONDON]

Discussion of a report of refugee situation. [THE TERM WIDELY USED WAS "DP" FOR DISPLACED PERSON.]
    Great crowd outside upon arrival. After a short wait, we were admitted to the Gallery reserved for Distinguished Visitors. The crowd seems quieter and not so restless as usual. I do not know what has gone on during the past two or three days, but the meetings are drawing to a close.
    Mrs. [ELEANOR] Roosevelt comes to the platform to speak for the U.S. delegation. She comes to oppose an amendment to a proposal by Russians. She sets a background for a negative viewpoint by explaining that our viewpoint is different. She objects to a report that soldiers should be sent back to their country. She says that these soldiers may have fought for their country & yet do not choose to return because they are not in sympathy with the present gov't. She talks as a school teacher telling the assembly [THAT IT] must have an international point of view rather than thinking of themselves.
    2nd Point: She opposes an amendment which would prevent propaganda against the UNO to be allowed to enter refugee

[CAMP ?]. "Are we so weak as to prevent people from hearing another point of view?" (Her voice is very high and seems on the point of breaking at times. ([HOWEVER] [s]he speaks with force). "We hope to be right, but we are not always sure of being right."

She rejects their amendment which would restrict human rights and human freedom. She received an ovation from the crowd, and the gallery is abuzz with discussion as the speech is now translated into French. The speech was a minor bomb shell, and I am happy to hear a stand taken by our delegation.

Delegation from UK comes again with apology for their objection to the report.

Again the term "propaganda" is declared elusive and subtle.

Mrs. Roosevelt is seated next to the Russian delegation for a purpose, I think.

U.K. opposes the leader of a refugee camp being of the nationality of the camp itself. No objection to returning traitors and war criminals. Reference to UNO Charter as the mandate: "The lamp which lights the Assembly"; "worth of common man." The UK will not lose sight of the ideal of the individual man – toleration. We are proud of our refugees and are proud of no one more than Karl Marx, who came to the UK, studied in libraries here, in an attempt to destroy the very walls of the country in which he found refuge. A powerful speech and well delivered.

The speaker corrected his opening statement by saying that he did not regret opposing the amendment. He regretted that he must take so firm a stand against the Russian delegation, but he was proud to take the stand which he did. At one point the speaker waxed eloquent by saying that when such terms as "tolerance," "human rights" were taken out, the language would no longer be English.

Delegation from Czechoslovakia favored amendment.

Vyshinsky (Rus.) wishes to explain point of view in regard to questions raised by Mrs. R. (The one translator is taking the Russian down & translating into both French & English.) Unlimited freedom does not exist & cannot exist. Men must be limited. Unlimited freedom impossible. Impossible not to limit the freedom of the individual. Must be limited by laws—criminal laws which prevent crimes. The will of men is limited by others—by the good of all. A State is limited—cannot be an aggressor or [IT] goes against the rights of others. Democracy is limitation of tyranny. Principle here is that unlimited freedom is impossible. Not necessary to examine question on such a high point of view. Not question of limiting propaganda but that against the UNO.

Tens of thousands who have festered minds & oppose the present gov't (ex. of Poland). All have paid too much for tolerance w/ German propaganda. Statement of all that Russia has suffered. What is propaganda? Enemy propaganda. " I would like to turn the question of suspicion to the speaker who used it first—Frazier, New Zealand. One of the most powerful speakers. Quotes Emerson. Absolute freedom is most certainly impossible. We cannot fear fear.

Are Polish boys who fought at Catania [?] to lose their freedom because they oppose the present government? It wasn't tolerance that brought [ON] this war. It was intolerance.

To say that men must be subjected is entirely counter to all ideals of freedom.

---

* Letter from Art to Dotty
London
Feb. 12, 1946 [752-759]

Darling,

Today has been far more exciting than I had anticipated. It began when I arose at the very early hour of 0820 for breakfast—my first in the cafeteria in several days. I found out by chance that it is possible to attend the Lichfield trials being held here in London, and so I rounded up Devers.

We dashed down to 44 Grosvenor Square when the trials are being held and walked in without difficulty during a recess. I do not know how much publicity these trials have had in the States but over here it has been a big event. Starting out as a trial of Sgt. Judson Smith (Ky.) of brutality in relation to his treatment of prisoners, the proceedings have developed into a "trial of the U.S. Army' as Time so aptly put it. The trials have made Sgt Smith a forgotten man and at the present Col. Kilian (former commanding officer of the 10th Replacement Depot), is in the limelight. It seems most likely that the investigations will go a great deal higher.

Today was the fifth or sixth day of the cross examination of Col. Kilian. During the entire day, the Colonel resorted over and over to the excuse that he does not remember certain observations, conversations, incidents, etc.

An attempt was made to end the cross examination today, but it will be continued tomorrow. I thought that I would leave tomorrow morning but I am happy to find that it will be tomorrow night. Thus, I will be able to get back to the trials tomorrow morning.

My letter was interrupted last night by an unexpected trip to UNO. I found out that there was to be an evening meeting open to the public. There were no tickets available, but Devers and I managed to get in after standing in line for a short while. The meeting was the most interesting which I attended.

We sat in the Gallery for Distinguished Visitors, although it really isn't so good a spot as the public gallery. Three amendments had been proposed by the Russian delegations to a report on the refugee situation in Europe. We missed the first few minutes in which Vyshinsky spoke, but were in time to hear a very fine speech by Mrs. Roosevelt. She drove more than one sharp wedge into the Russian stand and her speech was really a powerful one. The British delegate came forward with an eloquent speech also which took the same stand. We did hear the rebuttal by Mr. Vyshinsky but it was a weak reply from our point of view. Another outstanding speech was then made by a certain Mr. Frazier from New Zealand. It was the second time that I was impressed by his forcefulness and vigor.

We left a few minutes before midnight hoping to catch the last bus or subway home. However, we were a bit too late and so walked to Marble Arch—fifty minute stroll. A heavy London fog veiled the city as we passed by No 10 Downing St. the dock and somber Buckingham Palace, and Hyde Park.

Today I spent part of both morning and afternoon at the trials again, but finally left in disgust. The evidence was repetitious and seemed to prove nothing. Tried to get into Parliament, but it was very crowded and a long line awaited.

Within an hour I will leave the Club for Victoria Station. We go from there to New Haven, thence across the channel to Dieppe, and to Paris tomorrow morning.

From a fellow just coming over from the 71st, I understand that 50 points and above are out; 48-49 expected to leave shortly. 45-47 will be next, My Love!

I shall write a full account of the situation as soon as I get back. Should arrive in Augsburg Friday night and Memmingen Saturday.

Hope that there isn't too much of a gap in my mail after I leave here, but these letters should get to you much faster than those from Germany. Even though letters are delayed, you may know in your heart that each and every day I repeat over and over to you and to myself that Our Love is eternally strong and everlastingly true.

I love you,
Bushy
P.S. Sorry I failed to get a Valentine for you, My Dear. You will be my Valentine, I hope?

———

Feb. 13
Lichfield Courtroom
Grosvenor Sq.

Questions concern conversation between Col. Kilian & Lt. Col. Hummel. Kilian admits that he had thought of the possibility of being tried. Feeling that Smith's case is a key one. Mutual defense recalled, and Kilian admitted plan for an organized defense—individual council but all under one head. Kilian admits that a conviction of Sgt. Smith would ultimately lead to him. He admits that he has gone to the aid of any other men who have been tried in his command.

Question pertaining to the opinion of Kilian regarding the outcome of Smith's trial. Kilian burst out with the statement that Carroll has driven into him time after time that he (Kilian) must stand trial. That if Carroll had anything to do with it, he would be tried. Kilian testified that shortly after arriving here, he was advised to gather data for his defense in case his own trial was held. Kilian now says that the outcome of the trials of EM [ENLISTED MEN] and officers would not affect his trial. Kilian stated that he thinks the Gov't. should have tried him first (when confronted with the question, "Are you not aware that the CO of a post is always last to be tried in a case of this kind?" Kilian spoke of the Smith case and the case of the other EM & officers as being hurdles to be overcome. Carroll immediately took up the figure and laid out pencils on the table to represent the hurdles. (Kilian often attempted to crack a joke and smiles with self-satisfaction. Letter written by Lt. Col. Hummel regarding 11 Jan. '46, which included bits of conversation and incidents gathered by Kilian & copied later by Lt. Cabage. Kilian states that he talked with Lt. Col. Hummel but not as a complaint, & that the letter was an independent action. Kilian is extremely evasive & appears to be playing a game. Much repetition. I wonder if Carroll is playing a game also. What sort of a marathon race is this? Kilian is a fox with effective defense tactics.

[RE-READING THIS DETAILED ACCOUNT, I HAVE NO IDEA WHY I WAS SO FASCINATED WITH THE TRIAL. IT MUST HAVE MADE HEADLINES AT THE TIME.]

Last night Devers and I waited to hear Mr. Frazier (New Zealand) deliver a powerful speech at the UNO. We missed the last bus and the subway and walked back to Marble Arch. The fog was heavy, the street lights dim as we walked past Buckingham Palace, Hyde Park, etc. We slept very late.

Feb. 14
Victoria Station

With some regret I sit in the train on my way back to the Continent. We go to New Haven, across the Channel to Dieppe, arriving in Paris tomorrow morning. A dense fog covered the city this afternoon, and tonight the street lights cast an eerie glow. The people that I have met here have been most cordial—far more than I would expect after being in contact with the GIs for lo these many years. The way the volunteer workers come day after day to the American Clubs to wait on us and make our leave pleasant is really heart warming.

Back to the Continent

Feb. 14
Paris

I would hardly think that the time might come when I would pass up the opportunity to spend a day or two in Paris. Almost all of the fellows on pass to England stop here.

I arrived at Gare St. Lazare at 4:30 this afternoon and will leave Gare d L'Est at 7:30. Had time to shave, wash a bit, eat a hearty supper, and read the paper. Two reasons are really responsible for my desire to continue on immediately. First is the news which awaits me at the unit—both letters from home and recent events in the 71st itself Second is the fact that I am terribly tired. Slept only three hours last night on top of the ventilator over the engine room aboard the boat & under the open sky. But more than that I traveled more than 1,200 miles within the UK and have covered almost 3.000 miles since I left Memmingen. I still have more than 800 miles to go. I could really appreciate little that I saw or did here in Paris.

Memmingen, Germany
February 16, 1946 [760-761, typed]

Darling,

At 12:30 this morning Devers and I ended a trip which had taken me over three thousand miles. We roused the CQ out of bed and also the 1st Sgt. before we were able to get the key for our room. At the same time we got the key to the mail. Joy of joys! I should go on furlough more often! I had a total of SIXTEEN big, wonderful letters from my wonderful wife. Four or five others from Mother and Dad were also most welcome. As late as was the hour, and as sleepy as I was after travelling from England nonstop, I sat on the corner of my bed and began to read. I did not stop until I had read every single line, My Love. By that time it was two o'clock, and I hardly felt like sitting down and writing you at that time. Tonight I sat down at seven o'clock to re-read your letters and begin to answer them. After two hours and a couple of interruptions, I have almost a full page of typed notes in reference to points which I wish to cover in answering all of these. Since there is so much to write about, I had better bring you up to date on my activities and the situation which I found here upon arrival.

I wrote last from London, shortly before leaving. We took a taxi to Victoria [Station] and left about ten-thirty. The train ride was a short one and the coaches were comfortable. At New Haven we passed through customs and on to the boat. The crowd seemed to be never-ending and the bunks and deck chairs were soon gone. Devers and I ended up by sleeping under the open sky and on top of the ventilators above the engine room. Hot air was coming up from the engines and we were warm enough, that is, until the warm air ceased about six. We did not leave the port until about seven o'clock when the tide was in. In view of the fact that frequent gales have raged on the Channel for the past several weeks, I had expected rough weather. However, the water was as calm as a very calm lake. The boat made the only ripples to be seen. Behind us the white wake marked our trail and the smoke from the engines hung in a line. The sun was bright and the channel breeze most pleasant. From Dieppe we were put on another troop train and soon were moving swiftly toward Paris. (Dieppe shows the scars of war and the great rocks jut out to sea as if defying the god Mars to destroy it. A church stands high on the rock looking out to sea, outliving the ravage of the destruction which passed.)

I never thought that the time would come when I would not choose to remain in Paris for a couple of days. We could very easily have spent two or three days there. However, the train brought us into the city about 4:30 and at 7:30 we were on the train again heading for Germany. Three reasons influenced my decision: first, I was very, very tired of so much travel and so much sight-seeing; second, I was anxious to get the latest news at the outfit (rumors of which had reached our ears in England); third, and most important was the stack of letters which I knew awaited me. We arrived in Augsburg at 8:30 last night. I had planned to spend the night with Ted and collect my travel money from Division Finance. I found that Ted had left yesterday afternoon for Switzerland and Italy, and that all elements of the 71st Div. Hq. were no longer around. Thus, when we found a Lt. with a jeep coming right down to Memmingen, we loaded on.

The hour passes and I must get out of the office and let the CQ get to bed right away, but I must give you some inkling of the general situation here. Only yesterday all men with 46 points and above left the unit. There were a couple who left with 45. If Devers had not been in England he would have been in Le Harve today getting ready to ship home. However, both of us will leave on the next shipment. The Sgt. Major in Personnel is a very good friend of ours and he remained behind with 48 points. He did not choose to go to the 66th Regt., and there may be a reason for that. I think that he may do us a special favor and get us a good deal. As I say, we will both leave on the next shipment which will probably be next week. I do not know how long it will take us to process, and of course that will depend on the outfit to which I go. However, I do not think that I will spend as much time as we spent in the 94th. All of the units seem to be moving out much faster now. Unless I am very much mistaken, I will not be here when this letter reaches you even though it come fast airmail. I will probably leave next week, My Love, and this time there will be no stops. Long delays, perhaps, but no turning back.

Darling, your letters bring you very close to me (two more tonight), and I grow more excited each day that brings me nearer to you.

I love you,
Bushy
P.S. Letters from 7th Jan thru 5th Feb. (postmarked 7th)

Darling,

I had intended to make this a nice long letter attempting to catch up with the twenty letters which I have had from you since my return from England. (Really, My Love, it is wonderful! Two yesterday and two more today!) However, at Church today I found that it would be wise for me to make another little excursion this afternoon instead of writing. As I have told you before, my beloved chess set has been scattered in a variety of places. Alsup and Ch. Webb would have taken care of it had they been here longer. When they left they tried to leave complete instructions with the fellows left here in the Chaplains' section, but it was not done. This afternoon I went with Chaplain Bowman to Neu Ulm. My box and leather board is not yet completed, but it will be done on Wednesday. I have most of my men here, the others being with the lady who is making the box. It seems that eventually I will have all of these things together and get them in the mail.

The best news in your letter today written on the 8th and telling me that the source of Mom's trouble has been found. I do hope that the operation affects a cure and that she is well on the road to recovery by now. Give her my love and my best wishes. If possible I will write her tomorrow. Also happy to hear that the records arrived, and only hope thy [they] brought half the pleasure which you describe. You do say such nice things, Darling!

Letter from Ted tonight which was written just before he left for Switzerland. It seems that the 66th has a special mission to perform prior to going home, and that may explain why a few 46 to 50 pointers went to that unit. He thinks that we may go there together within a couple of weeks. After hearing about the general situation, I am inclined to think that I may remain here until the 1st of March. There should be few delays however, when I do leave.

By the way, the jacket which you mention receiving was one which I captured from the Germans during combat. There is an interesting tale hanging thereby which I shall later relate. I carried it as an extra bit of equipment during the remainder of combat. The package came to the post office while I was in the 94th and supposedly on my way home. Therefore, the PO forwarded it on. Glad that it reached you.

Happy to hear more details of your trip to Jamestown both from you and from Mother and Dad. They were certainly very much pleased that you were able to visit with them even if only for a short week-end. Perhaps when you quit work and before I come you could spend a bit longer with them.

I have to get up for a reveille tomorrow morning and so I must get to bed earlier than usual tonight. Back to the RSO to my old job again. Should have more interesting news in a few days. But the most interesting thing that I can think of tonight is the mere fact that with all of my heart,

I love you,
Bushy

Letter from Art to Dotty
Memmingen, Germany
February 18, 1946 [764-765]

My Dearest,

My first day at the office since my return was spent in introducing a new man to the work in order that he may take over when I leave. He is from the 66th Regt. and has been doing the same work before. Thus there is little to worry about along that line. However, one thing did give me cause for a few minutes worry this morning. I went over to Personnel before lunch to check up on my travel money still pending. By chance I inquired about shipping, and I found that my name was not on the list for shipment with 45 pointers. Upon investigation we found that someone had given me a mere 41 points. The mistake was soon rectified but it could easily have cost me another delay. Fate seems determined to keep us apart as long as possible, My Love.

I spent most of my evening getting a package of "junk" ready to send home (Jamestown), and in wrapping a bottle of perfume to send to Uldene. I failed to send her anything for Christmas and I must write and thank Odell and her for the wedding present. Since there was no first class mail of any sort today, I shall try to catch up with a few of the letters which I received from you upon my return. The list certainly looks formidable!

My mind was much relieved to learn that all of the packages, at least most of them, arrived. After reading about your difficulty unlocking the typewriter, I dreamed of the button which must be pushed but after awaking I could not recall it. I am sure that you have long since found the solution though. By the way, the clamps should be put on the skiis (if you have opened them) with the bottoms facing each other and the tiny block of wood placed in the middle. I wish that I could have had those cathedral pictures bound by the lady in Ulm who does such nice leather work. She could have made a lovely book of those, but of course it is too late now. Perhaps I can have that done later. In reference to the letters, I had intended to sort them, but my time ran short before I left the 94th. Sorry that there was so much "junk" to be sent, but we can make a bon fire with all of it when I get there. In addition to the $40 money order which you received, I sent one for $35 and one for $30, the first in late Oct. or early Nov. and the second sometime in Nov. Perhaps you wrote of receiving these but the letter failed to arrive. (If these do not come we can put in a claim for I have the stubs.) I intended to mention that I sent $50 MO to Dad to be in our account at Jamestown. That brings our account there to almost $100, which helps. My trip to England took almost that much out of our savings, but I believe that it was well worth it to me. (Even if I wanted to I could hardly say anything about your "extravagant purchase of music", Darling. I really don't want to anyway, and I am really happy that you bought it if it will be of any help whatsoever with your lessons.)

From the news which you seem to be hearing concerning the 71st I note that it is still as totally incorrect as ever. How can the 71st come home in May, if there is no such thing as the 71st? I don't know who this Commander Krum happens to be, but he is certainly off the beam. You asked about Ted's points and I think that I failed to say that he was 45. For a while he had 46, but the mistake was found. He thinks that we will both still go to the 66th, but I may leave before he returns. (He will get back from Rome about the 26th or 27th.) As I wrote last night, I will probably not get out as quickly as I had thought at first. Unless I leave in a great rush, I shall try to send you a radiogram of anything important which happens. I shall always regret that I did not send one to you when I found that I was leaving the 94th (However, it would not have gotten there much before my letter which reached you on the 7th.) Glad that the one telling you of my trip to England arrived within a few days.

I have covered less than a third of the letters, Darling, but I must shave tonight before going to bed. What a difference a shave makes! Nicht wahr? (Mother suggests that we make a bonfire with my mustache. Hmmm!) No matter how much you may agree with her,
I still love you,
Bushy

Dearest Heart,

There is not a great deal that is new today, but we did find that Devers will be leaving on Thursday or Friday. A large number of men have been found with 48 to 51 points, and these will go out on the next shipment. I presume that I will get in one sometime and this can't go on forever. (or can it?) He will go to the 83rd Div. which will soon be on its way to the States. As time goes on I am sure that the boys who went to the 66th Regt. will not be leaving as soon as they had thought or hoped.

The new man on my job is catching on quickly to the work, but I think that I will be hear plenty long enough for him to get everything down pat. The driver for the RSO jeep is going to take me to Augsburg tomorrow when I hope to collect my Calif. travel money. Remember? "It's been a long, long time!" I hope to come back by way of Ulm and get my chess men and perhaps see some of Ted's friends in the 5th to get the latest rumors.

Tonight I had a long letter from Mary Ruth telling me all about the student government at Maryville [College]. She mentioned a number of familiar names such as Ray Swartzback, Scapeletti, Bob Hunter, etc. Just in case you see any of these fellows give them my very best regards. Perhaps I will be able to see them before they graduate yet. As I understand the new system, it applies only to the girls, but it is certainly a start. Hope to hear that it meets with success.

In all my excitement about the letters which I found awaiting me, I think that I failed to mention that I had about five or six copies of Sat. Review of Lit. and a couple of Encores. I should have plenty of reading material for a while. I must write to Time and the other publishers and get them to stop sending them overseas.

I don't think that I mentioned the new snack bar which we have since I went away. We can get pie, cake, ice cream, cocoa, and sandwishes (That was really an accident!) in addition to the coffee and doughnuts. There is a slight charge, but it makes a very nice addition to the facilities here. I will have to get around to see a show sometime, but in the evening I seem to be able to do little besides write a couple of letters, wrap a package, or take a bath.

I must get a little sleep tonight, since I have not been doing so well for the past two nights. Gotta lota dreamin' to do, and it is all to do with
Our Love, Bushy

P.S. Think I forgot to say that Pratt is back in school again—this time in Biartiz, France. Lucky guy! I'm happy for his sake for he expects to be around for a while yet.

Letter from Art to Dotty
Memmingen, Germany
February 22, 1946 [768]

Darling,

Today being Washington's birthday we were supposed to have a holdiay [holiday]. I only had to work during the afternoon, and so I slept very late this morning. After spending two and a half hours writing to you last night and then reading for an hour or so, I was rather sleepy, and it was nice not to have to get up for reveille.

In my letter last night I was preoccupied with other things, and I failed to mention a few recent events. On Wednesday I went to Augsburg to collect the money which I have waited for so long. The office was kind enough to let me have the RSO jeep and the driver. After cutting through considerably more red tape I collected my money. We came back by way of Ulm where I was able to get at last my complete chess set. When Chaplain Bowman saw my men last Sunday he offered me twice what I paid for them, and yesterday I could have sold the set for four times the cost. I am hardly interest[ed] in the selling of it, and I think that you will agree when you see it. I have it all ready for shipment, and I shall mail it next week.

Devers leaves tomorrow for the 83rd Division. I shall surely leave on the next shipment which should be next week sometime. Do not stop writing until I give you further word. We heard direcly from the 66th Regt. today. They have been issued rifles, steel helmets, ammunition, and are on some secret mission. Needless to say they are not ready to leave immediately for home.

I have been doing some tall financial figuring during the past few days, and I am pleased to find that we should have between $1500 and $2,000 after I receive my mustering out pay and all that is due me at present. This includes bonds, of course—approximated at $750 cash value. I would like to plan to keep at least a $500 reserve on hand for an emergency. I think that we will need $400 or $500 for running expenses during first year while we are getting settled in school, waiting for allotment checks from the Gov't, etc. We will have left well over $500 for which there will be no immediate use. I have been seriously thinking of some way in which we can invest such a sum in order to draw somesort of a return. I would like to find some sound business in which we could put our money and expect to get some sort of an annual return. I do not want to take any needless risks, and so we will choose as wisely as possible. We need to be in no rush about this, but can keep our eyes and ears open. It should be an established business and not one which is just opening. I shall talk about this more at a later time, but I wanted to give you something to think about.

The hour is again late. My eyes droop in weariness. I go to sleep to dream of
Our Love,
Bushy
[written in side margin]
MO enclosed for $100

* Letter from Art to Dotty
Memmingen, Germany
February 21, 1946 [768-769]

My Dearest Heart,
Truth comes slowly to us, like the dripping of the warm spring rain through the foliage of the trees or the soft rays of early October sunshine through the same foliage. Truth comes slowly as the days of our years until suddenly we are in its presents. We stumble in darkness, we wander outside the walls of Truth, but little by little we gather wee bits of wisdom here and there. Suddenly and without warning our eyes are cleared: we see, we know, we feel the warm rain of spring and the soft caress of sunshine through the trees.

It was just one month ago tonight you wrote, "...I somehow believe that you will be almost a different person when freed from the dark shadow of Army regimentation and Army every thing else...you will enjoy life more deeply and fully...."

Your words stirred thoughts which had been latent in my mind for some time. Good thoughts are like good wines: both must age in some deep, dark recess for a long, long time. I thought my own thoughts, and I made your thinking a part of mine. Tonight I saw Miss Jennifer Jones in a lovely portrayal of a childlike girl. The picture (Love Letters) was a story based on the complete loss of memory of the young girl. In forgetting her past she lost the inhibitions and restraints of formal society. As she expressed it, she found complete happiness by being merely herself.

The picture took me apart to the extent that I was able to do a bit more thinking along these lines of happiness, maladjustment, individuality, and "the dark shadow of Army regimentation". I suddenly became aware in a new way of the fact that I have something more than an intense dislike for my life in the Army; I have little less than a deep hatred for the life which I have been forced to live.

When I first put on the uniform of a soldier, I realized that I was entering something new and different from anything I had known before. I possessed an intense desire to adjust myself to the extent of becoming a good soldier. It was not necessary in this adjustment to curse, and drink, and think as those with whom I worked. However, it was imperative that I accept them, my fellow soldiers, as co-workers. As all of us seek social approval, I sought to become thought of as a hale-fellow, well-met, without lowering the ethical and moral standards which I had set up. If nothing else, I learned something of the important lesson of co-operating with the inevitable. I found men like myself, lost and out of sorts with the world around them. I made friends and I proved to my own satisfaction that all men have redeeming features. I learned a few things about life in the army and I kidded myself along. Sometimes I almost convinced myself that I had adjusted to it.

For my general state of mind, I think that it was best that I should have been able to think that I adapted myself. At least from day to day I was not obsessed with the frustration of my existence. Nevertheless, I know now that the day I donned my uniform I stifled a part of my life. Along side my suits of clothing I placed a part of my soul, my creative spirit.

I trust that the same fresh air and bright sunshine which takes the must and cobwebs from my clothing will also set free that intangible portion of my inner self. Darling, I know that as I return to a more normal way of living, and, most important, as I return to the satisfying joy of Our Love, I shall find again that which I have lost. I shall indeed be "almost a different person when freed..."

Truth comes slowly to us, like the dripping of the warm spring rain through the foliage of the trees or the soft rays of early October sunshine through the same foliage. Truth comes slowly as the days of our years until suddenly we are in its presents. We stumble in darkness, we wander outside the walls of Truth, but little by little we gather wee bits of wisdom here and there. Suddenly and without warning our eyes are cleared: we see, we know, we feel the warm rain of spring and the soft caress of sunshine through the trees.

Thine Own,
Bushy

My Dearest Heart,
Outside the wind rages and the snow continues to fall. It seems
that the winter which I thought almost passed has only begun for we
are having the worst snow storm which we have yet had. Snow is
reported four feet deep in Oberstdorf. I was perfectly happy to stay
inside tonight, take my bath, shave, play a little ping pong, and write to
my lovely wife. (Before I go any further, let me stop long enough to say
that I love her very dearly.) Spent an hour and a half going over old
negatives and selecting a few for enlargement as well as making a few
notes on my pictures taken in England and Scotland. Two rolls came
back today, and I thought it interesting that on these two rolls were
pictures taken in three, or rather, four countries. I shall try to send a
few of these at a time as per my usual habit. (I hope that this manner of
sending the pictures is more interesting than if I sent them all at once.)
Devers left today and I am alone in my room at least for a day or two. I
am selfish enough that I wish I could keep it this way, but I fear that I
will be unable to offer any objection to a new roommate. I shall miss
loquacious John. We were diametrically opposed in many respects, but
almost never did difficulties arise.
I spent part of my afternoon with Bill Myers at the Regt. PX. He is
still working there and is one of the few old friends left in the regiment.
We were in Paris together you remember. Found out tonight that
MacIntosh left in a recent shipment—we had been together since Camp
Roberts. Managed to get another filter for my camera, my stock should
soon be complete! In the library I browsed through parts of Noel
Coward's Middle East Diary (think mine is also interesting); Darwin's
Origin or Species (was hardly in the mood, but found it interesting and
readable); and a book on play production. As you see, I have my
difficulties when it comes to sitting down and concentrating on one
thing for any length of period.
The news today (or I should say rumor) did not help my spirits.
According to Personnel, no more shipments are expected until after the
coming move, slated to come sometime before the 10th of March. I
must admit that I had hoped to move from the 14th before that time.
However, there is nothing to be done about it. I wish that I could get
away to Rome on a furlough, but I think that such a thing would be out
of the questions.

The more delays that come up, the harder it is for me to make any definite plans regarding our immediate future when I return. I would like to be able to say that we would do such and such a thing, then such and such another thing, etc. I am wondering just what chance I will have of getting into not just Yale but any good school for graduate work. I would be happy to think that I could get into Chapel Hill (NC) or Duke, but the reports which I read are hardly encouraging.

I recognize full well the problem that we face in trying to find an apartment in Knoxville, and that too will be conditioned to a certain extent on the date of my arrival and our plans for the first few months. It is terribly difficult to get the proper perspective for planning from this side of the Atlantic, and so I intend to wait for the most part until we can talk everything over together. We are sure of what we want and the only questions to be settled will relate to the "how".

In this very regard I want to say something which is not intended as a confession but rather as a statement of fact. After three years in the service, My Love, I think that you can understand how accustomed one becomes to relying on others for many of the essentials. There are no such things as worry about rent, or taxes or grocery bills, or apartments, or a new suit, etc. All these things are provided. As a result I fear that I may appear to show some lack of the responsibility of a husband during the early adjustment period to civilian life. I believe that to a certain extent this is inevitable, but I shall attempt to cut it to the very minimum. I think that you will understand.

Was glad to get your reaction to the trailer question. I have asked a few questions since writing about it, and the general impression leads me to agree with your own conclusions. However, it will bear further investigation and discussions. As I think Mother pointed out, the initial expense would be quite large, and as you mention in one of your letters rent is high and such things as bathing and water difficult. I think that such a venture would only be advisable as a last resort, but it may come to that.

Last night I enclosed a money order for $100 which I trust arrives safely. My pay is still very much confused (and has been since last June), but I figure that I am due almost a hundred dollars more at the end of February. Unless I am radically wrong, we are going to have a tidy little sum tucked away when I get home—shall certainly need it.

Darling, I do hope that you are not doing too much. I would feel much better, if, while Mom is sick, you would drop some of your work. After all when I get there, you will have to drop almost all immediately —if not sooner. Now you are working night and day and that isn't good for you. It's detrimental to your health, and certainly not fair to your own state of happiness. I urge you for your own sake, if not for mine, to begin at once to find some one else to take over some of the extra work that you are doing. I know that there is a tremendous amount of work to be done, but you can't do it all, My Love, as much as you may try.

I do not mean to reprimand, but I love you so very much! I do not like to think of you working yourself to death, particularly since I am over here doing almost nothing. If my hours are not always filled with labor, they are always filled with thoughts and plans for the most wonderful thing in my life,

Our Love,
Bushy

Letter from Art to Dotty
Memmingen, Germany
February 24, 1946 [773-774]
Sunday Evening

My Dearest,

As I have stroked my beard and recounted before, I have had a number of thrilling experiences since I came to the ETO. However, allow me to stroke my mustache this time and say for me the most recurrent thrill has been the receipt of your letters. My heart always beats a bit faster, and my morale always shoots up when I see the familar [familiar] envelope, the familar handwriting, familar words and thoughts from you.

Between flurries of snow the sun shown today, and I wandered out after lunch to get a couple of pictures. I fainally ended up at the postoffice and stepped in for a chat with the boys. Before I left the mail arrived truck with three days mail for us. Instead of going to the library as I had planned, I stayed to sort mail (a la Devers). The reward of your two letters of the 10th and 11th were well worth my effort. Your question regarding which year is very well put. Under the existing circumstances, I hesitate to answer that. I do think that the cabin in April should be very close to heaven itself, and the anniversary will be well worth postponing a few days. I had once hoped that such a postponement would not be necessary, but I fear now that no such miracle will occur in the Army soon.

I always treasure your pictures and those which I received today added nuggets to my collection. Thank you very much, My Dear. I particularly like the "model", and incidentally, I'll buy that dream! The hat is very becoming, but I like the one with the Paris gloves a little better. (It isn't the same one, is it?) By the way, sometime take a look at the picture with the Paris gloves taken as you were coming down the steps. Glance at the sleeve of your left arm, and perhaps you will see why I looked several times in somewhat immodest concern. Such flowering sleeves can give strange effects at times and I still wonder sometimes about that particular picture.

Awfully glad to hear that Mother's operation will be performed soon. If we can help in any small way, don't hesitate to do so. Also, if she is to be at the hospital, why not get some flowers for the room with my love. I sent a money order a couple of days ago ($100), and I think that we can afford a bouquet of nice flowers, Darling.

Glad the typewriter is in operation again. I wonder if Dad could get the "y" and the "z" interchanged for me. The entire key cannot be changed, but just the head has to be cut off and welded again. I think that the case is also in need of repair and I think that this could be done at the shop. If so, it is possible to get that Gruen watch fixed for awhile, but I have a wrist watch from the PX which will do until parts are more easy to obtain.

I was terribly behind in my writing, but I did manage to write Mom tonight. Hope to get a letter to Mary Ruth this week as well as Tom, Hargrave, and a few others. I can't get over the fact that Hargrave is married. He still seemed to be uncertain when he wrote to me from Calif. I shall try to write him a proper letter of congratulation. Tom's situation sounds very good, and I think that he is just as lucky to remain in the States. There is something to be said for travel, but far more to be said about home. (Don't I know!) Yes, Tom writes always in a most interesting manner. Our correspondence has been a very long one as you know. Since Bill attended Notre Dame and MIT I was a bit surprised that he should wish to return to Tenn. to school. Wish he could make it though. We could have lots of fun together. I wonder if you have heard from the Roblene lately. I wrote Bob a long letter before leaving from the 94th, and told him to write to 607. If you haven't heard, wish you could write to Arlene sometime. Haven't written Dick or Hal in ages, but perhaps I can catch up at the cabin—Huh!!

I was happy to read in recent letters of your visit with Margaret Messer McClure. I remember Scott very well, but I can't seem to recall Margaret. Does she live in Knoxville? Bamberg is not far from Nurnberg, and there is a small possibility that we will come home with the same unit. Just in case I get in that vicinity I would like to look him up. Let me have his rank and unit if you happen to know it. I can imagine that it is lots of fun for two temporary widows to get together for a conference!

We have a new Warrant Officer in the RSO, and he has plans of making many changes in the bookkeeping. My department has been sadly neglectly for many months, and this new man has intentions of doing something about.it. Lucky for me, the new man who is taking my place, has done this sort of work before. Both of us will be keep very busy until the new set-up has been completed along with the move to another location. Rumors still seem to indicate that we are to go near Frankfurt, and I suppose that we will move out of here within the next ten days. Wish I could have left first, for it will mean an extra move among many moves. Methink I careth little for this nomadic, gypsy life!

Think I mentioned before how happy I was that you were able to get over to Jamestown again. Mother and Dad enjoy your visits so much. I intended to make a little explanation about the water colors. I found out about them in Oberstdorf and went for a sitting. When the first one was finished, I took it back to my room and tried to make up my mind to whom I should send it. I wanted to send it to you, but then I thought that when I get home you would have me and the folks would have neither me nor the picture. The only solution was to have another made. I never cared for either very much, but glad that you like yours.

Since I have a big day's work tomorrow, I must get to bed, Darling. Never forget that with all my heart,
                    I love you,
                    Bushy

Letter from Art to Dotty
Memmingen, Germany
February 25, 1946 [775-776]

Darling,

To receive mail two days in a row is most unusual and most heartening. Today I received your letters of the 12th and 14th, and both were filled with interesting tidbits of news. My heart filled with pride when I read of the invitation which you received to join the Civic Opera Assoc. I do wish that you could do it, My Love, for I know how much your music means to you. However, you were perfectly right in turning down the offer, since, as I reiterated last night, you are doing far too much at the moment. Sounds good to hear that you were able to get a pair of nylons. I had hoped to get a pair in New York on my way home, but I seriously wonder if it would be possible. I suppose you had to sign up for these months ago. Was surprised to find in another letter that sugar is still so hard to get. Is it still rationed?

It was something of a coincidence that I should have asked you last night about the Roblene. I wonder if Bob received my letter over here.

Do write them if you have the time, at least a note, and give them my best regards. I think that most of our friends will forgive me for not writing more when they hear of all the things I have done and places I have been during the past three or four months. Glad that you ordered the silver, although a bit surprised. Your choice would have been mine anyway, so it really matters little. The $100 money order which I sent a few days ago will pay for the set, and we can consider that our anniversary present to each other. How about it? We had talked of buying records from time to time, also of buying silver piece by piece. Your idea was a good one I think to wait until the plastic ones come out, and we will save a great deal from this new plan.

Because of the unsettled state in which we will be for the next three or four years, I think it wise for us to buy only the more essential things, such as silver, china, bedding, etc., and wait until we can settle down before we buy such things as furniture and other large itmes [items] of household fixtures. That will be the glorious day, Darling, when we settle in our more or less permanent home!

The room which has been my semi-permanent home since last Oct. (with a couple of notable exceptions) will be vacated by me tomorrow. We had an inspection today by Major Gen. McBride, Commander Officer of the 9th Div. He object[ed] to a number of things in this hotel, the main one being the fact that civilians live in the hotel with us. The owner and his wife will come into this room, and all others (being girls who work here) will have to leave. (Some of the GIs will regret this for personel reasons.) It seems useless to make many changes now, since we are to leave within such a short time, but when a General says something there is no question raised.

I spent most of my evening packing my treasured chess set which I must mail very soon. Each piece is in a separate compartment, but I wrapped each one in Kleenex so that it would fit tightly. I doubt if many mummies themselves received more care and attention from the Egyptians than did my chess men.

Yes, I remember Patsy and Jack Mehaney, having met them at the cabin more than once. I think that I understand your concern, My Love. When things are not what they seem, that is, prove contrary to our original conception, questions arise in our minds. I recall crossing a stream as a child by hopping from one stone to another. At first I was rather careless and stepped on any stone which seemed convenient. After one or two stones proved precarious, I moved with more caution. When I saw others fall into the water as a result of choosing a rolling stone, I took great care. When a mountain proves to be a mirage, we stop to question our vision in regard to other things. There is no reason to suppose that it represents a loss of faith in our eyesight, but perhaps it would be correct to say that doubt and pessimism are present in their embryonic stages. What I am driving at is that when you see another couple, apparently perfectly suited, break up their home, deep down you begin to wonder if rougher water is ahead for us than you had expected.

Forgive me if this analysis is a bit pointed. I do think that this unhappy ending reveals the difference which may arise as a result of a husband being away and in the service. I think that life in the service tends to strain to the utmost the weakest link in the chain of a man's character. Sometimes that weakest link breaks. (Read E.A. Robinson's "Richard Cory" sometime.) I know that I am changed in some respects, although I sincerely believe that no radical changes have resulted. I certainly do not think that our adjustment will be as complete in our first week together as though we had never been apart. At the same time, I am positive that nothing whatsoever will arise which patience, frankness, and prayer will not solve. Our reliance upon these three sources of strength has been proven of utmost worth before, and we shall certainly rely upon them still. Questions and concern over such failures can always be of great value, Darling, if we but face squarely and positively the application to our own lives.

May patience, frankness, and prayer continue to be solid cornerstones upon which we base the towering glory of

> Our Love,
> Bushy

* Letter from Art to Dotty
Memmingen, Germany
February 27, 1946 [777-778]

Darling,

Many years ago I developed a philosophy from Mother's teaching that everything happens for the best—if we choose to profit by the experience of the events. Many, many times over here I have thought that something more than my puny power of choice guided the path which I followed. I think that I have another case in point of a Guiding Power ordering our lives to our advantage, though we sometimes question this.

As I wrote, I missed the shipment to the 66th by a matter of hours. The boys in the 66th may reach home before I do, but some of them may not. I mentioned before that they have drawn gas masks, guns, steel helmets, etc., etc. Their mission was secret, and it remains officially off the record. However, I have had news of this "mission" which is not at all pleasant. I shall save the details until later for security reasons, but I can say that is was considered necessary to use ex-combat men for the job. Considering the fact that I was an inglorious BAR man in combat, I would probably have been given one of these weapons. Frankly, I am in no mood to make application for the position of a hero in combat at this late stage of the game. I have too much to come home to. (That means you, My Love, in case you were wondering!)

I don't think I mentioned that I am getting a leather bound album from the lady in Ulm. I may not be able to get it for some time, but she will probably send it to Alsup's home with some other things which she has for him. However, I would like to use it to put our shots of Bavaria. You haven't mentioned working on our pictures, and I presume that you have been far too busy. If nothing has been done, I think that we should wait until we can get the entire group (of several hundred) together, sort and select, and put together an album of which we can be justly proud. The more work we put into it the nicer it should be. I still have some enlargements of the best mountain pictures which I think are the best of my collection. I shall send these along shortly.

Talked with Ted today. He just came back from Italy, and had a marvelous time. He doesn't expect us to move out for several days yet. Nothing much new with him, except that Dave has a job in Washington (clerical) and is playing on Sunday in one of the churches. Both Dave and Mr. Kidder are working on a school for Ted. I wonder if I am going to be caught napping. Think that we had better get catalogues from Chapel Hill, Vanderbilt, Duke, in addition to Yale. Post-graduate field should not be so crowded as the undergraduate, but still it will be no snap to gain entrance in Sept.

I have intended to tell you about the new situation in the RSO. We are operating under the 9th Div. now, and many changes resulted. We are reorganizing our entire set of books, and a tremendous amount of work is envolved [involved]. Speaking of bookkeeping, I wish that I could think that our income tax next year would be no more than this. By the way, I favor some sort of a bookkeeping system for us, simple in form, but sufficient to show us our financial standing from time to time. This is the type of thing that we can look into during the transition period.

Darling, I would give a great deal to be able to hear you sing some of the solo numbers which you are doing from time to time. I can hardly wait for the time when I can hear you, and my heart will be a bustin' with pride and love.

Yesterday I moved into my new room (as a result of Gen. Mcbride's visit and special request). The owner of the hotel and his wife have occupied this room since we came here last Oct., but they were right along side the rooms occupied by the GIs. Since my room was somewhat withdrawn, they were moved there, and I came here. This room has steam heat, good lighting, plenty of room, and seems already far more homey than the other place. I am a little disappointed in my roommate, but we will not be here very long. That is the one thing I regret about moving next week, but I may have nice quarters there also. We are supposed to be going in the vicinity of Manneheim according to the latest rumor, and will probably leave here on or before the 10th.

I am very tired tonight, and the hour is late. Have a half day off tomorrow (unless work prevents), and I shall try to get off a very long letter to you without feeling so rushed. At least in sleep I can dissolve the time and distance which separates us and be with you again. With every fiber of my being,

I love you,
Bushy

* Letter from Art to Dotty
Memmingen, Germany
February 28, 1946 [779-780]

Dearest Darling,
....In proving foresight may be vain:
The best laid schemes o' micc en' men
Gang aft a-gley...." (Go oft amiss)

My old friend, Bobby Burns was right. Almost nothing that I had planned for this, my free afternoon and evening, has been accomplished. However, I have accomplished much that I had not expected. I had planned to shave, sleep, collect my pay, visit the Mil. Gov't Office. I did shave, but I also played ping pong and ate ice cream at the Red Cross rather than sleep. The other things I accomplished in one manner or another. On my return fromthe MG, I stopped in to see Myers at the PX. He was having a bargain day in an attempt to sell out all of the items on hand before the move. Always able to enjoy a chance to do a bit of high pressure selling, I began to clear out a bunch of stuff.

After getting through with all of the other things, I found that there were a number of special items which struck my fancy. I bought a swell leather brief case for less than $3. One like it in the States would cost at least $12 or $14. I will be able to use it at school a great deal. Another item of less practical value was a very nice pair of opera glasses. Yes, My Love, I recall that I have already sent a pair to you. These, however, would make a very nice gift for some of our operatic friends (perhaps Flo and Carl, or Aunt Carol and Uncle West.) We can decide upon their disposition later.

My reason for going to the MO was to get some information for an article. I had made an outline of a number of topics which I wanted to cover, and hoped to get an interview. I found the place rather busy, but did get a bunch of restricted reports of the activities and a promise that I could visit the officers in their quarters almost any evening and get additional information. I shall have to work fast, but I hope to get this done before we leave. You flattered me with your comments on the other article. I made no attempts to get it to a magazine, but I ask Mother and Dad to show it to Sgt [Alvin C. York] and indicated that if he like it I would like for him to send it to Congressman Gore or some one else in Washington. I of course would like to get it to a magazine also, but I really do not think that it warrants that. I am trying to get enough information together now to be able to speak or write with some degree of intelligence on certain phases of the Occupation, conditions in Germany, etc.

I have been delving into Louis Nizer's book, What To Do with Germany, written sometime in '44. Reading this ten months after the fighting has ceased gives an interesting slant to the contents. Facts and ideas are thoughtfully presented and I am enjoying the moments that I have been able to spend so far with the book.

A short month was made shorter for me as a result of my travel during the first two weeks. I hope that the coming month will also be filled with travel, a great deal of it! Received my first normal pay in months today, and will put most of it in the form of a money order before I ship from the 14th.

The weather here during the past two days has been like Spring. When the snow stopped, the temperature shot up and the roads became canals of slush. Had a nice letter from Harriet which I don't think I mentioned before. She speaks of coming to Tenn. in July rather than April. Guess I should be able to see her—maybe things will speed up, My Love. I can always be hopeful. When do they plan to sail? I hate to think of them going to India now with all of the unrest and discontent that fills that land. From the papers yesterday and today I gather that even in Columbia, Tenn., riots are going on. The wake of war is truly not smooth.

Don't think that I mentioned in a previous letter a book which may be on its way home to me from England. I found while in London a new book by Palmer on <u>The Political Figures in Shakespeare</u> (perhaps it was "Political Characters"). I wanted to buy it but decided to wait until the last minute to see if my funds were sufficient. Well, they were not. But at the last second (perhaps it was the last ten), I managed to exchange some French francs with a kind soul. I left the money along with a note to one of the ladies working in the Red Cross Club (she worked with the RC in the first world war, so you really don't need to worry, Darling!) I asked her to send it to 607 if and when she had time to get it for me. I am sure that it will come eventually, but I wanted you to know what the story was when it arrives.

Your pictures and letters remind me over and over the burning fact that I should be eternally gratefully and humble for the gift of your Love. God is truly kind. You are very lovely, very wonderful, and

> I love you,
> Bushy

Letter from Art to Dotty
Memmingen, Germany
March 1, 1946

Darling,

And here is your latest news from the rumor factory. As we go to press the hotest rumors say the move expected to take place next week has been delayed. There is a possibility that the move anticipated by the 14th Inf. will be postponed for an unknown period of time, perhaps cancelled. "Oh the joy of the soldier's life!" This news is good as far as I am concerned individually. It seems entirely possible now that I could ship out sooner than if we had moved as planned. Here's hoping.

I talked to Ted again tonight, and he plans to come down tomorrow. There will be much for us to talk about since both have been away on furlough since seeing each other. I have some pictures for him and others which I wanted to show him. Also wanted him to see the chess set before I mail it home early next week. One of the several things which I like very much about my camera is that the enlargements are usually good. I have a number of the Garmisch pictures enlarged now, and I shall send them to you along with other "junk" next week.

I am beginning to have a bit of tooth trouble—my first in some time. During combat my gold tip worked loose and finally came out. I saved the tip however, and was later able to get it replaced. Within the past two or three weeks the tip has again loosened and fallen out. It is hurting me a bit, and I think that I shall go to the dentist tomorrow morning. I have the usual apprehension concerning dentists, but perhaps the blonde assistant will hold my hand while the work is being done!

Devers left a number of bits of odds and ends around and among these were three or four watches which I suppose were picked up during combat. At any rate, I have found that two or three of them are rather good watches. The market here is hardly to be compared with the one in Berlin, but I did see a very foolish GI pay three hundred dollars for a Swiss watch which cost less than $40 in the PX, and could probably be had in the States for $100. So far I have realized a nice profit on a couple of these watches and I think that I can sell the others. This money will help to make up that which I spent on my furlough.

I shall enclose an enlargement of a picture taken last July prior to my trip to Paris. Some of the other enlargements whcih I have are too large for an envelope and will have to be sent in a package. Gotta get to sleep now; but, if I may repeat myself,

I love you,
Bushy
PS. Hope Mom is improving rapidly. Give her my love.

Letters from Art to Dotty
Memmingen, Germany
Mar 3 '46 (Sun. [782-785, handwritten]

Darling,

Ted and I have just come over to the Red Cross Club to write and thus the pen (for a change). Of course, the pen is supposed to be mightier than the sword but I will still take a typewriter.

After a hectic session in which I tried to arrange transportation for Ted, he finally managed to get down here yesterday. We had a lot of pictures to show off and lots more to talk about. Saw a picture last night and then came back to talk some more. This morning to church and more bull sessions. As usual we have had a swell time talking over MC, our lovely wives, (one each!) etc.

Yesterday came your wonderful Valentine, and, Darling, it's simply wonderful. I really think that it is the best picture which you have had made in a long, long time, and I have been showing it off a great deal.

Thank you very much for being so thoughtful as to send it to me. I can easily see now that my suspicions were correct. You are getting more beautiful all the time!

Today came two more letters written on the 18th & 19th. I am surprised that my mail from England had not begun to arrive at that time; I wrote two or three letters from Camp Wings before crossing the channel. My mail from England certainly should not have been delayed so long.

Both Ted and I enjoyed the note concerning Roy Crawford. We agree wholeheartedly that it would have been a great mistake to have delayed our marriage so long. I do admire that girl's patience.

Monday night [typed]

I didn't have time enough to finish the letter last night as the Red Cross was closing. Ted and I talked as hard as we could for some time afterward, the talk always seeming to come back to our plans concerning home, family, and our very wonderful wives. Wonder why? Ted left this morning on the mail truck, and arrived in Augsburg without mishap. We talked on the phone again tonight, and he gave me some information concerning a filter which I shall try to get for him here in town. Latest news with him is that the 5th will not move in this area until about the 15th. However, it is expected that we will leave next Monday and Tuesday. I guess that we are definitely going to Mannheim, and I can only hope that the billets are good.

Another letter from you today, this one written on the 21st. Glad that my letters from England finally began to come thru. Devers pronounces his name with a short "a", by the way. I believe that you told of a $40 dollar money order coming. I shall check up and be sure. From the best that I can gather, there are two MO which never arrived and I shall began a tracer on them from here as soon as I am sure which two it was. Only a few days ago, I sent you another for $100 which I hope will come through without difficulty. I shall try to send another before I leave here.

I am surprise that you seem tothink that I have too many colds. Really about the first one th t I have had this winter came when I went to England, and I think that that was due to the lack of fruit juice in my diet and the unusual hours which I kept. Of course, I like to think that you are even interested in my colds, and it will be a real pleasure to have Nurse Bushing taking careof me. Oh joy, oh Happy Day!

632

Spent most of my evening working on my chess set again and wrapping a couple of other things. We have a fire drill at six o'clock in the morning (what a horrible hour to get up!) and I will have to get some sleep. Promise a much longer letter tomorrow, at which time I can promise that I will have far more to say concerning the vitally important subject of
Our Love,
Bushy
PS. Still think your picture is nothing short of wonderful, Love ya!

* Letter from Art to Dotty
Memmingen, Germany
March 5, 1946 [786, typed]
Dearest Heart,
This matter of mail requiring so long to go back and forth is most provoking. There are so many things which we need to talk about, and it takes so very long to get answers to questions and discussions! I will be interested in getting your reaction to my suggestion that we invest a small amount in some sound business that would provide still another cord of security to our financial future. I have no idea what the set up is with Uncles West and Ben, but I am sure that there firm is booming and will continue with plenty of business for some time. Perhaps they have no desire to sell shares of stock, but theirs is the type of business in which I think that we could and should invest. There is no need for us to say very much along these lines to anyone else, but we can continue to keep our eyes and ears peeled.

Some one brought to my attention the fact that jeeps are going to be on sale to vets at a greatly reduced rate. Now, I am sure that a jeep is not the smoothest looking car on the road, but I know something of their power and durability. I think that a good looking body could be put on a jeep, and make a fairly respectable looking automobile of it. With a trailer (jeep trailer—not house), a great deal can be carried by one of these little jobs. I do think that a new car would be entirely out of our reach at the moment and a good used car may be difficult to find. Perhaps you would hardly be interested, but I thought that we might consider the purchase of a jeep in lieu of something better. (It would be ideal for mountain travel.)

By the way, I think that I forgot to mention that someone made an error last week. By the kindness of Mr. Hurley, the new Warrant Officer in the RSO, my rating came through as T/4. I am grateful. By doing abit of work with a paper and pencil, I find that we are no [now] drawing the equivalent pay of a Master Sgt., single and in the States. My base pay is now $78. In addition I draw 20% of this base over and above for overseas service, 5% of it for longevity (more than 3 years service), plus $10 Combat Infantry pay, and you draw $28 directly from the Gov't. That means that our gross income from the Army is $135 plus your earnings from the church (which I have never known, My Love.). Do you think I should remain in the service and hold on to my stripes. Don't answer that question! The stripes of course mean very little at this late stage, but my ego is boosted a bit. T/4 means Technician, 4th grade, or the same as a buck sergeant in pay level.

[handwritten] My typewriter just left and so rather than hold this until tomorrow I shall send it incomplete. Chess set mailed today. Tonight I mail

> All my Love,
> Bushy

P.S. Note new APO 173. Hope you don't have to use it long. I will wire when I leave or perhaps my new address.

* Letter from Art to Tom
Memmingen, Germany
March 5, 1946

Dear Tom,

Dotty sent your letter on to me, your letter written on the 13th January. Needless to say, the conditions under which it was received were somewhat at variance with those which I had expected when I wrote you last. The 94th Incident has long since past, but it has left an indelible scar on my good nature. [editor's underline]

I was most happy to learn that your expected trip to the Pacific did not materialize, and Charleston sounds rather wonderful to me. I am anxious to hear more about your job in the Public Works Dept. I wouldn't want to make a dirty crack, but it sounds to me as though you have gone Democratic, Tom! You speak of wanting to see Europe, but I strongly recommend that you wait a few years. Europe is not a pleasant place just now, and it is so often in the service that one does not get to take advantage of the travel which one does. Speaking from a worm's eye view, I believe that almost all of the experience which we gain in the service can be advantageous; profitable for oursleves in many, many cases. I do hope that your work there proves both interesting and profitable.

Your continued interest in liberal arts indicates to me the proof of a theory which I have long held. I sincerely believe that an injustice would be done both to yourself and to the field of arts should you make a final decision to pursue a technical or scientific course of work. The discoveries which science has made in the past ten years have truly revolutionized our modern life, and nothing short of a New Reformation will bring us abreast in the field of spiritual, cultural, and moral values. The victories which Labor and Industry have experienced will hardly tend to drive intelligent men and women to liberal arts. The world of cultural values and intelligent thought will gain when you decide that rewards of happiness and service lie in the direction of liberal arts.

The long conversation which you suggest sounds inviting, and I look forward to the time when it is possible. At the moment those conversations seem long ago and far away—in the future. Do want to talk with you more about the Far Easter Highway subject, which I think has a real future. The history of the next few decades will be made in Asia and the Far East, and we know far too little concerning China, India, Russia, and the surrounding areas.

I am always glad to get your impressions concerning politics from the Stateside, for as I have mentioned before our sources of information over here are seriously limited. As you suggest, the labor situation is deplorable, and I can see little positive progress. I am disappointed by the total absence of a[n] effective program in Washington. Speaking of Harry, I am sure that his theme song must be, "Hail, Hail, the Gang's All Here". I wonder how soon the Missouri mule will replace the street cars in D.C. I fear that his down hill run can only end up in a crash at the bottom of the hill, i.e. '48., if not before.

My stay with the 94th was of short duration, but not before I had completed the lengthy process of clearing everything for shipment. As you know, I had received credit for ten months of ERO time. Some fellows were able to get all the way home with these points, but Bushing was not so lucky. I was cut a full ten, and thus came a delay of two and a half to three months. [editor's underline] From Sonthofen I was sent to the 66th Regt. (third Regt. in the 71st Div.), only to find that I was supposed to return to the 14th. I arrived at the 66th located in Garmisch-Partenkirchen just before the New Year and was given the opportunity to remain in the Rest Center Hotel there for five days. Celebrations were in full swing there—in Garmisch, the winter sports center for all of Europe. I had a chance to see my first hockey game, skating exhibitions by Olympic Champions, and the Zugspitz (highest peak in Germany). Upon my return to the 14th, I was placed in the Regimental Supply Office. My job has been that of keeping the books for all regimental supplies, and I have enjoyed the work more than my other army jobs.

In the latter part of January, a long delayed dream was realized for me when I left at last on my furlough to England. I think you know how much I had wanted to see England: it was to be the high-light of my European tour. I was not disappointed. I forgot to mention that I tried for school again in England, earlier in the month of Jan, but disappointment along this line had become habitual. Most of my ten days (actually extended to 15 as a result of the shipping situation) were spent in London, but I did visit Edinburgh, Cambridge, and Stratford. In the City itself, I saw the usual points of interest, and a number of fine plays. The UNO meeting was in full swing, and this too I attended for three or four meetings. I thought of you and wished that you could have been there. At the time the DP problem was in the limelight, I heard Mrs. Roosevelt and Mr. Vyshinsky in hot debate. It was the first time that I had heard Mrs. R., and I must say that I was proud of her power of speech and argument. (While I was in London, she made a speech at a Pilgrim Club Dinner. One of the papers reported that she spoke "with hardly a trace of that accent we call American". I felt as though she were acting as a traitor to our American English.) Wish that I had more time for much greater detail concerning the procedure and some of my impressions (UNO and otherwise), but I will save these accounts for that long conversations to come. At the very end of my stay, I managed to sit in for four or five sessions of the Lichfield trials. I do not know how much publicity these trials have received in the States, but GIs are very much interested in their proceedings. By the time I reached Memmingen again, I had covered 1,200 miles in the UK, and 3,500 miles during the entire trip. It was thoroughly wonderful and I am convinced more than ever that I should return to school in England for at least a year. I found a warm welcome for GIs both in England and Scotland, but only the good breeding of these people can account for this. Few GIs seem to appreciate the many things for which we must thank England.

Thanks for the invitation to visit you in Charleston, and I only hope that I can take advantage of it. (I am expecting to ship out at almost any time, and should be in the States by mid-April. We are moving next week to Mannheim and in this area the 14th will take up permanent occupation duty.) I shall also plan very definitely to visit your parents when I get back to Knoxville. You know full well that wherever Dotty and I happen to be, you will always be welcomed with open arms. Do plan to visit with us at the earliest possible moment.

As ever,
Art
Again I suggest that you write to 607 W. Glenwood, rather than here. I will probably spend the next six or eight weeks travelling, but it can't be helped.

Darling,
Tomorrow a furlough leaves for Switzerland and Italy, but I will not be on it. I will also be here when these fellows return from this furlough, and no one is leaving from Service Company. Furthermore, the man who will eventually take my place is doing most of my work, while I work with Mr. Hurley on reports and requisitions which are flooding our office. Such is life, but I do become unhappy at times, even though I really have no ground to complain. Ted had convinced me that I should take the trip if it were possible to do so, since in all probability it would be my one and only chance to see Switzerland and Rome. When I found that I could go and get back before the next shipment, I wanted very much to go. The Sergeant in charge of the RSO decided that I had already been on enough furloughs.

A great deal of discussion came up about a week ago when we received a liquor ration in the Regiment. Supposedly there was to be a quart of American whiskey for every man, but the colonel decided that that was too much. Instead of passing it around by the bottle, the ration was put in the blubs (Privates' and Non-coms') and sold by ration tickets, allowing each man only a couple drinks each evening. The entire proceedings held no interest to me, except that I thought the colonel acted wisely in spreading the whiskey out in such a manner. We have had little difficulty from drunk and disorderly conduct among the men, but had all of that stuff been passed out at once there would very likely have been trouble. There are still a few of us over here, My Love, that refuse to drink this junk.

I heard some interesting information today which is in line with what I wrote last night concerning a jeep. Some fellow wrote to his brother over here that when he was released fromthe Service he was given the choice of a jeep for about $250 or a command car for about $400. The latter cars are merely are used for generals, etc., and are usually Buicks, Chevrelets, or some other middle priced car. Of course, they are painted OD (olive drab), but could always be repainted at a minimum cost. I think that if such an opportunity presents itself to me that I shall surely take advantage of it. I do not want to over-emphasize this matter of a car, for we can certainly do without one very easily. However, I think that we would find it very practical since bus travel is still so unsatisfactory and since we will want to go back and forth between Knoxville and Jamestown very frequently as long as we are in Tennessee.

[handwritten] I wrote the other page while at work today and now tonight I find myself without a machine. Saw a light comedy tonight, played ping pong and bathed. Rather full evening, and my first night out this week.

Talked with Regt. Sgt. Major tonight and learned that absolutely no shipments go out until after we move even though there are quotas. That makes me very unhappy, but of course these days might possibly merely be wasted elsewhere. If I can only get to a unit well on its way! But it is always possible that I will have other long delays. It really can't go on forever, Darling, no matter what we think.

My heart is numb and I feel "Lost between a distant star-haven and the long, dark moon…" I need your smile and your presence, I need
  Your Love,
  Bushy
[In side margin] Note new APO 173

Letter from Art to Dotty
Memmingen, Germany
March 9, 1946 [789]

My Dearest Heart,

The clock tells me that it is almost midnight and I should be sleeping at this hour. However, I also must get a letter written, even if it is only a brief note. For three days now we have had to work late in the RSO, and my evenings have been spent in getting several packages wrapped and on their way. Well, now I was wrong when I said that I had worked late for three days. Thursday afternoon I went to Augsburg with Sgt. Smith (Supply Sgt.) to turn in some excess equipment. We saw Ted for a few minutes, exchanged rumors, and returned by way of Ulm. Smith wants to get a chess set and I wanted to pick up a couple of things which the lady there had made for me. By the time we had returned here it was almost nine o'clock. Both last night and tonight we worked late, and we thought that it would be necessary to work tomorrow. However, we were able to get all of our reports completed and ready to go to Division on Monday morning.

This morning I sent a large envelope containing pictures to you, and also another small package. Both are coming first class, and should not take too long to get there. Tomorrow I must get up early and get a couple of more boxes up to the POst Office before the trucks leave for Augsburg. One large package contains the leather photo album for our European pictures. This was done by the lady in Ulm. Among other odds and ends there is a scarf for you, and the opera glasses which I spoke about in another letter. The leather bag will do very nicely as a pack for some of the innumberable hikes which we shall surely take. The leather brief case I bought some time ago for a song at the PX. It will be very practical for school, and I think that such a one would be rather expensive in the States. At the very last moment before our eve comes, I was able to get my skii shoes made, and these I am sending to Jamestown in a package of (junk) things. (Darling, I really think that I should have sent more of these odds and ends to Jamestown. They are really rather useless, many of them, and we shall certainly dispose of them when I get there.) I found a small wooden box with an inlay atop which I am sending to Mother. I haven't been able to find very much for her over here so far.

There is a great deal of confusion with the move coming up next week, and the town to which we are supposed to go has been changed several times each day. Wineheim is the latest, being just outside of Mannheim. Still supposed to move out about Tuesday or Wednesday. Latest rumor is that the next shipment will go out to the 4th Armored Div. after we make the Regt. move. The story goes that that will be about the 20th of the month, but it remains on the list of rumors and there is nothing official.

I receive more compliments every day on how beautiful you are, My Darling, and everyone likes the new picture I have almost as much as I do. It is certainly nothing new to me to hear that you are beautiful for I have been telling both you and myself that for six years now (that is, six years, tomorrow night!) I love you with all of my heart.

Thine own,
Bushy

New APO 173

My Dearest Heart,

As though it were yesterday I remember in perfect detail this night six years ago. I had just returned from a week-end at home; I came to supper at Pearsons (dining hall at Maryville College), and there you were at my table. Your bright smile, your quick wit, your loveliness— these things attracted me, even as I had been attracted long before I met you. After finishing my meal I waited outside in the lovers' lobby. One thing I cannot recall, and that is the exact number of fellows I had to knock down to reach you first. I am sure that it must have been six or seven, but anyway I did. After more fun and laughter during those hallowed minutes between six-thirty and seven I managed to insist that you should attend the Vesper service (with me!). After returning you to Baldwin and me to Carnegie, I recall telling "Preacher", my roommate, what a lovely creature I had accompanied to the services, and I mentioned that I must see more of her. I have and I will! Darling, I love you so very much. I have only begun my attempt to prove myself worthy of you, and I shall go on all of my life trying to be worthy of your love. Would that I could at this moment hold you close to me and whisper something of the meaning to me of Our Love.

Word came today that the RSO crew will leave here very early on Tues. morning for our new location. Tomorrow we will have to break down rations after they come in late tomorrow afternoon. That will mean that I will have little time tomorrow night to pack my things. I did most of it tonight. The latest story is that we have a nice town near Mannheim and that the billets [a nonmilitary facility] are good. It will make little real difference as far as I am personally concerned for I should be leaving very soon after the Regt. is settled in the new area. As I think I wrote last night, we will go to the 4th Armored Division I believe.

Last night I had a call from Wallace who went to the 66th. They are to leave for the port area between the 20th and 25th of March, and should be on a boat by the end of the month. I only hope that the 4th Armored will be fast on their heals. Devers tried to call me once when I was away, and I have expected a call almost daily since that time. However, I rather think that he is well on his way also by now.

I did something today that was most unusual for me on a Sunday morning: I arose shortly past eight o'clock. The reason was that I had to get my packages to the Post Office before eight-thirty or suffer the consequences of carrying them with me on the trip. I just made the deadlined and had time to write Mother and Dad before church. This afternoon I planned to lie down for an hour or so and then spend the afternoon packing and writing. I went to sleep as soon as I had finished lunch, and I arose just in time to get to supper. What a lovely way to spend a damp, rainy afternoon in Bavaria.

I think I told you about all of the packages which I have sent during the past two days—six I think in all, but part of them are going to Jamestown. The one which I mailed today to you contains the leather photo album from Ulm, the leather brief case, and a few other odds and ends. I was unable to insure it due to the move that we are making, but I think that it should arrive without mishap.

We had a new chaplain holding services for us today. The 47th Regt. is moving into town, and so their chaplain held a joint service for both units. He was very young and told us that he had only been with the 47th for a week. I am sure that he is just out of seminary, and I thought of Hal, Dick, Olson, and the other classmates of mine who are just starting out as ministers.

Sometime I want to discuss with you the broad scope of behavior connected with the escape drive. It seems to me that agreat deal can be explained in this way, and I would like to read a bit about it. I am sure that much of the activity of the GIs overseas is a direct result of their conscious or unconscious desire to get away from the reality of the present. Under these circumstances in which we live, under these unnatural surroundings, many are unable to adjust and still maintain their old standards of morals and ethics. The warped results of adjustment are to be seen all around, and the effects will continue to reveal themselves for the next decade (perhaps I should say the next several decades.)

There are so many things about which I want to talk with you, but none more important that the depth of my love for you. Sickened as I am by the continued delays which began three months ago, I still feel my pulse quicken when the slightest bit of goods news is heard. God will surely hasten the day when we are again united in

Our Love,
Bushy

PS. As I started to send this, Ted called. He is leaving Tuesday for the 4th Armored. I should leave very soon thereafter I think. Hope we are close enough together to see each other.

Letter from Art to Dotty
Memmingen, Germany
March 11, 1946 (Monday) [792-793]

Darling,

I begin this letter not knowing how far I will be able to get with it. It is now almost nine-thirty and I returned from work less than an hour ago. I have a fire going full blast in the hope that I will be able to get a bath and a necessary shave tonight, and I also expect another call from Ted momentarily. We leave here at eight o'clock tomorrow morning, and so everything is in something of turmoil tonight.

Today I have been tired and somewhat out of sorts, but my morale shot sky-high again when I found that I had five wonderful letters from you, a copy of "Hearth-Log", and a letter from Van. The first letter from you was dated on Jan. 6th, having crossed the ocean for the third time. It contained the first news which I had received concerning Dad's operation. Since you have not mentioned it in other letters, I presume that everything is all right now and that there were no ill-effects. I certainly hope that you do not follow suit and get an operation just to be in style or something. Another letter told of David's operation, and still others told of Mother's condition. So glad that she is getting along all right also, and I do hope that you bought some flowers for her as I had suggested.

* Later

Well, my call did come through from Ted, and I did get my bath and shave. Now, of course, it is very late, and I do not have too much time left for sleeping. Ted leaves tomorrow morning for a unit in the 4th Armored located near Regensburg. He has already heard a wild rumor that the outfit is supposed to sail early in April. I only hope that they leave a little early.

Glad to hear what you have to say about "Lost Weekend", and hope that I can see it soon. I have read two or three very good comments about it. "Mildred Pierce" is to show here on Wed. and Thurs. and I wanted to see that. That is Joan Crawford's picture, you know. I have put away three or four good books which I will probably have time to read as I begin to process. I think I read more while I was in the 94th than at any other time during my overseas stay.

As I was coming out of the bathroom I had an interesting conversation with another fellow who was shaving. In speaking of the move, he asked me if I was taking my "women" with me. In anyother situation I would of course been insulted. I did not take offense in this case, since with 75% of the fellows the question would be perfectly normal. Upon further questions, the fellow could hardly believe that I had not been with a women since coming overseas. He came over only last November, and like most of the new men came rapidly under the influence of Hitler's low moral standards. As much as I regret to say it, I do not believe that more than 10% of the GIs in Europe would claim to be ETO virgins. I get terribly disgusted sometimes, but there seems to be no help for it. It hardly tends to increase my faith in fellow men.

I do believe that we are at last straight on those back Money Orders which I sent. In a recent letter I stated the amounts and the approximate times which I sent these, and if you received two or three in December that should just about cover those early ones. There was another $100 one which I sent some time in February which should have reached you by this time. I know what you mean about these confusing letters, but I must admit that the mail system [h]as been in better order during recent weeks. It still takes a terrible long time it seems, but when they do come most of the time they are in order. I still can't understand why there should have been such a long delay in my letters reaching you fromEngland. I thought that they would come in four or five days.

It looks as though I am in for some sightseeing during the next three weeks. Tomorrow to the Rhine, and with a few days back to the Danube. Very shortly thereafter I should be on the last long leg of the journey—HOME! I shall have difficulty in writing as regularly as I should but I shall always find time to whisper each night,

I love you,
Bushy

Letter from Art to Dotty
Weinheim, Germany
March 14, 1946 [794]

Darling,

The big news came at six o'clock TONIGHT (that really wasn't supposed to be capitalized), when we received word that we are to move out again within a couple of days. Why can't this Army make up its mind? I am really not too surprised, but it does seem so silly that we should move in to this town, unpack, begin to get things in shape for decent living, only to have someone decide that we should not remain. A billeting party leaves tomorrow morning, and I presume that we will leave about Sunday. At least the move will come in time to disrupt any plans for a quiet, restful day that we might plan.

We worked most of the day getting our RSO fixed up, and the billets are just beginning to appear livable and almost pleasant. I was able to sneak in time enough to write a note to Ted and also a brief letter to Mom. I have had no late news concerning her condition after the operation, but I do hope that everything went along well.

Sgt. Smith (supply sgt.) and I came over to the Red Cross tonight for a little game of chess. He wiped me out but we did have an enjoyable game. He beats me consistently in ping pong, and I had hoped that I could succeed in beating him in chess. However, I shall be happy to try again at any other time. I was off from work early this afternoon, and I was over here then to get a haircut (long delayed by moving, etc.) Found that there is a very nice library here, and I spent an enjoyable hour brousing through a few books of poetry.

By the way, I haven't mentioned it before, but I would like to make one small request concerning the first few weeks of my return. I would like very much to spend a little time at Jamestown during the time for planting the garden. I would like very much to put out the garden for Mother this year. Perhaps we can plan to get to Jamestown in the fall and late summer to do a bit of canning for our winter supply of food. What say?

The news continues to look black in regard to the Anglo-Russian relationship. I continue to believe that we have every reason to get along withthe Kremlin and very, very few reasons to create friction. We have done many things to create suspicion, and of course she has done the same. Frank talk and open discussion is the only thing which can ever settle international problems.

Rumors persist that our shipment is to be made the 20th, and that date can not come too soon to suit me. I hope that very soon I will have good news to report. Tonight the only news I know is that I love you with all of my heart.

> Eternally thine,
> Bushy

[The following is handwritten on this letter by someone else. Perhaps it is a note to Art.]

Dear _____

Enclosed is list of people in for group I, which you & _____ are vespens' for dining every Mo—

It occurs to me you might like to get in touch with Mr. _____, & between 2 of u divide the list and telephone everyone on it, urging them to bring their signed pledge cards to Sun. morn. Service. If you do this, it might materially cut down on no. of calls you will be making Sun. afternoon.

Letter from Art to Dotty
Weinheim, Germany
March 13, 1946 [795-796]

Darling,

It is 10:30 AM and we already have our office and regimental supply room set up and ready for operation. After and [an] eight hour ride, during which time we covered about two hundred and seventy-five miles, we arrived here at four-thirty yesterday afternoon. Although there had been a vicious rumor that we would unload the trucks as soon as we arrived, this was soon dispelled. We managed to get together a bit of food, walked a bout the town for a few minutes, and then "hit the sack". (In Army slang, sack is not a drink but a bed!) I was in bed by 8:45, the earliest inlong weeks.

The long ride up was made more enjoyable by a nice day. I rode in the front seat of an open truck, and had a perfect view of the country side through which we passed. The route was very much the same that I had taken several times by train, but the outlook was entirely different. From Ulm we came by way of the autobahn to Heidleberg. A number of bridges are still "kaput", bridges which we blown up by the retr eating Army just about a year ago. From Ulm the autobahn winds out of the valley of the Danube, passes through parts of the Swartzwald, or Black Forest, and outside of Karlsruhe, passes into the valley of the Rhine. Everywhere we saw entire families working on their farms, preparing for the spring planting. There was some snow still on the ground, but after we reached the Rhine area, the snow was no more. With few incidents we reached Heidelberg, and from there it is but about fifteen kilometers to Weinheim. I had looked forward to seeing the little university town on the River. It is a lovely town, situated just at the base of a range of low hills. The river runs through the town, and the flat, open plain stretches westward. As you know, the town was untouched by war, and I certainly want to go back to see more of it before I leave here. I can see why this town is called Weinheim for the surrounding hills are literally covered with vineyards.

Of course, everything is still very much unsettled, and most of the company will not arrive until today. We have a location for our billets in the middle of the town, and our RSO is in a large factory not too far fromwhere we live. The rooms seem fairly decent on the whole, and I really don't think that I will have to worry too long about my room in this town, but I still have had no further rumors concerning when I will move out.

I am back now from lunch, having relieved the CQ in order that he can go eat. On the desk beside me is an interesting letter, telling me somethingabout theplant here. The name of it is the Freudenberg Plant, and it is "extremely important to essential civilian supply in the American Area. It is the largest leather factory in American area and is engaged in U.S. Army contracts as well." It is so important that never before have soldiers been allowed to occupy the factory area. I rather think that if another place can be found, we will move out. Alarge number of small units are located here in town, and we understand that some of them will be taken out shortly. If and when this takes place, still another shift may take place.

Still later

It is almost time to go home, and I had better finish this letter before I leave. Have to move my room a couple of times tonight, shave, bathe, get a haircut, and a couple of other things. Guess I will try to see a movie tonight if there is anything half decent one playing. I will give you the latest rumors as fast as they come off the press, but at the moment there seems to be a stalemate. However, there is never a stalemate on the reports of one thing. Nothing whatsoever will ever stop or even slow down the progress of

> Our Love,
> Bushy

Letter from Art to Dotty
Weinheim Germany
March 15, 1946 [896-898, handwritten]

My Darling,

I have just been told in subtle terms that typing is improper for personal letters, of course, I know, but a pen seems so much more awkward than a nice, comfortable typewriter. I really should apologize for writing to you on a machine, My Love. I flatter myself to think that perhaps I can make my letter personal though not written by hand, but that is not based purely on biased egotism.

The fellow who made this remark was Sgt. Bruns, by the way, my new roommate. Sgt. Bruns, my wife! My wife, Sgt. Bruns! Bruns is to take over the position of First Sgt. when Findlay leaves next Monday morning at 8:00 for a unit of the 4th Armored Div. He is one of the nicest and the cleanest fellows I have met over here. We attend church together all of the time, and play a bit of ping pong now and then. Just returned from a show with him, before which I was defeated in another game of chess with Sgt. Smith.

Did almost exactly nothing today. Everything is held up because of the move again. As I wrote last night, we are moving again. I only hope it isn't over the week-end.

Had a letter from Mother & Dad last night. Mother never received the birthday telegram which I sent her from London. I found a little present for her last week and mailed it, but of course that is a bit late. Sounds like Jamestown is blooming with building and I understand that a daily round trip schedule to Knoxville is being planned. Not bad, eh? We could certainly give them a great deal of trade, should we decide not to buy a car.

Oh, by the way, I almost forgot, My Love, at four-thirty this afternoon I listened while the First Sgt. took down the names of those men who are to leave for the 4th Armored Division. Mine happens to be among them. We are to go to a small town, (I can't recall the name) South East of Ingolstadt, and I think the unit will be the 126 Armored Oxd. Bn, APO 254, I shall wire you the correct address upon arrival, but I think it will be Ted's outfit. We leave Monday morning. What a joy to start out once more.

> "O Mistress mine, where are you roaming?
> O stay and hear! Your true-love's
> That can sing both high and low;
> Trip no further pretty sweeting'
> Journeys end in lovers meeting
> Every wise man's son doth know."
> (The third line is in very serious question!)

I love you,
Bushy

Letter from Art to Dotty
Weinheim Ger.
Mar 17, 1946 [799-802]

My Darling,

Well, it's about time I began to use nice paper on which to write my lovely wife. Bruns (my roommate) allowed me to use this since all that have is packed.

My day was made bright by three letters from you dated on Feb 25th, Mar 1st, and Mar 7. It was my first mail in several days and most welcomed. This morning I arose late and weathered a very cold shower —my first bath in several days. (Our bathing facilities have been nil here.) After shaving, Bruns and I found our way to church and a communion service.

After lunch, Brums, Smith, and I managed to get a jeep and rode about for a couple of hours seeing the town. In the process we visited a couple of old castles on nearby hills and saw a good many of the back streets.

Late in the afternoon, Bob Mulford came up to spend the night here, prior to leaving with us tomorrow morning. He had to make a run out to a nearby town. We had a chance to go through Mannheim which I was anxious to see. It is thoroughly destroyed.

Leaving tomorrow morning at 8 o'clock for Mainburg and the 126 Armored Oxd. Bn. APO 254. Will try to wire address upon arrival. Continue to write here until I wire otherwise. I must get to bed, but not before telling you in no uncertain terms,

I love you,
Bushy

Letter from Art to Dotty
Mainburg, Germany
March 19, 1946 [803-805]

Darling,

I will not have too much time to write here, but at least I can get aletter started. We arrived here about eight-thirty last night after riding for almost twelve hours on the back of a 2½ ton truck. We returned the same way we traveled on a week before until we passed Ulm. There we took to the side roads, the same being extremely dusty and uncomfortable for riding over. Through Donaworth, Dillingen, Ingolstadt, etc. until finally we reached here.

The town itself is rather small, and the entire battalion is located here, but scatttered all over the place. We have central mess, on the far side of town, making an appetite merely a matter of course after walking all the way to the hall. As my address shows I was put in Company "B", and our rooms are very nice. Ted is in Company "A", and is located very near to where I am. He is working in headquarters where I am supposed to come. It seems that the office is in need of typists, and my MOS numbers shows that I am a typist. I will probably be called up here tomorrow. I would much rather have a definite job and steady work to keep me busy during the next few days, and I will welcome whatever work I get. Do hope that I can land something with Ted though. Our record continues to amaze me when I think that we have separated five times in the Army and rejoined again.

The so-called "pipe-line" seems somewhat familar, as do most of the processes of processing. We had a clothing check today, in the same old fashion. Rumors are hot as usual, and the usual delays can be anticipated. There remain many things yet to do before we are ready to move toward the port, but this is a wonderful beginning. There is some talk of going out through Bremenshaven. I certainly hope so for that would give me a chance to see something of the northern section of Germany which I have never seen. Le Harve is seventy hours from here by train and Bremenshaven only sixty. I presume that we will know where we are going before we leave.

I don't know when this letter will arrive, but I do not think that you need write to me after April 6 or 7th. I put those dates down arbitrarily, only hoping and think that a letter written after that would not have time to reach me before we pull out. It may be that within a few days I will revise that, as I see how things develop here. I think that we can easily count on one or two delays, at least. You know a little of how the Army operates in such matters. I am still trying to send you a cablegram as I promised, but so far I have been unable to do so. Perhaps I will still be able to get one out, and I shall continue to try.

Ted and I are doing a little work here in the office tonight, but are going to a USO show at eight o'clock. Will report on that later. Until tomorrow, goodnight, and may God continue to Bless
Our Love,
Bushy

[all handwritten from here to end]
We have just returned from the show, put on in our mess hall. It was a German affair and strictly on the corny side. It passed a couple of hours and we came out to my place to write.

Yesterday before leaving the 14th, everyone was given a quart of Am. whiskey. It was part of a Special Service Issue and is sold for $2.00

per qt. I gave mine to some of the fellows remaining behind, allowing them to pay for it, of course. Tonight the fellows here are making the most of their wiskey. I must say, however, that most of the boys feel that they are too close to the boat to act up much. Today the young girls paraded up and down the streets all day trying to flirt now and then with the GIs. I heard a number of fellows remark that they are going to stay away from the women from now on. It's a pity they didn't decide that months ago.

As we passed the CP tonight, I stopped to read the bulletin board. I am to report to the Bn. CP. as soon as possible. This will be for some sort of work in the office with Ted. Will find out early tomorrow morning.

I still want to write a lengthy discussion as to why I think we should have two or three days to ourselves before seeing everybody else. (You really don't know what a wolf I am—now!) I shall save my discussion for a later time.

As the time draws near for my departure, I find my mind crowded in delightful confusion with thought of our reunion. Allow me to repeat myself by saying, again and again, and again

I love you,
Bushy

March 20
Mainburg, Germany
(About 30 Km SE of Ingolstadt)

Between my last notes (written in Paris) and the present ones, there is a long gap covering more than a month. It seems far longer than that since Devers and I arrived in Memmingen at 12:30 on the morning of the 16th of Feb. I had planned to spend the night in Augsburg [with Ted K.], but found that he had left the same day for the Rome-Swiss tour. We secured a ride to Memmingen where I found sixteen letters from Dotty. Tired as I was I read each one avidly before going to bed. Our men down to 46 points, plus a few 45 pointers, had left the previous day for the 66th Regt. Devers left within a few days for the 102nd Inf. and almost all the old Service Company had left. I continued to work in RSO as stock records clerk with a promising understudy who soon took over. Mr. Hurley, our new Asst. S-4, put through my promotion, and I became a T/4 on the 27 Feb. Same grade, same job Capt. Garner offered me last Nov.

Men in 45 point bracket were supposed to move out much earlier, but a general shifting within the 9th Div. delayed the shipment. Ted and the men in the 5th moved to Mainburg and the 126th Armored Ord. Maint. Bn on the 12th of March, the same day for Sv. Co. and most of the 14th [REGT.] moved by truck and train to the Karlsruhe – Heidelberg area. Sv. Co. landed in Weinheim near the latter city [AND NORTHEAST OF MANNHEIM]. I traveled by truck enjoying the scenic ride very much though I knew full well that it must be repeated in reverse very soon.

We took the autobahn outside of Ulm and began to wind and climb through the Schwarzwald. Over the autobahn we traveled swiftly, but many bridges are still out, bridges blown up by the retreating Wehrmacht less than a year ago. In some cases long detours are necessary. We skirted Suttgart, passed through Pforzheim, and Karlsruhe. Outside of the latter city we found ourselves in the flat plain area of the Rhine and sped rapidly north to Heidelberg.

Letter from Art to Dotty
Mainburg, Germany
March 22, '46 [806-815]

Darling,

I must confess that I have allowed the rush and excitement of these days to distract me to the point of writing far too little. Forgive me, My Love, if I write less I think more of you each passing day. I am again beginning to feel the real excitement of being in the "pipe-line."

As I wrote before. I was called to Bn. Hdq and found a somewhat confused situation. S-1, S-2, S-3 (the administrative branches with the exception of S-4, which is supply), Personnel, Message Center, and a couple of other nameless functions are being carried on in a room and a half, while the entire Battalion of men is being processed in the same room at the same time. By some unknown freak of fate the work is being done and we are making progress toward that final readiness date of departure.

Ted and I are working together in the office, which makes the work more pleasant. Since my billets are far on the other side of the town, I leave my mess kit with his things and seldom return to my room between breakfast and night fall. We have been having variety shows every night, and Ted and I usually attend. He is in the habit of seeing everything that comes for the sake of seeing the few good pictures or shows which come. I am in the habit of seeing almost nothing because I had rather miss a good show now and then as to see some of the trash that comes along.

We stood in line for an hour and a half tonight to get our PX rations—probably over lost on these side for we received them for several weeks in advance.

There are times in the office when the work is very slack for we have a number of clerks assisting. At these times I manage to do a bit of reading and I have just finished a very fine biography of Shelley.

You know, when I return to my studies, I would like to keep a small notebook at hand in which I could record place names to be visited. It could be divided into geographical sections and as I read of places I could jot down the names and their significance. Then, when we come to England, spend a few weeks in Scotland, or even visit the Continent again, we shall have a handy reference of places and things to see. I still want to work out plans for a filing system at which you can be of invaluable aid.

I am wondering if you could not help me out a great deal with a bit of German between now and Sept. I have picked up a bit over here and my Dutch background will help. Now, I would like to spend some time with you studying rudiments of grammar. Think it would be lots of fun to learn to speak together in German as we used to do in Dutch and Malay.

It is most surprising and encouraging to realize that I will be eligible for more than forty-six months of schooling under the GI Bill. That amounts to more than $4,000 for living expenses and $2,000 for tuition. Darling, I am sure that we can get the PhD now. For a very long time it was really a pipe dream. I was hoping! Now, we can plan!

My Love, I do not want to appear stubborn about an old subject, but I do want to express my views once more concerning the question of my homecoming. I still wish that we could plan to be alone for a couple of days.

In the first place, we will need to adjust ourselves to being together again. In my letters from day to day it is impossible to reflect the gradual changes which take place. I cannot tell you how I have changed for I do not know myself. It is inevitable that both of us should find it necessary to make certain adjustments to each others thoughts and actions. During the first days of our reunion, I am convinced that this can best be done while we are alone!

In the second place, we are entitled, after these terrible months of separation, to find complete joy in happiness on what will truly be our second honeymoon. To be brutally frank, My Sweetest Heart, I don't want to be troubled with anyone else. I want to spend hours just holding you in my arms, looking at you, talking to you, and telling you in no uncertain terms of the depth of my love for you. I know as well as you that no matter how hard we try, there are certain to be social obligations to fulfill. People will call up, perhaps come to visit, perhaps there will be a party or a young people's skating party. I would like to think that you would be, that we would be completely free from any social obligations during those first precious moments and hours during which we are together again.

In the third place, I think that it would be less difficult for everyone else concerned. Mother wrote me that though I was supposed to report to the Draft Board within ten days after being discharged, they would grant any extension that I wished. Now, I agree that we should get to Jamestown as soon as possible, but I would still like to have two or three days with my wife—alone.

If I have labored the points, it is merely because I love you and long to be with. Forgive me for bringing it up again. It's merely the Irish in me. I am keeping my roommates awake, although I would love to talk to you all night. There is so much to say and pen and ink are so inadequate. Goodnight and God Bless

Our Love,

Bushy

P.S. As I wrote before, there is no need to write to me now for the letters will not catch me now.

Mar 24
Mainburg, Germany

To continue the above story, we found our billets not too uncomfortable, but hardly had we begun to settle down when we found that we must move to another town. The Regt. CO had moved into Weinheim, our new town, without proper authorization. The RSO had been located in the largest leather factory in the Am. Zone of Occupation, and the setup was suitable. However, the move had to be made. Luckily for me, I left for the home-bound 254 Armd. Ord. Maint. Bn before we found a new location.

Dearest Dotty,

How well I recall the events of one year ago this date! It was on the second day of Spring (22nd) that I just set foot on Germany. From Bitche we had moved into positions near Pirmasens. Our squad occupied the crest of a long, steep hill, and at the foot of the hill ran a small stream separating France and Germany. On the 22nd we moved forward across the draw and on a few miles into Germany. (I well recall the blank, unbelieving stares that we received as we passed from one small town to the next.) Late in the afternoon we arrived in a town, somewhat larger than most, where our company was to stop—for the moment. We spent the entire day of the 23rd, searching houses for weapons and soldiers, resting, washing, shaving. It was the first time that we had been under a roof since entering combat. Shortly before midnight we waited with our equipment on our back. As my birthday began, I rolled forward through the impregnable Siegfried Line on top of a truck load of gasoline. The moon was bright and the white dragon teeth stretched out, row on row, no longer defying our advance but seeming to be completely indifferent to our passage. Pill boxes and other blockades could be seen against the hillsides. (Extremely steep hills are in this area, but there are few trees.) As daylight dawned we had reached the edge of the Rhine plain and the hillsides were covered with vineyards. By noon we were near London and here we stopped for more transportation.

In this area, the Germans had had time for some scanty preparation. Forced laborers had dug extensive networks of trenches which zigzagged across fertile fields. At many strategic spots along the road, fox holes and embankments had been constructed, but no snipers were left to harass us.

Late in the afternoon as we moved forward we did learn that one unit from the 5th Inf. had been ambushed in town where civilians opened with machine guns from behind white flags. We saw streams of people come back from the areas where the heavier fighting was going on. Some had carts, other bicycles or wagons. Many had nothing but a pack on their back. There was tearful anguish in their faces but I thought of the millions of other Europeans who had been driven from their homes by the German soldiers in the earlier days of the war. These people were reaping what others had sown.

We passed through the large city of Speyer and on to a smaller town nearby. Complete darkness had fallen by the time we took up our positions along a dyke outside the town. As swiftly and as silently as possible we dug our fox holes and began our "Watch on the Rhine." Thus ended my birthday 1945, and thus began one of the most exciting phases of my combat experiences, ours was diversionary activity intended as a feint across the Rhine while the 3rd Army made it's famous crossing farther north.

Today has been entirely different and yet is has hardly been an ideal way to spend one's birthday. I arose at my usual hour (now) of 7:25 and reached Ted's barracks about 7:55. We went over for breakfast and then to work. With the exception of about an hour and a half during which I slept, I was at the office all day. This afternoon we began our separation-center rosters. There was no church service in town and so I was unable to attend service anywhere. Tonight, Ted and I will go to the USO show which will be very mediocre at best. Oh by the way, I'm scheduled to go to Camp Atterbury for separation. It is in Indiana and about 100 miles from Cincinnati I understand. Other camps are closer, but all Tenn boys are supposed to go thru Atterbury. We still have no idea when we are to leave here, and the delay does little to raise our morale.

Yesterday, during a lull in the work, Ted and I slipped away from the office to get a few pictures of local color. We have taken together about three rolls here in Mainburg which is more or less typical of a small town in this area. I shall not try to get these developed before I get home.

Since we arrived last Monday, the weather has been almost perfect. Yesterday there were just enough fast-flying clouds to give good backgrounds for our photography. Today, however, has been cloudy, and a light rain is beginning to fall. It will really be a wonderful season to get home (as if any season would not be wonderful). Spring is a wonderful season of the year!

Last night I packed what I think will be my last box in the ETO. It contains a number of your letters (Nov-Jan) some extra socks and underwear, a SRL issue on music, and a few other odds and ends. There is also a small anniversary present, Darling. I would have liked to have carried it and given it to you in person, but I decided it would be wise to mail it instead. It isn't much, but I hope that it will provide many hours of enjoyment for both of us.

I suppose that the ideas expressed in my last letter (concerning my home-coming) were a little extreme. Forgive me if I appeared to be stubborn on the one little point. As perhaps you know, Cordy is going to Washington to meet Ted. He will be released at Fort Meade, only a few miles from his home.

Later

The variety show was much better than I had expected, but I only attend these things to pass the time more quickly. Such things are like a narcotic for me: during the time that I attend I can sometimes lose myself for the moment. I can forget momentarily my loneliness and laugh, but when the show ends I always feel the let-down that comes when the effect of the narcotic as [has] worn away.

Need I tell you that there is an ever present loneliness in my heart that overpowers my spirit as does a deep and impenetratible fog on a somber winter's day. My spirit will ever be moored, tied down among earthly surroundings while I am yet apart from you. When we are together again, my spirit will be unleashed and will fly again unto heights that only Life and Love can know. [editor's underline]

The first summer that we were apart I recall that a poem to you came tumbling out almost as fast as I could put down the words. As a poem, it was very poor, but the idea expressed arose from a deep and heart-filled love which even then had begun to blossom. If you still have a copy of the poem, reread it tonight. What I want to say in that poem, what I want to say in this letter, what I want to say all of my life is merely this, My Darling:

> "I love thee to the depth and breadth
> and height
> My soul can reach.....
> .... I love thee with the breath,
> Smiles, tears, of all my life! – and,
> if God choose,
> I shall but love thee better
> after death."
> [Art quotes Elizabeth Barrett Browning's work.]

Eternally thine,
Bushy

Homeward Bound

On the 18th we made a long twelve-hour ride from Weinheim to Mainberg. From Ulm to our new location we traveled over narrow, dusty roads, but there were few complaints. We were on our way! When I joined this new unit, I could count five times that Ted and I had been separated only to rejoin again. [(1) WE REPORTED TO FORT OGLETHORPE, GA., FOR ACTIVE DUTY JUNE 1, 1943. FROM THERE WE SHIPPED TO CAMP ROBERTS, CALIF., WHERE WE BEGAN OUR BASIC TRAINING. (2) BECAUSE I WAS OUT OF TRAINING FOR LESS THAN A WEEK, I WAS SENT TO ANOTHER TRAINING GROUP TO COMPLETE BASIC. WHEN HIS TRAINING WAS OVER, TED SHIPPED OUT, BUT IN EARLY JANUARY, 1944, (3) WE MET AGAIN AT STANFORD UNIVERSITY FOR THE ARMY SPECIALIZED TRAINING PROGRAM (ASTP) – HE IN THE CHINESE LANGUAGE TRAINING PROGRAM, I IN DUTCH. (4) WHEN THE CHINESE PROGRAM WAS TERMINATED AFTER THREE MONTHS, HE WAS SENT TO THE 5TH INFANTRY REGIMENT FOR MANEUVERS. I REMAINED AT STANFORD, AFTER WHICH I REPORTED TO FORT BENNING, GEORGIA, AND ASSIGNED TO THE 14TH REGIMENT, WHICH ALONG WITH THE 5TH WERE IN THE 71ST INFANTRY DIVISION. (5) WHEN THE ARMY CONTINUED TO LIST MY POINTS AT 55, I LEFT THE 71ST TO JOIN A HOME-BOUND UNIT. BUT THEN WAS SHIPPED BACK TO THE 71ST. TED BEING STILL THERE. (6) WHEN THE TIME ACTUALLY CAME FOR US TO COME HOME, WE WERE BOTH SENT TO THE 254 ARMD. ORD. MAINT. BN.] As a result of my 405 Specialist No. (Clerk Typist), I was called immediately to Bn Hq. to work on the many forms and papers connected with going home. Ted is in the office also, and so we had much time together.

Though the day has been Sunday and my birthday, it has been spent at work. I did sleep for a couple of hours in the afternoon, and I saw a USO [SHOW] tonight. The only highlight of the day was a twelve-page letter to Dotty. I trust that my birthday next year will be somewhat different.

Darling,

The office is quiet this afternoon: a couple of guys are working, others are reading, others are absent. The climax to our work came yesterday when we worked until almost midnight to get the separation rosters out of the way. In two days time we typed more than 168 rosters, one for each company for each separation center in the States. We worked in pairs and Ted and I worked together most of the time. When we finished more than twenty stencils yesterday afternoon, we found that every single one had been done incorrectly. We did not have to do them over, but we did have to correct the lot of them. As I say, the job of completing everything was done shortly before midnight.

Although we are now ready from an administrative angle, there is still no indication as to when we are to leave here. When we first came, we were told that we were to move out on Monday, the 25th. That was yesterday and we seem no nearer the port than we were a week ago. The S&S carried a story last week that twenty thousand troops scheduled to leave in April would be shipped in March, but I am sure that we have nothing to do with this group. Of course, if the backlog of troops in the ports are cleared out early, then there should be little to hold us up when we do get started.

Last night Ted received the good news concerning Dave's proud bundle of charm. It's a girl, Katheleen Mary, weight six pounds, thirteen ounces, born on a Sunday. Mary and Dave are living with the Kidders, awaiting an apartment which they are supposed to get shortly. It seems that the housing shortage is not confined to Knoxville.

Cordy will meet Ted in Washington, but they will soon return to her home in order than she can complete her school term. They hope to get to Maryville for commencement, and I have been wondering if that would be a good time to take them up to the cabin. Ted and I have talked a great deal about spending some time up there. Of course, I don't mean, My Dear, that this should be our first vacation at the cabin. For us, I have long dreamed of spending several days up there, completely and delightfully alone. Now, perhaps commencement time would be a bit early for us to plan to invite them up, but I do hope that we can manage it before the summer is gone. After that we will be tied down, as will they. Think it over, and we can decide later.

Have just returned from the show given as usual in the Mess Hall. These shows are always German talent and so often are not very entertaining. Of course, a GI body of troops, homeward bound is not an easy thing [to] please at any time. Generally speaking any sort of sexy dance or act goes over in a big way.

From my observations over here, I have developed a few new ideas concerning sex. When we read in psychology that it was one of the basic drivers, I hardly knew what the statement meant. I have a clearer conception now I think for I have seen how far it can drive men as they drop their moral standards to a lower and lower level. As I am about to leave the ETO, I think I have begun to realize how some men have been able to go as far as they have. I have never and could never separate illicit sex relations from moral and religious sinning. This is, I believe, what many have done. By crushing their moral and religious training until they think nothing of sleeping with one woman after another. It is a sad state of affairs.

By the way, I wonder if you should not make inquiry concerning the shield of which we talked before. We should have one I think, since it is considered one of the best methods. After we have had a chance to talk over our plans, we will be able to act regarding the family. For a few months we shall certainly want to make the most of complete freedom. Don't get the wrong idea, My Love. I am still as anxious to become a proud father as ever—only more so. However, we certainly want nothing to interfere with the joy of enjoying life to the fullest. Perhaps this can best be accomplished if we do not plan for a blessed event immediately.

I shall never be able to tell you of the anticipation with which I look forward to our reunion. Days seem to go on endlessly and all meaning is taken from them except as they bring me closer to you. I can but gather dust on the shelf until I enter the presence of my Kindred Soul who alone can bring out the best and highest within me. I need you, My Darling.

I do hope that you can cut yourself loose from the responsibilities of your many activities when I return. I do not want to appear selfish, but there will be so many things which we will want to do together. We will want to spend at least two or three weeks at Jamestown, a week at the least at the cabin, visits to Maryville, etc. Hope we can still rent a car from Hadley.

Hope Mother is completely well by this time, Give her my love. For you, I can only say Goodnight, sweetest dreams and remember always.

      I love you,

      Bushy

P.S. The golf balls in one box which I sent are for Hargrave. I didn't have time to make up a separate box.

Letter from Art to Dotty
Mainburg, Germany
March 27, 1946 [833-839]

Dearest Heart,

What a beautiful day this has been! Spring is such a terribly time for us to be apart but for that there is no help. There was very little to be done today in the office, and so Ted and I went for a long walk in the afternoon.

Everyone is on tender hooks, awaiting something definite as to when we will leave. We still no [know] absolutely nothing concerning the date of our departure, so we sit and twiddle our thumbs.

We saw a new phase of the AO today when a portion of the District Constabulary passed through. This new arm of the Army of Occupation is motorized and is intended as a swift, powerful striking unit. Light tanks, armored cars, jeeps and half tracks make up part of the vehicular strength, and these pass through various sections from time to time for the purpose of training but really more for the purpose of impressing the German people with the fact that we are here to do more than fraternize.

We are beginning to get GI again with reveille starting in. We are also cursed with billet guard every night. Last night more men were shipped in, but these were sent back since our records and rosters are all packed. One could almost think that we are settling down for a summer's stand.

Ted received a letter from home tonight which was postmarked on the 21st. It came direct and I certainly wish that I could have sent you a radiogram when we moved here, of course, such speed is very unusual and we would probably not have been so lucky. I will certainly be very far behind on the news when I do get home, for I hardly expect any more letters to get through to me. I shall try to telegraph when I reached the States to let you know when to expect me. I should be a civilian within two weeks after we sail, but when that will be remains the $64 question. I'm still "bidin' my time."

Ted and I went to the USO show again tonight for want of anything else to do. Now and then we have a fairly decent show. There is always a large number of popular songs that are played and something like "Rum & Coca-Cola" goes over with the GIs.

You know, I still don't like the idea of a trailer home, but a great many schools offer entrance if the student can find a place to stay. From that standpoint, a trailer would be a great advantage. By the way, when Harriet & family come down in the summer, I hope that we have been able to find an apartment. It seems to me that 607 would be a little crowded by that time.

Think I wrote once about catalogues from Yale, Chapel Hill, Princeton, Chicago, etc. I hope that you have been able to get for I must get to work immediately on my applications. I think that the best plan for me will be to take a few courses at UT during the summer and then get started on my MA in the fall. I also want to clear with USAFI (Armed Forces Institute) for my Stanford credit and also my Sorbonne credit. I think that these credits have been standardized, and I can certainly use them. By the time another year rolls around I should well be on my way to a degree.

Since I have to shave and get some sleep in preparation for an early reveille tomorrow, I shall tell you, My Darling,

I love you,
Bushy

Mar. 29
Mainburg, Germany

I read the following passage today and was profoundly affected. That is to say, the passage caused me to think, and I was inadvertently saddened by the thought. The speaker here is reminiscing about his return from Europe after the last war:

"'...What happened when you got back home'?"

"'That's the funny thing,' I answered, 'the most curious thing about it. Nothing happened. Nobody really seemed to understand that I'd been away. It just seemed to everyone that I had been around the

corner. They just asked what I was doing—that was all.'

"And that was true. Life means so very little, most of it—particularly someone else's life."

Marquand, Wickford Point, (AS Edition), p. 247

* Letter from Art to Dotty
Mainburg, Germany
March 29, '46 [840-847]

Darling,

For the second time we have corrected the 168 stencils which were made out earlier this week. It was decided that some minor error was sufficient reason and in addition we prove the durability of the stencils to withstand many corrections. I really do not mean to be bitter, for it is really good to have a job and have something to do while we wait.

Another silly thing happened today when we moved our offices to another building. There is more room for the big boys to have nice office space, but far less space in which the work will be done.

Last night I broke my usual routine of attending the USO show to come home early, spend almost an hour soaking in a full bath tub of water, and in going to bed early. The rest afreshed me for the day's work, and tonight I was entertained by the film at the German theater. "You were Never Lovelier" is an old film I understand, but it was quite new to me. I enjoyed the music as well as the routine story.

Far more important was a short passage which I read in Wickford Point (Marquand). The book itself is written in an unusual, leisurely style which sometimes seems interesting and other times seems less interesting. At any rate this portion of the book was extremely interesting for me because it described in a very brief passage the feelings of a young man returning from the last war.

"'What happened when you got back from home'?

"'That's the funny thing! I answered, 'the most curious thing about it. Nothing happened. Nobody really seemed to understand that I'd been away. It just seemed to everyone that I had been around the corner. They just asked what I was doing—that was all!

"And that was true. Life means so very little, most of it—particularly someone else's life."

The passage was so startling that it aroused thought (which, of course, is always a good thing.) It gave me a new slant on my homecoming which I really needed to get. Now, Darling, I know that you will be happy to see me and so will the folks. We must realize and admit, however, that very few others will even be interested in the fact that your husband has returned from the ETO. I say this not from self pity or in criticism. I certainly want no bands out. It is merely a fact that more than five million other men have already returned to civilian life, to their homes, and to their loved ones. My return is like a birth or a wedding: it will be truly a soul-thrilling event for us. Otherwise, not a ripple will appear outside our little circle.

Saturday Morning

Our lives go on here in an existence not unlike suspended animation. Here we find ourselves hanging between two entirely different lives. Most of us in this unit have been in the Army for almost three years and have adjusted ourselves to one extent or another to this mode of living. Soon, very soon we hope, we are to return to a more normal life, at least a more individual one.

I suppose that almost all ranges of feeling are found here. Of course, everyone, almost everyone, is filled with anticipation at the thought of getting out of Europe and to the States. Some of the men consider the Army as almost a phobia and think of the States as a virtual utopia where all problems will be automatically solved. Others look upon the States with some eager anticipation yet realizing that many problems exist there, as they do everywhere. There are even those few who look with dread upon the responsibilities of civilian life. A few men have even volunteered to remain in the ETO after getting this far in the pipe-line.

With our many moods and varied feelings, all anxiously await some definite word as to our immiediate future. My anticipation knows no bounds, My Dear, for soon I know that we will be together once again.

Thine own,
Bushy

* **Letter from Art to Dotty**
Mainburg, Germany
March 30, 1946 [848-849]

Dearest Heart,

The path to progress is littered with the remains of those who have dreamed and yet who have been unable to fulfill their dreams. Appalling figures are given to discourage returning vets from launching out into business ventures of their own. The divorce rate is rising, and literary trends in America seem to point to mass production of trash.

Nevertheless, progress in made only as a result of someone dreaming. Individuals only make individual progress as they dare to dream and make plans by which their dream may be realized. I would sometime like to count up the number of plans which I have dreamed, and which have fallen by the wayside of all dreams. There have been many and yet there have been a few which have been realized. I still believe that one must "hitch ones wagon to a star." We never reach all of the goals which we set, and yet should we fail to set goals as a result, we would accomplish very little.

All of this rambling leads me to my point, of course, that I have another plan in mind. This one just occurred to me this morning while I was writing another letter to you. For some time I have been wondering just how I should attempt to put some of my experiences overseas into writing. I had thought of short stories as being perhaps the best medium for me during the next ten years or so, since I will need at least that much time if not longer to develop my own style. The idea which suddenly popped into my head was to rewrite my letters to you—that is the letters written since I came into the Army, perhaps since I came overseas.

My idea would be to comb my letters for pertanent passages from my letters reflecting my experiences, my thoughts, conditions in the Army, etc. Within a letter-medium, I would have more latitude for putting across views and observations, and my novice style would not be so prominent. In additions to my letters to you, I could use my journal, letters to Mother and Dad, and an overflowing journal of notes, I think that I would have a wide choice of source material. The big job would be to choose and delete. [Boy, he isn't kidding! We have fallen in love with them all!]

Such a compliation might have more of a chance as a book than anything else I would be likely to produce for sometime to come, and yet that is of minor importance. I do hope to find some success in writing—someday, but I know full well that I have absolutely no talent for writing. I have that feeling way down inside of me that I will find myself in writing someday, but I suppose most people experience the same thing at one at time or another. To work over our letters and put them in some sort of consolidated form would be to at least provide a source for my own use at some future time. This, by the way, is another little project I have thought about for the summer. (Boy what a schedule I have planned for the months between now and September!)

I don't think that I have mentioned the little group in which I have been associating since I came here. In the office there are two other fellows who came with Ted from the 5th Inf. One worked in Personnel inthe 5th and the other fellow was in the supply room in Hq. Co. Bob Busek is a young college fellow from Cincinnati, and C.B. Groce was a freshman attending the university in Texas when he came into the service. The four of us work together, eat together, attend the shows together. It is the closest to being a Maryville [College] crowd that I have found in a long time in the Army, and I enjoy the association. As I think back over my friends in the Army, there are very few with whom I would care to correspond after I return to civilian pursuits. I do not think that I am snobbish, but it is very true that there are a relatively few people we meet with whom we can continue to associate or to correspond over a long period of time.

By accident I found out yesterday that the commanding officer of the Battalion, a certain Major John Ridley, hails from Smyrna, Tenn., not far from Jamestown. Mother taught school there at one time. I have actually had contact with very few people from my own section of the country since I came into the Army.

I hope that you have begun to write to this address, even though I told you when I came tostop writing. Just in case my mail is coming through in a hurry, say eight or nine days, you may as well write a few letters to this address. I think that I might get them at the port—even if not here.

Lots of love,
Bushy

Mar. 31
Mainburg, Germany

Services held today in all BN Hq Building. Interesting chaplain conducted – Lt. Co. who had been in the Army for 29 years. Had a number of interesting stories to relate and a good message. After the service, Ted and I (along with friend C. B. Groce) watched a soccer game played by civilians for the remainder of the afternoon. The game was mediocre but the crowd was large. The Germans do not have much entertainment, and they seem to enjoy this sort of thing. We have been attending the German movie each time it changes (once a week), and the civilians seem to attend these in large numbers. The shows, of course, are American with German subtitles and are usually some of the older films. Tonight "The Bells of St. Mary" was shown in the mess hall for the GIs.

April 1

Very dusty ride to Munich in the back of a ¾ ton truck. Almost entire Personnel staff (actually six of us) including Ted. Beautiful day and city cleaned up a great deal since I was there last. Enjoyed getting away from here, but this waiting is beginning to get intolerable.

Letter from Art to Dotty
Mainburg, Germany
April 1, 1946 (Mon.) [850-857]

Darling,

After another long and dusty ride. I managed to get part of the dust washed off before going down to the office. Nothing is going on there, and so I came back to Ted's room to write. Shortly after we reached the office this morning, we found that a truck had to go into Munich. Almost everyone wanted to go along, and almost everybody did. As far as Freising, the roads were extremely dusty, but from on we were on the hard surface. Didn't do much, actually although we had lunch in the Red Cross Club where Hitler's Beer Hall was once located. (I was there once before last summer.) The hall in which Hitler first started trouble has been converted into a gym with a large basketball court, seats, etc. It was here that the Mardi Gras was held last week. Much of the rubble is being cleared away in the city of Munich, and some buildings are being rebuilt. However the evidence of war, the bombgutted buildings, and the bleak walls left standing,—these things will not be erased for many, many years to come.

Saturday night I slept the round of the clock, arising about 10:30 Sunday morning. When I came down for lunch, I was happy to find that church services would be held in the afternoon. Ted, Genece, and I joined with a room full of other men in singing (without a piano or organ) and in listening to a chaplain (Lt. Col.) who had been in the Army for 29 years. What a man! His stories were interesting, and he had a good message.

After the services we wandered over to a soccer game which was being played at a field near town. The crowd was large and the game was enjoyable. Last night a new element was added on our field of entertainment when we saw a movie at the mess hall. As you no doubt know, "The Bells of St. Mary" is a very fine picture even when the projector is a 16 mm and the screen is a couple of table clothes. Bergman's performance is very fine as a nun and Crosby is as usual serious enough to retain the dignity of a Catholic priest and yet humorous enough to be completely human. I really think that this was the first time I had seen Bergman perform, but I can no believe all I have heard concerning the quality of her performance.

Later

Another variety show tonight which was one of the best we have seen. Great many acrobats and jugglers over here it seems, and some of them are good.

Tuesday Morning

Spent the morning getting a haircut—how exciting! My letters are surely very monotonous these days for I have so little about which to write.

Oh, I just thought about something else to ask about, Darling. I wonder if cabins are available out at Norris. You know, I have never been out there and perhaps it would be a nice place to spend a few days, of course, we should be busy enough I suppose with trips to Jamestown, Emert's Cove, Maryville, etc.

I suppose that my homecoming will be entirely different than anything I have imagined. You will never know the hours that I have spent thinking of each step, each move, each bright smile, each heavenly kiss. Perhaps you disagree but I don't think that the train station is the most appropriate plan for us to me (Remember San Francisco). Certainly wish that I could get some word from you in order to know what is going on, both in your thoughts and in your activities.

Though delays come and my letters do not come through as they should, of this you may be ever sure, with all my heart,
I love you,
Bushy

P.S. Encouraging news came in today, indicating that we are not completely forgotten. Unless there is further delay, we should leave here before the week is out. Oh joyous day!

April 2

Upon our return from the afternoon movie ("Weekend at the Waldorf"), Ted and I found that the big news had reached Bn. Hq. about three o'clock. We are to move out Thursday at 1600 (4 o'clock). Apparently we are to go to Le Havre, although this does not seem to be definite. When we told most of the fellows, the news was met with disbelief. The long delay here and week postponement have led to much restlessness and excessive drink on the part of many men. A number of former "girl friends" from Augsburg and Ingolstadt have arrived by this time, and the former good intentions of taking no more chances seem to have been cast aside.

Almost everyone can be heard counting the days and estimating the time it will take to get home now that we know we are to leave on the 4th. We allow three days for the trip to the port and another six or seven crossing. It will be extremely difficult for me to get home in time for me to hear Dotty sing for Easter. My longing for her has increased with each passing day, and I miss her presence intensely.

April 5
Mainz, Germany

At 4:30 yesterday afternoon we loaded on our deluxe cars at Mainburg. Although there is an order that no troops will be transported except in heated coaches, we had 45 boxcars for the 725 men in our battalion. Rather than going with our respective companies, all of us in Personnel are traveling in a single car. In addition to our nineteen men, we have three extra for a total of twenty-two. Needless to say we are slightly crowded. This hardly compares with the first train ride which Ted and I took together across another continent when we first came into the Army. [WE WERE SHIPPED FROM FORT OGLETHORPE, GEORGIA, TO SAN FRANCISCO IN A LUXURY COACH WITH PRIVATE COMPARTMENTS AND AN OBSERVATION LOUNGE ON ONE END.] However, it makes the trip far more interesting to be traveling with a group with whom I have some acquaintance. From Ingolstadt we may have come north thru Nuremburg, but the first town through which we came this morning was Aschaffenburg and later Darmstadt. Luckily enough we are wearing fatigues, and so the dirt and grime are not soiling our ODs [SLANG FOR OLIVE DRAB].

Aschaffenburg, Germany, April 5, 1945

[SHORTLY AFTER BOARDING OUR "40 AND 8" BOX CAR (40 MEN OR 8 HORSES) ONE OF THE GIs DISCOVERED THAT I HAD BEEN AN ENGLISH MAJOR. HIS FIRST QUESTION WAS, "DO YOU THINK HAMLET WAS MAD?" THAT DISCUSSION OCCUPIED OUR TIME FOR SEVERAL MILES.]

April 7
Sargueux, France

Yesterday on my wedding anniversary I could do no more than think of my lovely wife—not even a chance to write her a letter. Friday, after we crossed the Rhine at Mainz, we continued westward to Bad Kreuznach and thence south. This leg southward was thru a beautiful valley through which a small stream flowed. The hillsides were covered with vineyards, and the valley floor was intensively cultivated. Small country villages were located along the stream, and in them ancient bridges joined either bank. The voices of spring had called forth early buds, and light green hue was over the landscape. In some places this color ranged from dark green thru light grays, orange, and delicate reddish browns.

At one small town we stopped for no apparent reason. Civilians surged out of the town and along the tracks. We estimated that at least three hundred people of all ages crowded around our train. Most of them had something to sell—rings, cameras, eggs, schnapps, wine, bracelets, etc...—and everyone wanted cigarettes. 200 German marks or 2,000 Fr. francs were offered for a carton. I have seen many forms of the black market, but nothing that would compare with this. We halted in Homburg for a chow stop, having passed thru some of the supply area of the Siegfried line. It was at Homburg that the rain began, and when we awoke the following morning the rain was still coming down. We crossed into France sometime after midnight (thus on the 6th) and not far from the point where I made my initial entry [INTO GERMANY MORE THAN A YEAR BEFORE]. It was very cold and uncomfortable, and I remained in bed most of the time. In the late morning we passed through Charleville (north of Ardennes), and by noon we stopped in Tournes for another meal. From Tournes to Laon and thru La Fere to Chauny (outside of Amiens) for another chow stop about 10:30. Ted and I found two other bridge players (at about our speed), and we spent most of our time playing bridge. [I PLAYED SO MUCH THAT I NEVER AGAIN HAD INTEREST IN THE GAME.]

Sunday night
Camp Philip Morris
(near Le Havre, France)

After the rain began and as we neared the coast, our car became increasingly colder. However, we were heading homeward, and there were very few complaints. We traveled very little during Saturday night and were stopped in the small town of Serqueux for chow. More delays and finally speeded toward the coast via Yvetot (71st Div. Hdq. when we first landed). All along the way children and grownups waved to us, and we tossed cigarettes, candy, and other bits from our "K" rations.

We arrived in Le Havre about 2:45 and loaded on trucks to ride to Camp Philip Morris about four miles away. Personnel is in one hut. No news as yet but strong rumors that we may leave here on Wednesday. That sounds too good.

Letter from Art to Dotty
Camp Philip Morris
Near Le Harve, France
April 8, 1946

Darling,

I began a letter last night but was unable to finish it, and so I will begin again. We arrived in Le Harve about three o'clock yesterday afternoon and came immediately to the camp here. Our trip from Mainburg took a full 72 hours and I have traveled in greater comfort.

Personnel section came in one box car—twenty-two of us in one car. I thought of the first trip which Ted and I made together across another continent in a private compartment. We awoke Friday morning outside of Darmstadt and in the afternoon crossed the Rhine just south of Frankfurt at Mainz. We continued westward as far as Kreuznach and then southward into France. Sometimes during the wee small hours of the sixth we crossed into France. I spent a great deal of time during the day thinking of our anniversary, but there was not even a chance to write you. Ted and I found two other fellows who played bridge, and we spent most of our trip on the floor of the car.

As we came toward the coast, the signs of spring were in evidence everywhere. Trees are budding and the hillsides are green. I can well imagine how beautiful will be the Smokies and the Cumberlands when I arrive.

When we arrived here, the Pers. Sec. was again put together in a single quonset hut. Most of the fellows are in tents, and I think our situation is a bit better. Ted and I are sleeping side by side, and Groce & Burzek are at the other end of the room. One of the fellows has a radio working and we put up a stove in this morning. The latter is much needed as we discovered last night.

There is little news here so far. We found this morning that our separation center rosters are correct while the other units of C.C.R. (Combat Command Reserve) have theirs made incorrectly. That means less work for us. If we are lucky, we may be on the boat by next Monday, but the 66th Regt. left here on Ap 2. (These fellows left the 14th on the 15th of Feb.) I have given up all hope of reaching home by Easter.

Not much to do here, but I understand that there are two theaters. Our lighting here is very poor and I hope that I can find a library or a writing room in which to spend a few spare hours.

Most of my spare hours will be spent in thinking and dreaming of
Our Love, Bushy

Letters from Art's parents to Dotty
Monday 4-8-46

Dear Dorothy

Yesterday brought our latest news from Sgt. Bushing still in Mainburg as of Mar. 30. Records and equipment all packed and ready to move when some "big stiff" (my quotation—not his) gives the word. Today's New York Times, Sun issue, says that some over 9000 troops from ETO are landing in the states today. That must mean that the deployment centers are clearing out, and there won't be a long delay when the 126th moves in—Via LaHarve is the shortest route.

The crossing time is usually 8 to 13 days—depending on the weather and port. Our boys are going from New York to Camp Atterbury, Indiana for discharges, and it takes from 1 1/2 to 3 days in Camp.

We know we will want to visit over in Knoxville, but we are wondering how soon you will come on to see us.

Two of our nearest neighbor's boys are on the way home—one from China the other from India.

Last week we got out about 1000 letters to our returned veterans, and was real busy all week. We hope for a quiet week this week— Regular routine work.

Hope you are not so rushed with work, and that it won't be long until we see you.

Trust your mother is improving in health, and that the cure will be entirely successful.

Love from us both
Mother B.

I guess we'll have to forget about that suit. Don't want you to have too much trouble about it, and I may be able to get one for Fall wear. We're to have through buses from here to Knoxville in the next few weeks.

4 pm
Dear daughter Dorothy:

I'll just a line to Mother's letter. Arthur wanted us to try & reach him with one more letter A.P.O. 254 just in case he might be unduly delayed. So we wrote him a long newsy letter, trusting he will receive, but better pleased if it misses him because shipped out. About our new Consolidated Bus Schedule. Beginning tomorrow we are to have 3 through Buses to Chattanooga 6:00 am 10:30 am and one other but don't know time. The early Bus will allow 3 to 3 1/2 hrs for shopping in

Chattanooga—returning here 7:00 to 7:30 P.M. of conise connections at Crossville should mean a better schedule to connect with Greyhound at Crossville. But, praise be, the Consolidated is looking to running straight on to Knoxville—meaning that shopping may be done there with return here same day. So tell Mother Barber, that when you & Sgt Art come to live with us, when she gets lonesome for you & you get lonesome for your other home, you'll run down for the day, and back to your mountain home. Art & I can shop down there, Mother Bushing & you can go shopping in the big city and will combine Country & city life —as long as the money holds out. Kind regards and love aplenty

from Daddy no 2

P.S. Our last mail leaves here at 4:30 PM daily. New schedule.

April 10
Camp Philip Morris

Rumors were current yesterday that we were to leave tomorrow. However, it seems that our luck is not so good. We have worked at Personnel for the last two nights, and all of our rosters are typed and ready. We should leave by Friday or Saturday since we do not have to go with the rest of the CCR [?].

The sun has been out most of the time since we arrived, but a strong wind continues almost constantly, and almost everyone has a bad cold. We have a great deal of paper work to clear with our individual companies. We have signed five or six papers declaring that we have no ammunition, five or six others regarding our pistols. A recent ruling makes it necessary for us to have a bill of sale for all cameras. Of course, many fellows "liberated" [A GI EUPHEMISM FOR STEALING] their cameras, and many bought theirs from other GIs. The officer told us to make up our own bill of sale. The Army certainly makes it difficult for a fellow to remain strictly honest.

April 11

Hot rumor came down yesterday that we were to load aboard ship last night. However, it seems that the rest of CCR is leaving and we remain. Some of our rosters were made from very poor stencils, and these came back for corrections. It is thought that this caused our delay while others think that the dogs which are being taken with us are the cause. However, the real reason seems to be that no ships are available for a unit this large.

We spend our time wondering when the real news will come. Played bridge for about four hours last night with Ted and a couple of others. One must go to Le Havre (10 km.) for a shower, riding in an open truck both ways. With a bad cold, I am afraid to take a chance on a shower at this state of the game.

I was suddenly struck tonight with a new thought and a question. Mother and Dad have been working in the office since Oct. of 1940, and both are very tired. Rather than being stopped in May, the draft will probably be continued for another year. For the past few months I have thought and planned only of getting back home and to school as soon as possible. I have not considered the possibility of my active responsibility to my parents. I know that Dad's health is not the best, and I may find that I should delay my education for awhile. I must not fail to consider them and their needs in my planning. [LOOKING BACK, I AM GLAD THAT I CONSIDERED THIS POTENTIAL, BUT TWO OR THREE THINGS HAPPENED UNEXPECTEDLY. FIRST, THE DRAFT WAS TO CONTINUE FOR SEVERAL YEARS MORE. SECOND, MY FATHER AND MOTHER CONTINUED TO WORK IN THE OFFICE UNTIL DAD RETIRED IN 1959, AT AGE 83. THIRD, I WAS ASKED TO TEACH IN THE UNIVERSITY OF TENNESSEE SUMMER SCHOOL SHORTLY AFTER I ARRIVED HOME AND THEN ASKED TO APPLY FOR AN ASSISTANTSHIP IN THE DEPARTMENT.]

April 12
[CAMP PHILIP MORRIS]

The full news came yesterday when I found that we will sail tomorrow on the "USSR Victory." The boat has a capacity of only 1,000 men, and the trip will probably take a full nine days. I sent a telegram to Dotty yesterday giving her the latest, and it was supposed to reach her within six hours. Not bad!

Slept late again this morning and went through a "short arm" examination this afternoon (the so-called "short-arm" is intended to reveal any cases of VD). My company of 200 men went thru the line in less than five minutes, and the companies were examined in fifteen minutes. Spent most of the afternoon at the Club reading. There is nothing to do now but to wait.

Ted, Groce, Buzek, and I went to the show tonight – "The Lady Objects." It was not such a good movie, but the scenery was good and in Technicolor. This is our last night in the ETO, and we are rather excited. At the moment, we (about half of the hut) sit around the fire listening to AFN Paris. One fellow reads, another cleans his mess kit, another eats a "K" ration. Outside, the moon shines bright and clear, the night is warm. The sea should be calm, and the end of the trail leads to the end of my rainbow. For fifteen months I have been separated from the one who makes my life complete. During these months, I have lived but half a life. It will be as though rising from a coma to be again with my lovely wife, to share again with her the joy of living.

It was one year ago tonight that President Roosevelt passed away. The world still mourns its loss.

April 13
Aboard Ship En Route

At 12:05 we loaded on great semi-trailers in Camp Philip Morris and rode to the docks at Le Havre. Without undue confusion or delay we received the traditional coffee and doughnuts from the Red Cross girls, and at 1:40 I struggled across the gangplank of the "USSR Victory," one of the famed Victory ships of this war. Luckily I found myself in the same compartment as Ted, and we have adjacent bunks. Shortly after we boarded, another Victory ship docked alongside us with re-enlistees and rookies from the States. One could have thought that they were German soldiers during combat to have heard the cracks and insults that bombarded the air between the two ships.

At 6:45 we pulled anchor and rode swiftly through the harbor channel. Much has been done in Le Havre to clean up the wreckage of war, but much still remains to be done. Certainly a vast amount of work has been done since I was here in Feb. of 1945. By 7:50 the last shadows of the continent faded into the multi-colored haze. Being a sentimentalist, I took a fond last look at the Continent from which I had gleaned a few secrets during the past fifteen months. I glanced at it with a mere glimmer of regret; and then my eyes swept westward to bits of gold dust left behind in the sky by the sun. There in the sunset was my gold and my future. The moon is fair tonight; the sea is calm; I'm going home!

April 18
At Sea

Our fifth day at sea and for four of these I have been too sick to enjoy very much. Every time I remain on my feet for any length of time, I rush to the rail and feed the fish. It is not pleasant, and so I remain in my bunk most of the time. Ted too is sick. Tonight we felt good enough to lie on the edge of our bunks and talk about Maryville [COLLEGE] for four solid hours. Not a bad subject to discuss when there are so many pleasant personalities and memories. Sea has been relatively smooth, but the Victory model tosses like a canoe. Day before yesterday we averaged only about 10 knots an hour, but we are more than half way now. Tonight I enjoyed the rare privilege of standing on the deck and watching a moon just past the full shine fair upon the water. The sea is almost without a ripple, and we are gliding along swiftly.

Ap 20
At Sea

At about two o'clock this afternoon we heard from the loud speaker that we were but 700 miles from N.Y. Speculation began anew concerning our probable time of arrival. The ocean has been calm for most of our journey, and we have made fair speed for a vessel of this type (max sp. 17 knots). Yesterday the "Queen Mary" glided past like a swan, and our tub seemed to be standing still. With luck, we should arrive in port early enough Mon. to reach Kilmer in the evening—we fervently hope!

Pictures almost every night have provided welcome diversion for otherwise drab and ageless days. A daily paper has been our avidly read source of news, and an active PA system has provided frequent programs of recorded music. We have a plentiful supply of books from Special Services, and a gambling table on one of the middle decks has been an almost continual scene of the galloping dominoes galloping. As a result of the urging of my friend Groce, I have read a book on Jazz by a Belgian addict (Robt. Goffin). The book is not well written, but I gained a new tolerance of this music, so ultra-American. Of course, it does have a place in our culture, growing from a strong Negro background.

Yesterday was Good Friday and about fifty of us packed into the officers' mess for services. Tomorrow is Easter, and it would be *wonderful to be with Dotty for services at home. However, we will have our service aboard ship, and then next Easter...!*

Ap 21
Easter, At Sea

Rough sea & USSR Victory tosses atop the water as tho she had no weight at all aboard. Gallery was filled for church service and good service built around Ten Commandments. I missed the Communion Service which Baptist minister was not permitted to administer. [NO EXPLANATION; PERHAPS I WAS FEEDING THE FISH AGAIN.] Topside in time to see the sky clear for the sunset. Very beautiful.

Ap 22
H.Y. Harbor, USA

After good sleep I awoke at 5:30 to find the ship moving with unusual smoothness. On deck I found the sky cloudless and the sea with hardly a motion on the glassy surface. Played bridge on deck for a couple of hours & [THEN] packed my bags. At 3:20 we sighted Ambrose Lighthouse (18 mi. out), and at 3:40 the dim outline of the Jersey coast was sighted through the haze. At reduced speed we proceeded up the channel while the land we have longed so very long to see became clear. The front of the boat was crowded, and Ted and I went to the poop deck in the rear to watch the personal dramas unfold. As we came closer in, a welcoming boat came out to meet us. The deck was crowded with Am. flags & and twenty or thirty girls crowded the rail to wave to us. No one jumped overboard, and some Joe pointed these out as a species called "Amerkanish Fraulein." With the aid of a couple of tugs we moved into one of the Trans. Corp docks on Staten Island. We now await D-hour when we disembark for Kilmer.

Ap 23
Camp Kilmer

At 7:51 last night I skipped down the gang plank of the USSR Victory with as much speed as I could maintain and still retain control over myself and the duffel bag on my shoulder. We landed on Staten Island and took the ferry to a Jersey train. I went up on the top deck to receive the real climax to my landing. I looked out over the darkened bay to see the well-known lady with the lights, and she never looked lovelier. I voiced a silent prayer for this my country, my native land, and for the Light held aloft to the world. I prayed that it might ever be thus. I looked out over the harbor again to see the lights of lower Manhattan and found that oft-photographed scene a new thrill. We loaded from the ferry to the train and sped swiftly to Kilmer. After a short orientation, a shave, and chow, I tried to sleep but failed miserably until 3:30. Today I worked in Personnel and completed our processing here. We now wait until Thur. to go to Separation Center.

Ap 24
Kilmer

Just returned from wonderful visit with a great bunch of Maryville folk located down at Princeton. Ted and I left with passes at noon today, and after waiting for an hour and a half in New Brunswick managed to get a bus to Princeton. Talked with the gang at the Seminary, ran out to see Olson & Jean Pemberton & baby, back to Benham Club for supper, and then back to see Olson & Jean for the remainder of the evening. Wonderful to be in decent atmosphere again. Baby is nine weeks old, and Olson shows wear and tear. My interest in babies during school term dropped, but the prospects of Princeton as a source for my M.A looks bright. Think it has swell possibilities.

Ap 26
Fort Meade, MD

Left Kilmer about 1:30 yesterday and came by way of the back roads to Meade, arriving about 2:30. Immediately we turned in all excessive clothing and equipment, much to our happiness.

Today processing went on apace, and we are to be finished at 2:40 tomorrow. Tonight I was shocked, yes stunned, when I called Dotty and found out that Mother Barber passed away last week. I have not yet recovered from the news and can hardly believe it. She had suffered throughout the winter from arthritis and heart trouble. Mother and Dad came to Knoxville for the service.

April 29
Knoxville, 607 W. Glenwood Ave.

On Saturday morning, Ted and I rushed around from one spot to another finishing the last portions of our processing. The climax came, I think, when we were marched into a long room where two rows of fully equipped shoe shining equipment was set up for our use. At another place, we were given any clothing needed; PWs [PRISONERS OF WAR] sewed stripes and emblems on our uniforms; and our clothing was pressed by PW help. The complete process at Fort Meade moved with remarkable efficiency—for the army! At 2:40 we marched into a little chapel with a flag-bedecked platform. A brisk breeze unfurled a large American flag, and I looked upon it with burning pride. A major gave the same speech that I suppose he has given for several hundred times. However, it was an impressive speech concerning the need for leadership in the ranks of civilian activity. By 3:00 we were marching up to the platform one by one to salute and receive the pass to freedom and individual living. Cordelia (Ted's wife), and Mr. and Mrs. Kidder were waiting for Ted when we came out, and they rushed me into Washington to catch my 4:30 train. My coach was half-filled with young fellows going home, preparatory to shipment overseas. Their talk was light and frivolous, and they made disparaging remarks about colored folk. I slept little and arrived in Knoxville on Sunday morning in time to awaken Dotty with a kiss.

MY BEAUTY, ASLEEPING

Moon-beams of midnight,
Moon-beams and starlight,
Steal to her gently,
My beauty, asleeping,
Go gently creeping
And whisper my love;

Wind in the pine-tree,
Wind ever kind t' me,
Touch her so lightly,
The Queen of my Isle,
Yes, linger awhile
And whisper my love.

"My Beauty, Asleeping," by Art Bushing

Dotty and Art, home

Letter from Art to Tom
The Barber Cabin
Near Gatlinburg
May 12, 1946

Dear Tom,

From over a nearby range of hills, the sun has just peeped; Mt. LeConte is shrouded in morning fog; every leaf and every blade of grass reflect the myraid rays of light; the song of the river provides a mellow background for the songs of the birds. If I wax in a romantic vein, it is only because this is such a logical place in which to wax. Dotty and I came to the mountains on Wednesday, and as always we have found this spot a veritable paradise where we are able to withdraw completely from the world. Yesterday, Dad Barber and three cousins arrived to spend the weekend, and this afternoon we will have to return to Knoxville. Just two weeks ago this morning at this hour I arrived at 607 to greet my wife, and this trip to the cabin has been a fitting climax to my reconversion period to civilian life. (I assure you that the process is by no means a difficult one!)

I believe that my last letter to you was written in Mainburg, Germany, shortly before leaving that spot on the long road home. Our trip to the coast (eight hundred miles) was made in three days via box cars, but we were going in the right direction and there was little complaint. After more delay, we sailed from Le Havre on the 13th of April aboard the U.S.S.R. Victory. I don't suppose you have had the questionable pleasure of riding a Victory ship which does not have sufficient ballast in the hold. Don't! Although the sea was relatively calm, we spent nine days bobbing up and down, back and forth, end to end; now and then we moved forward. I could hardly appreciate Kaiser's efforts.

We landed in New York on the 22nd and rushed to Kilmer where we encountered more waiting and delay. From there I came to Meade (just outside of D.C.) to become a glorified civilian on the 27th. I will not try to describe my feelings upon becoming something more than a member of his majesty's forces. I caught the first train out of Washington and reached home in time to awaken Dotty with a kiss. I had not had mail since leaving Weinheim (near Heidelberg), and so I had missed a great deal of news. However, I did call Dotty from Fort Meade, and was shocked to learn of Mrs. Barber's death. This happened just before Easter, and the services we held just eight days before I arrived. Mrs. Barber was a very wonderful person, and it is extremely difficult to become accustomed to the home without her.

After two or three days in Knoxville, we went over to Jamestown to remain until the following Monday. Tom, I hardly recognized the place, but more of that later. Upon our return to Knoxville, we made a quick dash over to Maryville and thence to the mountains.

As to the future, my plans remain a bit unsettled. Since Mrs. Barber's sickness began last fall, Dotty has been taking care of the household, and of course will continue to do so until we leave Knoxville. I want to spend more time over at Maryville until the graduation exercises are held on the 22nd, and we will then plan to return to Jamestown for a longer visit. I want to help Dad get the house painted and do a number of other odd jobs around the place. We will probably try to spend two or three weeks in all at home during the summer. After that I will find some sort of temporary work for the remainder of the summer. As to school, my plans are in the process of being revised. Dr. Hunter, Dean at Maryville and head of the English Department, is a very close friend of mine, and his advice is that I should not waste my time with a refresher course (which I had not contemplated up to now). His advice is to go on without delay, and this I will hope to do in the Fall. Princeton will be my first choice, with Chapel Hill (N.C.) being perhaps my second. These choices will naturally be conditioned by the possibility of being admitted for the Fall term. I am still under the impression that the graduate schools are not so crowded as are the undergraduate departments.

Tuesday Night

My sincere apologies are in order for I have been unable to finish this letter started on Sunday. Our wonderful stay in the mountains ended all to soon, and we returned very late Sunday afternoon.

There are so many things that I want to discuss with you, but I certainly can't wait to write about all of them before finishing this letter. Your letter of the 6th and 21st of March we[re] here to greet me, and I was most happy to learn of your work. Sounds like a job with plenty of experience attached. Perhaps you can solve some of my housing problems, Mr. Anthony! I can imagine that even playing second fiddle has its compensations, and I am glad that you are able to practice a bit. I was afraid that you were not keeping up with the music, and that would be definitely bad. Sorry to hear that your parents are planning to move, and I hope that I can get in touch with them before they do so. Maryville Commencement will be held next Tuesday, and we are going to be going back and forth a great deal between here and there until then. However, I am going to write your folks immediately and make plans to visit them as soon as possible. (By the way, Dotty and I came by way of Oak Ridge on our return from Jamestown, but were unable to get off the bus without a pass.)

I have a number of opinions about politics, but I am counting on seeing you soon. My hope is that you will be getting a leave sometime soon—or has the Navy quit that sort of thing? After consultation with my lovely wife, I find that nothing would prevent you spending two or three days with us here—or longer if possible. It would be really wonderful if you could stop by here, Tom, and spend a few days with us. What are the possibilities?

In regard to the article which I sent you, I am seriously thinking of rehashing it and sending it to one of the magazines—Collier's or Sat. Evening Post. Which would you sugguest? Perhaps another magazine would be better, but I am a bit out of touch with the general list of current literature (?).

Am following with interest the editorials by our friend Lippman concerning the European cauldron. Am beginning to wonder how far we can drift before 1948 when the Rep. president takes office and attempts to right the hundredfold wrongs which have been committed. Poor Harry is in a mess, and I see no immediate way out for him. Byrnes is doing what should have been done months ago as he sits at the Paris Conference, but Russia is acting in a most disappointing manner. I am beginning to wonder if my optimism has been without foundation. I don't like the fatalism which marks people over here—the same sort which I found prevailing among the GIs overseas. I am just about ready to go all out for Stassen, as I think I wrote before, but would value your estimation of him.

I could go on like this for two or three hours, but I will have to stop now. Am counting on having you here soon, and will certainly try to see your folks as soon as possible.

As ever,
Art

THAT'S AMERICA

We live in a land
Where freedom's free,
A land that belongs to
To you and me,
A land our own
From sea to sea.
That's America;

The Turk may come
From a foreign shore,
The Swede may come
To our front door,
But passing that--
Foreigner no more,
That's America;

No class nor clan
Will bar the way
As they work ahead
From day to day,
As on they forge
They laugh and say,
"That's America!"

We're brothers all
In states united,
And here we live
Where wrongs are wrighted,
For Liberty's flame
Has long been lighted,
That's America;

But now again
The questions come
Of our right to live
As in past we've done,
But we'll answer again,
Each father, each son,
That's America!

We pray to God
That blood we'll spare,
But the Libery we love
Demands our care,
For a world that's free
We'll strive, we'll dare,
That's America!

In conclusion, a poem, "That's America," by Art Bushing

Lisa Soland and Dotty Bushing.
One of our last visits prior to COVID-19
and the isolation of all retirement communities.

EDITOR'S NOTE
AND ACKNOWLEDGMENTS

I had the pleasure of first meeting Dotty Bushing during the technical week of my new one-man play *Sergeant York*, which opened in Knoxville on April 20, 2018. My friend, Mary Bogart, arranged the meeting because Dotty knew Alvin York, and Mary thought that Dotty might offer some personal insight into the WWI hero. It was during that initial meeting that Dotty informed me of her late husband's WWII diary and her unfulfilled desire to have his diary published.

Our initial approach to the publication began only with Art's diary of Army life from January 1945 to April of 1946, but because of their fine collection of artifacts, it was difficult to be content with this well-told, but partial story. As Art writes in the author's preface, "The big job would be to choose and delete." Well, the "big job" was mine, and Art wasn't kidding! The two lovebirds were prolific to say the least, setting the goal of writing to each other every day they were apart. Over three and a half years, that is a lot of letters! Though I tried to be ruthless in my editing responsibilities, it was an impossible task because, through their letters, I had quickly fallen in love with them both, as I know you will too.

The history buffs will enjoy a few references to Sgt. Alvin York as told from the viewpoint of Art's father, who worked as Sgt. York's personal secretary. Art and Dotty attended Maryville College together, and throughout this two-volume set, there are countless references to their alma mater as well as to their friendships forged there.

Volume I: 1943 to 1944 covers Art's experience in the Army prior to leaving for the European Theatre. Volume II: 1945-1946 covers Art's time overseas, before and after his four months in actual combat. I find the time following combat most compelling, while Art waits patiently (and sometimes not so patiently) for his redeployment and his return home to Dotty's arms. Though this time period appears to be less action-packed, it is an aspect of WWII not adequately explored in other history books or non-fiction art forms.

Enormous gratitude must be paid to Martha Hess and Dotty for their original work editing Art's diary entries from January 1945 through April of 1946. Throughout these writings, the capitalizations in the brackets are Art's later added notations. All the chapter divisions and titles are his as well. Chapter 1 has been published in Volume I, and Chapters 1 through 9 in Volume II. As editor, I did not have access to the original diary—only Dotty's and Martha's fine revision.

I also cannot emphasize enough how grateful I am for my assistant, Tonya Hobbs, who joyfully participated in transcribing the letters. Without her supportive spirit and willingness to serve, this collection would have taken much longer to complete. Also, it was wonderful to work alongside Dotty's daughter, Jennifer, as well as all the other Bushing children who have been very kind and accommodating in every way. I would also like to personally thank writer Darnell Arnoult who made herself available to me as a friend and consultant.

Think about publishing a two-volume set, totaling about 1200 pages, and asking busy folks to read them and write promotional quotes. That was tough to do—to ask. But I was completely surprised at the enthusiasm. Not one person declined. Their response alone warmed my heart to such an extent, that it made the entire two years of working on the books worth it. This had everything to do with Art and Dotty Bushing's legacy, of course. But still, 1200 pages?! Here are their precious names: Sam Venable, Michael F. Dilley, Gerald York, Dave Tabler, Tom Bogart, Gerald W. Gibson, Douglas Mastriano, Joanie Latorre, and Charles Hubbard. I'm very grateful. But I am especially grateful to Dotty who entrusted me with her late husband's writings.

The 1943 and 1944 diary entries have been transcribed in their entirety and without revision. Like all the letters, no errors in spelling or punctuation have been fixed. Those diaries and every letter have been presented as close to how they were originally written or typed as possible. I especially enjoyed reading the letters Art typed on a faulty typewriter as we have the privilege to watch his frustration grow in battle with two obstinate typewriter keys! Capturing the language as it was originally executed offers a clearer portrayal of the writer's personality, mindset, and environment. Even under the conditions in which they were living, with all their challenges—the war, and separation from each other—the reader can clearly see how intelligent, kind, loving, and expressive they both were, as also were their family and friends. These volumes capture the sweetest of exchanges on every front, and I have been honored to play a role in bringing these values back to the forefront of whatever public is drawn to them.

The diary, letters, and photographs have been arranged chronologically. The diary entries are italicized and justified; the letters are not, with a page divider placed between them. When "Maryville" is mentioned, the writers are referring to either Maryville College located in Maryville, Tennessee, or the town of Maryville. When Art Bushing returned from Europe, he taught at Maryville College for 50 years, so one can understand the impact that institution had on the two of them.

We were in the deepest throes of transcribing the letters when COVID-19 hit our world of publishing and the world at large. Up to this point, I had been trying to visit with Dotty regularly, but on March 12, 2020, that all came to a screeching halt. I could not help but find it all so profound how each of the letters, the struggles, the fears, and the unknowns that Art and Dotty were facing, we too were now experiencing to some degree.

In the letter dated February 25, 1945, Art wrote to Dotty: "I am trying to keep up with my notes reflecting something of the life of the G.I., my surroundings, and my own thoughts and feelings regarding these things.... I hope that I shall be able to return with my little black book filled to the brim. The squad already expects me to publish what I am writing and they are extremely curious as to what I put down. I hope that it will prove of interest to our little ones." It is to these "little ones," Art and Dotty's descendants, that I dedicate my part in bringing these two books—their story—into your hands. And to Art, who "hitched his wagon to a star" when he married you, Dotty. May these books honor your husband, your children, and the generations to come, creating the lasting legacy for Art your heart desired. Another "dream" of his complete.

Lisa Soland, Senior Editor
Climbing Angel Publishing
June 2020
Knoxville, Tennessee

A look at journal of 50 years ago

**Arthur S.
Bushing**

Friday, August 11, 1995

On the 50th anniversary of the dropping of the atomic bomb on Hiroshima, sermons, discussions, and debates have provided a full-range of opinions and emotions regarding that historic event. As a combat veteran of World War II in Europe, I have tried to sort through my own reactions to Hiroshima both then and now. At the time, I was studying at the Sorbonne in Paris.

From journal notes, Aug. 6: "The news of the new atomic bomb was announced today. This new bomb is based on the principle of smashing the atom, and it is claimed to be as powerful(one bomb) as 20,000 tons of TNT. Another comparison is that it would take 2,000 Superforts to carry the destruction equal to that of one [atomic] bomb.

"Of course, the immediate effect in the war against Japan is being played up in the papers. One city, Hiroshima, is reported to have been wiped out by the bomb. However, the long range use of such power is not hidden from view. Such tremendous [power] diverted to peace time utility can revolutionize the world just as its discovery will revolutionize the world of science. What hath man wrought? What hath man wrought against man?"

Aug. 8: "Rumors fly tonight that Russia has declared war on Japan. This [is] of very great significance along with continued reports of atomic bomb (One bombing mission by 25 bombers loaded with atomic bombs could have done the same damagewhich the Air Corps accomplished during the entire ETO [European Theater of Operation] —or so the story goes]. . . .'

Aug 10: "After lunch. . . [a fellow

student] and I went to the American Library to study and read. A GI told us that peace rumors were in the air but we merely laughed [in disbelief]. After we had finished we started to walk down Haussmann Boulevard to the metro. A young boy passed us with a newspaper announcing that Japan had offered to surrender. The boy's words were 'Japan kaput!' Suddenly I seemed to be walking on very light air. I seemed to hear the birds singing and I wanted to dance and shout.I thought seriously of dashing up to kiss a few mademoiselles, but decided to refrain. . . .In front of the Madeleine [Church] we saw a jeep loaded with GIs and WACs bearing a sign 'Japan Licked.' We let off a little steam with a healthy yell.

"The French smiled at our outburst. The soldiers standing around the Red Cross seemed to hardly know what was going on. There was little sign of rejoicing. A few began a parade in the direction of the Opera House, but the large majority merely watched in silence. I was forced to agree with Miss Stein that the American soldier is a bit glum." [Gertrude Stein had met informally with a number of us the night before, sharing her wide-ranging opinions on politics, literature, the war, and Ameri-

can soldiers.]

In order to understand my views 50 years later, one must remember America's collective shock after the attack on Pearl Harbor. With some reason, we had fears of the Japanese landing troops on the West Coast. Their submarines were ranging close to shore in both oceans. During the early months following, we continued to lose men, matériel, and strategic outposts in the Pacific.

The Japanese soldiers were tenacious, some actually holding out in island caves for many months after the war ended. Their view of human life was very different from ours, witness the Kamikaze pilots who trained to fly their bomb-loaded suicide missions into our ships. Records showthat more than 2,000 Kamikaze missions flew against our fleet at Okinawa.

One third of the civilian population was killed in the defense of Okinawa, and we had every reason to expect that in defense of the home islands the Japanese people would be intransigent. Perhaps their reactions to an invasion would have been similar to that of the Vietnamese civilians in their later struggle against the French, the Japanese, and the Americans.

Had the bomb not been used, most historians agree that:

■ The war would have continued for many more months.

■ A significantly larger number of Japanese soldiers and civilians would have died.

■ Many, many more Americans would have died.

Few if any involved in making the decision to use the bomb had any idea of its devastating power, immediately or long range. The prolonged

effects of radiation were not well understood. With the belief that the war could be brought to a close quickly, few argued that the new weapon should not be tried.

When we consider the evils perpetrated in the Nazi concentration camps, the surprise attack on Pearl Harbor, the inhumanity demonstrated on the Bataan Death March, the fire bombing of Dresden by the RAF and the USAAF, we have overpowering evidence that war brings out the very worst in human behavior, both collectively and individually. Americans were not immune.

On the other hand, what we did through the Marshall Plan to rebuild Europe was, I believe, unheard of in the annals of war. Our contribution to a new political system in Japan changed Far Eastern history. Furthermore, after the war, I witnessed numerous acts of kindness that GIs proffered to the German civilian population, reflecting an American spirit of individual outreach and forgiveness.

Obviously, the perspectives from which we review Aug. 6, 1945, differ widely. Although Hiroshima remains a blot on human history, I believe it was the lesser among the evils available at that time. The full effects of the decision to develop atomic energy are the least among those we are still struggling to understand.

Dr. Arthur S. Bushing, a Maryville resident and semi-retired professor of English at Maryville College, earned his undergraduate degree at Maryville College, his masters ■■■■■■■ at UT. He saw combat with the 71st Infantry Division in Europe.

The Daily Times article "A Look at Journal of 50 Years Ago,"
Opinions, published August 11, 1995

Art & Dotty Bushing

AUTHOR'S BIOGRAPHY

Dr. Arthur Story Bushing (March 24, 1922 – October 29, 2008) was born in Oroville, Washington, but spent much of his childhood in Jamestown, Tennessee. His father, Arthur Samuel Bushing, was personal secretary to WWI hero Sgt. Alvin C. York and in 1939 Art "Junior" graduated from the Alvin C. York Institute. Art began his teaching career in 1943 as instructor of physics at Maryville College, where he had received his undergraduate degree and met his wife, Dorothy "Dotty" Bushing. During WWII, he served in the United States Army in the European Theatre and earned the Bronze Star, the Battle of the Rhineland, and the Battle of Central Europe medals. In 1947, he returned to his alma mater as an assistant professor of English, while completing his master's degree from the University of Tennessee. Over the fifty years of teaching at Maryville College, countless students were taught from his *Manual of Outlining and Research*, and he enjoyed touring and lecturing on the life of Sgt. Alvin C. York. Dr. Bushing retired from teaching in 1996, but he and Dotty continued to be active in the life of the College, which included serving as historians. Dr. Bushing was also an active member of Highland Presbyterian Church, serving as Elder and Sunday School teacher for many years. In 1991 Art was recognized by the College with an honorary doctor of letters degree and in 2000 he was presented the Maryville College Medallion, the highest honor bestowed by the College. Art and Dotty enjoyed 64 years of marriage and were the proud parents of four children: Stuart, Barbera, Kathryn, and Jennifer.

ABOUT CLIMBING ANGEL PUBLISHING

Climbing Angel Publishing exists for the purpose of sharing stories of hope and encouragement, aiding in the gathering together of community, and supporting the process of betterment. The following books are available at ClimbingAngel.com and major bookstores.

Adult Books: *(Romans 8:28-30)*

In His Image
By Faith
My Birthday Gift to Jesus
Without Ceasing
SonLight
Corona Victus: Conquering the Virus of Fear
Art Bushing: His Diary, Letters, & Photographs of WWII
Art & Dotty: His Diary, Their Letters & Photographs of WWII

Children's Books: *(Philippians 4:8)*

The Christmas Tree Angel
The Unmade Moose
Thump
Somebunny To Love